Islamic Intellectual History in the Seventeenth Century

Scholarly Currents in the Ottoman Empire and the Maghreb

For much of the twentieth century, the intellectual life of the Ottoman and Arabic-Islamic world in the seventeenth century was ignored or mischaracterized by historians. Ottomanists typically saw the seventeenth century as marking the end of Ottoman cultural florescence, while modern Arab nationalist historians tended to see it as yet another century of intellectual darkness under Ottoman rule. This book is the first sustained effort at investigating some of the intellectual currents among Ottoman and North African scholars of the early modern period. Examining the intellectual production of the ranks of learned *ulema* (scholars) through close readings of various treatises, commentaries, and marginalia, Khaled El-Rouayheb argues for a more textured – and text-centered – understanding of the vibrant exchange of ideas and transmission of knowledge across a vast expanse of Ottoman-controlled territory.

Khaled El-Rouayheb is James Richard Jewett Professor of Arabic and of Islamic Intellectual History in the Department of Near Eastern Languages and Civilizations at Harvard University. He specializes in Arabic and Islamic intellectual history, especially in the period from the thirteenth to the eighteenth centuries. He is the author of *Before Homosexuality in the Arab-Islamic World, 1500–1800* (2005) and *Relational Syllogisms and the History of Arabic Logic, 900–1900* (2010). He is also coeditor of the forthcoming *Oxford Handbook of Islamic Philosophy*.

Islamic Intellectual History in the Seventeenth Century

Scholarly Currents in the Ottoman Empire and the Maghreb

KHALED EL-ROUAYHEB
Harvard University

CAMBRIDGE
UNIVERSITY PRESS

CAMBRIDGE
UNIVERSITY PRESS

32 Avenue of the Americas, New York, NY 10013-2473, USA

Cambridge University Press is part of the University of Cambridge.

It furthers the University's mission by disseminating knowledge in the pursuit of education, learning, and research at the highest international levels of excellence.

www.cambridge.org
Information on this title: www.cambridge.org/9781107042964

First published 2015

Printed in the United States of America

A catalog record for this publication is available from the British Library.

Library of Congress Cataloging in Publication Data
El-Rouayheb, Khaled.
Islamic intellectual history in the seventeenth century : scholarly currents in the Ottoman Empire and the Maghreb / Khaled El-Rouayheb.
pages cm
Includes bibliographical references and index.
ISBN 978-1-107-04296-4 (hardback : alkaline paper)
1. Turkey – Intellectual life – 17th century. 2. Africa, North – Intellectual life – 17th century. 3. Learning and scholarship – Turkey – History – 17th century. 4. Learning and scholarship – Africa, North – History – 17th century. 5. Muslim scholars – Turkey – History – 17th century. 6. Muslim scholars – Africa, North – History – 17th century. 7. Muslim philosophers – Turkey – History – 17th century. 8. Muslim philosophers – Africa, North – History – 17th century. I. Title.
DR511.E57 2015
956′.015 – dc23 2015010600

ISBN 978-1-107-04296-4 Hardback

O reader! There may occur in our work things with which you are not familiar and that you will find nowhere else. Do not hurry to condemn this, whimsically heeding the call of the one who merely relays what others have said and stitches it together, and for whom the ultimate in knowledge and the aim of all effort is to say "So and so has said." No by God! . . . We seek refuge in God from blackening folios and stuffing quires with what people have said and meant, following the well-trodden path of imitation (*taqlīd*) as the dull-witted do . . . There is no difference between an imitator being led and a pack-animal being led. So know, o reader, that we have not included in this or other compositions anything besides what we believe to be correct, viz. concepts and propositions that are evident or correctly argued for.

– al-Ḥasan al-Yūsī (d. 1691)

Had it not been for imitation (*taqlīd*), no one of the ignorant would have been deprived of the truth, and no one could be heard saying, "We have not heard this from our first forefathers." The one whom the Lord wishes to make a consummate scholar, He will guide by making him understand that "Wisdom is the stray camel of the believer" and will make him commit to take what is pure and leave what is adulterated . . . O you, who are brimming with intelligence, do not look to *who* is saying something but to *what* is being said, for this is the way of the verifiers (*muḥaqqiqīn*) and the custom of those who delve deep (*mudaqqiqīn*) into scholarly matters!

– Ḳara Ḫalīl Tīrevī (d. 1711)

Contents

Figures, Maps, and Tables *page* xi
Acknowledgments xiii
Note on Transliteration, Dates, and Translations xv

Introduction 1

PART I: "THE PATH OF THE KURDISH AND PERSIAN VERIFYING SCHOLARS"

1 Kurdish Scholars and the Reinvigoration of the Rational Sciences 13
The Myth of the "Triumph of Fanaticism" 14
Opening the Gate of Verification in Damascus 26
Opening the Gate of Verification in the Hejaz, Istanbul, and Anatolia 37
Conclusion 56

2 A Discourse on Method: The Evolution of *Ādāb al-baḥth* 60
An Explosion of Interest in Dialectics (*Ādāb al-baḥth*) 61
Seventeenth-Century Ottoman Contributions to *Ādāb al-baḥth* 70
Ādāb al-baḥth and Relational Syllogisms 85

3 The Rise of "Deep Reading" 97
Traditional Manuals on the Acquisition of Knowledge 99
Ādāb al-baḥth and "The Proprieties of Reading" 106
Müneccimbāşī on "the Proprieties of Reading" 109
Sāçaḳlīzāde on the Acquisition of Knowledge 115

Deep Reading and Textual Criticism 120
Ottoman Education and the Ideal of Deep Reading 125
Conclusion 128

PART II: SAVING SERVANTS FROM THE YOKE OF IMITATION

4 Maghrebī "Theologian-Logicians" in Egypt and the Hejaz 131
Maghrebī Logicians in Egypt 131
The Seventeenth-Century Efflorescence in the Maghreb 147
Four Maghrebī Scholars in the East 153
The End of an Era 170

5 The Condemnation of Imitation (*Taqlīd*) 173
Sanūsī on Imitation (*Taqlīd*) 175
Sanūsī's Influence in the East 188
Sanūsī-Inspired Creedal Works 193
A Forgotten Chapter in Islamic Religious History 200

6 al-Ḥasan al-Yūsī and Two Theological Controversies in Seventeenth-Century Morocco 204
The Controversy Concerning the "Imitator" (*Muqallid*) 204
Ḥasan al-Yūsī's Defense of Logic 215
Ḥasan al-Yūsī on the Controversy Concerning the Islamic Profession of Faith 221
Epilogue: Zabīdī's Criticism 230

PART III: THE IMAMS OF THOSE WHO PROCLAIM THE UNITY OF EXISTENCE

7 The Spread of Mystical Monism 235
Sixteenth-Century Arab Sufi Scholars on Ibn ʿArabī 237
The Shaṭṭārī Order in the Hejaz 249
The Naqshbandī Order in the Hejaz and Syria 257
The Khalwatī Order in Syria 261
Conclusion 270

8 Monist Mystics and Neo-Ḥanbalī Traditionalism 272
Kūrānī on Figurative Interpretation (*Taʾwīl*) 275
Kūrānī and Nābulusī on the Value of Rational Theology (*Kalām*) 285
Kūrānī and Nābulusī on Occasionalism and Human Acts 294
Conclusion 305

9 In Defense of *Waḥdat al-Wujūd* 312
Taftāzānī's Criticism of *Waḥdat al-Wujūd* 313
Kūrānī's Defense of *Waḥdat al-Wujūd* 320

Nābulusī's Defense of *Waḥdat al-Wujūd* 332
Conclusion 344
Conclusion 347

References 363
Index 391

Figures, Maps, and Tables

Map of the Near East *page* 12

Beginning of a manuscript of Jalāl al-Dīn al-Dawānī's *Risāla fī ithbāt al-wājib* with a commentary by Mullā Ḥanafī Tabrīzī (fl. 1516) and a gloss by Mīrzā Jān Bāghnavī (d. 1586), copied in Mardin in 1042/1632 by the Kurdish scholar ʿAbd al-Raḥmān b. Ibrāhīm Āmidī (d. 1656) 123

Map of the Maghreb 130

Title page of Egyptian manuscript, dated 1137/1724, of al-Ḥasan al-Yūsī's gloss on Sanūsī's handbook on logic. A note by a later hand indicates where in the manuscript readers will find the discussion of the ten Aristotelian categories 146

Autograph certificate by Muḥammad al-Rūdānī, dated 1083/1673, to the Damascene scholar Ibrāhīm Ibn al-Naqīb al-Ḥusaynī (d. 1708) 167

Map of India and Arabia 234

Autograph certificate by Ibrāhīm Kūrānī, dated 1089/1678, to the Damascene Ḥanbalī scholar ʿAbd al-Qādir al-Taghlibī (d. 1723), written on the title page of a manuscript copy of Kūrānī's *Maslak al-sadād fī masʾalat khalq afʿāl al-ʿibād* 308

Autograph dedication by Kūrānī to the Damascene Ḥanbalī scholar Abū l-Mawāhib al-Ḥanbalī (d. 1714), written on the title page of a manuscript copy of Kūrānī's postscript to his *Maslak al-sadād fī masʾalat khalq afʿāl al-ʿibād* 309

Acknowledgments

The greater part of the present book was drafted while I was a Fellow of the Wissenschaftskolleg zu Berlin in the academic year 2011–2012. I would like to thank that wonderful institution for its support, and for providing me with an ideal environment in which to ponder, research, and write. I am also grateful to Harvard University for granting me a sabbatical leave in that year, thus allowing me to accept the fellowship in Berlin.

While working on the book, I benefited greatly from discussions with (in alphabetical order): Shahab Ahmed, Michael Cook, Patricia Crone, Edhem Eldem, Th. Emil Homerin, Cemal Kafadar, Roy Mottahedeh, Reza Pourjavady, Adam Sabra, and Himmet Taşkömür. Michael Cook and an anonymous reader for Cambridge University Press kindly agreed to read the entire manuscript in draft and saved me from a number of factual errors and stylistic infelicities.

I would also like to extend my thanks to Marigold Acland of Cambridge University Press for initial encouragement, and to William Hammell and Kate Gavino, also of Cambridge, for seeing the manuscript through the later stages of review and production.

The images from manuscripts that appear in this book are reproduced with the kind permission of Princeton University Library. Chapter 3 of the present work is a revised and expanded version of my contribution to K. Chang, B. Elman, and S. Pollock (eds.), *World Philologies* (Harvard University Press, 2015), 201–224. I thank Harvard University Press for permission to reprint that contribution in revised and expanded form. Brill kindly granted me permission to use excerpts from my article "The Myth of the Triumph of Fanaticism in the Seventeenth-Century Ottoman

Empire," *Die Welt des Islams* 48(2008): 196–221. Cambridge University Press kindly granted me permission to use excerpts from my article "Opening the Gate of Verification: The Forgotten Arab-Islamic Florescence of the Seventeenth Century," *International Journal of Middle East Studies* 38(2006): 263–281.

I am greatly indebted to the Turkish Ministry of Culture for allowing me to access their online collection of digitized manuscripts (www.yazmalar.gov.tr). I am equally indebted to the curators/directors and staff of the Rare Books and Special Collections division of Princeton University Library, of Süleymaniye Kütüphanesı in Istanbul, and of the Orientabteilung of the Berlin Staatsbibliothek for graciously allowing me access to their invaluable manuscript collections.

My research assistants Caitlyn Olson and Shahrad Shahvand provided valuable assistance with the preparation of the manuscript. My wife Manja Klemenčič offered her support and encouragement throughout, from the earliest stages of thinking through the basic idea of the book to the final submission of the manuscript.

Note on Transliteration, Dates, and Translations

I have followed the transliteration system of the *Journal of Islamic Studies* for Arabic, Persian, and Ottoman Turkish respectively, with one exception: for Ottoman Turkish I use Ḫ/ḫ (instead of H/h) to render the letter خ.

One obvious problem in a book such as this is how to transliterate personal names. Adopting a single transliteration system (say Arabic or Turkish) for all scholars of the period is both unsatisfactory and offensive to modern national sensibilities. I have instead elected to follow the Arabic transliteration system for Arabic-speaking scholars from North Africa, Arabia, and the Levant; the Ottoman Turkish transliteration system for Turkish-speaking scholars from Anatolia, southeastern Europe, and Crimea; and the Persian transliteration system for Kurdish, Persian, and Indo-Muslim scholars. My solution to the problem may not be to the liking of all, and there will be liminal cases where it is admittedly arbitrary (e.g., the case of a scholar born in Herat but active most of his adult life in the Hejaz, or a Kurdish scholar who was active mostly in Istanbul). But I can think of no other solution that avoids unsatisfactory transliterations such as "Abdülġanī Nāblusī" or "Muḥammad al-Sājaqlīzāda."

I have retained the Arabic transliteration system for scholars active before the establishment of the Ottoman, Safavid, and Mughal Empires, regardless of ethnicity. I have retained the Ottoman Turkish rendering of epithets such as "Çelebī" and "Efendī," not varying the spelling when these are used of Arabic- or Kurdish-speaking scholars. In a few cases, a scholar's name is already widely used in the secondary literature in a form that does not correspond to a strict application of these transliteration rules. In such cases I have retained the more familiar form, for example, Ibrāhīm Kūrānī (not Gūrānī), Shāh Waliyullāh (not Valiyullāh), and Muḥammad ʿAbduh (not ʿAbdu). I have not transliterated terms that are already widely used in English, such as Quran, hadith, madrasa, Sufi, Sunni, Shiite, and Hejaz.

Especially in cases of very common names such as "Muḥammad" and "Aḥmad" I have sometimes added the father's name to facilitate the proper identification of a person. In such cases, I have used a simple "b." for *ibn* ("son of"). I have retained the full "Ibn" only when it is followed by the name of a more distant ancestor, the construction "Ibn X" functioning in such cases as a family name that is passed on through the generations, as in the case of "Ibn ʿArabī," "Ibn Taymiyya," and "Ibn Khaldūn."

I have in the main given all dates according to the Gregorian calendar only. In a few cases, especially in footnotes discussing the dates of manuscripts, I have given the date according to both the Islamic calendar and the Gregorian, thus: "Hijri date/Gregorian date." A year in the Hijri calendar will usually begin in one Gregorian year and end in the following year. Unless the source also gives the month of the year, I have given the Hijri date followed by the two Gregorian years that it spans, for example, 1078/1667–1668.

All translations are my own unless otherwise indicated.

Introduction

Dominant narratives of Islamic intellectual history have tended to be unkind to the seventeenth century in the Ottoman Empire and North Africa. Three independent narratives of "decline" – an Ottomanist, an Arabist, and an Islamist – have converged on deprecating the period as either a sad epilogue to an earlier Ottoman florescence or a dark backdrop to the later Arab "renaissance" and Islamic "revival." Until recently, Ottomanists typically located the heyday of Ottoman cultural and intellectual achievement in the fifteenth and sixteenth centuries. After the death of Süleymān the Magnificent in 1566, the Empire was supposed to have entered a period of long decline that affected both its political-military fortunes and its cultural-intellectual output.[1] Scholars of Arabic literature and thought were inclined to view the seventeenth century as yet another bleak chapter of cultural, intellectual, and societal "decadence" (*inḥiṭāṭ*) that began with the sacking of Baghdad by the Mongols in 1258 and came to an end only with the "Arab awakening" of the nineteenth and twentieth centuries.[2] Historians who study self-styled Islamic

[1] For classic statements of this view, see Halil İnalcık, *The Ottoman Empire: The Classical Age, 1300–1600* (London: Weidenfeld & Nicholson, 1973), 179–185, and S. J. Shaw, *History of the Ottoman Empire and Modern Turkey, Vol. 1: Empire of the Gazis: The Rise and Decline of the Ottoman Empire, 1280–1808* (Cambridge: Cambridge University Press, 1976), 169ff.

[2] A classic statement of this view is R. Nicholson, *A Literary History of the Arabs* (Cambridge: Cambridge University Press, 1930), 442ff. For more recent reiterations, see G. El-Shayyal, "Some Aspects of Intellectual and Social Life in Eighteenth-Century Egypt," in P. M. Holt (ed.), *Political and Social Change in Modern Egypt* (Oxford: Oxford University Press, 1968), 117–132, and P. M. Holt, "The Later Ottoman Empire in Egypt and the Fertile Crescent," in P. M. Holt, A. K. Lambton, and B. Lewis (eds.), *The Cambridge History of Islam* (Cambridge: Cambridge University Press, 1977), I, 374–393.

"reformist" and "revivalist" movements of the eighteenth and nineteenth centuries have often portrayed the immediately preceding centuries as marked by unthinking scholarly "imitation" (*taqlīd*), crude Sufi pantheism, and "syncretic" and idolatrous popular religious practices.[3]

To be sure, such assessments are no longer accepted unquestioningly in academic circles. But their influence is still felt in the woefully underdeveloped state of research into the intellectual history of the seventeenth century in the Ottoman Empire and North Africa. The tide is turning, though, and recent years have seen a number of valuable monographs, doctoral dissertations, and editions of scholarly works.[4] The present book is intended as a contribution to the ongoing reassessment of the period. Its focus is on a number of hitherto unnoticed intellectual trends among the scholarly elite – the *ulema* – in the Ottoman Empire and North Africa in the seventeenth century. Though the *ulema* are mentioned in almost any history of the period, our knowledge of their intellectual preoccupations is still much more meager than our knowledge of their institutional contexts and their potential political role as intermediaries between rulers and ruled.[5] This gap in our knowledge has tended to be reinforced by a number of factors. Most scholarly writings by seventeenth-century Ottoman *ulema* are in Arabic (not Turkish) and tend to be dense and technical – neither characteristic endearing them to Ottomanists. Modern historians have also tended to assume that the interests of the Ottoman *ulema* were by the seventeenth century quite narrow (largely confined to Islamic law, Quran exegesis, and grammar), and that their writings overwhelmingly consisted of unoriginal and pedantic commentaries

3 This view forms an important part of the rhetoric of Muslim self-styled reformers such as Muḥammad ʿAbduh (d. 1905), Muḥammad Rashīd Riḍā (d. 1935), and Muḥammad Iqbāl (d. 1938). Two influential expositions of it are to be found in Abū l-Ḥasan Nadwī's *Mādhā khasira al-ʿālam bi-inḥiṭāṭ al-muslimīn*, first printed in 1950 and going through numerous reprints, and Aḥmad Amīn's *Zuʿamāʾ al-iṣlāḥ fī l-ʿaṣr al-ḥadīth*, first printed in 1948 and also frequently reprinted. A more sophisticated expression of the view is to be found in Fazlur Rahman, *Islam* (1st ed., 1966; 2nd ed., 2002; Chicago: University of Chicago Press,), 196–211.

4 See, for example, the articles, monographs, or dissertations by Ralf Elger, Dina LeGall, Stefan Reichmuth, Derin Terzioglu, and Barbara von Schlegell listed in the bibliography; see also the editions of the works of Nābulusī, Yūsī, and Kūrānī by Samer Akkach, Bakri Aladdin, Oman Fathurahman, and Hamid Hammani.

5 For a good sense of recent scholarship on the Ottoman and North African *ulema*, see M. Zilfi, *The Politics of Piety: The Ottoman Ulema in the Postclassical Age (1600–1800)* (Minneapolis: Bibliotheca Islamica, 1988); D. Klein, *Die osmanischen Ulema des 17. Jahrhunderts: eine geschlossene Gesellschaft?* (Berlin: Klaus Schwartz, 2007); J. Hathaway, *The Arab Lands under Ottoman Rule, 1516–1800* (Harlow, UK: Pearson Education, 2008), 114–137, 262–266.

and glosses on earlier works –assumptions that have not exactly invited closer study.[6] Furthermore, intellectual history has itself been under something of a cloud in recent years. The tendency of historians of ideas to focus on the intellectual elite and to situate ideas in the context of other ideas (as opposed to social and political realities) is sometimes seen as unfashionable.[7] Many historians now prefer to explore new avenues of research untainted by suspicions of elitism and old fashion, for example, popular culture and mentalities. Some of this new research is impressive and very welcome.[8] Less welcome, I think, is an unintended consequence of this shift in academic focus. "High" intellectual life in the Ottoman Empire and North Africa largely remains unexplored territory. Resting satisfied with this state of affairs and simply shifting research to other topics risks reinforcing the impression that on one side of the Mediterranean in the seventeenth century one encounters Galileo, Kepler, Bacon, Newton, Descartes, Malebranche, Spinoza, Locke, and Leibniz, whereas on the other side one encounters popular chroniclers, Sufi diarists, popularizers of medical or occult knowledge, and the like. Studies of popular chroniclers, Sufi diarists, and popularizers of medical or occult knowledge are of course most welcome, but the present book is written with the assumption that there is still a legitimate place for the study of the ideas, issues, and controversies that preoccupied the "academics" of the period.

6 For a clear expression of this view, see Ali Uğur, *The Ottoman Ulema in the Mid-17th Century: An Analysis of the Vekāʾiʿ ül-fużalā of Meḥmed Şeyḫī Efendī* (Berlin: Klaus Schwarz Verlag, 1986), lxxii–lxxiii. The intellectual preoccupations of the post-sixteenth century Ottoman *ulema* are still routinely depicted as having been narrow and dogmatic by comparison to their Safavid and Mughal colleagues; see, e.g., F. Robinson, "Ottomans-Safavids-Mughals: Shared Knowledge and Connective Systems," *Journal of Islamic Studies* 8(1997): 151–184, esp. 155ff. and 172; S. F. Dale, *The Muslim Empires of the Ottomans, Safavids, and Mughals* (Cambridge: Cambridge University Press, 2010), 196.

7 See the editors' introduction to D. M. McMahon & S. Moyn (eds.), *Rethinking Modern European Intellectual History* (Oxford and New York: Oxford University Press, 2014), 4–5. See also the thoughtful discussion by D. M. McMahon in his contribution to that volume: "The Return of the History of Ideas?" 13–31, esp. 15–21.

8 See, e.g., L. Berger, *Gesellschaft und Individuum in Damaskus, 1550–1791* (Würzburg: Ergon, 2007); J. Grehan, *Everyday Life & Consumer Culture in 18th-Century Damascus* (Seattle and London: University of Washington Press, 2007); N. Hanna, *In Praise of Books: A Cultural History of Cairo's Middle Class, Sixteenth to the Eighteenth Century* (Syracuse, NY: Syracuse University Press, 2003); C. Kafadar, "Self and Others: The Diary of a Dervish in Seventeenth Century Istanbul and First-Person Narratives in Ottoman Literature," *Studia Islamica* (1989): 121–150; D. Sajdi, *The Barber of Damascus: Nouveau Literacy in the Eighteenth Century Ottoman Levant* (Stanford: Stanford University Press, 2013).

The book is divided into three parts, each consisting of three chapters. The first part deals with the influx into the Ottoman Empire of scholars from the Kurdish and Azeri areas, in part due to the conquest of these areas by the Shiite Safavids under Shah ʿAbbās I (r. 1588–1629). This westward movement seems to have had a profound impact on Ottoman scholarly culture. Contemporary observers spoke of the "opening of the gate of verification," the introduction of new works and teaching techniques, and the reinvigoration of the study of the rational and philosophical sciences. Two consequences are explored in some detail: the first is the explosion of interest in the science of dialectics (*ādāb al-baḥth*) among Ottoman scholars from the seventeenth century; the second is the closely related rise of conscious reflection on the proper manner of perusing scholarly books (*ādāb al-muṭālaʿa*).

Part II deals with the eastward movement of scholars and works from the Maghreb, connected both to the turmoil in Morocco that followed the collapse of the Saʿdid dynasty in 1603 and to the institution of the Hajj which brought North African scholars eastward, some settling in Egypt or the Hejaz. Again, this development had significant consequences. It led to the spread of the influence of the fifteenth-century North African scholar Muḥammad b. Yūsuf al-Sanūsī (d. 1490), whose works came to dominate the teaching of theology and logic in the Azhar college in Cairo from the seventeenth century to the end of the nineteenth. One of the hallmarks of this tradition is that it insisted on the inadequacy of "imitation" (*taqlīd*) as a basis for assent to the Islamic creed and instead stressed the necessity for the "verification" (*taḥqīq*) of the creed through demonstrative argument. This in turn led to the writing of creedal works explicitly aimed at nonscholars, conveying the amount of rational theology (*kalām*) that every believer should know. Another characteristic of this tradition was an enthusiasm for logic (*manṭiq*) and an extensive use of logical concepts and argument forms in the field of rational theology – leading one eighteenth-century observer to complain of the predominance in Cairo in his time of what he called "theologian-logicians" (*al-mutakallimīn al-manāṭiqa*).

Part III deals with the spread of Sufi orders from India and Azerbaijan into the Arabic-speaking areas of the Near East in the seventeenth century. This development led to the strengthening of the influence of the idea of "the unity of existence" (*waḥdat al-wujūd*) associated with the followers of Ibn ʿArabī (d. 1240) – an idea that until then had enjoyed little support from members of the *ulema* class in Syria, Hejaz, and Egypt. This led to the weakening of the hold of Ashʿarī and Māturīdī theology in these areas and to the reassertion of more "traditionalist," near-Ḥanbalī positions on a range of core theological issues. Paradoxical as it may sound, seventeenth-century supporters of mystical monism seem to have played an important role in rehabilitating the ideas of the Ḥanbalī thinker Ibn Taymiyya (d. 1328), for centuries an object of suspicion or neglect on the part of Ashʿarī and Māturīdī theologians.

Some of the better-known scholars of the seventeenth century, such as Aḥmed Müneccimbāşī (d. 1702), al-Ḥasan al-Yūsī (d. 1691), Ibrāhīm Kūrānī (d. 1690), and ʿAbd al-Ghanī al-Nābulusī (1641–1731), feature prominently in the pages that follow. But my aim has been to discuss them as representatives of larger intellectual trends within the *ulema* class in their time, not as heroic figures who somehow managed to stand out in an otherwise bleak century. After all, even older studies that perpetuated the image of seventeenth-century intellectual stagnation or decline were sometimes prepared to admit that there were "exceptions."[9] More recent scholarly literature has not succeeded in properly laying this idea to rest; indeed it has often succumbed to the temptation to underline the importance of an individual figure by portraying his background and opponents in dark colors.[10] The list of "exceptions" has simply become too long for the idea to be taken seriously: Aḥmad al-Maqqarī, al-Ḥasan al-Yūsī, Yaḥyā al-Shāwī, and Muḥammad al-Rūdānī in the Maghreb; Ibrāhīm Kūrānī and his student Muḥammad Barzinjī in Medina; ʿAbd al-Qādir al-Baghdādī in Cairo; Khayr al-Dīn al-Ramlī in Palestine; Qāsim al-Khānī in Aleppo; ʿAbd al-Ghanī al-Nābulusī in Damascus; Aḥmed Müneccimbāşī, Ḳara Ḫalīl Tīrevī, and Meḥmed Sāçaḳlīzāde in Ottoman Turkey; Muṣṭafā Mōstārī in Bosnia; and Aḥmad Ḥusaynābādī and his son Ḥaydar Ḥusaynābādī in the Kurdish

9 For example, in H. A. R. Gibb and H. Bowen, *Islamic Society and the West* (London and New York: Oxford University Press, 1957), ʿAbd al-Ghanī al-Nābulusī is conceded to have been an "exception" in an age of "compilation and imitation" (Vol. 1, part II, 164). In J. Spencer Trimingham's *The Sufi Orders in Islam* (first published in 1971; 2nd ed. New York and Oxford: Oxford University Press, 1998), Nābulusī is said to have been "among the few original writers within the Arab sphere" (70) and "one of the few Arab Sufis of the age who possessed any insight" (95).

10 For example, Muḥammad al-Ḥajjī has portrayed Muhammad al-Rūdānī as a lone genius in a civilization that had passed its prime and descended into "ignorance" and "resignation"; see the introduction to his edition of Rūdānī's *Ṣilat al-khalaf bi-mawṣūl al-salaf* (Beirut: Dār al-Gharb al-Islāmī, 1988), 13. Similarly, Ibrāhīm Kūrānī has recently been portrayed as a "revivalist" in an age marked by "extremist" Sufism and "trivialized ulema discourse" that "could no longer go any further"; see B. Nafi, "Taṣawwuf and Reform in Pre-Modern Islamic Culture: In Search of Ibrāhīm al-Kūrānī," *Die Welt des Islams* 42(2002): 307–355.

regions.[11] It is high time to stop expanding the list of purported "exceptions" and to embark instead on an overall reappraisal of the period. What follows is an attempt to contribute toward this task. The three developments that I discuss are of course not exhaustive of the intellectual concerns of seventeenth-century *ulema* in the Ottoman Empire and North Africa. Nevertheless, they should hopefully be sufficient to belie received views of the seventeenth century as intellectually barren or stagnant, passively awaiting "revival" and "reform," and encourage further research on a rich intellectual tradition that has been overlooked for too long.

Each of the three parts of the book opens with a chapter that traces scholarly lineages and the diffusion of works based on contemporary biographical and bibliographical sources. In each case, this is followed by chapters that discuss the contents of illustrative works belonging to the intellectual trends in question: on dialectic, on the proper manner of reading, on rational theology, and on mystical metaphysics. Some of these works are dense and technical, and the chapters that discuss their contents will to some extent have to engage with this density and technicality – this is simply unavoidable in any serious probing of the intellectual life of the *ulema*. Members of this group underwent years of arduous training in a range of scholarly disciplines, and their concerns were often abstruse and highbrow – not less so than those of present-day academics in the humanities and non-applied sciences. To recover these concerns means not glossing over the contents of their works or treating them simply as epiphenomena of social context or political structures. It is all very well to complain that intellectual historians treat ideas as if they were divorced from institutional, social, and economic realities.[12] But such worries seem

11 Most of these figures will be discussed to some extent in the chapters that follow. Those who will not be discussed are the literary scholar ʿAbd al-Qādir al-Baghdādī, the jurist Khayr al-Dīn al-Ramlī, and the logician Muṣṭafā Mōstārī. For the first of these figures, see M.G. Carter, "al-Baghdādī, ʿAbd al-Qādir b. ʿUmar," in J. E. Lowry and D. Stewart (eds.), *Essays in Arabic Literary Biography, 1350–1850* (Wiesbaden: Otto Harrassowitz, 2009), 69–77. For the second figure, see H. Gerber, "Rigidity versus Openness in Late Classical Islamic Law: The Case of the Seventeenth-Century Palestinian Muftī Khayr al-Dīn al-Ramlī," *Islamic Law & Society* 5 (1998): 165–195. For the third figure, see A. Ljubovic, *The Works in Logic by Bosniac Authors in Arabic* (Leiden, the Netherlands: Brill, 2008), 36–48.

12 The complaint is made by David Gutelius in his valuable "Sufi Networks and the Social Context of Scholarship in Morocco and the Northern Sahara, 1660–1830," in S. Reese (ed.), *The Transmission of Learning in Islamic Africa* (Leiden, the Netherlands: Brill, 2004), 15–38, at 15. I have learned a good deal from Gutelius' work and I see our approaches as complementary rather than opposed. I agree that attention to social and

misplaced when we know much more about the institutional, social, and economic realities than about the ideas. It is hardly controversial to point out that the study of the institutional, social, and economic history of the Ottoman Empire is significantly more developed than the study of its intellectual history. The more pressing danger, as I see it, is the tendency to think that the study of social, political, and institutional context somehow makes the close study of scholarly works superfluous – that intellectual history can simply be read off social and institutional history.[13]

Two aspects of the present book may occasion some surprise or concern. One is that there will be next to no discussion of Islamic law or jurisprudence.[14] Surely, one might object, those two fields were a major concern of the ulema class. The response to this is twofold: First, as already mentioned, I do not pretend that this book is an exhaustive survey of the intellectual history of the period. Second, it is precisely one of the points of the book that the question of "stagnation" and "decline" in Islamic intellectual history has unhelpfully tended to be associated with the development (or lack of development) of Islamic law and specifically with the question of *ijtihād* – whether "the gate of *ijtihād*" was closed or remained open (or at least slightly ajar). This focus has, or so I would suggest, tended to elide the centrality of the ideal of "verification" (*taḥqīq*) for premodern Islamic scholarly culture.[15] To put it bluntly, *ijtihād* – the derivation of legal rulings directly from the acknowledged sources of Islamic law without being bound by legal precedent – was of little or no import for logicians, dialecticians, mathematicians, astronomers,

economic context can enrich our understanding of Islamic intellectual history. I merely argue that close attention to the contents of scholarly works is also legitimate, and that there has been a tendency not to do so when it comes to Ottoman and North African intellectual history in the early-modern period.

13 For two studies of early modern Islamic scholars that focus on political and social context while largely avoiding any in-depth engagement with the contents of scholarly works, see J. Berque, *Al-Yousi: Problèmes de la culture marocaine au XVIIème siècle* (Paris: Mouton, 1958) and P. Gran, *The Islamic Roots of Capitalism, Egypt 1760–1840* (1st ed., 1979; 2nd ed., 1998 Syracuse, NY: Syracuse University Press). Both studies are unreliable when it comes to the intellectual context within which their central characters (al-Ḥasan al-Yūsī and Ḥasan al-ʿAṭṭār respectively) operated.

14 For an important study showing the dynamism of Islamic legal thinking in this period, see Haim Gerber, *Islamic Law & Culture, 1600–1840* (Leiden, the Netherlands: Brill, 1999).

15 This point has also been made, from a somewhat different perspective, by William Chittick in his *Science of the Cosmos, Science of the Soul: The Pertinence of Islamic Cosmology in the Modern World* (Oxford: Oneworld, 2007).

grammarians, theologians, philosophers, and mystics. Even if one were to assume, for the sake of argument, that the "gate of *ijtihād*" was in fact closed, this would tell us nothing about the dynamism or stagnation of nonlegal fields of Islamic scholarship.

The present book also eschews the use of terms such as "enlightenment" and "humanism." The study of Islamic and Ottoman intellectual life in the early modern period has been stimulated by the works of Reinhardt Schultze and Stefan Reichmuth – scholars who have contributed toward the rising interest in this period within the field of Islamic Studies.[16] Nevertheless, their deployment of Western historical concepts such as "enlightenment" and "humanism" to characterize Islamic intellectual traditions in the seventeenth and eighteenth centuries must, I think, be rejected. To apply with even a minimum of plausibility to the Islamic early modern period, the meanings of such terms have to be stretched to such an extent that they arguably become devoid of historical content and become free-floating "ideas" not associated with any particular region or period. Any emphasis on the need for critical reflection on received views or any rhetoric of praise for novelty and individual "illumination" is equated with "enlightenment"; any concern with letter-writing, collating manuscripts, and polymathy is equated with "humanism"; any fideist rejection of rationalist or mystical speculation is equated with "pietism," and so on. Furthermore, the whole enterprise of attempting to capture a "zeitgeist" seems highly questionable, especially at a time when European historians are stressing the heterogeneity of intellectual and cultural pursuits in the early modern period and hence rethinking the usefulness of terms such as "the enlightenment" and "the scientific revolution."[17] Even apart from this point, the broad characterizations involved in speaking of an early modern Islamic "enlightenment" or "humanism" must surely be premature given just how little the period has been studied. In light of all this, it seems better to leave aside stimulating but overhasty attempts at capturing the age by a few "isms" imported from Western European historiography, and to start afresh by focusing on a number of intellectual

[16] R. Schultze, "Das islamischen achtzehnte jahrhundert" *Die Welt des Islams* 30(1990): 140–159; R. Schultze, "Was ist die islamischen Aufklärung?"*Die Welt des Islams* 36(1996): 276–325; S. Reichmuth, *The World of Murtaḍā al-Zabīdī (1732–1791): Life, Networks and Writings* (Oxford: Bibb Memorial Trust, 2009).

[17] See, e.g., S. Shapin, *The Scientific Revolution* (Chicago: University of Chicago Press, 1996) and J. G. A. Pocock, *Barbarism and Religion, Volume One: The Enlightenments of Edward Gibbon 1737–1764* (Cambridge: Cambridge University Press, 1999), 1–10.

currents and works, and describing these as far as possible in a language that would have been recognizable to the scholars whose outlook we as historians seek to understand. Once reasonably grounded narratives of the intellectual history of the period have been established, it may be fruitful to go further and ask comparative and "global" questions.[18] But to let research in the fledgling field of Ottoman and North African intellectual history be guided from the outset by the desire to relate it to the much more advanced field of European intellectual history is sure to lead to lopsided emphases and tendentious readings of the sources.[19] Instead of genuinely developing our sketchy knowledge of the intellectual history of the period, we would be stuck in a situation that development theorists once referred to as "the development of underdevelopment."

Having said this, preliminary methodological discussions and polemics will not take us far. At the end of the day, a historical approach is vindicated if it yields accounts of the past that are deemed instructive and

[18] For "global intellectual history," which has generated some excitement in recent years, see S. Moyn and A. Sartori (eds.), *Global Intellectual History* (New York: Columbia University Press, 2013).

[19] For example, in an otherwise informative and stimulating monograph on ʿAbd al-Ghanī al-Nābulusī, Samer Akkach interprets Nābulusī's rejection of the idea of the soul as an immaterial substance as an "anti-Cartesian" position even though Islamic theologians routinely – at least since Ghazali's *The Incoherence of the Philosophers* in the eleventh century – rejected the idea of the soul as an immaterial substance (associating it with heresies such as the denial of bodily resurrection and belief in the transmigration of souls). There is no reason to think that Nābulusī had ever heard of Descartes. Akkach also attributes to Nābulusī a concern with safeguarding the "relative autonomy of natural processes" and "the predictability inherent in the consistency and uniformity of natural laws," invoking a treatise by Nābulusī that defends the appropriateness of attributing effects to worldly causes in everyday speech (even though strictly speaking only God is believed to have causal powers). But the purpose of Nābulusī's treatise was explicitly to defend saint and grave veneration against purist attacks. He wished to establish that it is not idolatrous in everyday situations to say, "Visiting the shrine of so-and-so conferred such-and-such a benefit." As will become clear in Chapters 8 and 9 of the present study, Nābulusī was an occasionalist and panentheist and he would not have agreed that "natural processes" are "autonomous" in any interesting sense of that word, and there is no reason to think that the issue of the "consistency and uniformity of natural laws" was at stake in the controversies in which he was involved. These concerns are simply read into the text by Akkach in his eagerness to draw parallels between Ottoman and Western European intellectual concerns; see S. Akkach, *ʿAbd al-Ghanī al-Nābulusī: Islam and the Enlightenment* (Oxford: Oneworld Publications, 2007), 86–88, 99. For a similar critique of Akkach's reading, see J. Stearns, "All Beneficial Knowledge is Revealed: The Rational Sciences in the Maghrib in the Age of al-Yūsī (d.1102/1691)," *Islamic Law and Society* 21 (2014): 49-80, at 66–72, 79–80.

worthwhile. To put it more proverbially, "the proof of the pudding is in the eating." The chapters that follow are themselves my main argument for taking the intellectual preoccupations of seventeenth-century Ottoman and North African *ulema* seriously, on their own terms.[20]

[20] My project is very much in the spirit of Benjamin Elman's call for studying early modern Chinese scientists and scholars "on their own terms rather than speculate about why they did not accomplish what the Europeans did"; see his *On Their Own Terms: Science in China, 1550–1900* (Cambridge, MA: Harvard University Press, 2005), xxvi.

PART I

"THE PATH OF THE KURDISH AND PERSIAN VERIFYING SCHOLARS"

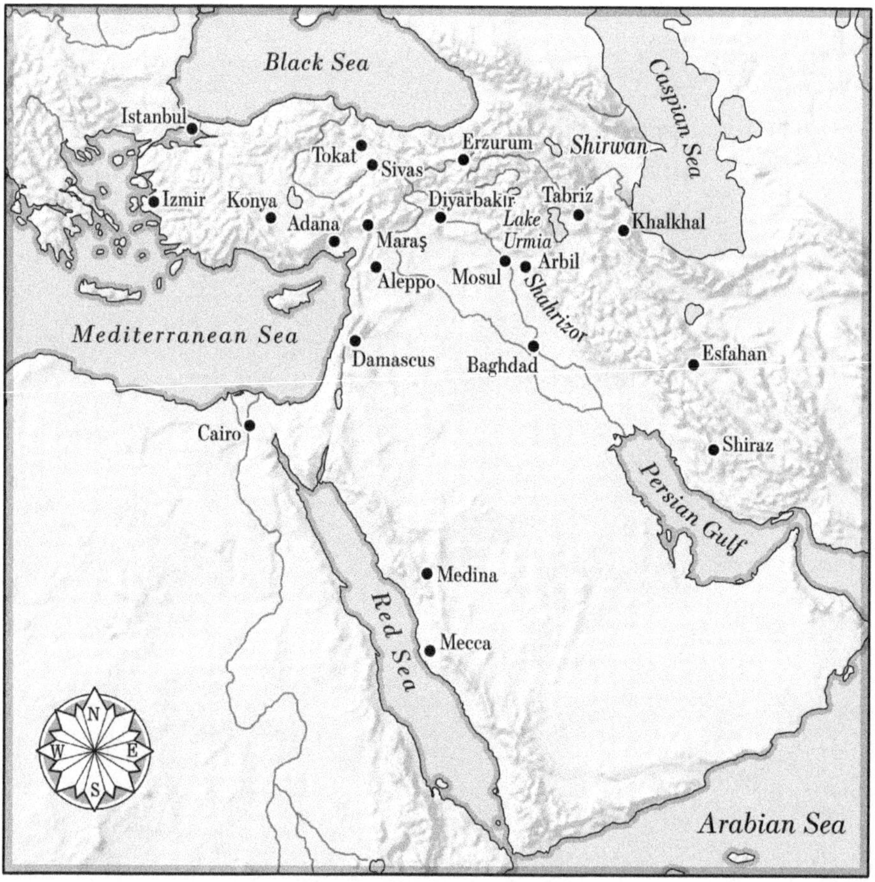

Map of the Near East

1

Kurdish Scholars and the Reinvigoration of the Rational Sciences

Since at least the early 1970s, the prevalent view among historians has been that the Ottoman tradition of studying the rational sciences came to an end in the seventeenth century. This development (which has been dubbed "the triumph of fanaticism") was thought to have been a consequence of the violently puritan Ḳāḍīzādelī movement, named after the fiery preacher Meḥmed Ḳāḍīzāde (d. 1635) and inspired by the ideas of the uncompromisingly strict religious scholar Meḥmed Birgevī (d. 1573).[1] The truth of the matter, or so I argue in this chapter, is very different. The "rational sciences" were cultivated vigorously in the Ottoman Empire throughout the seventeenth and eighteenth centuries. An important transformation in Ottoman scholarly life did indeed occur in the first half of the seventeenth century, but this had nothing to do with a suppression of the rational sciences by fanatical Ḳāḍīzādelīs. It was rather that works on philosophy, logic, dialectics, rational theology, semantics, rhetoric, and grammar by Persian scholars of the fifteenth and sixteenth centuries began to be studied intensively in Ottoman scholarly circles during this period. At first, such works were taught by Azeri and Kurdish scholars who made an impression on local scholars with their mastery of the "books of the Persians" and their manner of lecturing that heeded the discipline of dialectic. Ottoman scholarly culture was profoundly influenced by this development. From around the middle of

[1] An influential expression of this view is in Halil İnalcık, *The Ottoman Empire: The Classical Age, 1300–1600*, 179–185. İnalcık's view is followed by Marshall Hodgson, *The Venture of Islam* (Chicago: Chicago University Press, 1974), III, 123, and by Francis Robinson, "Ottomans-Safavids-Mughals: Shared Knowledge and Connective Systems," *Journal of Islamic Studies* 8 (1997): 151–184, esp. 155ff., 172.

the seventeenth century to the end of the Empire in the early twentieth, it seems to have been the norm for Ottoman Turkish scholars to trace their intellectual pedigree back to scholars who had been involved in this transformation in the first half of the seventeenth century.

The Myth of the "Triumph of Fanaticism"

The evidence presented for the "triumph of fanaticism" thesis consists in (1) the appearance of the violently puritan Ḳāḍīzādelī movement toward the end of the sixteenth century; (2) the destruction of the Istanbul observatory in 1580, just a few years after its construction; and (3) remarks by the Ottoman scholar and judge Aḥmed Ṭāşköprīzāde (d. 1561) and the Ottoman scribe and bibliographer Kātib Çelebī (d. 1657) lamenting the declining interest in the rational sciences in their time. A closer look at this evidence will show that it is far from conclusive.

The Ḳāḍīzādelīs are described both by contemporaneous observers such as Kātib Çelebī and the historian Muṣṭafā Naʿīmā (d. 1716) and by more recent scholarship as constituting a minority within the class of Ottoman religious scholars.[2] In light of this, one should not simply assume that the appearance of the Ḳāḍīzādelīs meant a decline in all the practices of which the Ḳāḍīzādelīs disapproved. Furthermore, it is not even clear that the Ḳāḍīzādelīs were uniformly opposed to all the "rational sciences." Kātib Çelebī attributed to Meḥmed Ḳāḍīzāde lines such as "Who'd give a farthing for philosophy?" and "Who sheds a tear if a logician dies?" during his lectures.[3] But this may not have been a considered or uniform opinion in Ḳāḍīzādelī circles. Kātib Çelebī himself related that he had attended the lectures of Ḳāḍīzāde on, among other things, the commentary of al-Sayyid al-Sharīf al-Jurjānī (d. 1413) on *al-Mawāqif*, a summa of rational theology by ʿAḍud al-Dīn al-Ījī (d. 1355), more than half of which is devoted to a thorough and dispassionate discussion of topics such as the ten Aristotelian categories, essence and existence, the nature of time and space, and the cosmology of the Islamic philosophers.[4]

[2] Madeleine Zilfi, *The Politics of Piety: The Ottoman Ulema in the Post-Classical Age, 1600–1800*, chapter 4, esp. 190; G. L. Lewis (trans.), *The Balance of Truth by Kātib Chelebī* (London: George Allen & Unwin, 1957), 137 ("It is unnecessary to point out that the followers of Qâdîzâde at the present time are notorious for their extremism and have earned general reproach.")

[3] G. L. Lewis (trans.), *The Balance of Truth*, 136.

[4] G. L. Lewis (trans.), *The Balance of Truth*, 136. More than half of *Sharḥ al-Mawāqif* is devoted to epistemology, metaphysics, and physics, with traditional creedal dogmatics

Kātib Çelebī also related in passing that he himself had taught mathematics and astronomy to the son of Aḥmed Rūmī Āḳḥīṣārī (d. 1632), a prominent early Ḳāḍīzādelī figure.[5] The later Ḳāḍīzādelī leader Vānī Meḥmed (d. 1685) was said by contemporary sources to have been well versed in the rational sciences.[6]

Hard evidence for Ḳāḍīzādelī hostility to all rational sciences is in fact surprisingly elusive and seems to be more of an assumption than a conclusion of historical research. Historians have tended to assume that the Ḳāḍīzādelīs were simply followers of the earlier Damascene Ḥanbalī scholar Ibn Taymiyya (d. 1328), and that one may therefore impute to them the latter's well-attested hostility to, for example, rational theology and logic.[7] There can be little doubt that on a range of issues the Ḳāḍīzādelīs were in agreement with Ibn Taymiyya and his disciple Ibn Qayyim al-Jawziyya (d. 1350): the condemnation of monistic Sufism, the opposition to the veneration of shrines, and the valorization of moralist activism. But these similarities do not preclude the existence of important differences. The sixteenth-century scholar Meḥmed Birgevī, whose legacy the Ḳāḍīzādelīs claimed to represent, was a staunch adherent of the Māturīdī school of rational theology, and he explicitly stated that anyone who claims that God is in the direction of "above" is an infidel (*kāfir*) and that anyone who claims that God's attributes undergo change is likewise an infidel.[8] The two positions that Birgevī considered to be tantamount to unbelief had been endorsed by Ibn

merely taking up approximately the last third of the work (see al-Sayyid al-Sharīf al-Jurjānī, *Sharḥ al-Mawāqif* (Istanbul: Maṭbaʿa-yi ʿĀmire, 1239/1824) or the numerous later editions).

5 G. L. Lewis (trans.), *The Balance of Truth*, 142. On Aḥmed Rūmī Āḳḥiṣārī, see the introduction to Yahya Michot (ed. and trans.), *Against Smoking: An Ottoman Manifesto* (Markfield, UK: Kube Publishing, 2010).

6 S. Çavuşoğlu, "The Ḳāḍīzādelīs: An Attempt at Şerīʿat-Minded Reform in the Ottoman Empire" (Unpublished PhD dissertation, Department of Near Eastern Studies, Princeton University, 1990), 155–156. Çavuşoğlu cites the near-contemporary biographers Uşāḳīzāde (d. 1724) and Şeyḫī (d. 1733).

7 The most detailed study of the Ḳāḍīzādelīs in English, S. Çavuşoğlu, "The Ḳāḍīzādelīs: An Attempt at Şerīʿat-Minded Reform in the Ottoman Empire," is pervaded by the assumption that the Ḳāḍīzādelīs were simply exponents of a timeless "Salafism" whose most prominent earlier advocates had been Ibn Ḥanbal (d. 855) and Ibn Taymiyya. Michot has also characterized the Ḳāḍīzādelīs as constituting a "Taymiyyan" school; see the introduction to his edition and translation of Aḥmed Rūmī Aḳḥiṣārī's tract against tobacco, *Against Smoking*.

8 Ḫādimī, Ebū Saʿīd, *Barīqa maḥmūdiyya fī sharḥ al-Ṭarīqa al-muḥammadiyya* (Cairo: Muṣṭafā al-Bābī al-Ḥalabī, 1348/1929–30), I, 113, 151–153.

Taymiyya.[9] In other words, Birgevī was committed to the view that Ibn Taymiyya's positions on a number of central theological issues were not only mistaken but also beyond the pale of Islam altogether. This had in fact been the explicit position of ʿAlāʾ al-Dīn al-Bukhārī (d. 1438), a Ḥanafī-Māturīdī scholar whose *Faḍīḥat al-mulḥidīn*, a lengthy and vituperative attack on the Andalusian mystic Ibn ʿArabī (d. 1240) and his followers, seems to have been widely read in Ḳāḍīzādelī circles (judging by the numerous manuscripts of the work that survive in Turkish libraries).[10] Bukhārī had in his day claimed that Ibn Taymiyya was an anthropomorphist and an infidel and that anyone who described him as "Shaykh al-Islām" was likewise an infidel.[11] This severe Māturīdī censure of Ḥanbalī theological positions was still current in the seventeenth and eighteenth centuries. The Ottoman scholar and judge of Istanbul Aḥmed Beyāżīzāde (d. 1687) was opposed to Sufi monism and played a leading role along with the Ḳāḍīzādelī leader Vānī Meḥmed in the notorious case of public stoning for adultery in Istanbul in 1680, but he nevertheless considered the Ḥanbalīs to be heretics who were outside the ranks of Sunni Islam (Sunnism for Beyāżīzāde being confined to Ashʿarīs and Māturīdīs).[12] The later Turkish scholar Dāvūd Ḳārṣī (fl. 1739–1755), a follower of Birgevī and a shrill critic of Sufi monism, expressed the same opinion concerning the Ḥanbalīs: they are "among the wayward sects" (*min al-firaq al-ḍālla*) and hence not Sunnis at all.[13] The position of Birgevī

[9] See K. El-Rouayheb, "From Ibn Hajar al-Haytami (d. 1566) to Khayr al-Din al-Alusi (d. 1899): Changing Views of Ibn Taymiyya amongst Sunni Islamic Scholars," in S. Ahmed and Y. Rapoport (eds.), *Ibn Taymiyya and His Times* (Karachi: Oxford University Press, 2010), 303–304.

[10] On Bukhārī's work, see the discussion by Bakri Aladdin in the introduction to his edition of ʿAbd al-Ghanī al-Nābulusī, *al-Wujūd al-ḥaqq* (Damascus: Institut Francais de Damas, 1995), 16–30. As shown by Aladdin, Bukhārī's work came to be misattributed to Saʿd al-Dīn al-Taftāzānī (d. 1390) and was printed in Istanbul in 1294/1877 as a work of Taftāzānī's in a collection entitled *Rasāʾil fī waḥdat al-wujūd*.

[11] Bukhārī's charge elicited a lengthy response by the Damascene scholar Ibn Nāṣir al-Dīn (d. 1438) entitled *al-Radd al-wāfir ʿalā man zaʿama anna man sammā Ibn Taymiyya Shaykh al-Islām kāfir*; see the edition of Z. al-Shāwīsh published by al-Maktab al-Islāmī in Damascus in 1393/1973–1974.

[12] Aḥmed Beyāżīzāde, *Ishārāt al-marām min ʿibārāt al-Imām*, ed. Yūsuf ʿAbd al-Razzāq (Cairo: Muṣṭafā al-Bābī al-Ḥalabī, 1949), 141ff. On the role of Beyāżīzāde and Meḥmed Vānī in the incident of public stoning, see Zilfi, *The Politics of Piety*, 203–204.

[13] Dāvūd Ḳārṣī, *Sharḥ al-Qaṣīda al-Nūniyya* (Istanbul: Meḥmet Ṭālib b Ḥüseyn, 1318/1900–1901), 41. Ḳārṣī in the same work denounced "the infidel atheistic panentheists (*al-wujūdiyya al-malāḥida al-kafara*)" (on p. 17). Ḳārṣī wrote a commentary on Birgevī's *Uṣūl al-ḥadīth* (repeatedly printed in Istanbul in the nineteenth century), as well as works on logic, dialectics, and astronomy.

concerning the study of logic, rational theology, mathematics, astronomy, and medicine in his major work, *al-Ṭarīqa al-muḥammadiyya*, is certainly much closer to the position of the venerable Ghazālī (d. 1111) than to that of Ibn Taymiyya. Birgevi considered rational theology (*kalām*) to be a *farḍ kifāya* – in other words, studying and teaching the discipline is incumbent on some within the Muslim community (but not on each and every Muslim). Like Ghazālī, Birgevī thought *kalām* should not be cultivated as an end in itself but had been necessitated by the appearance of heresies after the earliest generations of Islam.[14] This qualified endorsement of the discipline is still noticeably different from the traditional Ḥanbalī view that *kalām* is a heretical innovation to be avoided. In Chapter 5, it will be seen that some Ḳāḍīzādelī figures endorsed the idea that knowing the rational justifications for the tenets of the Islamic creed is an individual duty (*farḍ ʿayn*) and that Muslims who neglect to do so and simply take the creed on trust are sinners (see Chapter 5, the section "Sanūsī's Influence in the East"). It is hard to imagine a position that is more opposed to the early Ḥanbalī mistrust of the entire enterprise of rational theology.

The study of mathematics (*ḥisāb*) for Birgevī is also a *farḍ kifāya*.[15] He held medicine (*ṭibb*) to be "commendable" (*mandūb*) but without being a duty.[16] Birgevī's verdict concerning what he called the "sciences of the philosophers" (*ʿulūm al-falāsifa*) is unexpectedly nuanced. The status of logic (*manṭiq*) is similar to that of *kalām*, that is, it is a *farḍ kifāya* – a verdict that is in stark contrast to that of Ibn Taymiyya and Ibn Qayyim al-Jawziyya, who had poured scorn on the idea that studying logic could be a religious obligation.[17] As for metaphysics (*ilāhiyyāt*), parts of it conflict with religion and are therefore prohibited, unless one studies them to refute them (*illā ʿalā wajhi l-radd*) – a significant qualification. Other parts of metaphysics do not conflict with revelation and these have been incorporated into the discipline of rational theology. Physics or natural philosophy (*ṭabīʿiyyāt*) can likewise be divided into claims that conflict with religion and claims that have been incorporated into

[14] Ḫādimī, *Barīqa maḥmūdiyya*, I, 258.
[15] Ibid., 255.
[16] Ibid., 266.
[17] Ibid., 262. For Ibn Taymiyya's attack on logic, see especially W. Hallaq, *Ibn Taymiyya against the Greek Logicians* (Oxford: Clarendon Press, 1993). Ibn al-Qayyim's vehement denial of the position that studying logic is a *farḍ kifāya* is quoted in Muḥammad Murtaḍā al-Zabīdī, *Itḥāf al-sāda al-muttaqīn* (Cairo: al-Maṭbaʿa al-Muyammaniyya, 1311/1894), I, 176.

kalām.[18] Birgevī was here obviously alluding to the fact that the standard works of rational theology studied in the Ottoman Empire such as the aforementioned *al-Mawāqif* of Ījī with the commentary of Jurjānī included a great deal of physics and metaphysics.[19] Birgevī prohibited astrology but he was careful to distinguish this from astronomy. He wrote:

> I say: what is prohibited of the science of the stars (*ʿilm al-nujūm*) is what is related to judgments such as "If a lunar or solar eclipse or an earthquake or something like this occurs at such-and-such a time then such-and-such will occur." As for knowing the direction to which prayer should be made (*qibla*) and the times of prayer (*al-mawāqīt*) – which is the science called *hayʾa* – since these are conditions for prayer they must be known by thorough investigation of phenomena, and this science is one of the conditions of investigation and knowledge, and hence it is permissible to study it.[20]

The fact that even one of the strictest of Ottoman scholars, and the person who inspired the Ḳāḍīzādelī movement, did not have a problem with the science of astronomy invites a reconsideration of the motives behind the demolition of the Istanbul observatory in 1580. A number of studies have made it clear that the main motive for building the observatory in 1577 had been astrological, and that likewise the motive for destroying it a few years later was apprehension of astrology and not astronomy. The historian of science Aydin Sayılı has noted that "the reason and purpose for the foundation of the Observatory . . . appears to have been almost completely astrological."[21] In one of the lengthiest contemporary accounts of the career of the observatory, according to Sayılı, "astrological activities are mentioned in detailed fashion, both in praising him [the court astronomer-astrologer who headed the observatory] and in trying to justify the act of the demolition of the Observatory."[22] The historian of Arabic astronomy D. A. King has noted that the leveling of the observatory seems to have been a consequence of the Ottoman court astrologer's

[18] Ḫādimī, *Barīqa maḥmūdiyya*, 1: 262–265.

[19] For a discussion of the physics and metaphysics of this work, see A. I. Sabra, "Science and Philosophy in Medieval Islamic Theology: The Evidence of the Fourteenth Century," *Zeitschrift für Geschichte der Arabisch-Islamischen Wissenschaften*, 9(1994): 1–42. Birgevī had studied the work in his student days (Çāvūşoğlu, "The Ḳāḍīzādelīs," 51–52).

[20] Ḫādimī, *Barīqa maḥmūdiyya*, 1: 260–261.

[21] A. Sayılı, "Alā al-Dīn al-Manṣūr's Poems on the Istanbul Observatory," *Belleten* 20(1956): 429–484. The quotation is from p. 445. See also A. Sayılı, *The Observatory in Islam*, 2nd ed. (Ankara: Türk Tarih Kurumu Basimevi, 1988), 303–304.

[22] Sayılı, "Alā al-Dīn al-Manṣūr's Poems," 446.

"incorrect prediction of an Ottoman victory over the Safavids following the appearance of the famous comet of 1577."[23]

The quotations from Ṭāşköprīzāde and Kātib Çelebī adduced in support of the idea of a "triumph of fanaticism" are also far from conclusive. Lamenting the "decline of the times" is a well-known *topos*. It is risky to treat such laments as anything more than this unless they offer, or are supported by, other evidence.[24] Ṭāşköprīzāde and Kātib Çelebī may indeed have had the impression that there was a decline of interest in the "rational sciences" in their day by comparison to bygone times. However, both scholars were themselves enthusiastic about the "rational sciences" and might well have been prone to exaggerate the extent to which these sciences were respected and cultivated in an idealized past. Perhaps the most telling reason for not taking the laments of Ṭāşköprīzāde and Kātib Çelebī at face value is that it is possible to adduce quotations from seventeenth-century Ottoman scholars who were under the impression that there had been a significant *rise* in interest in philosophy in their time. For example, the Meccan scholar Muḥammad ʿAlī ibn ʿAllān al-Ṣiddīqī (d. 1648), in his commentary on Birgevī's *al-Ṭarīqa al-Muḥammadiyya*, wrote:

> It has become prevalent in this time, and the time just before it, to study the idiocies of the philosophers among most people (*wa-qad ghalaba fī hādhā l-zamāni wa qablahu bi-qalīlin al-ishtighālu bi-jahālāti l-falāsifa ʿalā akthari l-nās*), and they call it "wisdom" (*ḥikma*) and consider as ignorant those who are innocent of it. They think that they are accomplished people and persist in studying it, and you hardly find any of them who have memorized any Quran or Hadith from the Prophet. They are more appropriately described as ignorant and ignoble rather than "wise," for they are the enemies of the prophets, and corrupters of Islamic law, and they are more harm to the Muslims than the Jews and Christians.[25]

A contemporary of Ibn ʿAllān, the Egyptian scholar and belletrist Aḥmad al-Khafājī (d. 1658), made similar comments after a brief stay in Istanbul in 1642. Khafājī had been recalled to the Imperial capital after what appears to have been controversial spells as Ottoman Judge of

[23] D. A. King, "Taḳī al-Dīn b. Muḥammad b. Maʿrūf," *Encyclopaedia of Islam*, 2nd edi. (Leiden, the Netherlands: Brill, 1960–2002), Vol. 10, 132–133.

[24] The pitfall of treating such laments as straightforward observations of fact, rather than literary contributions to a genre, has been noted by D. A. Howard in his "Ottoman Historiography and the Literature of 'Decline' of the Sixteenth and Seventeenth Centuries," *Journal of Asian History* 22(1988): 52–77.

[25] The passage is quoted in the later commentary of Rajab Āmidī (fl. 1649–1676) on Birgevī's *Ṭarīqa*; see Ḫādimī, *Barīqa maḥmūdiyya*, 1:80 (the commentary of Rajab Āmidī is printed on the margins).

Salonika and Cairo – his opponents accused him of corruption.[26] He had a falling out with the then *Şeyḫülislām* Yaḥyā Zekeriyāzāde (d. 1644); was forced into retirement in Egypt; and promptly wrote a number of epistles in ornate, rhyming prose decrying what he claimed was a steep fall in academic standards since his first visit to Istanbul some forty years earlier.[27] Some modern historians have taken Khafājī's epistles at face value, as yet another piece of evidence for Ottoman "decline," but this is frankly preposterous.[28] Khafājī's rambling epistles are all too clearly self-serving and motivated by personal animosity and sour grapes. In any case, Khafājī's remarks offer no support to the idea of a "triumph of fanaticism." On the contrary, he portrayed the situation as one in which philosophers and astrologers had gained the upper hand at the expense of jurists and Quran exegetes. He wrote:

> One of the philosophers (*ḥukamāʾ*) said to the Sultan: "If you make your philosophers your viziers and your viziers your philosophers you will do right, for your philosophers make reason the measure of things (*yuḥakkimūna l-ʿaql*)[29], whereas your viziers cannot do this." People have now done as this philosopher advised, and so astrologers and philosophers (*al-munajjimūn wa-l-ḥukamāʾ*) have been made the heads of the religious law of the Chosen Prophet, and their leader has expelled and banished the religious scholars (*al-ʿulamāʾ*) [...] The witness [in a court of law] used to be asked about prayer and devoutness and religious obligations; now he is asked about modal syllogisms and logical propositions [...] The examinations used to be conducted on the basis of books of Quran exegesis and the commentaries of the *Hidāya* [a book on Ḥanafī law], whereas now they are conducted to lead astray on the basis of the astrological divinations (*zāʾirja*) of al-Sabtī and the philosopher al-Kindī's *Nuqāya*.[30]

26 On Khafājī, see Muḥammad Amīn al-Muḥibbī, *Khulāṣat al-athar fī aʿyān al-qarn al-ḥādī ʿashar* (Cairo: al-Maṭbaʿa al-Wahbiyya, 1284/1867–1868), I, 331–343; Uğur, *The Ottoman Ulema*, 219–220.

27 Aḥmad al-Khafājī, *Rayḥānat al-alibbā wa-zahrat al-ḥayāt al-dunyā*, edited by ʿAbd al-Fattāḥ Muḥammad al-Ḥilū (Cairo: Muṣṭafā al-Bābī al-Ḥalabī, 1967), II, 283–354.

28 A point well made by Rifaat Abou El-Hajj, *Formation of the Modern State: The Ottoman Empire, Sixteenth to Eighteenth Centuries* (Albany: SUNY Press, 1991), 25–27.

29 I read يحكّمون العقل instead of يحكمون القتل in the printed text. The latter (meaning "they kill well") makes little sense in the context, whereas the accusation that philosophers and Muʿtazilī theologians *yuḥakkimūna l-ʿaql*, i.e., rely to an improper extent on reason unaided by revelation, was standard in mainstream Sunni rhetoric. See, e.g., ʿAbdullāh al-ʿAyyāshī, *Riḥla*, edited by Aḥmad Farīd al-Mazyadī (Beirut: Dār al-Kutub al-ʿIlmiyya, 2011), I, 342.

30 Khafājī, *Rayḥānat al-alibbā*, II, 334. The *Hidāya* is a widely used manual of Ḥanafī law by al-Marghīnānī (d. 1197). Abū l-Abbās al-Sabtī is a thirteenth-century Moroccan scholar famed for his knowledge of *zāʾirja*, see T. Fahd, "Zāʾirdja," EI2, Vol. 11, 404. Kindī is the well-known ninth-century philosopher and astrologer (see on him J. Jolivet and R. Rashed, "al-Kindī," EI2, Vol. 5, 122–123). I have not been able to find other

Almost a century after Ibn ʿAllān and Khafājī, the Turkish scholar Meḥmed Sāçaḳlīzāde (d. 1732) was still lamenting what he considered the inordinate enthusiasm of many of his contemporary Ottoman scholars and students for philosophy.[31] Sāçaklīzāde emphasized that it was incumbent to declare as infidels Aristotle, Plato, and the Islamic philosophers who followed them such as Avicenna and Fārābī "and their likes." He then explicated this last phrase in the following manner:

If you say: "Who are their likes?" We say: Those who are fond of philosophy and indulge in it and call it "wisdom" (*ḥikma*) by way of extolling it... and are proud of what they have learned of philosophy, and who consider as ignorant those who are innocent of it. By the Lord of the Heavens and the Earth! These are the unbelieving philosophizers! One encountered their likes in the time of [the jurist] Āḫī Çelebī (d. 1495) and he said about them [...] "The desire to study jurisprudence is slight amongst the philosophizers whose lot in the afterworld is nothing but fire. Verily they will reach hell and what an end!" I say: Perhaps the philosophizers in our time are more numerous than they were in his time (*wa laʿalla l-mutafalsifīna fī ʿaṣrinā aktharu minhum fī ʿaṣrihi*).[32]

Sāçaḳlīẓaḍe thus believed that there was *more* rather than less interest in philosophy – under the guise of the name *ḥikma* – among Ottomans in his own time than there had been in the fifteenth century. He suggested that this impious state of affairs exposed the Ottoman polity to the danger of divine punishment in the form of further military defeats by Christian Europe:

Philosophy has become widespread in the Ottoman lands in our times (*wa qad shāʿat al-falsafatu fī bilādi l-Rūmi fī zamāninā*), the year 1130/1717. Before that by some eighty years or more the Christians conquered many of the Ottoman lands and defeated the soldiers of the Sovereign (*Malik*) of Islam several times and took countless Muslims and their families captive. It is now feared that there will be a general conquest by the Christians, and so we ask of God that He remove this cause from [the realm of] the Sovereign of Islam and his viceroys, and thus

references to a work by him entitled *al-Nuqāya*. Khafājī was clearly less concerned with verisimilitude than with rhyme, rhetorical effect, and showing off his knowledge of obscure titles. There is no reason whatsoever to believe that Ottoman scholars were being examined on the basis of the works of al-Sabtī and al-Kindī.

31 On Sāçaḳlīzāde, see S. Reichmuth, "Bildungskanon und bildungreform aus der sicht eines islamischen gelehrten der Anatolischen provinz: Muḥammad al-Marʿašī as-Sāġaqlī (Saġaqli-zade, gest. um 1145/1733) und sein *Tartīb al-ʿulūm*," in R. Arnzen and J. Thielmann (eds.), *Words, Texts and Concepts Cruising the Mediterranean Sea* (Leuven, the Netherlands: Peeters, 2004), 493–522.

32 Meḥmed Sāçaḳlīzāde, *Tartīb al-ʿulūm*, edited by Muḥammad b. Ismāʿīl al-Sayyid Aḥmad (Beirut: Dār al-Bashāʾir al-Islāmiyya, 1988), 229.

that the scholars (*'ulamā'*) desist from teaching philosophy and that those who do not desist be punished.[33]

Sāçaḳlīzāde's fulminations against the study of philosophy, and its dire effects on the military strength of the Ottoman Empire, are of course also *topoi*. He explicitly modeled his statements on the suggestion of Ibn Qayyim al-Jawziyya that the study of philosophy under the 'Abbasids was punished by God in the form of the Mongol invasions.[34] However, there is good reason to believe that Sāçaḳlīzāde's complaints had some basis in contemporary realities and should not be dismissed as quixotic attacks on nonexistent enemies. Several Ottoman scholars who were active in Sāçaḳlīzāde's lifetime wrote extensive glosses on the handbook on physics and metaphysics entitled *Hidāyat al-ḥikma* by Athīr al-Dīn al-Abharī (d. 1265), its commentary by Qāḍī Mīr Ḥusayn Maybudī (d. 1504), and its gloss by Muṣliḥ al-Dīn Lārī (d. 1579). The fact that Ibn 'Allān and Sāçaḳlīzāde explicitly stated that many of their contemporary "philosophizers" chose to call the discipline *ḥikma* also suggests that Abharī's *Hidāyat al-ḥikma* was one of the books they had in mind when fulminating against the study of philosophy by Ottoman scholars and students. The list of Ottoman scholars who wrote extant glosses on this work in the seventeenth and eighteenth centuries is noteworthy:

- Zayn al-'Ābidīn Gūrānī (fl. 1656), dedicated to the Ottoman Grand Vizier Meḥmed Köprülü (d. 1661)
- Ḥüseyn Adanavī (fl. 1670s)
- 'Alī Nīthārī Ḳayṣerī (d. 1698)
- Müneccimbāşī Aḥmed Mevlevī (d. 1702)
- *Ḳara Ḫalīl Tīrevī (d. 1711)
- Ḥaydar Ḥusaynābādī (d. 1717)
- 'Abdullāh b. Ḥaydar Ḥusaynābādī (d. 1695)
- Ibrāhīm Şehirlīzāde Sīvāsī (fl. 1698)
- Muḥammad b. 'Abbās Kurdī (fl. 1705)
- Meḥmed b. Aḥmed Ṭarsūsī (d. 1732)
- Yūsuf 'Atāḳī (d. 1738)
- 'Abdullāh Yūsufefendīzāde (d. 1754)
- *Meḥmed b. Ḥamīd Kefevī (d. 1754)

[33] Sāçaḳlīzāde, *Tartīb al-'ulūm*, 234nA (the footnote reproduces a marginal annotation to the text by Sāçaḳlīzāde himself).

[34] Sāçaḳlīzāde, *Tartīb al-'ulūm*, 233–234, citing Ibn Qayyim al-Jawziyya's *Ighāthat al-lahfān*.

- *Ismāʿīl Gelenbevī (d. 1791)
- ʿAbdullāh Kānḳirī (d. 1823)[35]

The three glosses marked with an asterisk were printed or lithographed in Istanbul in the nineteenth century in editions clearly intended for *medrese* students.[36] Also printed in the nineteenth century was an Ottoman Turkish translation of Qāḍī Mīr's (Arabic) commentary by Meḥmed Āḳkirmānī (d. 1760).[37] The glosses and translation belie the idea of an Ottoman turning away from philosophy after the sixteenth century and instead suggest that this particular handbook on physics and metaphysics was widely studied in Ottoman medreses from the seventeenth century to the nineteenth.

Lest it be thought that the listed glossators were marginal or unrepresentative figures, it may be worthwhile to look more closely at two of the names:

1. Ḳara Ḫalīl Tīrevī.[38] This scholar's literary output was almost exclusively devoted to glosses on works of philosophy, dialectic, and logic. Some of these glosses were repeatedly printed in Istanbul in the nineteenth century, attesting to their continued and widespread use in education.[39] Despite his specialization in philosophy and logic, Ḳara Ḫalīl was hardly a marginal or disreputable figure of the *ulema* class. He rose to the position of *Ḳāżīʿasker* of Anatolia,

[35] For extant copies of these glosses see (in order but skipping the glosses marked with *): R. Mach, *Catalogue of Arabic Manuscripts (Yahuda Section) in the Garrett Collection* (Princeton, NJ: Princeton University Press, 1977), nr. 3052; MS: Süleymaniye Kütüphanesı, Istanbul: Çorlulu Ali Paşa 315; www.yazmalar.gov.tr/ 06MilYzA2486/1; www.yazmalar.gov.tr/ FE2154/2; Mach, *Catalogue*, nr. 3053; Mach, *Catalogue*, nr. 3054; Mach, *Catalogue*, nr. 3057; www.yazmalar.gov.tr/ 50Gül-Kara128; www.yazmalar.gov.tr/ 06MilYzA1579/5; www.yazmalar.gov.tr/ 34Ma266/2; www .yazmalar.gov.tr/ 28Hk3542; MS: Süleymaniye Kütüphanesı, Istanbul: Hasan Hüsnü Paşa 1274.

[36] Ḳara Ḫalīl, *Ḥāshiya ʿalā Ḥāshiyat al-Lārī* (Istanbul: Maṭbaʿa-yi ʿĀmire, 1271/1855); Meḥmed Kefevī, *Ḥāshiya ʿalā Ḥāshiyat al-Lārī* (Istanbul: Şirket-i Ṣeḥāfiye-yi ʿOsmāniye, 1309/1891–1892); Ismāʿīl Gelenbevī, *Ḥāshiya ʿalā Ḥāshiyat al-Lārī* (Istanbul: Maṭbaʿa-yi ʿĀmire, 1270/1853–1854).

[37] Printed in Istanbul by Maṭbaʿa-yi ʿĀmire in 1266/1849–1850.

[38] On Ḳara Ḫalīl, see Şeyḫī Meḥmed Efendī, *Veḳāʾiʿ ül-fużalāʾ*, IV, 329–330; Ismāʿīl al-Baghdādī, *Hadiyyat al-ʿārifīn: asmaʾ al-muʾallifīn wa athar al-muṣannifīn* (Istanbul: Milli Eğetim Basımevi, 1951–1955), I, 354–355.

[39] For example, Ḳara Ḫalīl, *Ḥāshiya ʿalā Ḥāshiyat Ḳūl Aḥmed ʿalā Sharḥ Īsāghūjī* (Istanbul: Maṭbaʿa-yi ʿĀmire, 1279/1862–1863 and Yaḥyā Efendī Maṭbaʿası, 1289/1872–1873); Ḳara Ḫalīl, *Ḥāshiya ʿalā Risālat Jihat al-waḥda* (Istanbul: Maṭbaʿa-yi ʿĀmire 1258/1842–1843 and 1288/1871–1872).

the third highest position to which an Ottoman scholar could rise.[40] The example of Ḳara Ḫalīl alone should be sufficient to cast doubt on the thesis of a "triumph of fanaticism" in the Ottoman Empire in the seventeenth century.

2. Meḥmed b. Aḥmed Ṭarsūsī likewise wrote a number of glosses on handbooks of logic and philosophy.[41] He also wrote an encyclopedic survey of the sciences entitled *Unmūdhaj al-ʿulūm*, covering the rational sciences (logic, dialectic, medicine, astronomy, and mathematics) as well as the religious and linguistic sciences.[42] He was also a prominent Ḥanafī jurist (and mufti of Tarsus) whose most esteemed work was an extensive gloss on *Mirʾāt al-uṣūl*, a handbook on Ḥanafī jurisprudence by Mullā Ḫüsrev (d. 1480) – a gloss that was printed at least twice in Istanbul in the nineteenth century.[43] Interestingly, Ṭarsūsī was in his youth a protégé of the Ḳāḍīzādelī leader Meḥmed Vānī, from whom he derived a certificate.[44] The example of Ṭarsūsī shows that prominence

40 For a list of Ottoman *Şeyhülislāms* and *Ḳāżīʿaskers* in the seventeenth and eighteenth centuries, see Zilfi, *The Politics of Piety*, 246ff. Ḳara Ḫalīl is listed on p. 252 (nr. 26).

41 On this scholar, see Yaşar Sarıkaya, *Abū Saʿīd Muḥammad al-Ḫādimī (1701–1762): Netwerke, Karriere und Einfluss eines osmanischen Provinzgelehrten* (Hamburg: Verlag Kovač, 2005), 46–50. See also Fındıḳlılı ʿİsmet, *Tekmiletü l-şeḳāʾiḳ*, in *Şaḳaiḳ-i Nuʿmaniye ve Zeyilleri* (Istanbul: Çağrı Yayinları, 1989), 62–63 and Būrsalī, *ʿOthmānlī Müelliflerī* (Istanbul: Matbaʿah-i ʿĀmire, 1333/1914–1342/1928), I, 348. Both mentioned sources agree on giving 1145/1732–1733 as the date of death. Ismaʿil Baghdādī (*Hadiyyat al-ʿārifīn*, II, 309) gives the date of death 1117/1705–1706, which cannot be correct and may be the date of death of the scholar's father Aḥmed b. Meḥmed Ṭarsūsī. His works on logic and philosophy include (1) *Ḥāshiya ʿalā Ḥāshiyat al-Lārī ʿalā Sharḥ Hidāyat al-ḥikma* (MS: Manisa İl Halk Kütüphanesı 2033). The gloss was completed in 1122/1710; (2) *Ḥāshiya ʿalā Ḥāshiyat Mīrzā Jān ʿalā Sharḥ Ithbāt al-wājib* (Mach 2403). The gloss was completed in 1110/1698; (3) *Ḥāshiya ʿalā Ḥāshiyat Ḳūl Aḥmed ʿalā Sharḥ Īsāghūjī* (Mach 3171 and Ormsby 361). The gloss was completed in 1106/1695.

42 Sarıkaya, *Abū Saʿīd Muḥammad al-Ḫādimī (1701–1762)*, 48–49.

43 By Maṭbaʿa-yi ʿĀmire in 1267/1851 and by Hācı Muḥarrem Bōsnavī Maṭbaʿası in 1289/1872. The gloss was completed in 1111/1699. I indicate the dates of completion to rule out the possibility that these works could have been written by the author's grandfather, also named Meḥmed b. Aḥmed Ṭarsūsī (d. 1067/1657). (On the grandfather, see Uğur, *The Ottoman Ulema*, 194–195.)

44 An extant manuscript of a work on dialectics (www.yazmalar.gov.tr/ 37 Hk 2727) dated 1090/1678 was, according to the colophon, written by Meḥmed b. Aḥmed Ṭarsūsī while "in the service of Meḥmed Vānī (*fī khidmat mawlānā Meḥmed Vānī*)." The work in question is a gloss on a handbook on dialectics by the sixteenth-century Ottoman scholar Ṭāşköprīzāde. This gloss has been attributed to both Meḥmed Ṭarsūsī himself (in which case the manuscript in question is an autograph) and to his father Aḥmed (in which case Meḥmed is just the copyist). For Vānī's certificate to Ṭarsūsī, see Sarıkaya, *Abū Saʿīd Muḥammad al-Ḫādimī (1701–1762)*, 47.

> as a Ḥanafī jurist, and even a close personal relationship with a Ḳāḍīzādelī leader, did not preclude a keen interest in rational sciences such as logic, astronomy, physics, and metaphysics.

It should be added that Sāçaḳlīzāde himself, despite his hostility to Neo-Platonic/Aristotelian philosophy, was far from being an obscurantist who condemned all "rational sciences." He went out of his way to condone the study of rational theology, astronomy, mathematics, medicine, logic, and dialectic. Sāçaḳlīzāde's hostility to philosophy did not extend to the two standard theological summas *al-Mawāqif* by Ījī with the commentary of Jurjānī and *al-Maqāṣid* by Sa'd al-Dīn al-Taftāzānī (d. 1390), despite the fact that both works devoted considerable space to a careful presentation and discussion of the physics and metaphysics of the Islamic philosophers. Indeed he repeatedly stressed that a student's mastery of theology is insufficient unless these works and their philosophical preliminaries had been carefully studied.[45] The disciplines of mathematics and medicine were unproblematic for Sāçaḳlīzāde, as they had been for Birgevī.[46] When it came to astronomy, he – like Birgevī – made a distinction between what he called *ha'ya*, that is, the study of heavenly bodies and their movements on the basis of observation, and what he called *aḥkām al-nujūm* – the effort to use the results of the former science to predict the course of future events on earth. The former he deemed a praiseworthy science useful for determining the direction and times of prayer; the latter he deemed a prohibited science. Sāçaḳlīzāde went on to contrast astronomy as mentioned by the philosophers, and incorporated into the theological works of Muslim scholars of the late medieval period, with "Islamic astronomy" (*al-hay'a al-islāmiyya*) as practiced by scholars such as the Egyptian Jalāl al-Dīn al-Suyūṭī (d. 1505), which attempted to derive the principles of cosmology from reported sayings of prominent figures from the earliest generations of Islam.[47] He explicitly stated that in case of conflict between rational and traditional cosmology, it was the latter that should be reinterpreted to accord with the former. It had, for example, been proven conclusively that the sun is many times larger than the earth, and hence it is not possible, as some early Islamic traditions asserted, that the sky rests on a great mountain range circumscribing the earth.[48] As for logic, Sāçaḳlīzāde

45 Sāçaḳlīzāde, *Tartīb al-'ulūm*, 148–149, 205.

46 Ibid., 180–181 (on mathematics and geometry), and 184–185 (on medicine and surgery).

47 See A.H. Heinen, *Islamic Cosmology: A study of* as-Suyūṭī's al-Hay'a as-sanīya fī l-hay'a as-sunnīya, with critical edition, translation, and commentary (Beirut: Orient-Institut, 1982).

48 Sāçaḳlīzāde, *Tartīb al-'ulūm*, 181–184.

wrote that studying it is a communal duty incumbent on the Muslim community as a whole (*farḍ kifāya*). Particularly, the study of inferences (*baḥth al-adilla*) is a duty, he stated, as it formed part of the skills needed in studying the principles of jurisprudence.[49] Sāçaḳlīzāde conceded that earlier scholars such as Ibn Qayyim al-Jawziyya and the Egyptian Ḥanafī jurist Ibn Nujaym (d. 1563) had prohibited logic, but insisted that this should be understood to relate to logic mixed with philosophy. The kind of logic that was studied in his time (*al-manṭiq al-mutadāwal al-yawm*) was by contrast free from the heretical doctrines of the philosophers.[50]

The evidence behind the idea of a "triumph of fanaticism" in the Ottoman Empire in the seventeenth century is, to sum up, far from compelling. The Ḳāḍīzādelīs were by all accounts a minority within the scholarly class, and in any case there is surprisingly little evidence that they were hostile to all the rational sciences. Sixteenth- and seventeenth-century Ottoman scholars who railed against Aristotelian/Neo-Platonic philosophy were at the same time careful to endorse disciplines such as rational theology, logic, medicine, mathematics, and astronomy. The destruction of the Ottoman observatory in 1580 seems to have been due to apprehension of astrology, not astronomy. The complaints of a few authors about a declining interest in the rational sciences are in line with a well-known topos of the "decline of the times" and cannot be taken simply as straightforward descriptions of facts. If some scholars bemoaned what they saw as a declining interest in the rational sciences, others bemoaned what they deemed the excessive and increasing study of philosophy. Such commonplace complaints cancel each other out and highlight the need to look elsewhere for more reliable indicators of what was going on at the time. Bio-bibliographic information suggests that the study of philosophy and the rational sciences continued unabated in Ottoman scholarly circles throughout the seventeenth century. As seen in the following sections, there is considerable evidence that the study of philosophy and the rational sciences was actually reinvigorated by an infusion of books and scholars from the Persian, Azeri, and Kurdish regions in the east.

Opening the Gate of Verification in Damascus

In the first decade of the seventeenth century, a Kurdish scholar known as Mullā Maḥmūd settled in Damascus. He achieved renown in the city

[49] Ibid., 139–140.
[50] Ibid., 114 and 235.

as a scholar and teacher, and by the time of his death in 1663 he had taught practically all Damascene scholars who achieved prominence in the mid- and late seventeenth century. The sources do not indicate why Mullā Maḥmūd should have left the Kurdish areas, but the first decade of the seventeenth century was a time of considerable unrest in the Kurdish borderlands between the Ottoman Empire and Safavid Iran. In a series of campaigns between 1603 and 1607, the Safavids under Shah ʿAbbās I (r. 1588–1629) managed to wrest the historic regions of Azerbaijan (in what is today northwestern Iran) and Shirwan (roughly corresponding to the present-day Republic of Azerbaijan) from the Ottomans.[51] This was accompanied by a "systematic and savage depopulation" of the border areas to forestall a potential Ottoman counteroffensive, with mass deportations of Kurds, Azeris, Armenians, and Georgians to more eastern areas of Iran.[52] In 1609–1610, a Kurdish revolt in the region south of Lake Urmia was crushed by the Safavids, an event commemorated in the traditional Kurdish ballad *Bayt-i Dimdim*.[53] Relations between the predominantly Sunni Kurds and the Shiite Safavids remained tense thereafter, and some of the most virulent anti-Shiite polemics from the seventeenth century were written by Kurdish scholars such as Zayn al-ʿĀbidīn Gūrānī (fl. 1656), Aḥmad b. Ḥaydar Ḥusaynābādī (d. 1669), and Muḥammad b. ʿAbd al-Rasūl Barzinjī (d. 1691).[54]

The arrival of Mullā Maḥmūd in Damascus was depicted by the local biographer Muḥammad Amīn al-Muḥibbī (1650–1699) as a significant event in the scholarly life of his city. He wrote:

He [i.e., Mullā Maḥmūd] mostly taught the books of the Persians (*kutub al-aʿājim*), and he was the first to acquaint the students of Damascus with these books, and he imparted to them the ability to study and teach them. It is from

51 R. Savory, *Iran under the Safavids* (Cambridge: Cambridge University Press, 1980), 85–87.

52 J. Perry, "Forced Migration in Iran during the Seventeenth and Eighteenth Centuries," *Iranian Studies* 8(1975), 199–215, at 206–207.

53 M. Gunter, *Historical Dictionary of the Kurds* (Landham, MD: Scarecrow Press, 2011), 50, 85, 201.

54 Zayn al-ʿĀbidīn al-Gūrānī, *al-Yamāniyyāt al-maslūla*, edited by M. M. al-Murābiṭ (Cairo: Maktabat al-Imām al-Bukhārī, 2000); Aḥmad b. Ḥaydar al-Ḥusaynābādī, *Ghusl al-rijlayn fī radd madhhab al-shīʿa*, extant manuscripts of which are listed in F. Schwarz, "Writing in the margins of empires – the Ḥusaynābādī family of scholiasts in the Ottoman-Safawid borderlands," in T. Heinzelmann and H. Sievert (eds.), *Buchkultur im Nahen Osten des 17. und 18. Jahrhunderts* (Bern: Peter Lang 2010), 183–184; Muḥammad b. ʿAbd al-Rasūl al-Barzinjī, *al-Nawāfiḍ li-l-Rawāfiḍ* described in Mach, *Catalogue*, nr. 2630.

him that the gate of verification (*bāb al-taḥqīq*) in Damascus was opened. This is what we have heard our teachers say.[55]

The passage is sufficiently arresting to merit some unpacking. The term *taḥqīq* is a central concept in Islamic scholarly culture. Its importance is attested as early as the tenth and eleventh centuries. Early Islamic theologians of that period often used the verbal noun *taḥqīq* to denote the rational demonstration of the truth of the Islamic creed, as opposed to *taqlīd*, that is, acceptance of the creed based on uncritical acceptance of what one has been told by elders, peers, and teachers.[56] A very similar understanding is to be found in the writings of the philosopher Avicenna (d. 1037), who also contrasted *taqlīd*, that is, the uncritical acceptance of received philosophical views, with *taḥqīq*, that is, the independent logical demonstration of the truth of such views.[57] Such an understanding of *taḥqīq* is still in evidence in the seventeenth century. The dictionaries of technical terms by ʿAbd al-Raʾūf al-Munāwī (d. 1622) and Ebū l-Beḳā Kefevī (d. 1684) both explained that *taḥqīq* is "to establish the proof of a scholarly question" (*ithbāt dalīl al-masʾala*)."[58] In practical terms, a scholar who was not a *muḥaqqiq* would confine himself to reiterating received views and perhaps also clarifying them for his students or readers. A *muḥaqqiq*, on the other hand, would critically assess received views. For example, the Afghan scholar ʿAbd al-Raḥīm Kābulī (d. 1723), who settled in Damascus, was once approached by a local student who wished to study the commentary of the prominent Egyptian scholar and judge Zakariyyā al-Anṣārī (d. 1519) on Abharī's aforementioned introduction to logic *Īsāghūjī*. Kābulī was not familiar with that particular commentary and was reportedly unimpressed when he discovered that the commentator had merely "explained the expressions and did not go the way of the verifiers (*awḍaḥa l-ʿibārata fīhi wa lam yasluk maslaka l-muḥaqqiqīn*)."[59]

55 Muḥibbī, *Khulāṣat al-athar fī aʿyān al-qarn al-ḥādī ʿashar*, IV, 329–330.

56 See R. Frank, "Knowledge and Taqlīd: The Foundation of Religious Belief in Classical Ashʿarism," *Journal of the American Oriental Society* 109(1989): 37–62, esp. p. 43 n18 (*taḥqīq*), p. 48B (*ahl al-taḥqīq*) and p. 55B (*al-muḥaqqiqūn min ahl al-naẓar*).

57 D. Gutas, *Avicenna and the Aristotelian Tradition* (Leiden, the Netherlands: Brill, 1988), 187–193.

58 ʿAbd al-Raʾūf al-Munāwī, *al-Tawqīf ʿalā muhimmāt al-taʿārīf*, ed. M. R. al-Dāya (Beirut and Damascus: Dār al-Fikr, 1990), 164; Ebū l-Beḳā Kefevī, *al-Kulliyyāt*, ed. M. al-Miṣrī and ʿA. Darwīsh (Damascus: Wizārat al-thaqāfa, 1975), II, 76.

59 Muḥammad Khalīl al-Murādī, *Silk al-durar fī aʿyān al-qarn al-thānī ʿashar* (Istanbul and Cairo: al-Maṭbaʿa al-mīriyya al-ʿāmira, 1291/1874–1301/1883), III, 9–10.

Muḥibbī's reference to the "books of the Persians" is particularly intriguing. The term had been used by the earlier Damascene scholar Badr al-Dīn al-Ghazzī (d. 1577) in his comprehensive educational manual *al-Durr al-naḍīd fī adab al-mufīd wa l-mustafīd*. Ghazzī was in that context introducing the budding student to widely used scribal abbreviations, both in compilations of hadith, such as writing خ for the esteemed compiler al-Bukhārī, and in "the books of the Persians," such as writing مح for "absurd" (*muḥāl*) or مط for "conclusion" (*maṭlūb*) or ح for "in that case" (*ḥīna'idhin*).[60] The nature of the abbreviations strongly suggests that the "books of the Persians" covered the instrumental or rational sciences. This is further supported by the fact that some of the Damascene students of Mullā Maḥmūd such as ʿAbd al-Ghanī al-Nābulusī (1641–1731) and Abū l-Mawāhib al-Ḥanbalī (1635–1714) are reported to have studied logic, semantics-rhetoric (*maʿānī wa bayān*), and grammar (*naḥw*) with the Kurdish scholar.[61] The handbooks mentioned in this connection were: *Īsāghūjī* by Abharī, an elementary exposition of logic, with the commentary of Ḥusām al-Dīn al-Kātī (d. 1359), and *Talkhīṣ al-miftāḥ*, a standard handbook on semantics and rhetoric by Jamāl al-Dīn al-Qazwīnī (d. 1338) with the short (*Mukhtaṣar*) and long (*Muṭawwal*) commentaries by the great Timurid scholar Saʿd al-Dīn al-Taftāzānī. Abharī, Qazwīnī, and Taftāzānī were all of Persian or Central Asian origin and their works could well have been referred to as the "books of the Persians." Muḥibbī claimed that Mullā Maḥmūd had been "the first to acquaint the students of Damascus" with such books, but this cannot be taken entirely at face value. The Damascene scholar Ḥasan al-Būrīnī (1556–1615), for example, had studied the aforementioned works on semantics-rhetoric in his student days.[62] Yet, there is reason to think that Mullā Maḥmūd did introduce other and later Persian-authored works that had not been taught in Damascus prior to his arrival in the city. Two other Damascene students of Mullā Maḥmūd, ʿUthmān al-Qaṭṭān (d. 1704) and ʿAbd al-Qādir Ibn ʿAbd al-Hādī (d. 1688), are known to have gone on to teach

60 Badr al-Dīn al-Ghazzī, *al-Durr al-naḍīd fī adab al-mufīd wa l-mustafīd*, ed. Nashʾat al-Miṣrī (Giza: Maktabat al-Tawʿiya al-Islāmiyya, 2006), 461; ed. ʿAbdullāh al-Kandarī (Beirut: Dār al-Bashāʾir al-Islāmiyya, 2006), 272.

61 Kamāl al-Dīn al-Ghazzī, *al-Wird al-unsī wa-l-wārid al-qudsī fī tarjamat al-ʿārif ʿAbd al-Ghanī al-Nābulusī*, edited by S. Akkach (Leiden, the Netherlands: Brill, 2012), 143; Abū l-Mawāhib al-Ḥanbalī, *Mashyakha*, ed. M. M. al-Ḥāfiẓ (Damascus: Dār al-Fikr, 1990), 86–87.

62 Ḥasan al-Būrīnī, *Tarājim al-aʿyān min abnāʾ al-zamān*, ed. S. al-Munajjid (Damascus: al-Majmaʿ al-ʿilmī al-ʿarabi, 1959–1963), II, 303.

works by later Persian scholars such as Jalāl al-Dīn al-Dawānī (d. 1502) and ʿIṣām al-Dīn al-Isfarāyinī (d. 1537).[63] These authors do not seem to have been studied in Damascus in the sixteenth century. There is no reference to their works in the quite detailed accounts available to us of the studies of Damascene scholars such as the just-mentioned Būrīnī or Najm al-Dīn al-Ghazzī (1570–1651).[64] It is also revealing that Najm al-Dīn al-Ghazzī did not mention either Dawānī or Isfarāyinī in his biographical dictionary of Muslim notables who died in the tenth Islamic century (1494–1591), whereas the younger Damascene scholar Ibn al-ʿImād al-Ḥanbalī (1623–1679) included entries on both scholars when he covered the same century in his general collection of obituaries covering the first millennium of Islamic history.[65] There is therefore some reason to believe that the works of scholars such as Dawānī and Isfarāyinī were indeed introduced into the scholarly milieu of Damascus in the early seventeenth century.

Neither Dawānī nor ʿIsām al-Dīn al-Isfarāyinī has received much attention by modern scholars (indeed the first two editions of *Encyclopedia of Islam*, the standard reference work in Islamic studies, does not have an entry on the latter figure at all). This is unfortunate, for it will emerge from the present chapter that the two scholars had a powerful impact on Ottoman intellectual life. Dawānī, active in western Iran (especially in Shiraz and Tabriz), is arguably the most significant Islamic philosopher active after the thirteenth century and before the seventeenth. Apart from his philosophical works, he also wrote widely studied works on logic and rational theology. Though some later Shiite traditions assert

[63] Ibn ʿAbd al-Hādī taught Isfarāʾīnī's *Sharḥ al-Risāla al-wadʿiyya* to the biographer Muḥibbī, see Muḥibbī, *Khulāṣat al-athar*, II, 438. Qaṭṭān taught Dawāni's commentary on the creed of al-Ījī to the chronicler Ibn Kannān al-Ṣāliḥī (d. 1740), see Ibn Kannān al-Ṣāliḥī, *al-Ḥawādith al-yawmiyya min tārīkh iḥdā ʿashar wa-alf wa-miʾa*, ed. A. Ḥ. al-ʿUlabi (Damascus: Dar al-Ṭabbāʿ, 1994), 84.

[64] On Būrīnī, see the entries on his teachers Ismāʿīl al-Nābulusī (d. 1585) and ʿImād al-Dīn al-Ḥanafī (d. 1578) in Būrīnī, *Tarājim al-aʿyān*, II, 61–79 and 302–310 which mention the books on grammar and semantics-rhetoric that they taught, the works of ʿIṣām al-Dīn Isfarāyinī being conspicuously absent. On Ghazzī, see Muḥibbī, *Khulāṣat al-athar*, IV, 189–200 (esp. 191–192).

[65] Najm al-Dīn al-Ghazzī, *al-Kawākib al-sāʾira fī akhbār al-miʾa al-ʿāshira*, ed. J. Jabbūr (Beirut: American University of Beirut Publications, 1945–1958). Ibn al-ʿImād al-Ḥanbalī, *Shadharāt al-dhahab fī akhbār man dhahab* (Cairo: Maktabat al-qudsī, 1351/1932–1933), VIII, 160 (on al-Dawānī) and 291 (on al-Isfarāyinī). Ibn al-ʿImād's biographical information on the two scholars is scanty, and his dates of death are wrong. However, it is significant that he still felt the need to include a reference to the two scholars.

that he converted to Shiism just before his death, his major works were written as a Sunni who claimed descent from the first Caliph Abū Bakr al-Ṣiddīq (reviled and cursed by the Shiite Safavids).[66] Perhaps helped by his Sunni credentials, he exerted a profound influence on later Ottoman and Mughal scholarship in philosophy, logic, and rational theology. His major works include

1. Three sets of glosses on *Sharḥ Tajrīd al-kalām*, a commentary by ʿAlī al-Qūshjī (d. 1479) on a handbook of philosophy and theology by Naṣīr al-Dīn al-Ṭūsī (d. 1274)
2. A commentary on *Hayākil al-nūr* by the Illuminationist (*ishrāqī*) philosopher Yaḥyā al-Suhrawardī (d. 1191)
3. A commentary on *Tahdhīb al-manṭiq*, a handbook on logic by the aforementioned Timurid scholar Taftāzānī
4. A commentary on *al-ʿAqāʾid al-ʿAḍudiyya*, a short creed by the Ashʿarī theologian ʿAḍud al-Dīn al-Ījī
5. *Risālat Ithbāt al-wājib*. Dawānī wrote two treatises with this title, known to the subsequent tradition as the "old" (*qadīma*) and the "new" (*jadīda*) treatises. In these, he discussed and evaluated various proofs for the existence of a Necessary Being.
6. *Risālat al-zawrāʾ*, a treatise defending the controversial mystical idea of the "unity of existence" (*waḥdat al-wujūd*).

ʿIṣām al-Dīn al-Isfarāyinī in turn was one of the most influential contributors to the disciplines of semantics-rhetoric and grammar after the fourteenth century and also contributed esteemed works on logic and on the "science of imposition" (*ʿilm al-waḍʿ*) dealing with the theory of conventional reference. He was active in Herat (in present-day Afghanistan) and later – after the Safavid conquest of the city in 1511 – in Sunni Uzbek-controlled Central Asia.[67] His major works include

1. A lengthy commentary, entitled *al-Aṭwal*, on Qazwīnī's aforementioned handbook *Talkhīṣ al-miftāḥ*
2. An extensive gloss on the commentary by the eminent Persian poet, mystic, and scholar Jāmī (d. 1492) on *al-Kāfiya*, a handbook on Arabic syntax by Ibn al-Ḥājib (d. 1248)

[66] On Dawānī and his works, see R. Pourjavady, *Philosophy in Early Safavid Iran* (Leiden, the Netherlands: Brill, 2011), 4–16.

[67] On ʿIṣām al-Dīn al-Isfarāyinī and his works, see C. Brockelmann, *Geschichte der Arabischen Litteratur* (Leiden, the Netherlands: Brill, 1937–1949), II, 410–411 and Suppl. II, 571.

3. A commentary on a treatise on metaphor (*istiʿāra*) by Abū l-Qāsim al-Samarqandī (fl. 1488)
4. A Persian treatise on figurative language (*majāz*)
5. A commentary on a treatise on "imposition" (*waḍʿ*) by ʿAḍud al-Dīn al-Ījī
6. An extensive gloss on the commentary by Quṭb al-Dīn al-Rāzī al-Taḥtānī (d. 1365) on the classic handbook of logic *al-Shamsiyya* by Najm al-Dīn al-Kātibī (d. 1277)

It is plain from Kātib Çelebī's great bibliographic compilation *Kashf al-ẓunūn* that these works by Dawānī and Isfarāyinī were widely studied in the Ottoman Empire in the mid-seventeenth century.[68] They were still being studied in the nineteenth century when many of them were printed by the early printing presses of Istanbul and Cairo in editions clearly meant for students at traditional madrasas. At least in the case of Damascus, there is reason to believe that their works began to be studied intensively and systematically only from the beginning of the seventeenth century.

Muḥibbī linked the arrival of Mullā Maḥmūd in Damascus and the teaching of the "books of the Persians" to what he called "opening the gate of verification (*taḥqīq*)." To understand why he did so, it is helpful to keep the following factors in mind:

1. The works of the fifteenth- and sixteenth-century Persian scholars were suffused with the rhetoric of *taḥqīq*, that is, of the need to critically assess received scholarly propositions as opposed to being satisfied with merely reiterating and explicating them. In the introduction to his commentary on *Tahdhīb al-manṭiq*, for example, Dawānī wrote:

> I have not heeded what is commonly accepted, for truth is more worthy of being followed, and I have not stood still at the station of what has already been said, for the pathway of reasoning is open. Instead, I have shown the unsullied way and churned the cream of plain truth. I have presented verified points (*taḥqīqāt*)

[68] Kātib Çelebī, *Kashf al-ẓunūn ʿan asāmī al-kutub wa-l-funūn* (Istanbul: Maarif Matbaasi, 1941–1943), 1372 (Jāmī's commentary on *al-Kāfiya* and the gloss of Isfarāyinī); 477 (*Talkhīṣ al-miftāḥ* and its commentary by Isfarāyinī); 898 (al-Ījī's *Risālat al-waḍʿ* and the commentary by Isfarāyinī); 845 (al-Samarqandī's *Risālat al-istiʿāra* and its commentary by Isfarāyinī); 516 (Taftāzānī's *Tahdhīb al-manṭiq* and its commentary by Dawānī); 1144 (al-Ījī's *ʿAqāʾid* and its commentary by Dawānī).

that are absent from commonly circulating books, and indicated subtle intricacies (*tadqīqāt*) not contained in lengthy tomes.[69]

Dawānī struck the same tone in the preamble and introduction to his commentary on the creed of ʿAḍud al-Dīn al-Ījī:

> O Thou who hast enabled us to verify (*taḥqīq*) the Islamic creed and shielded us from imitation (*taqlīd*) in the principles and corollaries of theology . . . I have not abandoned myself to the alleys of gathering quotes, as is often done by the disputatious (*ahl al-jidāl*) who are unable to take the highroad of proof (*istidlāl*). Rather, I have followed the plain truth even if it goes against what is commonly accepted (*al-mashhūr*), and I have held on to the exigencies of proof even if not bolstered by the statements of the majority (*al-jumhūr*).[70]

ʿIṣām al-Dīn al-Isfarāyinī likewise disparaged the uncritical acceptance of received views (*taqlīd*) in the introduction to his glosses on the commentary of Jāmī on *al-Kāfiya*, the handbook on syntax by Ibn al-Ḥājib. He wrote:

> These are glosses that, like the sun, put out the starlight of [other] books, adequate embroidery to *al-Fawāʾid al-Ḍiyāʾiyya* [the title of Jāmī's commentary]. May there not be anyone who withholds praise or who faults or defames it. May those who are high-minded and free from obstinacy not reject it because of what it contains of novelties (*ibtidāʿ*), and may the poet who can boast of having observed its depths come to its aid with pleasing literary inventions (*ikhtirāʿ*). He who does not throw off the shackles of mere imitation (*taqlīd*) may say what he pleases, for I do not address him.[71]

For much of the twentieth century, it was assumed that the genres of commentary (*sharḥ*) and gloss (*ḥāshiya*) were necessarily stale and unoriginal, confining themselves to pedantic explication. The examples of Dawānī and ʿIṣām al-Dīn show that on the contrary commentaries and glosses could be written by scholars keen on stressing their credentials as "verifiers" who moved beyond "imitation" and wished to critically assess the merits of scholarly propositions. And there is no reason to dismiss their self-presentation as empty posturing. Kātib Çelebī, the seventeenth-century bibliographer, noted that ʿIṣām al-Dīn in his glosses on Jāmī's

69 Jalāl al-Dīn al-Dawānī, *Sharḥ Tahdhīb al-manṭiq* (Istanbul: Hācı Muḥarrem Bōsnavī Maṭbaʿası, 1305/1887), 2 [printed with independent pagination along with Taftāzānī's *Tahdhīb al-manṭiq* and Mīr Abū l-Fatḥ's *Ḥāshiya ʿalā Sharḥ al-Dawānī*].

70 Jalāl al-Dīn al-Dawānī, *Sharḥ al-ʿAqāʾid al-ʿAḍudiyya* (Istanbul: ʿĀrif Efendī Maṭbaʿası, 1316/1899), 2.

71 ʿIṣām al-Dīn al-Isfarāyinī, *Ḥāshiya ʿalā Sharḥ al-Jāmī* (Istanbul: Hācı Muḥarrem Bōsnavī Maṭbaʿası, 1281/1864), 2.

commentary on *al-Kāfiya* had argued against Jāmī "on most points."[72] Even allowing for some exaggeration, it is obvious that ʿIṣām al-Dīn was doing much more than explicating Jāmī's commentary. Likewise, Dawānī's works on logic, philosophy, and theology to a large extent live up to their author's claim about departing from received views. His commentary on the Ashʿarī creed of Ījī was written from an ostensibly Ashʿarī position but departed from mainstream Ashʿarism on a number of substantial points. For example, Dawānī's discussion of the problem of the divine attributes ended by concluding that Ashʿarī arguments against the Muʿtazilīs on this point were inconclusive and that the Muʿtazilī position (which is to deny that there are divine attributes super-added to the divine essence) should not be deemed heretical.[73] He also argued that – contrary to the accusation traditionally leveled by theologians – the Aristotelian/Neo-Platonic philosophers were not in fact committed to the view that God does not know particulars in the sublunary world.[74] In the field of logic, Dawānī also presented a number of original and influential views. For example, he argued that relational inferences (such as "Zayd is the brother of ʿAmr, and ʿAmr is a writer, so Zayd is the brother of a writer") should be acknowledged as formally productive without the need to regiment them into the form of an Aristotelian syllogism with three terms.[75]

2. Muḥibbī not only credited Mullā Maḥmūd with introducing new works to Damascene students but also with "imparting to them the ability to study and teach them" (*qawwāhum ʿalā qirāʾatihā wa iqrāʾihā*). This ability would have been crucial from the perspective of the ideal of "verification," for the proper response to the "books of the Persians" would surely not have been merely to understand their contents but also to learn how to approach them in the same critical spirit with which they had originally been written. In other words, Damascene students were not only being exposed to new works but also inducted into a scholarly ethos emanating from Timurid and post-Timurid Persia. One of the distinctive features of this ethos appears to have been the extensive use of the discipline called "dialectics" (*munāẓara*) or "the rules of enquiry" (*ādāb al-baḥth*). There is some evidence that Kurdish and Persian scholars were thought to have a distinctive manner of teaching that consciously

72 Kātib Çelebī, *Kashf al-ẓunūn*, II, 1372.

73 Dawānī, *Sharḥ al-ʿAqāʾid*, 28.

74 Ibid., 27.

75 K. El-Rouayheb, *Relational Syllogisms and the History of Arabic Logic, 900–1900* (Leiden, the Netherlands: Brill, 2010), 92–102.

employed the principles of this science. In Istanbul, Muḥibbī met a Turkish scholar and teacher who, he noted, "was remarkable in his manner of lecturing and explicating, following the path of the Persian and Kurdish verifying scholars in heeding the rules of enquiry" (*jārin ʿalā ṭarīqati muḥaqqiqī l-ʿajami wa l-akrādi fī murāʿāti ādābi l-baḥth*).[76] A few years earlier, the Moroccan scholar ʿAbdullāh al-ʿAyyāshī (d. 1679) vividly described a class by a Kurdish scholar he had met during his stay in the town of Medina:

> His lecture on a topic reminded one of discussion (*mudhākara*) and parley (*mufāwaḍa*), for he would say "Perhaps this and that" and "It seems that it is this" and "Do you see that this can be understood like that?" And if he was questioned on even the slightest point he would stop until the matter was established.[77]

The science of *munāẓara* or *ādāb al-baḥth*, though it had roots in the earlier sciences of eristic (*jadal*) and logic, was a relatively recent science that had emerged in the writings of the Central Asian scholars Rukn al-Dīn al-ʿAmīdī (d. 1218) and Shams al-Dīn al-Samarqandī (d. 1303).[78] Even as late as the seventeenth century, it seems to have had little impact on the Maghreb (which might explain al-ʿAyyāshī's bafflement at the manner of lecturing of his Kurdish colleague). The Moroccan scholar al-Ḥasan al-Yūsī (d. 1691), for example, did not mention it in his encyclopedia of the sciences *al-Qānūn*.[79] In the eastern Arabic and Turkish-speaking lands, the discipline was certainly known prior to the seventeenth century. The Egyptian scholar and judge Zakariyyā al-Anṣārī had written a commentary on Samarqandī's epitome of *ādāb al-baḥth*, and the sixteenth-century Ottoman Turkish scholars Ṭāşköprīzāde and Birgevī had written their own short introductory overviews of the

[76] Muḥibbī, *Khulāṣat al-athar*, II, 242 (line 5).

[77] ʿAyyāshī, *Riḥla*, I, 396.

[78] On the early development of this science, see L. Miller, "Islamic Disputation Theory: A Study of the Development of Dialectic in Islam from the Tenth through the Fourteenth Centuries" (Unpublished PhD dissertation, Princeton University, 1984). Miller credits Samarqandī with the transformation of the earlier discipline of theological and juridical "disputation" (*jadal*) into a general, topic-neutral discipline called *munāẓara* or *ādāb al-baḥth*. The fourteenth-century historian Ibn Khaldūn credited Rukn al-Dīn al-ʿAmīdī with taking this step already a few generations earlier; see F. Rosenthal (transl.), *The Muqaddima of Ibn Khaldun* (New York: Pantheon Books, 1958), III, 33. Be that as it may, it was certainly Samarqandī's works that became the point of reference for the subsequent tradition. Ibn Khaldūn did not mention Samarqandī and observed that the discipline was neglected in his time.

[79] Al-Ḥasan al-Yūsī, *al-Qānūn fī aḥkām al-ʿilm wa aḥkām al-ʿālim wa aḥkām al-mutaʿallim*, ed. Ḥamīd Ḥammānī (Casablanca: Maṭbaʿat Shāla, 1998).

discipline.[80] But it is well to distinguish between (1) familiarity with a field and (2) its intensive cultivation as one of the core scholarly disciplines and the systematic use of its concepts when discussing other disciplines. The latter phenomenon was arguably something that in the fifteenth and sixteenth centuries was characteristic of Persianate scholars and was introduced into the Ottoman lands in the course of the seventeenth century. As shown in the following chapter, bibliographic evidence suggests that Ottoman writings on *ādāb al-baḥth* underwent a dramatic increase in quantity after the mid-seventeenth century.

It also seems that Timurid and post-Timurid Persianate scholars used the concepts and argument forms of logic and *ādāb al-baḥth* even when they were writing works in other fields. Meḥmed Sāçaḳlīzāde, the aforementioned scholar who was critical of the extensive study of philosophy in Ottoman madrasas but had no problem with other rational sciences, wrote of *ādāb al-baḥth* or *munāẓara:* "someone who has no share in this science will hardly be able to understand scholarly enquiries."[81] He also wrote that the commentary by Jāmī on Ibn al-Ḥājib's handbook on syntax *al-Kāfiya* – a commentary widely studied in Ottoman colleges (often with the critical glosses of ʿIṣām al-Dīn al-Isfarāyinī) – was only comprehensible to students "after they have acquired a share of logic and *munāẓara*."[82] The Egyptian scholar Jalāl al-Dīn al-Suyūṭī, notorious for his hostility to philosophy and logic, prided himself in knowing grammar, rhetoric, and jurisprudence "according to the principles of the Arabs and the erudite, not according to the way of the Persians and philosophers."[83] His remarks were almost certainly aimed at Timurid scholars such as Taftāzānī and Jurjānī who wrote influential works on grammar, rhetoric, and jurisprudence as well as on logic, *ādāb al-baḥth*, and philosophy. There can be little doubt that the books taught by Mullā Maḥmūd in Damascus, and the manner in which he taught them, exemplified the "philosophical and Persian" approach that Suyūṭī so despised.

[80] For Zakariyyā al-Anṣārī's commentary, see P. K. Hitti, N. A. Faris, and B. ʿAbd al-Malik, *Descriptive Catalog of the Garrett Collection of Arabic Manuscripts in the Princeton University Library* (Princeton, NJ: Princeton University Press, 1938), nr. 871. For relevant works by the other two scholars, see Mach, *Catalogue*, nrs. 3373–3374, 3384.

[81] Sāçaḳlīzāde, *Tartīb al-ʿulūm*, 141.

[82] Ibid., 115, 127.

[83] Jalāl al-Dīn al-Suyūṭī, *Ṣawn al-manṭiq wa-l-kalām ʿan fannay al-manṭiq wa-l-kalām*, ed. ʿA. S. al-Nashshar (Cairo: Maktabat al-Saʿāda, 1947), page *lam* of the editor's introduction, citing Jalāl al-Dīn al-Suyūṭī, *Ḥusn al-muḥāḍarafī akhbār Miṣr wa-l-Qāhira*, ed. M. Abū l-Faḍl Ibrāhīm (Cairo: ʿĪsā al-Bābī al-Ḥalabī, 1967–1968), I, 338.

Opening the Gate of Verification in the Hejaz, Istanbul, and Anatolia

In the cosmopolitan atmosphere of Mecca and Medina, where scholars from all parts of the Islamic world congregated for the Hajj and sometimes settled for shorter or longer periods, the works of ʿIṣām al-Dīn al-Isfarāyinī were being studied intensively already a few decades prior to Mullā Maḥmūd's arrival in Damascus. Two of ʿIṣām al-Dīn's grandchildren, Jamāl al-Dīn Muḥammad and Ṣadr al-Dīn ʿAlī (d. 1598), settled in Mecca and are known to have taught their grandfather's works there, as well as a number of other works by fifteenth-century Persian scholars, such as Jāmī's commentary on Ibn al-Ḥājib's *al-Kāfiya*.[84] It appears that Egyptian scholars first became familiar with ʿIṣām al-Dīn's works via such Persian scholars in western Arabia. The prominent Egyptian scholars Aḥmad al-Ghunaymī (d. 1634) and Aḥmad al-Khafājī both reportedly studied ʿIṣām al-Dīn's works while in Mecca.[85] Ghunaymī's student Ibrāhīm al-Maymūnī (d. 1669), who became renowned for his command of the field of semantics and rhetoric, was asked by a Moroccan scholar passing through Cairo which books he used to teach the discipline. Maymūnī singled out the short and long commentaries of the Timurid scholar Taftāzānī on Qazwīnī's *Talkhīṣ al-miftāḥ* as classic works that for centuries had been the staple handbooks on which numerous glosses had been written. He then added that ʿIṣām al-Dīn al-Isfarāyīnī had more recently written his lengthy *al-Aṭwal* in which he had critically synthesized the most important points raised by glossators.[86] From the perspective of Maymūnī in the mid-seventeenth century, ʿIṣām al-Dīn had been the most important contributor to the fields of semantics and rhetoric since the great Timurid scholars of the fourteenth century.

As for Istanbul and the Turkish-speaking parts of the Empire, one might at first sight suspect that at least the works of Dawānī were studied much earlier than the seventeenth century, for Dawānī dedicated several

[84] Muḥibbī, *Khulāṣat al-athar*, III, 147–148 (on ʿAlī al-ʿIṣāmī). See also the entry on ʿAbd al-Qādir al-Ṭabarī (d. 1623) in ibid., II, 457–464 in which it is detailed (on p. 458, lines 9–10) which works he studied with ʿAlī al-ʿIṣāmī. Jamāl al-Dīn Muḥammad features as a transmitter of the works of ʿIṣām al-Dīn in the chain of transmission given by Ibrāhīm Kūrānī in *al-Amam li-īqāẓ al-himam* (Hyderabad, Deccan: Matbaʿat majlis dāʾirat al-maʿārif al-niẓāmiyya, 1328H), 109. Jamāl al-Dīn's son ʿAbd al-Malik al-ʿIṣāmī (d. 1627) was also an important scholar in the fields of grammar, semantics-rhetoric, and logic; see the entry in Muḥibbī, *Khulāṣat al-athar*, III, 87–88.

[85] Muḥibbī, *Khulāṣat al-athar*, I, 313 (lines 11–12) and I, 332 (lines 20–21).

[86] ʿAyyāshī, *Riḥla*, I, 181. On Maymūnī, see Muḥibbī, *Khulāṣat al-athar*, I, 45–46.

of his works to the Ottoman Sultan Bāyezid II and a number of his students are known to have settled in Istanbul during that Sultan's reign (1481–1512).[87] Nevertheless, these indicators are not in fact decisive. To be sure, manuscripts of Dawānī's works must have circulated in the sixteenth century Ottoman Empire. But it is important to keep in mind the difference between (1) being familiar with certain works and reading them, and (2) studying these works intensively as a regular part of madrasa education. There is reason to believe that the latter was established in the Turkish-speaking parts of the Empire only in the course of the seventeenth century, and that the cases of Istanbul and Damascus were after all quite similar in this respect. The prominent Ottoman Turkish scholar and judge Aḥmed Ṭāşköprīzāde (1495–1561), for example, left behind detailed information about the books he studied and later taught, and he did not mention the works of Dawānī in that context.[88] By the time of Kātib Çelebī (1609–1657), this had clearly changed and Dawānī's works were being intensively studied by Ottoman students. Perhaps the most telling evidence for the claim that the intensive and systematic study of Dawānī's works in Ottoman Turkish scholarly circles started only in the seventeenth century is the absence of major extant Ottoman Turkish commentaries or glosses on these works from the sixteenth century. All the glosses on Dawānī's works mentioned by Kātib Çelebī in his *Kashf al-ẓunūn* were written by scholars who were ethnically Persian, Central Asian, Azeri, or Kurdish. Kātib Çelebī's list is, to be sure, not exhaustive, but supplementing it on the basis of other reliable sources merely yields additional glosses by scholars from the eastern regions. Ottoman Turkish glosses on Dawānī's works start to be written only toward the end of the seventeenth century and the beginning of the eighteenth. One may consider the following works.

1. Dawānī's commentary on Taftāzānī's *Tahdhīb al-manṭiq*

The first major gloss on the work that is extant and authored by an Ottoman Turkish scholar appears to have been that by Ḳara Ḫalīl Tīrevī (d. 1711). This was followed by numerous other Ottoman Turkish glosses in the eighteenth century, by, for example, Veliyüddīn Ḥamīdī (fl. 1718), ʿAlī Marʿaşī (fl. 1723), Meḥmed b. Ḥamīd Kefevī (d. 1754),

[87] Pourjavady, *Philosophy in Early Safavid Iran*, 11–12, 15–16.

[88] Ṭāşköprīzāde, *al-Shaqāʾiq al-nuʿmāniyya fī ʿulamāʾ al-dawla al-ʿUthmāniyya*, edited by Sayyid Muḥammad Ṭabaṭabāʾī Behbehānī (Tehran: Kitābkhāne-yi Majlis-i Shūrā-yi Islāmī, 1389/2010), 471–477.

Ḥafīd ül-Nīthārī (d. 1774), Ismā'īl Gelenbevī (d. 1791), and 'Abdullāh Kānḳirī (d. 1823).[89] By comparison, the numerous earlier glosses on the work (or at least the glosses that are known and extant) appear all to have been written by scholars who were Persian, Azeri, or Kurdish:

- Ghiyāth al-Dīn Dashtakī (d. 1542)
- Jamāl al-Dīn Shīrāzī (d. 1554)
- Mīr Abū l-Fatḥ 'Arabshāhī (d. 1568)
- Mullā 'Abdullāh Yazdī (d. 1573)
- Fakhr al-Dīn Sammākī Astarābādī (d. 1576)
- Muṣliḥ al-Dīn Lārī (d. 1579)
- Ḥusayn Khalkhālī (d. 1604)
- Nūrullāh Shūshtarī (d. 1610)
- Ṣadrüddīnzāde Meḥmed Emīn Şirvānī (d. 1627)
- Zayn al-'Ābidīn Gūrānī (fl. 1656)

2. Dawānī's commentary on Ījī's *'Aqā'id*

Again, this is a work that was intensively glossed by eighteenth- and nineteenth-century Ottoman Turkish scholars such as Ḳara Ḫalīl Tīrevī, Yūsuf 'Atāḳī (d. 1738), Meḥmed b. Ḥamīd Kefevī, Ismā'īl Gelenbevī, 'Abdullāh Kānḳirī, 'Abd ül-Raḥīm Menteşevī (d. 1836), and Meḥmed Fevzī, known as "Edirne Müftisī" (d. 1890).[90] Known and extant glosses on the work from the sixteenth and seventeenth centuries appear again to have been written by Persian, Central Asian, Indian, Azeri, or Kurdish scholars:[91]

89 MS: Süleymaniye Library, Istanbul: Laleli 2583 (Ḥamīdī), Laleli 2586 (Kefevī); Mach, *Catalogue*, nrs. 3238–3242.

90 Mach, *Catalogue*, nrs. 2296–2297 (Kefevī and Gelenbevī); www.yazmalar.gov.tr /19Kh4030/1 ('Atāḳī); www.yazmalar.gov.tr /Raşid Efendi 468 (Menteşevī); www .yazmalar.gov.tr /19Hk914 (Kānḳirī); Meḥmed Fevzī's gloss was printed in Istanbul in 1306/1888–1889 (by Esad Efendi Matbaasi) – for an extant copy see Süleymaniye Library, Istanbul: Tirnovali 1062. Ḳara Ḫalīl wrote super-glosses on the glosses of Aḥmad Ḥusaynābādī, Maḥmūd Ḥasan and Ḥusayn Khalkhālī listed below; see Süleymaniye Library, Istanbul: MS Süleymaniye 763 fols. 1–25 and 35–48; MS Nurosmaniye 2125: fols. 25–42.

91 Brockelmann listed a gloss by the Ottoman scholar Aḥmed Ḫayālī (d. 1465) on Dawānī's commentary. This makes no chronological sense, for Dawānī's work was completed in 906/1500, decades after the death of Ḫayālī. Kātib Çelebī listed a gloss by Ḫayālī on Jurjānī's commentary on the creed of Ījī, and Ḫayālī also wrote esteemed glosses on Taftāzānī's commentary on the creed of Nasafī. It may be that one of these works was confused by a cataloguer with a gloss on Dawānī's commentary. Alternatively, "al-Khayālī" (الخيالي) could have been confused by a scribe or cataloguer with "al-Khalkhālī" (الخلخالي) who did write a gloss on Dawānī's commentary. Brockelmann's *Geschichte der*

- Ḥakīmshāh Muḥammad Qazwīnī (d. 1521)
- Ḥusayn Khalkhālī (d. 1604)
- Yūsuf Qarabāghī (d. 1621)
- Jāmī Marvazī (fl. before 1668)[92]
- Maḥmūd Ḥasan Kurdī (fl. before 1672)[93]
- ʿAbd al-Ḥakīm Siyālkūtī (d. 1657)
- Aḥmad b. Ḥaydar Ḥusaynābādī (d. 1669)
- Ibrāhīm Kūrānī (d. 1690)
- Ḥaydar b. Aḥmad Ḥusaynābādī (d. 1717)

3. Dawānī's *Ithbāt al-wājib*

Commentaries and glosses on this work follow the same pattern. Until the late seventeenth century all known and extant commentaries and glosses are by Persian, Azeri and Kurdish scholars:[94]

arabischen Literatur is a monumental work but often relies on uncritical hand-lists of manuscripts and must therefore be used with caution. Florian Schwartz, in his valuable survey of works by the Ḥusaynābādī family of scholars, follows Brockelmann and lists an extant gloss by Ḥaydar Ḥusaynābādī (d. 1717) on Ḫayālī's gloss on Dawānī's commentary. An inspection of the manuscript in question (Süleymaniye Kütüphanesi, Istanbul: MS Hamidiye 728) reveals it to be a gloss on Ḫayālī's gloss on Taftāzānī's commentary on the creed of Nasafī.

92 This scholar (from Merv in Central Asia) must have been active prior to 1079/1668, which is the date of a manuscript copy of his gloss (www.yazmalar.gov.tr /Raşid Efendi 465).

93 Most manuscripts refer to the author simply as "Maḥmūd Ḥasan" or "Maḥmūd b. Ḥasan." The colophon of MS Edirne Selimiye Yazma Eser Kütüphanesi 568 [www.yazmalarl.gov.tr /22 Sel 568], copied in 1083/1672, adds the attributive "al-Kurdī" to the name. It is possible that he is none other than Mullā Maḥmūd Kurdī, the scholar who settled in Damascus and was said by Muḥibbī to have opened "the gate of verification" there.

94 Brockelmann attributed a gloss on this work to the famed Ottoman *Şeyḫülislam* Kemālpāşāzāde (d. 1534), referring to an extant copy in the Bibliothèque Nationale in Paris (De Slane, 2399). Such a gloss is not mentioned by Ṭāşköprīzāde in his detailed list of works by Kemālpāşāzāde, nor by Kātib Çelebī in his list of glosses on Dawānī's *Ithbāt al-wājib*. An inspection of the manuscript in question is inconclusive: The work itself bears no indication of authorship. It is attributed to Kemālpāşāzāde on the title page, but this is written in a distinctly different hand from that of the work itself. The gloss covers fols. 113b–130b of the extant manuscript. It is written in a different hand from that of the two preceding works that are bound with it, both of them also attributed to Kemālpāşāzāde. It must be kept in mind that Kemālpāşāzāde was a prolific scholar to whom works were often mistakenly attributed in later times (a famous case is the attribution to him of the erotic work *Rujūʿ al-shaykh ilā ṣibāh* which is actually a thirteenth-century work). Even if one supposes Kemālpāşāzāde to have authored the gloss, it is clear that this was not one of his more well-known works, and the fact that neither Ṭāşköprīzāde nor Kātib Çelebī knew of it also indicates that it was not nearly as widely studied as some of the glosses that I list here.

- Mullā Ḥanafī Tabrīzī (fl. 1516)
- Muḥyī al-Dīn Qarabāghī (d. 1535)[95]
- Maḥmūd Nayrīzī (fl. 1499–1522)
- Ḥusayn Ardabīlī (d. 1543)
- Aḥmad b. ʿAbd al-Awwal Qazwīnī (d. 1558)
- Naṣrullāh Khalkhālī (a student of Jamāl al-Dīn Shīrāzī [d. 1554])
- Mīr Abū l-Fatḥ ʿArabshāhī (d. 1568)
- Mullā ʿAbdullāh Yazdī (d. 1573)
- Mīrzā Jān Bāghnavī (d. 1586)
- Yūsuf Qarabāghī (d. 1621)
- ʿAlā al-Dīn Qāḍīzāde Karahrūdī (a student of Bahāʾ al-Dīn al-ʿĀmilī [d. 1621])
- Ḥaydar Ḥusaynābādī (d. 1717)

Again, Ottoman Turkish glosses on the work only appear in the late-seventeenth and eighteenth centuries, by scholars such as Meḥmed b. Aḥmed Ṭarsūsī (d. 1732), Aḥmed Ḳāzābādī (d. 1750), and Meḥmed b. Ḥamīd Kefevī.[96]

The pattern of extant glosses outlined above strongly suggests that the study of Dawānī's works in the sixteenth and early-seventeenth centuries

[95] Kātib Çelebī attributed a gloss to "al-Mawlā al-Ḥanafī" and another gloss to "ʿIzz al-dīn Muḥammad al-Qarabāghī al-Rūmī, who died in 942/1535." He only cited the incipit of the former gloss, however. The former scholar would seem to be the same as "Mawlānā Muḥammad al-Ḥanafī al-Tabrīzī" to whom Kātib Çelebī attributed a standard and much-glossed commentary on Ījī's treatise on *ādāb al-baḥth*. He was active in Herat in the early decades of the sixteenth century and may have been one of the many Sunni scholars of the town who left for Central Asia after the Safavid conquest, for Kātib Çelebī stated that he died in Bukhara, though his estimated date of death – "around 900/1494" – is a bit off; the scholar was still alive in the second decade of the sixteenth century (see the mention of him in W. Thackston (trans. and ed.), *Khwandamir: Habibu l-siyar* (Cambridge, MA: The Department of Near Eastern Languages and Civilizations, Harvard University, 1994), III, 529–530). The other scholar mentioned by Kātib Çelebī would seem to be Muḥyī al-Dīn (not ʿIzz al-Dīn) Muḥammad al-Qarabāghī (d. 1535) whom Ṭāşköprīzāde mentioned a century earlier as having written a commentary on Dawānī's treatise. Qarabāghī studied in Persia and later settled and died in the Ottoman Empire (see Ṭāşköprīzāde, *al-Shaqāʾiq al-nuʿmāniyya*, 395). However, it seems that extant copies attributed in manuscript catalogues to "al-Qarabāghī" contain the same text as the glosses attributed to "Mullā Ḥanafī Tabrīzī." The issue is complicated further by the fact that the commentary attributed to "Mawlānā Ḥanafī" by Kātib Çelebī was referred to by later glossators as having been written by "Mawlānā al-Ḥanafī al-Qarabāghī" (see, e.g., the introduction to Ḥaydar Ḥusaynābādī's gloss which is extant in numerous manuscripts). It may be that there are not two different glosses but one gloss whose authorship is uncertain. The gloss appears to have been completed in 922/1516, which is compatible with it being written by either of the two mentioned scholars.

[96] See Mach, *Catalogue*, nrs. 2403–2404, 2406.

was associated with teachers of Persian, Central Asian, Azeri or Kurdish background. This association was apparently only broken toward the end of the seventeenth century when a sustained Ottoman Turkish tradition of glossing these works emerged. The case of Mullā Maḥmūd in Damascus thus seems to have been part of a more general trend in the Ottoman Empire.

Two scholars in particular played a role in Istanbul analogous to that of Mullā Maḥmūd in Damascus: Ḫōca ʿAbd ül-Raḥīm (d. 1656) and Mullā Çelebī Āmidī (d. 1656). Ḫōca ʿAbd ül-Raḥīm was born in Adana but went east to study "the philosophical sciences: mathematics, physics and metaphysics" in the Kurdish areas.[97] He then settled in Istanbul and was teaching regularly in the city from the year 1620. From April 1647 to July 1648 he occupied the post of Şeyḫülislām of the Empire.[98] According to the later biographer Şeyḫī Meḥmed (d. 1733), he received the honorific "Ḫōca" because he was the teacher of so many students who went on to become prominent scholars in their own right. At least three of his students in turn became Şeyḫülislāms: Behāʾī Meḥmed (1603–1654), Muṣṭafā Bōluvī (d. 1675), and Yaḥyā Minḳārīzāde (d. 1677).[99] One of Ḫōca ʿAbd ül-Raḥīm's extant works is a treatise dedicated to Sultan Murād IV (r. 1623–1640) on a problem in each of nine scholarly disciplines (Quran exegesis, prophetic tradition, law, semantics, rhetoric, metaphysics, logic, astronomy, and geometry). In the introduction to this treatise Ḫōca ʿAbd ül-Raḥīm gave his scholarly genealogy:[100]

97 Muḥibbī, *Khulāṣat al-athar*, II, 411–412. The Arabic text has: *raḥala fī mabdaʾi amrihi ilā bilādi l-akrādi wa qaraʾa bihā l-ʿulūmaʾ l-ḥikmiyyata wa l-riyāḍiyyata wa l-ṭabīʿiyyata wa l-ilāhiyya*. My rendering assumes that the *wa* after *ḥikmiyyata* is an error.

98 Şeyḫī, *Veḳāʾiʿ ül-fużalāʾ*; A. Uğur, *The Ottoman Ulema in the Mid-17th Century*, 176–178.

99 On Behāʾī Meḥmed, see Muḥibbī, *Khulāṣat al-athar*, IV, 2–9 (see esp. p. 3 line 1ff for his relation to Ḫōca ʿAbd ül-Raḥīm) and Uğur, *The Ottoman Ulema*, 153–155. On Bōluvī, see Muḥibbī, *Khulāṣat al-athar*, IV, 371–372 (he is mentioned as a student of Ḫōcā ʿAbd ül-Raḥīm in the entry on the latter in ibid., III, 412, line 2) and Uğur, *The Ottoman Ulema*, 427–429 (who mentions that Bōluvī was a student of Uzun Ḥasan (d. 1671), a student of Mullā Çelebī Āmidī). On Minḳārīzāde, see Muḥibbī, *Khulāṣat al-athar*, IV, 4:477–478 (see esp. p. 477 line 6) and Uğur, *The Ottoman Ulema*, 450–452.

100 Ḫōca ʿAbd ül-Raḥīm, *Ajwiba ʿan tisʿ masāʾil* (MS: Princeton University Library: Yahuda 4070), fols. 18b–19a. Ḫōca ʿAbd ül-Raḥīm also studied with Ṣadrüddīn Şirvānī's son, Ṣadrüddīnzāde Meḥmed Emīn (d. 1627). This is stated by both Muḥibbī (*Khulāṣat al-athar*, II, 411) and Şeyḫī (Uğur, 177) and it is confirmed by the later scholar Muḥammad Hibatullāh al-Tājī (d. 1808), who gave the chain of transmission through which he related the works of Ṣadrüddīnzāde Meḥmed Emīn; see Muḥammad Hibatullāh al-Tājī, *al-ʿIqd al-farīd fī ittiṣāl al-asānīd* (MS: Princeton University Library,

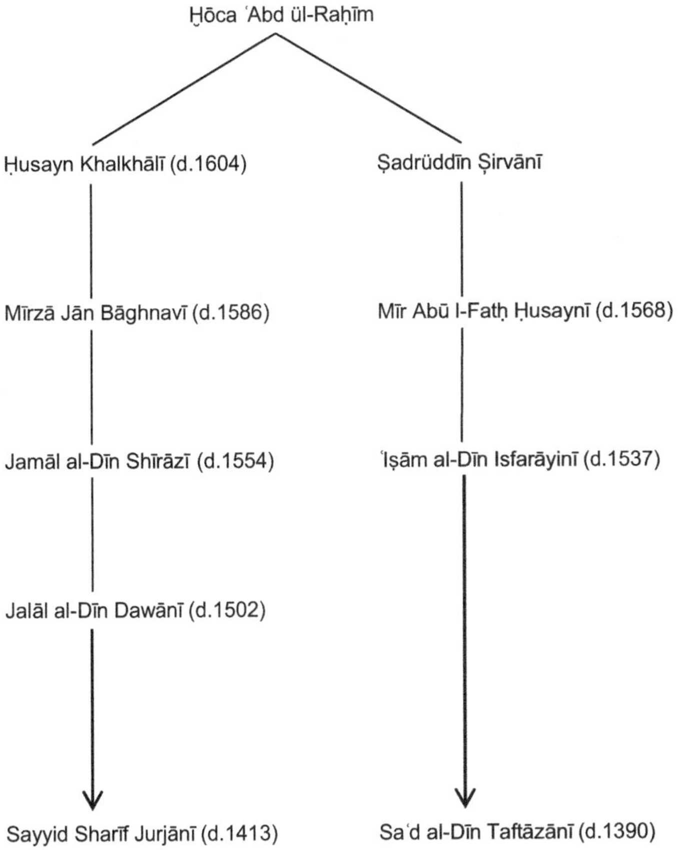

Ḫōca ʿAbd ül-Raḥīm's student Yaḥyā Minḳārīzāde, who was Şeyḫülislam from 1662 to 1674, gave the same scholarly genealogy in his certificate to the Medinan scholar Ibrāhīm al-Khiyārī (d. 1672).[101] As will be seen later, this genealogy – especially the left branch – reappears regularly in Ottoman scholarly genealogies from the mid-seventeenth century to the early twentieth. It will therefore repay closer attention. One striking feature is that it circumvents Ottoman scholars from the fifteenth and sixteenth centuries such as Mollā Fenārī (d. 1431), Aḥmed Ḫayālī

Yahuda 3723), fols. 66b–67a. However, Ḫōca ʿAbd ül-Raḥīm apparently also obtained a certificate from Ṣadrüddīn himself and hence Ṣadrüddīn's son was "skipped" in the lineage. This phenomenon seems to have been quite usual in scholarly lineages.

101 Ibrāhīm al-Khiyārī, *Tuḥfat al-udabāʾ wa-salwat al-ghurabāʾ*, ed. R. M. al-Sāmarrāʾī (Baghdad: Wizārat al-thaqāfa, 1969), I, 310–311.

(d. 1465), Kemālpāşāzāde (d. 1534), Ṭāşköprīzāde, and Ebū l-Su'ūd (d. 1574). Instead, Ḫōca 'Abd ül-Raḥīm and Yaḥyā Minḳārīzāde traced their scholarly pedigree to sixteenth- and fifteenth-century Persian scholars. Another remarkable feature of the genealogy is that it offers what is surely a decisive refutation of the idea that seventeenth-century Ottoman scholars turned away from the rational sciences. Ḫōca 'Abd ül-Raḥīm and Minḳārīzāde – two of the most influential Şeyḫülislāms of the seventeenth century – traced their intellectual ancestry to fourteenth-, fifteenth-, and sixteenth-century Persian scholars who were primarily esteemed for their contributions to the rational sciences, including logic and philosophy.

The adduced genealogy led back to the great Timurid scholars (and rivals) al-Sayyid al-Sharīf al-Jurjānī and Sa'd al-Dīn al-Taftāzānī, who wrote a number of works on semantics-rhetoric, jurisprudence, rational theology, logic, and philosophy that by all accounts dominated the curricula of Ottoman madrasas. The later Sunni Persian scholars Dawānī and 'Iṣām al-Dīn Isfarāyinī and their works have already been presented. Other scholars in the genealogy who wrote works that came to be widely studied in Ottoman madrasas are

1. Mīr Abū l-Fatḥ b. Makhdūm Ḥusaynī 'Arabshāhī (d. 1568). Unlike his teacher 'Iṣām al-Dīn Isfarāyīnī, Mīr Abū l-Fatḥ embraced Shiism and thus made peace with the new order in Persia.[102] As was not unusual in the sixteenth century, he nevertheless had Sunni students and two of his works in particular came to be intensively studied in later Ottoman circles:

102 He wrote a commentary, dedicated to Shāh Ṭahmāsp (r. 1524–1576), on a popular Shiite handbook of theology by Ibn Muṭahhar al-Ḥillī (d. 1325); see Mīr Abū l-Fatḥ, *Miftāḥ al-Bāb*, ed. M. Mohaghegh (Tehran: Institute of Islamic Studies, 1986). This Mīr Abū l-Fatḥ, who gave his own name as "Abū l-Fatḥ b. Makhdūm al-Ḥusaynī al-'Arabshāhī," is often confused in manuscript catalogues with Abū l-Fatḥ b. Amīn al-Sa'īdī, a fifteenth-century scholar who studied with Qāḍīzāde al-Rūmī (fl. 1412), one of the prominent astronomers in the circle of Ulugh Beg (d. 1449) in Samarqand. The confusion goes back to Kātib Çelebī, who attributed to this Abū l-Fatḥ al-Sa'īdī a gloss on his teacher Qāḍīzāde's commentary on *Ashkāl al-ta'sīs*, a standard handbook on geometry, and then attributed to the same scholar glosses on Dawānī's commentary on *Tahdhīb al-manṭiq* and on Mullā Ḥanafī's commentary on *Ādāb al-baḥth*, noting that the glossator died "around the year 950/1543." The Mīr Abū l-Fatḥ who glossed Dawānī in fact died in 976/1568 and he obviously cannot have been a student of an early-fifteenth century scholar. In my *Relational Syllogisms*, 109 (n.80) I noted the confusion of the two Mīr Abū l-Fatḥ's. At the time, I overlooked the fact that the first modern scholar to do so was Rosemarie Quiring-Roche, *Verzeichnis der orientalischen Handschriften in Deutschland: Arabischen Handschriften, Teil III* (Stuttgart: Franz Steiner Verlag, 1994), 258.

   a. A gloss (known in later Ottoman circles as *Mīr al-Tahdhīb*) on Dawānī's commentary on Taftāzānī's manual of logic *Tahdhīb al-manṭiq*
   b. A gloss (known in later circles as *Mīr al-Ādāb*) on the commentary of Mullā Ḥanafī Tabrīzī on Ījī's manual of dialectics (*ādāb al-baḥth*)
2. Mīrzā Jān Ḥabībullāh Bāghnavī (d. 1586).[103] Perhaps the last major Sunnī Persian philosopher, Mīrzā Jān, like ʿIṣām al-Dīn Isfarāyini, left Persia and settled in Uzbek Central Asia. He exerted a profound influence on Ottoman and Mughal intellectual life through both his students and his works, which include the following:
   a. A gloss on the gloss of Quṭb al-Dīn al-Rāzī on the commentary of Naṣīr al-Dīn al-Ṭūsī on Avicenna's famous epitome of philosophy *al-Ishārāt*
   b. A gloss on the commentary of Ibn Mubārakshāh al-Bukhārī (fl. 1360) on *Ḥikmat al-ʿayn*, a widely studied handbook on physics and metaphysics by Kātibī (d. 1277)
   c. A gloss on a commentary by Mullā Ḥanafī Tabrīzī on Dawānī's "older" treatise on proving a Necessary Existent
   d. A gloss on Qūshjī's commentary on Ṭūsī's *Tajrīd al-kalām* discussing some of the major points of dispute in previous glosses by Dawānī and Dawānī's inveterate rival Ṣadr al-Dīn Dashtakī (d. 1498)
   e. A gloss on the commentary of Quṭb al-Dīn al-Rāzī al-Taḥtanī on the handbook of logic entitled *Maṭāliʿ al-anwār* by Sirāj al-Dīn al-Urmawī (d. 1283)
3. Ḥusayn Khalkhālī (d. 1604).[104] The attributive "Khalkhālī" suggests that he hailed from the town or province of Khalkhāl in

103 On Bāghnavī, see Mīrzā Muḥammad Bāqir Khwansārī, *Rawḍāt al-jannāt fī aḥwāl al-ʿulamāʾ wa-l-sādāt* (Qum, 1391/1971–1972), III, 12; and C. Brockelmann, *GAL*, Suppl. II, 594. Note that Brockelmann misread 'Bāghnavī' as 'Bāghandī' following a confusion that goes back to Kātib Çelebī's *Kashf al-ẓunūn* between الباغنوي and الباغندي. Bāghnaw or Bāgh-i naw ("New Garden" in Persian) is an area in present-day Shiraz. On the works listed in the text that follows, see Mach, *Catalog*, nrs. 2401, 3071, 3076, 3228, and 3232. Work (a) was printed in Istanbul by Maṭbaʿa-yi ʿĀmire in 1290/1873–1874 and work (b) was printed in Kazan by al-Maṭbaʿa al-Mīriyya in 1321–2/1903–1904.

104 Muḥibbī, *Khulāṣat al-athar*, II, 122; Kātib Çelebī, *Sullam al-wuṣūl ilā ṭabaqāt al-fuḥūl*, edited by Ekmeleddin İhsanoğlu, Maḥmūd ʿAbd al-Qādir al-Arnāʾūṭ, and Ṣāliḥ Saʿdāwī Ṣāliḥ (Istanbul: IRCICA, 2010), II, 59. Kātib Çelebī gives the date of death 1030/1620. On the works listed in the text that follows, see Mach, *Catalog*, nrs. 2293, 2415, 3243,

what is today the Iranian province of Eastern Azerbaijan (which for much of the sixteenth century was under Ottoman control). He was one of the most prominent students of Mīrzā Jān Bāghnavī and in turn was a teacher of a number of scholars (such as Ḫōca ʿAbd ül-Raḥīm) who came to enjoy renown in the Ottoman Empire. His works include

a. A gloss on Dawānī's commentary on the Ashʿarī creed of Ījī
b. A gloss on Dawānī's commentary on Taftāzānī's handbook of logic *Tahdhīb al-manṭiq*
c. A treatise on the existence and attributes of the Necessary Being
d. A gloss on Maybudī's commentary on the handbook of philosophy *Hidāyat al-ḥikma*
e. *Sharḥ al-dāʾira al-hindiyya*, a commentary on a passage in a standard manual of Ḥanafī law dealing with a matter of astronomy

Another scholar who achieved prominence as a teacher in the Ottoman lands and helped promulgate the scholarly lineage that has just been presented was Mullā Çelebī Āmidī.[105] Of Kurdish origin, he studied with Ḥusayn Khalkhālī and achieved renown as a teacher, first in the town of Āmid (or Diyarbakır) in what is today southeastern Turkey. He came to the attention of the Ottoman Sultan Murād IV when the latter passed through the town in 1638 on his way to reconquer Baghdad and southern Iraq from the Safavids, and the Sultan brought the Kurdish scholar back with him to Istanbul. Apparently, the Sultan asked Mullā Çelebī to examine the scholars of Istanbul, and the Kurdish scholar promptly wrote a collection of difficult questions in nine scholarly disciplines – Quran exegesis, prophetic tradition, law, semantics, rhetoric, metaphysics, logic, astronomy, geometry – and then evaluated the answers submitted by the major scholars of Istanbul. (Ḫōca ʿAbd ül-Raḥīm's aforementioned treatise was a response to this challenge.)[106] Incidentally, this must have occurred just a couple of years before the Egyptian scholar Khafājī came to Istanbul in 1642 and wrote his complaints – cited in the earlier section

3059, and 4994. The last work has been printed (Baghdad: Wizārat al-Awqāf, 1981, edited by D. ʿA. Nūrī).

[105] Muḥibbī, *Khulāṣat al-athar*, IV, 308; Şeyḫī, *Vekāʾiʿ ül-fużalāʾ*, Uğur, *The Ottoman Ulema*, 174–175.

[106] Muḥammad Zāhid al-Kawtharī, "Ṭuraf min anbāʾ al-ʿilm wa-l-ʿulamāʾ," in his *Maqālāt* (Cairo: al-Maktaba al-Azhariyya li-l-turāth, 1994), 575–576.

"The Myth of the 'Triumph of Fanaticism'" – about how the "leader" of the "philosophers" had the Sultan's ear and was lording it over the religious scholars and examining them on logic and astrology. Since Khafājī's invective also includes a number of unfavorable mentions of Kurds, there can be little doubt that he had Mullā Çelebī in mind.[107] According to the biographer Meḥmed Şeyḫī, Mullā Çelebī was particularly well versed in the rational sciences (*'ulūm-i 'aḳliye*) and astronomy (*felek*).[108] According to the Damascene biographer Muḥibbī, Mullā Çelebī counted as his students practically all prominent Ottoman Turkish scholars active in the second half of the seventeenth century. One of these students was Ders-i 'āmm Ṣāliḥ Żihnī (d. 1681), the scholar who had impressed Muḥibbī in Istanbul with his manner of teaching that "followed the way of the Persian and Kurdish verifying scholars in heeding the science of dialectic." This Ṣāliḥ Żihnī, in turn, "taught most of the scholars of the age" according to the biographer Şeyḫī writing a generation later.[109]

So far, the focus has been on Damascus, Hejaz, and Istanbul. The pattern is very similar in more eastern parts of the Ottoman Empire such as eastern Anatolia and the Kurdish areas. One may consider the scholarly genealogies of the following three prominent seventeenth-century scholars:

1. Tefsīrī Meḥmed b. Ḥamza Debbāġī (d. 1699).[110] Born in the city of 'Ayntāb (present-day Gaziantep in southeastern Turkey), he studied the rational sciences in Diyarbakır with the Kurdish scholars 'Alī Gūrānī (d. 1681) and Zayn al-'Ābidīn Gūrānī.[111] He later

[107] See Khafājī, *Rayḥānat al-alibbā*, II, 335 (l.5): *fa-qara'a fī dākhilihi 'alā l-akrādi wa-l-zunūj*; 335 (l.16): *wa-sharaḥa Dīwān al-Mutanabbī bi-i'jāzi l-lughati al-kurdiyya*; 336 (l.11): *wa-ḥakama fī l-mas'alati l-zunbūriyyati bayna Sībawayh wa-l-Kisā'ī fa-ṭarada naḥlahā wa-farraqa 'alā l-akrādi 'asalahā.*

[108] According to Şeyḫī, Mullā Çelebī wrote annotations on standard handbooks on geometry (Qāḍīzāde al-Rūmī's commentary on *Ashkāl al-ta'sīs*) and mathematical astronomy (the works of 'Abd al-'Aliyy al-Birjandī on *hay'a*, presumably either his commentary on Ṭūsī's *Tadhkira* or his gloss on Qāḍīzāde al-Rūmī's commentary on al-Jaghmīnī's introduction to astronomy). These works are a far cry from the more colorful divinatory-astrological works mentioned by Khafājī but apparently close enough for Khafājī, who was more interested in writing a rhetorically effective lampoon rather than historical accuracy.

[109] Uğur, *The Ottoman Ulema*, 507–508.

[110] Şeyḫī, *Veḳā'i' ül-fużalā'*, II, 158.

[111] There is an entry on the former in Muḥibbī, *Khulāṣat al-athar*, III, 203. I have not come across entries or obituaries of the latter. Three of his extant works are *al-Yamāniyyāt*

settled in the town of Sivas in eastern Anatolia and gained renown as a scholar and teacher. Again, his scholarly genealogy goes back to the Persian philosophers Mīrzā Jān Bāghnavī and Dawānī:[112]

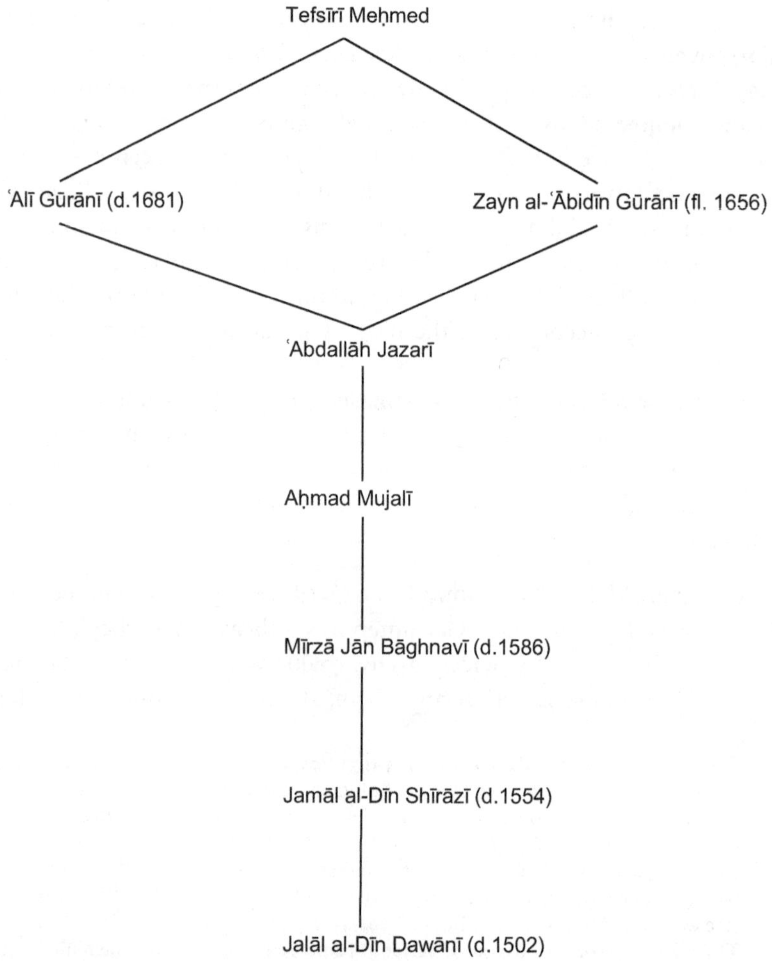

al-maslūla (an anti-Shiite tract); a gloss on the gloss of Lārī on Qāḍī Mīr Maybudī's *Sharḥ Hidāyat al-ḥikma* (on philosophy); and a gloss on the gloss of Mīr Abū l-Fatḥ on Dawānī's *Sharḥ Tahdhīb al-manṭiq* (on logic). All three were dedicated to the Ottoman Grand Vizier Meḥmed Köprülü (v. 1656–1661).

112 See the sources for the lineages of Ebū Saʿīd Ḫādimī (d. 1762) and Ismāʿīl Gelenbevī in the text that follows. The Kurdish scholar Aḥmad Mujalī features in several important

To get a sense of the significance of this particular scholarly genealogy, it may be pointed out that some of the most prominent Ottoman scholars of the eighteenth century – for example, Ebū Saʿīd Ḫādimī (d. 1762) and Ismāʿīl Gelenbevī (d. 1791) – had scholarly genealogies going back to Tefsīrī Meḥmed, as will be seen shortly.

2. Ḥaydar b. Aḥmad Ḥusaynābādī (d. 1717), a Kurdish scholar who was based in the village of Māwarān near the town of Irbil in present-day Iraq.[113] He studied with his father Aḥmad Ḥusaynābādī (d. 1669), himself a prominent scholar who wrote among other things an esteemed gloss on Dawānī's commentary on *al-ʿAqāʾid al-ʿAḍudiyya*. In turn, Ḥaydar wrote a number of philosophical works that appear to have been widely studied in the Ottoman Empire:
   a. A gloss on the gloss of Muṣliḥ al-Dīn Lārī on the commentary by Dawānī's student Qāḍī Mīr Ḥusayn Maybudī on *Hidāyat al-ḥikma*, the aforementioned handbook of physics and metaphysics by Abharī
   b. A gloss on the gloss of Mīrzā Jān Bāghnavī on the commentary of Ibn Mubārakshāh al-Bukhārī on *Ḥikmat al-ʿayn*, the aforementioned handbook on physics and metaphysics by Kātibī

scholarly lineages and was obviously an important link in the transmission of the works of Dawānī and Mīrzā Jān but little is known of him. The vocalization of his attributive is given in Muḥibbī, *Khulāṣat al-athar*, II, 474 on the authority of the Kurdish scholar Ibrāhīm Kūrānī, who was a student of a student of Mujalī. On the other hand, Kātib Çelebi gives the vocalization "Mijalī" and explains that the attributive derives from a Kurdish tribe in Rowandoz near Irbil in Iraq; see Kātib Çelebī, *Sullam al-wuṣūl*, V, 282. In numerous sources his attributive appears as المنجلي (see, e.g., Khiyārī, *Tuḥfat al-udabāʾ*, 310; Muḥibbī, *Khulāṣat al-athar*, II, 411). This form appears too often in early and independent sources to be dismissed without further ado, but it may simply be a variant of the same attributive (just as "Mullā" and "Munlā" can be used interchangeably). Some genealogies have him as a student of Mīrzā Jān's student Mīrzā Makhdūm Ḥusaynī (d. 1587); see, e.g., Ibn Sanad al-Baṣrī, *Maṭāliʿ al-suʿūd*, 399. It may be that he had studied primarily with Mīrzā Makhdūm but also obtained a certificate from an aging Mīrzā Jān himself and hence Mīrzā Makhdūm came to be "skipped" in some lineages.

113 On this scholar and his family in general, see Schwartz, "Writing in the margins of empires." The works of Ḥaydar b. Aḥmad are listed on pp. 184–186. See also Mach, *Catalogue*, nrs. 3053, 3079, 2402.

c. A gloss on the gloss of Mīrzā Jān Bāghnavī on the commentary of Mullā Ḥanafī Tabrīzī on Dawānī's "older" treatise on proofs for the existence of a Necessary Being.

According to an eighteenth-century Iraqi source, Ḥaydar's scholarly reputation was such that students flocked to the village of Māwarān even from as far away as Dagestan and Khorasan.[114] His scholarly genealogy is as follows:[115]

Ḥaydar b. Aḥmad Ḥusaynābādī (d.1717)

Aḥmad Ḥusaynābādī (d. 1669)

Muḥammad b. Shirwīn

Aḥmad Mujalī

Mīrzā Jān Bāghnavī (d.1586)

Jamāl al-Dīn Shīrāzī (d.1554)

Jalāl al-Dīn Dawānī (d.1502)

[114] ʿUthmān al-ʿUmarī, *al-Rawḍ al-naḍir fī tarjamat ʿulamāʾ al-ʿaṣr*, edited by S. al-Nuʿaymī (Baghdad: al-Majmaʿ al-ʿilmī, 1975), III, 9.

[115] Ibn Sanad al-Baṣrī, *Maṭāliʿ al-suʿūd*, ed. Raʾūf and Qubaysī (Baghdad: Wizārat al-thaqāfa, 1991), 133. The twentieth-century scholar Muḥammad Zāhid al-Kawtharī

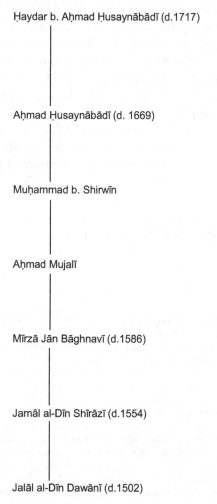

3. Ibrāhīm Kūrānī (d. 1690). Kūrānī was one of the towering figures of seventeenth-century Sufism whose ideas will be discussed in more detail in later chapters. In this context, it may be noted that his scholarly formation fits into the pattern just outlined. He hailed from the town of Shahrān in the Kurdish region of Shahrizor.[116] He studied with a number of Kurdish teachers the works of Taftāzānī, Jurjānī, Dawānī, and later Persian-Azeri scholars.[117] He then settled in Medina, where he is known to have taught philosophical works such as *Ḥikmat al-ishrāq* by the Illuminationist philosopher Suhrawardī and the standard handbook on physics and metaphysics *Hidāyat al-ḥikma* by Abharī.[118] It was his classes, incidentally, that so impressed the Moroccan scholar al-ʿAyyāshī for their dialectical manner. Kūrānī left behind quite detailed information about his teachers and their teachers in his record of studies entitled *al-Amam li-īqāẓ al-himam*, allowing us to reconstruct the following genealogy:[119]

assumed that "Muḥammad b. Shirwīn" was Ṣadrüddīnzāde Meḥmed Emīn Şirvānī, see Muḥammad Zāhid al-Kawtharī, *al-Taḥrīr al-wajīz fīmā yabtaghīhi l-mustajīz*, ed. ʿAbd al-Fattāḥ Abū Ghudda (Aleppo: Maktab al-Maṭbūʿāt al-Islāmiyya, 1993), p. 20 (where Aḥmad b. Ḥaydar is mentioned as a student of Meḥmed Emīn Şirvānī). But this is doubtful. Kātib Çelebī gives the name of this scholar as "Muḥammad Shirwīnī" and states that the attributive derives from a Kurdish tribe (and hence not from the province of Shirwan); see Kātib Çelebī, *Sullam al-wuṣūl*, V, 61. As was seen earlier in the case of the genealogy of Ḥōca ʿAbd ül-Raḥīm, Meḥmed Emīn Şirvānī would have traced his own scholarly genealogy via his father Ṣadrüddīn Şirvānī to Mīr Abū l-Fatḥ and ʿIṣām al-Dīn Isfarāyīnī.

116 See ʿAyyāshī, *Riḥla*, I, 383ff.

117 Kūrānī, *al-Amam*, 101–104.

118 ʿAyyāshī, *Rihla*, I, 396. ʿAyyashi studied both works with Kūrānī in Medina.

119 On Muḥammad Sharīf Gūrānī, see Kūrānī, *al-Amam*, 128; Muḥibbī, *Khulāṣat al-athar*, IV, 280–281. On ʿAbd al-Karīm Gūrānī, see Kūrānī, *al-Amam*, 129; Muḥibbī, *Khulāṣat al-athar*, II, 474. Muḥibbī gives the date of death as 1050/1640. On Yūsuf Gūrānī, see Muḥibbī, *Khulāṣat al-athar*, IV, 508. On Ibrāhīm Hamadānī, see Muḥibbī, *Khulāṣat al-athar*, I, 63–64. He is mentioned as a student of Mullā ʿAbdullāh Yazdī in the entry on the latter ibid., III, 40. On ʿAbdullāh Yazdī, see Khwānsārī, *Rawḍāt al-jannāt*, IV, 228–230. Khwānsārī's entry is much fuller than that of Muḥibbī, *Khulāṣat al-athar*, III, 40. Muḥibbī gives Yazdī's date of death as 1015/1606–1607, as opposed to Khwānsārī's 981/1573–1574, but the latter source – though later – is clearly much better informed about the life of Yazdī and gives details about his studies alongside Mīrzā Jān Bāghnavī with Dawānī's student Jamāl al-Dīn Maḥmūd Shīrāzī.

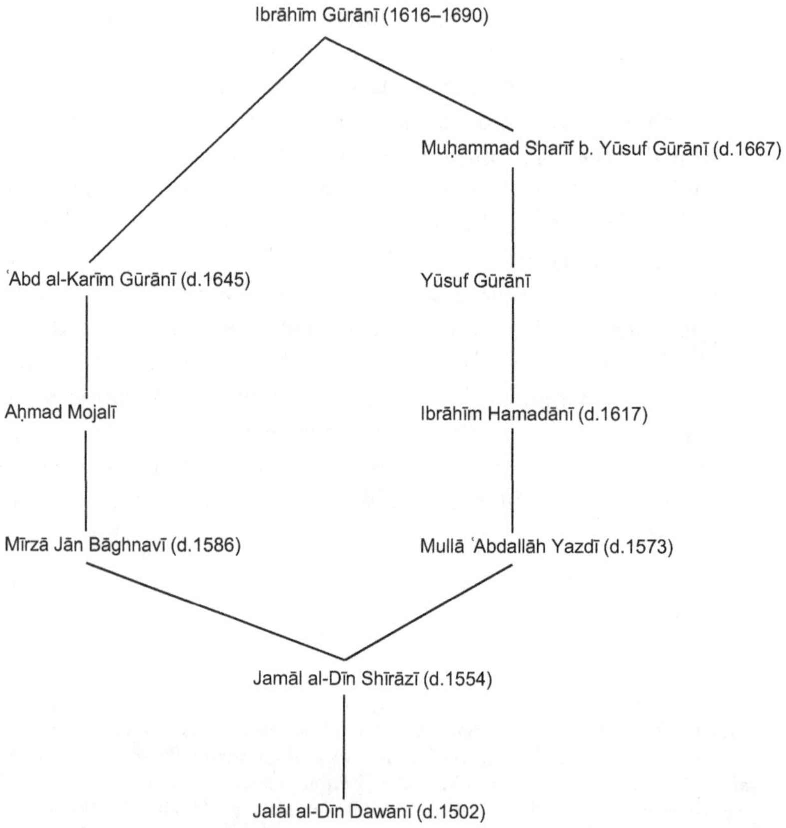

Scholarly genealogies, to be sure, usually involve a good deal of idealization and simplification. They are typically presented as if a scholar had only one or two teachers and this of course does not correspond to what is known of premodern Islamic education. Yet, even allowing for idealizations, such genealogies still reveal scholars' sense of who their most important teacher or teachers were. Again, it is striking that Ottoman scholars began in the seventeenth century to trace their intellectual genealogies to fifteenth- and sixteenth-century Persian, Kurdish, and Azeri scholars and in the process bypassed Ottoman scholars of the fifteenth and sixteenth centuries. The works of earlier Ottoman scholars such as Ebū l-Suʿūd, Ṭāşköprīzāde, Ḫayālī, and Mollā Fenārī continued to be studied after the sixteenth century, but the evidence is overwhelming that Ottoman scholars from the seventeenth, eighteenth, and nineteenth centuries did not trace their intellectual lineage to them but rather to Persian scholars such as Dawānī, ʿIṣām al-Dīn Isfarāyinī, and Mīrzā Jān Bāghnavī. Apart from the seventeenth-century lineages presented earlier, one may consider the intellectual lineages of three prominent eighteenth-century Ottoman Turkish scholars. The first is that of Ebū Sa'īd Ḫādimī, a prominent scholar and mystic based in Konya who wrote among other things an extensive commentary on Birgevī's *al-Ṭarīqa al-muḥammadiyya*, an innovative handbook of logic entitled *'Arā'is al-nafā'is*, and an esteemed compendium of Ḥanafī jurisprudence entitled *Majāmi' al-ḥaqā'iq*:[120]

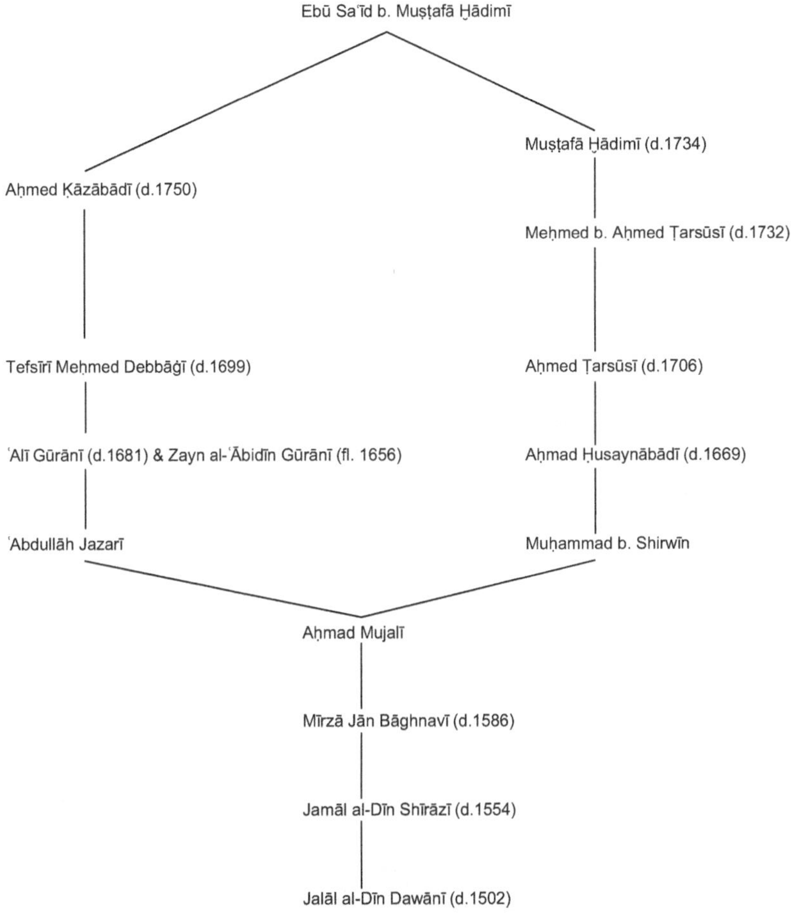

120 On Ḫādimī, see Sarıkaya, *Abū Sa'īd Muḥammad al-Ḫādimī (1701–1762)*. His intellectual lineage is given in an autograph certificate (*ijāza*) available at www.yazmalar.gov.tr/ 06 Mil Yz FB543, fols. 7–8. Ḫādimī also adduced a line of transmission for the canonical collection of hadith by Bukhārī (d.870). This lineage was very different, featuring Syrian and Egyptian scholars such as Muḥammad al-Kāmilī (d. 1719), Khayr al-Dīn al-Ramlī (d. 1671) and Ibn Ḥajar al-'Asqalānī (d. 1449) rather than Kurdish and Persian scholars whose focus was the rational sciences. It seems to have been common at the time to give distinct scholarly pedigrees for the rational and the "transmitted" sciences.

The second lineage is that of arguably the greatest Ottoman philosopher, theologian, logician, and mathematician of the eighteenth century, Ismāʿīl Gelenbevī:[121]

Ismāʿīl Gelenbevī (1730–1791)

Meḥmed Emīn Anṭālī (1700–1797)

Aḥmed Ḳāzābādī (d.1750)

Tefsīrī Meḥmed Debbāġī (d.1699)

ʿAlī Gūrānī (d.1681) & Zayn al-ʿĀbidīn Gūrānī (fl. 1656)

ʿAbdullāh Jazarī

Aḥmad Mujalī

Mīrzā Jān Bāghnavī

Jamāl al-Dīn Shīrāzī

Jalāl al-Dīn Dawānī

[121] Muḥammad Zāhid al-Kawtharī, "Tarjamat al-ʿallāma Ismāʿīl al-Kalanbawī wa-lumʿa min anbāʾ baʿḍ shuyūkhihi" in Muḥammad Zāhid al-Kawtharī, *Maqālāt* (Cairo: al-Maktaba al-Azhariyyali-l-turāth, 1994), 553–561.

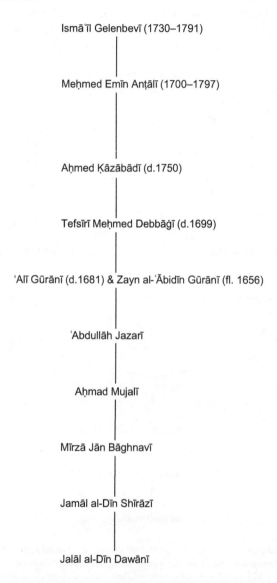

The third lineage is that of Ismāʿīl Ḳōnevī (d. 1781), best known for his monumental gloss on the widely studied Quran commentary of Bayḍāwī (fl. 1284):[122]

Ismāʿīl Ḳōnevī (d.1781)
|
ʿAbd al-Karīm Ḳōnevī
|
ʿOthmān Devrekī
|
ʿAlī Nīthārī Ḳayṣerī (d.1698)
|
Rajab Āmidī (fl.1649–1676)
|
ʿAbd al-Raḥmān Āmidī (d.1656)
|
Mullā Çelebī Āmidī (d.1656)
|
Ḥusayn Khalkhālī (d.1604)
|
Mīrzā Jān Bāghnavī
|
Jamāl al-Dīn Shīrāzī
|
Jalāl al-Dīn Dawānī

[122] On Ḳōnevī, see Murādī, *Silk al-durar*, I, 258. On Nīthārī, see Baghdādī, *Hadiyyat al-ʿārifīn*, I, 764. Rajab Āmidī is the author of a commentary, completed in 1087/1676, on Birgevī's *al-Ṭarīqa al-muḥammadiyya*. His other major work, a miscellany entitled *Jāmiʿ al-azhār wa laṭāʾif al-akhbār*, was completed in 1060/1649. On ʿAbd al-Raḥmān Āmidī, see Muḥibbī, *Khulāṣat al-athar*, II, 345 and Uğur, *The Ottoman Ulema*, 176.

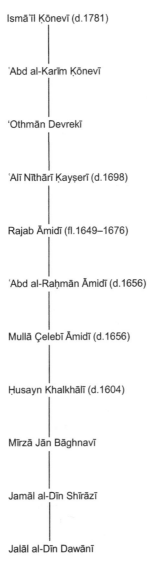

The prominent early twentieth-century Ottoman scholar Muḥammad Zāhid al-Kawtharī (d. 1951) traced his own intellectual lineage back to Ismāʿīl Ḳōnevī and via him to sixteenth- and fifteenth-century Persian specialists in the rational sciences.[123]

A noteworthy feature of these lineages is that the ethnicity of the scholars shifts in the course of the seventeenth century. The fifteenth- and sixteenth-century scholars are Persian; in the early seventeenth century they are Kurdish or Azeri; and in the second half of the seventeenth century scholars of Ottoman Turkish background begin to appear. Starting with scholars such as Tefsīrī Meḥmed (d. 1699), Aḥmed Ṭarsūsī (d. 1706), and ʿAlī Nīthārī (d. 1698) the lineages become predominantly Ottoman Turkish (or "Rūmī" to adopt the language of the time).[124] This pattern fits well with the bibliographic evidence presented above, suggesting that an Ottoman Turkish tradition of glossing the works of Dawānī first emerged toward the end of the seventeenth century. By the eighteenth century, the Ottoman Turkish scholarly tradition in the rational sciences seems to have come into its own and to have outgrown its dependency on Kurdish and Azeri teachers. A scholar such as Gelenbevī became renowned for his works on logic, dialectic, rational theology, and philosophy and yet had studied with Turkish teachers. Indeed, his works became esteemed enough to be studied and commented on in the Kurdish regions in the nineteenth century,[125] and for that to happen Kurdish students must at some point have obtained certificates to teach these works from Turkish teachers.

Conclusion

Historians who have cited Kātib Çelebī's writings in support of the idea of a seventeenth-century "triumph of fanaticism" have overlooked the

[123] Kawtharī, *al-Taḥrīr al-wajīz*, esp. 18; and *idem*, *Maqālāt*, 561.

[124] The term "Rūmī" (i.e., "Roman") was used by early Muslims of the inhabitants of the Byzantine Empire, and it continued to be used thus in later times, even after Asia Minor and Constantinople had become predominantly Muslim and Turkish-speaking. Especially when juxtaposed to "Kurd," "Persian," and "Arab," the term Rūmī tended to be used until the nineteenth century of the settled, Turkish-speaking Muslims of Anatolia and southeastern Europe. The terms "Turkī" and "Atrāk" were often slightly pejorative in this period and tended to be used of nomadic or semi-nomadic Turcomans. See on this topic, C. Kafadar, "A Rome of One's Own: Reflections on Cultural Geography and Identity in the Lands of Rum," *Muqarnas* 24(2007): 7–25.

[125] For example, his handbook on logic *al-Burhān fī ʿilm al-mīzān* was printed by the Kurdish press of Farajullāh Zakī al-Kurdī in Cairo in 1347/1929 with the glosses of the Kurdish scholars ʿAbd al-Raḥmān Panjiyūnī (d. 1901) and ʿUmar Ibn al-Qaradāghī (d. 1936). Gelenbevī's handbook on *ādāb al-baḥth* was printed by the same press in 1353/1934 with glosses by the same Kurdish scholars.

fact that he explicitly noted that the study of the philosophical sciences had continued uninterruptedly in the Kurdish provinces of the Empire and that students of Kurdish scholars who came to Istanbul in his lifetime were influential teachers in these sciences. It is worth quoting his testimony in full:

From the beginning of the Ottoman Empire till the time of the late Sultan Süleymān [r. 1520–1566] whose abode is Paradise, scholars who combined the study of the sacred sciences with that of philosophy (*ḥikmet*) were held in high renown. The Conqueror Sultan Meḥmed [r. 1451–1481] had built the eight colleges and had written in his endowment deed: "Let work be carried on in accordance with the Qanun" and had appointed lessons in the Glosses on the *Tajrīd* and the Commentary on the *Mawāqif* [both on philosophical theology]. Those who came after put a stop to these lessons as being 'philosophy' (*felsefiyāt*) and thought it reasonable to give lessons on the *Hidāya* and the *Akmal* [two standard works on Ḥanafī law]. But as restriction to these was not reasonable, neither 'philosophy' (*felsefiyāt*) nor *Hidāya* and *Akmal* was left.[126] Thereupon the market of learning in Rūm slumped, and the men of learning were nigh to disappearing. Then the novices of scholars who were working in accordance with the Qanun in some outlying places here and there in the lands of the Kurds came to Rūm and began to give themselves tremendous airs (*baʿẓ-i kenārda Ekrād diyārında yer yer Ḳānūn üzere şuġul eden ṭāliblerin mübtedīleri Rūm'a gelūb aẓīm ṭafra ṣatar oldı*). Seeing them, some capable men in our time became students of philosophy (*ḥikmet*).[127]

Modern historians have tended to take the first part of the quote as evidence for the "triumph of fanaticism" and to ignore the latter part about the reinvigoration of philosophical studies as a consequence of the influx of students from the Kurdish regions.[128] If the argument of the present chapter is sound, then this is to get things precisely the wrong way round. When Kātib Çelebī lamented the declining fortunes of the rational sciences after Sultan Süleymān he seems to have been indulging in a well-known topos current among Ottoman authors of his age. The claim that the study of Jurjānī's works on philosophical theology ceased after the reign of Süleymān is not a first-hand observation (Kātib Çelebī was not born until 1609) and cannot be corroborated by other sources, and it moreover flies in the face of clear evidence that Jurjānī's commentary on

126 The idea here seems to be that knowledge of the philosophical sciences is crucial even for a scholar who studies Islamic law, and that stopping the study of such sciences caused even the quality of scholarship in Islamic law to decline.

127 Lewis, *The Balance of Truth*, 26; Kātib Çelebī, *Mīzān ül-ḥaḳḳ fī iḫtiyār il-eḥaḳḳ* (Istanbul: Ebū l-Żiyā' Maṭbaʿası, 1306/1888–1889), 10–11.

128 For example, Çavuşoğlu cites the first part of Kātib Çelebī's remarks as evidence for a Ḳāḍīzādelī-inspired change in the Ottoman madrasa curriculum and leaves out the second part altogether; see "The Ḳāḍīzādelīs," 269–274.

the *Mawāqif* was still being taught in Meḥmed II's "Eight Colleges" in the 1670s.[129] It is also well to remember that Kātib Çelebī enjoyed the support of Şeyhülislām Ḫōca ʿAbd ül-Raḥīm who was well-versed in the rational sciences, traced his intellectual lineage to sixteenth- and fifteenth-century Persian philosophers and trained an entire generation of Ottoman scholars, including at least three later Şeyḫülislāms.[130] Even if one does not wish to discount Kātib Çelebī's remarks entirely, it should hopefully be plain from the evidence presented in this chapter that whatever current of hostility to the rational sciences he had in mind cannot plausibly be seen as a prevalent or consequential trend.

By contrast, when Kātib Çelebī was noting the reinvigoration of the rational and philosophical sciences by students from the Kurdish regions in the early decades of the seventeenth century, he was one of the first to describe – at first hand – an important and hitherto unnoticed development in Ottoman scholarly culture that was occurring in the early decades of the seventeenth century and that left its clear imprint on Ottoman scholarly pedigrees until the final days of the Empire. Kurdish and Azeri scholars such as Mullā Maḥmūd, Ḥusayn Khalkhālī, and Aḥmad Mujalī as well as their first- and second-generation students such as Ḫōca ʿAbd ül-Raḥīm, Mullā Çelebī Āmidī, and Aḥmad Ḥusaynābādī played an important role in linking the Ottoman intellectual tradition to Persian scholars of the fifteenth and sixteenth centuries. As shown by the examples of Mullā Maḥmūd and Mullā Çelebī, Kurdish scholars who settled in Istanbul and Damascus in the seventeenth century were esteemed as teachers of the rational sciences and the "books of the Persians." Several Turkish scholars are also known to have traveled to the Kurdish areas to complete their education in the rational sciences.[131] The examples of Ḫōca ʿAbd ül-Raḥīm and Tefsīrī Meḥmed, who went to the eastern provinces to study the philosophical sciences, have already been mentioned. Another example is Ṣarī ʿOthmān (d. 1678), who was born in Amasya in central

[129] For example, Muḥibbī wrote the following in his entry on Mullā Çelebī Āmidī's student Ṣāliḥ Żihnī Ders-i ʿāmm: "He then [after 1087/1676] moved to one of the Eight Schools and started to teach there the commentary on the *Mawāqif* in accordance with the stipulation of its [the school's] founder" (*Khulāṣat al-athar*, II, 242). The historian Şeyḫī confirms that Ṣāliḥ Żihnī taught at one of the Eight Schools (the so-called *Ṣaḥn*) from 1678 to 1680 (Uğur, 508).

[130] Ḫōca ʿAbd ül-Raḥīm's supportive attitude to Kātib Çelebī is mentioned by the latter in *Mīzān ül-ḥakḳ* (see Lewis, *The Balance of Truth*, 142).

[131] Especially Diyarbakır seems in the seventeenth century to have been an important intellectual center, but Mosul and even the village of Māwarān near Irbil also attracted students from far and wide.

Anatolia, studied in Istanbul, and *then* went to the Kurdish areas to complete his education (*tekmīl-i ʿilm*) and studied with notable scholars of that region such as Aḥmad Ḥusaynābādī before returning to the capital and becoming tutor to the famed Vizier Köprülüzāde Fāżil Aḥmed Pāşā (1635–1676).[132] Of the two phenomena mentioned by Kātib Çelebī, *this* was undoubtedly the more significant and consequential. It led to the incorporation of works by scholars such as Dawānī, Qāḍī Mīr Maybudī, ʿIṣām al-Dīn Isfarāyinī, Mīr Abū l-Fatḥ, and Mīrzā Jān Bāghnavī into the Ottoman madrasa curriculum, where they remained until the end of the Ottoman Empire. It also led a seventeenth-century Damascene observer to speak of the "opening of the gate of verification" in his city, and a host of prominent Ottoman Turkish scholars from Ḫōca ʿAbd ül-Raḥīm in the seventeenth century to Muḥammad Zāhid al-Kawtharī in the twentieth to trace their intellectual lineage to the people involved in this process rather than their own Ottoman forebears from the fifteenth and sixteenth centuries.

[132] Uğur, *The Ottoman Ulema*, 469–470.

2

A Discourse on Method

The Evolution of Ādāb al-baḥth

The rhetoric of "verification" (*taḥqīq*) as opposed to "imitation" (*taqlīd*) was central to the post-Timurid Persian tradition of studying the rational sciences and to their Ottoman successors from the seventeenth and eighteenth centuries. The concept of "verification" was neither novel nor confined to this particular scholarly tradition. As will be clear in later chapters of this book, it plays a prominent role in the works of Muḥammad b. Yūsuf al-Sanūsī (d. 1490), the influential North African Ashʿarī theologian and logician, and later scholars in Sanūsī's tradition, such as the Moroccan al-Ḥasan al-Yūsī (d. 1691). What seems to have been distinctive about the Timurid Persian and later Ottoman traditions was the overt connection between the ideal of "verification" and the intense interest in the discipline of *ādāb al-baḥth*. For the Damascene scholar Muḥibbī, it was a distinctive feature of "Persian and Kurdish verifying scholars" (*muḥaqqiqī al-ʿajam wa l-akrād*) and their Ottoman students that they heeded the science of *ādāb al-baḥth*.[1] For the Ottoman Turkish scholar Sāçaḳlīzāde, familiarity with *ādāb al-baḥth* was indispensable for following scholarly discussions, especially in logic, theology, and jurisprudence but also for understanding a standard handbook on Arabic syntax such as Jāmī's *Sharḥ al-Kāfiya*.[2] By contrast, there appears not to have been a single extant work on *ādāb al-baḥth* by a scholar from the Maghreb up to the eighteenth century, and – as mentioned in the previous chapter – the science is conspicuously absent from Yūsī's encyclopedia of the sciences entitled *al-Qānūn*. For Yūsī – a contemporary of

[1] Muḥibbī, *Khulāṣat al-athar*, II, 242.

[2] Sāçaḳlīzāde, *Tartīb al-ʿulūm*, 115, 127, 141; Sāçaḳlīzāde, *Taqrīr al-qawānīn*, 3.

Muḥibbī and Sāçaḳlīzāde – there was obviously no connection between *taḥqīq* and *ādāb al-baḥth*.

As indicated in the previous chapter, the science of *ādāb al-baḥth* or *munāẓara* emerged relatively late in Islamic history. Its roots, to be sure, lay in the earlier science of eristic (*jadal* or *khilāf*) that had developed among early Islamic theologians and jurists (with some influence from Aristotelian topics and Late Antique rhetoric). In the writings of the Central Asian scholars Rukn al-Dīn al-ʿAmīdī (d. 1213), Burhān al-Dīn al-Nasafī (d. 1288), and Shams al-Dīn al-Samarqandī (d. 1303), the elements of theological and juridical *jadal* or *khilāf* became generalized into a topic-neutral discipline of general applicability and infused with formal modes of argumentation derived from Aristotelian and Stoic logic.[3] The writings of Samarqandī on the new discipline of *ādāb al-baḥth* served as a point of departure for the later tradition, and especially his short epistle (*Risāla*) became a standard handbook that was often commented on and glossed by later scholars. By the early seventeenth century, *ādāb al-baḥth* or *munāẓara* had long been recognized in eastern Islamic lands as an independent scholarly discipline related but not reducible to logic and jurisprudential eristic. In the course of the seventeenth and eighteenth centuries, the field experienced a noticeable efflorescence in Ottoman scholarly circles. As shown in the next section, Ottoman contributions to the field became noticeably more numerous and more lengthy in the period from around the middle of the seventeenth century to the end of the eighteenth. As shown in the section after that, Ottoman works were not merely becoming more numerous and detailed. The new handbooks that were written by Ottoman scholars in this period testify to a substantial development of the field. In the final section of the chapter it is argued that these developments in turn had noticeable effects on the Ottoman tradition of logic.

An Explosion of Interest in Dialectics (*Ādāb al-baḥth*)

Writing in the mid-seventeenth century, Kātib Çelebī noted that the most common handbook on *ādāb al-baḥth* used in his day was Samarqandī's treatise along with the commentary of Masʿūd al-Shirwānī (d. 1499), a scholar who seems to have been active in Herat (in present-day Afghanistan).[4] However, this handbook was soon to be eclipsed by other

[3] See especially Miller, "Islamic Disputation Theory."

[4] Kātib Çelebī, *Kashf al-ẓunūn*, I, 207.

presentations of the field. The Ottoman tradition of writing glosses on it seems largely to have ceased by the mid-seventeenth century. Instead, the treatise of ʿAḍud al-Dīn al-Ījī, with the commentary of Mullā Ḥanafī Tabrīzī and the gloss of Mīr Abū l-Fatḥ, began to elicit a steady stream of Ottoman superglosses. Some of the major extant glosses are by the following scholars[5]:

- ʿAbd al-Raḥmān Āmidī (d. 1656), a student of Mullā Çelebī Āmidī
- ʿUmar Chillī (fl. 1655), a scholar active in Diyarbakır
- Muḥammad b. ʿAbdullāh Kurdī (d. 1673)
- Yaḥyā Minḳārīzāde (d. 1677), a student of Ḫōca ʿAbd ül-Raḥīm
- Tefsīrī Meḥmed Debbāġī (d. 1699), a student of ʿAlī Gūrānī and Zayn al-ʿĀbidīn Gūrānī
- Ḥamza Dārendevī (fl. 1688), a student of Tefsīrī Meḥmed
- Aḥmed Ḥācī-ʿÖmerzāde (fl. 1695), also a student of Tefsīrī Meḥmed
- Esʿad Yānyavī (d. 1729), a second-generation student of Tefsīrī Meḥmed
- Cārullāh Veliyüddīn (d. 1738), a second-generation student of Minḳārīzāde
- ʿAbdullāh Yūsufefendīzāde (d. 1754), another second-generation student of Minḳārīzāde
- Meḥmed Kefevī (d. 1754)
- ʿAbdullāh b. Ebī Saʿīd Ḫādimī (d. 1778)
- Ismāʿīl Gelenbevī (d. 1791)

Two features of these superglosses are worth emphasizing. First, the ethnicity of the glossators shifts over time and corresponds to the pattern outlined in the previous chapter. The earlier glosses (the first three) were written by Kurdish scholars; this is followed by a number of glosses written by Turkish first- or second-generation students of Kurdish or Azeri scholars; and by the eighteenth century an independent Ottoman Turkish tradition of glossing the work had taken hold. Second, there is a

[5] Mach, *Catalogue*, nr. 3356 (Āmidī); Mach, *Catalogue*, nr. 3354 (Chillī); www.yazmalar.gov.tr /19Hk4722 (Kurdī); Mach, *Catalogue*, nr. 3352 (Minḳārīzāde); www.yazmalar.gov.tr /43Va693 (Tefsīrī Meḥmed); Mach, *Catalogue*, nr. 3350 (Ḥamza); Mach, *Catalogue*, nr. 3353 (Ḥācī-ʿÖmerzāde); www.yazmalar.gov.tr /19Hk2313 (Yānyavī); Süleymaniye Library, Istanbul: MS: Kılıç Ali Paşa 877 (Carullāh); www.yazmalar.gov.tr /19Kh4689 (Yūsufefendīzāde); Mach, *Catalogue*, nr. 3351 (Kefevī); www.yazmalar.gov.tr /45AkZe1493/2 (Ḫādimī); Mach, *Catalogue*, nr. 3361 (Gelenbevī).

noticeable tendency for the glosses to become lengthier over time. The glosses of Cārullāh Veliyüddīn, Yūsufefendīzāde, and Gelenbevī are massive works (the last was printed in Istanbul in the nineteenth century in 609 pages).[6]

Alongside the tradition of writing superglosses on Mīr Abū l-Fatḥ's gloss, two influential new handbooks on *ādāb al-baḥth* were written by Ottoman Turkish scholars in the second half of the seventeenth century and the early decades of the eighteenth. A certain Ḥüseyn Adanavī, of whom more is said later, wrote a condensed treatise that came to be known as *al-Ḥusayniyya* and was the subject of numerous glosses by later Ottoman scholars. Particularly esteemed (judging by the number of extant manuscripts) were the glosses written by[7]

- ʿAlī Ferdī Ḳayṣerī (d. 1715)
- Ḫalīl Fāʾid Yedīḳūlelī (d. 1722)
- Meḥmed Dārendevī (d. 1739)
- Aḥmed Yegān Marʿaşī (d. 1751)
- Meḥmed Kefevī (d. 1754)
- Meḥmed Āḳkirmānī (d. 1760)
- Meḥmed Ṣādiḳ Erzincānī (d. 1808), printed in 216 pages in Istanbul in 1307/1890

Meḥmed Sāçaḳlīzāde wrote an independent summa entitled *Taqrīr al-qawānīn al-mutadāwala fī ʿilm al-munāẓara* that may be the lengthiest independent exposition of *ādāb al-baḥth* (i.e., a work that was not a commentary or gloss) ever written in Arabic (it was printed in Istanbul in the nineteenth century in 128 pages).[8] Sāçaḳlīzāde also wrote a shorter epitome entitled *al-Waladiyya* that became widely studied and elicited numerous commentaries by later Ottoman scholars, for example[9]

6 Ismāʿīl Gelenbevī, *Ḥāshiya ʿalā Mīr al-Ādāb* (Istanbul: Maṭbaʿah-i ʿĀmireh, 1234/1818–1819).

7 Mach, *Catalogue*, nrs. 3394–3400.

8 Sāçaḳlīzāde, *Taqrīr al-qawānīn al-mutadāwala fī ʿilm al-munāẓara* (Istanbul: n.p. 1289/1872–1873).

9 The commentaries of Behisnī and ʿAbd al-Wahhāb Āmidi have been printed repeatedly together in Cairo, for instance, by al-Khānjī press in 1329/1911 and by al-Maṭbaʿa Azhariyya in 1331/1912–1913. For extant manuscripts of the other commentaries, see Mach, Catalogue, 3403–3406; www.yazmalar.gov.tr /60Zile231 (ʿUmar Āmidī).

- Ḥüseyn b. Ḥaydar Bertizī,[10] a student of Sāçaḳlīzāde
- Meḥmed b. Ḥüseyn Behisnī,[11] another student of Sāçaḳlīzāde
- Ḫalīl Āḳvirānī (fl. 1163/1750)
- ʿUmar b. Ḥusayn Āmidī (d. 1776)
- ʿAbd al-Wahhāb Āmidī (fl. 1181/1767)
- Ḥasan Nāzikzāde İslimyevī (fl. 1199/1784)

The writing of new handbooks on *ādāb al-baḥth* continued throughout the eighteenth century. Extant handbooks were written by, for example, Meḥmed b. Vāʿiẓ Velīcānī Marʿaşī (d. 1746), Ebū Naʿīm Aḥmed Ḫādimī (d. 1747), Dāvūd Ḳārṣī (fl. 1739–1752), Meḥmed b. Ḥamīd Kefevī and Ismāʿīl Gelenbevī, though it seems that only the last of these came to be widely studied.[12] Older Ottoman handbooks from the sixteenth century were also extensively commented on and glossed in this period. Kātib Çelebī in his bibliographic survey *Kashf al-ẓunūn* mentioned a handbook by the prominent scholar and judge Ṭāşköprīzāde but did not mention any glosses on it, and indeed there appears not to be an extant gloss authored prior to the mid-seventeenth century. After that time, however, the handbook elicited numerous extant glosses by, for example[13]

- Ḳara Ḫalīl Tīrevī (d. 1711)
- Ismāʿīl Nāṣiḥ Üskūbī (fl. 1090/1678)[14]
- Aḥmed Ṭarsūsī (d. 1706) or his son Meḥmed (d. 1732)
- Aḥmed Ḥācī-ʿÖmerzāde (fl. 1695)
- Ibrāhīm Şehirlīzāde Sīvāsī (fl. 1698)

[10] The attributive "Bertizī" (برتزي) has often been mistaken by later scribes, cataloguers, and typesetters for "Tebrīzī" (تبريزي). Bertiz (now also called Yeniyapan) is a town near Maraş in southeastern Anatolia, where Sāçaḳlīzāde was active. On this scholar, see Ismāʿīl Baghdādī, *Hadiyyat al-ʿārifīn*, I, 327.

[11] Again, the attributive "Behisnī" (بهسني) has often been mistaken for "Bihishtī" (بهشتي). The scholar in question hailed from the town of Behisni (now Besni) east of Maraş. There is an entry on him in ʿĀkifzāde, *al-Majmūʿ fī l-mashhūd wa l-masmūʿ* (MS: Süleymaniye Kütüphanesi: Ali Emiri Arabi 2527), fols. 91a–b. ʿĀkifzāde does not give a date of death but mentions that the scholar wrote a commentary on Sāçaḳlīzāde's *Waladiyya* and that he was a Muftī in Behisnī for fifty-four years.

[12] Gelenbevī's treatise was printed in Istanbul in 1868 (by Maṭbaʿah-i ʿĀmireh) with the commentary of his student Meḥmed Saʿīd Ḥasanpāşāzāde (d. 1780) entitled *Fatḥ al-wahhāb fī sharḥ Risālat al-ādāb*. It was also printed in Cairo in 1934 (by the press of Farajullāh Zakī al-Kurdī) with the glosses of the Kurdish scholars Panjiyūnī (d. 1901) and Ibn al-Qaradāghī (d. 1936).

[13] Mach, *Catalogue*, nrs. 3375–3382; www.yazmalar.gov.tr /10Hk335/2 (Şehirlīzāde).

[14] This glossator has apparently been confused in numerous catalogues with the prominent mystic Ismāʿīl Ḥaḳḳī Būrsevī (d. 1725), for all the manuscripts that catalogues attribute to the latter scholar and that I have inspected are actually by the former scholar.

- Abū l-Suʿūd al-Kawākibī (d. 1725)
- Mūsā Niğdevī (d. 1729)
- Meḥmed Sāçaḳlīzāde (d. 1732)
- Meḥmed b. Ḥüseyn Sīnūbī (fl. 1141/1728)

A short treatise on *ādāb al-baḥth* by Birgevī also elicited a number of commentaries after the mid-seventeenth century, by scholars such as[15]

- Ibrāhīm Şehirlīzāde Sīvāsī (fl. 1698)
- Meḥmed Emīn Üsküdārī (d. 1736)
- Cārullāh Veliyüddīn (d. 1738)
- Meḥmed Ūlavī (fl. 1724)
- Aḥmed Ḳāzābādī (d. 1750)
- Meḥmed b. Ḥamīd Kefevī (d. 1754)
- Ḥafīd ül-Nīthārī (d. 1774)

The Ottoman scholarly literature on dialectics from the mid-seventeenth century to the end of the eighteenth dwarfs the Ottoman output from the fifteenth, sixteenth, and early seventeenth centuries. Kātib Çelebī in his *Kashf al-ẓunūn* mentioned a few short epitomes of dialectics by Ottoman Turkish scholars such as Kemālpāşāzāde and Ṭāşköprīzāde. He also mentioned around half a dozen relatively short glosses or superglosses written by Turkish Ottoman scholars on Samarqandī's treatise and its standard commentary by Masʿūd Shirwānī:[16]

- ʿAbd al-Muʾmin Nehārīzāde (fl. 1460s)
- Aḥmed Dīñḳōz (fl. 1460s)
- Şucāʿüddīn Ilyās (d. 1522)
- Lüṭfüllāh b. Şucāʿüddīn Ilyās (d. 1540)
- Sünbül Sinān (d. 1530)
- Emīr Ḥasan Çelebī (d. 1534)
- Ramażān Beheştī (d. 1571)
- Şāh Ḥüseyn Urfalī (fl. 1617)

This literature does not even begin to compare with the massive output after the mid-seventeenth century. It is not only that the number of

15 Mach, Catalogue, nrs. 3385–3388; www.yazmalar.gov.tr /06Hk168 (Üsküdārī); www .yazmalar.gov.tr /55Hk60/4 (Kefevī) and 55Hk60/6 (Nīthārī).

16 Kātib Çelebī, *Kashf Ẓunūn*, I, 39–40; Kātib Çelebī mentioned a few other glosses, but these were written by scholars of either Persianate or indeterminate origin. The mentioned glosses are those that can be attributed with confidence to Ottoman Turkish ("Rūmī") scholars.

Ottoman works on dialectics seems to have risen dramatically. Equally noticeable is the tendency for individual works to become lengthier and more detailed. The sixteenth-century handbook of Ṭāşköprīzāde, for example, is only a fraction of the length of Sāçaḳlīzāde's summa from the early eighteenth century. Similarly, the aforementioned fifteenth- and sixteenth-century glosses on Mas'ūd al-Shirwānī's commentary are considerably shorter than the mammoth glosses on Mīr Abū l-Fatḥ by Cārullāh Veliyüddīn, Yūsufefendīzāde, or Gelenbevī.

The Ottoman Turkish interest in *ādāb al-baḥth* in the seventeenth and eighteenth centuries seems also to have been noteworthy compared to that in other regions of the Islamic world. The prominent Egyptian scholar Ḥasan al-'Aṭṭār (d. 1835), who spent some years in Istanbul in the first decade of the nineteenth century, noted that there was much more interest in the discipline among Ottoman Turkish scholars than among Egyptian.[17] His observation is supported by bio-bibliographic evidence. The contribution of Egyptian scholars to the field is meager until the eighteenth century. The prominent scholar and judge Zakariyyā al-Anṣārī had written a commentary on Samarqandī's treatise on *ādāb al-baḥth*, but this work appears very much to have been an exception. Of the numerous handbooks, commentaries, glosses, and superglosses on *ādāb al-baḥth* mentioned in Carl Brockelmann's monumental *Geschichte der arabischen Literatur* (and conveniently listed together by Rob Wisnovsky), no other work can securely be attributed to an Egyptian scholar until such figures as Yūsuf al-Ḥifnī (d. 1764), Muḥammad b. 'Alī al-Ṣabbān (d. 1791), and Aḥmad b. Yūnus al-Khulayfī (d. 1795).[18] Even prolific and polymath Egyptian scholars such as 'Abd al-Ra'ūf al-Munāwī (d. 1622), Aḥmad al-Ghunaymī (d. 1635), Yāsīn al-'Ulaymī (d. 1651), Aḥmad al-Mallawī (d. 1767), and Aḥmad al-Damanhūrī (d. 1778), all of whom wrote on a wide range of rational and linguistic sciences (including logic), appear not to have written on this discipline.[19] As will be seen in subsequent chapters of the present work, scholarly life in Cairo in the second half of the seventeenth century and first half of the eighteenth was very much under

[17] Peter Gran, *The Islamic Roots of Capitalism, Egypt 1760–1840* (Syracuse, NY: Syracuse University Press, 1st ed., 1979; 2nd ed., 1998), 149.

[18] Rob Wisnovsky, "The Nature and Scope of Arabic Philosophical Commentary in Post-classical (ca. 1100–1900 A.D.) Islamic Intellectual History," in *Philosophy, Science and Exegesis in Greek, Arabic and Latin Commentaries*, ed. P. Adamson, H. Balthussen, and M. W. F. Stone, II (London: Institute of Advanced Studies, 2004), 169–173.

[19] See the list of works cited in Muḥibbī, *Khulāṣat al-athar* I, 312–315 (for Ghunaymī); II, 412–416 (for Munāwī); IV, 491–492 (for 'Ulaymī).

the influence of intellectual currents emanating from the Maghreb and, as noted previously, Maghrebi scholars appear not to have been familiar with the discipline of *ādāb al-baḥth* at all. It would seem that a sustained Egyptian interest in *ādāb al-baḥth* started only in the second half of the eighteenth century and, judging from the comments of Ḥasan al-ʿAṭṭār, was stimulated by exposure to the keen attention given to the discipline in Ottoman Turkey. The *Waladiyya* of Sāçaḳlīzāde apparently came to be adopted as a standard handbook in Egyptian scholarly circles after ʿAṭṭār, and was repeatedly printed by the scholarly presses of Cairo in the early twentieth century in editions obviously meant for local madrasa students.[20]

In Mughal India, an interest in *ādāb al-baḥth* is well attested for the seventeenth and eighteenth centuries. The standard handbook studied there appears to have been a treatise known as *al-Ādāb al-Sharīfiyya* and sometimes attributed to the illustrious Timurid scholar al-Sayyid al-Sharīf al-Jurjānī.[21] The treatise elicited a number of commentaries by Indo-Muslim scholars, of which two commentaries in particular appear to have been widely studied and glossed: one by ʿAbd al-Bāqī Ṣiddīqī Jawnpūrī (d. 1673) and the other by ʿAbd al-Rashīd Jawnpūrī (d. 1672).[22] The latter commentary was part of the influential curriculum (the so-called *Ders-i Niẓāmī*) laid down by Niẓām al-Dīn Sihālavī (d. 1748) in the Farang-i Maḥall College in Lucknow.[23] It is nevertheless noteworthy that the *Ders-i Niẓāmī* curriculum only included a single work on *ādāb al-baḥth*. A number of eighteenth-century sources clearly indicate that Ottoman students were in the habit of studying several works in this field.[24] The Indo-Muslim literature on *ādāb al-baḥth* also seems to have been considerably smaller in volume than the Ottoman. In the well-informed survey

20 For example, Sāçaḳlīzāde's *Waladiyya* was printed by the press of Muhammad Amīn al-Khānjī in 1329/1911 and by Maṭbaʿat al-Wājib in 1925. It was also printed with the commentaries of Behisnī and ʿAbd al-Wahhāb al-Āmidī by al-Khānjī press in 1329/1911 and by al-Maṭbaʿa Azhariyya in 1331/1912–1913.

21 I am skeptical of the attribution and the matter bears further investigation.

22 Wisnovsky, "The Nature and Scope of Arabic Philosophical Commentary," 172.

23 ʿAbd al-Ḥayy al-Ḥasanī, *al-Thaqāfa al-islāmiyya fī l-hind* (Damascus: al-Majmaʿ al-ʿilmī al-ʿarabī, 1958), 16.

24 Ömer Özyılmaz, *Osmanlı Medreselerinin Eğetim Programları* (Ankara: Kültür Bakanlığı, 2002), 35–36, 40–42, 57–58. The cited eighteenth century sources give – with some slight variations – the following list: (1) Ṭāşköprīzāde's introductory handbook; (2) Samarqandī's treatise with the commentary of Masʿūd Shirwānī, the gloss of ʿImād al-Dīn Yaḥyā al-Kāshī, and the supergloss of Şāh Ḥüseyn Urfalī; (3) Ījī's treatise with the commentary of Mullā Ḥanafī and the gloss of Mīr Abū l-Fatḥ; (4) the handbook of Ḥüseyn Adanavī; and (5) the lengthy summa of Sāçaḳlīzāde.

of Indo-Muslim scholarship by ʿAbd al-Ḥayy Ḥasanī (d. 1923), less than a single page is devoted to listing Indo-Muslim contributions to *ādāb al-baḥth*, compared to more than six pages devoted to Indo-Muslim contributions to logic.[25] A comparable listing of the Ottoman output on *ādāb al-baḥth* would certainly be much longer than a page and would probably not have been shorter than a listing of the Ottoman output on logic. There does not seem to have been any lengthy Indo-Muslim summa of the field comparable to the summa of Sāçaḳlīzāde, nor any new Indo-Muslim handbooks that came to be widely studied and commented on, comparable to the Ottoman handbooks of Adanavī, Sāçaḳlīzāde, and Gelenbevī. This is all the more noteworthy in light of the appearance of a number of Indo-Muslim handbooks on logic in the seventeenth and eighteenth centuries.[26] The conclusion seems unavoidable that the Indo-Muslim interest in the field of *ādāb al-baḥth* was less strong than it was in the central Ottoman lands in the seventeenth and eighteenth centuries.

In Safavid Iran, one might have expected the interest in *ādāb al-baḥth* to have been at least as strong as it was in the Ottoman Empire. After all, Iranian scholars stood for the greater part of the literature in this field until the sixteenth century, and the intensified interest in the discipline among Turkish Ottoman scholars was itself a consequence of the influence of Persian, Kurdish, and Azeri scholars in the course of the seventeenth century. It is therefore very surprising to be faced with what appears to be a dearth of relevant Safavid Iranian works after the sixteenth century. The major online resource for manuscripts extant in Iran (www.aghabozorg.ir) includes numerous works on *ādāb al-baḥth*, but it is very conspicuous that almost all listed works that postdate the sixteenth century are actually by Ottoman authors – manuscripts of these works somehow having made their way into Iranian libraries. Judging from this source, the Iranian tradition would seem to have largely petered out after Mīr Abū l-Fatḥ Ḥusaynī ʿArabshāhī (d. 1568) and Fakhr al-Dīn Sammākī Astarābādī (d. 1576). The article on *ādāb al-baḥth* in the standard Iranian historical reference encyclopedia *Dāʾirat al-Maʿārif-i Buzurg-i Islāmī* is based on Kātib Çelebī's *Kashf al-ẓunūn* from the mid-seventeenth century, supplemented with information on availability of manuscripts in the major Iranian

[25] Ḥasanī, *al-Thaqāfa al-islāmiyya*, 252–253 (on munāẓara) and 255–261 (on logic).

[26] Especially *Sullam al-ʿulūm* by Muḥibbullāh Bihārī (d. 1707) and *al-Mirqāt* by Fażl-i Imām Khayrābādī (d. 1828) came to be widely studied and elicited numerous commentaries.

manuscript libraries.[27] The article suggests that the standard handbook in Iran remained Samarqandī's handbook but this may have been simply copied from Kātib Çelebī – it mentions no later Iranian commentaries or glosses on that handbook. The article also mentions a handful of treatises by relatively unknown seventeenth- and eighteenth-century Iranian scholars, none of which seem to have elicited commentaries or glosses by later scholars. Of the numerous works on *ādāb al-baḥth* listed by Brockelmann and Wisnovsky, only a single work is ascribed to a post-sixteenth century Iranian scholar: a gloss by Muḥammad Bāqir Majlisī (d. 1689) on Mullā Ḥanafī Tabrīzī's commentary on the treatise of Ījī.[28] Most of the prominent specialists on the rational and philosophical sciences in Iran in the period from the seventeenth century to the nineteenth appear not to have written on the field at all: Mīr Dāmād (d. 1631), Mullā Ṣadrā Shīrāzī (d. 1635), Āqā Ḥusayn Khwānsārī (d. 1687), Mahdī Narāqī (d. 1795), and Mullā Hādī Sabzavārī (d. 1878).[29] There appear to have been no handbooks on *ādāb al-baḥth* or *munāẓara* in the curriculum of the Shiite madrasas of Najaf at the beginning of the twentieth century.[30]

The apparent decline of interest in the field in Iran after the sixteenth century is so dramatic and unexpected as to invite a more thorough investigation. If it did occur, then it may have been related to a tendency among some prominent Safavid Iranian logicians such as Ghiyāth al-Dīn Manṣūr Dashtakī (d. 1542), Mullā Ṣadrā Shīrāzī, and Muḥammad Yūsuf Ṭihrānī (fl. 1692) to distance themselves from the post-Avicennan

27 "Ādāb al-baḥth" in *Dā'irat al-ma'ārif-i buzurg-i islāmī*, ed. Kāẓim Mūsawī Bujnūrdī (Tehran, 1991–), I, 159–160.

28 Wisnovsky, "The Nature and Scope of Arabic Philosophical Commentary," 170 (the gloss is listed as C2, nr. c).

29 The article in *Dā'irat al-ma'ārif-i buzurg-i islāmī* attributes a treatise to Mullā Ṣadrā and lists one extant copy. The attribution is doubted in Sajjad Rizvi, *Mullā Ṣadrā Shīrāzī: His Life and Works and the Sources for Safavid Philosophy* (Oxford and New York: Oxford University Press on behalf of the University of Manchester, 2007), 111. There is no such treatise included in the edition of the collected philosophical treatises of Mullā Ṣadrā prepared by Ḥāmid Nājī Iṣfahānī in 1996 (see *Majmū'at-i rasā'il-i falsafī Ṣadr al-muta'allihīn*, ed. Ḥāmid Nājī Iṣfahānī [Tehran: Intishārāt Hikmat, 1996]). It is clear from this collection that Mullā Ṣadrā was a figure to whom treatises were often misattributed, sometimes due to a persistent confusion between him and his namesake Ṣadr al-Dīn al-Shīrāzī al-Dashtakī. One of the treatises in the collection edited by Ḥāmid Nājī Iṣfahānī (on the liar's paradox) is by this earlier figure (as noted by Rizvi, *Mullā Ṣadrā Shīrāzī*, 113).

30 A. M. Kirmili, "Le programme des etudes chez les chiites et principalement ceux de Nedjef," *Revue du monde musulman* XXIII (1913): 268–279. I am grateful to Professor Roy Mottahedeh of Harvard University for alerting me to this source.

tradition of logic and to reengage with the works of Avicenna himself and even with the more orthodox Aristotelian tradition of Fārābī and Averroes.[31] As had been observed by the great North African historian Ibn Khaldūn (d. 1406), the "later logicians" (*al-muta'akhkhirūn*) led by Fakhr al-Dīn al-Rāzī (d. 1210) and Afḍal al-Dīn al-Khūnajī (d. 1248) had narrowed the scope of logic, ceasing to be interested in all the books of the Peripatetic *Organon* and focusing instead on the formal study of definitions, propositions, and inferences.[32] The aforementioned Safavid scholars explicitly tried to reverse this trend. The theory of demonstration (*burhān*) in particular began to receive renewed interest from later Iranian scholars, and the space allocated to it in Safavid and Qajar handbooks on logic is substantially larger than was usual in the post-Avicennan tradition.[33] Several of the mentioned Safavid and Qajar scholars also adopted the self-image of older philosophers who had presented themselves as engaged in indubitable "demonstration" as opposed to what they claimed was the hollow and disputatious "eristic" (*jadal*) of the Islamic theologians (*mutakallimūn*).[34] It may well be that both the wish to return to the ways of "the ancients" (*al-qudamā'*) and the revival of interest in Aristotelian demonstration translated into a decreased interest in the relatively recent and dialectical discipline of *ādāb al-baḥth*. Be that as it may, there is good reason, at least pending further research, to believe that the keen interest in *ādāb al-baḥth* in the central Ottoman lands in the seventeenth and eighteenth centuries was unrivaled elsewhere in the Islamic world.

Seventeenth-Century Ottoman Contributions to *Ādāb al-baḥth*

The dramatic increase in the number and length of Ottoman writings on *ādāb al-baḥth* in the course of the seventeenth and eighteenth centuries

31 See El-Rouayheb, *Relational Syllogisms and the History of Arabic Logic*, 103–104, 145–148.

32 Rosenthal (transl.), *The Muqaddima of Ibn Khaldun*, I, 142–143.

33 The greater part of Muḥammad Yūsuf Ṭihrānī's *Naqḍ al-uṣūl wa talkhīṣ al-fuṣūl* (edited by A. Faramarz Karamaleki, S. Kavandi, and M. Jahed [Zanjan, Iran: Dānishgāh-i Zanjān, 2010]) is dedicated to demonstration. Even the less idiosyncratic and much more widely studied handbook of Sabzavārī devoted much more attention to demonstration than was usually the case in the post-Avicennan tradition, see Sabzavārī, *Sharḥ al-Manẓūma*, ed. Mas'ud Ṭālibī and with annotations by Ḥasanẓāde Āmulī (Qom: Nashr-i Nāb, 1416/1995), 323–338.

34 See, e.g., the introduction to Ghiyāth al-Dīn Dashtakī's *Mīzān al-'adl* (MS: Mashhad: Kutubkhāneh-i Quds-i Riżawī, 23596), fols. 1a–b in which the *jadal* and *khaṭāba* of the later logicians is contrasted to the *burhān* of the earlier logicians.

is a noteworthy phenomenon, but it does not by itself show that there was any substantial development of ideas within the discipline. Given the widespread twentieth-century denigration of the genres of epitome, commentary, and gloss, it remains an open question whether this voluminous literature amounted to more than "comment-mongering" or "reworking of existing discussions, constantly crossing and re-crossing the same familiar ground in the same familiar way."[35] Answering this question requires going beyond the bio-bibliographic evidence and engaging with the content of some of this literature. As it turns out, suspicions of "comment-mongering" and endless reiteration are misguided. The Ottoman literature on *ādāb al-baḥth* can be shown to have undergone a noticeable development in the course of the seventeenth century. This can be brought out by comparing two Ottoman handbooks, one from the mid-sixteenth century by Ṭāşköprīzāde and the other from the second half of the seventeenth by Ḥüseyn Adanavī. Both handbooks comprise a short epitome plus the author's own commentary.[36] Both were lithographed in Istanbul in the nineteenth century, the earlier work in 1895 in thirteen pages, the later in 1850 in thirty-one pages.[37]

The handbook by Ṭāşköprīzāde is described in Kātib Çelebī's bibliographic compilation as "comprehensive of the important elements of the discipline and very useful."[38] It is not, nor does it claim to be, particularly original or controversial. Few if any elements of the work would have been novel to a reader familiar with earlier presentations, in particular Samarqandī's treatise or that of Sinān al-Dīn Gancī (d. 1516), an

35 Nicholas Rescher, *The Development of Arabic Logic* (Pittsburgh: University of Pittsburgh Press, 1964), 73, 81–82.

36 There can be no doubt that in both cases the commentator is the author himself. In the case of Ṭāşköprīzāde, the commentator explicitly wrote that he was writing a commentary on his own work. In the case of Adanavī, the commentary itself has no introduction, but the commentator repeatedly used the first person when citing the text of the handbook itself, leaving no doubt that the commentator is the author himself. See, e.g., p. 17 (lines 8–9), p. 17 (l. 20), and p. 18 (l.3) of the lithograph edition published in Istanbul in 1267/1850. Eighteenth-century Ottoman scholars were well aware that the commentator of *al-Ḥusayniyya* was the author himself. ʿUmar Āmidī referred at one point to *Ḥüseyn Efendī ṣāḥib al-matn wa-l-sharḥ fī ʿilm al-ādāb* (*Sharḥ al-Waladiyya*, MS: www.yazmalar.gov.tr/ 60Zile231, p. 153 [margin]). ʿAbdullāh Kānḳirī also referred to *Ḥüseyn Adanavī fī sharḥ risālatihi l-ādābiyya*, see his *Nafāʾis ʿarāʾis al-anẓār wa laṭāʾif fawāʾid al-afkār* (Istanbul: Maṭbaʿah-i ʿAmire, 1313/1896), 188 (margin).

37 Ṭāşköprīzāde, *Sharḥ al-Risāla fī ādāb al-baḥth* (Lithograph: Istanbul, n.p. 1313/1895); [Ḥüseyn Adanavī,] *Ḥusayniyya* (Lithograph: Istanbul, n.p. 1267/1850). I have used copies in Princeton University Library, with call numbers 2262.21.387 and 2264.1191.348 respectively.

38 Kātib Çelebī, *Kashf Ẓunūn*, I, 41.

Azeri scholar who settled and died in the Ottoman Empire.[39] It was presumably appreciated as a useful handbook that covered the same ground as Samarqandī's treatise but nevertheless made less demands on the student, largely because it left out the rather abstruse examples given by Samarqandī of debates in theology, philosophy, and law to which the dialectical principles he outlined could be applied.[40]

Ṭāşköprīzāde presented the basic outline of the discipline by describing the proper role of respectively the claimant (*mu'allil*) and the questioner (*sā'il*). The questioner may offer an objection (*man'*) to the claimant's argument in one of three ways:

1. *Munāqaḍa*:[41] This is to object to a premise of the argument. This would be legitimate only if the premise is neither evidently true nor conceded by both parties. The questioner may adduce corroboration or support (*shāhid* or *sanad* or *mustanad*) for his objection or he may not. In either case, it is incumbent on the claimant to respond. The questioner should, however, take care not to go beyond adducing support to preemptively trying to prove that a premise is false, for this would be tantamount to becoming a claimant and constitute usurpation (*ghaṣb*) of his opponent's role.
2. *Naqḍ*:[42] This is to object that the claimant's proof is faulty in a general way and does not in fact establish the truth of the purported conclusion. The questioner should in this case adduce corroboration in support of the objection – merely making the bald statement that the adduced argument does not prove the point would be sheer obstinacy (*mukābara*). The corroboration might be that the same argument could be made for a conclusion that the claimant himself does not accept, or that the argument is circular or leads to absurdity (*muḥāl*).
3. *Mu'āraḍa*:[43] This is to supply an argument for a conclusion that contradicts that of the claimant. In this case, the questioner assumes the role of claimant and tries to adduce premises that entail the alternative conclusion.

The claimant's proper response to each of these objections will vary.

[39] On Gancī, see Ṭāşköprīzāde, *al-Shaqā'iq al-nu'māniyya*, 269–270. For an extant copy of his treatise, see www.yazmalar.gov.tr/ 26Hk576, fols. 67b–76a.

[40] These debates are the most demanding parts of Samarqandī's work and become even more so when the pros and cons of the various positions came to be discussed by later commentators and glossators.

[41] Ṭāşköprīzāde, *Sharḥ al-Risāla*, 5–7.

[42] Ibid., 7–8.

[43] Ibid., 8–9.

In the case of *munāqaḍa* (nr. 1 above),[44] the claimant should either adduce an argument for the premise or remind the questioner that the premise is evident or conceded by the questioner himself. The questioner may have adduced corroboration or support (*shāhid* or *sanad*) for his objection to the premise. If so, the claimant should attempt to refute the questioner's corroboration only in a case in which it is the only possible ground for rejecting a premise. Otherwise, refuting the given corroboration leads nowhere because the questioner may legitimately respond that the corroborating reason he had given for doubting a premise is only one of several possible reasons, and the claimant would still be bound to establish the premise. This is an important and subtle point that is related to the principle that if a premise used by the claimant is not evident or conceded, then he may legitimately be asked to supply a proof for it. The fact that the questioner may have given a specific reason for doubting the premise does not change this basic obligation to supply a proof. The claimant should therefore not attempt to refute the given reason unless he can show that it is the only possible reason for rejecting the premise. To put the point in a language closer to that of the dialecticians: the corroboration (*sanad*) offered by the questioner should be refuted only if it can be shown to be logically equivalent (*musāwī*) to the denial of the original claim.[45]

In the case of *naqḍ* (nr. 2 above),[46] the claimant may either supply a different proof or refute the corroboration (i.e. the questioner's reason for rejecting the claimant's proof). Refuting the corroboration is in this context legitimate because it shifts the burden of proof: the questioner is left in a position of having to offer another corroborating reason for rejecting the claimant's proof because an unsupported rejection of the proffered proof is deemed obstinacy. Refuting the corroboration of the questioner may take the form of accepting the further consequences of the argument (in modern parlance, "biting the bullet") or showing that the circularity or absurdity pointed out by the questioner is only apparent.

In the case of *muʿāraḍa* (nr. 3),[47] the original questioner has become a claimant arguing for a conclusion that contradicts the thesis of the original claimant. The original claimant in turn becomes a questioner

44 Ibid., 9–10.

45 If the corroboration is logically equivalent to the denial of the original claim then proving that the corroboration is false would show that the denial of the original claim is false (and therefore that the original claim is true).

46 Ṭāşköprīzāde, *Sharḥ al-Risāla*, 10.

47 Ibid., 10.

who can object to the counter-proof in one of the three mentioned ways: *munāqaḍa, naqḍ*, or *mu'āraḍa*.

Ṭāşköprīzāde, in line with practically all presentations of *ādāb al-baḥth*, held that the debate must end with either the claimant forcing the questioner to concede (this was called *ilzām*) or the questioner refuting the claimant (this was called *ifḥām*).[48] These were held to be the only possible outcomes of the debate, as the failure of the claimant to prove his point would in itself constitute a refutation by the questioner. The burden of proof rested on the claimant and his failure to prove his case in a discussion was tantamount to defeat. One assumes that, in practice, debates rarely ended in a clear-cut defeat of one side. There would surely, for example, have been ample opportunity to disagree over whether a premise is evident or not, or over whether a given argument's consequences were absurd or not. Also, the crucial question of the time that should be allocated to a debate seems to have received little or no attention in the literature. The fact that such issues were rarely if ever explicitly discussed in works on *ādāb al-baḥth* is significant. It suggests that the purpose of the discipline was not so much to secure a clear-cut outcome for a scholarly discussion as to set up rules that would help avoid such a discussion degenerating into an unruly clash (*khabṭ*). Also, a great deal of the scholarly interest in *ādāb al-baḥth* seems to have derived from its perceived usefulness, not in winning or resolving debates, but in understanding scholarly works that were often densely argumentative and made extensive use of the concepts of the discipline. When Muḥibbī noted that a contemporary Turkish Ottoman scholar heeded the principles of *ādāb al-baḥth* he was referring to his manner of teaching, that is, to a didactic rather than agonistic context. When Sāçaḳlīzāde commended the discipline to budding students, he stressed its helpfulness for reading and understanding scholarly works, not for winning debates. This point is dealt with at greater length in the following chapter.

The basic principles outlined by Ṭāşköprīzāde continued to be accepted in later centuries, and this is presumably why his handbook continued to be used until the final days of the Ottoman Empire. The development of the discipline in the seventeenth and eighteenth centuries did not involve a rejection of these principles but rather an incorporation of additional elements and distinctions. This is apparent from the new handbook on *ādāb al-baḥth* that came to be known simply as *al-Risāla al-Ḥusayniyya*. The early twentieth-century scholar Meḥmed Ṭāhir Būrsalī, in his

48 Ibid., 11.

standard survey of Ottoman authors entitled *'Othmānlī Müelliflerī*, attributed the work to a certain Şāh Ḥüseyn Amāsyavī who supposedly died in 1512.[49] By contrast, Būrṣalī's contemporary Ismā'īl al-Baghdādī, in his equally standard bio-bibliographic survey *Hadiyyat al-'ārifīn*, attributed the work to a certain Şāh Ḥüseyn Anṭāḳī who died in 1718.[50] Neither of the proposed identifications seems accurate, though the latter suggestion is significantly closer to the mark. Būrṣalī's identification obviously cannot be correct, for there are references in the work itself to Mīr Abū l-Fatḥ (d. 1568), Ḥusayn Khalkhālī (d. 1604), and – most revealingly – to 'Umar Chillī, who authored a gloss on Mīr Abū l-Fatḥ's gloss on Mullā Ḥanafī Tabrīzī's commentary on Ījī's treatise on *ādāb al-baḥth*.[51] This 'Umar Chillī is known to have been active in the predominantly Kurdish town of Diyarbakır in the 1650s and 60s, and his gloss on Mīr Abū l-Fatḥ is dedicated to Şeyhülislām Yaḥyā Minḳārīzāde (who occupied the position from 1662 to 1674), though there is evidence that the glosses had been authored first and then some years later prefaced with the dedication.[52] The *Risāla al-Ḥusayniyya* can therefore

49 Meḥmed Ṭāhir Būrsalī, *'Othmānlı Müellifleri* (Istanbul: Matba'ah-i 'Amire, 1333/1914–1342/1928), I, 274.

50 Baghdādī, *Hadiyyat al-'ārifīn*, I, 325. Baghdādī is followed by Brockelmann, *GAL* II, 467, SII, 482.

51 *al-Risāla al-Ḥusayniyya* (Lithograph: Istanbul 1267/1850), 12. Adanavī refers to "one of the glossators" but the identification with Chillī is made in the gloss of 'Alī Ferdī Ḳayṣerī (d. 1715); see his *Ḥāshiya* (www.yazmalar.gov.tr/ 06MilYzA 2614), fol. 11b (last line). Marginal annotations to a manuscript copy of *al-Ḥusayniyya* also identifies Chillī with the *ba'ḍ al-fuḍalā' wa fuḥūl al-'ulamā'* mentioned a bit earlier in the text (on p. 9 of the lithograph edition), see www.yazmalar.gov.tr/ 06MilYzA6484, fol. 7b.

52 An autograph copy of Chillī's commentary on the Persian epitome of philosophy *Jām-i gītī-namā* is dated 1066/1655 (see www.yazmalar.gov.tr/ 45Hk2732). The colophon of an extant manuscript of his commentary on *Khulāṣat al-ḥisāb* (on mathematics), copied from the autograph in 1074/1664 (www.yazmalar.gov.tr/ 06Hk2006) also mentions the author as alive at the time of copying (*kutiba min nuskhati muṣannifihi 'Umar b. Aḥmad al-Chillī ṭawwala llāhu 'umrahu*). Chillī's student Ḥasan Nūreddīnī died in 1078/1667–1668 at the age of forty; he must therefore have been born around 1628 and studying with Chillī in Diyarbakır in the 1650s (see Muḥibbī, *Khulāṣat al-athar*, II, 63–64). In the entry on this scholar in *Osmanlı Matematik Literaturu Tarihi*, ed. E. İhsanoğlu (Istanbul: IRCICA, 1999), 1, 112–118, his date of death is given as 1613 or ca. 1640. This seems to be based on a confusion with 'Umar Chillī's father Aḥmad Mā'ī Chillī who finished a commentary on *Risālat al-'ilm* by Mullā Ḥanafī Tabrīzī in 1612. (See www.yazmalar.gov.tr/ 45Hk8266: the colophon indicates that the commentary was completed by Aḥmad in 1021/1612 and then copied by an anonymous scribe in 1078/1668.) This commentary has been misattributed to the son 'Umar (e.g., in Mach, *Catalogue*, nr. 3268), apparently leading to some confusion concerning the lifetime of the son. The preface of an early manuscript (dated 1084/1673) of 'Umar Chillī's gloss on Mīr Abū l-Fatḥ contains a dedication to Yaḥyā Minḳārīzāde but also states that the

hardly have been written much earlier than 1660.[53] At the same time, a number of extant manuscripts date from the 1680s, and annotations and glosses begin to be written in the 1690s and 1700s.[54] It is therefore possible to date the work to between 1660 and 1680.[55] Most extant manuscripts do not give the author's name at all or refer to him simply as "Ḥüseyn Efendī." A few early manuscripts, however, give the name "Ḥüseyn Adanavī," and this is also the name given to the author of the treatise by the prominent Ottoman scholar and specialist in the rational sciences ʿAbdullāh Kānḳirī.[56] Like so many provincial Anatolian scholars, little is known of this Ḥüseyn Adanavī, as most Turkish Ottoman biographical sources are heavily biased toward scholars who went through the Istanbul-centered system of higher education and the consequent graded promotions through the higher echelons of the Ottoman educational and judicial institutions. It is very likely that he is identical to Ḥüseyn b. Pīrī Adanavī, who was a student of Tefsīrī Meḥmed in Sivas – the scholar mentioned in Chapter 1 as an important link in the scholarly lineage of later Ottoman scholars such as Sāçaḳlīzāde, Ḫādimī, and Gelenbevī. This Ḥüseyn b. Pīrī Adanavī wrote, in the lifetime of

glosses had been written some years earlier (see www.yazmalar.gov.tr/ 60Mü115, fol. 72a). Most copies of Chillī's gloss do not contain the dedication. The earliest dated manuscript of the gloss that I have managed to locate is from 1078/1667–1668 (see MS: Süleymaniye Kütüphanesı, Istanbul: Ayasofya 4426). İhsanoğlu et al. vocalize the scholar's attributive as "Çullī," whereas I presume he hailed from the town of Çille in Adıyamin province near Diyarbakır.

53 To clear up a possible confusion: Three manuscripts of Ḥüseyn Adanavī's work are listed in www.yazmalar.gov.tr as substantially earlier than this date: (1) 03 Gedik 17652/1, SN 4–19, dated 1021/1612; (2) 55 Hk 288/3, SN 85–100, dated 959/1552; and (3) 55 Vezirköprü 515/5 SN 94–107, dated 1010/1601. An inspection of manuscripts (2) and (3) shows that the colophons are not dated at all – the dates given must be cataloguing errors. The colophon of manuscript (1) is indeed dated 1021/1612 but this must be a scribal error, for the work is followed by Ferdī's gloss in the same handwriting and Ferdī completed his gloss in 1115/1703 and died in 1715. In the gloss, Ferdī mentioned his teacher ʿAlī Nīthārī (d. 1698) and also mentioned ʿUmar Chillī who – as was just established in the previous footnote – was active in the 1650s and 1660s.

54 The earliest dated extant manuscripts of the work (including the auto-commentary) appear to be from 1092/1681; see Mach, *Catalogue*, nr. 3393 (nr.1) and www.yazmalar.gov.tr/ MilYzA1549/3. The gloss of Meḥmed Dārendevī was completed in 1110/1698 (see the colophon of www.yazmalar.gov.tr/ 43Va702). The gloss of ʿAlī Ferdī Ḳayṣerī was completed in 1115/1703 (see the colophon of www.yazmalar.gov.tr/ 06MilYzA2614).

55 For simplicity, I have not made a distinction in this context between the handbook itself (the *matn*) and the author's own commentary on it (the *sharḥ*). The reference to Chillī occurs in the commentary and hence strictly speaking it is the commentary that can be dated to between 1660 and 1680. The handbook itself could have been written earlier, though this is unlikely if the author was a student of Tefsīrī Meḥmed.

56 Kānḳirī, *Nafāʾis ʿarāʾis al-anẓār wa laṭāʾif fawāʾid al-afkār*, 188 (margin).

his teacher, an extant gloss on the gloss of Lārī on Maybudī's commentary on Abharī's handbook of philosophy *Hidāyat al-ḥikma*.[57] The date of death given by Ismā'īl al-Baghdādī – 1718 – is at first sight plausibly true of a student of Tefsīrī Meḥmed, but it should be noted that one early manuscript of *al-Risāla al-Ḥusayniyya* dating from 1103/1691 refers to the author as deceased, suggesting that Ḥüseyn Adanavī actually predeceased his teacher.[58] The attributive "Anṭāḳī" is often used of the author of *al-Risāla al-Ḥusayniyya* in modern catalogues of manuscripts, but this finds no support in manuscripts themselves and would seem to be a result of the influence of Ismā'īl al-Baghdādī on later cataloguers. The honorific "Şāh" before the proper name Ḥüseyn also finds no support in manuscripts (or in Kānḳirī's valuable reference to the author) and may be due to a later confusion with Şāh Ḥüseyn Urfalī (fl. 1617), who authored an esteemed supergloss on Mas'ūd Shirwānī's commentary on Samarqandī's treatise on *ādāb al-baḥth*.[59]

Like Ṭāşköprīzāde, Adanavī explicitly presented his handbook as one that avoided the extremes of terseness (*ījāz*) and prolixity (*iṭnāb*). But his handbook is twice as long as Ṭāşköprīzāde's and significantly more densely written. Adanavī obviously felt the need to cover more in his presentation, and he explicitly stated that he was not confining himself to the familiar or generally accepted aspects of the discipline. In his introduction, he also adopted a combative tone that is entirely absent from Ṭāşköprīzāde's work, anticipating that what he would say might encounter resistance and expressing his wish that the discerning reader should read it charitably even though it might meet hostility from the common run of scholars for whom the value of what is said depends on who says it (the quintessence of *taqlīd*). He wrote:

O Thou who hast enabled us (*yā man waffaqanā*) to know the proper roles in inquiry as regards both clarifications (*taḥrīrāt*) and verifications (*taḥqīqāt*) . . . This is a hurried work (*'ujāla*) that is sufficient for those who seek the proper roles of

57 See MS: Süleymaniye Kütüphanesı, Istanbul: Çorlulu Ali Paşa 315. The manuscript was endowed by Çorlulu Ali Paşa (d. 1711) during his Grand Vizierate (1706–1710).

58 A manuscript dated 1103/1691 (www.yazmalar.gov.tr/ 67 Saf 286/3) closes with the words: *tammat al-risālatu l-ādābiyyatu li-l-fāḍili Ḥusayn Efendī al-Adanavī 'alayhi raḥmatu llāhi l-ghanī*.

59 An autograph manuscript of Şāh Ḥüseyn's supergloss on the gloss of 'Imād al-Dīn Yaḥyā al-Kāshī on Mas'ūd Shirwānī's commentary is dated 1027/1617 (see www.yazmalar.gov.tr/ 01Hk898, fol. 151b). The glossator gave his name as "Shāh Ḥusayn b. Aḥmad al-Ruhāwī." The colophon contains a dedication to a certain Shaykh Maḥmūd, presumably the prominent Sufi active in Diyarbakır, whose following was so large that he was deemed a threat by the Ottomans and executed in 1639; see M. van Bruinessen, *Mullas, Sufis and Heretics: The Role of Religion in Kurdish Society* (Istanbul: Isis Press, 2000), 90–102.

discourse... It does not confine itself to what is well-known (*mashhūr*) amongst students even though I wrote it while I was so busy I could not find time to sleep... I ask of the great enquirers and noble experts to look [at it] with the eye of charity even if it is rejected by the obstinate amongst commoners (i.e. those amongst contemporaries who are inept and know [the value of] what is said by means of who says it).[60]

The model for Adanavī's introduction seems to be the introductions to Dawānī's commentaries on *al-ʿAqāʾid al-ʿAḍudiyya* and *Tahdhīb al-manṭiq*. The former commentary starts with the exact same words as *al-Ḥusayniyya*: "O Thou who hast enabled us (*yā man waffaqanā*)."[61] In the later commentary, Dawānī had written:

This is a hurried but useful work (*ʿujāla nāfiʿa*) and a magnificent yield that quenches the desires of those who seek the discipline of logic... I have not confined myself to what is well-known (*mashhūr*), for truth is more worthy of being followed... even though I dictated it hurriedly, in the manner of improvisation... Even if it is rejected by the inept it will be accepted by the skilled, and even if it is faulted by the ignorant it will be praised by the consummate.[62]

Adanavī's text, unlike Ṭāşköprīzāde's, takes its point of departure from the kinds of discourse that someone might make in a dialectical situation: (1) a claim, (2) a proof, (3) a definition, or (4) a division.

1. A straightforward claim[63] poses a problem for the standard threefold division of objections. Because a proof has yet to be given, the questioner can hardly engage in *munāqaḍa* (i.e., objecting to a premise) or *naqḍ* (objecting that the argument is faulty and does not establish the truth of the conclusion) or *muʿāraḍa* (conceding that the claimant has an argument for the claim but proceeding to construct another argument for the opposite claim). Nevertheless, a questioner can use objections that are reminiscent of these strategies. He can (a) object to the claim, a move that Adanavī terms *munāqaḍa* "in a linguistically extended sense" (*majāzan lughawiyyan*); or (b) object that the claim is not consistent with the claimant's overall position, while offering a specific reason/corroboration for this charge, a move called "quasi-*naqḍ*" (*naqḍ shabīhī*); or (c) object that even if the claimant should have a proof for the offered claim, he – the questioner – already has a proof for the opposing claim, a move called "anticipatory" or "suppositious" *muʿāraḍa* (*muʿāraḍa taqdīriyya*).

60 Adanavī, *al-Risāla al-Ḥusayniyya*, 2–5.
61 Dawānī, *Sharḥ al-ʿAqāʾid al-ʿAḍudiyya*, 2.
62 Dawānī, *Sharḥ Tahdhīb al-manṭiq*, 2.
63 Adanavī, *al-Risāla al-Ḥusayniyya*, 5–7.

To these objections, the claimant may respond in a number of ways.[64] If faced with a straightforward objection to the claim (i.e., *munāqaḍa* "in a linguistically extended sense"), he may supply a proof (*dalīl*) or clarify the sense in which he intends the claim to be understood (*taḥrīr*) or refute the questioner's corroboration (*sanad*) if the latter can be shown to be logically equivalent (*musāwī*) to the denial of the original claim. If the questioner has offered a quasi-*naqḍ* or anticipatory *mu'āraḍa* then the claimant may disarm the objections in the same way as he would disarm a straightforward *naqḍ* or *mu'āraḍa*: refuting the corroboration in the case of *naqḍ* and refuting the counter-proof in the case of *mu'āraḍa*.

2. If the claimant gives a proof for a claim,[65] then the situation is the one envisaged in earlier handbooks. The questioner may object in one of the three familiar ways: (a) that he does not concede a specific premise; (b) that the argument is faulty because it leads to absurdity or circularity or conclusions that the claimant himself does not accept; and (c) that a compelling case can be made for the opposite claim. Adanavī envisages two further possibilities: (d) The questioner may charge that the claimant's proof is deficient in the sense that it lacks a necessary premise or is otherwise invalid. This deficiency is termed *dakhl* – Adanavī notes that there is some disagreement concerning whether making the charge should be classified as a form of *naqḍ* or *munāqaḍa*.[66] (e) The questioner explicitly rejects the conclusion of the argument *after* a proof has been offered for it. This might appear to be dangerously close to "obstinacy" (*mukābara*) and not all scholars allowed it. Those who considered it legitimate argued that it amounted to objecting to an unspecified premise of the proof and should be allowed on the grounds that the claimant could be asked to prove all premises.[67] In such a case, the questioner's objection is overtly directed at the conclusion of the argument but is in an extended

64 Ibid., 8.

65 Ibid., 8ff.

66 Ibid., 17. The uncertainty seems to betray a tension resulting from the importation of formal-logical notions into a conceptual scheme that originated in the nonformal modes of argumentation acknowledged in early theological-legal eristic. *Munāqaḍa* was originally to object to the "ratio legis" (*'illa*) offered for a claim, with no clear conception of the difference between objections to the logical form of the argument and objections to the premises of the argument. Similarly, *naqḍ* was to object that the "ratio legis" led to further consequences that the claimant himself would not want to accept. It is not clear in this scheme of things where to place, for example, the objection that the claimant's argument is formally invalid and does not imply its purported conclusion at all.

67 Adanavī, *al-Risāla al-Ḥusayniyya*, 7, 11–12.

sense directed at one or more premise. If the disputed premise was explicitly stated by the claimant then Adanavī terms the questioner's objection *munāqaḍa* "in a rationally extended sense" (*majāzan ʿaqliyyan*). If the premise was implicitly assumed, then Adanavī terms the objection *munāqaḍa* "in an elliptically extended sense" (*majāzan ḥadhfiyyan*).

Another novel feature of Adanavī's handbook is that the questioner's *naqḍ* and *muʿāraḍa* are presented in syllogistic form. For example, the questioner may charge that the claimant's proof is faulty because the same proof could be made in another case in which the conclusion does not follow. This, explains Adanavī, can be put into syllogistic form thus:[68]

> Your proof is a proof that can equally be made in cases where the conclusion does not follow.
> Every proof that can equally be made etc. is faulty.
> Your proof is faulty.

Adanavī points out that the first (minor) premise actually comprises two distinct propositions: "Your proof can equally be made in another instance" and "The conclusion does not follow in that instance." The claimant may deny either one of these propositions. In the case of the charge that the claimant's argument is circular or leads to infinite regress, the syllogistic presentation is as follows:[69]

> Your proof is a proof that leads to circularity or an infinite regress.
> Every proof that leads to circularity or an infinite regress is faulty.
> Your proof is faulty.

The claimant may respond by denying either the first (minor) premise or the second (major) premise. He may also offer a disjunctive conditional denial (*tardīd*), for example, replying that if the questioner means by "circularity" or "infinite regress" a vicious circularity or infinite regress then he denies the first premise and concedes the second, and that if he means "circularity" or "infinite regress" as such then he concedes the first premise and denies the second on the ground that not all circularity or infinite regress is vicious.

The syllogistic presentation of *naqḍ* and *muʿāraḍa* is not attested in earlier handbooks of *ādāb al-baḥth*, nor in non-Ottoman works such as the commentary of Adanavī's Indo-Islamic contemporary ʿAbd

[68] Ibid., 15. Adanavī referred to this as *qiyās al-takhalluf*.
[69] Ibid., 15. Adanavī referred to this as *qiyās al-istilzām*.

al-Rashīd Jawnpūrī on *al-Ādāb al-Sharīfiyya*.[70] Some of the important consequences of this novel practice for Ottoman logic are explored in the following section.

3. The claimant may be putting forward a definition (*taʿrīf*).[71] In this case, Adanavī makes a distinction between lexical definition on the one hand and real or nominal definition on the other. If the claimant offers a lexical definition (*taʿrīf lafẓī*), that is, is explaining an unfamiliar word by means of one or more familiar words that mean the same thing, then he is seeking to bring about the questioner's assent to a claim (about the meaning of words). The questioner may then respond in the same ways as he responds to a claim without an explicit proof, that is, by means of asking for a proof (*munāqaḍa majāzan lughawiyyan*), or pointing out that the lexical definition is not consistent with what the claimant otherwise holds (*naqḍ shabīhī*), or that he has a proof for a contrary claim (*muʿāraḍa taqdīriyya*).

If the claimant offers a real or nominal definition (*taʿrīf ḥaqīqī aw ismī*), then he is not seeking to elicit an assent to a claim but rather to bring to the questioner's mind a concept. One might imagine, for example, a teacher acquainting a student with the concept of "triangle" or "legal contract" or "nominal sentence." In this case, asking for a proof of the definition or countering it with an alternative definition betrays a lack of understanding of the purpose of a non-lexical definition, which is precisely to elicit and fix a conception (*taṣawwur*) and not an assent (*taṣdīq*). Adanavī accepted the view, voiced by some earlier scholars, that a non-lexical definition superficially looks like a straightforward judgment that can be true or false but is in fact not a judgment at all.[72] One might still, Adanavī wrote, object to a proffered definition by way of "quasi-*naqḍ*" (*naqḍ shabīhī*), pointing out that, for example, it is circular or includes ambiguous words or that it is too inclusive (*ghayr māniʿ*) or too exclusive (*ghayr jāmiʿ*). Again, Adanavī presented these "quasi-*naqḍ*" objections in syllogistic form, for example:[73]

> Your definition is a definition that includes ambiguous words.
> Every definition that includes ambiguous words is faulty.
> Your definition is faulty.

[70] ʿAbd al-Rashīd Jawnpūrī, *Sharḥ al-Risāla al-Sharīfiyya* (Cairo: Muḥammad ʿAlī Ṣubayḥ, 1929).

[71] Adanavī, *al-Risāla al-Ḥusayniyya*, 20ff.

[72] See al-Sayyid al-Sharīf al-Jurjānī, *Ḥāshiya ʿalā Sharḥ Mukhtaṣar Ibn al-Ḥājib* (Būlāq: al-Maṭbaʿa al-Amīriyya, 1316–1317/1898–1900), 85 (main text, lower column).

[73] Adanavī, *al-Risāla al-Ḥusayniyya*, 22–23.

The claimant may respond by denying either premise or, again, offering a disjunctive conditional denial: If by "ambiguous words" you mean ambiguous words without a disambiguating indicator (*qarīna*) then I deny the first premise, and if you mean ambiguous words as such then I deny the second.

The questioner may also object to implicit claims underlying a definition.[74] For example, if the claimant offers a *ḥadd*, that is, a definition per proximate genus and differentia, then the questioner may properly ask for a proof that what is implicitly claimed to be the proximate genus or differentia is indeed so, or he may counter the proposed definition with another definition that adduces an alternative proximate genus or differentia. Adanavī pointed out that such objections are exceedingly difficult to answer in the case of real definitions but less so in the case of nominal definitions in which appeal can be made to convention (*iṣṭilāḥ*).[75] The point that real definitions were very difficult to establish whereas nominal definitions were relatively straightforward was widely accepted by logicians since Avicenna.[76]

4. A claimant may also be putting forward a division (*taqsīm*)[77] of a universal into its parts. If the parts are mutually exclusive in reality then the division is real (*ḥaqīqī*). If the parts are merely conceptually distinct but can be true of the same things then the division is projective (*iʿtibārī*). Adanavī's position (from which some of his commentators demurred) was that the purpose of division too was primarily to determine and distinguish concepts, not to elicit assent. The primary objection to a division would on this account be to point out a general or formal defect of the division (*naqḍ shabīhī*) by indicating, for example, that it is not exhaustive or that it absurdly makes a counterpart (*qasīm*) of the divided universal a part (*qism*) of it. An example of this last charge was included in a classic handbook on logic that was widely studied by Ottoman students, namely the commentary of Quṭb al-Dīn al-Rāzī on *al-Risāla al-Shamsiyya* by Najm al-Dīn al-Kātibī. The handbook discussed at some length the problems associated with the standard division of "knowledge" (*ʿilm*) into

74 Ibid., 25.

75 Ibid., 25–26.

76 A-.M. Goichon, *Avicenne: Livre des definitions* (Cairo: Institut Français d'Archéologie Orientale, 1963), 2ff; Fakhr al-Dīn al-Rāzī, *Manṭiq al-Mulakhkhaṣ*, ed. A. F. Karamaleki and A. Asgharinezhad (Tehran: ISU Press, 2003), 118; Afḍal al-Dīn al-Khūnajī, *Kashf al-asrār ʿan ghawāmiḍ al-afkār*, ed. K. El-Rouayheb (Tehran and Berlin: Iranian Institute of Philosophy and Institute for Islamic Studies, 2010), 60.

77 Adanavī, *al-Risāla al-Ḥusayniyya*, 28.

"conception" (*taṣawwur*) and "assent" (*taṣdīq*). One particular problem is that knowledge was often defined as "the occurrence of the form of a thing to the mind." As pointed out by the commentator, "knowledge" on this definition seems indistinguishable from "conception," and hence the division seems absurdly to make "assent" both a counterpart (*qasīm*) and a part (*qism*) of knowledge/conception.[78] Adanavī again presented the quasi-*naqḍ* in syllogistic form, for example:[79]

> Your division is a division that makes a counterpart into a part.
> Every division that makes a counterpart into a part is faulty.
> Your division is faulty.

In most instances of quasi-*naqḍ*, the claimant may deny only the first (i.e., minor) premise and not the second.

Like a definition, a proffered division – though in a sense not a judgment at all – is nevertheless committed to implicit claims (e.g., that the division is exhaustive) to which the questioner may legitimately object. The questioner may ask for a reason to accept these implicit claims (*munāqaḍa majāzan lughawiyyan*) or propose an alternative division (*mu'āraḍa taqdīriyya*). The claimant would attempt to disarm these objections in the by now familiar ways: clarify the division, supply a reason, refute the questioner's corroboration if it is the only reason for rejecting the implicit claim, or fault the alternative division in the same ways as the questioner objected to the original division.

Adanavī's handbook is a good deal more complex than the foregoing discussion might have implied. Yet, even this somewhat abridged outline should be sufficient to bring out some of the conspicuous ways in which *al-Ḥusayniyya* differs from Ṭāşköprīzāde's handbook and indeed all earlier handbooks. The extensive discussion of claims, definitions, and divisions, the proliferation of technical terms involving subtypes or extended senses of *munāqaḍa*, *naqḍ*, and *mu'āraḍa*, and the presentation of dialectical exchanges in syllogistic form are all noticeably novel features. One of the early commentators on *al-Ḥusayniyya* seems to have had good grounds for writing that the handbook includes "principles and verifications that are absent from the works of the olden scholars until this

[78] Quṭb al-Dīn al-Rāzī, *Taḥrīr al-qawā'id al-manṭiqiyya bi-sharḥ al-Risāla al-Shamsiyya* (Istanbul: Aḥmed Efendī Maṭba'asī, 1325/1907), 7–8.

[79] Adanavī, *al-Risāla al-Ḥusayniyya*, 28–29. Adanavī did not explicitly present this syllogism, but noted that its "formation" (*taṣwīr*) would be clear from the preceding discussion of definitions and proceeded to discuss when the claimant may deny the first premise and when he may deny the second.

day" (*uṣūlin wa taḥqīqātin khalat ʿanhā zuburu l-awwalīna ilā hādhihi l-ayyām*).[80]

Despite such hyperbolic praise, it is unlikely that all of the mentioned novelties were due to Ḥüseyn Adanavī himself. Indeed, only on a few occasions did Adanavi explicitly claim that a specific point or suggestion was his own. It is clear from his numerous references to "glossators" that he was in conversation with a tradition of glossing and superglossing earlier handbooks on dialectics and logic, especially it seems Mīr Abū l-Fatḥ's two sets of glosses (on Dawānī's commentary on *Tahdhīb al-manṭiq* and on Mullā Ḥanafī's Tabrīzī's commentary on Ījī's treatise on *ādāb al-baḥth*) along with some superglosses on these, as well as glosses and superglosses on Masʿūd al-Shirwānī's commentary on Samarqandī's treatise. Establishing the exact relation of Adanavī's handbook to these glosses and superglosses would require a separate and very technical study. But even if almost all ideas in Adanavī's handbook derived from earlier scholars, it would still remain the case that his critical synthesis is strikingly different from – and considerably more complex and detailed than – earlier handbooks of dialectics. And the most plausible explanation for this is the accumulation of novel problems and distinctions in the course of the sixteenth and seventeenth centuries. In turn, the perceived need for new syntheses continued into the eighteenth century. Sāçaḳlīzāde's summa *Taqrīr al-qawānīn al-mutadāwala fī ʿilm al-munāẓara*, completed in 1705, is a monumental work that has yet to be studied adequately, but even a cursory examination shows it to have been an attempt to give a critical and unprecedentedly comprehensive presentation of the field.[81] Certain aspects of the work are clearly prefigured in Adanavī's handbook: the overall distinction between disputes relating to conception (*taṣawwur*) and disputes relating to assent (*taṣdīq*); the organization of the work according to the kinds of statements that a disputant might make; the extensive discussion of claims, definitions,

80 Meḥmed Dārendevī, *Sharḥ al-Risāla al-Ḥusayniyya*, MS: www.yazmalar.gov.tr/45AkZe672, fol. 3b. Dārendevī's commentary should not be confused with his earlier gloss on the author's own commentary.

81 Mehmet Karabela, in his "The Development of Dialectic and Argumentation Theory in Post-Classical Islamic Intellectual History" (unpublished PhD dissertation, McGill University, 2010), rightly points to the importance of Sāçaḳlīzāde's work but does not note the clear ways in which it is indebted to Ḥüseyn Adanavī's handbook. Karabela never mentions Adanavī's treatise – a drawback in an otherwise welcome and pioneering exploration of the later literature on *ādāb al-baḥth*.

and divisions; and the syllogistic presentation of dialectical exchanges. Nevertheless, Sāçaḳlīzāde's summa is significantly more detailed and discusses issues and defines technical terms that even Adanavī had not addressed. Sāçaḳlīzāde was also critical of some of the explicitly original suggestions that Adanavī had offered.[82] The new Ottoman handbooks on *ādāb al-baḥth* after the mid-seventeenth century cannot plausibly be dismissed as "reworking of existing discussions, constantly crossing and re-crossing the same familiar ground in the same familiar way." Rather, they are – as indeed anyone unencumbered with prejudices about "decline" might have suspected – indicative of significant developments in the field. The Yemenī jurist Muḥammad al-Shawkānī (d. 1834), who was lukewarm toward the rational sciences, was very much on target when he cautioned the budding student that "the issues of the science of *munāẓara* have become knotty in recent times" (*qad tasha''abat masā'ilu 'ilmi l-munāẓarati fī l-azminati l-akhīra*).[83]

Ādāb al-baḥth and Relational Syllogisms

The predilection for giving syllogistic presentations of dialectical exchanges, a novel feature common to the works of Adanavī and Sāçaḳlīzāde, led to important developments in Ottoman logic in the course of the eighteenth century. It motivated a renewed interest in applied logic, after centuries of neglect in the post-Avicennan logical tradition, and an interest in so-called "unfamiliar syllogisms," that is, formally valid relational inferences that had not been recognized in classical Aristotelian logic.

82 For example, in his *al-Risāla al-Waladiyya*, Sāçaḳlīzāde rejected the idea that a questioner might respond to an unproven claim by means of *naqḍ shabīhī* and *mu'āraḍa taqdīriyya*, dismissing both as "usurpation" (*ghaṣb*). See *al-Risāla al-Waladiyya* (Cairo: Maṭba'at al-Khānjī, 1329/1911), 8; 'Abd al-Wahhāb al-Āmidī, *Sharḥ al-Waladiyya* (Cairo: Maṭba'at al-Khānjī, 1329/1911), 97. Curiously, in his *Taqrīr al-qawānīn*, which seems to have been written earlier (there are references to it in *al-Risāla al-Waladiyya*), Sāçaḳlīzāde allowed for both of these strategies; see *Taqrīr al-qawānīn*, 32. For another riposte to Adanavī, see 'Umar Āmidī, *Sharḥ al-Waladiyya*, p. 153 (margin).

83 Muḥammad al-Shawkānī, *Adab al-ṭalab* (Beirut: Dār al-Kutub al-'ilmiyya, 2008), 98. Shawkānī's remark was elicited by an unnamed Indo-Muslim handbook that he had encountered. From his description of the work (he says it is approximately three quires in length and consists of an introduction and nine sections), this is almost certainly one of the Indo-Muslim commentaries on *al-Ādāb al-Sharīfiyya*. Though this handbook justifies Shawkānī's assessment, the Ottoman handbooks by Adanavī and Sāçaḳlīzāde (of which he seems to have been unaware) are unquestionably even more "knotty."

The way in which Ottoman *ādāb al-baḥth* provoked these developments can be brought out by considering the commentary on Sāçaḳlīzāde's short epitome *al-Waladiyya* by his student Ḥüseyn Bertizī, a commentary written during Sāçaḳlīzāde's lifetime, that is, before 1732.[84] Sāçaḳlīzāde had inverted the order of Adanavī's handbook, starting with a discussion of dialectical exchanges relating to definitions, then divisions, and then straightforward propositional claims. Like Adanavī, he presented the *naqḍ*-objection to a definition in syllogistic form, for example:[85]

> Your definition is a definition that is not exhaustive of the instances of the definiendum.
> Every definition that is not exhaustive etc. is faulty.
> Your definition is faulty.

In the following section devoted to divisions, Sāçaḳlīzāde did not present *naqḍ* objections in syllogistic form, but the fact that he had just done so with definitions invited commentators to fill in the gap, and this Bertizī proceeded to do. For example, Sāçaḳlīzāde noted that a *naqḍ* objection may be directed at a proposed division on the ground that it makes the part of a thing its counterpart. Bertizī presented the argument as an enthymeme with only the minor premise explicitly mentioned and with a "suppressed" (*maṭwiyya*) major premise (italicized in what follows):[86]

> This division is a division that makes a part of the divided thing into a counterpart.
> Every division that makes a part of the divided thing etc. is faulty.
> This division is faulty.

84 This is clear from the words *ṣānahu llāhu ta'ālā 'an kulli āfatin* that follow the mention of Sāçaḳlīzāde's name in Bertizī's introduction. Bertizī referred to Sāçaḳlīzāde as "my teacher" (*ustādhī*) in the preface. The sources differ significantly with respect to Sāçaḳlīzāde's date of death: The Ottoman scholar 'Ākifzāde (d. 1815) gave the year 1125/1713, which is obviously wrong because Sāçaḳlīzāde completed *Tartīb al-'ulūm* in 1128/1715 and also wrote annotations to that work in 1130/1718. Ismā'īl Baghdādī gave the date 1150/1737–1738, whereas Meḥmed Ṭāhir Būrṣalī gave the year 1145/1732–1733. The latter date seems preferable, as Būrṣalī cited a chronogram composed at the occasion of Sāçaḳlīzāde's death. The statement by Ismā'īl Baghdādī (*Īḍāḥ al-maknūn*, I, 357) that Bertizī finished his commentary in 1176/1762–1763 cannot be true. One extant manuscript of the commentary that I have inspected is dated 1161/1748, see Berlin Staatsbibliothek: Hs.Or. 4687.

85 Sāçaḳlīzāde, *Waladiyya*, 3 (lines 1–2).

86 Sāçaḳlīzāde, *Waladiyya*, 5 (lines 22ff); Bertizī, *Jāmi' al-kunūz* (www.yazmalar.gov.tr/06 Mil Yz A 4812), fol. 42a (lines 21ff).

Similarly, when Sāçaḳlīzāde wrote that a division could also be faulted for having parts that were not mutually exclusive, Bertizī regimented the statement into a syllogism with a "suppressed" major premise:[87]

> This division is a division whose parts are not mutually exclusive.
> Every division whose parts are not mutually exclusive is faulty.
> This division is faulty.

At first sight, such syllogistic presentations might appear as nothing but pedantic statements of the obvious, but this would be to miss some important points. First, the regimentations clarified the possible rejoinders to such objections. For instance, in the case of the second of the aforementioned syllogisms a disputant might contest the first premise and concede the second, or alternatively concede the first premise and contest the second on the ground that a projective division – as opposed to a real division – might have parts that are merely conceptually distinct but not exclusive in extension. Furthermore, the penchant for syllogistic regimentation led to a heightened awareness of formally valid arguments that did not naturally fit into the mold of a standard Aristotelian syllogism with three terms. An example of this is afforded by Bertizī's attempt at casting into syllogistic form the following formulation by Sāçaḳlīzāde of a *naqḍ*-objection to a definition: "This definition leads to circularity and this is absurd and every definition that leads to the absurd is faulty." Bertizī wrote that there are two ways of regimenting the argument. The first would be to take the Arabic "and this is absurd" (*wa-huwa muḥāl*) as an interjection within a lengthy predicate all of which reappears as a subject of the second, major premise:

> This definition is a definition that leads to circularity (and this is absurd).
> Every definition that leads to circularity (and this is absurd) is faulty.
> This definition is faulty.

Alternatively, the argument could be presented – as Sāçaḳlīzāde had himself done in his lengthy summa *Taqrīr al-qawānīn* – as a complex of two syllogisms, the first of which is "unfamiliar":[88]

> *This definition is a definition that leads to circularity.*
> *Circularity is absurd.*

[87] Sāçaḳlīzāde, *Waladiyya*, 6 (lines 5 ff). Bertizī, *Jāmiʿ al-kunūz*, fol. 46b (lines 16ff).

[88] Bertizī, *Jāmiʿ al-kunūz*, fol. 20b (l. 17ff). Sāçaḳlīzāde had offered this regimentation in his *Taqrīr al-qawānīn* (p. 16) but without mentioning the term "unfamiliar syllogism."

This definition is a definition that leads to the absurd.
Every definition that leads to the absurd is faulty.
This definition is faulty.

The "unfamiliar syllogism" (*qiyās ghayr muta ʿāraf*) – italicized in the preceding lines – is in effect a relational syllogism (or what Medieval Latin logicians called an "oblique" syllogism).[89] Though intuitively formally valid, such arguments were not recognized in classical Aristotelian logic. Beginning with Fakhr al-Dīn al-Rāzī in the late twelfth century, some Arabic logicians had proposed that such inferences were productive without the need for analyzing them into standard Aristotelian syllogisms.[90] The topic had elicited controversy in the wide-ranging debates between the fifteenth-century Persian philosophers Dawānī and Ṣadr al-Dīn Dashtakī. Dawānī had argued, against Dashtakī, that an inference such as the following was productive as it stood, without the need for rewriting it into the form of a standard Aristotelian syllogism:[91]

Zayd is the brother of ʿAmr.
ʿAmr is the leader of the town.
Zayd is the brother of the leader of the town.

Dawānī's point was repeated by some of his later followers and glossators, including some of the figures who appear regularly in scholarly chains linking Dawānī to the Ottoman scholarly tradition: Mīrzā Jān Bāghnavī (d. 1586), Ḥusayn Khalkhālī (d. 1604), Meḥmed Emīn Ṣadrüddīnzāde (d. 1627), Zayn al-ʿĀbidīn Gūrānī (fl. 1656), and Ḳara Ḥalīl Tīrevī (d. 1711).[92] Yet, up until the early eighteenth century, the point had simply been reiterated in certain ad hoc contexts and had left little influence on overall presentations of syllogisms in handbooks of logic. The fact that "unfamiliar syllogisms" came to be employed by Ottoman dialecticians in their attempts to regiment arguments into syllogistic form brought the concept to the forefront and led to further developments of the basic idea formulated by Dawānī. Most importantly perhaps, the idea emerged in the early decades of the eighteenth century that "unfamiliar syllogisms" can occur in all four syllogistic figures and that these have conditions of productivity that may or may not be similar to those of standard

[89] See Paul Thom, "Termini Obliqui and the Logic of Relations," *Archiv für Geschichte der Philosophie* 59(1977): 143–155.
[90] Khaled El-Rouayheb, *Relational Syllogisms and the History of Arabic Logic*, 39–48.
[91] Ibid., 92–104.
[92] Ibid., 104–107, 158–163.

syllogisms. This idea would later be incorporated into the new handbook on logic, entitled *al-Burhān fī ʿilm al-mīzān*, written by Ismāʿīl Gelenbevī in the 1760s. In that work, and in its numerous later commentaries, the logic of relational syllogisms in the four figures began to be explored for the first time in the history of Arabic logic.[93] The following are Gelenbevī's examples of the four figures, depending on whether the recurrent part (boldfaced in the examples) is part of the subject or predicate of the first, minor premise and the subject or predicate of the second, major premise:

(Figure 1)	
This is the slave of a **man.**	["Man" is part of the predicate.]
Every **man** is human.	["Man" is the subject.]
This is the slave of a human.	
(Figure 2)	
This is the slave of a **man.**	["Man" is part of the predicate.]
No woman is a **man.**	["Man" is the predicate.]
This is not the slave of a woman.	
(Figure 3)	
The slave of a **man** is a human.	["Man" is part of the subject.]
Every **man** is an animal.	["Man" is the subject.]
The slave of some animal is a human.	
(Figure 4)	
The slave of a **human** is an animal.	["Human" is part of the subject.]
Every Rūmī is a **human.**	["Human" is the predicate.]
The slave of some Rūmī is an animal.	

Bertizī's commentary, written at least 30 years before Gelenbevī's handbook, is one of the earliest attested occurrences of the idea that an unfamiliar syllogism can occur in a number of syllogistic figures. At one point, Sāçaḳlīzāde had presented the argument that it is not legitimate to ask for a proof as a whole (only to ask for a proof for a specific premise used in a proof) "since asking for proof is only appropriately directed at what can be proven and a proof as a whole cannot be proven" (*liʾanna al-manʿa innamā yaṣiḥḥu ʿalā mā yumkinu l-istidlālu ʿalayhi wa l-dalīlu lā yumkinu l-istidlālū ʿalayhi*). Bertizī regimented the argument into an

[93] Khaled El-Rouayheb, *Relational Syllogisms and the History of Arabic Logic*, 196–201. Gelenbevī's *Burhān* was written shortly after 1177/1763; see A. Bingöl, *Gelenbevi İsmail* (Ankara: Kültür ve Turizm Bakanliği, 1988), 5.

"unfamiliar syllogism of the second figure" (*qiyās ghayr muta'āraf min al-shakl al-thānī*):[94]

> Asking for proof is legitimately directed at what **can be proven.**
> It is not the case that a proof taken as a whole **can be proven.**
> It is not the case that asking for proof is legitimately directed at a proof taken as a whole

A pivotal work for the widespread recognition of the idea of "unfamiliar syllogisms" and their occurrence in the four figures of the syllogism was a short treatise by the little-known Ottoman scholar Mūsā Pehlivānī. This strikingly original treatise came to be widely studied and commented on in the eighteenth and nineteenth centuries and inspired a number of similar works by later scholars.[95] Despite this impact, Pehlivānī largely escaped the notice of the standard Ottoman biographical sources – in this respect he is similar to Ḥüseyn Adanavī. The known facts about his life are few. He hailed from the Turcoman tribe Pehlivan and taught in the town of Tokat in north-central Anatolia in the early decades of the eighteenth century. He authored at least two short works: the aforementioned treatise on unfamiliar syllogisms and another treatise on the vexed theological issue of free will. Other aspects of his life are uncertain. We have no information about his teachers, though two of his students had lifespans from 1700–1768 and 1693–1780 respectively, confirming that he must have been teaching in the early decades of the eighteenth century.[96] The early-twentieth century scholar Ismā'īl Baghdādī, in his abovementioned dictionary of Arabic and Islamic authors, gave 1133/1720–1721 as his date of death, whereas the earlier Ottoman scholar 'Abd ül-Raḥīm 'Ākifzāde (d. 1815) gave his date of death as "a bit after 1170/1756."[97] Unfortunately, neither source inspires full confidence. Baghdādī's dates

94 Bertizī, *Jāmi' al-kunūz*, fol. 70a (lines 8 ff). There is a problem with the validity of this inference (which I presume to be in the first mood of the second figure of the unfamiliar syllogism), see Khaled El-Rouayheb, *Relational Syllogisms and the History of Arabic Logic*, 206–208.

95 It was printed in Istanbul with the commentary of Meḥmed Ṭāvūskārī (d. 1780) and two glosses by later Ottoman scholars (by Maṭba'ah-i 'Āmireh, 1281/1864–1865). Also printed in Istanbul in the nineteenth century were *al-Risāla al-Istidlāliyya*, a somewhat expanded version of Pehlivānī's treatise by a certain 'Othmān b. Muṣṭafā Ṭarsūsī (Istanbul: Maṭba'at Dār al-Khilāfa,1258/1842) and a versification of Pehlivānī's treatise by Muṣṭafā Kāmil Yemlīḫāzāde (d. 1877) together with a commentary by the versifier's nephew Ḫalīl Es'ad, see Ḫalīl Es'ad Yemlīḫāzāde, *Jilā' al-'uyūn: Sharḥ al-Qiyāsiyya min Naẓm al-funūn* (Istanbul: Cemal Efendī Maṭba'asī, 1308/1890).

96 The two students are 'Abdullāh Amāsī and Meḥmed Erżurūmī, see 'Ākifzāde, *al-Majmū' fī l-mashhūd wa l-masmū'*, fols. 55a and 54a.

97 HA II, 482; 'Ākifzāde, *al-Majmū' fī l-mashhūd wa l-masmū'*, fol. 29a–b.

of death are often estimates or based on the time at which an author's work was completed.[98] ʿĀkifzāde's work is also not always reliable with respect to obituary dates.[99] Manuscript evidence suggests that Ismaʿīl Baghdādī's date of death for Mūsā Pehlivānī is too early. The colophon of a manuscript copy of his treatise on free will, dated 9 Rajab 1160/17 July 1747, refers to the author as alive at the time the copy was prepared.[100] On the other hand, the estimate of ʿĀkifzāde seems too late, for a commentary by Pehlivānī's student Ṭāvūskārī, completed in April 1748, seems to refer to Pehlivānī as no longer alive.[101] This might suggest that

98 For example, for the influential sixteenth-century Iranian logician and dialectician Mīr Abū l-Fatḥ, he gave the date of death 950/1543 even though two further works by the same scholar can be dated with confidence to 953/1546 and 972/1564 respectively. For Pehlivānī's student Meḥmed Ṭāvūskārī, Baghdādī gave 1161/1748 as the date of death, for no apparent reason except that this was the year in which he completed an influential commentary on Pehlivānī's treatise on syllogisms. Ṭāvūskārī completed a commentary on Birgevī's handbook on morphology *Kifāyat al-mubtadiʾ* in 1165/1752 (see the extant manuscripts of the commentary in Süleymaniye Kütüphanesı, Istanbul: Laleli 3096 and Esad Efendi 3133). He appears to have died as late as 1194/1780 – he is probably identical to the "Meḥmed Erżurūmī" mentioned by ʿAkifzāde, *al-Majmūʿ*, fol. 54a. Tavusker is a small town in the province of Erzurum in eastern Anatolia. Outside of his home region, the attributive "Ṭāvūskārī" might not have been recognized and the scholar would accordingly have been known as Meḥmed Erżurūmī – he is known by that name in the Istanbul printing of his commentary on Pehlivānī's treatise.

99 For example, he gave 1115/1703 or 1125/1713 as the date of death of Sāçaḳlīzāde (fol. 75a), even though that scholar's *Tartīb al-ʿulūm* can be dated securely to 1128/1715 and some of the author's own annotations to that work were written two years later. For the dating of *Tartīb al-ʿulūm*, see Sāçaḳlīzāde, *Tartīb al-ʿulūm*, 240 and 234 fn (A). One of Sāçaḳlīzāde's teachers, Ḥamza Dārendevī, is said by ʿĀkifzāde to have died at the age of seventy in 1167/1753, which obviously cannot be true: Sāçaḳlīzāde was already an established scholar in the 1690s and his teacher can hardly have been born later than 1650, and in any case one of Ḥamza Dārendevī's extant works was already written by 1099/1688 and there is reason to think that he was already deceased by 1113/1702. See Mach and Ormsby, *Handlist of Arabic Manuscripts (New Series) in the Princeton University Library* (Princeton, NJ: Princeton University Press, 1987), nr. 1014 for an extant manuscript of Ḥamza Dārendevī's supergloss on *Mīr al-Ādāb* dated 1099/1688. The colophon of another manuscript of the supergloss, dated 1113/1702, adds the phrase "May he rest in peace" (*raḥmatu llāhi ʿalayhi*) after the glossator's name (see www.yazmalar.gov.tr/ 50OrHis70, fol. 112a). Sāçaḳlīzāde referred to Ḥamza Dārendevī as his teacher in his gloss on Tāşköprīzāde's handbook on *ādāb al-baḥth*, see Sāçaḳlīzāde, *Ḥāshiya ʿalā Risālat al-ādāb* (MS: www.yazmalar.gov.tr/ 45Hk2007, fol. 53b [margins]). This is also confirmed by the scholarly genealogy given in Kawtharī, *al-Taḥrīr al-wajīz*, 19.

100 The colophon of MS www.yazmalar.gov.tr/ 01Hk1141 adds *ṣānahu l-maliku l-qawī* after the name of the author (see fol. 171a).

101 According to the colophons of at least two manuscripts (Süleymaniye Kütüphanesı, Istanbul: MS Yazma Bağislar 348 and www.yazmalar.gov.tr/ 43Va958), Ṭāvūskārī completed his commentary on Pehlivānī's treatise in the town of Gaziantep in Rabīʿ II, 1161/April 1748. The first mention of Pehlivānī in the commentary is followed by the

Pehlivānī died in late 1747 or early 1748. On that account, the year 1720 would be closer to the date on which Pehlivānī completed his innovative treatise on enthymematic and relational syllogisms.

Pehlivānī's treatise appears to be the first work to present all four figures of the "unfamiliar syllogism" and to suggest that each figure can be further subdivided into various moods. The details of Pehlivānī's treatment of "unfamiliar syllogisms" have been described elsewhere.[102] In the present context, the more important point is that, like Bertizī, Pehlivānī was clearly interested in "unfamiliar syllogisms" as part of an overall concern with casting arguments into explicit syllogistic form. The presentation of the four figures of the "unfamiliar syllogism" occurs only at the end of his treatise, almost as an afterthought, whereas the bulk of it is devoted to showing how one could reconstruct a complete syllogism from an argument with only one explicitly mentioned premise and the other premise "suppressed" (*maṭwiyya*). Some sense of Pehlivānī's approach to this issue will be helpful for bringing out the way in which his work was related to earlier discussions.

Pehlivānī's starting point was the question whether the explicitly mentioned premise had terms in common with the conclusion.[103] If, for instance, it had no terms at all in common with the conclusion, then the complete syllogism would either be a hypothetical syllogism (modus ponens, modus tollens, or disjunctive syllogism) or a complex of two or more simple syllogisms. For example, suppose that the explicitly mentioned premise is "A is B" and the conclusion is "J is D":

A is B.
J is D.

In that case, the two obvious ways of "extracting" a complete syllogism would be (1) to adduce a suppressed hypothetical premise, for example:

If A is B then J is D.
A is B.
J is D.

phrase *ja'ala llāhu mathwāhu min riyāḍi l-jinān* and regularly thereafter references to Pehlivānī are followed by the phrase "may he rest in peace" (*raḥmatu llāhi 'alayhi*). It would not be odd that the first commentary on the treatise was written shortly after its author's death.

102 El-Rouayheb, *Relational Syllogisms and the History of Arabic Logic*, 163–174.

103 Meḥmed Erżurūmī, *Sharḥ al-Risāla al-Qiyāsiyya al-Mūsawiyya* (Istanbul: Maṭba'ah-i 'Amire, 1281/1864–1865), 3ff.

Or (2) adduce a complex syllogism, for example[104]:

J is A.
A is B.
J is B.
B is D.
J is D.

Alternatively, the explicitly mentioned premise may have a term in common with the conclusion, for example[105]:

J is B.
J is A.

In such a case, the explicitly mentioned premise contains the subject of the conclusion (in this case "J"), which means that the suppressed premise must contain the predicate of the conclusion (in this case "A"). This predicate ("A") can be either the subject or the predicate of the suppressed premise. If it is the *subject* of the suppressed premise then the middle term B must be the predicate of that premise, and the complete syllogism would be in the second figure of the syllogism, thus:

J is B.
A is B.
J is A

If A is the *predicate* of the suppressed premise then the middle term B would have to be subject of the suppressed premise, and the complete syllogism would be in the first figure, thus:

J is B.
B is A.
J is A.

104 For some reason, Pehlivānī specified that in the complex syllogism the first would be "hypothetical-combinatorial" (a purely hypothetical syllogism) and the second would be "hypothetical-reiterative" (modus ponens, modus tollens, or disjunctive syllogism). This is baffling, and his commentator Meḥmed Ṭāvūskārī explained that there are numerous possibilities, one of which is that the complex syllogism consists of categorical syllogisms, as here. See Erżurūmī, *Sharḥ al-Risāla al-Qiyāsiyya*, 5–6. Pehlivānī's point makes sense only if we suppose his meaning to be that if the suppressed premise is a hypothetical premise but does not yield a conclusion with the explicitly mentioned categorical premise, then that hypothetical premise must be a premise of another purely hypothetical syllogism that yields a hypothetical proposition that then does produce the desired conclusion with the explicitly mentioned categorical premise.

105 Erżurūmī, *Sharḥ al-Risāla al-Qiyāsiyya*, 6ff.

Because the second figure of the syllogism never yields an affirmative conclusion, the only way to derive "J is A" from "J is B" would be to choose the second option, that is, construct a first-figure syllogism with an added premise whose predicate ("A") is also the predicate of the desired conclusion.

If one focuses solely on the tradition of Arabic logic, then Pehlivānī's concern with enthymemes and suppressed premises, and the systematic way in which he discussed them, would appear to have no precedent whatsoever. The post-Avicennan tradition of Arabic logic had since the thirteenth century exhibited little or no interest in how to regiment ordinary arguments into explicit syllogistic form, and none of the classic logic handbooks that were studied in Ottoman madrasas addressed this issue in detail.[106] Avicenna himself, and more orthodox Aristotelian Arabic logicians such as Averroes, had – following Aristotle – devoted some attention to the application of syllogistics to ordinary argumentation. But Pehlivānī's work bears no trace of being influenced by such older works. When one compares Pehlivānī's work with Avicenna's discussion of how to regiment arguments into explicit syllogistic form in *al-Shifā'*, the differences are striking.[107] Avicenna's primary concern was how to regiment arguments that already have two premises and need to be ordered in a syllogistically productive way. For Pehlivānī, such cases were of no interest whatsoever – he breezily stated that when both premises of a syllogism were mentioned "then the matter is clear" (*fa-l-amru ẓāhirun*).[108] Avicenna also spoke very briefly of supplementing single-premised arguments with a missing premise, but his discussion is very different from Pehlivānī's. His starting point was that the conclusion could be universal affirmative (Every J is A) or particular affirmative (Some J is A) or universal negative (No J is A) or particular negative (Some J is not A). In each case, Avicenna was content with giving an example. For instance, if the desired conclusion is "Every J is A" and the single premise is "Every D is A" then, if the proposition "Every J is D" is "conjoined" (*ittaṣala*), a complete syllogism would "obtain" (*ḥaṣala*).[109] There is no attempt to give a systematic view of possibilities depending on whether the term shared by the single premise and the conclusion is a predicate or subject.

[106] The only classic handbook familiar in Ottoman circles to broach this issue at all was Quṭb al-Dīn al-Rāzī, *Sharḥ Maṭāliʿ al-anwār* (Istanbul: Maṭbaʿah-i ʿAmire, 1277/1860–1861), 247–248. This gives a summary version of the discussion in Avicenna's *Shifā'*.
[107] Ibn Sīnā, *al-Shifā': al-Qiyās*, ed. S. Zāyid and I. Madkour (Cairo: n.p., 1964), 460–468.
[108] Erżurūmī, *Sharḥ al-Risāla al-Qiyāsiyya*, 4 (line 6).
[109] Ibn Sīnā, *al-Shifā': al-Qiyās*, 467–468.

The language is also very different from Pehlivānī's: Avicenna termed the regimentation of an argument into explicit syllogistic form "analysis" (*taḥlīl*), and he repeatedly spoke of a further premise being "conjoined" (*ittiṣāl*) so that a syllogism would "obtain" (*ḥaṣala*), all terms that are absent from Pehlivānī's treatise. Avicenna called the missing premise in an enthymeme an "implicit" (*muḍmara*) premise, whereas Pehlivānī – along with the dialecticians of his time – called it a "suppressed" (*maṭwiyya*) premise. Avicenna's discussion of enthymemes was of course innocent of the idea of "unfamiliar syllogisms."

It is when one looks at works on *ādāb al-baḥth* that Pehlivānī's interest, approach and terminology begin to appear recognizable. The closest precursor to the first part of Pehlivānī's treatise seems to be the final section of Sāçaḳlīzāde's summa *Taqrīr al-qawānīn*. Sāçaḳlīzāde had ended his work with the following words:

> A single premise of a categorical syllogism, if it contains the subject of the desired conclusion, then it [i.e., the explicit premise] is a minor premise and the major premise has been suppressed (*maṭwiyya*). If it contains the predicate of the desired conclusion then it is the major premise and the minor premise has been suppressed. If it contains neither of the two [i.e. neither the subject nor the predicate of the conclusion] then know that the syllogism is complex [...] And knowledge of suppressed premises (*al-maṭwiyyāt*) would require a detailed treatment.[110]

Both the approach and the language of this section are strongly continuous with Pehlivānī's treatise. Indeed, if Pehlivānī's treatise was in fact written around the year 1720, then it may be seen as following up on Sāçaḳlīzāde's recommendation fifteen years earlier that the topic of "suppressed premises" be discussed in greater detail.

The fact that Pehlivānī discussed "unfamiliar syllogisms" in a treatise devoted to "suppressed premises" might at first sight seem surprising but becomes more understandable when one considers the contemporary literature on *ādāb al-baḥth*. According to Pehlivānī's student Ṭāvūskārī, Pehlivānī wrote his treatise in response to requests from students to show how to form complete syllogisms from ordinary arguments *and* to explain the notion of unfamiliar syllogisms. Ṭāvūskārī's exact words were:

> It has been heard from him [i.e. Pehlivānī] – may he rest in peace – that the reason for his writing this treatise was the request of some of his students that he explain the way of extracting syllogisms from expressions and explain the unfamiliar syllogism ...[111]

110 Sāçaḳlīzāde, *Taqrīr al-qawānīn*, 93.

111 Erżurūmī, *Sharḥ al-Risāla al-Qiyāsiyya*, 3 (lines 16–18).

The suggestion is clearly that Pehlivānī treated the two topics together because they were already felt to be closely connected, and the most obvious source for this connection would have been the works of his contemporary dialecticians. As has been seen previously, there are already indications that the connection is present in Sāçaḳlīzāde's own works, and it is explicitly and indubitably established in the commentaries on *al-Waladiyya* by Sāçaḳlīzāde's students Bertizī and Behisnī – commentaries that exhibit the same systematic interest in supplementing single-premised arguments with "suppressed" premises and in employing "unfamiliar syllogisms" for that purpose.[112]

The roots of some of the most conspicuously novel developments in Ottoman logic in the eighteenth century – the interest in casting ordinary arguments into syllogistic form and the recognition of "unfamiliar" relational syllogisms – are clearly to be sought, not in the works of the older Islamic philosophers, but in Ottoman works on *ādāb al-baḥth* from the seventeenth and early eighteenth centuries.

[112] See, e.g., the use of "unfamiliar syllogisms" in Meḥmed b. Ḥüseyn Behisnī, *Sharḥ al-Waladiyya* [printed with the commentary of ʿAbd al-Wahhāb Āmidī] (Cairo, Maṭbaʿat al-Khānjī, 1329/1911), 29 (lower rubric). The attributive "Behisnī" (البهسني) is corrupted in the Egyptian printing to (البهتي). Behisnī refers to Sāçaḳlīzāde as "the teacher" (*al-ustādh*) in his commentary. Mentions of Sāçaḳlīzāde in the printed edition of his commentary are followed by the phrase "may he rest in peace," suggesting that the commentary was written after 1732, but there is at least one extant manuscript of his commentary that is listed in a manuscript catalog as being significantly earlier than that date, specifically www.yazmalar.gov.tr/ 19Hk2319 purporting to be from 1122/1709. I have not been able to consult this manuscript. As *Taqrīr al-qawānīn* was written in 1117/1705 and *al-Waladiyya* refers to it and was therefore presumably written after that date, such an early dating of Behisnī's commentary strikes me as doubtful.

3

The Rise of "Deep Reading"

Premodern Islamic education has often been characterized as personal rather than institutional, and as oral rather than textual. A student would ideally seek out a respected teacher, become part of his entourage, attend his classes, and "hear" knowledge from him. It is from cultivating this personal, oral–aural relationship with one or more teachers that a student would hope eventually to get recognition as a scholar in his own right and be sought out by a new generation of seekers of knowledge – in effect becoming a link in a chain of transmitters of knowledge extending back to early Islamic times. In this pedagogic model listening, discussing, repeating, memorizing, and reciting were of paramount importance. The private reading of texts, by contrast, played a subordinate and auxiliary role, and was sometimes even the source of anxiety and censure.

The model is of course an ideal type, and the actual process of acquiring knowledge would only have approximated it. There is abundant evidence for the existence in various times and places of students who were intractable or who by virtue of their intelligence and private reading came to surpass their teachers in scholarly accomplishment. Nevertheless, as a depiction of a widely held cultural ideal, the model does arguably reflect the character of education in many parts of the medieval Islamic world. A number of modern historical studies have emphasized the highly personal and noninstitutional character of the educational process in Baghdad, Damascus, and Cairo from the eleventh to the fifteenth centuries.[1]

[1] J. Berkey *The Transmission of Knowledge in Medieval Cairo: A Social History of Islamic Education* (Princeton, NJ: Princeton University Press, 1988), Chapter 2; M. Chamberlain, *Knowledge and Social Practice in Medieval Damascus, 1190–1350* (Cambridge: Cambridge University Press 1994), Chapter 2; D. Ephrat, *A Learned Society in a Period*

It was from teachers, and not from any institution, that a student obtained recognition as well as a certificate (*ijāza*) to teach. Contemporary biographers regularly felt it important to indicate with whom a scholar had studied, and almost never in which institutions he had done so. The madrasa functioned as a college that often provided accommodation and food for students, and kept one or more teachers on its payroll. But it did not issue degrees, nor was it a necessary part of the educational process, for some teachers conducted classes in mosques, or Sufi lodges, or at home. The transmission of knowledge and authority from teacher to student was basically face-to-face, with private reading and study playing an unofficial and complementary role. This model also seems applicable to the remnants of traditional Islamic education studied by anthropologists in the twentieth century.[2] For example, Brinkley Messick has distinguished between various ways in which twentieth-century Yemeni students at traditional madrasas interacted with texts: memorization (*ḥifẓ*), recitation (*qirāʾa*), listening (*samāʿ*), and private reading (*muṭālaʿa*).[3] He noted, however, that *muṭālaʿa* was commonly used to describe interaction with books on topics not formally studied at the madrasa, such as history and poetry.[4] The other three modes of textual interaction, by comparison, were central to the pedagogic process, or at least to the ideal-typical representation of that process.

In what follows, I present evidence for the emergence of a more impersonal and textual model of the transmission of knowledge in the central Ottoman lands in the seventeenth and eighteenth centuries. It is not just that the time-honored, oral–aural ideal did not fully correspond to actual educational realities; the ideal itself appears to have been supplemented with a newly articulated ideal of the acquisition of knowledge through "deep reading." This development may, I will suggest, have been related to two factors: the increased importance of the instrumental and rational sciences, especially the discipline of dialectics (*ādāb al-baḥth*), and the far-reaching reforms that the Ottoman learned hierarchy underwent in the sixteenth century.

of Transition: The Sunnī ʿUlamaʾ of Eleventh-Century Baghdad (Albany: SUNY Press, 2000), chapter 3.

2 Classic studies are D. Eickelman, *Knowledge and Power in Morocco: The Education of a Twentieth-Century Notable* (Princeton, NJ: Princeton University Press 1985), chapters 3 and 4; and B. Messick, *The Calligraphic State: Textual Domination and History in a Muslim Society* (Berkeley: University of California Press 1993), chapters 4–6.

3 Messick, *The Calligraphic State*, 84–92.

4 Ibid., 90–91.

Traditional Manuals on the Acquisition of Knowledge

On January 4, 1691, a prominent Ottoman scholar residing in Mecca completed a treatise in Arabic on a topic that, as far as he knew, had never before received extended attention: the proper manner (*ādāb*) of perusing books (*muṭālaʿa*). The scholar's name was Aḥmed b. Lütfullāh Mevlevī, now better known as Müneccimbāşī.[5] He was born in Salonika in 1631 or 1632, and began his education in his hometown, where he was also initiated into the Mevlevī Sufi order. He went to the Ottoman capital Istanbul in the mid-1650s and attended the lessons of, among others, the later Şeyhülislām Yaḥyā Minḳārīzāde and Ders-i ʿāmm Ṣāliḥ Żihnī (who, as mentioned in Chapter 1, had impressed the Damascene scholar Muḥibbī with his manner of teaching that "followed the path of the Persian and Kurdish verifying scholars in heeding the science of *ādāb al-baḥth*"). Aḥmed b. Lütfullāh apparently had a particular aptitude for mathematics, astronomy, and astrology, and in the year 1668 he was appointed to the post of court astrologer to Sultan Meḥmed IV (r. 1648–1687) – hence the title "Müneccimbāşī." When Meḥmed IV was deposed in 1687, Müneccimbāşī fell from grace and was exiled to Cairo. In 1690 he went to Mecca and took up a position as head of the local Mevlevī lodge. He died in the city twelve years later, in 1702. Though possibly best known today for his universal chronicle *Ṣaḥāʾif al-akhbār* (written in Arabic but later abridged and translated into Ottoman Turkish), he also wrote a number of other works, some of which appear – from the number of extant manuscripts – to have been widely copied and read in later times. These include

1. A lengthy commentary on a treatise on ethics (*akhlāq*) by ʿAḍud al-Dīn al-Ījī
2. A treatise on arithmetic, entitled *Ghāyat al-ʿudad fī ʿilm al-ʿadad*
3. A treatise on logical predication (*ḥaml*)
4. An extensively annotated translation into Arabic of a Persian treatise on figurative language (*majāz*) by ʿIṣām al-Dīn Isfarāyinī
5. A gloss on the gloss of Muṣliḥ al-Dīn Lārī on Qāḍī Mīr Maybudī's commentary on Abharī's *Hidāyat al-ḥikma*, covering the section on natural philosophy
6. The mentioned treatise on the "proper manner of perusing books" (*ādāb al-muṭālaʿa*)

[5] On his life and works, see Şeyḫī, *Veḳāyiʿü l-fużalāʾ*, II, 206–207; J. Kramers, "Münedjdjim Bashi," *EI2*, VII, 572; A. Ağırakça, "Müneccimbāşī, Aḥmed Dede," *İslam Ansiklopedisi* (Istanbul: Türkiye Diyanet Vakfı, 2006), XXXII, 4–6.

In the introduction to the last-mentioned work, which he completed just a few months after having arrived in Mecca from Cairo, Müneccimbāşī wrote that he had hesitated before venturing to write on a topic that no one had treated before.[6] When he decided to write nonetheless, he entitled the treatise "The Inspiration of the Sanctuary" (*Fayḍ al-ḥaram*). Without the guidance of previous authors, reliance would have to be placed on the divine inspiration and munificence (*al-fayḍ wa l-inʿām*) that one could hope would be forthcoming in the presence of the Sanctuary in Mecca.

Müneccimbāşī's remark about the absence of any previous extended treatment of the "art of perusing books" appears to be true. Since the ninth century, there had been a tradition of Arabic works partly or entirely devoted to the proper ways of acquiring knowledge, but these works had said very little about studying and perusing books on one's own. Their focus was invariably on the proprieties of student–teacher interaction, and the proper demeanor and conduct expected of student and teacher inside and outside of class. This can be seen in two typical and influential educational treatises from earlier centuries: *Taʿlīm al-mutaʿallim ṭuruq al-taʿallum* by the Central Asian jurist Burhān al-Dīn al-Zarnūjī (fl. 1203) and *Tadhkirat al-sāmiʿ wa l-mutakallim fī adab al-ʿālim wa l-mutaʿallim* by the Syrian scholar and judge Badr al-Dīn Ibn Jamāʿa (d. 1333).[7] A brief overview of these two works will be helpful for bringing out the novel emphasis of Müneccimbāşī's treatment.

The title of Zarnūjī's treatise can be translated as "Instructing the student in the pathways of learning." It begins with emphasizing the importance of knowledge, both of religious law and of ethics, adducing to this effect a number of quotations from the Quran as well as from the Prophet and venerable figures and scholars of the past.[8] It goes on to emphasize

[6] In the colophon of Müneccimbāşī, *Fayḍ al-ḥaram fī ādāb al-muṭālaʿa* (MS: Istanbul, Süleymaniye Kütüphanesi, Laleli 3034), fols. 160b–188b it is stated that a draft of the work was completed in Mecca "on the third of the third of the fourth of the third of the second of the second." I take this to mean "on the third hour of the third day of the fourth month of the third year of the second century of the second millennium," i.e., the 3rd of Rabīʿ II, 1102, corresponding to January 4, 1691.

[7] For the centrality of these two works, see F. Rosenthal, *Knowledge Triumphant: The Concept of Knowledge in Medieval Islam* (Leiden, the Netherlands: E. J. Brill, 1970), 294–298.

[8] Zarnūjī, *Taʿlīm al-mutaʿallim ṭuruq al-taʿallum*. Printed with the commentary of Ibrāhīm b. Ismāʿīl (Cairo: Dār Iḥyāʾ al-Turāth al-ʿArabī, no date), 4–9; G. von Grunebaum and T. M. Abel, *Az-Zarnūjī's Instruction of the Student: The Method of Learning* (New York: King's Crown Press 1947), 21–24.

the importance of acquiring knowledge with the right intentions – not to win worldly fame and glory but to obey God and maintain the religion of Islam.[9] The student should choose his teacher carefully, and once having made his choice should submit to the authority of that teacher and venerate him.[10] He should not walk in front of his teacher, or speak to him without permission, or seek him out at inopportune times, and he should show respect to the teacher's children.[11] The student should be careful to avoid idle chatter and too much eating and drinking, which may induce laziness and forgetfulness.[12] Instead he should devote himself to the task of learning with single-mindedness and diligence, and should in general lead an upright, modest, and pious life. Classes should preferably start on Wednesdays, for a number of religious traditions state that that day of the week is particularly auspicious.[13] In the early stages of education, a teaching session should cover as much material as is amenable to "apprehension" (*ḍabt*) by repeating twice. A sixteenth-century commentator on Zarnūjī's treatise glossed the word "apprehension" with "memorization and learning."[14] The gloss seems very much in the spirit of Zarnūjī's work. On the one hand, the centrality of "memorization" (*ḥifẓ*) for the learning process as described by Zarnūjī is undeniable. The work is full of practical advice on how to improve one's memory, and exhortations to avoid activities that may have an adverse effect on it. On the other hand, Zarnūjī clearly believed that there is more to "learning" (*ta'allum*) than mere memorization. He emphasized the importance of understanding (*fahm*), considering (*ta'ammul*), and thinking things over (*tafakkur*).[15] Especially at a more advanced stage of studies, a student should make a habit of "considering" the more intricate problems of individual disciplines and of "considering" before venturing to speak about scholarly

9 Zarnūjī, *Ta'līm al-muta'allim*, 10–13; Grunebaum and Abel, *Az-Zarnūjī's Instruction of the Student*, 25–27.

10 Zarnūjī, *Ta'līm al-muta'allim*, 13–15; Grunebaum and Abel, *Az-Zarnūjī's Instruction of the Student*, 28–29.

11 Zarnūjī, *Ta'līm al-muta'allim*, 17; Grunebaum and Abel, *Az-Zarnūjī's Instruction of the Student*, 32–33.

12 Zarnūjī, *Ta'līm al-muta'allim*, 27; Grunebaum and Abel, *Az-Zarnūjī's Instruction of the Student*, 44.

13 Zarnūjī, *Ta'līm al-muta'allim*, 28; Grunebaum and Abel, *Az-Zarnūjī's Instruction of the Student*, 46.

14 Zarnūjī, *Ta'līm al-muta'allim*, 28. The commentator wrote during the reign of the Ottoman Sultan Murād III (r. 1574–1595). The English translators have "retained in his memory" (Grunebaum and Abel, *Az-Zarnūjī's Instruction of the Student*, 46).

15 Zarnūjī, *Ta'līm al-muta'allim*, 29; Grunebaum and Abel, *Az-Zarnūjī's Instruction of the Student*, 47.

matters.[16] To aid the process of "understanding," Zarnūjī urged the student to "repeat" (*tikrār*) his lessons after class and to engage in discussion (*mudhākara*), disputation (*munāẓara*), and exchanges (*muṭāraḥa*) with his fellow students.[17] By contrast, the private reading and studying of books does not feature as an aid to "understanding," and in general plays a very marginal role in Zarnūjī's work. The term *muṭālaʿa* occurs only once in passing: books should be square in format because that was the shape preferred by the venerable Abū Ḥanīfa (d.767), founder of the Ḥanafī school of law to which Zarnūjī belonged, and because it is the shape most conducive to lifting, placing, and *muṭālaʿa*.[18] Zarnūjī considered books and writing to be a normal part of the educational process. Students must, he wrote, show respect for books, touching them only in a state of ritual purity and not extending the soles of their feet toward them.[19] He also urged students not to "write anything down" without understanding it first, clearly considering the taking of notes or dictation by students to be perfectly normal.[20] Nevertheless, the solitary reading and study of books was not something he emphasized. Tellingly, he advised the student to always have ink on hand so that he could write down what he "hears" (*yasmaʿu*) of unfamiliar scholarly points, and to leave generous margins on his own copies of handbooks so that he could write down what he "has heard" (*samiʿa*) of helpful comments and elucidations.[21] Knowledge, Zarnūjī explicitly declares, is something that is obtained "from the mouths of men" (*al-ʿilm mā yuʾkhadh min afwāh al-rijāl*).[22]

[16] Zarnūjī, *Taʿlīm al-mutaʿallim*, 30; Grunebaum and Abel, *Az-Zarnūjī's Instruction of the Student*, 49.

[17] Zarnūjī, *Taʿlīm al-mutaʿallim*, 30; Grunebaum and Abel, *Az-Zarnūjī's Instruction of the Student*, 48.

[18] Zarnūjī, *Taʿlīm al-mutaʿallim*, 19; Grunebaum and Abel, *Az-Zarnūjī's Instruction of the Student*, 35–36. Incidentally, the translators' reference to "silent reading" of the Quran (Grunebaum and Abel, *Az-Zarnūjī's Instruction of the Student*, 67) is based on a misunderstanding of the Arabic *qirāʾat al-Quran naẓaran*, which means "reciting the Quran while looking at the page" as opposed to reciting it from memory (*min ẓahri l-qalb*) – as explained by the sixteenth-century commentator; see Zarnūjī, *Taʿlīm al-mutaʿallim*, 41.

[19] Zarnūjī, *Taʿlīm al-mutaʿallim*, 18; Grunebaum and Abel, *Az-Zarnūjī's Instruction of the Student*, 34–35. The translators assume that the "book" (*kitāb*) is the Quran, but the thrust of Zarnūjī's point is clearly general.

[20] Zarnūjī, *Taʿlīm al-mutaʿallim*, 29; Grunebaum and Abel, *Az-Zarnūjī's Instruction of the Student*, 47.

[21] Zarnūjī, *Taʿlīm al-mutaʿallim*, 38 and 41; Grunebaum and Abel, *Az-Zarnūjī's Instruction of the Student*, 63 and 66.

[22] Zarnūjī, *Taʿlīm al-mutaʿallim*, 38; Grunebaum and Abel, *Az-Zarnūjī's Instruction of the Student*, 63.

The treatise by Ibn Jamāʿa, completed in 1273, evinces the same indifference to the private reading of books. The view that the imparting of knowledge is primarily an aural and oral matter is revealed already in the title, which translates as "The Memento to the Listener and Speaker of the Manner of the Scholar and the Student." The work is divided into five chapters. The first adduces a number of quotations from the Quran and traditions from the Prophet in praise of knowledge.[23] The second presents the manners proper to the scholar.[24] He should be pious and God-fearing and not use his knowledge for the sake of worldly gains. He should be clean and ritually pure when he comes to class, start by reciting some verses from the Quran, and invoke blessings on the students and all Muslims. He should lecture clearly and pause to allow questions. He should not be afraid to admit it when he does not know an answer to a question. He should behave in a kind and fatherly manner to his students and avoid undue favoritism. He may occasionally test his students' grasp or "apprehension" (*ḍabt*) by posing questions relating to the material covered. The third chapter deals with the manners proper to the student.[25] He should seek knowledge with the proper motives and live a diligent and pious life centered on his studies. He should eat and sleep moderately. He should seek out a pious and reputable teacher and show him respect and veneration at all times. For instance, he should be clean and neatly dressed before entering the presence of the teacher, should avoid addressing the teacher in the second person, and be courteous in his manner of posing questions. He should keep his eyes focused on the teacher during class, sit still and upright, and avoid fiddling with his hands, stroking his beard, picking his nose, leaning against a pillar or wall, or presenting his back to the teacher. The student should begin his studies by memorizing the Quran and learning its meaning, then move on to the study of hadith (reports about the sayings and doings of the Prophet Muḥammad), creedal theology, jurisprudence, and grammar. In each field he should memorize a short introductory manual and then attend the classes of a reputed teacher to hear the manuals explained and commented on. Before memorizing, however, he should make sure his copy of a manual is correct. He should therefore read out his own copy in the presence of the teacher or the teacher's assistant and incorporate corrections. He should behave toward his fellow students in a mild

[23] Ibn Jamāʿa, *Tadhkirat al-sāmiʿ wa l-mutakallim fī adab al-ʿālim wa l-mutaʿallim*, ed. Muḥammad al-ʿAjamī (Beirut: Dār al-Bashāʾir al-Islāmiyya, 2008), 33–39.

[24] Ibid., 44–78.

[25] Ibid., 80–114.

and brotherly fashion, and should not get into acrimonious debates with them or bicker over seating order. Like Zarnūjī, Ibn Jamāʿa stressed the importance of *mudhākara*: after class, the students should discuss among themselves the points that have been covered. Should a student find no one to discuss with, he should discuss with himself, repeating both the meaning (*maʿnā*) and the wording (*lafẓ*) of "what he has heard" (*mā samiʿahu*) so that both are taken to heart. The fourth chapter concerns a student's proper behavior with books.[26] He should treat books with respect, for example, not placing them on the floor, nor using them to fan himself or to squash bedbugs. When copying a book he should be in a state of ritual purity and face in the direction of the Kaʿba in Mecca. His copy should start with the standard pious formulae, and every time the copied text mentions God, prophets, or respected predecessors, standard expressions of respect should be added by the copyist in full – even if these are not to be found in the text of the exemplar. He should collate his copy carefully, and introduce needed corrections and disambiguations in the text or in the margins. The fifth and final chapter concerns the behavior proper to those residing in a college (*madrasa*).[27] For example, they should not be idle or engage in frivolous chatter. Noise levels should be kept to a minimum, as should unnecessary visits to and from the outside world.

As is clear from the preceding overview, the role of private study and reading is also marginal in Ibn Jamāʿa's presentation. There are a dozen passing references to *muṭālaʿa* in the work, but most of these references place the activity *outside* the context of a student's acquisition of knowledge. For instance, Ibn Jamāʿa wrote in his preamble that he had gathered the material included in the book from what he had heard from his teachers and from what he had come across in his readings (*muṭālaʿāt*). He also noted that he aimed to be succinct so that the work would not be deemed too long or boring to its reader (*muṭāliʿ*).[28] *Muṭālaʿa* is also presented as one of the things expected of an established and advanced scholar: a teacher-scholar should not rest content with his level of knowledge but seek to develop it by means of thinking, discussion, memorization, writing, and *muṭālaʿa*.[29] Writing scholarly works requires the *muṭālaʿa* of numerous texts.[30] A student should not interrupt his teacher if he

26 Ibid., 116–124.
27 Ibid., 126–134.
28 Ibid., 29.
29 Ibid., 52.
30 Ibid., 54.

finds him engaged in prayer or writing or *muṭālaʿa*.[31] A copyist should disambiguate a word in the margin if it is of a sort that may be perplexing to the *muṭāliʿ*.[32] Only a handful of occurrences of *muṭālaʿa* relate it specifically to the process of a student's acquisition of knowledge: nights are especially suitable for peer discussion (*mudhākara*) and *muṭālaʿa*.[33] After having memorized and mastered the introductory manuals, a student should move on to longer and more advanced works, and regularly engage in *muṭālaʿa*.[34] A student should not omit the introductory pious formulae, whether he is engaged in *muṭālaʿa* or in recitation (*qirāʾa*).[35] A teacher at a college should make himself available at set periods of the day for students who are preoccupied with the task of *muṭālaʿa* in their own copies of the handbook studied.[36] Ibn Jamāʿa was well aware that students engaged in *muṭālaʿa*, just as they engaged in peer discussions outside of class. Nevertheless, he gave only passing attention to the activity, highlighting instead the teacher–student relationship in the process of the acquisition of knowledge. Like Zarnūjī, he stressed that knowledge should be taken from scholars, not from books. A student should seek out recognized and pious scholars who themselves had studied with recognized and pious scholars. He should avoid those teachers who "take knowledge from the insides of folios" (*man akhadha min buṭūni l-awrāq*).[37] "Knowledge should not," he writes, "be taken from books, for this is one of the most harmful of vices" (*inna l-ʿilma lā yuʾkhadhu min al-kutubi faʾinnahu min aḍarri l-mafāsid*).[38] Following a tradition that was already centuries old in his time, Ibn Jamāʿa presented the transmission and acquisition of knowledge as taking place primarily in the presence of a teacher, and as being brought about by the activities of listening, reciting, memorizing, posing questions, and grasping orally delivered answers and explanations.

The works of Zarnūjī and Ibn Jamāʿa were paradigmatic for a number of later treatments of education. For example, the discussions of the topic by the Damascene scholar Badr al-Dīn al-Ghazzī, the Syrian Shiite scholar Zayn al-Dīn al-ʿĀmilī (d. 1558), and the Ottoman scholar and judge

[31] Ibid., 94.
[32] Ibid., 122.
[33] Ibid., 83.
[34] Ibid., 106.
[35] Ibid., 113.
[36] Ibid., 127.
[37] Ibid., 90.
[38] Ibid., 105.

Aḥmed Ṭāşköprīzāde are clearly in the same tradition.[39] There are some differences between these later authors that might be worth pursuing in a different context, but they all shared with Zarnūjī and Ibn Jamāʿa the emphasis on teacher–student interaction at the expense of activities such as peer-learning and private reading. It is precisely the shift in emphasis toward the latter two activities that is so conspicuous in Müneccimbāşī's work.

Ādāb al-baḥth and "The Proprieties of Reading"

Müneccimbāşī was not the first to write on *ādāb al-muṭālaʿa*. As he acknowledged in his introduction, he was familiar with one previous work on the topic, written by "one of the later scholars." It was, he wrote, very short ("a single folio-sheet") and consisted mainly of advice derived from the discipline of *ādāb al-baḥth*.[40] The work in question can be identified with some confidence as the treatise on *ādāb al-muṭālaʿa* by a certain Ḥāmid b. Burhān al-Dīn al-Ghaffārī that survives in numerous extant manuscript copies. Unfortunately, no obituaries or biographical notices of this scholar have been found yet. Two other works by him are extant: (1) a gloss on the commentary of Masʿūd al-Shirwānī (d. 1499) on Samarqandī's treatise on *ādāb al-baḥth*, and (2) a gloss on the gloss of Mullāzāde al-Khiṭāʾī (d. 1495) on the Short Commentary (*Mukhtaṣar*) of Taftāzānī on Qazwīnī's handbook on semantics and rhetoric *Talkhīṣ al-Miftāḥ*.[41] An extant manuscript of the first of these two glosses appears to have been copied in 895/1490 in Shiraz by a certain Tāj al-Dīn Muḥammad b. Shams al-Dīn but with marginal corrections and annotations by Ḥāmid b. Burhān al-Dīn himself.[42] This would place him in Shiraz in the final years of the fifteenth century. The attributive "Ghaffārī" suggests that he

39 Ghazzī, *al-Durr al-naḍīd fī adab al-mufīd wa l-mustafīd*; ʿĀmilī, *Munyat al-murīd fī adab al-mufīd wa l-mustafīd*, ed. Riḍā al-Mukhtārī (Beirut: Dār al-Amīra, 2006); Ṭāşköprīzāde, *Miftāḥ al-saʿāda wa-miṣbāḥ al-siyāda*, ed. Kāmil Kāmil Bakrī and ʿAbd al-Wahhāb Abū l-Nūr (Cairo: Dār al-Kutub al-Haditha, 1968), I, 6–70.

40 Müneccimbāşī, *Fayḍ al-ḥaram* (MS Nafiz Pāşā 1350), fol. 2a; (MS Laleli 3034), fol. 161a.

41 For extant copies of the first work, see www.yazmalar.gov.tr/ 19Hk2328, SN 7–64 and www.yazmalar.gov.tr/ MilYzA7379, SN 104–133. The latter manuscript leaves out the introduction in which the glossator gives his name as "Ḥāmid b. Burhān al-Dīn b. Abī Dharr al-Ghaffārī," and the colophon states that the gloss is known as "the gloss of Abū Ḥāmid." Kātib Çelebī listed a certain "Abū Ḥāmid" as the author of a commentary on Samarqandī's treatise but without giving an incipit. For an extant copy of the second work, see Āghā Buzurg Tehrānī, *al-Dharīʿa ilā taṣānīf al-Shīʿa,* VI, 365.

42 The manuscript is extant in the Kitābkhāneh-i Markazī-yi Dānishgāh-i Tehran, nr. 9216. It is described in http://www.aghabozorg.ir/showbookdetail.aspx?bookid=65089.

belonged to the Persian Ghaffārī family that has produced a number of distinguished figures – historians, painters, governors, and statesmen – since the sixteenth century.[43] The fact that the preambles of some of Ḥāmid Ghaffārī's works are explicitly Sunni also suggests that he was writing prior to the establishment of the Shiite Safavid dynasty in Iran in 1502.[44] The evidence thus indicates that Ḥāmid Ghaffārī was one of several Persian scholars active in the fifteenth and sixteenth centuries whose works were to have a profound influence on Ottoman scholarly culture in the course of the seventeenth century.[45]

Ghaffārī's work is very much as Müneccimbāşī described it. It is very short (around two folio-leaves of text) and is in the main an application of the principles of dialectics to the art of reading.[46] Ghaffārī wrote that a statement in a text is either a definition of some sort or a straightforward propositional claim. In the former case, the reader must consider whether the formal requirements of definitions are met: Is the definition adequate? Is it circular? Does it use terms that are more familiar than the

I thank Reza Pourjavady for drawing my attention to the existence of this manuscript, which I have not been able to inspect.

43 On the Ghaffārī line of painters in the eighteenth and nineteenth centuries, see W. Floor, "Art (*Naqqashi*) and Artists (*Naqqashan*) in Qajar Iran," *Al-Muqarnas: An Annual on the Visual Culture of the Islamic World* 16(1999): 125–154, at 141–145. See also various figures of the Ghaffārī family in *Encyclopaedia Iranica*, ed. E. Yarshater (New York: Bibliotheca Persica Press, 2001), X, 249–252. The family came to trace their descent back to the venerable Companion Abū Dharr al-Ghifārī. There is nevertheless reason to think that the attributive originally derived from the prominent Shāfiʿī jurist ʿAbd al-Ghaffār al-Qazwīnī (d. 1268); see S. Naficy, "al-Ghaffārī, Aḥmad b. Muḥammad," *EI2*, II, 994–995. The fact that the attributive is vocalized "Ghaffārī" and not (as one would expect) "Ghifārī" also suggests that the claim to descent from ʿAbd al-Ghaffār al-Qazwīnī was original and then adjusted at a later time since descent from a Sunni Shāfiʿī jurist ceased to carry any prestige in Safavid Iran.

44 For example, the preamble to his treatise on *ādāb al-muṭālaʿa* (www.yazmalar.gov.tr/45AkZe822, fol. 63a) confers peace and blessings on the Prophet, his family and all his companions (*wa-ālihi wa-ṣuḥbihi ajmaʿīn*). Some manuscripts of the work have a somewhat different and slightly less conspicuously Sunni wording (*wa-ṣuḥbihi wa-ālihi*) but the former reading seems to be original for *ajmaʿīn* is clearly intended to rhyme with the preceding *muṭāliʿīn*, *ʿālamīn* and *nāẓirīn*. The preamble to his gloss on Masʿūd's commentary also confers peace and blessings on the Prophet, his family and his companions (MS: 19 Hk 2328, SN 7).

45 This, incidentally, offers a qualification of the opinion of the eminent Iranian bibliographer Āghā Buzurg Tehrānī (d. 1970), who estimated that Ḥāmid b. Burhān al-Dīn al-Ghaffārī was a slightly younger relative of the Persian historian Qāḍī Aḥmad Ghaffārī (d. 1567), see Tehrānī, *al-Dharīʿa*, VI, 365. He would appear instead to have been an older relative of the sixteenth-century historian.

46 The following is based on two manuscripts of Ghaffārī's work: www.yazmalar.gov.tr/45AkZe822, SN 77–80 and MS: Harvard University, Houghton: MS Arab SM 4335–4339, fols. 1v–6v. Both manuscripts are very generous with margins and spacing. The text of the treatise could quite easily have been fitted onto two folio-leaves.

definiendum? Does it use figurative or unclear terms? In the latter case, the reader must consider whether the premises are themselves justifiable, or whether they actually imply the conclusion, or whether the argument is defective in a general way (e.g., if it is circular or leads to implausible conclusions when applied in other cases), or whether it is possible to construct a counterargument for the opposing conclusion. The reader is enjoined to read a certain issue in the text from beginning to end in such a way that the overall meaning is grasped. Then he ought to proceed as just mentioned: considering whether any dialectical objection can be raised and what if any answer can be given to such objections. It may be that the reader fails to find any objections, this being because either the given argument is beyond reproach or the reader is not sufficiently experienced. Ghaffārī urged the reader to attempt to read texts in this way again and again if necessary, for by sustained effort and practice it is possible to "ascend in reading in such a manner as to be able to distinguish between what is to be accepted and what is to be rejected." In general, becoming a consummate reader depends both on mastery of the science of dialectics (*uṣūl al-munāẓara wa-qawānīn al-baḥth*) and on familiarity with the technical terms of the specific discipline to which the work belongs. A student may not meet the second requirement, and in such a case he should resort to the guidance of more advanced scholars. Ghaffārī ended his brief work by warning the student against memorizing without understanding and against reading swiftly and summarily without stopping to consider the details of the argument, for both habits will entrench dull-wittedness and undo the potential for learning.

Ghaffārī's treatise shows that the first written reflections on "the proper rules of reading" were deeply influenced by the discipline of *ādāb al-baḥth*. It also shows the intimate link between the novel scholarly field of *ādāb al-muṭālaʿa* and the ideal of "verification." Ghaffārī explicitly wrote in his introduction that he had composed the work as an aid "to all those who seek to ascend in degrees of exactitude and who prepare to embark on the roads of verification" (*al-ṭālibīna li-l-taraqqī fī l-tadqīqi wa-l-mutaṣaddīna li-sulūki ṭarāʾiqi l-taḥqīq*). To be a "verifier" meant to be able to read closely, discern the structure of the argument in the text, and anticipate dialectical objections and replies. There is a clearly discernible continuity between this assumption underlying Ghaffārī's treatise and the observation (cited in the previous chapters) of the seventeenth-century Damascene scholar Muḥibbī that "Persian and Kurdish verifying scholars" heeded the science of *ādāb al-baḥth*, and Sāçaḳlīzāde's remark in the early eighteenth century that a student who is not well-versed in the science of dialectics "will hardly be able to understand scholarly enquiries" and that knowledge of logic and dialectics is necessary even for comprehending standard handbooks on, say, grammar.[47]

Müneccimbāşī on "the Proprieties of Reading"

Müneccimbāşī may well have derived the idea of writing on *ādāb al-muṭāla'a* from Ghaffārī's treatise, but he derived little else. His own contribution is significantly (more than ten times) longer and deals with a range of issues and problems not broached in his predecessor's brief work. It was with some justification that he claimed to be treading new ground and having to rely on "inspiration" rather than following in the footsteps of earlier authors. After the aforementioned preamble in which he expressed his hesitation about writing the treatise at all, Müneccimbāşī introduced his book with a proposed working definition of *muṭāla'a*. Lexically the verbal noun means "examination" or "perusal." In its technical sense, however, it refers specifically to the examination or perusal of texts, or as he proposed: "Perceiving writing so as to obtain an understood meaning," and more expressly: "Perceiving written utterances whose conventional meaning is familiar to arrive thereby at the intention behind their use."[48] The ability to engage in *muṭāla'a* is not, he wrote, present in the beginner:

> "A student in the earliest stages of seeking knowledge is not in a position to engage in *muṭāla'a* and derive meanings from written expressions; rather his concern is to take what he seeks from the mouths of men."[49]

Müneccimbāşī was not referring in this passage to a lack of literacy on the part of the beginning student. The ability to "derive" meanings and authorial intentions from the written text is, he wrote, dependent on "learning the principles of the instrumental sciences and being able to call their most important parts to mind" (*bi-itqāni l-uṣūli min al-'ulūmi l-āliyyati wa bi-istiḥḍāri l-muhimmāti minhā*).[50] In other words, the inability to engage in *muṭāla'a* is not due to sheer illiterate incomprehension of the writing. It is rather because, without a grounding in a range of "instrumental disciplines" – syntax, logic, dialectic, semantics-rhetoric (*'ilm al-ma'ānī wa l-bayān*) – a beginning student would not go beyond a reading that Müneccimbāşī characterized as "superficial"

47 Muḥibbī, *Khulāṣat al-athar*, II, 242; Sāçaḳlīzāde, *Tartīb al-'ulūm*, 115, 127, 141.
48 Müneccimbāşī, *Fayḍ al-ḥaram* (MS Nafiz Pāşā 1350), fol. 2b; (MS Laleli 3034), fol. 162a.
49 Ibid., fol. 3a; (MS Laleli 3034), fols. 162b–163a.
50 Ibid., fol. 3b; (MS Laleli 3034), fols. 163a–b.

(*saṭḥī*), "crudely literal" (*ẓāhirī*) and "uncritical" (*ḥashwī*).[51] The terms *ẓāhirī* and *ḥashwī* were often used by Muslim scholars who were open to logic and the rational sciences to disparage more literalist and fideist currents associated with the defunct Ẓāhirī school of law (which rejected analogy in jurisprudence) and the minority Ḥanbalī school of law (which rejected rational theology as well as figurative interpretations of anthropomorphisms in the Quran and hadith). The idea that *ḥashwī* groups are led to crudely literal and anthropomorphic readings of scriptural texts because of their ignorance of the rational and instrumental sciences was an old accusation, made, for example, by the influential North African Ashʿarī theologian Sanūsī, whose works were known in Ottoman scholarly circles.[52] However, the terms *ḥashwī* and *ẓāhirī* were often used in a broader and less determinate sense, and Müneccimbāşī need not have had any particular religious groupings in mind.[53] He may simply have thought that a reader equipped with nothing more than literacy in classical Arabic was unlikely to make much headway with the highly technical handbooks on theology, jurisprudence, and Quran exegesis that would have been studied by more advanced Ottoman students.

After having gained a familiarity with the basics of the instrumental and rational sciences, a student develops "the ability to engage in derivation" (*malakat al-istikhrāj*) of meanings from written scholarly handbooks, that is, the ability to do *muṭālaʿa*. The intermediate and advanced student who engages in this manner with a scholarly text is seeking one of four things: (1) to obtain knowledge that he does not have but for which he is prepared; (2) to move beyond knowledge taken on trust and uncover the evidential basis for scholarly propositions; (3) to deepen his evidentiary knowledge by repeated perusal, thus obtaining a thorough familiarity with the evidence and "the ability to call to mind at will" (*malakat al-istiḥḍār*); and (4) to deepen his evidentiary and consolidated knowledge by strengthening it through refreshing his acquaintance with familiar texts or through exposure to new texts and alternative presentations and proofs.[54]

[51] Ibid., fol. 19b; (MS Laleli 3034), fol. 184b.

[52] Sanūsī, *ʿUmdat ahl al-tawfīq*, 140. See the reference to Sanūsī in Sāçaḳlīzāde, *Tartīb al-ʿulūm*, 233.

[53] The only example he gave of *ḥashwīs* and *ẓāhirīs* are the *quṣṣāsīn* [sic], i.e., popular story-tellers; see Müneccimbāşī, *Fayḍ al-ḥaram* (MS Nafiz Pāşā 1350), fol. 19b; (MS Laleli 3034), fol. 184b).

[54] Müneccimbāşī, *Fayḍ al-ḥaram* (MS Nafiz Pāşā 1350), fol. 3a; (MS Laleli 3034), fol. 162b.

In the first chapter Müneccimbāşī presented the proprieties that are relevant to all four categories of readers.[55] Before commencing, a reader should mention the name of God and invoke blessings on His Prophet, followed by some choice prayers asking for divine inspiration and guidance. If he is reading a handbook on a scholarly discipline, he should have some initial conception of this discipline: its definition, its subject matter, and its aim. The reader may also be consulting the discussion of a particular issue (*mabḥath*) in a work, in which case he should have a clear initial conception of this issue. Should he, for example, wish to read a section on the proof for the existence of prime matter (*hayūlā*), he should know from the start that philosophers (*ḥukamāʾ*) believe that there is an externally existing substance called "matter" which, along with "form" (*ṣūra*), is a constituent of every body (*jism*). He should then consult the relevant section of books on philosophy. On encountering a passage, he should start by paying attention to its language: lexically, morphologically, syntactically, semantically, and rhetorically. He should then turn to the level of "second intentions" (*al-maʿqūlāt al-thāniya*), that is, second-order concepts, which are the province of logic. He should pay attention to what kind of definitions are being adduced, what kinds of propositions, and the logical structure of any arguments. In general, Müneccimbāşī noted, a student would find the disciplines of logic and syntax to be especially helpful in his efforts to understand demanding scholarly texts. He wrote: "The truth is that these two disciplines are like the parents of the student with regard to his education and his reaching perfection. So every student should strive to obtain a thorough ability in these two fields by heeding them in all his perusals."[56] It is telling that Müneccimbaşī should compare two *disciplines* to a student's parents. In the older educational literature it was typically the *teacher* who was cast in a paternal role.

Muṭālaʿa for Müneccimbāşī was obviously more than just reading. It is rather a close examination of a scholarly text that starts with paying attention to its syntactic, semantic, rhetorical, and logical features. Having done this, the reader should sum up the relevant issue by conceiving in his mind the claim (*mabdaʾ*), the argument (*wasaṭ*), and the principles on which the argument rests (*maqṭaʿ*). A sign that he has achieved this is that he is able to express the issue briefly and in his own words (*an yaqtadira ʿalā l-taʿbīri ʿanhu bi-ayyi ʿibāratin shāʾa wa bi-awjazi l-ʿibārāt*).

[55] Ibid., fols. 5b–10b; (MS Laleli 3034), fols. 166a–173a.
[56] Ibid., fol. 8b; (MS Laleli 3034), fol. 170a.

In his endeavors to thus unlock a scholarly handbook, a reader should heed and follow the example of an acknowledged commentary (*sharḥ*) on the relevant work and of an acknowledged gloss (*ḥāshiya*) on that commentary. Müneccimbāşī made it clear, however, that one should not get into the habit of consulting such commentaries and glosses before trying to understand the handbook oneself.[57]

The second chapter presents the techniques of reading that are relevant to readers of the aforementioned category (1), that is, those who examine the text with the aim of acquiring (*taḥṣīl*) new knowledge.[58] Such a reader should keep in mind whether the text he is reading affords "imitative" (*taqlīdī*) knowledge devoid of proof or "verified" (*taḥqīqī*) knowledge in which proofs are supplied. If he is reading a text on an instrumental science such as grammar or logic, then he may be content in the first instance with "imitative" knowledge – though he should at some point return to the discipline and become familiar with the evidence underlying its claims. If the text belongs to a discipline that is sought for its own sake, such as theology (*kalām*) and philosophy (*ḥikma*), then he should not be satisfied with merely "imitative" knowledge. Rather, he should have a distinct idea of claims, proofs, and basic principles and consider these carefully. He should turn these over in his mind without remaining bound to the particular linguistic utterances used to express them. A way to accomplish this is to express to oneself the basic points in different ways or in different languages.

The third chapter deals with the techniques relevant to the reader who falls into category (2): the one who seeks to obtain knowledge of the evidential basis of scholarly propositions.[59] In fact, much of the introduction and the second chapter already dealt with this task. At this stage, Müneccimbāşī added that the reader should heed the different nature of various disciplines with respect to proofs. In linguistic sciences proofs will take the form of attestations in works by canonical authors and poets, and analogy on the basis of this. In the sciences of Quran commentary and hadith a "proof" would be to adduce a report with an acceptable chain of transmitters. Some disciplines do not admit of "proof" at all, such as literary anecdotes (*muḥāḍarāt*), poetry and belles-lettres, and – curiously – history (*ta'rīkh*). The mention of belles-lettres, poetry, and history is somewhat puzzling. The first chapter dealing with general techniques for engaging in *muṭāla'a* had emphasized the pivotal importance of the

57 Ibid., fol. 20a; (MS Laleli 3034), fol. 185a.
58 Ibid., fols. 10b–12a; (MS Laleli 3034), fols. 173a–174b.
59 Ibid., fols. 12a–13b; (MS Laleli 3034), fols. 174b–176b.

instrumental and rational sciences. It may well have been Müneccimbāşī's view that one needed morphology, syntax, and semantics-rhetoric for a proper reading of poetry and history, but did he really believe that logic is relevant in that context too? Does it make sense to say that one should carefully separate claim, argument and axioms while reading poetry, or that a criterion for understanding a poem is that one can express the point succinctly and in one's own words, or that before starting to read a poem or chronicle one should have an initial conception of the issue discussed? It is clear that the focus of Müneccimbāşī's treatise is on the perusal of the technical and tightly argued handbooks studied intensively by Ottoman students, and that works on poetry, belles-lettres, and history are mentioned in this particular context merely for the sake of comprehensiveness. This is in marked contrast to the situation in the traditional Yemeni colleges described by Messick. There the object of *muṭālaʿa* tended to be precisely works belonging to fields such as belles-lettres and history that were not normally the subjects of formal instruction in colleges.

The fourth chapter presents the techniques appropriate to readers of category (3): those who seek to develop "the ability to call to mind at will."[60] Such a reader has already been exposed to and understood the evidential bases for particular scholarly propositions, but has yet to obtain familiarity with these to the point of being able to expound them independently and at will. This ability results from repeated *muṭālaʿa*. If the ability relates to an "instrumental" science such as grammar or logic, then one can also deepen one's knowledge by regularly "making use" (*istiʿmāl*) of it when reading texts that belong to other fields, for instance, noticing the grammar or logic of a text on jurisprudence or theology. This consolidated knowledge of all the issues of a discipline does not yet amount to consolidated knowledge of the discipline. A person who has the former but not the latter is not able to give a summary and yet comprehensive account of the discipline. A reader who thinks he has a consolidated knowledge of all the issues of a discipline must consider whether he also has a consolidated knowledge of the discipline as such. If not, he must reexamine his supposed knowledge of particular issues or consider whether the proper ordering principle that governs the many issues is still unclear to him.

The fifth and last chapter presents the proper manner of reading for a student who seeks to strengthen his consolidated and evidentiary knowledge.[61] Such a reader should strive to approach an issue in a

[60] Ibid., fols. 13b–15a; (MS Laleli 3034), fols. 176b–179a.
[61] Ibid., fols. 15a–17b; (MS Laleli 3034), fols. 179a–182a.

number of different ways, and from a number of different sources. He should also carefully consider whether the thesis advanced in a text admits of an objection, and what an answer to that objection would be. He should ask himself, preferably aloud, "If an objector were to say such and such, what would the answer be?" In effect, the reader at this stage should consider himself a participant in an organized disputation. Müneccimbāşī counseled this type of reader not to rely entirely on his own *muṭālaʿa* but to listen as well to what his teachers and fellow students have to say about the texts in question.

In the conclusion, Müneccimbāşī discussed various sources of error relating to language.[62] These can be errors with respect to individual words, for example, confusion between homonyms, or between figurative and literal meaning. They can also be errors relating to single propositions, both on the level of utterance, such as a preposition whose referent is not clear, or on the level of meaning, such as confusing various forms of predication (e.g., asserting that a phoenix exists when it only does so possibly). They can be errors relating to a complex of propositions, such as fallacious or circular arguments, or mistaking for example "Only humans are rational" for a single proposition whereas it is in fact two (All humans are rational and No non-human is rational). Müneccimbāşī's account of various types of error seems to be indebted to the commentary of Naṣīr al-Dīn al-Ṭūsī on *al-Ishārāt wa l-tanbīhāt*, an epitome of logic and philosophy by Avicenna – a commentary he cited earlier in his treatise.[63]

As an appendix, Müneccimbāşī discussed the proprieties of discussion (*mudhākara*) with fellow students.[64] *Mudhākara,* he wrote, is distinguished from "disputation" (*munāẓara*) by the fact that there may be more than two parties involved, and the roles of claimant and questioner are not fixed and may shift in the course of the exchange. One should be modest and friendly with the interlocutors, and as much as possible avoid being in a position of claimant "for all difficulty and hardship lie in that role." If he cannot get out of assuming the role, then he should express himself cautiously, emphasizing that he is merely expounding the author's views, and drawing in his fellow students by means of such questions as "What do my brothers think?" and "What is your opinion?"

[62] Ibid., fols. 17b–20b; (MS Laleli 3034), fols. 182a–186a.

[63] Ṭūsī, *Sharḥ al-Ishārāt wa l-tanbīhāt* (Tehran: Maṭbaʿat al-Ḥaydarī, 1957–1958), I, 225–227 and 313–321.

[64] Müneccimbāşī, *Fayḍ al-ḥaram* (MS Nafiz Pāşā 1350), fols. 20b–22a; (MS Laleli 3034), fols. 186a–188b.

The differences between the work of Müneccimbāşi and those of Zarnūjī and Ibn Jamāʿa are conspicuous. In Müneccimbāşī's treatise, especially *muṭālaʿa* but also *mudhākara* are at the center of attention. The student–teacher relationship is acknowledged in passing as important, but otherwise plays a subordinate role in a discussion of the proper means of "extracting" meanings from texts. In the works of Zarnūjī and Ibn Jamāʿa it is precisely the other way around: the existence of *muṭālaʿa* and *mudhākara* is acknowledged in passing, but the authors' focus is on the teacher–student relation and the oral–aural transmission of knowledge. Also noteworthy in Müneccimbāşī's work is the emphasis on logic, dialectic, semantics and rhetoric, as well as the prominent and positive references to "philosophy." These disciplines are not mentioned in the works of Zarnūjī and Ibn Jamāʿa, who clearly assume that a student's studies would focus on the core religious disciplines: Quran recitation and exegesis, hadith and law, supplemented with Arabic grammar.

Sāçaḳlīzāde on the Acquisition of Knowledge

The emphases on the student–text relationship and on the rational and instrumental sciences do not seem to be an effect of mere idiosyncrasy on the part of Müneccimbāşī. Both emphases are also to be found in an educational work by Müneccimbāşī's younger contemporary Meḥmed Sāçaḳlīzāde, who has already been mentioned on a number of occasions in the present study, both as a severe critic of what he deemed the excessive study of philosophy in Ottoman *ulema* circles (Chapter 1) and as the author of important works on dialectics (Chapter 2). Sāçaḳlīzāde was one of the prominent Ottoman scholars of his age, despite being active far from the imperial capital Istanbul, in or near his home town of Maraş in southeastern Anatolia.[65] In his *Tartīb al-ʿulūm* (The Ordering of the Sciences), a fair copy of which he completed in 1716, he criticized what he considered the wrong-headed ways in which the students of his time went about their studies. The proliferation of sometimes demanding commentaries and glosses on scholarly handbooks, he wrote, meant that students were often lost in a maze of subtleties and failed to get an initial overview of a discipline. Another evil that Sāçaḳlīzāde bewailed

[65] On Sāçaḳlīzāde, see Meḥmed Ṭāhır Būrsalī, *ʿOthmānlī Müellifleri*, I, 325–328. His work *Tartīb al-ʿulūm* has been discussed from a somewhat different perspective in Reichmuth, "Bildungskanon und Bildungreform."

was the related tendency to spend too much time on a particular work and its commentaries, glosses and superglosses, even while neglecting more important fields of learning. He gave as an example the treatise by Dawānī that discusses and critically assesses proofs for the existence of a Necessary Being (*ithbāt al-wājib*). Sāçaḳlīzāde wrote that students "waste" up to a year studying this work and its commentaries and glosses even though they are apt, with their dense web of arguments and counter-arguments, to do nothing but weaken faith.[66] Yet, despite his disapproval of the study of such works, Sāçaḳlīzāde was no fideist. As mentioned in Chapter 1, he went out of his way to declare astronomy, mathematics, and medicine to be commendable sciences.[67] He also considered the study of logic and dialectic to be commendable and indeed a *farḍ kifāya*, that is, a collective duty incumbent on the Muslim community (but not on each and every Muslim). Sāçaḳlīzāde's hostility to philosophy was also modified by his repeated stress on the importance of studying classical handbooks of rational theology such as *al-Mawāqif* of Ījī and *al-Maqāṣid* of Taftāzānī. These handbooks devoted considerable space to epistemological and metaphysical preliminaries, including rebuttals of skepticism, the nature of modality, the relationship between essence and existence, the soul and its relation to the body, and the Aristotelian categories of substance and nine types of attribute.

Like Müneccimbāşī, Sāçaḳlīzāde considered a working knowledge of the instrumental and rational sciences to be a necessary condition for engaging in *muṭāla'a*. He wrote:

> The student is not prepared for *muṭāla'a* after just gaining knowledge of lexicography, morphology and syntax; only after also gaining knowledge of logic, dialectic, rational theology, semantics, and the principles of jurisprudence... And I do not mean by "rational theology" (*kalām*) the creedal issues alone, but rather the discussions of substances and attributes, as included in works like *al-Maqāṣid* and *al-Mawāqif*.[68]

Sāçaḳlīzāde recommended that the student, after learning Arabic, the Quran, and the basics of the faith, should study the sciences in the following order: morphology, syntax, basic positive law (*al-aḥkām*), logic, dialectic, rational theology, semantics-rhetoric, and jurisprudence. Again, he specified that by "rational theology" he did not mean basic creedal

66 Sāçaḳlīzāde, *Tartīb al-'ulūm*, 150. Dawānī wrote two treatises on *Ithbāt al-wājib*. The older treatise is the one that tended to be studied in Ottoman colleges, with the commentary of Mullā Ḥanafī and the gloss of Mīrzā Jān.

67 Sāçaḳlīzāde, *Tartīb al-'ulūm*, 180–185.

68 Ibid., 205.

works, but the aforementioned summae of philosophical theology with their extensive epistemological and metaphysical preliminaries. Only then should the student venture to study hadith and Quran exegesis.[69] This order tallies well with what we know of the curriculum of Ottoman education, in which instrumental and rational sciences were typically studied at basic and intermediate levels, whereas jurisprudence, hadith, and Quran exegesis would be reserved for the most advanced levels.[70] But it is very different from the order envisaged by Zarnūjī and Ibn Jamāʿa who, like the venerable Ghazālī, assumed that the student will focus on the core religious disciplines and study these in the order of their importance.[71] It is particularly striking that in Ghazālī's *Iḥyāʾ ʿulūm al-dīn* – which is cited on a number of occasions in Sāçaḳlīzāde's work – the student is advised to begin by studying the Quran, then hadith, then the Quranic sciences (including Quran exegesis), then the hadith sciences, then positive law, then jurisprudence, and only then other sciences.[72] Ghazālī elsewhere explicitly rejected the suggestion that one should study rational theology before jurisprudence.[73]

The increased importance of the rational and instrumental sciences in Ottoman education was part of a more general trend in the Islamic world. After the twelfth century, and helped by the endorsement of prominent religious scholars such as Ghazālī and Fakhr al-Dīn al-Rāzī, logic started to feature regularly in the education of Muslim students.[74] The trend was reinforced by the immensely influential fourteenth-century Timurid scholars Taftāzānī and Jurjānī, whose works in a number of fields – including logic – were standard fare in Ottoman education. It is not only that logic was widely studied by Ottoman students, but a familiarity with the discipline was assumed by later authors writing on other fields. Jurists, theologians, and grammarians increasingly made conscious use of

69 Ibid., 210. A similar ordering is recommended by Zayn al-Dīn al-ʿĀmilī (d. 1558); see ʿĀmilī, *Munyat al-murīd*, 385–389.

70 S. Ahmed and N. Filipovic, "The Sultan's Syllabus: A Curriculum for the Ottoman Imperial Medreses Prescribed in a *Fermān* of Qānūnī I Süleymān, Dated 973/1565," *Studia Islamica* 98/99(2004): 183–218, at 191–193.

71 Ibn Jamāʿa, *Tadhkirat al-sāmiʿ wa l-mutakallim*, 103–106. Zarnūjī's narrowly religious conception of what a student should study is noted in Grunebaum and Abel, *Az-Zarnūjī's Instruction of the Student*, 3–4 and 15–16.

72 Ghazālī, *Iḥyāʾ ʿulūm al-dīn* (Cairo: Muʾassasat al-Ḥalabī, 1967), I, 5.

73 Ghazālī, *al-Mustaṣfā min ʿilm al-uṣūl* (Cairo: al-Maṭbaʿa al-Tijāriyya al-Kubrā, 1937), I, 58.

74 K. El-Rouayheb, "Sunni Muslim Scholars on the Status of Logic, 1500–1800," *Islamic Law and Society* 11(2004): 213–232; A. Spevack, "Apples and Oranges: The Logic of the Early and Later Arabic Logicians," *Islamic Law and Society* 17(2010): 159–184.

Greek logical concepts and argument-forms in their writings.[75] For example, a standard work on creedal theology studied by Ottoman students, Taftāzānī's commentary on the Creed (*'Aqā'id*) of Najm al-Dīn al-Nasafī (d. 1142), assumes as a matter of course that the reader would – in a discussion on the problem of divine foreknowledge and universal fatalism – understand the statement that "the impossibility of the consequent implies the impossibility of the antecedent" (*inna istiḥālata l-lāzimi tūjibu istiḥālata l-malzūm*).[76] A reader who has not been exposed to logic might think, like the English translator E. E. Elder, that *malzūm* in Taftāzānī's statement refers to the consequent and *lāzim* to the antecedent, thus imputing a plain fallacy to Taftāzānī and mistaking the sense of the passage as a whole.[77] The science of semantics-rhetoric, in which the writings of Taftāzānī and Jurjānī played a central role, also became increasingly important in later centuries. Ghazālī, Zarnūjī and Ibn Jamā'a had not felt the need to mention this discipline, but for a scholar such as Sāçaḳlīzāde it was a precondition for the mastery of jurisprudence and Quran exegesis.[78] The most widely studied Quran commentaries in Ottoman scholarly circles were those by al-Zamakhsharī (d. 1144) and al-Bayḍāwī, and both works – as well as their standard glosses by later scholars – are indeed practically incomprehensible to a reader who has had no exposure to semantics-rhetoric.[79] It should perhaps be added that in modern times there has been a backlash against this emphasis on the rational and instrumental sciences. This would seem to be due – at least in part – to the rising influence of the fundamentalist Salafī-Wahhābī current in Sunni Islam in the nineteenth and twentieth centuries. Salafīs typically reject the disciplines of logic and rational theology and have little sympathy with the later literature on jurisprudence and semantics-rhetoric that is suffused with logical and philosophical-theological

[75] This has been shown in the case of Islamic jurisprudence in W. Hallaq, "Logic, Formal Arguments and Formalization of Arguments in Sunni Jurisprudence," *Arabica* 87 (1990): 315–358.

[76] Taftazānī, *Sharḥ al-'Aqā'id al-Nasafiyya*, edited by Klūd Salāma (Damascus: Wizārat al-Thaqāfa, 1974), 96.

[77] E. E. Elder (trans.), *A commentary on the creed of Islam: Sa'd al-Dīn al-Taftāzānī on the creed of Najm al-Dīn al-Nasafī* (New York: Columbia University Press 1950), 92.

[78] Sāçaḳlīzāde, *Tartīb al-'ulūm*, 161. Sāçaḳlīzāde at this point merely stated that studying semantics should precede the study of law and jurisprudence, but he elsewhere (p. 163) made it clear that studying law and jurisprudence should precede the study of Quran exegesis.

[79] For the popularity of these two Quran commentaries, see Sāçaḳlīzāde *Tartīb al-'ulūm*, 165–166; Ahmed and Filipovic, "The Sultan's Syllabus," 196–198.

terminology. The Quran commentaries that they tend to prefer – for example, the one by Ibn Kathīr (d. 1373) – are indeed more straightforwardly readable by those who are innocent of the scholastic "instrumental" disciplines.[80]

The other basic point on which Müneccimbāşī differed conspicuously from previous authors was his focus on the student-text relationship as opposed to the teacher–student relation. Saçaḳlīzāde's work betrays the same novel emphasis. He regularly exhorted the student to study particular works, to avoid others, and to read works in a particular order. At one point, he recommended his own handbook on Quran recitation (*tajwīd*), *Juhd al-muqill*, together with his own commentary, stating: "He who has perused (*iṭṭalaʿa ʿalā*) these two works [i.e. the handbook and its commentary] will not be in need of most other works on this topic, and will become a recognized authority in this discipline."[81] This would seem to be a quite straightforward exhortation to take knowledge "from the insides of folios." Sāçaḳlīzāde repeatedly singled out particular works as especially useful and advised the budding scholar to have a copy of them.[82] He followed Ghazālī in distinguishing between three levels of proficiency in a discipline – basic (*iqtiṣār*), intermediate (*iqtiṣād*), and advanced (*istiqṣāʾ*) – and recommended works appropriate to each level. He then added that one need not memorize these handbooks; the aim should rather be to correct one's own manuscript copies and examine their contents, either by formal instruction (*taʿallum*) or – tellingly – by looking over and reading (*muṭālaʿa*) them so that one can consult whatever issue one needs.[83] To be sure, it may well have been Sāçaḳlīzāde's assumption that the student, particularly in his younger years, would study such works with a teacher. The point is not that Sāçaḳlīzāde (or Mūneccimbāşī) thought good teachers to be unimportant or dispensable. Nevertheless, the emphasis of Sāçaḳlīzāde's work is conspicuously on the student choosing the right texts, not the right teacher. In general, he had few kind words to say about the teachers of his day: they often impose advanced issues and discussions on students who are not prepared for

80 On Ibn Kathīr, see E. S. Ohlander, "Ibn Kathīr," in J. E. Lowry and D. J. Stewart (eds.), *Essays in Arabic Literary Biography, 1350–1850* (Wiesbaden: Harrassowitz Verlag, 2009), 147–159, especially 156–157 (for his Quran commentary). The first modern edition was published in 1924–1930 by the famous Salafī reformist Rashīd Riḍā (d. 1935).

81 Sāçaḳlīzāde, *Tartīb al-ʿulūm*, 130.

82 See, e.g., Sāçaḳlīzāde, *Tartīb al-ʿulūm*, 102, 120, 121, 167.

83 Sāçaḳlīzāde, *Tartīb al-ʿulūm*, 216.

them, and in their eagerness to have a large number of students they often do not put students in their place when they want to study works that are above their level.[84] Many teachers are also, he claims, woefully ignorant of core religious sciences, while vaunting their grasp of issues such as "species and genus, matter and form, and circularity and infinite regress."[85] In light of Sāçaḳlīzāde's low opinion of his colleagues' manner of teaching, it is perhaps not surprising that he appears to have been less troubled than Zarnūjī and Ibn Jamāʿa by students learning from books rather than "from the mouths of men."

Deep Reading and Textual Criticism

Yet another noteworthy feature of the treatises of Müneccimbāşī and Sāçaḳlīzāde deserves some consideration. This is their almost exclusive focus on understanding and evaluating the contents of works. By contrast, the aforementioned works of Zarnūjī and Ibn Jamāʿa offered the budding student advice on how to interact not only with teachers and fellow students but also with manuscripts as physical objects and scribal artifacts. In the sixteenth-century educational manual of Badr al-Dīn al-Ghazzī, such earlier discussions are expanded into a fairly lengthy treatment of what one might call "philological" tools, a treatment that underlies the presentation in Franz Rosenthal's classic *The Technique and Approach of Muslim Scholarship* (1947).[86] Ghazzī underlined the importance of the collation (*muqābala*) of one's manuscript with others, especially with an autograph, or a copy that has been collated with the autograph, or at least a copy owned by one's teacher. He then described in some detail how to proceed with the results of such careful collation. Potentially unclear words should be disambiguated, for example, by vocalizing the word fully and adding the relevant diacritical points, or indicating by means of a number of conventional signs that a letter should be read without diacritical points (e.g., adding three points under the س to indicate that it should not be read as a ش). A potentially problematic word that has been ascertained to be correct should be marked with a small (صح). A mistake in the manuscript that seems to be original should be marked with a small (كذا). If the scribe/student finds a reading in the manuscript

[84] Ibid., 196.
[85] Ibid., 162; see also 138.
[86] What follows is based on Ghazzī, *al-Durr al-naḍīd*, 421–466. F. Rosenthal, in his *The Technique and Approach of Muslim Scholarship* (Rome: Pontificium Institutum Biblicum, 1947), 7–18, used an epitome of Ghazzī's work published in 1930.

possibly correct but not certainly so, he may indicate this by marking it with a (صـ). Passages in the main text that are erroneous additions should be marked by means of, for example, crossing out the passage, or drawing a line over it, or adding a small (لا or من) over the word that begins the passage that should be deleted and an (الى) over the last word. An omission (*saqṭ*) should be indicated in the main text by a vertical line whose top is angled toward the margin where the missing word or passage (*al-laḥaq*) should be supplied with a clear indication that it is a correction (صح) as opposed to a marginal comment or explication. Ghazzī also introduced some of the more important scribal abbreviations with which the student should be familiar. In the science of hadith it was, for example, common to abbreviate the phrase "he related to us" (حدثنا) to (نا) or the title of an authoritative collection such as that of Muslim b. al-Ḥajjāj (d. 875) to (م). In works on the rational sciences, it was common to abbreviate, for example, "absurd" (محال) to (مح) or "in that case" (حينئذ) to (ح), or "the proposition to be proved" (المطلوب) to (المط).

It is conspicuous that there is no analogous discussion in the treatises of Müneccimbāşī and Sāçaḳlīzāde. The absence might appear particularly puzzling given their marked (and novel) emphasis on private reading, as opposed to "hearing" knowledge from a teacher. The reason is, I would suggest, that Müneccimbāşī and Sāçaḳlīzāde were addressing a more advanced type of student – a student who was presumed to know how to read manuscripts and to be familiar with the conventional signs and abbreviations used by scribes. Certainly, there is no reason to believe that Ottoman scholars in their time had ceased to pay attention to manuscript variants or to scribal conventions, and it is difficult to see how – in a manuscript culture – they could have afforded to do so. Rather, it seems that they considered familiarity with such matters to be something that a student would acquire in the earlier parts of his education, and that more advanced students would focus on the task of interpreting and discussing the contents of scholarly works with the aid of a thorough grounding in the auxiliary disciplines of grammar, semantics-rhetoric, logic, and dialectic. Sāçaḳlīzāde did in fact counsel the reader to collate his manuscript copy, but he did so in passing, noting that the reader might waste time trying to make sense of a corrupt text unless care was taken to make sure that the manuscript copy was free from scribal misreading and omissions. This, however, was clearly a preliminary step before the student/reader moved on to other, more advanced tasks: "Then," Sāçaḳlīzāde wrote, "he [the student] can proceed with deep reading (*al-muṭālaʿa al-ʿamīqa*) and exploring subtle aspects (*al-istiṭlāʿ ʿalā l-wujūh al-daqīqa*) and raising questions and suggesting answers (*wa-ithārat al-as'ila wa l-ajwiba*)."[87]

The assumption that attention to manuscript variants belongs to the preliminary stages of scholarship is illustrated by an influential scholarly work by an Ottoman contemporary of Müneccimbāşī and Sāçaḳlīzāde, Ḳara Ḫalīl Tīrevī, the Ottoman Military Judge (*Ḳāżī'asker*) mentioned in Chapter I who was keenly interested in philosophy, logic, and dialectics and left a number of works in these fields that continued to be widely studied until the early twentieth century. The work in question, completed in May 1694, is an extensive gloss (*ḥāshiya*) on a treatise by the Azeri scholar Meḥmed Emīn Ṣadrüddīnzāde on what makes the numerous enquiries of logic one discipline.[88] Ḳara Ḫalīl's glosses illustrate the kind of scholarly work that resulted from the reading strategy described and commended by Müneccimbāşī, with its emphasis on attentiveness to grammar, semantics-rhetoric, logic, and dialectic. Few aspects of the glossed text were considered unworthy of attention, ranging from the semantic and rhetorical aspects of the florid preamble in rhymed prose, to intricate metaphysical discussions of "second intentions." Ḳara Ḫalīl also sometimes cast the author's argument into explicit syllogistic form or gave the dialectical structure of a certain extended piece of reasoning. There are also sophisticated discussions of the philosophical contents of the work, and Ḳara Ḫalīl – though in general charitable – not infrequently expressed reservations or criticism of the author's substantive views on the topic. Ḳara Ḫalīl obviously felt it to be his task to cover any issue that might arise in the reading of the work: grammatical, semantic, rhetorical, logical, philosophical, or theological. In this respect, his glosses are typical of the Islamic scholastic genres of commentary (*sharḥ*) and gloss (*ḥāshiya*) after Taftāzānī and Jurjānī. Indeed, the very consolidation of the genre of the gloss as a standard vehicle for scholarly writing in Islamic civilization seems to date from the fourteenth century.[89]

[87] Sāçaḳlīzāde, *Tartīb al-'ulūm*, 204.

[88] Ḳara Ḫalīl, *al-Risāla al-'awniyya fī īḍāḥ al-ḥāshiya al-Ṣadriyya* (Istanbul: al-Maṭba'a al-'āmira, 1871). The treatise of Meḥmed Emīn Ṣadrüddīnzāde is itself a commentary on a passage from the commentary of Mollā Fenārī on Abharī's *Īsāghūjī*.

[89] The genre of commentary (*sharḥ*) is of course older, but again the fourteenth-century seems to have witnessed a substantial transformation of the genre. Pre-fourteenth century commentators tended in the main to confine their interventions to the subject-matter of the main text, whereas post-Timurid commentators tended increasingly to disregard disciplinary boundaries and, for example, engage in discussions of grammatical, semantic, rhetorical, philosophical and theological issues raised by a text on logic.

FIGURE 3.1 Deep reading: The introduction of Jalāl al-Dīn al-Dawānī's *Risāla fī ithbāt al-wājib* with the commentary of Mullā Ḥanafī Tabrīzī (fl. 1516), with extensive marginalia. Copied in Mardin in 1042/1632 by the Kurdish scholar ʿAbd al-Raḥmān b. Ibrāhīm Āmidī (d. 1656). (Muḥammad Mullā Ḥanafī, *al-Risālah al-Ḥanafiyya ʿalā Ithbāt al-wājib li-l-Dawānī*, fol. 1b. Islamic Manuscripts, Garrett Y3256. Manuscripts Division, Department of Rare Books and Manauscripts, Princeton University Library. Reproduced with permission.)

As mentioned earlier, the genre of glosses has been much disparaged by modern historians as inherently pedantic and unoriginal. More recent scholarship is beginning to question this assumption, and as was seen in Chapter 1, the glosses of Dawānī and ʿIṣām al-Dīn Isfarāyinī were in fact animated with a keen sense of the ideal of "verification," that is, the critical assessment of the claims being made in the glossed text, as opposed to "imitation," that is, the uncritical acceptance and exposition of scholarly theses. Ḳara Ḫalīl too invoked – indeed waxed eloquent about – this ideal in his gloss:

> Had it not been for imitation, no one of the ignorant would have been deprived of the truth, and no one could be heard saying "We have not heard this from our first forefathers." The one whom the Lord wishes to make a consummate scholar, He will guide by making him understand that "Wisdom is the stray camel of the believer" and will make him commit to take what is pure and leave what is adulterated... O you, who are brimming with intelligence, do not look to who is saying something but to what is being said, for this is the way of the verifiers and the custom of those who delve deep into scholarly matters![90]

What makes Ḳara Ḫalīl's work particularly relevant to the present context is that he was aware of significant variations among the manuscripts of the treatise of Ṣadrüddīnzāde. In the introduction to his glosses, he mentioned that the "most correct" (*aṣaḥḥ*) manuscript, in terms of both sense and transmission (*dirāyatan wa riwāyatan*), was the one in the possession of the author's grandson Meḥmed Ṣādiḳ b. Feyżullāh b. Meḥmed Emīn Ṣadrüddīnzāde (d. 1708) – himself a prominent Ottoman scholar and judge.[91] What did Ḳara Ḫalīl mean by the manuscript that "was most correct in terms of transmission"? He apparently faced a situation in which numerous and significant variants in available manuscripts resulted from the fact that the author had himself revised the work. Merely finding a single autograph would therefore not resolve the problem of adjudicating between these variants. The manuscript in question apparently stood out, not by being an autograph, but by indicating which revisions represented the author's final and considered version. This is clear from the fact that Ḳara Ḫalīl twice argued that a particular passage should be removed from the text on the grounds that it was crossed out in the manuscript "that is relied upon" (*al-muʿawwal ʿalayhā*).[92] To this extent, Ḳara Ḫalīl's approach seems similar to the "best-text" theory of textual

90 Ḳara Ḫalīl, *al-Risāla al-ʿawniyya,* 23.
91 Ibid., 3–4.
92 Ibid., 62, 116.

criticism associated in modern times with Joseph Bédier.[93] Nevertheless, there are important differences. Ḳara Ḫalīl frequently indicated that he preferred – on the grounds of sense or grammar – a reading present in other manuscripts and not in the manuscript "that is relied upon."[94] He also on a number of occasions adjudged a word or phrase to be a result of scribal error, even when it was attested by all available manuscripts.[95] Most importantly, it is clear that Ḳara Ḫalīl's interest in manuscript variants was part of an enterprise whose main aim was not that of establishing a text but of assimilating and critically assessing the content of a work. Knowledge of manuscript variations played an ancillary role in this task, whereas an intimate knowledge of the instrumental and rational sciences was absolutely central. The emphasis on careful collation of manuscripts and special attention to early or autograph copies, evinced in the earlier works of Ibn Jamāʿa and Ghazzī, had not disappeared. Rather, it had been supplemented with an increased emphasis on the use of logic, dialectic, syntax, semantics, and rhetoric for achieving "verification" through "deep reading." Though the ideal of "deep reading" was not novel – its roots can be traced back to the Timurid age – it appears that it was in the seventeenth- and eighteenth-century Ottoman Empire that the ideal first began to be fully and consciously articulated in educational manuals. As will be argued in the following section, this development may well have been related to the specific character of the early-modern Ottoman educational system.

Ottoman Education and the Ideal of Deep Reading

Two Ottoman works on education by Müneccimbāşī and Sāçaḳlīzāde, written independently of each other between 1691 and 1716, are markedly different from the classical Arabic-Islamic pedagogic literature. They both evince a distinct shift of emphasis away from the student–teacher relationship and the oral–aural model for the transmission of knowledge, and focus instead on the proper reading of texts. This novel focus may conceivably have been related to the increased importance of the rational sciences. The oral–aural model of the transmission of knowledge was developed in early Islamic times when "knowledge" (*ʿilm*)

93 J. Thorpe, *Principles of Textual Criticism* (San Marino, California: The Huntington Library, 1972), 114; D. C. Greetham, *Textual Scholarship: An Introduction* (New York and London: Garland Publishing, 1994), 324–325.

94 Ḳara Ḫalīl, *al-Risāla al-ʿawniyya*, 16, 33, 56, 57, 64, 66.

95 Ibid., 52, 130, 146.

paradigmatically consisted of reports (about the sayings and doings of the Prophet and other venerable figures or about Quranic readings and exegesis) whose acceptability was largely a function of the personal reputation of their transmitters. It is perhaps not surprising that the hold of this model weakened when the greater part of students' education was spent poring over dense scholastic handbooks on syntax, semantics, rhetoric, logic, dialectic, rational theology, and jurisprudence. The aural–oral ideal depicted by classical educational manuals had by the seventeenth century ceased to do justice to the role of careful reading in the acquisition of knowledge.[96] A more realistic sense is given by passing remarks in biographical dictionaries of scholars revealing, for example, that by the seventeenth century in al-Azhar College in Cairo it was usual for advanced students or teaching assistants to hold preparatory sessions in which the relevant section of a handbook would be read carefully and critically (*muṭālaʿat baḥth wa-taḥqīq*) with students before the teacher's class so that they would be prepared for the lecture.[97]

The shift in focus may also be related to the peculiar situation (from an Islamicate perspective) of Ottoman students after the sixteenth century. Starting with a series of measures instituted by the famed Ottoman *Şeyḫülislām* Ebū l-Suʿūd, the character of Ottoman education was transformed in significant ways.[98] One aspect of these reforms that is particularly relevant in the present context is that access to higher teaching or judiciary posts came to depend on the obtaining of a certificate (*mülāzemet*). Significantly, only relatively few scholars occupying the higher echelons of the judicial and educational apparatus were entitled to grant these, and only at specific times. It is generally recognized in modern scholarship that this led to a "bottleneck" situation in which the number of certificates granted was relatively small in relation to the number of students seeking them. This novel feature of Ottoman education must

96 A point also made in K. Hirschler, *The Written Word in the Medieval Arabic Lands: A Social and Cultural History of Reading Practices* (Edinburgh: Edinburgh University Press, 2012), 17–22. Hirschler's book is mainly concerned with the progressive "textualisation" of society and the popularization of reading practices in Egypt and Syria from the eleventh to the fifteenth centuries.

97 Muḥibbī, *Khulaṣat al-athar*, II, 202–203.

98 On the sixteenth-century reforms, see especially R. C. Repp, *The Müfti of Istanbul: A Study in the Development of the Ottoman Learned Hierarchy* (London: Ithaca Press 1986) and M. Zilfi, "Sultan Süleymān and the Ottoman Religious Establishment," in H. Inalcik and C. Kafadar (eds.), *Süleymān the Second and His Time* (Istanbul: The Isis Press 1993). On the Ottoman learned hierarchy in the seventeenth century, see A. Uğur, *The Ottoman ʿUlemā in the mid-17th Century* and D. Klein, *Die osmanischen Ulema des 17. Jahrhunderts. Eine geschlossene Gesellschaft?* (Berlin: Klaus Schwartz Verlag 2007). For what follows I have relied mainly on Klein, pp. 45–63.

have meant that for many students, the person who taught them and the person who granted them a formal certificate were no longer the same.[99] The most coveted *mülāzemet*s were those granted by the highest-ranking authorities in the learned hierarchy, the *Şeyḫülislām* and the military judges of Rumelia and Anatolia, learned scholars to be sure but usually no longer directly involved in teaching. Ambitious Ottoman students would usually seek to become part of the entourage of such high-ranking dignitaries, serving as clerks or scribes or teaching assistants. Obtaining such connections certainly involved a great deal of networking, ingratiation, and sometimes outright bribery, but it is unlikely that assessments of academic abilities were entirely irrelevant in this sharpened competition for certificates. In fact, it was not unknown in the seventeenth century for the granter of a *mülāzemet* to ask an applicant to take an examination (*imtiḥān*). After having received a *mülāzemet*, a young scholar would start teaching at lower-ranking colleges and usually get promoted to higher-ranking colleges according to a fixed and graded pattern. Before obtaining a teaching position at higher colleges paying more than 40 akçe per day, he would often be examined again. There is scattered evidence for such examinations in the seventeenth century; for example, in 1658 the scholar and judge Yaḥyā Minḳārīzāde – later to be *Şeyḫülislām* – was appointed to the position of "examiner of the *ulema*" (*mümeyyiz-i ʿulemā*ʾ).[100] After an imperial edict of 1703 they became the rule. One such examination in 1754, for which we have vivid evidence in the form of an extant diary by one of the examinees, was administered at the office of the *Şeyḫülislām*, and only twenty-six of ninety-nine applicants passed.[101] Ottoman social historians have given some attention to these educational reforms and the extent to which they may have made it easier for the higher echelons of the learned hierarchy to consolidate their control and perpetuate "dynasties" of scholarly families.[102] For the present purposes, however, what is striking is just how different the resultant educational

99 An edict of 1715, designed to curb abuses, stipulated that seekers of a *mülāzemet* should be required to state how old they were and with whom they had studied (Repp, *The Müfti of Istanbul*, 54–55), the assumption clearly being that an applicant's teacher was not normally the same as the person from whom a *mülāzemet* was sought.

100 Uğur, *The Ottoman ʿUlemā in the mid-17th Century*, 451.

101 M. Zilfi, "The Diary of a Müderris: A New Source for Ottoman Biography," *Journal of Turkish Studies* 1(1977): 157–173, at 169.

102 See especially M. Zilfi, "The ʿIlmiye Registers and the Ottoman Medrese System Prior to the Tanzimat," in J-L. Bacqué-Grammont and P. Dumont (eds.), *Contributions à l'histoire économique et sociale de l'Empire Ottoman* (Louvain: Peeters, 1983); M. Zilfi, "Elite Circulation in the Ottoman Empire: Great Mollas of the Eighteenth-Century," *Journal of the Economic and Social History of the Orient* 26(1983): 309–327.

system was from that which had prevailed in previous centuries, and still prevailed in Islamic regions beyond the central Ottoman lands. The reforms meant that an ambitious student's academic abilities would at crucial stages be evaluated by a scholar who was not his own teacher, sometimes even by means of the "modern" and impersonal institution of the centrally administered examination. In such a situation, the older literature that set forth the proprieties of student–teacher relationships may have appeared less timely and relevant, particularly for more advanced Ottoman students, than works that focused on how to peruse demanding works and gave advice on what texts to study and in what order.

Conclusion

Modern Ottomanists have often lacked the inclination (or training) to study in any in-depth manner the more technical, scholastic writings in Arabic of the Ottoman ulema. At the same time, specialists in Arabic and Islamic studies have often proceeded as if Ottoman history did not belong within their purview at all, inheriting the older Orientalist orientation toward the study of Arabic texts from the earlier, formative period of Islamic civilization. Between them, the biases of these two curiously disconnected fields have resulted in some glaring blind spots. Scholars such as Müneccimbāşī, Ḳara Ḫalīl and Sāçaḳlīzāde are now obscure figures – even to specialists in Islamic and Ottoman studies – belonging to an intellectual tradition whose details are little known and whose general features are often disparaged. For this very reason, the fact that their works attest to, and are reflective of, a novel development within Islamic education and scholarly culture appears to have been entirely overlooked. It is widely assumed that the "Islamic" model for the transmission of knowledge remained largely personal, informal, and oral–aural until the modern period, and it has even been suggested that this might have been one of the reasons for the "failure" of Islamic civilization to develop modern science and modern scientific institutions.[103] The fact of the matter is that, after the sixteenth century, a more formal and text-centered model for the transmission of knowledge emerged in the core areas of the Ottoman Empire, resulting in centralized examinations and certification as well as a marked shift in educational manuals from the proprieties of teacher–student interaction to strategies for "deep reading."

[103] T. Huff, *The Rise of Early Modern Science: Islam, China, and the West* (Cambridge: Cambridge University Press 1993), 155–156, 163–169, 220–222.

PART II

SAVING SERVANTS FROM THE YOKE OF IMITATION

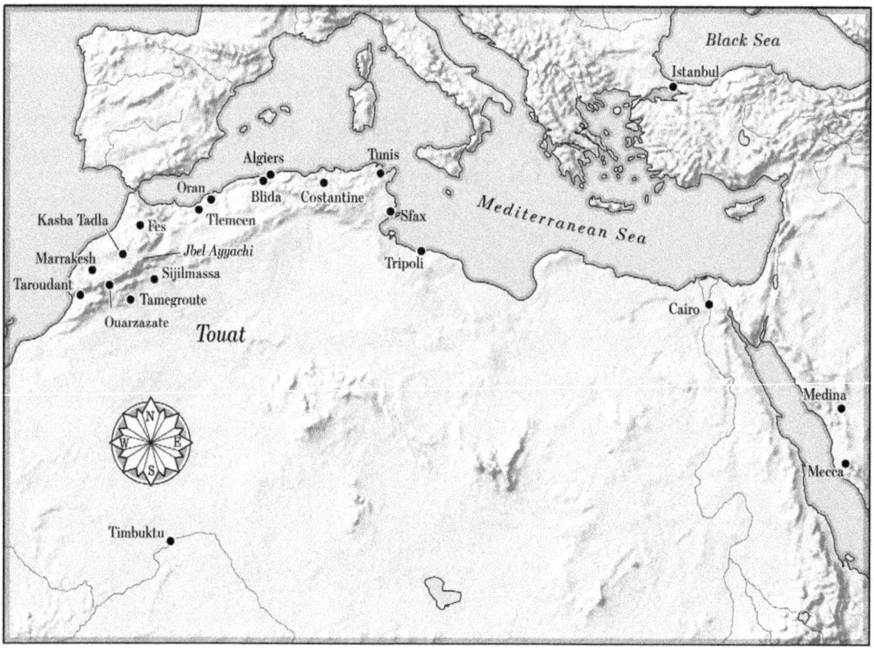

Map of the Maghreb

4

Maghrebī "Theologian-Logicians" in Egypt and the Hejaz

In the course of the seventeenth century, the study of the rational sciences in Cairo was stimulated by incoming scholars from the Maghreb. These scholars gained a reputation and were sought out by local students for their mastery of especially logic and rational theology (*kalām*). Particularly the theological and logical works of Muḥammad b. Yūsuf al-Sanūsī (d. 1490) from Tlemcen (in what is now western Algeria) and his later Maghrebī commentators and glossators came to be studied intensively in Egyptian scholarly circles, and this continued to be the case until the early twentieth century. The development parallels in a curious way that of seventeenth-century Istanbul where, as has been shown in previous chapters, Kurdish and Kurdish-trained scholars rose to prominence as teachers of the rational sciences. In both cases, a major center of Islamic scholarship (Cairo, Istanbul) fell under the influence of scholarly trends emanating from Kurdistan or the Berber highlands of Morocco – regions that one might have supposed, falsely as it were, to have been intellectual backwaters.

Maghrebī Logicians in Egypt

The prominent eighteenth-century scholar Muḥammad Murtaḍā al-Zabīdī (d. 1791) has sometimes been mentioned alongside Shāh Waliyullāh Dihlavī (d. 1762), Muḥammad al-Shawkānī (d. 1834), and Muḥammad b. ʿAbd al-Wahhāb (d. 1792) as a representative of an autochthonous Islamic revival predating the Napoleonic invasion of Egypt in 1798. He was born in Bilgram in India, studied primarily in Yemen and western Arabia, and then settled in Cairo where he wrote his two most famous works: his voluminous and magisterial commentaries on Fīrūzābādī's dictionary *al-Qāmūs* and on Ghazālī's seminal religious work *Iḥyā' 'ulūm al-dīn*.[1] Like the other eighteenth-century "revivalists" with whom he is often classed, Zabīdī had little sympathy for rational theology, logic, and other "rational sciences," and consciously set about revitalizing the study of Prophetic reports (hadith).

In the first volume of his commentary on Ghazālī's *Iḥyā'*, Zabīdī discussed the various fields of knowledge and among other things revisited the long-standing dispute about the religious status of studying disciplines such as logic.[2] Zabīdī mentioned a number of Islamic scholars who held that the discipline is forbidden, including Ibn Ṣalāḥ al-Shahrazūrī (d. 1245), Ibn Taymiyya (d. 1328), and Jalāl al-Dīn al-Suyūṭī (d. 1505), as well as a number of prominent scholars who rejected this opinion and held that the study of logic is licit and even commendable: people like Ghazālī himself, the later prominent Shāfiʿī jurist Taqī al-Dīn al-Subkī (d. 1355), as well as the seventeenth-century Moroccan scholar al-Ḥasan al-Yūsī (d. 1691). Zabīdī's own view was closer to that of the first group. Logic, he opined, is a worldly discipline with no religious use. Those preoccupied with the discipline were exercising themselves in matters of no religious import and therefore neglecting more important matters. In the course of the discussion, Zabīdī made an arresting historical observation. After quoting at length from the defense of logic by the Moroccan scholar Yūsī, he noted that enthusiasm for logic was characteristic of scholars from the Maghreb, where the works of the fifteenth-century theologian and logician Muḥammad b. Yūsuf al-Sanūsī were held in high regard. He wrote:

> After him [Sanūsī] came scholars and eminent notables who were enamored of his path given his righteousness and miracles and the esteem he enjoyed in that region [i.e., the Maghreb]. It was handed down from generation to generation and they [i.e., Maghrebī scholars] became engrossed with it [logic] to such an extent that they became leaders in this field who are singled out for their proficiency ... The study of logic and other such disciplines became like nourishment for them and they would not listen to any criticism or blame, to such an extent that this made them devoid of the narration of hadith.[3]

Zabīdī went on to note that incoming Maghrebī scholars had infected Egyptian scholars with enthusiasm for the discipline "in the time of the

[1] On Zabīdī, see S. Reichmuth, *The World of Murtaḍā al-Zabīdī (1732–1791): Life, Networks, and Writings* (Cambridge: Gibb Memorial Trust, 2009).

[2] Zabīdī, *Itḥāf al-sāda al-muttaqīn bi-sharḥ Iḥyā' ulūm al-dīn* (Cairo: al-Maṭbaʿa al-Muyammaniyya, 1311/1894), I, 175–184.

[3] Zabīdī, *Itḥāf al-sāda al-muttaqīn*, I, 179.

teachers of our teachers" – that is, roughly two generations before his time:

Thus you see that those who came to Egypt in the time of the teachers of our teachers had little knowledge of narrations. Because of this, it [i.e., logic] became popular in Egypt and they [i.e., local students] devoted themselves to studying it, whereas prior to this time they had only cultivated it occasionally to sharpen their wits. This is the reason for the decline of the science of hadith.[4]

Zabīdī's impression that the study of logic in Egypt had been stimulated by incoming scholars from the Maghreb around two generations before his time is supported by bio-bibliographic evidence. He first arrived in Egypt in 1753 at the age of twenty-one and dutifully attended the classes of some of the leading Egyptian scholars of his day and referred to them later as "our teachers" (*shuyūkhunā*), though it must be added that the teachers who were most important for his intellectual formation appear to have been those with whom he had studied during his sojourns in Yemen and the Hejaz. These prominent Egyptian "teachers" included three scholars whom Zabīdī referred to in other contexts as "the three Shihābs" (*al-shuhub al-thalāth*): Shihāb al-Din Aḥmad b. ʿAbd al-Fattāḥ al-Mallawī (1677–1767), Shihāb al-Dīn Aḥmad b. al-Ḥasan al-Jawharī (1684–1768), and Shihāb al-Dīn Aḥmad b. ʿAbd al-Munʿim al-Damanhūrī (1688–1778).[5] All three scholars left behind detailed accounts of their studies, and these confirm that they had studied logic with incoming scholars from the Maghreb.

Aḥmad al-Mallawī (from the Upper Egyptian town of Mallawī) was arguably the most important logician of Ottoman Egypt (1517–1882).[6] His logical works include[7]

4 Ibid., 179–180.

5 Zabīdī, *Tāj al-ʿarūs fī sharḥ jawāhir al-Qāmūs*, edited by ʿA. Farrūj et al. (Kuwait: Maṭbaʿat Ḥukūmat Kuwayt, 1965–2001), XV, 371; XVI, 455–456.

6 On him, see Muḥammad Murtaḍā al-Zabīdī, *al-Muʿjam al-mukhtaṣṣ*, edited by Yaʿqūbī and ʿAjamī (Beirut: Dār al-Bashāʾir al-Islāmiyya, 2006), 80–83. Zabīdī's account is followed by ʿAbd al-Raḥmān al-Jabartī, *ʿAjāʾib al-āthār fī l-tarājim wa l-akhbār* (Būlāq, n.p. 1297/1880), I, 286–287.

7 For works (1)–(3), see Fuʾād Sayyid, *Dār al-Kutub al-miṣriyya: Fihris al-makhṭūṭāt al-latī iqtanathā al-dār min sanat 1936 ilā 1955* (Cairo, 1961), 1:43, 1:84, 3:122. Work (5) is listed in Y. Zaydān and M. Zahrān, *Fihris makhṭūṭāt baladiyyat al-Iskandariyya: al-manṭiq* (Alexandria, 2001), nr. 193. Works (6) and (7) are mentioned in *Fihris al-kutub al-ʿarabiyya al-mahfūẓa bi-l-kutubkhāneh al-khedīviyya al-miṣriyya* (Cairo: Maṭbaʿat ʿUthmān ʿAbd al-Razzāq, 1305/1888–1311/1893), 59 and 87. Work (8) is mentioned in E. Fagnon, *Catalogue Generale des Manuscrits des Bibliotheque Publiques d'Alger* (Paris: Bibliothèque Nationale, 1893), nr. 1411. A manuscript of the long commentary on the *Sullam* is extant in the Bibliothéque Nationale in Paris, see M. Le Baron de Slane, *Catalogue des Manuscrits Arabes* (Paris, 1883–1895), nr. 2403.

1. A treatise on the logical relations (*nisab*) between modal propositions (*al-muwajjahāt*)
2. A didactic poem on modal propositions with commentary
3. A didactic poem on modal syllogisms (*mukhtaliṭāt*), with commentary
4. A treatise showing that all modality reduces to the four notions of necessity and its negation, and perpetuity and its negation
5. A didactic poem on the immediate inferences (*lawāzim*) of hypothetical propositions (*al-sharṭiyyāt*), with commentary
6. A gloss on a commentary by Zakariyyā al-Anṣārī (d. 1519) on the introductory handbook on logic *Īsāghūjī* by Athīr al-Dīn al-Abharī (d. 1265)
7. A versification of Sanūsī's *al-Mukhtaṣar fī l-manṭiq*
8. A didactic poem on the logical differences that result from understanding the subject of the proposition to have extramental existence (*al-qaḍiyya al-khārijiyya*) or merely supposed existence (*al-qaḍiyya al-ḥaqīqiyya*), with commentary
9. A long commentary on the didactic poem on logic *al-Sullam al-murawnaq* by ʿAbd al-Raḥmān al-Akhḍarī (d. 1546)
10. A short commentary on the *Sullam*
11. A didactic poem with commentary on the logical relations that can obtain between two propositions and between one proposition and the negation of the other.

As mentioned in previous chapters, modern historians have tended to be dismissive of didactic poems or commentaries, often assuming that works in such literary formats must have constituted nothing but "vulgarization" or "commentary-mongering." It can be shown that at least some of Mallawī's logical works were in fact substantial contributions to the Arabic logical tradition. For example, his work on the immediate implications of hypothetical propositions (nr. 5 in the list), completed in 1696, is arguably the most extensive and critical treatment of the topic in Arabic since the early fourteenth century. Mallawī in the work repeatedly invoked the concepts of "verification" (*taḥqīq*) and divine "inspiration" (*fatḥ*) to raise novel questions and propose novel answers.[8]

[8] See my "Aḥmad al-Mallawī (d. 1767): The Immediate Implications of Hypothetical Propositions," in K. El-Rouayheb and S. Schmidtke (eds.), *Oxford Handbook of Islamic Philosophy* (Oxford: Oxford University Press, forthcoming).

Quite apart from the question of the content of these works, their sheer number is noteworthy. Mallawī also wrote works on grammar, semantics-rhetoric, and rational theology, but logic appears to have dominated his oeuvre. Like most of his contemporaries, he had studied with a large number of scholars, but in his writings he repeatedly singled out as most important the Maghrebī scholars ʿAbdullāh al-Kinaksī and Aḥmad al-Hashtūkī (d. 1716).[9] Both of these scholars were students of al-Ḥasan al-Yūsī, the Moroccan scholar against whom Zabīdī had argued in his discussion of the status of studying logic.[10]

Aḥmad al-Jawharī also studied with Kinaksī and Hashtūkī, but his closest teacher appears to have been Muḥammad al-Ṣaghīr al-Warzāzī (d. 1726) with whom he studied rational theology and logic.[11] Warzāzī (from Ouarzazate in southern Morocco) in turn was a student of, among others, Yūsī's star pupil Ibn Yaʿqūb al-Wallālī (d. 1716).[12] A Moroccan scholar who later met Jawharī in Cairo noted that he was particularly interested in rational theology and had mastered the discipline with Warzāzī "and he used to be proud of this."[13] Jawharī's numerous works are indeed mostly contributions to rational theology, including a number of treatises on specific theological problems as well as a handbook entitled "The salvation of servants from the yoke of imitation (*Munqidhat*

[9] Aḥmad al-Mallawī, *Thabat* (MS: Princeton University Library: Yahuda 3786, fols. 1–29). See also the mentions of ʿAbdullāh al-Kinaksī in the introductions to Aḥmad al-Mallawī, *Sharḥ al-Sullam*, printed on the margins of Muḥammad b. ʿAlī al-Ṣabbān, *Ḥāshiya ʿalā Sharḥ al-Sullam li-l-Mallawī* (Cairo: al-Maṭbaʿa al-Azhariyya, 1319/1901), 34 (margins); and Aḥmad al-Mallawī, *Sharḥ al-Samarqandiyya*, printed on the margins of Muḥammad al-Khuḍarī, *Ḥāshiya ʿalā Sharḥ al-Samarqandiyya li-l-Mallawī* (Būlāq: Dār al-Ṭibāʿa al-ʿĀmira, 1287/1870), 15 (margin).

[10] On Hashtūkī, see Muḥammad al-Ḥudaygī, *Ṭabaqāṭ*, ed. A. Bū Mazgū (Casablanca: Maṭbaʿat al-Najāḥ al-Jadīda, 2006), I, 89–90 and ʿAbbās al-Simlālī al-Marrākushī, *al-Iʿlām bi-man ḥalla Marrakush wa Aghmāt min al-aʿlām* (Rabat: al-Maṭbaʿa al-Malakiyya, 1974), II, 352–353. The attributive "Hashtūkī" refers to the region south of Taroudant in southern Morocco, present-day Chtouka Ait Baha. I have not found biographical entries on Kinaksī. He features regularly in the chains of transmission listed in ʿAbd al-Ḥayy al-Kattānī, *Fihris al-fahāris* (Beirut: Dār al-Gharb al-Islāmī, 1982), 213, 749, 932. These reveal that he was an influential disciple of the Shādhilī Sufi ʿAbdullāh al-Sharīf al-Yimlaḥī (d. 1678). Manuscripts tend to vocalize the attributive الكنكسي very differently; I follow the vocalization given by Zabīdī, *Tāj al-ʿarūs*, XVI, 455–456. Zabīdī there gives his first name as Muḥammad b. ʿAbdullāh, but all other references give his name as ʿAbdullāh b. Muḥammad.

[11] On Jawharī, see Jabartī, *ʿAjāʾib al-āthār*, I, 309–310.

[12] Mallawī, *Thabat*, fol. 27a. On Warzāzī, see Jabartī, *ʿAjāʾib al-āthār*, I, 74; al-Simlālī al-Marrākushī, *al-Iʿlām*, VI, 33–34.

[13] Ḥudaygī, *Ṭabaqāt*, I, 115–116.

al-ʿabīd min ribqat al-taqlīd)." As will be seen in the following chapter, this rhetoric of denigrating "imitation" (*taqlīd*) in theology was typical of the North African Ashʿarī tradition of Sanūsī and his commentators and glossators.

Aḥmad al-Damanhūrī was perhaps the most prolific and polymathic of the "three Shihabs," contributing to a wide range of disciplines such as logic, rhetoric, imposition (*waḍʿ*), rational theology, Quran recitation, law (he prided himself in mastering all four schools of Sunni Islamic law), medicine, anatomy, mirrors for princes, arithmetic, and the occult sciences.[14] Damanhūrī left behind particularly detailed information about his studies from which it is clear that he was taught logic by Kinaksī. Kinaksī appears furthermore to have been Damanhūrī's main teacher: Damanhūrī gave a long list of central works on logic, rational theology, semantics-rhetoric, grammar, mathematics, hadith, and Quran exegesis that he had studied with his Maghrebī teacher. Kinaksī also initiated Damanhūrī into the Shādhilī order, teaching him the litany of his Sufi master ʿAbdullāh al-Sharīf al-Yimlaḥī (d. 1678).[15] One of Damanhūrī's earliest works, a didactic poem on rational theology with commentary written when he was fourteen years old, contains an acknowledgment of his debt to Kinaksī.[16] Damanhūrī became Rector of al-Azhar College (Shaykh al-Azhar) in the year 1768 and occupied the position until his death ten years later.

Egyptian scholars from the seventeenth and eighteenth centuries seem not to have shared the habit of their Ottoman Turkish contemporaries of giving neat scholarly genealogies.[17] Yet, because they routinely singled out certain teachers as particularly important for their formation, constructing such a genealogy for the "three Shihābs" is quite straightforward, and it would look like this:

[14] On Damanhūrī, see Zabīdī, *al-Muʿjam*, 83–90; Jabartī, *ʿAjāʾib al-āthār*, II, 25–27; J. H. Murphy, "Aḥmad al-Damanhūrī (1689–1778) and the Utility of Expertise in Early Modern Egypt," *Osiris* 25(2010): 85–103.

[15] Damanhūrī, *al-Laṭāʾif al-nūriyya fī l-minaḥ al-Damanhūriyya* (MS: Princeton University Library: Garrett 797H), fol. 6b.

[16] Damanhūrī, *al-Qawl al-mufīd fī sharḥ Durrat al-tawḥīd* (MS: Berlin Staatsbibliothek: Wetzstein 1734), fol. 30a.

[17] Of course, Egyptian scholars routinely gave chains of transmission of particular works or of Sufi orders into which they were initiated. What seems to have been absent is the habit of giving general chains of the form: I took knowledge (or the rational sciences) from X, who took it from Y who took it from Z, etc.

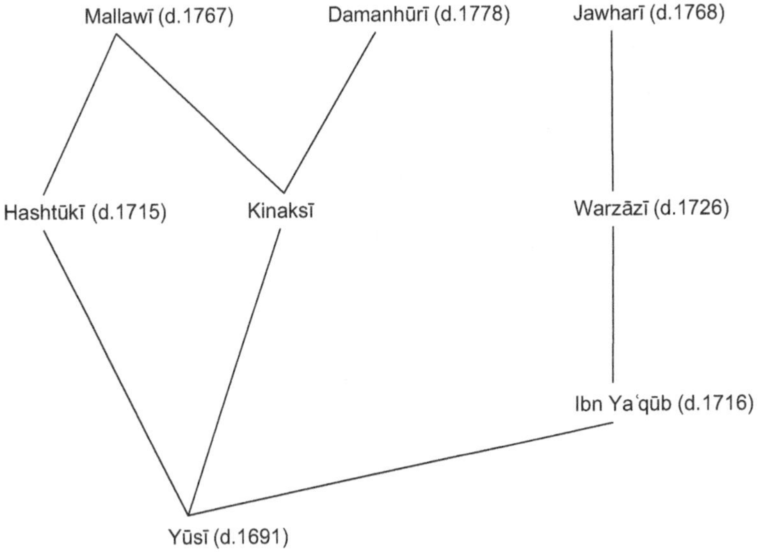

The works on logic that were taught to Egyptian students by Maghrebī scholars in the sevnteenth century were also of Maghrebī provenance. Two works in particular were regularly studied:

1. *al-Sullam al-murawnaq*, the aforementioned introductory didactic poem by al-Akhḍarī with Akhḍarī's own commentary and the glosses of the Algerian scholar Sa'īd Qaddūra (d. 1656)[18]
2. *al-Mukhtaṣar*, a more advanced handbook by the aforementioned Muḥammad b. Yūsuf al-Sanūsī, with Sanūsī's own commentary and the extensive glosses of al-Ḥasan al-Yūsī.[19]

Two other works, longer and more advanced, are also known to have been taught by incoming Maghrebī scholars in Egypt and western Arabia, though this was presumably only to the few advanced students who had a special interest in logic:

3. *al-Jumal* by Afḍal al-Dīn al-Khūnajī (d. 1248) with the commentaries of North African scholars such as Muḥammad al-Sharīf al-Tilimsānī (d. 1370), Sa'īd al-'Uqbānī (d. 1408), and Ibn Marzūq al-Ḥafīd (d. 1439)[20]

[18] Kinaksī taught this work to Damanhūrī; see later.

[19] Kinaksī taught this work to Damanhūrī, see later. Warzāzī taught it to Jawharī, see Jabartī, *'Ajā'ib al-āthār*, I, 310.

[20] The Maghrebī scholar 'Īsā al-Tha'ālibī (d. 1669) taught this work in the Hejaz to Aḥmad Ibn Bā-Qushayr (d. 1664) (see 'Ayyāshī, *Riḥla*, II, 302). The Maghrebī scholar Yaḥyā

4. *al-Mukhtaṣar* by Ibn ʿArafa al-Tūnisī (d. 1401) with the commentary of Sanūsī.[21]

It is therefore not surprising that Zabīdī should have thought that Maghrebī scholars had played an important role in spreading interest in logic in Egypt two generations prior to his own time. Some of the most prominent Egyptian scholars of the preceding generation had been taught logic by Maghrebī scholars using Maghrebī handbooks.

Why were Maghrebī scholars esteemed as teachers of logic in Cairo? Zabīdī himself suggested that Maghrebī scholars cultivated the discipline much more intensively than had hitherto been the custom in Egypt, and there is reason to accept this assessment. To be sure, logic was routinely studied in Egypt even before the arrival of Yūsī's students. Three handbooks are known to have been regularly studied by Egyptian students throughout the seventeenth century:

1. *Īsāghūjī*, the short, introductory handbook by al-Abharī that was usually studied with the commentary of the widely respected Egyptian scholar and judge Zakariyyā al-Anṣārī (d. 1519)[22]
2. *al-Risāla al-Shamsiyya* by Najm al-Dīn al-Kātibī (d. 1277) with the commentary of Quṭb al-Dīn al-Rāzī (d. 1365), a longer and more advanced handbook.[23]
3. *Tahdhīb al-manṭiq* by the Timurid scholar Saʿd al-Dīn al-Taftāzānī (d. 1390), covering approximately the same ground as Kātibī's *Shamsiyya*. In Egypt, the handbook was usually studied with the commentary of the Central Asian scholar ʿUbaydullāh Khabīṣī (fl. 1540)[24]

al-Shāwī (d. 1685) taught it at the Azhar; see Muḥibbī, *Khulāṣat al-athar*, IV, 487 (l. 2).

21 Mallawī referred regularly to this handbook in works that he wrote in his late teens while presumably still a student of Kinaksī; see El-Rouayheb, "Aḥmad al-Mallawī (d.1767)" for additional details and references.

22 Glosses on this commentary were written by the Egyptian scholars Aḥmad al-Ghunaymī (d. 1634) and Aḥmad al-Qalyūbī (d. 1659); see Muḥibbī, *Khulāṣat al-athar*, I, 314 (l. 16) and I, 175 (l. 22). It was printed in Cairo with the glosses of Yūsuf al-Ḥifnī (d. 1764) in 1302/1884–1885 by al-Maṭbaʿa al-ʿĀmira al-Sharafiyya.

23 The work was taught by the Egyptian scholars Ṣāliḥ al-Bulqīnī (d. 1606) and ʿAlī al-Ujhūrī (d. 1656), see Muḥibbī, *Khulāṣat al-athar*, II, 237 (l. 18) and III, 176 (l. 3–4). It was printed in Cairo in 1311/1894 (al-Maṭbaʿa al-Azhariyya) and 1323/1905 (al-Maṭbaʿa al-Amīriyya) and 1948 (Muṣṭafā al-Bābī al-Ḥalabī).

24 A gloss on this commentary was written by the Azharī scholar Yāsīn al-ʿUlaymī (d. 1651); see Muḥibbī, *Khulāṣat al-athar*, IV, 492 (l. 2). For an extant copy of this gloss, see Mach nr. 3253. Khabīṣī's commentary was printed in Cairo in 1296/1879 (Būlāq), 1327/1909 (al-Maṭbaʿa al-Azhariyya), 1328/1910 (Maṭbaʿat Kurdistān al-ʿIlmiyya) and 1936 (Muṣṭafā al-Bābī al-Ḥalabī).

The first of these handbooks is comparable in length and level to Akhḍarī's *Sullam* and the latter two to Sanūsī's *Mukhtaṣar*. But there seems to have been no handbook studied in Egypt prior to the mid-seventeenth century that is comparable to the more comprehensive and advanced textbooks taught by Maghrebī scholars: the aforementioned *Jumal* of Khūnajī and *Mukhtaṣar* of Ibn ʿArafa. In Ottoman Turkey and Safavid and Qajar Iran, a comparably extensive and detailed treatment of logic was afforded to advanced students by the handbook *Maṭāliʿ al-anwār* of Sirāj al-Dīn al-Urmawī (d. 1283) with the commentary of Quṭb al-Dīn al-Rāzī.[25] But this work seems not to have been well known in Egypt. The Egyptian scholar Ḥasan al-ʿAṭṭār (d. 1835), who played an important role in introducing eastern Islamic logical and philosophical works to Egyptian students, described it in terms that suggest he did not expect his readers to be familiar with it.[26] When eighteenth-century Egyptian logicians discussed the legal status of studying logic they regularly made a distinction between logic that was mixed with philosophy and logic that was not so mixed, adding that the second category is clearly licit. In such cases, they often listed works that exemplified non-philosophical logic: Abharī's *Īsāghūjī*, Akhḍarī's *Sullam*, Kātibī's *Shamsiyya*, Taftāzānī's *Tahdhīb*, Ibn ʿArafa's *Mukhtaṣar* and Sanūsī's *Mukhtaṣar*, but left out Urmawī's *Maṭāliʿ*.[27] The lack of mention of Urmawī's *Maṭāliʿ* cannot be because it was deemed "philosophical" – it covers more or less the same ground as Khūnajī's *Jumal* or Ibn ʿArafa's *Mukhtaṣar* – but must have been because it was simply less

25 Glosses on this commentary were written by Persian scholars such as Mīrzā Jān Bāghnavī (d. 1586) and Mullā Mīrzā Shirwānī (d. 1687); see Mach, nrs. 3228, 3232 and Ormsby, nr. 580. It was lithographed in Iran in 1274/1857 and 1315/1897. In Ottoman Turkey, the work was listed as an advanced handbook in *Kevākib-i Sebʿa*, a poem composed in the 1730s on works studied in Ottoman colleges; see Ö. Özelyımiz, *Osmanlı Medreselerinin Eğetim Programları*, 40. It was printed in Istanbul in 1277/1861 (Maṭbaʿah-yi ʿĀmireh) and in 1303/1885 (Ḥāc Muḥarrem Bōsnavī Maṭbaʿasī).

26 Ḥasan al-ʿAṭṭār, *Ḥāwāshī ʿalā Maqūlāt al-Bulaydī wa-l-Sijāʿī* (Cairo, al-Maṭbaʿa al-Khayriyya, 1328/1910–1911), 46 (lowest rubric). At one point, the text he was glossing mentioned *al-Ṭawāliʿ*. ʿAṭṭār explained that this is a handbook of philosophy and rational theology (*ʿilm al-ḥikma wa-l-kalām*) by al-Bayḍāwī. It should not be confused, he added, with *al-Maṭāliʿ* "which is a handbook on logic by Urmawī that is longer than the *Shamsiyya* and has been commented on by Quṭb al-Dīn al-Rāzī and glossed by al-Sayyid al-Sharīf al-Jurjānī."

27 See the lists of logical works mentioned in Mallawī, *Sharḥ al-Sullam*, 36–37 (margin); Aḥmad al-Damanhūrī, *Īḍāḥ al-mubham min maʿānī al-Sullām* (Cairo: Muṣṭafā al-Bābī al-Ḥalabī, 1948); Muḥammad ʿIllaysh, *Ḥāshiya ʿalā Sharḥ Īsāghūjī* (Cairo: Maṭbaʿat al-Nīl, 1329/1911), 19.

familiar to Egyptian students.[28] The situation may thus be summarized as follows:

	Maghrebī tradition of logical studies (mid-seventeenth century)	**Egyptian tradition of logical studies (mid-seventeenth century)**
Introductory level	Akhḍarī: *Sharḥ al-Sullam al-murawnaq*	Zakariyyā al-Anṣārī: *Sharḥ Īsāghūjī*
Intermediate level	Sanūsī: *Sharḥ Mukhtaṣar al-manṭiq*	Quṭb al-Dīn al-Rāzī: *Sharḥ al-Shamsiyyah* Khabīṣī: *Sharḥ al-Tahdhīb*
Advanced level	Sanūsī: *Sharḥ Mukhtaṣar Ibn ʿArafa* Khūnajī: *al-Jumal* + commentaries of al-Sharīf al-Tilimsānī or ʿUqbānī or Ibn Marzūq	

In light of this table, the reputation of Maghrebī teachers of logic among Egyptian students is understandable. It is also worth noting that in the case of Maghrebī scholars such as al-Ḥasan al-Yūsī and his students Ibn Yaʿqūb and Hashtūkī logic occupied a significant and even predominant part of their oeuvres. One of Yūsī's two most widely studied works was his extensive gloss on Sanūsī's commentary on his *Mukhtaṣar*, and one of his lengthiest treatises was on a specific problem in logic: the difference between the differentia (*faṣl*) and the unique property (*khāṣṣa*).[29]

[28] ʿIllaysh's gloss mentioned in the previous footnote does list the *Maṭāliʿ* among the works that mix logic and philosophy, along with Avicenna's *Shifāʾ*, Bayḍāwī's *Ṭawāliʿ*, Ījī's *Mawāqif* and Taftāzānī's *Maqāṣid*. Despite appearances, this inclusion actually confirms that Urmawī's work was not widely studied in Egypt. Urmawī's *Maṭāliʿ* initially consisted of a section on logic followed by a section on philosophy (see Kātib Çelebī, *Kashf al-ẓunūn*, II, 1715). This seems to be the reason why ʿIllaysh mentions it as a work that mixes logic and philosophy. But the later philosophical section was hardly ever studied and the commentaries on it by Shams al-Dīn al-Iṣfahānī (d. 1348) and Quṭb al-Dīn al-Rāzī only cover the part on logic. ʿIllaysh seems not to have been aware of this. Urmawī was a younger associate of Khūnajī and the logic section of his *Maṭāliʿ* is basically an epitome of Khūnajī's summa *Kashf al-asrār*. There is no reason whatsoever to think that the logic expounded in the *Maṭāliʿ* is somehow more "philosophical" than that of Khūnajī's *Jumal*.

[29] Muḥammad al-Maghribī al-Khaṭṭāb, *Fahāris al-Khizāna al-Ḥasaniyya bi-al-qaṣr al-malakī bi-l-Rabāṭ* (Rabat, n.p. 1985), IV, nr. 1314. The two listed manuscripts of Yūsī's treatise, entitled *al-Qawl al-faṣl fī tamyīz al-khāṣṣa ʿan al-faṣl*, consist of fifty and fifty-six folios respectively, making it longer than the standard elementary introductions

Yūsī is also reported to have written an incomplete commentary on a didactic poem on logic by Muḥammad al-ʿArabī al-Fāsī (d. 1642) and a short treatise on the nexus between subject and predicate in a judgment (*al-nisba al-ḥukmiyya*).[30] Ibn Yaʿqūb wrote four major works on logic: a commentary on Akhḍarī's introductory *Sullam*; a commentary on Sanūsī's intermediate *Mukhtaṣar*; a commentary on Khūnajī's advanced *Jumal*; and his own didactic poem on logic with prose commentary.[31] It is difficult to point to an Egyptian scholar prior to Aḥmad al-Mallawī who similarly wrote numerous advanced works on logic and for whom logic could be said to have been something of a *specialization*. There is, to sum up, good reason to believe that seventeenth-century Maghrebī scholars were indeed studying and writing on logic more intensively, and at a more advanced level, than was usual in Egypt in the sixteenth and early seventeenth centuries.

Maghrebī teachers in Egypt did not only teach logic, of course. Kinaksī and Warzāzī were also prominent teachers of the *kalām* works of Sanūsī, especially Sanūsī's three Ashʿarī creeds known as the Short (*al-Ṣughrā*), the Medium (*al-Wusṭā*), and the Long (*al-Kubrā*).[32] To each of these creeds, Sanūsī had himself written a commentary, all of which were widely studied in Islamic Africa until the modern period and elicited a large number of glosses by later Maghrebī scholars. Particularly esteemed were the glosses of the Moroccan scholar ʿĪsā al-Sugtānī (d. 1652) on Sanūsī's commentary on the Short Creed, and al-Ḥasan al-Yūsī's extensive gloss on Sanūsī's commentary on the Long Creed. Kinaksī and Warzāzī are known to have taught these glosses to their Egyptian students.[33]

In addition, Kinaksī is known to have taught semantics-rhetoric, grammar, mathematics, Sufism, and – contrary to what one might expect from Zabīdī's comments cited in the previous section – some of the canonical collections of Prophetic hadith along with their standard commentaries. For example, the works he taught to Damanhūrī are as follows:[34]

to the whole field of logic and probably the most extensive treatment of this particular issue ever to have been written in Arabic.

30 Muḥammad Ḥajjī, *al-Zāwiya al-Dilāʾiyya wa dawruhā l-dīnī wa-l-ʿilmī wa-l-siyāsī* (Casablanca: Maṭbaʿat al-Najāḥ al-Jadīda, 1988), 110.

31 Muḥammad b. al-Ṭayyib al-Qādirī, *Nashr al-mathānī li-ahl al-qarn al-ḥādī ʿashar wa-l-thānī*, ed. Ḥajjī and Ṭawfīq (Rabat: Maktabat al-Ṭālib, 1977–1986), III, 229–233.

32 C. Brockelmann, *GAL*, II, 323–326, Suppl. II, 352–356.

33 Kinaksī taught Sugtānī's gloss to Damanhūrī (see reference that follows). Warzāzī taught Yūsī's gloss to Jawharī, see Jabartī, *ʿAjāʾib al-āthār*, 1:310.

34 Damanhūrī, *al-Laṭāʾif al-nūriyya fī l-minaḥ al-Damanhūriyya*, fol. 5b–6b.

Grammar	Ibn Hishām (d. 1360): *Qaṭr al-nadā*; Ibn Hishām: *Shudhūr al-dhahab*; Ibn Mālik (d. 1274): *Tashīl al-fawā'id*; Ibn Mālik: *al-Alfiyya* with the commentary of Ibn Hishām
Logic	Abharī (d. 1265): *Īsāghūjī* with the commentary of Zakariyya al-Anṣārī (d. 1519); Akhḍarī (d. 1546): *Sharḥ al-Sullam*; Sanūsī (d. 1490): *Sharḥ al-Mukhtaṣar* with the gloss of Yūsī (d. 1691)
Semantics-rhetoric	Jamāl al-Dīn al-Qazwīnī (d. 1338): *Talkhīs al-Miftāḥ* with the Short (*Mukhtaṣar*) and Long (*Muṭawwal*) commentaries of Taftāzānī (d. 1390) and the glosses on the latter commentary by Jurjānī (d. 1413) and Ḥasan Çelebī Fenārī (d. 1481)
Prosody	Aḥmad al-Qinā'ī (d. 1454): *al-Kāfī*; Diyā' al-Dīn al-Khazrajī (d. 1228): *al-Qaṣīda al-Khazrajiyyah*
Mathematics	'Abd al-Qādir al-Sakhāwī (fl. 1591): *al-Risāla al-Sakhāwiyyah*; 'Alī al-Qalaṣādī (d. 1486): *Kashf al-asrār*; Ibn Ghāzī (d. 1513): *Munyat al-ḥussāb*; Ibn al-Bannā' (d. 1321): *Talkhīs a'māl al-ḥisāb*; Ibn al-Bannā: *Raf' al-ḥijāb*
Inheritance laws	The section on inheritance in the *Mukhtaṣar* of Khalīl b. Isḥāq (d. 1365) with the commentary of al-Qalaṣādī; Ibrāhīm al-Tilimsānī (d. 1291): *al-Manẓūma al-Tilimsāniyya* with the commentary of al-Qalaṣādī
Hadith terminology	Zayn al-Dīn al-'Irāqī (d. 1404): *Alfiyyat al-muṣṭalaḥ*; the introduction of Shihāb al-Dīn al-Qasṭallānī (d. 1517) to his commentary on *Ṣaḥīh al-Bukhārī*.
Hadith collections	*Ṣaḥīḥ al-Bukhārī* with the commentary of al-Qasṭallānī; *Ṣaḥīh Muslim*; al-Tirmidhī (d.892): *al-Shamā'il*
Jurisprudence	Tāj al-Dīn al-Subkī (d. 1370): *Jam' al-jawāmi'* with the commentary of Jalāl al-Dīn al-Maḥallī (d. 1459) and the gloss of Ibn Abī l-Sharīf al-Maqdisī (d. 1500)
Rational theology	The creeds of Sanūsī; Sanūsī's commentary on his Short Creed with the gloss of Sugtānī (d. 1652)
Sufism	Ibn 'Aṭā'ullāh al-Iskandarī (d. 1309): *al-Ḥikam*; Ibn 'Aṭā'ullāh: *al-Tanwīr fī isqāṭ al-tadbīr*; 'Abd al-Wahhāb al-Sha'rānī (d. 1565): *al-Ṭabaqāt*
Quran exegesis	*Tafsīr* of Bayḍawī (fl. 1284)

The absence of "the science of imposition" (*'ilm al-waḍ'*) and *ādāb al-baḥth* from the list is conspicuous. As noted in previous chapters, there was little interest in these two disciplines in the Maghreb at the time.[35]

[35] Neither science is mentioned in Yūsī's encyclopedia of the sciences *al-Qānūn*; see Yūsī, *al-Qānūn fī aḥkām al-'ilm wa aḥkām al-'ālim wa aḥkām al-muta'allim*.

Also noteworthy is the absence of the works of Dawānī (d. 1502) and ʿIṣām al-Dīn Isfarāyinī (d. 1537) that figured prominently in the study of the rational sciences in Ottoman Turkey by the time Kinaksī was teaching Damanhūrī. In fact, with the exception of semantics-rhetoric, prosody, hadith, and Quran exegesis, the listed handbooks were not widely studied by Ottoman Turkish students of the period. In some cases, this is what one would have expected: Ottoman Turkey was overwhelmingly Ḥanafī in law and would have used other handbooks of jurisprudence or law; it was also inclined to Māturīdī theological positions rather than the radical and uncompromising Ashʿarism of Sanūsī; Shādhilī Sufism was much less common in the Turkish-speaking world than in North Africa. In other cases, the differences are not so readily explicable through such juridical and creedal differences. As has already been noted, Maghrebī handbooks on logic were not widely studied outside North Africa. The *Kāfiya* of Ibn al-Ḥājib (d. 1248) with the commentary of Jāmī (d. 1492), which was a staple handbook of syntax in Ottoman Turkey and Mughal India, is conspicuous by its absence; there are indications that Maghrebī scholars thought it insufficient in its coverage compared to their own handbooks.[36] In mathematics, Maghrebī scholars had a different tradition from that which was current in the Islamic East, a fact noted already by the fourteenth-century Egyptian scholar Ibn al-Akfānī (d. 1348).[37] Most of the handbooks on mathematics taught by Kinaksī appear to have been unknown to the Ottoman bibliographer Kātib Çelebī.[38]

Yūsī and his students also appear to have played an important role in a noticeable rise of interest in eighteenth-century Egypt in the ten Aristotelian categories (*al-maqūlāt*): (1) substance (*jawhar*), (2) quantity (*kamm*), (3) quality (*kayf*), (4) relation (*iḍāfa*), (5) where (*ayn*), (6) when (*matā*), (7) posture (*waḍʿ*), (8) possession (*milk*), (9) action (*fiʿl*), and (10) passion (*infiʿāl*). The early Arabic Aristotelians of Baghdad had given considerable attention to this topic and had followed the Greek philosophical

36 On the centrality of Jāmī's *Sharḥ al-Kāfiya*, see ʿAbd al-Ḥayy al-Ḥasanī, *al-Thaqāfa al-Islāmiyya fī l-Hind*, 16; Ö. Özyılmaz, *Osmanlı Medreselerinin Eğetim Programları*, 25, 35, 40. ʿAyyāshī noted that an Indo-Muslim scholar with whom he had studied in Medina did not have a thorough grasp of Arabic syntax. He thought this was due to the fact that he had not studied anything longer than the *Kāfiya*; see ʿAyyāshī, *Riḥla*, I, 535.

37 Ibn al-Akfānī, *Irshād al-qāṣid ilā asnā al-maqāṣid*, edited by J. J. Witkam (Leiden: Ter Lugt Pers, 1989), 61 (l. 802). Ibn al-Akfānī is followed by Ṭāşköprīzāde, *Miftāḥ al-saʿāda wa miṣbāḥ al-siyāda fī mawḍūʿāt al-ʿulūm*, I, 390.

38 Of the works mentioned, only Ibn al-Bannā's *Talkhīṣ* is listed in Kātib Çelebī's *Kashf al-ẓunūn*.

tradition in considering Aristotle's *Categories* as part of the books of the logical *Organon*.[39] But Avicenna (d. 1037) had influentially argued that the categories did not belong to logic, and post-Avicennan logicians after the twelfth century largely ceased to discuss them.[40] This did not mean that interest in the categories ceased entirely; discussions of substance and the various types of attribute were included in works of philosophical theology such as *Ṭawāliʿ al-anwār* by Bayḍāwī (fl. 1284), *al-Mawāqif* by Ījī (d. 1355) and *al-Maqāṣid* by Taftāzānī.[41] The treatment of the categories in these works, though, tended to be dispersed throughout the early sections devoted to philosophical preliminaries. Yūsī, in both his gloss on Sanūsī's *Mukhtaṣar* on logic and his gloss on Sanūsī's commentary on the Long Creed, had given a short and concentrated account of the ten categories.[42] This may well have encouraged a number of eighteenth-century Egyptian scholars to write works devoted exclusively to this topic. The first such Egyptian work seems to have been *Nayl al-saʿādāt fī ʿilm al-maqūlāt* by Muḥammad al-Bulaydī (1683–1763). This may have been the first Arabic work exclusively devoted to the categories to have been written outside of Iran since the twelfth century. Bulaydī hailed from a North African family of Andalusian origin that settled in Egypt. The attributive "al-Bulaydī" (some sources vocalize it as "al-Balīdī") probably derives from the town of Blida near Algiers.[43] He studied with a number of scholars in Cairo, including Yūsī's first- and second-generation students Kinaksī, Hashtūkī, and Warzāzī, but the available biographical

39 See the Long Commentary on the *Categories* by Abū l-Faraj b. al-Ṭayyib (d. 1043) edited by C. Ferrari, *Der Kategorienkommentar von Abū l-Farağ ʿAbdullāh ibn aṭ-Ṭayyib: Text und Untersuchungen* (Leiden, the Netherlands: Brill, 2006). See also the Short Commentary of Fārābī (d. 950), edited and translated by D. M. Dunlop, "Fārābī's Paraphrase of the Categories of Aristotle," *Islamic Quarterly* 4(1957): 168–197 and 5(1959): 21–54.

40 For Avicenna's view that the *Categories* did not belong to logic, see A. I. Sabra, "Avicenna on the Subject Matter of Logic," *Journal of Philosophy* 77(1980): 746–764, at 764. There is no discussion of the topic in the standard madrasa handbooks of logic from the thirteenth and fourteenth centuries.

41 See the table of contents of the English translation of Bayḍāwī's *Ṭawāliʿ* with the commentary of Shams al-Dīn al-Iṣfahānī (d. 1348): E. E. Calverley and J. W. Pollock (transl.), *Nature, Man and God in Medieval Islam* (Leiden, the Netherlands: Brill, 2002).

42 Yūsī, *Nafāʾis al-durar fī ḥawāshī al-Mukhtaṣar* (MS: Bibliotheque Nationale, Paris: Arabe 2400), fols. 141a–142b; Yūsī, *Ḥawāshī ʿalā Sharḥ Kubrā al-Sanūsī*, edited by Ḥamīd Ḥammānī (Casablance: Dār al-Furqān, 2008), 333–336.

43 On him, see Zabīdī, *Muʿjam*, 800; Jabartī, *ʿAjāʾib al-āthār*, I, 259; Murādī, *Silk al-durar*, IV, 110–111. Murādī gave the date of birth 1096/1684–1685 but Zabīdī wrote that he had been told by Bulaydī himself that he was born in 1094/1683. For the vocalization of the attributive "Bulaydī," see ʿAṭṭār, *Ḥawāshī*, 11 (upper rubric).

entries do not indicate which of his many teachers were particularly important to him. Nevertheless, his work on the categories does reveal his indebtedness to the Maghrebī tradition of theologian-logicians. Not only did he repeatedly cite from the works of Sanūsī and his later Maghrebī glossators, there are also numerous passages that are unacknowledged paraphrases from Yūsī's works, as pointed out by Bulaydī's later glossator Ḥasan al-ʿAṭṭār.[44] Another indicator of the Maghrebī stimulus to this new interest in the categories is an Egyptian manuscript of Yūsī's gloss on Sanūsī's *Mukhtaṣar* on logic, copied in 1724. On the title page, the scribe has added a note indicating where in the manuscript the reader would find the discussion of the ten categories, a clear indication that this topic in Yūsī's work was thought to be of particular interest to readers (see Figure 4.1).

Two further works on the categories were written by Bulaydī's students Khalīl al-Maghribī (d. 1763) and Aḥmad al-Sijāʿī (d. 1783). The former was a short commentary, completed in 1739, on an anonymous couplet presenting the ten categories.[45] The latter was a somewhat longer commentary, completed in 1768, on Sijāʿī's own short didactic poem on the categories.[46] The works of Bulaydī and Sijāʿī were widely studied throughout the nineteenth and early twentieth centuries. Sijāʿī's work was printed in Cairo in 1886 with the gloss of Ḥasan al-ʿAṭṭār.[47] It was then printed together with the treatise of Bulaydī in 1910, along with glosses on both works by ʿAṭṭār.[48] It would seem that these works on the categories served as the main handbooks on "philosophy" (*ḥikma*) in Egypt in the nineteenth and early twentieth centuries. Sijāʿī's didactic poem (minus his commentary) was regularly included in the collections of manuals (*mutūn*) printed in Cairo in the nineteenth and twentieth centuries for the benefit of Azharī students, and it was there classified as

44 ʿAṭṭār, *Ḥawāshī*, 75, 121, 125, 166. ʿAṭṭār characteristically complained about Bulaydī's reliance on relatively introductory theological works such as Sanūsī's commentary on the Short Creed and its later glosses while neglecting philosophical works from the Persianate tradition (p. 180).

45 On Khalīl al-Maghribī, see Jabartī, *ʿAjāʾib al-āthār*, I, 262. He also studied with Aḥmad al-Mallawī, mentioned in the previous section as one of the prominent Egyptian scholars who had studied with Yūsī's students Kinaksī and Hashtūkī.

46 On Aḥmad al-Sijāʿī, see Jabartī, *ʿAjāʾib al-āthār*, II, 75–77 (for the vocalization of his attributive, see Zabīdī, *Tāj al-ʿarūs*, XXI, 182). The historian Jabartī characteristically emphasized the studies of Sijāʿī with his father Ḥasan al-Jabartī (d. 1774), but ʿAṭṭār's gloss brings out the reliance of Sijāʿī on "his teacher" (*shaykhuhu*) Bulaydī; see ʿAṭṭār, *Ḥāwāshī*, 98–99.

47 Būlāq: al-Maṭbaʿa al-ʿĀmira al-Sharafiyya, 1303/1886. 55 pp.

48 Cairo: al-Maṭbaʿa al-Khayriyya, 1910. 310 pp.

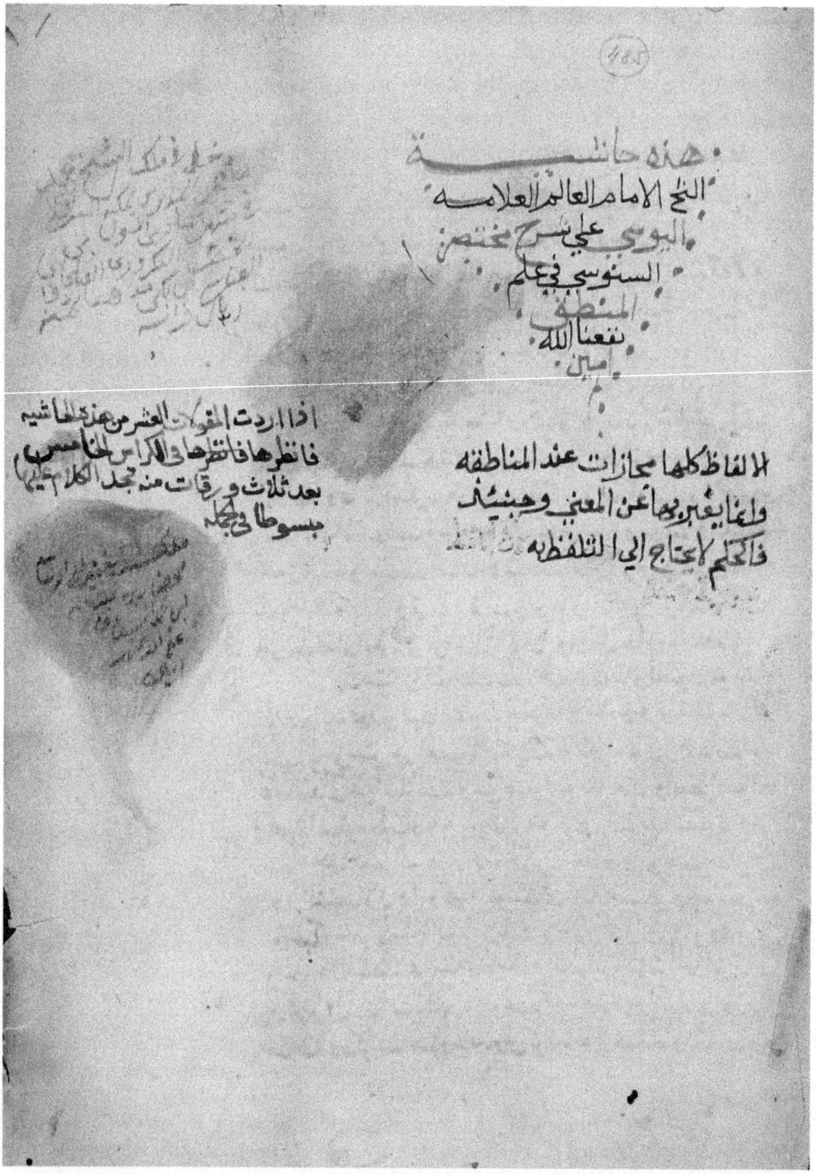

FIGURE 4.1 Title page of Egyptian manuscript, dated 1137/1724, of al-Ḥasan al-Yūsī's gloss on Sanūsī's handbook on logic. A note by a later hand indicates where in the manuscript the reader will find the discussion of the ten Aristotelian categories. (al-Ḥasan al-Yūsī, *Nafā'is al-durar fī ḥawāshī al-Mukhtaṣar*, title page. Islamic Manuscripts, Garrett 485H. Manuscripts Division, Department of Rare Books and Manuscripts, Princeton University Library. Reproduced with permission.)

a manual of *ḥikma*.[49] Manuscripts of Bulaydī's and Sijāʿī's works are extant in libraries in Syria, indicating that they elicited interest beyond Egypt.[50] But there are no indications that they came to be studied in the Turkish- or Kurdish-speaking parts of the Ottoman Empire. Conversely, Abharī's *Hidāyat al-ḥikma* with the commentary of Qāḍī Mīr Maybudī (d. 1504), the main handbook on "philosophy" (*ḥikma*) in Ottoman Turkish madrasas, appears not to have been part of the regular curriculum in Egypt.[51] There are no extant Egyptian glosses on the work (compared to the plethora of glosses by Ottoman Turkish scholars mentioned in Chapter 1), nor any Cairene printings of the work in the nineteenth or early twentieth century.

The Seventeenth-Century Efflorescence in the Maghreb

The fact that seventeenth-century Moroccan scholars were reputed teachers of the rational sciences in Cairo might at first sight appear surprising. There has been practically no modern study that acknowledges that the Maghreb may have been an important center for the study of disciplines such as logic. Morocco especially is often assumed to have been an intellectual backwater in comparison to more eastern regions such as Egypt, Syria, and Iraq, with any intellectual influence accordingly going from

49 See *Majmūʿ min muhimmāt al-mutūn al-mustaʿmala min ghālib khawāṣṣ al-funūn* (Cairo: al-Maṭbaʿa al-Khayriyya, 1306/1888–1889), 286; *Majmūʿ al-mutūn al-kabīr* (Cairo: al-Maṭbaʿa al-ʿUthmāniyya al-Miṣriyya, 1347/1928), 463–464. The didactic poem appears without any attribution in both anthologies.

50 See ʿA. Ḥasan, *Fihris makhṭūṭāt Dār al-Kutub al-Ẓāhiriyya: al-falsafa, al-manṭiq, ādāb al-baḥth* (Damascus: Majmaʿ al-Lugha al-ʿArabiyya, 1970), 169–172.

51 To be sure, Ḥasan al-Jabartī, the father of the historian ʿAbd al-Raḥmān, is reported to have taught Abharī's *Hidāyat al-ḥikma* to students, for example, to Muḥammad b. Ismāʿīl al-Nafarāwī (d. 1771), Aḥmad al-Sijāʿī, Abū l-Ḥasan al-Qalʿī (d. 1785), and Muḥammad b. ʿAlī al-Ṣabbān (d. 1792); see Jabartī, *ʿAjāʾib al-āthār*, I, 268 (l.11), II, 75 (l.8–9), II, 227 (l.31) and II, 99 (l.9). Jabartī had studied the work with an Indo-Muslim scholar who had stayed in Cairo for a while (see Jabartī, *ʿAjāʾib al-āthār*, I, 393 [ll.2–3]). But this is not sufficient to show that the work continued to be widely studied in the nineteenth and twentieth centuries. It is also revealing that the reports do not mention the commentary of Qāḍī Mīr. Ṣabbān studied Abharī's handbook with the shorter and less demanding commentary of Ibn al-Sharīf al-Jurjānī (d. 1434). Nafarāwī and Sijāʿī both reportedly studied the handbook with the commentary of "Qāḍīzāde." This could be a mistake for Qāḍī Mīr, but it could also be a reference to the commentary of Mullāzāde al-Kharziyānī or the commentary of Qāḍīzāde al-Rūmī, fourteenth- and early-fifteenth-century scholars known to have written commentaries on Abharī's handbook (for extant manuscripts of their commentaries, see Mach, *Catalogue*, nrs. 3046 and 3158). The absence of extant Egyptian glosses on Qāḍī Mīr's commentary is striking, as is the absence of an older Cairene printing.

east to west rather than the other way. This assumption, to be sure, may have been true of some periods of Islamic history. Morocco had admittedly experienced an intellectual and cultural florescence in the thirteenth and fourteenth centuries – this had been the period of, for example, the mathematician and astronomer Ibn al-Bannāʾ (d. 1321), the great traveler Ibn Baṭṭūṭa (d. 1368), and the logician and jurist Muḥammad al-Sharīf al-Tilimsānī (d. 1370) who was patronized by the court of the Marinid ruler Abū ʿInān al-Mutawakkil (r. 1348–1358) and was well versed in the works of Avicenna and post-Avicennan logicians as well as Averroes' Middle Commentaries on Aristotle.[52] But this is generally thought to have been followed by a period of intellectual and cultural retrenchment between the end of the Marinid dynasty in the early fifteenth century and the establishment of the Saʿdid dynasty in the mid-sixteenth.[53] There is certainly no evidence for a strong interest in rational theology and logic – the fields that so interested Yūsī and his students – in this period.[54] According to a seventeenth-century account, Morocco was practically devoid of the study of rational sciences (*al-maʿqūl*) such as rational theology, the principles of jurisprudence and logic until the Tunisian scholar Muḥammad Kharrūf al-Anṣārī (d. 1558) settled in Fes. Nonetheless, the account goes on to suggest that this scholar began to train local students in these neglected sciences. The report, which is to be found in a

52 On Ibn al-Bannāʾ, see H. Suter, "Ibn al-Bannāʾ al-Marrākushī," EI2, III, 731. The literature on Ibn Baṭṭūṭa is of course vast. For helpful overviews, see A. Miquel, "Ibn Baṭṭūṭah," EI2, III, 735 and M. Tolmacheva, "Ibn Baṭṭūṭah," in J. E. Lowry and D. Stewart (ed.), *Essays in Arabic Literary Biography, 1350–1850* (Wiesbaden: Otto Harrassowitz, 2009), 126–137. On al-Sharīf al-Tilimsānī, see Ibn Khaldūn, *al-Taʿrīf bi-Ibn Khaldūn wa riḥlatihi gharban wa sharqan*, edited by M. al-Ṭanjī (Cairo: n.p., 1951), 62–64, and Aḥmad Bābā al-Timbuktī, *Nayl al-ibtihāj bi-taṭrīz al-Dībāj* (Cairo: ʿAbbās b. ʿAbd al-Salām b. Shaqrūn, 1351/1932), 255–264 (margins).

53 Muḥammad Ḥajjī, in his valuable study of Moroccan intellectual life under the Saʿdid dynasty, suggests that the fifteenth and early sixteenth centuries formed a period of general intellectual inertness (*khumūl*); see his *al-Ḥaraka al-fikriyya bi-l-Maghrib fī ʿahd al-Saʿdiyyīn* (Rabat, Maṭbaʿat Faḍāla, 1977), I, 54. This seems unkind to the works of, for example, the Sufi Aḥmad Zarrūq (d. 1493), the jurist Aḥmad al-Wansharīsī (d. 1508), and the historian and mathematician Ibn Ghāzī al-Miknāsī (d. 1513). It may be more cautious to suggest that there was a retrenchment of scholarship and an orientation toward Sufism and the basic legal and practical sciences at the expense of belles-lettres and disciplines such as rational theology, the principles of jurisprudence, semantics-rhetoric, and logic.

54 No Moroccan work on theology or logic from the fifteenth or early sixteenth century appears to have been cited by seventeenth- and eighteenth-century Moroccan scholars such as Yūsī, Ibn Yaʿqūb, Hashtūkī and Aḥmad b. ʿAbd al-ʿAzīz al-Hilālī (d. 1761).

biographical entry on one of Muḥammad Kharrūf's students Muḥammad al-Qaṣṣār al-Gharnāṭī (d. 1603), is worth quoting:

The market of the rational sciences was stagnant in Fes, let alone the other regions of Morocco. So he [Muḥammad al-Qaṣṣār] began to sell briskly from the merchandise of rational theology, the principles of jurisprudence, logic, semantics and other such sciences that had hitherto found no buyers. For the people of Morocco had until that time lacked an interest in sciences other than grammar, law and Quran... Then Shaykh Kharrūf al-Tūnisī came and he was a leading scholar in these sciences... Shaykh Manjūr and Shaykh Qaṣṣār benefitted from him... The [later] scholars of Morocco can be traced back to him [al-Qaṣṣār] and al-Manjūr.[55]

The two prominent students mentioned in the passage were Aḥmad al-Manjūr (d. 1587) and the aforementioned Muḥammad al-Qaṣṣār. These two scholars in turn are reported to have trained the major Moroccan scholars of the early seventeenth century, such as ʿĪsā al-Sugtānī, the author of an esteemed gloss on Sanūsī's commentary on the Short Creed; Muḥammad al-ʿArabī al-Fāsī, who composed a didactic poem on logic that appears to have enjoyed some popularity in the seventeenth century (Yūsī's incomplete commentary on it has already been mentioned); and Ibn ʿĀshir (d. 1631), whose didactic poem *al-Murshid al-muʿīn* on the basics of theology, law, and Sufism was regularly studied and commented on in subsequent centuries.[56]

In the second half of the seventeenth century and the early decades of the eighteenth, the rational sciences seem to have flourished to an unprecedented extent. Yūsī's glosses on Sanūsī's theological and logical works were the most extensive and detailed Maghrebī contributions to these two fields since the fifteenth century. Manuscripts of these glosses survive in numerous copies throughout North Africa.[57] Yūsī's death in 1691 left his student Ibn Yaʿqūb in the position of arguably the leading scholar on logic, semantics-rhetoric, and rational theology in the whole of Islamic Africa, writing a number of works in these fields that enjoyed esteem well beyond seventeenth-century Morocco, as evidenced by the fact that some of them were printed in Cairo in the early twentieth century in editions

55 Muḥibbī, *Khulāṣat al-athar*, IV, 121.

56 See Muḥammad Makhlūf, *Shajarat al-nūr al-zakiyya fī ṭabaqāt al-Mālikiyya*, edited by ʿA. ʿUmar (Cairo: Makatabt al-Thaqāfa al-Dīniyya, 2006), II, 223 (on Sugtānī); II, 207–208 (on Muḥammad al-ʿArabī); and II, 203 (on Ibn ʿĀshir).

57 See the list of extant manuscripts of these two works in Ḥajjī, *al-Zāwiya al-Dilāʾiyya*, 109, 111. Note that even Ḥajjī's list is far from exhaustive.

obviously meant for madrasa students.[58] This period also saw the composition, by scholars such as Muḥammad b. Saʿīd al-Mirightī (d. 1678), Ibn Shuqrūn al-Miknāsī (fl. 1701), and Aḥmad al-Rasmūkī (d. 1721), of handbooks on chronology (*mīqāt*), medicine, and mathematics that continued to be studied in Morocco until the modern period.[59] Incidentally, Arabic belles-lettres and poetry also seem to have flourished in the period, especially in the works of Ibn Zākūr al-Fāsī (d. 1708) and Muḥammad al-ʿAlamī (d. 1721).[60]

This revival of the fortunes of the rational sciences in cities such as Fes, Marrakesh, and Meknes was supplemented by the remarkable rise of the Zāwiyas: Sufi lodges – often located in rural areas – that also afforded instruction in the exoteric Islamic and instrumental sciences. In the course of the seventeenth century, three such lodges in particular developed into leading centers of scholarship in Morocco to which even students from older established urban centers of learning such as Fes, Marrakesh, and Tlemcen came to study:

1. al-Zāwiya al-Dilāʾiyya, founded near Kasba Tadla in the Middle Atlas by Abū Bakr al-Dilāʾī (d. 1612) and expanded by his son Maḥammad[61] (d. 1636) and grandson Muḥammad al-Ḥājj

58 His commentary on Qazwīnī's *Talkhīṣ al-Miftāḥ* entitled *Mawāhib al-fattāḥ bi-sharḥ Talkhīṣ al-Miftāḥ* was printed in Cairo along with three other commentaries under the title *Shurūḥ al-Talkhīṣ* by ʿĪsā al-Bābī al-Ḥalabī in 1937. His commentary on Taftāzānī's *Maqāṣid* entitled *Ashraf al-Maqāṣid bi-sharḥ al-Maqāṣid* was published with the title *Falsafat al-tawḥīd* in Cairo by al-Maṭbaʿa al-Khayriyya, n.d. (the edition is incomplete and only includes the first half dealing with philosophical preliminaries). The esteem enjoyed by Ibn Yaʿqūb's commentaries in Cairo is recorded by the Syrian scholar Hibatullāh al-Tājī (d. 1808) in his *al-ʿIqd al-farīd fī ittiṣāl al-asānīd* (MS: Princeton University Library, Yahuda 3723), fol. 69a. Tājī mistakenly gave Ibn Yaʿqūb the first name Muḥammad and his date of death as "after 1150/1737" but the reference is nevertheless clear (he mentioned some of the works and that Ibn Yaʿqūb was a teacher of Warzāzī and a student of Yūsī).

59 For Mirightī, see Ḥajjī, *al-Zāwiya al-Dilāʾiyya,* 102–103 and Khayr al-Dīn al-Ziriklī, *al-Aʿlām* (Beirut: Dār al-ʿIlm li-l-Malāyīn, 1995), VI, 139–140. The sources differ considerably in vocalizing the attributive of this scholar. I follow Ziriklī, who did some careful research on this point and concluded that the attributive derives from a village or tribal settlement near Tiznit in southern Morocco. On Ibn Shuqrūn, see M. Lakhder, *La vie littéraire au Maroc sous la dynastie ʿAlawide (1664–1894)* (Rabat: Editions techniques nord-africaines, 1971), 161–166. On Rasmūkī, see Ḥudaygī, *Ṭabaqāt*, I, 114–115.

60 On Ibn Zākūr, see M. Hadj-Sadok, "Ibn Zākūr," EI2, III, 971–972. On ʿAlamī, see Lakhder, *La vie littéraire au Maroc*, 137–151.

61 This given name is not uncommon in Morocco. In Arabic script, it is written exactly as the more common "Muḥammad" and as a consequence it is not always easy to distinguish the two given names in written sources. In the case of this particular scholar,

(d. 1671).[62] Until its destruction in 1668 by the forces of Mawlāy Rashīd (r. 1666–1672), it may have been the leading center of Islamic scholarship in Morocco. Yūsī, for example, taught there in the 1650s and 60s and it is there that his students Hashtūkī and Ibn Yaʿqūb attended his lectures. Two other luminaries who spent time at the lodge were the prominent scholar Aḥmad al-Maqqarī al-Tilimsānī (d. 1632), famous for his literary history of Islamic Spain, who will be discussed in greater detail in the following section, and the grammarian Muḥammad al-Murābiṭ al-Dilāʾī (d. 1678) whose major work was a voluminous commentary on the widely studied grammatical handbook *Tashīl al-fawāʾid* by Ibn Mālik (d. 1274).[63]

2. al-Zāwiya al-ʿAyyāshiyya, founded in 1634 in Jbel Ayyachi in the High Atlas by Muḥammad b. Abī Bakr al-ʿAyyāshī (d. 1651), a disciple of Maḥammad b. Abī Bakr al-Dilāʾī.[64] ʿAyyāshī's son Abū Sālim ʿAbdullāh (d. 1679) was the author of a lengthy description of his pilgrimage to Mecca and his year-long sojourn in Medina, a valuable source for the intellectual life of Mecca and Medina in the mid-seventeenth century. He appears to have played a crucial role in expanding the library holdings of the lodge, thus helping to establish it as a major intellectual center. Abdullāh's son Ḥamza (d. 1717) enjoined such prominence that the lodge came to be called al-Zāwiya al-Ḥamziyya after him. Students were still being trained there into the eighteenth and nineteenth centuries, for example, the prominent Moroccan scholars Abū Madyan al-Fāsī (d. 1767) and Aḥmad b. ʿAbd al-ʿAzīz al-Hilālī (d. 1761).
3. al-Zāwiya al-Nāṣiriyya, in Tamagroute (or Tamgrut) in the Draa valley in southeast Morocco.[65] Originally founded in 1575, the lodge was transformed into a major center of scholarship, with

a number of sources take care to indicate that the given name is Maḥammad, not Muḥammad. In all other cases, I have opted for the form "Muḥammad."

62 See Ḥajjī, *al-Zāwiya al-Dilāʾiyya;* Ch. Pellat, "al-Dilāʾ," EI2, XII, 223.

63 For an extended discussion of teachers and students at the Zāwiya, see Ḥajjī, *al-Zāwiya al-Dilāʾiyya,* 92–137. The main figures of the Dilāʾ clan are discussed on pp. 79–91 (for Muḥammad al-Murābiṭ, see pp. 87–88). Muḥammad al-Murābiṭ's commentary on Ibn Mālik's *Tashīl* has been published – see Muḥammad al-Murābiṭ, *Natāʾij al-taḥṣīl fī sharḥ al-Tashīl*, ed. Muṣṭafā al-Ṣādiq al-ʿArabī (Tripoli: al-Kitāb wa-l-tawzīʿ wa-l-iʿlān wa-l-maṭābiʿ, 1980). The edition consists of 1,547 pages.

64 See Ḥajjī, *al-Ḥaraka al-fikriyya,* II, 508–510; and the introduction of Mohamed Zahi to his edition of Abū Sālim ʿAbdullāh al-ʿAyyāshī (d. 1679), *Itḥāf al-akhillāʾ bi-ijāzāt al-mashāyikh al-ajillāʾ* (Beirut: Dār al-Gharb al-Islāmī, 1999), 11–21.

65 See Muḥammad Ḥajjī, *al-Ḥaraka al-fikriyya*, II, 549–551; "Ibn Nāṣir" in EI2, XII, 395; E. Levi-Provencal, "Tamgrūt" in EI2, X, 170.

> a renowned library containing thousands of manuscripts, by the prominent Shādhilī Sufi Muḥammad Ibn Nāṣir al-Dar'ī (d. 1674) and his son and successor Aḥmad Ibn Nāṣir (d. 1717). Yūsī, for example, was a disciple of Muḥammad Ibn Nāṣir and spent time at the lodge in his youth.[66] Another prominent scholar who was a student and disciple of Muḥammad Ibn Nāṣir was Muḥammad Ibn Sulaymān al-Rūdānī (d. 1683), whose career and works are discussed in greater detail in the subsequent section. The important Berber author Muḥammad Awzāl (d. 1749) also spent a significant amount of time at the Zāwiya and was a student and protégé of Aḥmad Ibn Nāṣir.[67] The success of Muḥammad Ibn Nāṣir and his son in transforming a small lodge on the edge of the Sahara, far from the established urban centers of Morocco, into a major center of scholarship was connected to their success in establishing the lodge as a significant local power actively involved in the trans-Saharan trade.[68]

The economic activities of Muḥammad and Aḥmad Ibn Nāṣir highlight an important point: The rise of southern and southeastern Morocco as vibrant centers of scholarly life in the seventeenth century was presumably related to the trans-Saharan trade and the influx of gold, slaves and salt that had increased noticeably after the Moroccan conquests of Touat (in what is today southern Algeria) and Timbuktu during the reign of Sultan Aḥmad al-Manṣūr, nicknamed "the Golden" (r. 1578–1603).[69] The southern parts of Morocco gained in strategic and economic importance from this trade and it is only to be expected that its cultural and intellectual weight should have increased as well. The political turmoil that enveloped Morocco after 1603 may well have adversely affected economic life, but there is evidence that the trans-Saharan trade continued

[66] K. L. Honerkamp, "al-Yūsī, al-Ḥasan b. Mas'ūd," in *EALB, 1350–1850*, 410–419, esp. 414.

[67] N. van den Boogert, *The Berber literary tradition of the Sous: with an edition and translation of the "Ocean of Tears" by Muḥammad Awzāl (d. 1749)* (Leiden: Nederlands Instituut voor het Nabije Oosten, 1997), 127–135.

[68] See D. Gutelius, "The Path Is Easy and the Benefits Large: The Nāṣiriyya, Social Networks and Economic Change in Morocco, 1640–1830," *Journal of African History* 43(2002): 27–49; D. Gutelius, "Sufi Networks and the Social Contexts for Scholarship in Morocco and the Northern Sahara, 1660–1830," in S. Reese (ed.), *The Transmission of Learning in Islamic Africa* (Leiden, the Netherlands: Brill, 2004), 15–38.

[69] J. M. Abun-Nasr, *A History of the Maghrib in the Islamic Period* (Cambridge: Cambridge University Press, 1987), 215–217.

nonetheless throughout the seventeenth century, facilitated by the activities of local magnates such as Ibn Nāṣir who used parts of the proceeds to finance the activities of their lodges. The political situation stabilized under the reigns of Mawlāy Rashīd (r. 1666–1672) and Mawlāy Ismāʿīl (r. 1672–1727) and the demand for goods from across the Sahara presumably increased as a consequence – the latter Sultan reasserted Moroccan control over the entrepôts of the Saharan trade and famously established a sizeable army consisting of Black African slaves.[70]

The North African littoral also seems to have experienced urban and economic growth for much of the period from the sixteenth to the eighteenth centuries. The city of Algiers, under Ottoman control since 1529, grew spectacularly in the sixteenth and seventeenth centuries, outpacing the venerable towns of Tlemcen and Constantine to become the major urban center in what is today Algeria.[71] Tunis, under Ottoman control since 1574, enjoyed a renewed period of growth in the seventeenth and eighteenth centuries, after what seems to have been a period of economic and demographic decline since the late fifteenth century.[72] The intellectual life of the two cities in the Ottoman period is still severely underresearched, but there are indications that both cities were also important centers of scholarly activity. As will be seen in the following section, Algiers produced a number of prominent scholars in the seventeenth century, some of whom settled in the East and enjoyed considerable esteem there. Tunis also produced a number of scholars in this period whose works were esteemed well beyond the confines of their own city and lifetimes, such as ʿAlī al-Nūrī al-Safāqisī (d. 1706), Muḥammad Zaytūna (d. 1726), and Ibn Saʿīd al-Ḥajarī (d. 1785).[73]

Four Maghrebī Scholars in the East

The students of Yūsī who settled temporarily or permanently in Egypt were part of a larger eastward movement of Maghrebī scholars in the seventeenth century. The movement was in part a natural concomitant of the pilgrimage to Mecca and the pious habit of sojourning in Mecca

70 Abun-Nasr, *A History of the Maghrib*, 230–232.

71 R. Le Tourneau, "Al-Djazāʾir," EI2, II, 519; A. Raymond, *The Great Arab Cities in the 16th–18th Centuries: An Introduction* (New York: New York University Press, 1984), 8.

72 P. Sebag, "Tūnis," EI2, X, 629; A. Raymond, *The Great Arab Cities in the 16th–18th Centuries*, 8.

73 Muḥammad Makhlūf, *Shajarat al-nūr al-zakiyya*, II, 259–261 and II, 319.

and Medina for an extended period. It was also no doubt driven in part by the political turmoil that had affected Morocco after the disintegration of the Saʿdian dynasty in 1603. In what follows, the careers of four prominent Maghrebī scholars who settled in Egypt, Syria, or the Hejaz in the seventeenth century are sketched:

1. Aḥmad al-Maqqarī al-Tilimsānī (d. 1632)[74]

Born in Tlemcen in 1578 or 79, Maqqarī traveled to Fes and Marrakesh in his early twenties, possibly attracted by the prospects of patronage afforded by the court of the aforementioned Moroccan Sultan Aḥmad al-Manṣūr. He composed a number of celebrated works there, including one in rhymed prose interspersed with verse on the Prophet's sandals entitled *Fatḥ al-mutaʿāl fī madḥ al-niʿāl* and an extensive biography, with lengthy literary and historical digressions, of the venerable Maghrebī scholar al-Qāḍī ʿIyāḍ (d. 1149), entitled *Azhār al-riyāḍ fī akhbār ʿIyāḍ*.

Maqqarī also resided at the Zāwiya Dilāʾiyya, presumably sometime between 1604 and 1613, and he remained in correspondence with Maḥammad b. Abī Bakr al-Dilāʾī, the son of the lodge's founder, throughout his life. In 1618, he left Fes for the East: performing the pilgrimage and then settling in Cairo, whence he made several further trips to Mecca, Medina, Jerusalem, and Damascus. In Cairo, he obtained a reputation as a teacher of rational theology – an aspect of his career that has received very little attention from modern historians who have focused almost exclusively on his literary-historical works. He is known to have lectured on Sanūsī's Short Creed (*al-Ṣughrā*) and wrote an extant gloss on Sanūsī's own commentary on it.[75] He also wrote a versification of the Short Creed, entitled *Iḍāʾat al-dujunna fī ʿaqāʾid ahl al-sunna*. According to one of Maqqarī's students, the didactic poem arose in the context of Maqqarī's teaching the Short Creed in Cairo. After each lesson, Maqqarī would summarize the main points in verse until the entire poem had been

[74] Unless otherwise indicated, information on this scholar is taken from M. Fierro and L. Molina, "al-Maqqarī," *EALB, 1350–1850*, 273–283.

[75] Maqqarī's gloss is entitled *Itḥāf al-mughram al-mughrā fī takmilat Sharḥ al-Ṣughrā*; see Muḥammad al-ʿĀbid al-Fāsī, *Fihris makhṭūṭāt Khizānat al-Qarawiyyīn* (Casablanca: Dār al-Kitāb, 1979–1989), and the reference to an extant Tunisian manuscript of this work by Nizār Ḥammādī in his valuable edition of Sharaf al-Dīn Ibn al-Tilimsānī, *Sharḥ Maʿālim uṣūl al-dīn* [Beirut: Dār Maktabat al-Maʿārif, 2009], 13 n.1). Other sources indicate that Maqqarī wrote a commentary on the Short Creed rather than a gloss on Sanūsī's commentary. This has led some modern historians to attribute both a commentary and a gloss to Maqqarī but this is very unlikely. The title of the supposed commentary is *Itḥāf al-mughram al-mughrā fī sharḥ al-Ṣughrā* which simply leaves out the word *takmilat* in the previous title.

completed.[76] The versification enjoyed considerable popularity: Maqqarī claimed to have written around 200 copies of it in his own hand, and the work elicited commentaries by later scholars, including the famed Damascene scholar and mystic ʿAbd al-Ghanī al-Nābulusī (d. 1731) and the Azharī scholar Muḥammad ʿIllaysh (d. 1882).[77] Maqqarī was also interested in the occult sciences, writing a number of extant works on magic squares and talismans.

In 1628, Maqqarī visited Damascus, where he stayed for a little over a month, teaching hadith and *kalām* to widespread acclaim. It was apparently there that he was urged by local belletrists to write a work on the learned Andalusian Vizier Ibn al-Khaṭīb (d. 1375).[78] As with Maqqarī's biography of al-Qāḍī ʿIyāḍ, the resultant work, entitled *Nafḥ al-ṭīb fī ghuṣn al-Andalus al-raṭīb wa dhikr wazīrihā Lisān al-Dīn Ibn al-Khaṭīb*, contains extensive literary and historical information on Islamic Spain in general, making it much more than a simple biography of one man. He completed his magnum opus in Cairo in 1629. It has been widely esteemed ever since, and is one of the few works from the period that has retained its popularity through the nineteenth and twentieth centuries, despite the considerable shifts in literary tastes and the emerging modern prejudices about the sterility and "decadence" of the "post-classical" age. Even Jurjī Zaydān (d. 1914), who in general was scathing about the state of Arabic literature in the Ottoman period prior to the nineteenth century, praised the work in his influential literary history *Tārīkh ādāb al-lugha al-ʿarabiyya* (1911–1914).[79]

2. ʿĪsā al-Thaʿālibī (d. 1669)[80]

Born in Zouaoua in present-day Algeria, ʿĪsā al-Thaʿālibī went to Algiers to complete his education. He there attended the lectures of Saʿīd Qaddūra, the famous glossator of Akhḍarī's handbook of logic.

76 ʿAyyāshī, *Riḥla*, II, 396–397.

77 ʿAbd al-Ghanī Nābulusī, *Rāʾiḥat al-janna bi-sharḥ Iḍāʾat al-dujunna* (Cairo: Muṣṭafā al-Bābī al-Ḥalabī, 1958); Muḥammad ʿIllaysh, *al-Futūḥāt al-ilāhiyya al-wahbiyya ʿalā l-manẓūma al-Maqqariyya*, printed on the margins of Muḥammad ʿIllaysh, *Hidāyat al-murīd li-ʿAqīdat ahl al-tawḥīd* (Cairo: Maṭbaʿat Muḥammad Efendī Muṣṭafā, 1306/1888).

78 R. Elgar, "Adab and Historical Memory: The Andalusian Poet/Politician Ibn al-Khaṭīb as Presented in Aḥmad al-Maqqarī, Nafḥ al-Ṭīb," *Die Welt des Islams* 43(2002): 289–306.

79 Jurjī Zaydān, *Tārīkh ādāb al-lugha al-ʿarabiyya* (Cairo: Maṭbaʿat al-Hilāl, 1911–1914), III, 316–317.

80 Unless otherwise indicated, my source on Thaʿālibī is Muḥibbī, *Khulāṣat al-athar*, III, 240–243.

His most important teacher, though, was ʿAlī b. ʿAbd al-Wāḥid al-Sijilmāsī (d. 1647) who had studied in Morocco with scholars such as al-Maqqarī and Maḥammad b. Abī Bakr al-Dilāʾī before settling in Algiers.[81] Thaʿālibī left behind a detailed account of his studies with his teacher, revealing that he studied among other things the works of Sanūsī on theology and logic, as well as Khūnajī's *Jumal* on advanced logic with the standard North African commentaries. Thaʿālibī went on pilgrimage to Mecca in 1650 and stayed in the East, mainly in Mecca but with occasional trips to Medina and Egypt, until his death. As noted by his student ʿAbdullāh al-ʿAyyāshī, the aforementioned son of the founder of the Zāwiya ʿAyyāshiyya: "He devoted himself to spreading knowledge, and he had perfected the means to do this from amongst sciences such as syntax, morphology, logic, rational theology, semantics-rhetoric and the principles of jurisprudence."[82] One of the local scholars who studied with him was Aḥmad Bā-Qushayr (d. 1664). Thaʿālibī taught him rational theology, the principles of jurisprudence and logic. In the latter field, Bā-Qushayr carefully studied the commentary of Saʿīd al-ʿUqbānī on Khūnajī's *Jumal*.[83]

Despite his proficiency in the "rational sciences," Thaʿālibī showed a keen interest in the science of hadith, attending the lectures of the major scholars of the Hejaz and Egypt in this field. He was also a Shādhilī Sufi who in addition was initiated into a number of other Sufi orders then current in the Hejaz (such as the Shaṭṭārī and Naqshbandī) while retaining his primary allegiance to his original order. In the words of ʿAyyāshī: "He received instruction from several Sufi masters and took their path but never abandoned the litany of the Shādhilīs. For this reason he was acceptable to both the exoteric scholars and the esoteric mystics, as is usually the case with prominent Shādhilīs."[84] ʿAyyāshī also noted a revealing story relating to Thaʿālibī's reputation as a teacher of logic.[85] When ʿAyyāshī arrived in the Hejaz in 1662 he found that Thaʿālibī was not on speaking terms with a resident Indo-Muslim scholar, Badr al-Dīn al-Hindī, who also had a reputation as a teacher of logic and was a student of the prominent Indo-Muslim specialist in the rational sciences ʿAbd al-Ḥakīm Siyālkūtī (d. 1657). The break had occurred, ʿAyyāshī explained, when another Maghrebī scholar residing in the Hejaz wrote to

[81] On Sijilmāsī, see Muḥibbī, *Khulāṣat al-athar*, III, 173–174.
[82] ʿAyyāshī, *Riḥla*, II, 170.
[83] Ibid., 302.
[84] Ibid., 168.
[85] ʿAyyāshī, *Riḥla*, I, 536–537.

the Indo-Muslim scholar with a problem in logic relating to the hypothetical syllogism. The problem caused the Indo-Muslim scholar some difficulty and he asked for time to consult some books before responding. In the meantime, the question was presented to Thaʿālibī, who was familiar with this particular problem and answered with ease. The Indo-Muslim scholar then accused the Maghrebīs of having set up the entire affair to cast him in a negative light, a charge that Thaʿālibī strenuously denied. ʿAyyāshī in fact had a high opinion of Badr al-Dīn al-Hindī and studied logic with him during his sojourn in the Hejaz. The two works that he mentioned having studied were Abharī's *Īsāghūjī* with the commentary of Mollā Fenārī (d. 1431) and *al-Risāla al-Shamsiyya* by Kātibī with the commentary of Quṭb al-Dīn al-Rāzī, both widely used handbooks in the Islamic East (but not in the Maghreb).[86] Interestingly, the treatment of hypothetical syllogisms in both handbooks is perfunctory, whereas the North African commentaries on Khūnajī's *Jumal* dealt at great length with the topic.[87] It is therefore hardly surprising that Thaʿālibī had an easier time with the posed problem than his Indo-Muslim rival.

Thaʿālibī is supposed to have written a treatise in response to the logical query addressed to him, but this may not be extant and is not mentioned in his obituaries. His more well-known works include a record of his studies and certificates, an edition of the studies and certificates of the Egyptian scholar Muḥammad b. ʿAlāʾ al-Dīn al-Bābilī (d. 1666), and a collection of the names of the narrators (*ruwāt*) of the venerable Abū Ḥanīfa (d. 767).

3. Yaḥyā al-Shāwī (d. 1685)[88]

Yaḥyā al-Shāwī was born in 1620 or 1621 in the town of Miliana and went to nearby Algiers to complete his studies. He studied with ʿĪsā al-Thaʿālibī's teachers Saʿīd Qaddūra and ʿAlī al-Sijilmāsī and also with ʿĪsā al-Thaʿālibī himself. When the latter left Algiers on pilgrimage, Shāwī reportedly followed him part of the way so that he could complete his study of logic.[89] Shāwī himself left for the pilgrimage in 1663 and then

86 Ibid., 535–536.

87 Compare the discussion in Fenārī, *Sharḥ Īsāghūjī* (Istanbul: Maṭbaʿat Aḫter, 1294/1877), 23–25 and Quṭb al-Dīn al-Rāzī, *Taḥrīr al-qawāʿid al-manṭiqiyya* (Istanbul: Aḥmed Efendī Maṭbaʿasī, 1325/1907), 161–168 with a manuscript of al-Sharīf al-Tilimsānī's commentary on Khūnajī's *Jumal* (MS: British Library: Add. 9617) in which thirty-four folios are devoted to a discussion of the hypothetical syllogism (fols. 106b–140a).

88 On him, see especially Muḥibbī, *Khulāṣat al-athar*, IV, 486–488.

89 Muḥibbī, *Khulāṣat al-athar*, III, 241 (ll.17–18).

settled in Egypt where he taught Mālikī law, grammar, rational theology (the works of Sanūsī) and logic (Khūnajī's *Jumal*) at al-Azhar.[90] From Cairo, he traveled to Istanbul sometime between 1664 and 1666, meeting the Ottoman *Şeyḫülislām* Yaḥyā Minḳārīzāde (d. 1677) and participating in the celebrated *Ḥużūr Dersleri*, the scholarly gatherings conducted in the presence of the Sultan in the month of Ramadan, before returning to Cairo.[91] In Istanbul, he met the Damascene historian and belletrist Muḥammad Amīn al-Muḥibbī (d. 1699) who, along with a number of other Damascenes in the Ottoman capital, asked him to give lectures on a number of works of Quran exegesis, semantics-rhetoric, grammar, and rational theology. The young Muḥibbī was obviously impressed with Shāwī, pouring lavish praise on him in his voluminous biographical dictionary of notables who died in the eleventh Islamic century:

> He was one of the marvelous signs of God in Quran exegesis, and a visible miracle in lecturing and writing... In law (*fiqh*), he is the leader and its rulings are taken from his mouth. As for *uṣūl* [either theology or jurisprudence or both], it is a mere branch of his knowledge. The whole of logic is just an introduction to his sciences, and if grammar is what you desire then there is no one who should speak of it but him... In sum, thoughts are insufficient to attain the lowest reaches of his merits and the precedents of the tongue are incapable of capturing even the first of his distinctions.[92]

It is true that the biographical literature of the period was given to hyperbole, but the praise is fulsome even when compared to Muḥibbī's entries on his other teachers.[93]

Other seventeenth-century observers were more restrained in their assessment of Shāwī. The Moroccan traveler ʿAyyāshī was decidedly lukewarm in what he had to say of him.[94] This may well have been due to

[90] The printed edition of Muḥibbī's *Khulāṣat al-athar* states that Shāwī taught "the commentary of Khūnajī's *Jumal* by Ibn ʿArafa on logic" (*wa-sharḥ al-Jumal li-l-Khūnajī li-Ibn ʿArafa fī l-manṭiq*). Ibn ʿArafa almost certainly did not write a commentary on Khūnajī's *Jumal*. Muḥibbī was probably not too familiar with these works and may have been mistaken or, alternatively, the text of the edition is corrupt and should read *sharḥ al-Jumal wa Ibn ʿArafa fī l-manṭiq*.

[91] On the *Ḥużūr Dersleri*, see M. Zilfi, *The Politics of Piety*, 227–232 and M. Zilfi, "A Medrese for the Palace: Ottoman Dynastic Legitimation in the Eighteenth Century," *Journal of the American Oriental Society* 113(1993): 184–191.

[92] Muḥibbī, *Khulāṣat al-athar*, IV, 486.

[93] See, e.g., the entry on Muḥibbī's main teacher Ibrāhīm al-Fattāl (d. 1687), in Muḥibbī, *Khulāṣat al-athar*, I, 51–53.

[94] ʿAyyāshī, *Riḥla*, II, 472–473.

a particularly vicious controversy between Shāwī and the Medinan mystics Ibrāhīm Kūrānī (d. 1690) and Muḥammad b. ʿAbd al-Rasūl Barzinjī (d. 1691) concerning the question of the "satanic verses" – ʿAyyāshī had close personal relationships with Shāwī's opponents.[95] According to some early Islamic traditions, Satan had managed on one occasion to interpolate into the Prophet Muḥammad's recitation of the divine revelation a praise of some pre-Islamic Arabian gods.[96] The incident is supposed to have led to a short cessation of the ongoing hostilities between the Meccan polytheists and the early Islamic community until the interpolation was pointed out to the Prophet by the Archangel Gabriel and rectified. The question of the authenticity of these early reports appears to have elicited controversy from a very early period. The reports tended to be unequivocally dismissed by rational theologians (the *mutakallimūn*) for whom monotheism (*tawḥīd*) and the veracity and infallibility of the Prophet were truths of reason (they held it to be circular to attempt to establish these truths by appealing to revelation itself) and for whom traditional reports that conflicted with such necessary truths carried no weight. A number of mystics as well as fideist traditionalists opposed to rational theology were less sure about dismissing the reports out of hand on rationalist grounds. Ibrāhīm Kūrānī wrote a treatise based on the acceptance of the reports, and this elicited a strong reaction from contemporary North African Ashʿarī theologians, the tenor of which may be gathered from the title of Shāwī's riposte: "The fine arrow in the throat of the calumniating heretic (*al-Nabl al-raqīq fī ḥulqūm al-sābb al-zindīq*)."[97]

Shāwī's other works include

a. An extensive gloss on Sanūsī's commentary on the Short Creed[98]
b. A collection of answers, entitled *al-Tuḥaf al-rabbāniyya fī jawāb al-asʾila al-Lamadāniyya,* to miscellaneous questions in theology[99]

[95] For ʿAyyāshī's close relationship to Kūrānī, see ʿAyyāshī, *Riḥla*, I, 383ff.

[96] See Shahab Ahmed, "Satanic Verses," in J. D. McAuliffe (ed.), *Encyclopaedia of the Quran* (Leiden, the Netherlands: Brill, 2001–2006), V, 531–536.

[97] Kūrānī's treatise has been edited by A. Guillaume, "al-Lumʿat al-saniya by Ibrahim al-Kurani," *Bulletin of the School of Oriental and African Studies* 20(1957): 291–303. For Shāwī's riposte and Barzinjī's reply, see P. K. Hitti et al., *Descriptive Catalog of the Garrett Collection of Arabic Manuscripts in the Princeton University Library* (Princeton: Princeton University Press, 1938), 460–461.

[98] Yaḥyā al-Shāwī, *Ḥāshiya ʿalā Sharḥ Umm al-barāhīn* (Manuscript: Milli Kütüphane, Ankara: Afyon Gedik Aḥmet Paşa 17879). Available on-line at www.yazmalar.gov.tr (Arşiv Numarası: 03 Gedik 17879).

[99] Yahyā al-Shāwī, *al-Tuḥaf al-rabbāniyya fī jawāb al-asʾila al-Lamadāniyya*, edited by J. M. Faytūrī (Beirut: Dār al-Madār al-Islāmī, 2002).

c. A lengthy adjudication of the criticisms raised by the great grammarian and Quran exegete Abū Ḥayyān al-Gharnāṭī (d. 1344) against the earlier prominent exegetes Zamakhsharī (d. 1144) and Ibn ʿAṭiyya (d. ca. 1147)[100]

d. A short and reportedly unusual manual on "the principles of grammar" (*uṣūl al-naḥw*) dedicated to Sultan Meḥmed IV (r. 1648–1687) and entitled *Irtiqāʾ al-siyāda li-ḥaḍrat Shāhzāda.*[101] The "principles of grammar" is concerned, not with first-order grammar of Arabic, but with second-order reflection on grammatical methodology and reasoning. It was not a mainstream discipline and is not mentioned in the major overviews of Islamic sciences by Ikfānī (d. 1348) Ṭāşköprīzāde (d. 1561), or Kātib Çelebī (d. 1657). There are only a few known contributions to the field prior to Shāwī, notably *Lumaʿ al-adilla* by Ibn al-Anbārī (d. 1181) and *al-Iqtirāḥ* by Jalāl al-Dīn al-Suyūṭī. Interestingly, Shāwī's work on *uṣūl al-naḥw* was copied by Jirmānus Farḥāt (d. 1732), one of the pioneering figures in the awakening of interest in Arabic language and literature among the Christians of Syria in the eighteenth and nineteenth centuries.[102] Farḥāt presumably became acquainted with the work through his Muslim teacher in Aleppo Sulaymān al-Naḥwī (d. 1728) who had studied with Shāwī.[103] Farḥāt's copy was in turn copied as late as 1869 by a Maronite scribe, suggesting a continued interest in Shāwī's work in Christian Arabic circles until the modern period.[104]

4. Muḥammad Ibn Sulaymān al-Rūdānī (d. 1683)[105]

100 Yaḥyā al-Shāwī, *al-Muḥākamāt bayna Abī Ḥayyān wa Ibn ʿAṭiyya wa-l-Zamakhsharī*, edited by M. ʿUthmān (Beirut: Dār al-Kutub al-ʿIlmiyya, 2009).

101 Yahyā al-Shāwī, *Irtiqāʾ al-siyāda fī uṣūl naḥw al-lugha al-ʿarabiyya*, edited by ʿA. al-Saʿdī (Damascus: Dār Saʿd al-Dīn, 2010). The editor's introduction includes a helpful overview of the field of *ūṣūl al-naḥw*.

102 On Jirmānus Farḥāt, see K. Brustad, "Jirmānus Jibrīl Farḥāt," in *EALB, 1350–1850*, 242–251 and I. Kratschkowsky, "Farḥāt, Djarmānus," *EI2*, II, 795.

103 Murādī, *Silk al-durar*, II, 158–159.

104 See Shāwī, *Irtiqāʾ al-siyāda*, 158–159 (fn. 3). This late manuscript is one of the three used by the editor to establish the text of the printed edition (Manuscript ي).

105 The main sources for his life are Muḥibbī, *Khulāṣat al-athar*, IV, 204–208; ʿAyyāshī, *Riḥla*, II, 81–101; ʿAlī b. Tāj al-Dīn al-Sinjārī, *Manāʾiḥ al-karam fī akhbār Makka wa-l-bayt wa wulāt al-ḥaram*, edited by Mājida Fayṣal Zakariyyā (Mecca: Jāmiʿat Umm al-Qurā, 1998), IV, 510–521; Muṣṭafā b. Fatḥullāh al-Ḥamawī, *Fawāʾid al-irtiḥāl wa-natāʾij al-safar fī akhbār al-qarn al-ḥādī ʿashar*, edited by ʿAbdullāh al-Kandarī (Damascus, Beirut and Kuwait: Dār al-Nawādir, 2011) II, 84–97. A modern study by a Moroccan scholar is Muṣṭafā al-Maslūtī, *Muḥammad b. Sulaymān al-Rūdānī: Ḥakīm*

Rūdānī was born in the town of Taroudant in southern Morocco in 1629 or 1630.[106] He went in his youth to al-Zāwiya al-Nāṣiriyya, where he stayed for four years, studying a range of disciplines with Ibn Nāṣir. He then spent time in Marrakesh, the Zāwiya Dilā'iyya, and Fes, studying with scholars such as the theologian 'Īsā al-Sugtānī, the chronologist Muḥammad b. Sa'īd al-Mirightī, and the grammarian Muḥammad al-Murābiṭ al-Dilā'ī.[107] He is reported to have been particularly eager to find teachers who were proficient in "the philosophical sciences: astronomy, astrology, mathematics and logic." His search eventually led him in the early 1650s to Algiers, where he studied with the logician Sa'īd Qaddūra. He then went to Istanbul by sea and from there to Egypt, before settling in the Hejaz. Already in his brief sojourns in Istanbul and Cairo he showed himself to be a somewhat inflexible purist. He reportedly argued with an unnamed Turkish jurist against the permissibility of coffee and tobacco. In Rūdānī's own words: "I had then just finished my studies and had mastered a good deal of jurisprudence and logic, so he did not bring forth an argument except that God permitted me to refute it until I defeated him."[108] In Egypt, he asked for a juridical verdict (*fatwā*) from

al-Islām wa mafkharat al-Maghrib (Rabat: Markaz al-dirāsāt wa-l-abḥāth wa-iḥyā' al-turāth, 2010). This is a useful compendium of information but hagiographic in tone and poor on analysis.

106 Ḥamawī, who studied with Rudānī, wrote that he had seen a note in Rūdānī's own hand stating that his father had told him that he was born in 1039/1629–1630; see his *Fawā'id al-irtiḥāl*, II, 84. The date of birth given in the modern printing of Muḥibbī's *Khulāṣat al-athar* (IV, 204) and reiterated by most secondary sources – 1037/1627–1628 – seems to be a mistake caused by a common confusion of "9" (تسع) with "7" (سبع) in manuscript sources. Ḥamawī took care to distinguish the two numerals (*bi-taqdīm al-tā'*). Sinjārī, who also received a certificate from Rūdānī, gave his date of birth as 1033/1623–1624 (*Manā'iḥ al-karam*, IV, 512).

107 These are the scholars he mentioned in his own record of studies and certificates (see Rūdānī, *Ṣilat al-khalaf bi-Mawṣūl al-Salaf*, edited by Muḥammad al-Ḥajjī (Beirut: Dār al-Gharb al-Islāmī, 1988), 453, 464, 465, 468). 'Ayyāshī also mentioned as one of Rūdānī's teachers al-Ḥakīm Aḥmad al-Murīd al-Marrākushī (*Riḥla*, II, 82), but this scholar reportedly died in 1048/1638–1639 when Rūdānī was not yet ten years old, see Muḥammad al-Ṣaghīr al-Ifrānī, *Safwat man intashara fī akhbār ṣulaḥā' al-qarn al-ḥādī 'ashar*, edited by 'Abd al-Majīd Khayālī (Casablanca: Markaz al-turāth al-thaqāfī al-Maghribī, 2004), 203–204. Curiously, there are no reports of Rūdānī having studied with the two most prominent astronomers in Morocco in his time: Aḥmad al-Walatī (d. 1651) in Marrakesh and Muḥammad al-Ṣabbāgh al-'Uqaylī (d. 1665) in Fes, even though he must have had an opportunity to do so. On Walatī and 'Uqaylī, see Ifrānī, *Safwat man intashara*, 282–283 and 259. Interestingly, the latter of these two scholars also seems to have combined expertise in the astronomical and mathematical sciences with a puritan streak – he wrote one work that to judge from its title is aimed at reprehensible "innovations" (*bida'*) in the city of Fes.

108 'Ayyāshī, *Riḥla*, II, 84.

the prominent and aging Maliki jurist ʿAlī al-Ujhūrī (d. 1656) concerning the woolen clothes imported from Europe and "worn by most scholars in Egypt, Cairo, Syria and the Hejaz." Rūdānī held such clothes to be ritually impure (*najis*) because they were made of wool shorn from living sheep, and he refused to concede Ujhūrī's response that they were permissible if for no other reason than that they were so widely worn and had become a general necessity (*li-ʿumūm al-balwā bihi*).[109] Once settled in the Hejaz, Rūdānī for pious reasons insisted on living by his own means, instead of – as most of the scholars of his age – receiving possibly tainted money from pious foundations established by rulers and notables. He earned a living by crafting astronomical instruments, metal- and glassware, and bookbinding.[110]

It is important to point out that Rūdānī's purism did not imply that he frowned upon the study of the rational sciences or was opposed to Sufism. He had received various forms of initiation from a number of masters of the Shādhilī order and recorded these in his record of studies and certificates.[111] He was also a prominent teacher of logic and especially astronomy in the Hejaz. The local scholar Aḥmad Ibn Tāj al-Dīn (d. 1670) studied with Rūdānī and went on to become the time-keeper of the Prophet's Mosque in Medina and a prominent scholar in the fields of astronomy, astrology, logic, mathematics, and the occult sciences.[112] It was incidentally Rūdānī who had posed the problem in logic that had caused such difficulty to the Indo-Muslim scholar Badr al-Dīn and led to a breakdown in relations between Badr al-Dīn and ʿĪsā al-Thaʿālibī. Badr al-Dīn's charge of collusion between Rūdānī and Thaʿālibī may or may not be true, but it is clear that the two Maghrebī scholars had studied in very similar milieus and using the same handbooks on logic (the works of Sanūsī and the standard Maghrebī commentaries on Khūnajī's *Jumal*).[113]

The Morrocan traveler ʿAyyāshī met Rūdānī in Medina in the years 1662–1664. He noted Rūdānī's intimate knowledge of astronomy, chronology, and astronomical instrumentation and added that Rūdānī, despite this expertise, did not engage in astrological predictions "out of

[109] Ibid., 84–85.
[110] Ibid., 91–92.
[111] See Rūdānī, *Ṣilat al-khalaf*, 466–476.
[112] Muḥibbī, *Khulāṣat al-athar*, I, 178–179.
[113] The works on logic mentioned by Rūdānī in his record of studies are those by Sanūsī and the North African commentators on Khūnajī's *Jumal*, more or less corresponding to the works studied by Thaʿālibī. See Rūdānī, *Ṣilat al-khalaf*, 181, 279.

piety."[114] ʿAyyāshī was particularly enthusiastic about a spherical astrolabe that Rūdānī had made:

One of the most subtle and precise of his innovative creations is the comprehensive instrument in the arts of chronology and astronomy. No one had preceded him in this; rather he thought it up himself with his superior mind and skilled craft. It is a spherical astronomical instrument smoothly polished... To the onlooker it looks like an egg made of gold due to its luminosity, overdrawn with circles and figures. Over this has been constructed another [instrument] that is hollow and divided into two halves with holes and perforations for the figures of the zodiac. This is spherical like the one underneath it, polished and dyed green... It makes unnecessary any other instrument in the art of chronology and astronomy while being easy to use since things on it are sensed and the imaginary astronomical circles and the cross-sections between them are seen. It can be used in all countries regardless of their longitude or latitude.[115]

ʿAyyāshī added that Rūdānī made copies of this instrument himself, selling them to interested buyers.

The Damascene biographer and belletrist Muḥibbī also mentioned this astronomical instrument in his obituary of Rūdānī, writing: "He invented (*ikhtaraʿa*) a great astronomical sphere (*kura*) that was superior to old spheres and astrolabes and that spread throughout the Hejaz, the Yemen and India."[116] Rūdānī's astrolabe also gained renown in Morocco. ʿAyyāshī brought one back with him and it was later used to confirm that the prayer-niche of the Zāwiya ʿAyyāshiyya was indeed facing the proper direction.[117]

Neither ʿAyyāshī nor Muḥibbī were astronomers and their enthusiastic appraisals cannot without further ado be taken at face value. The most detailed examination of Rūdānī's spherical astrolabe by a modern specialist concludes that the instrument was not a radical innovation and was continuous with the earlier Arabic-Islamic tradition of spherical astrolabes, but also that it included a modification that is not attested in earlier instruments and that significantly facilitated its use, specifically having two external rotating caps instead of the standard one.[118]

Despite his reputation as a teacher of logic and astronomy, Rūdānī was also esteemed as a scholar of hadith. One of his major works is

[114] ʿAyyāshī, *Riḥla*, II, 97.

[115] Ibid., 92.

[116] Muḥibbī, *Khulāṣat al-athar*, IV, 206 (ll. 3–4).

[117] See the introduction of Mohamed Zahi to his edition of ʿAyyāshī's *Itḥāf al-akhillā*ʾ, 15.

[118] Louis Janin, "Un texte d'ar-Rudani sur l'astrolabe sphérique," *Annali dell'Istituto e Museo di Storia della Scienza di Firenze* 3(1978), 71–75, esp. 72–73.

a voluminous topical collation of hadith recognized by Sunni Muslims, based on two earlier partial collections.[119] Rūdānī, described in a near-contemporary source as "the hadith-scholar of the Hejaz" (*muḥaddith al-Ḥijāz*), counted among his students ʿAbdullāh b. Sālim al-Baṣrī (d. 1722), who in turn would go on to become a prominent hadith scholar. Baṣrī's son related that his father had been initiated into the Shādhilī order by Rūdānī and had studied "all of the sciences" with him, "especially the science of hadith."[120] Baṣrī has been seen by some modern historians as foreshadowing an eighteenth-century reinvigoration of the study of hadith that was centered in Mecca and Medina and closely connected with "revivalist" tendencies.[121] The matter has yet to be studied thoroughly, but there is reason to qualify this thesis as it stands. There was clearly a great deal of interest in hadith in the Hejaz already in the mid-seventeenth century: both Thaʿālibī and Rūdānī are said to have developed their strong interest *after* settling there, and the same is related of their Kurdish-born contemporary Ibrāhīm Kūrānī.[122] The keen study of hadith in the Hejaz should therefore not be seen as a novel eighteenth-century phenomenon. It also should not automatically be equated with "reformist" or "revivalist" tendencies; it engaged scholars of different temperaments and inclinations. If Rūdānī was something of a contrarian purist, Thaʿālibī was explicitly described by ʿAyyāshī as the opposite: affable, sociable, and thinking well of all varieties of Sufis to such an extent that he was sometimes blamed for this.[123] Such an inclination did not

[119] Rūdānī, *Jamʿ al-fawāʾid min Jāmiʿ al-uṣūl wa Majmaʿ al-zawāʾid* (Medina: Maṭbaʿat al-Sayyid ʿAbdullāh Hāshim al-Yamanī, 1961) and (Kuwait and Beirut: Maktabat Ibn Kathīr and Dār Ibn Ḥazm, 1998). The two collections synthesized by Rūdānī are *Jāmiʿ al-uṣūl* by Majd al-Dīn Ibn al-Athīr (d. 1210) and *Majmaʿ al-zawāʾid* by Nūr al-Dīn al-Haythamī (d. 1405).

[120] Sālim b. ʿAbdullāh al-Baṣrī, *al-Imdād bi-maʿrifat ʿuluw al-isnād* (Hyderabad, Deccan: Maṭbaʿat Majlis Dāʾirat al-Maʿārif, 1328/1910), 68.

[121] J. Voll, "ʿAbdullāh ibn Sālim al-Baṣrī and 18th century Hadith Scholarship," *Die Welt des Islams* 42(2002): 356–372.

[122] For example, ʿAyyāshī wrote of Thaʿālibī "His desire to serve the noble hadith was reinforced [after settling in Mecca] and he had hitherto been one of those who were abstentious in this field" (*Riḥla,* II, 170). ʿAyyāshī also wrote that Kūrānī had been thoroughly trained in all sciences before settling in Medina except Sufism and hadith, and that he said that before coming to the countries of the Arabs (*bilād al-ʿarab*) he had not suspected that there were still people who said "It has been related to us . . . ,"; see *Riḥla,* II, 384. Ḥamawī's account suggests that Rūdānī developed an interest in hadith and began to collect relevant books after he started teaching in Mecca, see Ḥamawī, *Fawāʾid,* II, 93 (ll. 2–7).

[123] ʿAyyāshī, *Riḥla,* II, 89 (contrast between the retiring Rūdānī and the sociable Thaʿālibī), and II, 168 (Thaʿālibī's tendency to think well of Sufis of all stripes "and sometimes he would be blamed for this").

prevent Tha'ālibī from keenly engaging in the practice of listening to and relating hadith after settling in Mecca. Such activities may – sometimes at any rate – have indicated nothing more than a pious practice thought to be particularly appropriate to sojourning in Mecca and Medina. It might also be added that 'Ayyāshī's reports of Rūdānī's arguments concerning tobacco, coffee, and woolen clothes make no mention of Rūdānī arguing on the basis of hadith (and given the novelty of the disputed items it is difficult to see how he could have). Rather, he is portrayed as arguing rationally, using jurisprudence and logic and engaging in what 'Ayyāshī – who did not share Rūdānī's purism – thought was "oversubtle reasoning" (*tadqīqāt 'aqliyya*) that was out of place in law and could only lead to obsessive scruples (*waswasa*).

A few years after 'Ayyāshī returned to Morocco in 1664, Rūdānī moved from Medina to Mecca, apparently at the suggestion of the charismatic Sufi 'Abd al-Raḥmān al-Miknāsī (d. 1675), who was an enthusiastic admirer of Ibn 'Arabī and himself of North African origin.[124] In November 1668, the two North Africans started a soup kitchen for the poor of Mecca. In April 1669, Rūdānī set up a new sundial (*mizwala*) of his own making in the Holy Mosque.[125]

In 1670, Köprülü Fāżıl Muṣṭafā Pāşā, the younger brother of the famed Ottoman Grand Vizier Fāżıl Aḥmed Pāşā (v. 1661–1676), made the pilgrimage to Mecca. Reportedly interested in astronomy, Fāżıl Muṣṭafā met Rūdānī, was impressed with his command of the field, and asked him to travel back with him to Istanbul.[126] They traveled via Damascus and were accompanied on the trip by a number of Damascene scholars. One of these, 'Abd al-Qādir Ibn 'Abd al-Hādī (d. 1688), described Rūdānī in the following terms:

> His knowledge of hadith and *uṣūl* [again, theology or jurisprudence or both] is unequalled by anyone we have met. As for the science of belles-lettres (*adab*), he is the ultimate authority. In the philosophical sciences – logic, physics, and metaphysics – he was the teacher whose knowledge could not be acquired through natural means. And he was proficient in the sciences of mathematics: Euclid, astronomy, geometry, Almagest, calculus, algebra, arithmetic, cartography, harmony, and geodesy. His knowledge of these fields was unique, other scholars knowing only the preliminaries of these sciences rather than the advanced

[124] Sinjārī, *Manā'iḥ al-karam*, IV, 283–285. On Miknāsī, see Muḥibbī, *Khulāṣat al-athar*, II, 346–349.

[125] Sinjārī, *Manā'iḥ al-karam*, IV, 288.

[126] 'Abd al-Malik al-'Iṣāmī, *Simṭ al-nujūm al-'awālī fī anbā' al-awā'il wa-l-tawālī* (Cairo: al-Maṭba'a al-Salafiyya, 1960–1961), IV, 524.

issues ... In the occult sciences such as divination, magic squares, numerology and alchemy he was skilled to the utmost.[127]

The Grand Vizier also seems to have been impressed with Rūdānī and bestowed upon him the status of Supervisor of the religious endowments of Mecca and Medina. Rūdānī used his position to enact a number of controversial measures, including some that were of a markedly puritan nature and reminiscent of the attempted Ḳāḍīzādelī reforms in Istanbul at the time, such as banning musical instruments and women from popular religious festivals.[128] ʿAyyāshī had in 1662–1664 described Rūdānī as a retiring figure in Medina, only giving lessons at home to a select few. After his return from Istanbul he seems to have led a more public life in Mecca and attracted scores of students whom he taught subjects such as hadith, jurisprudence, *kalām*, grammar, and semantics-rhetoric.[129]

In 1682, after the death of the local ruler al-Sharīf Barakāt (whom he had helped accede to power ten years earlier), he was exiled from the Hejaz and went to Damascus. The biographer Muḥibbī recounted that he used to visit Rūdānī there along with the Ottoman court astrologer, polymath, and historian Müneccimbāşī.[130] It was in Damascus that Rūdānī completed his aforementioned compilation of hadith entitled *Jamʿ al-fawāʾid min Jāmiʿ al-uṣūl wa Majmaʿ al-zawāʾid*. He died shortly thereafter, on October 31, 1683.

Rūdānī's other works include

a. *Ṣilat al-khalaf bi-mawṣūl al-salaf*, an extensive record of the various chains of certifications he had received for relating a large number of scholarly works in especially the traditional sciences[131]
b. A treatise on the astrolabe entitled *Bahjat al-ṭullāb fī l-ʿamal bi l-asṭurlāb*[132]

127 Muḥibbī, *Khulāṣat al-athar*, IV, 207.
128 ʿIṣāmī, *Ṣimṭ al-nujūm al-ʿawālī*, IV, 525.
129 See Ḥamawī, *Fawāʾid al-irtiḥāl*, II, 93. Rūdānī's works that Ḥamawī mentions as having been written in this period presumably reflect his teaching: an epitome of *Talkhīṣ al-Miftāḥ* with commentary (on semantics-rhetoric) and glosses on *Tashīl al-fawāʾid* and on *Sharḥ al-Tawḍīḥ* (both on grammar). Ḥamawī studied with Rūdānī hadith and *Sharḥ al-Musāyara* by Ibn Abī l-Sharīf al-Maqdisī (d. 1500) (on *kalām*); see *Fawāʾid*, II, 97. Muḥibbī also attributed to Rūdānī an epitome with commentary of *al-Taḥrīr*, a handbook on jurisprudence by the Ḥanafī scholar Ibn al-Humām (d. 1457) that was also acceptable to Shāfiʿīs and Mālikīs.
130 Muḥibbī, *Khulāṣat al-athar*, IV, 205 (ll. 20ff).
131 Edited by Muḥammad Ḥajjī (Beirut: Dār al-Gharb al-Islāmī, 1988).
132 Mach, *Catalogue*, nr. 4950.

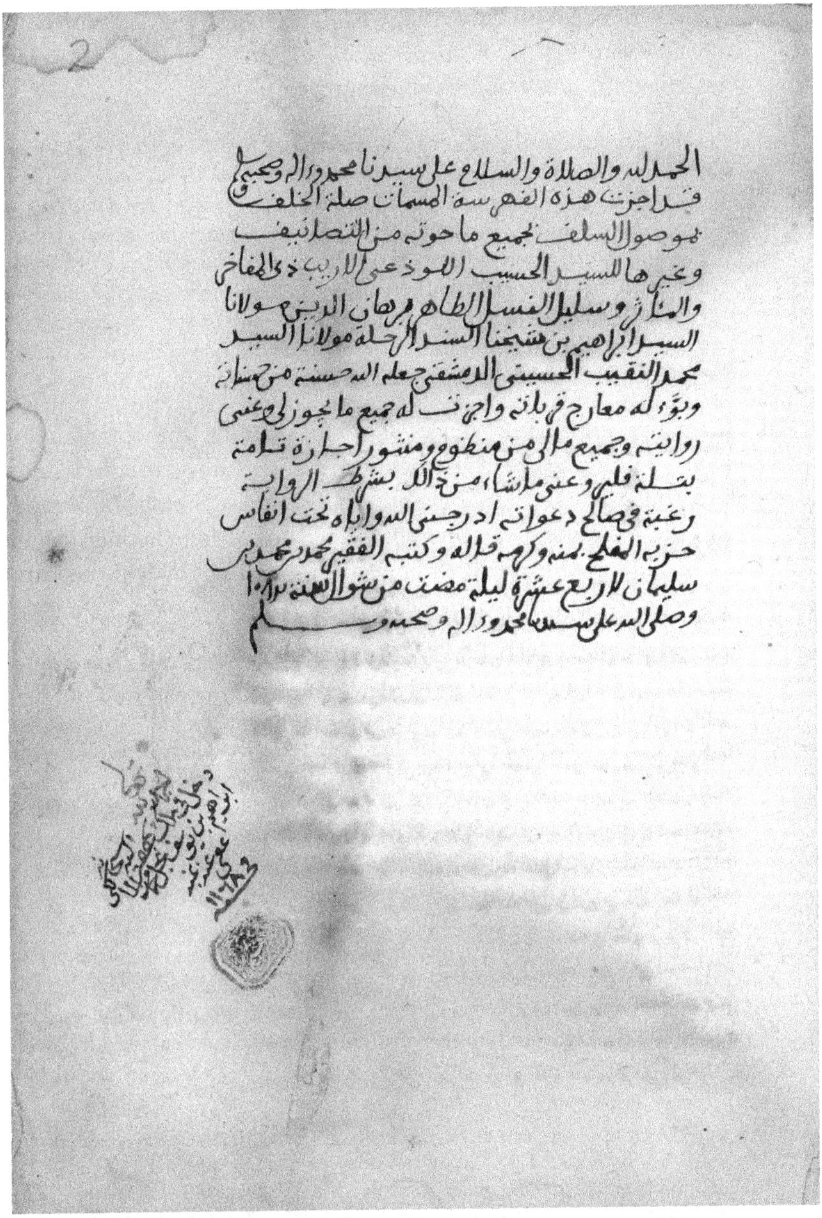
الحمد لله والصلاة والسلام على سيدنا محمد وآله وصحبه و
قد أجزت هذه الفهرسة المسماة صلة الخلف
بموصول السلف بجميع ما حوته من التصانيف
وغيرها للسيد الحسيب اللوذعي الأريب ذي المفاخر
والمآثر وسليل النسل الطاهر برهان الدين مولانا
السيد ابراهيم بن شيخنا السند الرحلة مولانا السيد
محمد النقيب الحسيني الدمشقي جعله الله حسنة من حسناته
وبوأه له معارج في بابه وأجزت له جميع ما يجوز لي وعني
روايته وجميع ما لي من منظوم ومنثور اجازة تامة
بتلقه قلبي وعني ما شاء من ذلك بشرطه الرواية
ورغبة في صالح دعواته أدرجني الله وإياه تحت أنفاس
حزب المفلح بمنه وكرمه قاله وكتبه الفقير محمد بن محمد بن
سليمان لأربع عشرة ليلة مضت من شوال سنة ١٠٨٣
وصلى الله على سيدنا محمد وآله وصحبه وسلم

FIGURE 4.2 Autograph certificate by Muḥammad al-Rūdānī (d. 1683), dated 1083/1673, to the Damascene scholar Ibrāhīm Ibn al-Naqīb al-Ḥusaynī (d. 1708). (Muḥammad al-Rūdānī, *Ṣilat al-khalaf bi-mawṣūl al-salaf*, fol. 2b. Islamic Manuscripts, Garrett 173B. Manuscripts Division, Department of Rare Books and Manuscripts, Princeton University Library. Reproduced with permission.)

c. A didactic poem on chronology (*ʿilm al-mīqāt*) with a prose commentary entitled *Maqāṣid al-ʿawālī bi-qalāʾid al-laʾālī*. ʿAyyāshī described the work in the following terms:

> He had a poem in the science of chronology which is longer than the *Rawḍa* [a didactic poem on chronology by ʿAbd al-Raḥmān al-Jādirī (fl. 1392), widely studied in the Maghreb]. He went to great lengths to craft this poem and presented the science with a great deal of exactitude. He went against many other authors in the field on a number of issues whose truth he made clear with proof and demonstration. He facilitated the use of it [the science of chronology] by means of rules and principles based on the correct astronomical observations in these late times such as the observations of Sultan Ulugh Beg [d. 1449 in Samarqand].[133]

d. A treatise, entitled *al-Nāfiʿa ʿalā l-āla al-jāmiʿa* and completed in 1661, describing the aforementioned spherical astrolabe that he had constructed.[134] Its purpose was to assist users who already had the instrument; it apparently does not include enough details to enable the instrument to be reconstructed now.[135] In the introduction, Rūdānī wrote:

> It is among the countless overflowing gifts of God... that He has inspired me to make an instrument from which benefit may be derived – if He so wills – in the sciences of astronomy and chronology by lowly people such as myself, and which gathers together what is dispersed in all chronological instruments... The one who has thorough knowledge of it has no need to resort to the *Almagest* for proof and demonstrations, since what is contained there [i.e. in the *Almagest*] is unseen (*ghayb*) whereas it [Rūdānī's instrument] is visible evidence (*shahāda*), and "an account is not like seeing for oneself." Furthermore, God Most High has opened up my breast to write this hurried piece about it... in order to bring out what it contains of useful lessons. Since it is my hope of the Most Generous that it will prove beneficial, I have entitled it "The Beneficial on the Comprehensive Instrument." It is God who suffices me, there is no other God but He, upon Him do I rely, and it is toward Him that I face repentantly wherever I turn...[136]

133 ʿAyyāshī, *Riḥla,* II, 97–98. For an extant manuscript, see Mach, *Catalogue*, nr. 5017.

134 The work has been edited by Ch. Pellat in his "al-Nāqiʿa ʿalā al-āla al-jāmiʿa li-l-Rūdānī," *Bulletin d'études orientales* 26(1973): 7–82. Pellat also translated the treatise into French in his "L'astrolabe sphérique d'ar-Rūdānī," *Bulletin d'Études Orientales* 28(1975): 83–165. Pellat mistook the title of the treatise on the basis of the single manuscript that he used. Further manuscripts of the work explored by Muḥammad Ḥajjī (see the introduction to his edition of Rūdānī, *Ṣilat al-khalaf*, 13 fn.9) give the title *al-Nāfiʿa ʿalā l-āla al-jāmiʿa* as does ʿAyyāshī, *Riḥla,* II, 93.

135 Janin, "Un texte d'ar-Rudani," 74.

136 Pellat, "al-Nāqiʿa ʿalā al-āla al-jāmiʿa li-l-Rūdānī," 80 (journal pagination), 3 (treatise pagination). The introduction is also given in ʿAyyāshī, *Riḥla,* II, 93.

It may be tempting to see in Rūdānī's emphasis on direct perception, as opposed to the rational proofs afforded by theoretical works on astronomy, an indication of "empiricism." But such an assessment based on a single passing passage would be premature. Whether there is a consistent and unusual image of science and scientific method in Rūdānī's astronomical works is a question that requires further study.

A noticeable aspect of the passage is the pious language of self-effacement and the appeal to the notions of divine "inspiration" (*ilhām*) and "opening up the breast" (*fatḥ*) in a work on astronomy. This rhetoric is not unusual for Maghrebī scholars of the time, but it is far less common in the works of Rūdānī's contemporary Ottoman or Iranian specialists in the rational sciences. The introduction to the widely studied treatise of the Azeri scholar Meḥmed Emīn Ṣadrüddīnzāde (d. 1627) on what makes the numerous enquiries of logic one discipline (mentioned in Chapter 3), strikes a distinctly self-aggrandizing note, the author making it clear to the reader that he has mastered all relevant issues and is divulging subtle and noble thoughts with which neither other humans nor jinn are familiar.[137] Even in the works of seventeenth-century Safavid scholars influenced by Neo-Platonic Illuminationist philosophy, the rhetoric of divine inspiration and illumination is often qualified by references to the author's own wide readings or powers of reasoning, the suggestion being that God's munificence is mediated by such factors, and the rhetoric of self-denigration is accordingly toned down.[138] By contrast, a commitment to Ashʿarī occasionalism (the view that only God has causal powers) and Shādhilī Sufism seems to have made Maghrebī scholars more inclined toward rhetorically emphasizing that God's assistance is not mediated or earned. They would have emphasized that, to modify an adage from Nietzsche, "a thought comes when He wants, not when I want."[139] Rūdānī struck this note when recounting how he began, at the invitation of a Sufi master in Tadla, to teach younger students when he himself was merely an older student who had not finished his education:

137 Meḥmed Emīn Ṣadrüddīnzāde, *Risālat Jihat al-waḥda* (Istanbul: Maṭbaʿah-yi Ḥāci Muḥarrem Bōsnavī, 1288/1871), 2–3.

138 See the prefaces to Mīr Dāmād, *al-Qabasāt*, ed. M. Mohaghegh (Tehran: Tehran University Publications, 1988), 1–2, and to Mullā Ṣadrā, *al-Shawāhid al-rubūbiyya*, in *Majmāʿah-i Rasāʾil-i falsafī-yi Sadr al-Mutaʾallihīn*, ed. Ḥ. N. Isfahānī (Tehran: Ḥikmat, 1996), 283–284.

139 Nietzsche, *Beyond Good and Evil*, §17: "a thought comes when 'it' wants, not when 'I' want" (translated by R. J. Hollingdale).

He said to me: Sit with us and teach any work that you choose in any discipline and we ask of God Most High to open up your breast (*an yaftaḥa ʿalayka*). So I sat down and taught a number of works that I had studied. If I hesitated on any point I would feel ideas (*maʿānin*) being cast into my heart as if they were tangible bodies (*kaʾannahā ajrām*), and most of these ideas were those that our teachers had expounded to us without our understanding them, and I had not remembered them before then.[140]

It is worth noticing that Rūdānī said that "most" (and by implication not "all") of the ideas that had been cast into his heart were those he had heard from his teachers. As seen in the case of his invented astrolabe and work on chronology, the rhetoric of self-effacement and divine inspiration could easily go hand in hand with a critical and independent-minded scholarly attitude.

The End of an Era

There is some reason to believe that the efflorescence of the rational sciences in Morocco slowly came to an end in the course of the eighteenth century, partly as a consequence of the political turmoil and economic retrenchment that followed the death of the powerful Mawlāy Ismāʿīl in 1727, and partly as the result of a deliberate policy of favoring the traditional sciences adopted by Sīdī Muḥammad III (r. 1757–1790).[141] The study of the rational sciences survived, to be sure, but the Moroccan logical works that were written in the nineteenth century seem to have consisted of commentaries and glosses on relatively introductory handbooks such as Akhḍarī's *Sullam* and another didactic poem entitled *al-Kharīda* by Ḥamdūn Ibn al-Ḥājj (d. 1817).[142] These handbooks

[140] Rūdānī, *Ṣilat al-khalaf*, 467.

[141] On the religious policy of Muḥammad III, see F. Harrak, "State and Religion in Eighteenth Century Morocco: The Religious Policy of Sidi Muḥammad b. ʿAbd Allāh, 1757–1790" (PhD thesis, University of London: School of Oriental and African Studies, 1989), 298ff. On Sultan Muḥammad's attempt at banning logic and *kalām* from the curricula of the schools, see ibid., p. 347 and pp. 352–354. The Sultan approved of mathematics and astronomy as religiously useful (p. 347).

[142] Works that I have seen from this period include the commentaries of Ibn Kīrān (d. 1812) and Muḥammad b. Ḥamdūn Ibn al-Ḥājj (d. 1858) on *al-Kharīda;* lithographed together in Fes in 1329/1911, and the gloss of ʿAlī Qaṣṣāra (d. 1843) on a commentary on Akhḍarī's *Sullam* by Muḥammad b. al-Ḥasan al-Bannānī (d. 1780), lithographed together with Bannānī's commentary in Fes in 1300/1883. Further glosses on Bannānī's commentary on Akhḍarī's *Sullam* were written by Muḥammad b. Manṣūr al-Shafshāwunī (d. 1816) and Muḥammad al-Mahdī Ibn Sūda (d. 1877); see Muḥammad Makhlūf, *Shajarat al-nūr al-zakiyya,* II, 381, 434. Muḥammad Aqaṣbī

are noticeably less demanding than Sanūsī's *Mukhtaṣar* and Khūnajī's *Jumal* that had elicited commentaries and glosses by earlier scholars such as Yūsī, Ibn Ya'qūb, and Hashtūkī.[143] There is also no indication that nineteenth-century Moroccan logicians had any influence in more eastern regions. On the contrary, in the early decades of the nineteenth century, the works of the Egyptian scholar Ḥasan al-'Aṭṭār, an advocate of the Indo-Muslim and Ottoman traditions of the rational sciences, began to elicit interest in Morocco.[144] The works of Persianate logicians such as Dawānī, 'Iṣām al-Dīn Isfarāyinī, and Khabīṣī also became familiar to Maghrebī scholars in the course of the eighteenth century.[145] The current of influence – at least in the rational sciences – seems again to have started to flow from east to west. Nevertheless, this should not obscure the fact

al-Fāsī (d. 1834) wrote an extant supergloss on the gloss of Sa'īd Qaddūra on Akhḍarī's own commentary on the *Sullam*; see M. al-Khaṭṭāb, *Fahāris al-Khizāna al-Ḥasaniyya bi-l-qaṣr al-malakī bi-l-Rabāṭ* (Rabat: n.p., 1985), IV, 35 (nr. 59). Contrary to the supposition of C. Brockelmann (*GAL* II, 615 and Suppl. II, 706), who is followed by R. Wisnovsky ("The Nature and Scope of Arabic Philosophical Commentary," 190), the poem entitled *al-Qaṣīda al-Shamaqmaqiyya* by Ibn al-Wannān (d. 1773) is not a work on philosophy or logic but a sprawling eulogy of Sīdī Muḥammad III that commentators considered a work of "belles-lettres" (*adab*); see the lithograph of the work in Fes in 1895–1897 (in two volumes) with the commentary of Aḥmad b. Khālid al-Nāṣirī (d. 1897) entitled *Zahr al-afnān min ḥadīqat Ibn al-Wannān*. For an overview of the contents of the work, see Lakhder, *La vie littéraire au Maroc*, 239–240.

143 The last extant Moroccan glosses on Sanūsī's *Mukhtaṣar* that I have managed to find are by 'Umar b. 'Abdullāh al-Fāsī (d. 1773) and Muḥammad b. al-Ḥasan al-Bannānī, see Khaṭṭāb, *Fahāris al-Khizāna al-Ḥasaniyya*, IV, nr. 10 and nr. 44. The last commentary on Khūnajī's *Jumal* is the one by Ibn Ya'qūb, see Khaṭṭāb, *Fahāris al-Khizāna al-Ḥasaniyya*, IV, nr. 17. My claim is made on the basis of the evidence from C. Brockelmann, *GAL* (summarized by Wisnovsky "The Nature and Scope of Arabic Philosophical Commentary," 168) as well as the catalogs of some of the major manuscript collections in Morocco: Khaṭṭāb, *Fahāris al-Khizāna al-Ḥasaniyya*, IV, 11–61; Ṣāliḥ al-Tādilī and Sa'īd al-Murābiṭ (eds. and rev.), *E. Levi-Provencal: Fihris al-makhṭūṭāt al-'arabiyya al-maḥfūẓa fī l-khizāna al-'āmma bi-l-Rabāṭ, al-juz' 1* (Rabat: al-Khizāna al-'āmma li-l-kutub wa l-wathā'iq, 1997–1998); Ḥamīd Laḥmar, *al-Fihris al-waṣfī li-makhṭūṭāt khizānat al-zāwiya al-Ḥamziyya al-'Ayyāshiyya* (Rabat: Wizārat al-awqāf, 2009), III, 879–927; 'Abd al-Raḥmān al-Ḥurayshī, *al-Fihris al-mūjaz li-makhṭūṭāt mu'assasat 'Allāl al-Fāsī* (Rabat: Mu'assasat 'Allāl al-Fāsī, n.d.), II, 259–271; M. Manūnī, *Dalīl makhṭūṭāt Dār al-kutub al-Nāṣiriyya bi-Tamagrūt* (Rabat: Wizārat al-awqāf, 1985).

144 Peter Gran, *The Islamic Roots of Capitalism*, 148.

145 For example, the Tunisian scholar Ibn Sa'īd al-Ḥajarī (d. 1785) wrote a gloss on Khabīṣī's commentary on *Tahdhīb al-manṭiq* in which he replied to the criticisms raised against Dawānī's commentary by 'Iṣām al-Dīn Isfarāyīnī; see Ibn Sa'īd, *Ḥāshiya*, 3 (margin). I have not come across any references to Dawānī or 'Iṣām al-Dīn in the works of Yūsī, Ibn Ya'qūb and Hashtūkī.

that during a remarkable interlude, from the early seventeenth century to the early eighteenth, the roles were reversed and Maghrebī scholars – many of them having studied in Sufi lodges in the Berber mountains and valleys of central and southern Morocco – had been lionized as particularly excellent teachers of the rational sciences in the venerable cities of Cairo, Damascus, Mecca, and Medina.

5

The Condemnation of Imitation (*Taqlīd*)

In their seminal *Introduction à la théologie musulmane: Essai de théologie comparée* (1948), George Anawati and Louis Gardet made a number of claims about Islamic rational theology (*kalām*) that have remained influential ever since. The authors suggested, among other things, that whereas theology in medieval Christianity was an instrument to understand and deepen faith in the "mysteries" of the creed, the Islamic discipline of *kalām* was an apologetic and defensive discipline whose task was merely to defend a creed already established by revelation against heretics and infidels.[1] This basic and widely accepted thesis has led to a number of subsidiary claims. One such is that the method of *kalām* was "dialectical": it sought to demolish the positions of heretics and infidels rather than engage in more constructive reflection or theological system building. In the words of the eminent scholar of Islamic theology Josef van Ess:

> From the beginning Muslim theology had to think in the categories of defense and attack. There was no time for silent reflection about eternal truth; unequipped with systematic consistency, the *mutakallimūn* had to join battle against Jewish, Christian and Manichean intellectual skill... Sometimes, and especially in the later scholastic phase of *kalām*, one merely fought an enemy who had long since left the field; easy victories were won, and the decision of the moment was lost. And even when there was still an enemy the system showed serious shortcomings: in many cases the premises had no absolute or intrinsic value, but were taken from the adversary, good only for negative refutation, and not for positive deduction. Many of the arguments were made for momentary success; they proved that one was right, but not always that one had the complete truth. They were critical but

[1] L. Gardet and G. Anawati, *Introduction à la théologie musulmane: Essai de théologie compare* (Paris: J. Vrin, 1948), esp. 305–315, 329–330.

not constructive, valid but not formally valid; *kalām* means the triumph of the *argumentum ad hominem*.[2]

The supposed "dialectical" and "apologetic" nature of *kalām* also led scholars to ponder why the tradition survived after the thirteenth century when the need for apologia and polemic was believed to be less pressing. By that time, mainstream Sunni thought had emerged victorious in its struggle against both the Muʿtazilī school and the adherents of Aristotelian–Neo-Platonic philosophy (*falsafa*), and non-Muslims had become an unthreatening minority in the Middle East. As *kalām* works continued to be written for centuries after that date, Anawati and Gardet inferred that this later literature must have constituted a "fossilized conservatism" (*conservatisme figée*): the old arguments were still reiterated but against long-vanquished foes who were no longer in a position to offer any resistance.[3] There are echoes of this unflattering assessment of later *kalām* in the previous quotation from van Ess. There are also echoes of it in William Montgomery Watt's influential *Islamic Philosophy and Theology* (1st edition, 1962; 2nd edition, 1985); the entire period from 1250 to 1850 is there dismissed in a short chapter of seven pages entitled "The Stagnation of Philosophical Theology."[4]

The interpretation of Anawati and Gardet seems to rest mainly on the testimony of the eminent eleventh-century religious thinker al-Ghazālī, who grew increasingly lukewarm toward *kalām* in his later years, and of the fourteenth-century historian Ibn Khaldūn, who thought that *kalām* was not much needed in his own day because the old heresies had been defeated. Nevertheless, their interpretation extrapolates too readily from this evidence and does not do justice to considerable stretches of Islamic religious history. Richard Frank has pointed out that early Ashʿarī theologians considered the kind of rational reflection in which they were engaged to be not only apologetic but also a necessary part of having religious faith (*īmān*) in the full sense of the word.[5] As will be seen in the present chapter, the same is true of the later North African Ashʿarī tradition represented by the influential fifteenth-century theologian Muḥammad b. Yūsuf al-Sanūsī. For him, *kalām* is a demonstrative, not a dialectical science, and a

[2] J. van Ess, "The Logical Structure of Islamic Theology," in G. E. von Grünebaum (ed.), *Logic in Classical Islamic Culture* (Wiesbaden: Otto Harrassowitz, 1970), 24–25.

[3] Gardet and Anawati, *Introduction à la théologie musulmane*, 76–78.

[4] W. M. Watt, *Islamic Philosophy and Theology: An Extended Survey* (Edinburgh: Edinburgh University Press, 1985), 133–141.

[5] R. M. Frank, "Knowledge and *taqlīd*: the foundations of religious belief in classical Ashʿarism," *Journal of the American Oriental Society* 109(1989): 37–62.

mastery of its essentials is a religious duty incumbent on every adult and sane Muslim, regardless of the presence or absence of infidels and heretics. A nominal Muslim who has no inkling of *kalām*, Sanūsī declared, is at best a sinner who is neglecting a religious duty and at worst not strictly a believer at all. Such radical views on the necessity of mastering at least the basics of rational theology and thus going beyond "imitation" in creedal matters exerted a profound influence for centuries throughout the Maghreb, sometimes with explosive consequences. As was shown in the previous chapter, Sanūsī's works also came to be studied regularly in Egypt, Syria, and the Hejaz in the course of the seventeenth century. Perhaps more surprisingly, his works can be shown to have had an influence on Turkish scholars associated with the militant Ḳāḍīzādelī movement in seventeenth-century Istanbul.

Sanūsī on Imitation (*Taqlīd*)

The reputation of Sanūsī has suffered dramatically in the course of the twentieth century. There can be little doubt that his theological and logical works were widely studied from the fifteenth to the nineteenth century throughout Islamic Africa and even beyond. Carl Brockelmann has listed more than two dozen commentaries and glosses on Sanūsī's works from this period. He also listed premodern Turkish, Javanese, and Malay translations of his creeds.[6] As late as the second half of the nineteenth century and the early decades of the twentieth, it is clear that Sanūsī's works were still studied in the prestigious Azhar College in Cairo, being printed on several occasions by the scholarly printing presses of Cairo, often with the commentaries and glosses of prominent Egyptian religious scholars such as Ibrāhīm al-Bājūrī (d. 1860), Muḥammad ʿIllaysh (d. 1882), and Ismāʿīl al-Ḥāmidī (d. 1898).[7] Despite this historic influence, Sanūsī has elicited very little interest from Western scholars of Islam in the twentieth century. He is a striking example of just how dramatically the canon of Islamic religious thinkers has shifted in modern times. Up until the end of the nineteenth century, Sanūsī was arguably a much more influential and mainstream figure in Sunni Islam than the fourteenth-century Ḥanbalī purist Ibn Taymiyya. Today, Ibn Taymiyya is widely considered to have

6 C. Brockelmann, *GAL*, II, 323–326 and SII, 352–356.

7 Ibrāhīm al-Bājūrī, *Ḥāshiya ʿalā matn al-Sanūsiyya* (Būlāq: Dār al-Ṭibāʿa al-ʿāmira, 1283/1866); Muḥammad ʿIllaysh, *Hidāyat al-murīd li-ʿAqīdat ahl al-tawḥīd* (Cairo: Maṭbaʿat Muṣṭafā Efendī, 1306/1888); Ismāʿīl al-Ḥāmidī, *Ḥawāshin ʿalā Sharḥ al-Kubrā* (Cairo: Muṣṭafā al-Bābī al-Ḥalabī, 1936).

been a central figure in Islamic religious history, whereas Sanūsī is little known even to specialists in Arabic and Islamic studies and often confused with the nineteenth century founder of the Sanūsiyya Sufi order.[8]

This reversal of fortunes is presumably due in part to the aforementioned assumption that Sanūsī was a representative of "fossilized conservatism" with nothing remotely original to say. The very fact that his creeds were so popular has led to the claim that they were "vulgarizations."[9] Such an assessment is quite simply baffling; no one who is even cursorily familiar with Sanūsī's commentary on the Long Creed could dismiss it as a work of popularization. It deserves to be recognized as a major work in the Ashʿarī tradition and is quite original in certain respects – for example in its systematic use of syllogisms in arguing for the truth of the creed. It is true that Sanūsī also wrote shorter and more accessible creedal works. But it will emerge from the present chapter that he did so for a significant reason: He was convinced – as few other Sunni Islamic theologians were – that it is the individual duty of every Muslim to master the essentials of Ashʿarī theology, and he accordingly wrote creeds that he hoped could be understood by the common people.

Sanūsī's views on the nature and purpose of *kalām* are presented in the opening parts of his theological works, most extensively in his commentary on the Long Creed. He there began by affirming that the first duty of the believer is to engage in what he called *naẓar*. This *naẓar* is defined as "positing a known or ordering two or more knowns in such a manner that they yield a desired conclusion."[10] Sanūsī's wording suggests that he was thinking of logical inferences from known concepts or propositions to unknown concepts and propositions, and this is confirmed by his subsequent explication:

If these [knowns] lead to the knowledge of a singular entity then they are called a definition (*taʿrīf*) or explicative discourse (*qawl shāriḥ*). If they lead to an assent,

[8] There is not a single reference to Sanūsī and his widely studied works on *kalām* in J. R. Halverson's *Theology and Creed in Sunni Islam: The Muslim Brotherhood, Ashʿarism and Political Sunnism* (New York: Palgrave Macmillan, 2010), which deals among other things with what the author mistakenly assumes to have been the demise of *kalām* in Sunni Islam after Ghazālī. There is also not a single reference to Sanūsī in Tilman Nagel's *A History of Islamic Theology: From Muhammad to the Present* (Princeton, NJ: Markus Wiener Publishers, 2000).

[9] H. Bencheneb, "al-Sanūsī, Muḥammad b. Yūsuf," *EI2*, IX, 21a. Despite a tenuous grasp of the contents of Sanūsī's works, Bencheneb's article is well informed about Sanūsi's life, times, and influence and remains a helpful starting point for further research.

[10] Muḥammad b. Yūsuf al-Sanūsī, *ʿUmdat ahl al-tawfīq wa l-tasdīd fī sharḥ ʿAqīdat ahl al-tawḥīd* [=*Sharḥ al-Kubrā*] (Cairo: Maṭbaʿat Jarīdat al-Islām, 1316/1898), 4.

which is knowledge of a relation between one thing and another in the sense of affirmation or negation, then they are called argument (*ḥujja*) or proof (*dalīl*).[11]

Sanūsī's language here is suffused with terminology from the discipline of logic. One might compare Sanūsī's remarks here with his discussion of the nature and purpose of logic in his *Epitome* of logic:

Acquired knowledge that is sought is limited to two kinds: conception (*taṣawwur*) and assent (*taṣdīq*). The way leading to knowledge of unknowns from conceptions is definition (*ta'rīf*), and the way leading to unknowns from assents is argument (*ḥujja*)... Since the mind is not immune from error as it uses these two ways on its own, due to the frequency with which error appears in the guise of truth, there is need for firm rules that the mind knows primarily and with necessity... and these principles are what is called the science of logic.[12]

The idea that the first duty of a believer is to engage in logical inferences is related to the basic principle – accepted by almost all practitioners of *kalām* – that proper knowledge of God and of basic religious truths is not innate but has to be acquired. Such knowledge could be acquired either through imitation (*taqlīd*) of one's elders and peers or through independent reasoning, that is, *naẓar*. The prior option was for Sanūsī – and here again he was typical of the theologians – distinctly inferior to the latter. What is unusual about Sanūsī is the degree to which he disparaged *taqlīd*. In his Long Creed, he wrote:

The first duty incumbent before anything else on the person who reaches the age of maturity is to exercise his mind on what will lead him with certain demonstrations and clear proofs to knowledge of his Lord [...] and not to be satisfied with the lowly occupation of *taqlīd*, for this does not avail him on the Last Day according to many verifying scholars.[13]

In the introduction to his commentary on the Middle Creed, Sanūsī wrote:

We praise and thank Him for countless bounties, the most precious of which is what He – may He be exalted – has bestowed of the bounty of faith (*īmān*) and coming forth from the darkness and prison of *taqlīd* concerning the creed to the spacious light of correct reasoning (*al-anẓār al-ṣaḥīḥa*) that reveals the quintessence of certainty (*yaqīn*).[14]

11 Sanūsī, *Sharḥ al-Kubrā*, 4.

12 Muḥammad b. Yūsuf al-Sanūsī, *Sharḥ Mukhtaṣar al-manṭiq* (Cairo: No publisher, 1292/1875), 5, 4.

13 Sanūsī, *Sharḥ al-Kubrā*, 3, 11. The quotation is from the creed itself, as opposed to the commentary. The creed is marked off in the printed text with a ص.

14 Muḥammad b. Yūsuf al-Sanūsī, *Sharḥ al-Wusṭā* (Tunis: Maṭba'at al-Taqaddum al-Waṭaniyya, 1327/1909), 2.

In his commentary on the Short Creed, he wrote:

> Lowly imitation (*al-taqlīd al-radī'*) is at the root of the unbelief of the idolaters, who say "We found our fathers upon a faith-community, and we are following upon their traces." For this reason, the verifying scholars (*muḥaqqiqūn*) have said: Imitation in the tenets of the creed is not sufficient. One of the religious dignitaries said: There is no difference between an imitator being led and an animal being led.[15]

Sanūsī delineated three options within the Ash'arī school concerning *taqlīd* in creedal matters:[16]

1. It is a perfectly acceptable way to acquire religious faith. Those who go beyond the stage of imitation and acquire faith through inferential reasoning (*naẓar*) are doing something that is commendable but not strictly a duty. Sanūsī attributed this view to a minority of earlier scholars such as al-Qushayrī (d. 1074) and al-Ghazālī.
2. Reasoning is the individual duty of every adult and sane person and the believer who remains at the stage of *taqlīd* is a sinner who is shirking a religious duty.
3. Reasoning is a condition (*sharṭ*) for faith (*īmān*). A person who is nominally a Muslim but remains at the stage of *taqlīd* is not only a sinner but also an infidel in the eyes of God. Such a person remains a Muslim legally but – as with a hypocrite (*munāfiq*) who utters the profession of faith – this will be to no avail on the Day of Judgment.

Of these options, Sanūsī unequivocally rejected the first. The question of whether it is the second or third option that is correct he seems to have left open – his various statements are studiedly compatible with either position:

> It [*taqlīd*] is insufficient for salvation in the view of many verifying scholars...
>
> In sum, that which has been related by many mainstream Sunnis and verifiers among them is that *taqlīd* is not sufficient in matters of religious creed...
>
> This is a short compendium the understanding of which will raise – if God wills – the legally responsible person from the stage of *taqlīd*, concerning whose sufficiency for faith there is disagreement, to correct reasoning, concerning whose sufficiency there is a consensus...[17]

[15] Muḥammad b. Yūsuf al-Sanūsī, *Sharḥ Umm al-barāhīn* [=*Sharḥ al-Ṣughrā*] (Cairo: Maṭba'at al-Istiqāma, 1934), 82.

[16] Sanūsī, *Sharḥ al-Kubrā*, 12–13; Sanūsī, *Sharḥ al-Wusṭā*, 21ff; Sanūsī, *Sharḥ al-Ṣughrā*, 14–15.

[17] Sanūsī, *Sharḥ al-Kubrā*, 11, 13; Sanūsī, *Sharḥ al-Wusṭā*, 9.

In his commentary on the Short Creed, he expressed a guarded preference for the position that the imitator is not strictly speaking a believer at all:

> The true position indicated by the Quran and Sunna is to hold that correct reasoning is incumbent [i.e., not merely supererogatory] while hesitating concerning whether it is a condition for faith or not, and the more plausible position (*al-rājiḥ*) is that it is indeed a condition for faith.[18]

Regardless of whether *taqlīd* is a sin or outright unbelief, Sanūsī considered it to be the duty of the individual believer to engage in theological reasoning and thus go beyond merely imitating elders and peers. The believer should not, Sanūsī emphasized, rest content with firmness of conviction, for such firmness of conviction could be found equally among non-Muslims. Rather, one should know each tenet of the creed along with at least one demonstration of it.[19] Sanūsī used the term "demonstration" (*burhān*) in its technical sense in logic: a valid inference from proven or indubitable premises. As Sanūsī was well aware, Arabic logicians typically recognized that there are formally valid inferences that are not demonstrative: for example, a dialectical (*jadalī*) inference would consist of premises that are accepted by all parties in an argument, and a rhetorical (*khaṭābī*) inference would consist of premises that elicit emotional assent from listeners. Theology for Sanūsī must rest on demonstrative inferences: its premises must not just be emotionally congenial or accepted for the purposes of the argument at hand but be indubitable or proven.[20]

Sanūsī's view that nominal Muslims who are unable to give any rational justification for their beliefs are either sinners or infidels in the eyes of God was by no means a dramatic departure from earlier Ashʿarism. As shown by Richard Frank, early Ashʿarīs routinely extolled the necessity of "reasoning" (*naẓar* or *baḥth*) or "verification" (*taḥqīq*) in assenting to the fundamental tenets of the Islamic creed, as opposed to reliance on mere "imitation" (*taqlīd*).[21] The theologian Abū Isḥāq al-Isfarāyinī (d. 1027), for example, wrote:

> When a person believes this [i.e., the fundamental articles of faith], the literalists (*ahl al-ẓāhir*) say that he truly has faith (*īmān*): that he is one of those on whose

[18] Sanūsī, *Sharḥ al-Ṣughrā*, 15.

[19] Sanūsī, *Sharḥ al-Kubrā*, 31–32; Sanūsī, *Sharḥ al-Wusṭā*, 28; Sanūsī, *Sharḥ al-Ṣughrā*, 16 (citing Abū Bakr Ibn al-ʿArabī).

[20] Sanūsī, *Sharḥ al-Kubrā*, 11: *wa bi-l-jumlatī fa-l-muʿtamadu min hādhihi al-aqsāmi fī taṣḥīḥi al-ʿaqāʾidi l-dīniyyati l-qismu l-awwalu l-ladhī huwa l-burhān.*

[21] Frank, "Knowledge and taqlīd."

behalf the Prophet will intercede and that he will ultimately achieve paradise. The expert theologians (*ahl al-taḥqīq*), however, say that this is not the case until his belief (*iʿtiqād*) in what we have set forth becomes, as we have explained, a real knowing (*maʿrifa*) and he thus belong to the number of those who know (*al-ʿārifūn*) and be no longer counted among those who simply repeat the statements of others (*al-muqallidūn*).[22]

Sanūsī may not have been directly familiar with works by Abū Isḥāq, but he had no difficulty in citing later Ashʿarī works in support of his views about the nature and purpose of *kalām*, for example, works by Abū Bakr Ibn al-ʿArabī (d. 1148), a prominent North African Mālikī jurist and (sometimes critical) student of Ghazālī; Ibn Dihāq (d. 1219), a scholar and jurist active in Almohad Spain; Sharaf al-Dīn Ibn al-Tilimsānī (d. 1260), a theologian and jurist based in Cairo; and Ibn ʿArafa (d. 1401), a prominent Tunisian jurist, theologian, and logician.[23]

The accusation that the Ashʿarīs deny the "faith of the imitator" (*īmān al-muqallid*) had repeatedly been raised by a number of opponents, ranging from conservative jurists of the Ḥanafī school in eleventh-century Khorasan to the Andalusian philosopher Averroes (d. 1198).[24] Some Ashʿarīs, such as Ghazālī and Fakhr al-Dīn al-Rāzī (d. 1210), rejected the charge and stated that an imitator is neither a sinner nor an infidel, and that engaging in rational theology is commendable but not an individual duty incumbent on each and every legally responsible Muslim.[25] Others tried to argue that the claim is not as radical as it may seem. Ghazālī's eminent teacher Imām al-Ḥaramayn al-Juwaynī (d. 1085), for example, opined that a Muslim who neglects familiarizing himself with *kalām* could be said to be a sinner or infidel only if he had the potential

[22] Ibid., 48–49. I have slightly modified Frank's translation. For the Arabic text, see R. M. Frank, "Al-Ustādh Abū Isḥāḳ: An ʿ*Aḳīda* together with selected fragments," *Mélanges de l'Institut Dominicain d'Études Orientales* 19(1989): 129–202, at 135.

[23] Sanūsī, *Sharḥ al-Ṣughrā*, 15–17 (reference to Abū Bakr Ibn al-ʿArabī's *al-Mutawassiṭ fī l-iʿtiqād*); Sanūsī, *Sharḥ al-Kubrā*, 12–13 (reference to Ibn ʿArafa's *al-Shāmil*), 32–34 (reference to Ibn Dihāq's *Sharḥ al-Irshād*), 41 (reference to Ibn al-Tilimsānī's *Sharḥ al-Maʿālim fī uṣūl al-dīn*).

[24] One of the accusations to which al-Qushayrī responded in his apologia for the Ashʿarīs, written in response to the (short-lived) persecution of Ashʿarīs in Seljuk Khorasan, was that al-Asharī denied the faith of the imitator and therefore considered the common people to be infidels; see Tāj al-Dīn al-Subkī, *Ṭabaqāt al-Shāfiʿiyya al-Kubrā*, edited by Ṭanāḥi and al-Ḥilū (Cairo: ʿĪsā al-Bābī al-Ḥalabī, 1964–1976), III, 418–420. Averroes repeated the charge in his *Faṣl al-maqāl wa-taqrīr mā bayna l-sharīʿa wa l-ḥikma min al-ittiṣāl*, edited by G. Hourani (Leiden, the Netherlands: Brill, 1959), 37.

[25] Ghazālī's opinion is cited in Sanūsī, *Sharḥ al-Ṣughrā*, 15; Rāzī's opinion is cited in Sanūsī, *Sharḥ al-Kubrā*, 28.

(*ahliyya*) for such an endeavor, a qualification that seems to have been understood to confine the duty to those who pursued a scholarly career. The average nonscholarly Muslim was according to Juwaynī charged only with having true belief, not with having the justified true belief that constitutes knowledge (*ma'rifa*).[26] Others argued that the ordinary believer is not an imitator at all for, if challenged, he could give reasons for his convictions even if he did not master the technical terms of *kalām*. For example, the prominent fourteenth-century Timurid scholar Taftāzānī held that it was only someone who, for example, lived in peripheral areas with no exposure to knowledgeable Muslims and who, if challenged about his reasons for believing, could only answer that this is what he had been told by his peers or elders who could properly be called an imitator.[27] Similarly, the Egyptian-based Māturīdī theologian and Ḥanafī jurist Ibn Humām (d. 1457) wrote that one almost never encountered "imitaters" in the creed, for people in the marketplace could often be heard to indulge in inferences from the creation to the Creator.[28] Yet other Sunni scholars argued that unquestioningly following the Quran and the hadith of the Prophet should not be considered *taqlīd* at all. Only the unquestioning following of fallible authorities could properly be termed *taqlīd*.[29]

These were all ways in which one could take the edge off the radical maxim that an imitator is either a sinner or an infidel. What is striking about Sanūsī is that he firmly opposed all such moderating suggestions, thus leaving intact the radical nature of the claim. He explicitly rejected the proposal that engaging in rational theology is not an individual duty and that commoners could therefore not be said to be sinners, let alone infidels. It is true, he conceded, that ordinary believers cannot be expected to master all the intricacies of the discipline, but a grasp of the basic

26 Frank, "Knowledge and taqlīd," 53–57.

27 Sa'd al-Dīn al-Taftāzānī, *Sharḥ al-Maqāṣid*, ed. 'A. 'Umayra (Cairo: Maktabat al-Kulliyyāt al-Azhariyya, 1984), V, 223.

28 Kamāl al-Dīn Ibn Abī al-Sharīf, *al-Musāmara fī sharḥ al-Musāyara fī l-'aqā'id al-munjiya fī l-ākhira*, edited by Ṣalāh al-Dīn al-Ḥimṣī (Damascus: Ṣalāḥ al-Dīn al-Ḥimṣī, 2009), 482–483 (top rubric).

29 This suggestion was made by the famous hadith scholar Ibn Ḥajar al-'Asqalānī (d. 1449), see the quotation from Ibn Ḥajar's monumental commentary on *Ṣaḥīh al-Bukhārī* in al-Ḥasan al-Yūsī, *Ḥawāshī 'alā Sharḥ Kubrā al-Sanūsī*, 301. This was also the position of the later Ḥanbalī scholar Muḥammad al-Saffārīnī (d. 1774), who cited Ibn Taymiyya as expressing the same view, see Muḥammad al-Saffārīnī, *Lawāmi' al-anwār al-bahiyya wa-sawāṭi' al-asrār al-athariyya sharḥ al-Durra al-muḍī'a fī 'aqīdat al-firqa al-marḍiyya* (Beirut and Riyadh: al-Maktab al-Islāmī and Dār al-Khānī, 1991), I, 267 (ll. 16–20), I, 275 (ll. 18–23).

tenets and arguments is well within their reach.[30] He also rejected in no uncertain terms the suggestion that ordinary Muslims are not imitators and that their beliefs and reasoning are basically sound. He wrote:

Even weaker than this is the statement of one of our contemporaries that there is no imitator amongst the believers, commoners as well as elite, and that justified knowledge (*ma'rifa*) obtains for them all, the sole difference being in the degree to which they can or cannot express what is in their hearts. We say that this is even weaker than the statements related of some Indians [i.e. Hindu ascetics who claim that justified knowledge is not obtained through ratiocination but through asceticism] since they at least impose a condition for the occurrence of justified knowledge, viz. renunciation of worldly attachments, and this person does not impose any conditions at all but makes justified knowledge obtain for anyone called a "believer" without the necessity of *naẓar*. There is no concealing the fact that this statement is false and that there is consensus that the opposite is true, for it is known without a shadow of doubt that the tenets of the creed are not all self-evident, rather some require subtle *naẓar*. How could this not be the case when this noble community alone has disagreed in matters of creed to such an extent that they have divided into 73 sects of which only one is right?[31]

The position that knowledge of the rational grounds for one's assent to the Islamic creed is a condition for having faith (*īmān*) might appear extreme insofar as it seems to imply that many ordinary nominal Muslims are in fact unbelievers. Sanūsī was willing to endorse this consequence. By contrast with Ibn Khaldūn, who a century earlier had stated that *kalām* was of little use because the older heresies had been vanquished, Sanūsī often returned to the theme of the evilness of his own day and the prevalence of ignorance and creedal error. For instance, he wrote in the commentary on his Long Creed:

As for our own times, the Right Path (*al-sunna*) is by comparison to reprehensible innovations as rare as a white hair on the skin of a black bull. One who does not expend himself today in acquiring knowledge and taking it from well-versed scholars – and how rare are these today, especially in this science [i.e. *kalām*]! – will die in a state of heretical innovation and unbelief without even realizing it. Most people today have not even attained the rank of believers by imitation, but rather remain in the rank of corrupt beliefs and heedless ignorance. This is due to nothing else but the approach of the Hour and the scarcity of knowledgeable, upright scholars and decent, clever students, as well as the abundance of the

30 Sanūsī, *Sharḥ al-Wusṭā*, 28–29. The suggestion that Sanūsī was rejecting had been made by Abū Yaḥyā b. al-Sharīf al-Tilimsānī (d. 1423) in his commentary on Juwaynī's *Irshād*.

31 Sanūsī, *Sharḥ al-Kubrā*, 36. According to Yūsī's gloss, the contemporary scholar against whom Sanūsī was arguing was his local rival Ibn Zakarī (d. 1493); see Yūsī, *Ḥawāshī*, 287.

people of the nether world who are impressed with what they think they know and who are misled and mislead.[32]

In the commentary on his Short Creed, he wrote:

The most important thing that a rational and thoughtful person can do in these difficult times is to seek that which will save his soul from eternal damnation, and this is only by mastering the tenets of the creed as it has been expounded by the leaders of the Sunni community. And how rare it is that someone masters this in these difficult times in which the sea of ignorance has overflowed, falsity has spread ever so widely and the waves of denying the truth, hating those who uphold it, and presenting falsity in the beguiling guise of truth have reached all corners of the land! And how blissful today is the one who verifies the tenets of his faith and then obtains knowledge of what is necessary for him of the derived principles of outward and inner conduct... and then cuts himself off from people and stays clear of their evil until his impending death releases him from this corrupt world.[33]

The pessimistic tone is a recurrent feature of Sanūsī's works, and it is tempting to relate it to the turmoil undergone by the Maghreb in the fifteenth century. Ibn Khaldūn had been writing during the heyday of the Naṣrid dynasty in Granada, the Marīnid dynasty in Morocco, and the Ḥafṣid dynasty in Tunisia. In Sanūsī's lifetime, a century later, the local dynasties of North Africa were in terminal decline, the Christian Reconquista of Spain was entering its final stages and the Spaniards and Portuguese were even making inroads into North Africa itself (within a few years of Sanūsī's death, the nearby ports of Oran and Melilla would fall to the Spaniards and Tlemcen itself would pay tribute to the Spanish crown).[34] Given Sanūsī's harsh verdict on his time and on what he perceived to be the creedal ignorance and waywardness of his contemporaries, there was little incentive for him not to push the Ashʿarī denigration of *taqlīd* and praise of reasoning (*naẓar* or *taḥqīq*) and justified conviction (*maʿrifa*) to its logical conclusion. If indeed "Every believer has *maʿrifa* of God" – a proposition for which there is some support in the Quran and hadith – then, Sanūsī noted, by "contraposition" (*ʿaks al-naqīḍ al-muwāfiq*) "No one who does not have *maʿrifa* of God is a

32 Sanūsī, *Sharḥ al-Kubrā*, 30–31.

33 Sanūsī, *Sharḥ al-Ṣughrā*, 6.

34 On the Portuguese and Spanish expansion along the Atlantic and Mediterranean coasts of North Africa in the fifteenth and sixteenth centuries, see J. Abun-Nasr, *A History of the Maghrib*, 144–147 and A. C. Hess, *The Forgotten Frontier: A History of the Sixteenth-Century Ibero-African Frontier* (Chicago: University of Chicago Press, 1978), 26–44.

believer." This proposition in turn can be combined syllogistically with the proposition "Every imitator does not have *ma'rifa* of God" to yield (by the syllogistic mood CELARENT) the conclusion "No imitator is a believer."[35]

Two factors should nevertheless be kept in mind to avoid misunderstanding: First, Sanūsī explicitly adhered to the view that anyone who utters the profession of faith is legally a Muslim and should be treated as such in this world; the question is whether the mere profession of faith will be sufficient on Judgment Day.[36] Second, Sanūsī expected the ordinary Muslim to be familiar with the basic tenets of the creed and at least one argument for each, but not to be familiar with all the issues and debates in *kalām* or to be able to refute heretical arguments – these were tasks for specialists.[37] His shorter, more popular creedal works accordingly do not place as many demands on the reader as his longer works. They do not present possible objections or the detailed arguments of non-Ash'arī sects, nor do they make systematic use of logical terminology such as "major premise" or "contraposition." The dogmatic nature of Sanūsī's shorter creedal works may indeed – if divorced from their context – fuel suspicions of a "fossilized conservatism." But Sanūsī did not write short and relatively simple creeds because he could not write anything more sophisticated. His longer theological works include detailed discussions of theological disagreements, both within Ash'arism and with opposing schools. He wrote more popular works because he believed it to be of ultimate importance that ordinary Muslims be given the means with which to acquire correct creedal beliefs and their evidential grounds, thereby going beyond unthinking imitation of their elders and peers.

Sanūsī went on to deal with possible objections to his position concerning the necessity of theological reasoning: One such objection is that it is absurd to make eternal salvation dependent on familiarity with the technical terms and subtle arguments of the discipline of *kalām*. The companions of the Prophet were not familiar with such technical terms and subtleties, and there is general agreement that they are models for later believers. Sanūsī replied that the Companions of the Prophet were far from being imitators: they had direct knowledge of the proofs of the prophecy of Muḥammad. It is unacceptable to suggest, as, for example,

35 Sanūsī, *Sharḥ al-Kubrā*, 39.
36 Sanūsī, *Sharḥ al-Kubrā*, 15.
37 Sanūsī, *Sharḥ al-Kubrā*, 31–32; Sanūsī, *Sharḥ al-Ṣughrā*, 17–18.

Fakhr al-Dīn al-Rāzī had done, that the venerable Companions – by consensus of Sunnis the best generation in human history – were mere imitators and thus at a lower degree of excellence than later theologians.[38] The most that one could say is that the Companions were not familiar with the later technical terms and distinctions of the field of *kalām*, just as they were not familiar with the technical terms and distinctions of, for example, the developed disciplines of Arabic grammar and rhetoric or the science of hadith. One should not infer from this that their understanding of Arabic or hadith was defective or that they were ignorant of the substance of *kalām*, viz. the rational proofs for the tenets of the Islamic creed. Salvation is not dependent on familiarity with the jargon of *kalām* but it is arguably dependent on knowledge of the tenets of the Islamic creed and of the rational grounds on which they rest.[39] Sanūsī was an uncompromising Ashʿarī occasionalist, that is, he held that only God possesses causal powers and that it is therefore strictly speaking God and not the so-called "cause" who brings about an "effect." It was well within His power to create knowledge of the tenets of the Islamic creed and their proofs without a formal training in *kalām*. Nevertheless, Sanūsī stated that in his day and age, it was God's habit to create such knowledge after the study of *kalām*, and prudence therefore dictated that this is how pious servants should attempt to acquire such knowledge.[40]

Sanūsī's distinction between the basic purpose of *kalām* and the later technical vocabulary of the discipline also enabled him to deal with another and related objection: that the discipline of rational theology is a reprehensible innovation (*bidʿa*) not known to the earliest generation of Islam who ought to serve as a model for later believers. Supporters of this position often invoked numerous sayings by early Sunni authorities condemning *kalām* and its practitioners. They often also cited anecdotes relating how prominent theologians had repented later in life and returned to the simple belief of "old women." Sanūsī associated this position with what he called the *Ẓāhiriyya* and the *Ḥashwiyya*. The former term straightforwardly referred to followers of the Ẓāhirī school of law who did not allow analogy in jurisprudence and insisted on adhering to the letter of the revealed law without any extrapolation. The school had enjoyed some support in Islamic Spain and North Africa from the eleventh century to the fourteenth, but largely died out thereafter, giving

38 Sanūsī, *Sharḥ al-Kubrā*, 28.
39 Ibid., 29.
40 Ibid., 16.

way to the Mālikī school of law and the Ashʿarī school of theology.[41] The term *Ḥashwiyya* is not so readily identifiable with any known sect, but Ashʿarīs and Māturīdīs in later centuries often used it disparagingly of the fideist Ḥanbalī school, which rejected the discipline of *kalām* and also disallowed any figurative reinterpretation of apparent anthropomorphisms in the Quran and hadith.[42] Sanūsī replied that the Companions did engage in the substantial aspect of *kalām*, just as they spoke Arabic and practiced Islamic law – it is just that the developed technical vocabulary of these sciences arose at a later stage. The condemnations of *kalām* by early venerable Sunni scholars were, or so Sanūsī claimed, aimed at the heretical Muʿtazilīs, for at the time when such condemnations were made only Muʿtazilīs described themselves as practitioners of *kalām* – it was only later that orthodox Sunnis adopted the technical terms and distinctions of *kalām* and used them against the Muʿtazilīs.[43] As for commending the faith of "old women," Sanūsī argued that this might have made sense in an earlier time when the creed had only just begun to be corrupted by heresy (so that older people could be trusted to have the uncorrupted creed). In later times, such a commendation would be of little use for now there were old women among the heretics too. Rather, the situation was precisely the opposite: Where, Sanūsī asked, would old women and other commoners be had it not been for the efforts and guidance of the Sunni scholars who protected the faith from heresy and vulgar misunderstanding?[44]

Yet another related objection is that the Quran and the hadith are themselves sufficient to establish the creed, without a need for the discipline of theology. Again, this was a view that Sanūsī imputed to the *Ẓāhiriyya* and the *Ḥashwiyya*. He rejected it on a number of grounds: Typically for the theologians, he argued that there were central tenets of the Islamic creed that it would be circular to try to establish by appeal to the Quran and hadith (e.g., the existence of God and the veracity of the Prophet). He also argued that the position is self-refuting because the Quran and hadith repeatedly urge believers to engage in reflection and

[41] Ibn Khaldūn referred to the Ẓāhirī school as defunct in his own time, and to Islamic North Africa as uniformly Mālikī; see F. Rosenthal, *The Muqaddima*, III, 5–6, 12–18.

[42] The Ashʿarī and Shāfiʿī scholar Taqī al-Dīn al-Subkī used the term of the radical Ḥanbalī Ibn Taymiyya; see his *al-Sayf al-saqīl fī l-radd ʿalā Ibn Zafīl* in *al-Rasāʾil al-Subkiyya fī l-radd ʿalā Ibn Taymiyya* (Beirut: ʿĀlam al-kutub, 1983), 84–85. The Ottoman Māturīdī scholar and judge Aḥmed Beyāżīzāde (d. 1687) used the term of the Ḥanbalīs in general; see his *Ishārāt al-marām min ʿibārāt al-Imām*, 141ff.

[43] Sanūsī, *Sharḥ al-Wusṭā*, 37–38 (citing the view of Ibn ʿArafa).

[44] Sanūsī, *Sharḥ al-Kubrā*, 20–22.

contemplation of natural phenomena and on the rational absurdity of, for example, idolatry or the Trinity. Furthermore, *kalām* is necessary to avoid errors arising from too literal an understanding of the Quran and hadith (which might lead, for example, to an anthropomorphic conception of God). He wrote:

As for the one who claims that the way unto knowing the truth has already appeared, viz. the Book and the Sunna, and that other ways are prohibited, the reply to him is that the fact that these two [the Book and the Sunna] are legitimate proofs cannot be known except through reasoning. Furthermore, in these two sources there are appearances that, if taken literally, lead to unbelief according to some or heresy.[45]

For Sanūsī, it was therefore emphatically *not* the case that *kalām*'s function is merely to defend a creed established independently by revelation; on the contrary, *kalām* is necessary for a proper understanding of the Quran and hadith.

Because theological reasoning is the individual duty of every legally responsible Muslim, Sanūsī concluded that theologians are duty bound to provide instruction in theology to the community. Judging from Sanūsī's polemical tone while discussing this point, it seems that his opinion encountered resistance from contemporary scholars who believed that ordinary believers should not be exposed to theology. He wrote:

As for the claim of some who have no insight (*baṣīra*) and no verification (*taḥqīq*) that the tenets of the creed should not be taught to the common people and their proofs should not be mentioned to them, without making a distinction between those proofs that are clear and understandable to them and those that are not, this is clearly wrong. If reasoned knowledge is an individual duty . . . then how can it not be the case that one should teach them what leads them to this? And if it is legitimate to recite the Quran and hadith of the Prophet in their presence without explication, even though there are apparent meanings there that by consensus must be understood non-literally and the literal understanding of which has led many people astray, then it is all the more legitimate to teach them the creed along with the proofs that they are able to comprehend.[46]

It would seem that his opponents cited the widely respected Ghazālī in support of their view. The way in which Sanūsī dealt with this invocation offers an instructive example of how a later scholar could in effect disagree with a venerable earlier authority while retaining the semblance of respect and agreement. Sanūsī wrote:

[45] Ibid., 36.

[46] Sanūsī, *Sharḥ al-Wusṭā*, 39–40.

Ghazālī has said: "The beliefs of the common people should not be meddled with" . . . He means by this – and God knows best – that this is the case as long as reprehensible beliefs are not apparent. But such reprehensible beliefs have become apparent in our times, and therefore it is obligatory to rectify this and to teach them the truth kindly and in a manner that their minds can comprehend.[47]

A few Western scholars writing on Islamic theology have taken note in passing of Sanūsī's Short Creed, and in general they have scoffed his "intellectualism" and his demand "that the average believer . . . be a philosopher!"[48] Such assessments are perhaps predictable; they betray the widespread anti-intellectualism and anti-rationalism among modern English-speaking (mainly Protestant) historians of religion. What *is* surprising is that the lopsided view that Islamic theology was exclusively apologetic, and therefore lost its raison d'être in later centuries, should have had so much currency in the Western study of *kalām* in the twentieth century, despite the dim acknowledgment of Sanūsī's "intellectualism" and of his extraordinary influence until the twentieth century.

Sanūsī's Influence in the East

Sanūsī's works did not have an immediate impact east of the Maghreb. There are hardly any explicit references to him in the theological works of sixteenth-century Egyptian scholars such as ʿAbd al-Wahhāb al-Shaʿrānī (d. 1565), Ibn Ḥajar al-Haytamī (d. 1566), Aḥmad b. Qāsim al-ʿAbbādī (d. 1585), and Ibrāhīm al-Laqānī (d. 1631).[49] This was to change in the

47 Sanūsī, *Sharḥ al-Kubrā*, 15.

48 A. J. Wensinck, *The Muslim Creed: Its Genesis and Historical Development* (Cambridge: Cambridge University Press, 1932), 248; W. M. Watt, *Islamic Philosophy and Theology*, 139. Wensinck repeats the commonplace distinction between the God of the philosophers and the God of Abraham (which goes back to the seventeenth-century Jansenist Blaise Pascal) and accuses Sanūsī of presenting the former rather than the latter, simply because Sanūsī tried to demonstrate the existence of God. It is clear that for Wensinck any attempt at rational grounding of religious belief will do violence to the "God of Abraham." The modern study of Islamic theology has been hampered by such a deep-rooted lack of sympathy with the entire enterprise of *kalām*.

49 ʿAbd al-Wahhāb al-Shaʿrānī, *al-Yawāqīt wa l-jawāhir fī bayān ʿaqāʾid al-akābir* (Cairo: Muṣṭafā al-Bābī al-Ḥalabī, 1959); Ibn Ḥajar al-Haytamī, *al-Taʿarruf fī l-aṣlayn wa l-taṣawwuf*, printed on the margin of Muḥammad ʿAlī Ibn ʿAllān al-Ṣiddīqī (d. 1648), *al-Talaṭṭuf fī l-wuṣūl ilā l-Taʿarruf* (Mecca and Cairo: Maṭbaʿat al-Taraqqī and Muṣṭafā al-Bābī al-Ḥalabī, 1912–1936). In a relatively lengthy discussion of the question of the faith of the imitator, Aḥmad b. Qāsim al-ʿAbbādī does not refer to Sanūsī and his opinion at all; see his *al-Āyāt al-bayyināt ʿalā Sharḥ Jamʿ al-jawāmiʿ* (Cairo: n.p,1289/1872), IV, 280ff. Laqānī's popular creedal poem *Jawharat al-tawḥīd* seems to be influenced in some ways by Sanūsī's creeds, but it is noteworthy that Laqānī did not

course of the seventeenth century. Due in large part to incoming scholars from the Maghreb, such as Maqqarī, Shāwī, Kinaksī, and Warzāzī, Sanūsī's works became a core part of the curriculum at the Azhar College in Cairo and remained very influential there until the early twentieth century. (This development, incidentally, is strikingly analogous to the simultaneous introduction of the works of Dawānī to the curriculum in Ottoman Turkey due to Kurdish and Azeri scholars.)

The cultural connections between the Maghreb and Cairo had traditionally been strong, and it is not surprising that Sanūsī's influence should eventually have moved eastward along with the many Maghrebī scholars who had a certificate to teach his works and settled in Cairo or passed through the city on their way to the pilgrimage. More unexpected, perhaps, is the influence of Sanūsī in the Turkish-speaking parts of the Ottoman Empire. At first sight, Sanūsī's uncompromising Ashʿarism should have elicited little interest among Ottoman Turkish scholars who overwhelmingly adhered to the Māturīdī school of theology. (Of course, Dawānī was also nominally an Ashʿarī, but his commitment to the school was less dogmatic and he was also profoundly influenced by the mystical monism of Ibn ʿArabī and the philosophical ideas of Avicenna and the Illuminationist school.) Admittedly, Sanūsī's works seem not to have become part of the curriculum in the central parts of the Ottoman Empire, but there is nevertheless evidence of an interest in them by around 1600.[50] The bibliographer Kātib Çelebī, writing in the first half of the seventeenth century, mentioned Sanūsī's three creeds, noting of the Short Creed that

explicitly mention Sanūsī in his own commentary on the poem; see Ibrāhīm al-Laqānī, *Hidāyat al-murīd li-Jawharat al-tawḥīd*, edited by Marwān al-Bajāwī (Cairo: Dār al-Baṣā'ir, 2009). Note, for example, the absence of any explicit mention of Sanūsī in Laqānī's lengthy discussion of the faith of the imitator (*muqallid*) on pp. 194–201. This is not because Laqānī systematically avoided citing earlier scholars. He mentioned, for example, the Timurid theologians Taftāzānī and Jurjānī, as well as the fifteenth-century Egyptian scholars Ibn Ḥajar al-ʿAsqalānī, Ibn al-Humām, al-Suyūṭī, and Zakariyyā al-Anṣārī (see pp. 82, 105, 106, 125, 132, 164–165, 204, 220–221, 499, 624). There is even mention of some of Sanūsī's North African contemporaries such as the Sufi Aḥmad Zarrūq and the jurist Muḥammad al-Tatāʾī (d. 1535); see pp. 448, 662.

50 It is possible that familiarity with Sanūsī's works in Istanbul was due to Tunisian scholars who fled there after the Spanish conquest of Tunis in 1535. For one such Tunisian scholar in Istanbul, see Ṭāşköprīzāde, *al-Shaqāʾiq al-nuʿmāniyya*, 391–392; Makhlūf, *Shajarat al-nūr al-zakiyya*, II, 135. Nevertheless, none of the available seventeenth- or eighteenth-century sources for the Ottoman Turkish madrasa curricula mentions Sanūsī's works (see the list of *kalām* works in Özyılmaz, *Osmanlı Medreselerinin Eğetim Programları*, 25, 35, 41, 58) and there appears to have been no Ottoman Turkish tradition of commenting or glossing them.

"it is a useful epitome that contains all the tenets of the creed."[51] The Bosnian scholar Ḥasan Kāfī (d. 1616) listed Sanūsī's creeds as one of the works on which he relied in his own theological work *Rawḍāt al-jannāt fī uṣūl al-iʿtiqādāt*.[52] Ḥasan Kāfī did not follow Sanūsī's radical views on "imitation." He explicitly stated that an "imitator" with regard to the creed should be considered a believer, and that the first duty of the believer is simply to affirm the truth of the creed rather than engage in *naẓar*.[53] Nevertheless, Ḥasan Kāfī did believe that going beyond the stage of imitation and knowing the rational justifications for the tenets of the creed is a duty incumbent on every believer and that it is therefore a sin to rest content with mere imitation. He wrote:

> Know that the faith of the imitator is correct (*ṣaḥīḥ*), for if a man relates a report and another believes him, there is nothing to prevent someone from saying "He believes him" ... and this is the meaning of assent by imitation. This is so, even if he [the imitator] is a sinner by not engaging in *naẓar*.[54]

He also wrote:

> It is incumbent (*wajaba*) on every rational person to expend his existence on acquiring and attaining it [i.e. faith (*īmān*)] through decisive proofs and to do his best to learn its specifics and generalities as far as human capacity allows, so that he may escape from the bonds of imitation in the tenets of the creed.[55]

The other creedal works that Ḥasan Kāfī mentioned as sources for his own work, in particular the early Māturīdī creed *al-Fiqh al-akbar* (falsely attributed to Abū Ḥanīfa), the creed of the early Ḥanafī jurist al-Ṭaḥāwī (d. 923), and the widely studied creed of Najm al-Dīn al-Nasafī (d. 1142), all lack this radical rhetoric concerning the duty of engaging in *naẓar* and thus going beyond *taqlīd*.[56] It is therefore very likely that this element in Ḥasan Kāfī's work was due to Sanūsī.

Ḥasan Kāfī was a severe critic of Sufis and other "innovators."[57] He therefore belonged, like his older contemporary Meḥmed Birgevī

[51] Kātib Çelebī, *Kashf Ẓunūn*, 170.

[52] Ḥasan Kāfī, *Azhār al-rawḍāt fī sharḥ Rawḍāt al-jannāt*, edited by ʿAlī Akbar Ḍiyāʾī (Beirut: Dār al-kutub al-ʿilmiyya, 2012), 158.

[53] Ḥasan Kāfī, *Azhār al-rawḍāt*, 151, 192–193.

[54] Ibid., 192–195 (the creed itself, boldfaced in the printed edition).

[55] Ibid., 152–153 (the creed itself, boldfaced in the printed edition).

[56] Ḥasan Kāfī lists these other sources for his work in *Azhār al-rawḍāt*, 155–159. The creeds mentioned have been conveniently translated in W. M. Watt, *Islamic Creeds: A Selection* (Edinburgh: Edinburgh University Press, 1994), 48–56 (Ṭaḥāwī), 62–68 (*al-Fiqh al-akbar*), and 80–85 (Nasafī).

[57] K. Süssheim and J. Schacht, "Āḳ Ḥiṣārī," *EI2*, I, 310a.

(d. 1573), to a current of Ottoman anti-mystic purism that would erupt with violence onto the streets of Istanbul in the early decades of the seventeenth century and that has come to be known as the Ḳāḍīzādelī movement after the fiery preacher Meḥmed Ḳāḍīzāde (d. 1635) and his vigilante followers. One of the most prominent seventeenth-century Ottoman authors belonging to this current of thought was Aḥmed Rūmī Āḳḥiṣārī (d. 1632), who wrote invectives against the veneration of shrines and against the novel phenomenon of smoking tobacco, as well as a number of other works of a sharply purist and moralist character.[58] It is of some interest to note that Aḥmed Rūmī also wrote a short treatise on "imitation" that consists almost entirely of quotations from Sanūsī. The treatise begins as follows:

> Know, o brothers, that what is necessary in the creeds of the faith is knowledge (*ma'rifa*) and this is certain conviction that corresponds to the truth and is based on proof. Imitation, i.e. certain conviction that corresponds to the truth but without proof, is not sufficient. The verification of this point according to what I have summarized from the words of al-Imām al-Sanūsī is... [59]

Aḥmed Rūmī's treatise is indeed mainly a patchwork of passages selected from Sanūsī's theological works concerning the necessity of going beyond *taqlīd* and ascertaining the rational proofs for the tenets of the creed. The passages quoted include Sanūsī's laments concerning widespread creedal ignorance among the common people and the necessity of teaching them the basics of the creed along with at least one proof for each tenet.[60] They also include Sanūsī's passionate polemics against those who argue that imitation in the creed is sufficient and that the enterprise of rational theology is an illegitimate innovation unattested among the earliest generations of Islam.[61] The fact that Aḥmed Rūmī embraced Sanūsī's position on these matters shows all too clearly the insufficiency of seeing the Ḳāḍīzādelīs as nothing but Ottoman exponents of a timeless "Salafism" along with earlier Ḥanbalī scholars such as Ibn Ḥanbal and Ibn Taymiyya.[62] Sanūsī's views on the nobility and necessity of *kalām* and his disparagement of *taqlīd* in matters of creed are radically opposed to the traditional position

[58] On this author and his works, see the introduction to Y. Michot, *Against Smoking*.

[59] Aḥmed Rūmī Aḳḥiṣārī, *Risāla fī l-taqlīd* (MS: www.yazmalar.gov.tr/ 45Hk2937/6), fol. 51b. For other manuscripts of this treatise, see Michot, *Against Smoking*, 7 (nr. 9).

[60] Aḳḥiṣārī, *Risāla fī l-taqlīd*, fol. 52b. The folio-sheet includes three distinct quotations from Sanūsī's works: lines 1ff (from Sanūsī, *Sharḥ al-Wusṭā*, 28); lines 6ff (from Sanūsī, *Sharḥ al-Kubrā*, 37–38); lines 12ff. (from Sanūsī, *Sharḥ al-Kubrā*, 15).

[61] Aḳḥiṣārī, *Risāla fī l-taqlīd*, fol. 59a (from Sanūsī, *Sharḥ al-Kubrā*, 34ff).

[62] This is the view of Michot, *Against Smoking* and Çavuşoğlu, "The Ḳāḍīzādelīs."

of the Ḥanbalīs. There can be little doubt that Sanūsī's attacks on what he called the "*Ḥashwiyya*" were at least in part aimed at the Ḥanbalīs. He associated the *Ḥashwiyya* with a condemnation of the discipline of *kalām* as a reprehensible innovation; with the view that simple appeal to Scripture is sufficient to establish the creed and repel heresy; with the belief that God's eternal Word consists of letters and sounds; and with a rejection of nonliteral interpretations of apparent anthropomorphisms in the Quran and hadith leading to the affirmation that God has hands and feet, sits on a throne and occasionally moves down to the lower heavens.[63] These were all characteristically Ḥanbalī positions.

To be sure, Ḥanbalī thinkers sometimes disparaged *taqlīd* and endorsed so-called *ijtihād* in matters of law. In other words, they might condemn the "imitation" of earlier jurists and call for basing legal judgments on a direct engagement with the sources of Islamic law. But in matters of creed (as opposed to law) the standard position of the Ḥanbalīs was very different and amounted to a rejection of the need for a scholarly discipline that deals with the rational proofs for the tenets of the Islamic faith and that purports to be fundamental in the sense that it precedes and underwrites appeal to the Quran and hadith. The creedal work of the seventeenth-century Damascene Ḥanbalī scholar ʿAbd al-Bāqī al-Baʿlī (d. 1661) illustrates the typical Ḥanbalī approach: there is no reference to the dangers of *taqlīd* or to the necessity of engaging in *naẓar* or *kalām*, nor is there any attempt at giving rational proofs for the tenets of the creed (though the author did cite rational arguments in support of his rejection of the Ashʿarī view that the uncreated Word of God does not consist of sounds and letters). On the contrary, ʿAbd al-Bāqī extolled the virtue of submissive acceptance (*taslīm*) and warned against the dangers of delving deep with one's reason (*al-taʿammuq fī l-fikr*) into matters divine.[64]

The Ḳāḍīzādelīs were indeed influenced by certain aspects of the writings of the radical fourteenth-century Ḥanbalī thinkers Ibn Taymiyya and his disciple Ibn Qayyim al-Jawziyya (d. 1350) – particularly their condemnation of the veneration of shrines and saints and their ideas about governance in accordance with religious law (*siyāsa sharʿiyya*). But the

[63] Sanūsī, *Sharḥ al-Kubrā*, 140; Sanūsī, *Sharḥ al-Wusṭā*, 31.

[64] ʿAbd al-Bāqī al-Baʿlī, *al-ʿAyn wa l-athar fī aqāʾid ahl al-athar*, edited by ʿIṣām Rawwās Qalʿajī (Damascus and Beirut: Dār al-Maʾmūn, 1987), 51–52. In the creedal work of the later Palestinian Ḥanbalī scholar Muḥammad al-Saffārīnī, there is a warning against *taqlīd* in matters of creed, but Saffārīnī explicitly stated that simple, unreflective reliance on the Quran and hadith should not be considered to be *taqlīd* at all. See Saffārīnī, *Lawāmiʿ al-anwār al-bahiyya*, I, 267 (ll. 16–20) and I, 275 (ll. 18–23).

Ḳāḍīzādelīs were clearly also open to influences from other sources. One such source was an old Ḥanafī-Māturīdī tradition of strong hostility to esoteric Sufism and the Karrāmiyya (the latter being influential opponents of the early Ḥanafīs in Khorasan and Central Asia some of whose ideas are thought to have influenced Ibn Taymiyya).[65] As mentioned in Chapter 1, there are traces of this older Ḥanafī tradition in the writings of the fifteenth century scholar ʿAlā al-Dīn al-Bukhārī (d. 1438), a virulent critic of the mystical monism of Ibn ʿArabī who nevertheless also considered Ibn Taymiyya an infidel, as well as in the writings of Birgevī – the spiritual forefather of the Ḳāḍīzādelīs – whose purism was often directed at Sufi "innovators" but who was also uncompromisingly hostile to the theological views of the Karrāmiyya, for example, that God is in the "direction" (*jiha*) of "above" (*fawq*) and that His attributes undergo change (both views shared by Ibn Taymiyya). And as has just been seen, some prominent Ḳāḍīzādelīs were also demonstrably influenced by the radical Ashʿarī (and very un-Ḥanbalī) position of Sanūsī concerning the necessity of rational theology and the dangers of imitation in matters of creed.

Sanūsī-Inspired Creedal Works

Sanūsī's view that it is incumbent on each adult and sane Muslim to know both the articles of faith *and* their rational proofs inspired a distinctive North African genre of theological literature in later times. This literature relied heavily on Sanūsī's own shorter theological works: The Short Creed known as *al-Ṣughrā*; its abridgment known as *Ṣughrā al-Ṣughrā*; and *al-Muqaddimāt* which presents the basic definitions and divisions of the science of *kalām*.[66]

The tradition of writing short and simple creeds was of course not new. Nevertheless, Sanūsī's shorter creeds and the later works that they inspired stand out in a number of ways, for example:

1. They include rational proofs for each article. This is what one would expect from the preceding exposition of Sanūsī's views on *taqlīd*. It was deemed insufficient just to assent to the articles of

[65] Wilfrid Madelung has noted the affinity between the position of the Karrāmiyya (against whom the early Ḥanafīs often argued) and Ibn Taymiyya; see his *Religious Sects in Early Islamic Iran* (Albany, NY: Persian Heritage Foundation, 1988), 43.

[66] Sanūsī, *Sharḥ Ṣughrā al-Ṣughrā*, edited by Saʿīd Fūda (Amman: Dār al-Rāzī, 2006), idem., *Sharḥ al-Muqaddimāt*, edited by Salīm Fahd Shaʿbāniya (Damascus: Dār al-Bayrūtī, 2009).

faith; one should also be familiar with at least one argument for each.

2. They tend to include explicit statements to the effect that *taqlīd* in matters of creed is insufficient and that it is incumbent on each legally responsible Muslim to go beyond this stage by mastering the contents of the work in question.
3. Their basic organizing principle is to present what is necessarily true of God, what cannot possibly be true of God, and what is contingently true of God; and then to present what is necessarily, impossibly, and contingently true of God's prophets. They typically begin by explaining the three modal notions "necessity," "impossibility," and "contingency." And they typically end by claiming that all the articles of faith that have been expounded are implicitly present in the Islamic profession of faith "There is no god but Allah, and Muhammad is His messenger." This organizing principle meant that numerous issues that loom large in earlier Sunni creeds were not mentioned at all or were dealt with as an aside. As one modern editor of Sanūsī's Commentary on the Short Creed has noted, there is no mention of a number of traditionally important articles of faith such as the belief in Hell and Paradise, the Last Judgment, the questioning in the grave, belief in angels and the divine Throne, belief in the heavenly Tablet and the heavenly Pen, the beatific vision of God in Paradise, and the fate of the cardinal sinner.[67] Even central questions of classical Islamic theology – such as the creation of human voluntary acts (do we create our own voluntary actions or are they created by God?), the nature of the Quran (is it created or uncreated?), and apparent anthropomorphisms in the Quran and hadith (should they be interpreted literally or figuratively?) – are dealt with as corollaries of the necessary attributes of God, not as independent articles.

One of the more influential later creedal works belonging to this genre is the didactic poem *al-Murshid al-mu'īn 'alā l-ḍarūrī min 'ulūm al-dīn* by the Moroccan scholar 'Abd al-Wāḥid Ibn 'Āshir (d. 1631). The work consists of 314 lines of verse and covers the basics of (1) the articles of faith according to the Ash'arī school, (2) Islamic law according to the Mālikī school, and (3) Sufism in the "sober" tradition of al-Junayd

[67] See the remarks of Muḥammad Ṣādiq Darwīsh in the introduction to his edition of Sanūsī's *Sharḥ al-Ṣughrā*, 8.

(d. 910). The work elicited a number of commentaries over the centuries, the earliest being by Ibn ʿĀshir's student Muḥammad Mayyāra al-Fāsī (d. 1661), who first wrote a lengthy commentary and then an abridgement of it.[68] The brief overview that follows will largely be based on the first section of Ibn ʿĀshir's poem, dealing with theology, along with the shorter of Mayyāra's two commentaries.

Ibn ʿĀshir's poem addresses itself explicitly to the "illiterate" (*ummī*). His commentator Mayyāra explained that the poem includes what even an illiterate person should know about the creed, the law, and Sufism.[69] The poem then proceeds, in the tradition of Sanūsī, to declare that the judgment of reason (*ḥukm al-ʿaql*), that is, judgments that are based on reason rather than revelation or sense-experience, can be divided into those that are necessarily true, not possibly true, and contingently true. Ibn ʿĀshir then briefly explained the notions of necessity (*wujūb*), impossibility (*istiḥāla*), and contingency (*jawāz*): the necessary is what reason judges cannot be false; the impossible is what reason judges cannot be true; and contingency is what reason judges can be true or false – whether it is one or the other being determined by revelation or experience.[70] Ibn ʿĀshir then stated that the first duty of the believer is to know God and His prophets with their attributes (*ṣifāt*) on the basis of proof. Mayyāra in his commentary explained that the condition that true knowledge (*maʿrifa*) be based on proof (*dalīl*) is to rule out conviction that is true but not so based, for this is called *taqlīd* and is deemed insufficient in matters of creed by the "verifiers" among theologians.[71]

The attributes that are necessarily true of God and that should be known by all believers are as follows:[72] (1) Existence (*wujūd*), (2) Uncreatedness (*qidam*), (3) Everlastingness (*baqāʾ*), (4) Self-sufficiency (*ghinā*), (5) Unlikeness to created things (*mukhālafat al-ḥawādith*), (6) Unity (*waḥdāniyya*), (7) Power (*qudra*), (8) Will (*irāda*), (9) Knowledge (*ʿilm*),

68 Mayyāra, *al-Durr al-thamīn fī sharḥ al-Murshid al-muʿīn* (Cairo: Maṭbaʿat al-taqaddum al-ʿilmiyya, 1323/1905); idem, *Mukhtaṣar al-Durr al-thamīn* (Rabat: Wizārat al-awqāf, 1981). Another esteemed commentary was written by the later Moroccan scholar al-Ṭayyib Ibn Kīrān (d. 1812). This has been published with the Gloss of Idrīs al-Wazzānī (fl. 1930) entitled *al-Nashr al-ṭayyib ʿalā sharḥ al-shaykh al-Ṭayyib* (Cairo: al-Maṭbaʿa al-Miṣriyya, 1348/1930–1352/1933). A more recent commentary is by Muḥammad al-Muwaqqit al-Marrākushī (fl.1925); see his *al-Ḥabl al-matīn ʿalā naẓm al-Murshid al-muʿīn* (Beirut: al-Maktaba al-thaqāfiyya, 1987).

69 Mayyāra, *Mukhtaṣar*, 14.

70 Ibid., 17–18.

71 Ibid., 20.

72 Ibid., 25–29.

(10) Life (*ḥayāt*), (11) Sight (*baṣar*), (12) Hearing (*sam'*), and (13) Speech (*kalām*). The commentator Mayyāra explained that the necessary divine attributes were usually divided by theologians – in the North African Ash'arī tradition, of course – into: (1) *Ṣifāt nafsiyya*, (2) *Ṣifāt al-ma'ānī*, and (3) *Ṣifāt salbiyya*.[73] The first category includes "attributes" that are not really attributes at all; for example "existence" can truthfully be said of God, but should not be regarded as a real attribute of the Divine Self. It is not as if there is a Divine Self that has the attribute of Existence superadded to it, for being a self (*dhāt*) is simply identical to existing. The Ash'arī position in general was that existence is not an attribute of entities – the distinction between essence and existence is merely mental and does not correspond to any real distinction in the extramental world. The second category, *Ṣifāt al-ma'ānī*, includes real attributes that are superadded to the divine essence, that is, attributes that cannot be reduced to each other or to God's essence. Traditionally, the last seven of the thirteen attributes, viz. Power, Will, Knowledge, Life, Sight, Hearing, and Speech were considered to belong to this category. The third category includes privative attributes. Attributes (2) to (5) were standard examples, for they were held to primarily assert that God is *not* created, will *not* cease to be, is *not* dependent on anything else, and is *not* similar to His creatures.

Is this division of attributes part of what Ibn 'Āshir and Mayyāra thought every believer should know? The question may not admit of a hard and fast answer. On the one hand, the division of attributes is not mentioned in Ibn 'Āshir's poem itself, suggesting that he may not have considered it to be part of what should be known by all. On the other hand, illiterate commoners were surely not expected just to memorize the poem and then go off and make as much sense of it as they could. They must have been expected to attend lectures by scholars who could expound the meanings and implications of the memorized verses. Extant commentaries are valuable for giving a sense of what kinds of further information were supplied in such lectures. Mayyāra, for example, explicitly drew out some of the implications of the necessary and impossible attributes of God: for example, that God is not a body, that He does not have spatial location, that there are no causes other than God, and that God's Speech is eternal and does not consist of letters and sounds.[74] Such implications must have been considered part of what

[73] Ibid., 32–33.
[74] Ibid., 18, 26–27, 29, 35.

ordinary believers should know, as Sanūsī and his followers vehemently denounced vulgar anthropomorphisms and popular belief in natural causation as heinous heresy or outright unbelief. What is explicitly stated in the popular creeds therefore hardly exhausts all that ordinary believers were expected to know.

Corresponding to the thirteen necessary attributes are thirteen attributes that are not possibly true of God. These are the opposites of the thirteen necessary attributes, for example (1) Non-existence (*ʿadam*), (2) Createdness (*ḥudūth*), (3) Cessation (*fanāʾ*), and so on. As for the attributes that are contingently true of God, these are everything that God freely chooses to do, such as creating the world, sending forth prophets, rewarding believers, and punishing unbelievers. These are, in the jargon of *kalām*, "the attributes of acts" (*ṣifāt al-afʿāl*) and are held to be beyond count and knowable by revelation alone.[75]

Having presented the necessary, impossible, and contingent attributes of God, Ibn ʿĀshir proceeded to provide rational proofs, so that – as the commentator Mayyāra wrote – "the legally responsible person (*al-mukallaf*) may by knowing these free himself from the noose of *taqlīd*."[76] The proof for the existence of God is as follows: Accidents are constantly coming-to-be and passing-away, and this implies that substances are themselves created in time since what cannot exist without accidents that are created in time must itself be created in time. Since the substances that make up the world are created in time, one must posit a creator. Otherwise, one would have to suppose that the world came into existence on its own without sufficient reason. In other words – closer to the original Arabic – one would have to suppose that the world came into existence without a preponderant factor (*murajjiḥ*) that causes the world to exist rather than not to exist.[77] The commentator Mayyāra expounded these arguments and regimented them into syllogistic form:

The world is created.
Everything created has a creator.
―――――――――――――
The world has a creator.

[75] Ibid., 34–35.
[76] Ibid., 36.
[77] Ibid., 36–37. This particular proof goes back to the Ashʿarī theologian Imām al-Ḥaramayn al-Juwaynī; see A. Shihadeh, "The Existence of God," in T. Winter (ed.), *The Cambridge Companion to Classical Islamic Theology* (Cambridge: Cambridge University Press, 2008), 197–217, at 209–211.

The proof of the first premise, viz. "The world is created" is another syllogism:

> The bodies of the world are implicates of created accidents.
> Everything that is an implicate of created accidents is created.
> The bodies of the world are created.

Mayyāra was aware that as its stands this second proof is open to doubt. The second premise is arguably not self-evident and must itself be established through further premises. Furthermore, the actual conclusion of the proof is "The bodies of the world are created" whereas the desired conclusion is "The world is created," and it is not immediately evident that these two claims are equivalent. He listed the additional propositions that are needed to circumvent such difficulties but, crucially, did not give the proofs for these propositions.[78] This again raises the question of just how much the ordinary, unlearned believer should know of these proofs, and it points to a deep tension in the Sanūsian genre of popular creeds. It may be recalled that Sanūsī thought that the ordinary believer should know at least one proof for each article of faith but was not required to deal with problems and doubts raised by heretics or anticipated by orthodox theologians. But it was also mentioned previously that Sanūsī and his followers demanded demonstrative certainty in matters of creed. Ibn ʿĀshir mentioned that the proof he gave is "decisive" (*qāṭiʿ*), and his commentator characterized it as a "demonstration" (*burhān*).[79] In one sense, this is perhaps understandable. Ibn ʿĀshir and Mayyāra believed that it *is* possible to supply the needed subproofs for the premises mentioned – they were familiar with Sanūsī's commentary on the Longer Creed in which such proofs are given.[80] In this sense, one might say that the proof is a demonstration – it is a valid argument with evident or demonstrable premises. Knowing the proof, the ordinary believer knows one demonstrative argument for an article of faith. But ordinary believers were apparently not expected to prove the premises of the demonstration themselves, and this implies that they were expected to have unwavering certainty on the basis of trust that learned theologians can establish these premises beyond doubt. One might wonder whether this is not simply *taqlīd* in another form.

78 Mayyāra, *Mukhtaṣar*, 38–39.
79 Ibid., 36.
80 Sanūsī, *Sharḥ al-Kubrā*, 59–70.

The proofs given by Ibn ʿĀshir – and explicated by Mayyāra – for the other necessary attributes, besides existence, almost all explicitly have the structure of a hypothetical syllogism in modus tollens (*istithnāʾ naqīḍ al-tālī*), with the following form:[81]

> If God did not have attribute X then such-and-such would be the case.
> Such and such is not the case.
> God has attribute X.

For the attributes of Sight, Hearing and Speech, the rational proofs are supplemented with the evidence of the Quran. One might at first sight wonder if such appeals to the Quran are legitimate at this stage, and – if they are – why they cannot be used across the board to establish all the attributes. But as Sanūsī and Mayyāra explicitly stated, there are attributes that must be proven rationally because it would be circular to attempt to prove them by appeal to Quran and hadith – for example, God's Existence. Once such central attributes have been established by reason, other attributes can be established by appeal to the Quran and hadith without any circularity.[82]

Ibn ʿĀshir's poem then gave the necessary, impossible, and contingent attributes of God's prophets. They must be truthful; cannot possibly lie or commit sins; and may be subject to human accidents such as disease, hunger, pain, and death.[83] The proofs again tend to take the form of hypothetical syllogisms in modus tollens: If they are not truthful then God would be lying, as God's creating miracles at their hands is tantamount to declaring them truthful. But God does not lie, so the prophets are truthful. If they commit sins, then committing sins would be incumbent on believers (since God has commanded believers to follow the example of the prophets). But God has not commanded humans to commit sins, so prophets do not commit sins. As for prophets being subject to human accidents such as disease, hunger and pain, that is proved – all too neatly perhaps – by showing that incontestable reports show that prophets were in fact afflicted with such human accidents. If they were actually afflicted with disease, hunger, pain, and death then it must have been possible for them to be subject to these accidents.[84]

81 Mayyāra, *Mukhtaṣar*, 40–45.
82 Mayyāra, *Mukhtaṣar*, 46; Mayyāra, *al-Durr al-thamīn*, 33; Sanūsī, *Sharḥ Ṣughrā al-Ṣughrā*, 77–81.
83 Mayyāra, *Mukhtaṣar*, 48–50.
84 Ibid., 51–53.

In the conclusion of the theological section of the work, it is claimed – following Sanūsī's Short Creed – that the articles that have been presented are all implicit in the Islamic profession of faith "There is no God but Allah."[85]

A Forgotten Chapter in Islamic Religious History

The almost complete neglect of the tradition of Sanūsī and his followers by Western scholarship for the greater part of the twentieth century might suggest that it constituted a marginal aberration in Islamic history – an aberration that one might simply disregard when giving overviews of or generalizations about the course of Islamic religious history. This is clearly not the case. Whatever one thinks of the "proofs" supplied by Sanūsī and his followers, or of the very idea of demanding that ordinary believers internalize such proofs, it is clear that Sanūsī-inspired popular creedal works played an important role in religious life for centuries in large swathes of the Islamic world. Sanūsī's shorter creeds appear to have been studied throughout Islamic Africa by virtually every student for centuries. As mentioned previously, there are also premodern translations or adaptations of these creeds into Berber, Fulfulde, Turkish, Javanese, and Malay.[86]

As noted previously, Sanūsī's works were introduced into the Azhar College in Cairo in the course of the seventeenth century, and dominated the teaching of theology there in the eighteenth and nineteenth centuries – the very same centuries in which the Azhar emerged as the major center of learning in the Arabic-Islamic world.[87] As mentioned in the previous chapter, three eminent Egyptian scholars who had studied with incoming Maghrebī scholars in the last decades of the seventeenth century and the first decades of the eighteenth were the "three Shihābs": Aḥmad al-Mallawī, Aḥmad al-Jawharī, and Aḥmad al-Damanhūrī. All three wrote shorter theological works that were explicitly inspired by Sanūsī and reminiscent in scope, length, and organization of the first section of Ibn ʿĀshir's didactic poem with Mayyāra's short commentary. The earliest of

[85] Ibid., 54–58.

[86] For Berber adaptations of Sanūsī's short creeds, see Boogert, *The Berber Literary Tradition of the Sous*, 153–154. For the influence of Sanūsī's *Ṣughrā* in Muslim West Africa and the translation of it into Fulfulde, see L. Brenner, "Muslim Thought in Eighteenth-Century West Africa; The Case of Shaykh Uthman b. Fudi," in N. Levtzion and J. Voll (eds.), *Eighteenth-Century Renewal and Reform in Islam* (Syracuse, NY: Syracuse University Press, 1987), 39–67, at 45–47.

[87] M. Winter, *Egyptian Society under Ottoman Rule 1517–1798* (London and New York: Routledge, 1992), 118–119.

these works seems to have been a short didactic poem plus commentary by Mallawī, completed in May 1701.[88] Damanhūrī's didactic poem plus commentary was completed in July 1703, when he was a mere fourteen years old.[89] Jawharī's creedal work was revealingly entitled *Munqidhat al-ʿabīd min ribqat al-taqlīd* (The deliverance of servants of God from the yoke of taqlīd); it elicited a commentary by his son Muḥammad b. Aḥmad al-Jawharī (d. 1801).[90] Perhaps the most influential of Egyptian works in this genre was the later prose work of Muḥammad al-Faḍālī (d. 1821), entitled *Kifāyat al-ʿawām fī-mā yajib ʿalayhim min ʿilm al-kalām* (The sufficiency for commoners with respect to what is incumbent upon them from the science of *kalām*). This was printed on at least four occasions between 1881 and 1911 in Cairo, along with the gloss of Faḍālī's student Ibrāhīm al-Bājūrī.[91] Writing during the First World War, the German orientalist Max Horten noted, with some exaggeration, that the creeds of Sanūsī and Faḍālī were known "throughout the Orient." He adduced their works in support of his claim that even semi-educated believers in the Islamic world were much more familiar with the theological dogmas of their religion and with Greek logical-philosophical concepts than the educated but nonscholarly classes of Europe in his day.[92]

In the hundred years since Horten wrote, the influence of Sanūsī and his epigones has declined steeply. In the twentieth century, both Islamic modernists and Salafīs rejected Ashʿarism in favor of either neo-Muʿtazilī or neo-Ḥanbalī positions. Predictably, these intellectual movements have sought to rewrite Islamic religious history in their own image, highlighting thinkers they find more congenial, such as the classical Muʿtazilī theologians and Islamic philosophers (for the modernists) or Ibn Taymiyya and

[88] There are three manuscripts of this in the Azhar library in Cairo, with the following call numbers: (1) Khuṣūṣi 3295, ʿUmūmī 42397; (2) Khuṣūṣi 2789, ʿUmūmī 33390; (3) Khuṣūṣī 40570, ʿUmūmī 53316 According to the colophons, Mallawī completed the work on 16 Dhū l-Ḥijja 1112/May 24, 1701.

[89] For Damanhūrī's work, entitled *al-Qawl al-mufīd bi-sharḥ Durrat al-tawḥīd*, see MS: British Library: Or. 11023), fols. 61a–70a; MS: Princeton University Library: Yahuda 2798, fols. 6b–13a. According to the colophons, it was completed "in the beginning of the third [month] of the fifth [year] of the second [decade] of the twelfth [century], i.e., 1 Rabīʿ I, 1115/July 15, 1703. Damanhūri was born in 1101/1689–1690.

[90] Jabartī, *ʿAjāʾib al-āthār*, I, 310 (l.26); III, 165 (ll.27–28). For extant copies of the commentary, see *Fihris al-kutub al-mawjūda bi-l-maktaba al-Azhariyya ilā sanat 1366/1947* (Cairo: al-Maṭbaʿa al-Azhariyya, 1947), II, 305.

[91] Printed by al-Maṭbaʿa al-Wahbiyya in 1298/1881; by al-Maṭbaʿa al-Khayriyya in 1310/1892; by Dār al-Kutub al-ʿArabiyya, 1328/1910; and by al-Maṭbaʿa al-Azhariyya in 1329/1911.

[92] M. Horten, *Muhammadanische Glaubenslehre: Die katechismen des Fuḍālī und Sanūsī* (Bonn: Marcus and Weber, 1916), 3–4.

his followers (for the Salafīs). This rewriting of history to serve modern ideological perspectives is in evidence already in the well-known *Risālat al-tawḥīd* by the Egyptian self-styled "reformer" Muḥammad ʿAbduh (d. 1905). The work is in some ways indebted to the tradition of Sanūsī that dominated the teaching of theology at the Azhar in ʿAbduh's student days, for example beginning by denigrating *taqlīd* in matters of faith, then explaining the concepts of necessity, impossibility, and contingency, and then presenting God's necessary attributes. ʿAbduh nevertheless dismissed, in a brief historical overview in the introduction to his work, the entire course of Islamic theology after Ghazālī as confused, misconceived, and pedantic.[93] He thus, with a few rhetorical flourishes and nebulous historical allusions, wrote off not just Sanūsī but even such recognized giants of Islamic religious thought as Fakhr al-Dīn al-Rāzī (d. 1210), Sayf al-Dīn al-Āmidī (d. 1231), Naṣīr al-Dīn al-Ṭūsī (d. 1274), Ibn Muṭahhar al-Ḥillī (d. 1325), and Ṣadr al-Sharīʿa al-Maḥbūbī (d. 1346). ʿAbduh's student Rashīd Riḍā (d. 1935), in his annotations to the work, also portrayed in dark colors the supremacy of the Ashʿarīs in "the middle ages" (*al-ʿuṣūr al-wusṭā*), merely taking his teacher to task for not mentioning "the great renewer" (*al-mujaddid al-ʿaẓīm*) Ibn Taymiyya.[94]

The new vision of Islamic religious history propounded by various self-styled "reformers" and "revivers" has tended to dominate both Islamic and Western scholarship for most of the twentieth century, and it has no place for Sanūsī and his later followers, except perhaps as a foil to be briskly dismissed. An important chapter in Islamic religious history was thus confined to obscurity, and the way was cleared for the construction of a number of "truths" by eminent historians of Islamic religious thought: Islamic theology is basically apologetic or dialectical (L. Gardet and G. Anawati); orthopraxy is more important in Islam than orthodoxy (W. Cantwell Smith, J. van Ess); law rather than theology is "Islam's ideal religious science" and anti-*kalām* traditionalism is Islam's "basic orientation" (G. Makdisi).[95] As the Italian author Italo Svevo perceptively observed in the 1920s:

93 Muḥammad ʿAbduh, *Risālat al-tawḥīd*, edited by Bassām ʿAbd al-Wahhāb al-Jābī (Beirut and Limassol: Dār Ibn Ḥazm and al-Jaffan wa l-Jābī, 2001), 76–78.

94 ʿAbduh, *Risālat al-tawḥīd*, 78 (fn. 2).

95 Gardet and Anawati, *Introduction à la théologie musulmane*, 305–315, 329–330; W. Cantwell Smith, *The Meaning and End of Religion* (New York: Macmillan, 1962), 179; W. Cantwell Smith, *On Understanding Islam: Selected Studies* (The Hague and New York, Mouton Press, 1981), 241; van Ess, "The Logical Structure of Islamic Theology," 24–25; van Ess, *The Flowering of Muslim Theology* (Cambridge, MA: Harvard University Press, 2006), 15; G. Makdisi, "Law and Traditionalism in the Institutions of

The past is always new; as life proceeds it changes, because parts of it that may have once seemed to have sunk into oblivion rise to the surface and others vanish without a trace because they have come to have such slight importance. The present conducts the past in the way a conductor conducts an orchestra. It wants these particular sounds, or those – and no others. That explains why the past may at times seem very long and at times very short... The only part of it that is highlighted is the part that has been summoned up to illumine, and to distract us from, the present.[96]

Learning of Medieval Islam," in G. von Grunebaum (ed.), *Theology and Law in Islam* (Wiesbaden: Otto Harrassowitz, 1971), 75–88, at 75.

96 Quoted in A. Assmann, *Cultural Memory and Western Civilization: Functions, Media, Archives* (Cambridge: Cambridge University Press, 2011), 7–8.

6

al-Ḥasan al-Yūsī and Two Theological Controversies in Seventeenth-Century Morocco

Sanūsī's view that neglect of rational theology is either a sin or outright unbelief and his pessimistic rhetoric about the creedal ignorance of commoners could easily have radical consequences. This can be seen from two theological controversies that erupted in southern Morocco in the second half of the seventeenth century. The first concerned the status of the "imitator" who is unable to give a theologically satisfying account of the creed and its rational grounding. The second, closely related, controversy concerned the proper understanding of the first part of the Islamic profession of faith "There is no god but Allah" (*lā ilāha illā Allāh*). Later Moroccan theologians who took seriously Sanūsī's denigration of "imitation" held that every Muslim must understand the meaning of the profession of faith and that this implies knowing what is denied and what is affirmed by it, as outlined in Sanūsī's Commentary on the Short Creed (*al-Ṣughrā*). Their radical position appears to have reignited an older controversy on this very point – what exactly *is* denied (*al-manfī*) by the statement "There is no god but Allah"? Is it the idols of the unbelievers and polytheists? Or is it any imagined equal of Allah? Or both? The present chapter takes a closer look at these controversies from the perspective of al-Ḥasan al-Yūsī, the eminent Moroccan theologian and logician who has already been mentioned on numerous occasions in the preceding chapters. Yūsī's interventions reveal the extent to which theological discussions in the later North African Ashʿarī tradition were intertwined with the discipline of logic.

The Controversy Concerning the "Imitator" (*Muqallid*)

In his *Muḥāḍarāt* – a collection of haphazardly organized literary, historical, and moral observations – Yūsī described the eruption of a controversy concerning the "faith of the imitator" in Sijilmāsa (in southeast Morocco) in the 1660s and 70s:

In the 1070s [= 1660s]... I passed by the town of Sijilmāsa and found that a great controversy had arisen amongst students and teachers concerning the meaning of "There is no god but Allah." [...] Then I passed by Sijilmāsa on a later visit and saw an even more disagreeable and untoward controversy. This had arisen because they had seen the works of those amongst the religious leaders who encouraged looking into the science of theology and warned against ignorance of that discipline and against *taqlīd*. So they began to ask people about their beliefs and demand an answer and an explication. If they encountered someone who was not articulate about what is in his heart or tongue-tied due to being caught off-guard or simply unaware of a matter of consequence – or so they imagined – in the creed, then they would charge him with ignorance and unbelief. They spread the word that corruption had appeared in the religious beliefs of the common people and started teaching them the creed. Among people, the word was that one who does not study the creed in this way is an infidel.[1]

Yūsī mentioned that he had tried to dissuade the leader of this party but to no avail:

He went to extreme lengths in explaining the tenets of the creed... to such an extent that he would fall into ways of speaking that are disrespectful to God the Exalted and intolerable to anyone with a sense of the majesty of God the Exalted. His classes would be attended by uncouth Bedouins... who would go back to their people and start posing questions of such a nature to base people like themselves: Where does God live? Where does He go? Where does He stay? Where is He? And what is He like?... Then they spread the word that the meat slaughtered by Muslim commoners should not be eaten and that one should not intermarry with them for fear that they do not know the true meaning of monotheism.[2]

The account in clearly colored by Yūsī's disapproval of this tendency, but it nevertheless attests to the explosive potential in Sanūsī's denigration of *taqlīd*. The fact that the party in question took their inspiration from the works of Sanūsī is clear from another account of this phenomenon in an early eighteenth-century obituary of the Moroccan scholar and traveler Abū Sālim al-ʿAyyāshī (d. 1679):

He wrote a number of fine works including... *The Judicious and Fair Judgment to End the Disagreement amongst the Jurists of Sijilmāsa*... i.e., on the issue of the unbelief of the imitator, for a man among the jurists named Ibn ʿUmar

[1] al-Ḥasan al-Yūsī, *al-Muḥāḍarāt*, edited by Muḥammad Ḥajjī and Aḥmad al-Sharqāwī Iqbāl (Beirut: Dār al-Gharb al-Islāmī, 1982), I, 226–227.

[2] Yūsī, *al-Muḥāḍarāt*, I, 229.

claimed that he who does not know the principles of monotheism in the manner mentioned by al-Sanūsī and who does not know what is being denied and what is being affirmed in the profession of faith has no share in Islam.[3]

Of course, to say that the radical party in Sijilmāsa in the 1660s and 70s invoked Sanūsī's name is not to imply that their actions followed in a straightforward manner from his works. There were a number of elements in Sanūsī's writings that could be emphasized by someone unwilling to countenance such extreme positions. As mentioned previously, Sanūsī had accepted the principle that anyone who professes the faith should be treated as a Muslim legally, and he had also stressed that the creed should be taught to the commoners with kindness and in easily comprehensible terms. It is at least doubtful that he would have approved of the kind of inquisition described by Yūsī or of the scruples about eating meat slaughtered by, or intermarrying with, the common run of Muslims. At the same time, it is not difficult to see how Sanūsī's views could have led to the radical positions described by Yūsī. This is especially the case if one considers the widely studied glosses of the Moroccan scholar ʿĪsā al-Sugtānī on Sanūsī's commentary on the Short Creed. On a number of occasions, Sugtānī considered possible objections to and qualifications of Sanūsī's position on *taqlīd*, but he showed little inclination to make use of such opportunities to soften Sanūsī's stance. For example, he cited Taftāzānī's point that the common run of Muslims could not be said to be "imitators" and that the term should be used only of someone in a very marginal area who describes himself as Muslim but has never been exposed to even the basics of the faith. Sugtānī rejected the suggestion and insisted that many commoners were obviously "imitators" and that Taftāzānī's point was at best an observation of how matters stood in his region and age and should not be generalized.[4] Similarly, Sugtānī anticipated the objection that Sanūsī's position would imply that the majority of nominal Muslims are in fact infidels and that this is clearly false and contradicts hadith reports that say that the followers of the

[3] Ifrānī, *Ṣafwat man* intashara, 325–326. For a helpful account of the identity of some of the scholars who had these radical views, including references to extant manuscript copies of their works and those of their opponents, see Ḥamīd Ḥammānī's introduction to his edition of Yūsī's *Mashrab al-ʿāmm wa l-khāṣṣ min kalimat al-ikhlāṣ* (Casablanca: Dār al-Furqān, 2000), 168–185. But the discussion is marred by Ḥammānī's assumption that the radical view is in some obvious sense contrary to "the spirit of Islam" and that Yūsī's opposition to it was due to his being close to "the people."

[4] ʿĪsā al-Sugtānī, *Ḥāshiya ʿalā Sharḥ Umm al-barāhīn* (MS: Princeton University Library, Yahuda 5500), fol. 19b.

Prophet Muḥammad will form the majority of the people of paradise. His reply was to take the objection as a hypothetical syllogism in modus tollens:

> If Sanūsī is right then the majority of nominal Muslims are infidels.
> It is not the case that the majority of nominal Muslims are infidels.
> It is not the case that Sanūsī is right.

He then responded by saying that one might respond by denying either the conditional premise, on the grounds that the majority of nominal Muslims had knowledge of the basics of rational theology even if they were unable to expound what they knew or defend it from objections, or the second premise (the negation of the consequent) on the grounds that it simply does not follow from the majority of nominal Muslims being infidels that the followers of the Prophet Muḥammad will not constitute the majority of the people of paradise.[5] One might be excused for thinking that this was Sugtānī's preferred option because he had only just dissented from Taftāzānī's optimistic view that "imitators" are rare even among unlearned commoners. There is in any case nothing to suggest that Sugtānī was particularly concerned to head off radical interpretations of Sanūsī.

Yūsī, unlike his teacher Sugtānī, would break decisively with Sanūsī's position on the question of *taqlīd*, perhaps partly as a consequence of the drastic uses to which it had been put in his own time. His position was much closer to that of Ghazālī's teacher Juwaynī: the common people are obliged to assent to the basics of the faith, not to be familiar with the proofs or terminology of the rational theologians. Yūsī related the following of his conversation with some unlearned people who were distressed by the demands of the radical party in Sijilmāsa:

> "Do you not profess that God the Exalted exists?" They said: "Yes!" "Do you not know that He is alone in his dominion and has no partner and that there is no other god besides Him and that all other objects of worship other than Him are null and void?" They said: "Yes, this is all certain for us without a doubt or hesitation." I said: "This is the meaning of the profession of faith that you are obliged to believe... It is the same with all the tenets of the creed. You are obliged to believe their meaning, not to know the terms used in the books of the scholars, nor to know the logical definitions and descriptions that are used there. The understanding of these expressions and mastery of these realities and explanations is another discipline the knowledge of which is not demanded of commoners."[6]

[5] Sugtānī, *Ḥāshiya*, fols. 19b–20b.
[6] Yūsī, *Muḥāḍarāt*, I, 228.

In a more scholarly context, Yūsī wrote:

Some theologians and the majority of hadith scholars are of the view that imitation is sufficient. Its essence is to be certain of what has been heard from the leaders of religion, without any doubt or perplexity or hesitation . . . I say: This, God willing, is the correct position, since the aim is to believe the truth and this has occurred. Even if one were to say that the aim is to have insight (*baṣīra*) then we say that this too has occurred, for we say that the meaning of having insight is to believe the truth while knowing that it is the truth in such a manner that one is not among those who merely surmise or guess.[7]

Yūsī managed to disagree with Sanūsī while maintaining a tone of respect toward the venerable theologian. In his Gloss on Sanūsī's Commentary on the Long Creed, he ended his lengthy discussion of the views concerning "imitation" in creedal matters with the following words:

The issue is, as you see, one concerning which contradictory views have been advanced by theologians. [. . .] The statements of the author [i.e. Sanūsī] in most of his works are not devoid of harshness and excess, and this may be due to his zeal on behalf of the religion of Islam on account of his seeing that the commoners had come to be enveloped in the dark night of ignorance, may God reward him.[8]

Yūsī acknowledged that one might on occasion find instances of egregious creedal error on the part of commoners, "especially amongst the rural people and the women and children." He himself related that in his youth he had heard one woman say to another "May God forgive our sins" and the other woman reply: "He will forgive us if He is enabled to do so by His own God who created Him."[9] He also remembered boys saying on the appearance of a mysterious line in the sky: "That's God or the sword of God!" and believing that God would descend to earth on Judgment Day and smite His enemies with His sword.[10] Yūsī noted that if even extremely crude notions such as these could be encountered among commoners then it was hardly surprising to find wayward beliefs such as the belief that God is in the direction of "above" or that created objects have causal powers to be "widespread" (*fāshiya*).[11] On this basis, Yūsī rejected the more rosy claims about the spiritual state of the commoners that could be found among some theologians (such as Taftāzānī and Ibn Humām). There were, he insisted, cases of frightful ignorance among some commoners,

7 Yūsī, *Mashrab al-ʿāmm wa l-khāṣṣ*, 490.
8 Yūsī, *Ḥawāshī*, 301f.
9 Ibid., 289.
10 Ibid., 291.
11 Ibid., 290.

and he therefore shared Sanūsī's view that the proper creed should be taught to them. At the same time, he was also eager that this point not be pushed to what he saw as the opposite extreme.[12] He believed that simple exposure to the basics of the faith, perhaps supplemented with proofs derived from the Quran and hadith, would be sufficient for the commoners, who in general were simply ignorant rather than corrupted by heresy or doubt.[13]

In general, Yūsī's assessment of his own age was significantly more optimistic than Sanūsī's. In a remarkable observation, especially given the prevalent commonplace of the "decline of the times" in Islamicate literature, Yūsī opined that complaints about the present and nostalgia for better times in the past are ubiquitous and grounded in the inevitable frustrations from the all too human behavior of contemporaries combined with an idealized impression of the past:

> The world has always been thus, and people have been people since they were created. It would be best for a person to acquiesce and even be content with his own time. In this way, he will show proper respect to God the Exalted and Wise who is the Lord of the first and the last, and find the way that leads toward thanking and praising Him, peace of mind, freedom from cravings and expectations, magnanimity to one's contemporaries, giving them their due, thinking well of them, deriving benefit from them, and seeing the good things and overlooking the bad.[14]

Yūsī's relatively optimistic assessment of his own time was not unusual for Moroccan writers of the late seventeenth and early eighteenth centuries. His student Ibn Yaʿqūb al-Wallālī and the scholar and biographer Muḥammad al-Ṣaghīr al-Ifrānī (fl. 1718–1724) both portrayed the reign of Mawlāy Ismāʿīl in glowing terms as an age of intellectual florescence that compared favorably with the immediately preceding past.[15] Ifrānī, for example, wrote:

> A number of our older teachers have said: In our youth we would seek knowledge and inquire about its issues, especially the rational sciences, but we would not find anyone who was thoroughly familiar with these issues. [...] Rather the didactic

[12] Yūsī explicitly invoked the principle of avoiding both excess (*ifrāṭ*) and deficiency (*tafrīṭ*) in assessing the state of the commoners with respect to the creed; see *Ḥawāshī*, 289.

[13] Yūsī, *Mashrab*, 477ff.

[14] Yūsī, *Muḥāḍarāt*, I, 364–365.

[15] See the preamble to Ibn Yaʿqūb al-Wallālī, *Falsafat al-tawḥīd [=Ashraf al-maqāṣid fī sharḥ al-Maqāṣid]* (Cairo: al-Maṭbaʿa al-Khayriyya, no date), 2–3; and Muḥammad al-Ṣaghīr al-Ifrānī, *Rawḍat al-taʿrīf bi-mafākhir mawlānā Ismāʿīl ibn al-Sharīf* (Rabat: al-Maṭbaʿa al-Malakiyya, 1962), 67–68.

poem *al-Sullam al-murawnaq* [on logic] was only known in Fes to one or two. When God bestowed the aegis of the present rule, and enhanced and renewed its standing, the sciences gushed forth upon people...and in this blessed era a number of notables have appeared who are well-versed and outstanding in science and write excellent works. [...] All those to whom I have alluded are so accomplished that they can discuss on an equal footing with the ancients and sometimes accept and sometimes reject what they have said. Well has a poet said:

> Say to the one who reckons contemporaries as naught
> And gives preferences to the ancients:
> That ancient was once new,
> And this new will in turn be ancient![16]

Such portrayals are obviously exaggerated by their panegyric intent but nevertheless betray a spirit of optimism that contrasts sharply with the weepy pessimism of Sanūsī in the second half of the fifteenth century. Yūsī, in another noteworthy departure from the regressive view of history that was so widespread in premodern Islamic civilization, wrote that whereas the period of the early Ashʿarī theologians had seen a profusion of heresies and popular uncertainty, this was no longer the case in his own time:

As for today, the religious law has become known in a plethora of independent ways and the Message has become so apparent that it is obscure to neither elite nor commoners, to such an extent that [belief in] the prophecy of Muḥammad has become almost innate to this noble community, just as [belief in] the existence of God the Exalted is innate, especially in our time, for though ignorance is widespread there is nothing now among the scholars except the truth to which the Sunni community adheres.[17]

The point that heresies were a thing of the past had been made in the fourteenth century by Ibn Khaldūn, who inferred from this that there is little remaining use for the science of *kalām*.[18] The point that belief in God and the prophecy of Muhammad is "inborn" (*fiṭrī*) had also been a prominent theme in the writings of earlier scholars such as Ibn Ḥazm (d. 1064) and Ibn Taymiyya who were opposed to the enterprise of *kalām* and its claim to ground the Islamic creed in subtle rational argumentation.[19] Yūsī did not draw the same conclusions and remained

16 Ifrānī was born ca. 1669 so the older of his teachers would have been born near the beginning of the seventeenth century.

17 Yūsī, *Ḥawāshī*, 214.

18 Rosenthal, *The Muqaddima*, III, 54.

19 C. Adang, "Islam Is the Inborn Religion of Mankind: The Concept of *fiṭra* in the Works of Ibn Ḥazm," *Al-Qantara* 21(2000): 391–410; W. Hallaq, "Ibn Taymiyya on the Existence of God," *Acta Orientalia* 52(1991): 49–69.

convinced of the value of *kalām*. Yūsī agreed with Sanūsī that anyone who is honest would concede that one's own theological beliefs before embarking on the study of *kalām* were unsatisfactory. Sanūsī had written with characteristic verve:

> As for the common people, most of them do not care to attend the classes of the scholars or attend the people who uphold rightness and one may verify amongst them belief in anthropomorphism, that God is in a certain direction, that natural entities have causal powers, that God's actions have a final cause, that His Word consists of letters and sounds, and that He like humans sometimes speaks and sometimes is silent... Some of these beliefs constitute unbelief by consensus of the learned scholars, while concerning the other beliefs there is disagreement [whether they constitute unbelief or are just erroneous]... By God! Had it not been for His kindness – may He be exalted – and His enabling us to engage with learning and its people we would have been wallowing in the valleys of the beliefs of the partisans of falsehood. How strange it is when a rational person is ignorant of necessary truths and does not recognize his own state before engaging with learning and does not recognize the state of the common people![20]

Yūsī commented thus: "There is no doubt that the one who is honest with himself knows this. Belief in the existence of God, even if it is innate, usually occurs in a manner and state that is corrupt due to the pressure of customs and habits."[21] In his encyclopedic *al-Qānūn*, Yūsī stated in no uncertain terms that the science of theology (*kalām* or *uṣūl al-dīn* or *ʿilm al-tawḥīd*) is the noblest and most exalted of the sciences. Its uses were manifold:

> As for its purpose... In this world it is to obtain certainty (*yaqīn*); rise from the depths of *taqlīd*; give guidance to the one who seeks it; refute the obstinate; preserve the principles of religion from the doubts sown by heretics; ensure the proper intention and devotion, and so forth. In the other world, it is to gain bliss, and this alone should suffice you.[22]

It may be noted that Yūsī listed the obtaining of true certainty and going beyond *taqlīd* as the first worldly purpose of kalām, even before the "apologetic" uses of allaying doubts and refuting heresies. The fact that *taqlīd* is sufficient for the commoners did not imply for Yūsī that there is no value in going beyond that station. On the contrary, mastering the discipline of *kalām* and thus the rational justification for the Islamic creed

[20] Sanūsī, *Sharḥ al-Kubrā*, 37.
[21] Yūsī, *Ḥawāshī*, 291.
[22] Ibid., 181.

is a communal duty (*farḍ kifāya*).[23] In other words, it is incumbent on some members of the Islamic community to go beyond simply accepting the creed in imitation of peers or elders and obtain the ability to verify the truth of the creed, expound it to "imitators" and allay any doubts or uncertainties that may arise.

One might ask whether rational theology is the only way to go beyond *taqlīd* and verify the truth of the Islamic creed. Is it not conceivable, for example, that straightforward appeal to the Quran and hadith could serve this purpose? On this account, one might still make a distinction between ordinary believers who simply accept the articles of faith by *taqlīd* and scholars who are intimately familiar with the Quran and hadith and can ground the articles of faith therein, without recourse to the discipline of *kalām* that had been repeatedly condemned by venerable figures of the early Islamic community. Yūsī, like Sanūsī, associated such a view with "literalists" (*Ẓāhiriyya*) and "fideists" (*Ḥashwiyya*), and he endorsed Sanūsī's insistence that there is need for a discipline that underwrites in rational terms appeals to Quran and hadith and that also provides some systematic basis for distinguishing between cases in which a literal understanding of the creedal pronouncements of the Quran and the hadith is mandatory and cases where such an understanding leads to anthropomorphism and other heresies.[24]

In his Gloss on Sanūsī's Commentary on the Long Creed, Yūsī anticipated two possible arguments for proscribing *kalām*: (1) that it involves citing and discussing heretical opinions, and (2) that it is an "innovation" (*bid'a*) unknown to the earliest generations of Islam. His response to the first worry was in part to invoke the precedent of the Quran, which often cites the arguments of the infidels and rebuts them. "In this," he wrote, "there is the greatest argument for those who practice *kalām*."[25] Of course, some heresies, such as those of the Aristotelian/Neoplatonic philosophers (*falāsifa*), arose at a later period but Yūsī argued that it is the theologians who undertake to refute their ideas who are following the precedent of the Quran, and not those who would simply ignore the philosophers. More generally, Yūsī held that expounding the truth and refuting falsehood are complementary endeavors. "How," he asked, "can the truth be known so that one confines one's attention to it and distinguishes it from falsity if falsity is not known?"[26]

[23] Ibid., 182.
[24] Ibid., 256ff.
[25] Ibid., 271.
[26] Ibid., 271.

As for the objection that *kalām* as a discipline is an "innovation" unknown to the earliest generations of Islam, Yūsī responded by showing that all scholarly disciplines in their full-fledged form were developed after the earliest generations of Islam.[27] The mere fact that theologians used technical terms and modes of presentation that were not attested in the earliest periods is therefore not grounds for proscription, for the same could be said of those who engaged in grammar, semantics-rhetoric, jurisprudence, mathematics, astronomy, and even the science of hadith. One might possibly object that the earliest generations of Islam did make use of those other disciplines *avant la lettre*: they distinguished between correct and incorrect speech and between rhetorically effective and ineffective discourse, gave juridical verdicts, related hadith, calculated, and made astronomical observations; it is just that the technical vocabulary of these disciplines developed later. Yūsī replied that this was precisely his (and Sanūsī's) point about rational theology and the closely related discipline of logic: the earliest generations of Islam had engaged in *kalām* and logic *avant la lettre*. He wrote:

> If it is said: Rational theology and logic are innovations and every innovation must be avoided, then we say: We do not concede that all innovations must be avoided, for some of them are commendable. Even if we were to concede this, then other sciences such as mathematics, medicine, astronomy, jurisprudence, the science of hadith and belles-lettres and the like are innovations. It may be said: But the earliest generations engaged in calculations, treatments, giving legal verdicts and relating hadith; it is only the terminology of these arts that is novel. To this we reply: Similarly, they would explicate and prove and give reasons, and there is no meaning to logic except this.[28]

The full-fledged science of Arabic grammar had, Yūsī remarked, arisen only after the pristine Arabic of the earliest generations had begun to be corrupted and certain explicit rules were felt to be necessary. The sciences of law and jurisprudence developed once a need was felt for general principles for the derivation of legal rulings as opposed to simply proceeding on a case-by-case basis. The science of hadith developed once it became apparent that some reports about the sayings and doings of the Prophet were not authentic. Similarly, the science of *kalām* developed once the unity of the early community had been sundered by creedal disagreements:

[27] Ibid., 273ff.
[28] Ibid., 278.

Creedal beliefs in early Islam were uncorrupted. When factions and whims became plentiful, and the community divided into sects as predicted by the Truthful One [the Prophet Muḥammad], and malice in matters of religion became abundant, and truth came to covered with doubts sown by the deceivers, the leaders and scholars of the community undertook to fight the deceivers with their tongues... They felt the need for general axioms and rational principles and a technical vocabulary to apply to the contested issues and with which to understand the arguments of their opponents during disputes. So they wrote this down and called it the science of *kalām* or principles of religion.[29]

With the rise of numerous individual sciences, a need was felt for a discipline that would regulate the manner in which unknowns are derived from knowns and distinguish proper from improper ways of doing this. This, wrote Yūsī, was the science of logic:

Since all the disciplines mentioned, and others besides, revolve around the apprehension of two things and the judgment with one of them upon the other, and since ratiocination is not always correct, as shown by the disagreement of rational people in the conclusions of their ratiocination, there was a need for that which leads to apprehension and distinguishes between correct and incorrect ratiocination and they wrote down the science of logic and translated it into Arabic so that this noble Arabic community would benefit from it... and it was one of the sciences that had been extracted by the Greeks.[30]

For Yūsī, this brisk survey of the rise of the various sciences in Islam should allay worries about theology and logic being innovations unknown to the earliest generations of Islam. "Let one who prohibits some of them prohibit them all," he noted, "for what is the difference otherwise?"[31] In his survey of the sciences *al-Qānūn*, Yūsī ended his survey of "the philosophical sciences" (*al-ʿulūm al-falsafiyya*) with the following assessment:

We do not heed those who prohibit the knowledge of some of these, for science in itself is nourishment for the mind, joy for the spirit and an attribute of perfect virtue... Even magic, which all jurists agree may not be used, if one were to learn it... just to know it, and be able to distinguish between it and miracles... studying it would be permissible, or even a duty, as has been stated already. And the science of belles-lettres, which is licit by common consent, if one were to study it with the view to becoming a poet who lampoons those whom it is not permitted to lampoon, or praise those whom it is not permitted to praise, studying it would not be permitted to him. "Acts are judged according to their intentions."[32]

[29] Ibid., 276.
[30] Ibid., 277.
[31] Ibid., 278.
[32] Yūsī, *Qānūn*, 177. Yūsī is quoting a well-known hadith.

Ḥasan al-Yūsī's Defense of Logic

Yūsī's discussion of the position of the literalists and fideists started with a defense of *kalām* and evolved into a defense of logic. The two disciplines were for Yūsī, and for Sanūsī before him, intimately linked. As noted in the previous chapter, Sanūsī held the position that *naẓar* is the first duty of a believer since knowledge of God is not innate (at least not in a fully actualized manner) and must be inferred from matters that are evident. It was also noted that Sanūsī's characterization of *naẓar* is shot through with logical terminology. For him, the science of logic expounded the rules of correct inference, and consequently the theologians who engage in *naẓar* should proceed in accordance with such rules. Sanūsī explicitly availed himself of syllogistic modes of presentation when constructing his argument for the existence of God. For example, he began his proof by inviting the reader to construct the following categorical syllogism[33]:

> I exist after not having existed.
> <u>Everything that exists after not having existed has been brought about by something else.</u>
> I have been brought about by something else.

He then proceeded to argue that this something else must be a voluntary agent rather than an impersonal natural cause, presenting the following syllogism[34]:

> You are in one of many possible ways.[35]
> <u>Everything that is in one of many possible ways has been brought about by a voluntary agent.</u>
> You have been brought about by a voluntary agent.

The conclusion of this syllogism was then used as a premise in the following syllogism in the second figure[36]:

> You have been brought about by a voluntary agent.
> <u>No natural cause is a voluntary agent.</u>
> You have not been brought about by a natural cause.

33 Sanūsī, *Sharḥ al-Kubrā*, 45.
34 Sanūsī, *Sharḥ al-Kubrā*, 53.
35 Meaning, you might have been a bit shorter or taller, or darker or fairer, or stouter or thinner, etc.
36 Sanūsī, *Sharḥ al-Kubrā*, 54.

Even more common was Sanūsī's use of hypothetical syllogisms, especially modus tollens, for example[37]:

> If God does not possess a Will, you would not be in one of many possible ways.
> You are in one of many possible ways.
> God possesses a Will.

Particularly striking are Sanūsī's references to modal logic. For example, in his discussion of the question of the possibility of the beatific vision in paradise, which Ashʿarīs affirm and Muʿtazilīs deny, Sanūsī mentioned that one argument adduced against the possibility was that when Moses asked God to let him see Him, he received the answer "You shall not see me" (Quran 7:143). Sanūsī responded by saying that since the request was clearly to see God in this life, the denial should also be understood to refer to this life, not the hereafter. He adduced in support of this response that the contradictory of the modal proposition known as "the temporal" (*al-waqtiyya*) – one of more than a dozen modality propositions recognized in post-Avicennan logic – is also temporally qualified. If one says, "Zayd possibly sees the moon at time *t*" then the contradictory is *not* "Zayd does not possibly see the moon" but rather "Zayd does not possibly see the moon *at time t*."[38]

In the ninth and tenth centuries, a number of Muslim theologians had expressed their distaste for Greek-derived logic (*manṭiq*). After Ghazālī in the eleventh century, however, theologians increasingly began to adopt the terminology and argument-forms of logic in their works. By the time of Sanūsī, this evolution was complete. It is difficult to find an Islamic scholar after the thirteenth century who approved of *kalām* but disapproved of logic, though there were still scholars who disapproved of both disciplines.[39] It was therefore natural for Yūsī to assume that the literalist-fideist attack on the legitimacy of *naẓar* was at once an attack on *kalām*

37 Ibid., 86 (l.2ff).

38 Sanūsī, *Sharḥ al-Kubrā*, 205, 211. The example I have given is of the "possible-temporal" (*mumkina waqtiyya*) not the "absolute temporal" (*waqṭiyya muṭlaqa*) because that seems to fit the theological issue better. For these two modal propositions, see Sanūsī, *Sharḥ al-Mukhtaṣar*, 38–39.

39 See my "Theology and Logic," in S. Schmidtke (ed.), *The Oxford Handbook of Islamic Theology* (forthcoming) [but available on Oxford Handbooks Online, http://www.oxfordhandbooks.com/view/ 10.1093/oxfordhb/9780199696703.001.0001/oxfordhb-9780199696703-e-009].

and on *manṭiq* and that a response to this attack involved a defense of both disciplines.

Yūsī concluded his polemic against those who condemned *naẓar* by discussing the objection to logic that had been advanced in a fatwa by the prominent Egyptian scholar Jalāl al-Dīn al-Suyūṭī.[40] Suyūṭī had been asked about the claim that studying logic is the individual duty of every Muslim because knowledge of theology is an individual duty and such knowledge presupposes knowledge of logic. Exactly who held such a view is not clear, though it may well have been a somewhat uncharitable rendering of views akin to those of Sanūsī. In any case, Suyūṭī angrily rejected the view, responding that logic is a "noxious" (*khabīth*) and forbidden discipline inextricably linked to the heresies of the philosophers. Furthermore, Suyūṭī noted, logic is of no use for theology at all since logic deals with inferences involving universals and universals do not exist outside the mind. Yūsī rejected the first part of Suyūṭī's response, viz. that logic is noxious and forbidden, as a mere claim, and moreover a claim he felt he had adequately answered in the preceding rebuttal of the position that *kalām* and logic are forbidden innovations.[41] The second part of Suyūṭī's response, viz. that logic deals with universals and these do not exist outside the mind, seems to be an echo of the opinion of Ibn Taymiyya, whose lengthy attack on Greek logic Suyūṭī abridged.[42] There is no indication that Yūsī was directly familiar with the writings of Ibn Taymiyya, whose positions on a range of issues would have been considered heretical by the North African Ashʿarī tradition to which Yūsī belonged. Yūsī was certainly not impressed by this particular argument against logic. He wrote:

> As for his claim that universals do not exist outside the mind etc., I wonder how such a claim can be made in such a context by a rational being, not to mention a scholar. I had thought that he [i.e. Suyūṭī] was of a higher scholarly rank, and that he was one of those who, though not a specialist, had an idea of the discipline, but such a statement shows that he has not an inkling of the rational sciences.[43]

The statement implies, wrote Yūsī, that there is no general scientific rule (*qānūn*) whatsoever, whether juridical or theological or grammatical.[44]

40 Jalāl al-Dīn al-Suyūṭī, *al-Ḥāwī li-l-fatāwā* (Cairo: Idārat al-Ṭibāʿa al-Munīriyya, 1352/1933), I, 255–257. Yūsī quotes this in *Ḥawāshī*, 279–280.

41 Yūsī, *Ḥawāshī*, 280.

42 Suyūṭī's abridgement has been translated by Wael Hallaq as *Ibn Taymiyya against the Greek Logicians* (Oxford: Clarendon Press, 1993).

43 Yūsī, *Ḥawāshī*, 281.

44 Ibid., 281.

The term *qānūn* refers to a general rule that has as its subject a universal rather than a singular term, for example "The subject of a nominal sentence (*mubtada'*) is in the nominative."[45] Such rules were clearly conceived by Yūsī to be essential to anything claiming to be a science. To say, as Suyūṭī did, that logic was of no worldly or religious use because it involved such universals, meant that all sciences were of no use.

It is important to note that Yūsī was *not* defending the view that universals exist outside the mind. He on a number of occasions clearly adhered to the view that everything that exists extramentally is a particular.[46] This is a point that bears emphasis because a lamentable number of modern studies of Ibn Taymiyya's criticism of logic simply assume it to be self-evident that nominalism is incompatible with the Greek-derived discipline of formal logic. As a matter of fact, a standard handbook of logic taught in Muslim colleges in later centuries, Kātibī's *al-Risāla al-Shamsiyya,* explicitly stated that the discussion of the extramental existence of universals had nothing to do with logic.[47] Especially in later centuries it was not uncommon for Muslim logicians to be nominalists – for example, the Illuminationist philosopher Suhrawardī (d. 1191), the influential thirteenth-century logician, dialectician and Māturīdī theologian Shams al-Dīn al-Samarqandī, the Tīmūrid polymath Taftāzānī, Yūsī's second-generation Egyptian student Aḥmad al-Mallawī, and the eighteenth-century Ottoman Turkish scholar Ismā'īl Gelenbevī.[48] Some of the most prominent logicians in the mediaeval Latin tradition, for example William of Ockham (d. 1348) and John Buridan (d. ca. 1360), were also nominalists.[49]

45 On the term *qānūn*, see al-Sayyid al-Sharīf al-Jurjānī, *al-Ta'rīfāt* (Beirut: Maktabat Lubnān, 1969 [reprint of the Flügel edition of 1895]), 177.

46 In *Mashrab al-'āmm wa l-khāṣṣ*, Yūsī explicitly wrote: *lā shay'a min al-kulliyyi bi-mawjūdin fī l-a'yāni min ḥaythu huwa kullī* (p. 246, ll. 16–17). In his gloss on Sanūsī's *Mukhtaṣar* he endorsed Taftāzānī's rejection of realism with respect to universals, see Yūsī, *Nafā'is al-durar fī ḥawāshī al-Mukhtaṣar*, fols. 131a–b.

47 Quṭb al-Dīn al-Rāzī, *Sharḥ al-Shamsiyya*, I, 289–294 (main text, top rubric).

48 H. Ziai and J. Walbridge (eds. and trans.), *Suhrawardī: The Philosophy of Illumination* (Provo, Utah: Brigham Young Press, 1999), 7–8; J. Walbridge, "Suhrawardī and Illuminationism," in P. Adamson and R.C. Taylor (eds.), *The Cambridge Companion to Arabic Philosophy* (Cambridge: Cambridge University Press, 2005), 207–210; Shams al-Dīn al-Samarqandī, *Sharḥ Qistās al-afkār* (MS: Yale University Library, Beinecke: Arabic 11), fol. 19b; Sa'd al-Dīn al-Taftāzānī, *Sharḥ al-Shamsiyya* (Lucknow: al-Maṭba' al-Yūsufī, 1317/1899), 21; Muḥammad b. 'Alī al-Ṣabbān, *Ḥāshiya 'alā Sharḥ al-Mallawī* (Cairo: Muṣṭafā al-Bābī al-Ḥalabī, 1938), 63 (main text ll. 6–7); Ismā'īl Gelenbevī, *al-Burhān fī 'ilm al-mīzān* (Cairo: Maṭba'at al-Sa'āda, 1347/1928–1929), 43, 46–48 (top rubric).

49 P. V. Spade (ed.), *The Cambridge Companion to Ockham* (Cambridge: Cambridge University Press, 1999); G. Klima, *John Buridan* (Oxford: Oxford University Press, 2008).

Yūsī's point was rather that Suyūṭī's remark about universals not existing outside the mind is simply irrelevant. Regardless of our position regarding the extramental existence of universals, it struck Yūsī as self-evident that universals are essential to any science. Grammar deals with "subject" and "verb" and "preposition"; law deals with "ritual purity" and "marriage" and "inheritance"; jurisprudence deals with "analogy" and "hadith" and "ijtihād," all of which are universals in the sense that they have numerous instances, as opposed to particulars like "ʿUmar b. al-Khaṭṭāb" or "The Prophet Muḥammad." Indeed, all propositional knowledge according to Yūsī involves universals, for they involve predication, and logical predicates are necessarily universal, for example: "x is *red*," "y is an *innovation*," "z is *forbidden*."[50] Subjects, by contrast, could be either particulars or universals, for example "*Zayd* is courageous" or "*Humans* are mortal." But even in the latter case, the universal subject-term should be understood as shorthand for the particulars to which it applies, which is precisely why universal subject-terms are regularly quantified: "*Every human* is mortal," "*Some humans* are literate."[51] Affirmative predications assert that universal properties are true of externally existing particulars. When such assertions are true, then the externally existing particular possesses a particular instance of the universal property.[52] There is nothing in this standard account – expounded in the handbooks on logic studied throughout the Islamic world at the time – that is incompatible with the position that all that exists in the extramental world are particular substances and their particular attributes.

Yūsī clearly thought that Suyūṭī simply did not know what he was talking about. He noted that he had initially planned to write an

50 Yūsī, *Mashrab al-ʿāmm wa l-khāṣṣ*, 245–251.

51 In Sanūsī's *Mukhtaṣar*, it is explicitly stated as a principle that in a standard categorical proposition the predicate is predicated of the instances falling under the subject-term (*ʿalā mā ṣadaqa ʿalayhi mawḍūʿuhā*), which is why subject-terms are normally quantified and predicate-terms are not (see Sanūsī, *Mukhtaṣar*, 43). In Kātibī's *Shamsiyya* and Quṭb al-Dīn al-Rāzī's standard commentary thereon, it is stated that the subject-term should normally be taken to refer to the individuals falling under it, and that propositions in which the subject-term stands for the universal itself and cannot be quantified (such as "Human is a genus") are of no interest to logic; see Quṭb al-Dīn al-Rāzī, *Sharḥ al-Shamsiyya,* II, 20–29 (main text, top rubric). The idea that logical subjects are particular and logical predicates are universal remains the prevalent view among modern philosophical logicians, see P. T. Geach, *Reference and Generality* (Ithaca and London: Cornell University Press, 1980), Chapter 2; P. F. Strawson, "Singular Terms and Predication," in P. F. Strawson, *Logico-Linguistic Papers* (Aldershot, UK: Ashgate, 2004), 41–56.

52 Yūsī, *Ḥawāshī*, 281.

independent rebuttal of the fatwa, but then decided it would be a waste of time. He would indeed have ignored Suyūṭī's view altogether were it not for the fact that the dull-witted (*al-buladā'*) sometimes thought that it was correct. Perhaps realizing that his response to the widely esteemed Egyptian scholar would be deemed excessively harsh, he added that he was drawing out the absurd consequences of Suyūṭī's verdict while realizing that of course Suyūṭī was too much of a scholar to actually believe these absurdities:

> We have not intended our discussion to be a depreciation of the status of any scholar, nor to treat Suyūṭī unfairly. We have merely drawn out the consequences of his words, while realizing that he is one of the eminent scholars and is not of the views that we have drawn out. Nevertheless, even if he is the object of respect and veneration, truth is after all more worthy of being followed. Among the words of Aristotle the Wise concerning his teacher Plato are the following: "We love the truth and we love Plato as long as the two coincide; if they part then truth takes precedence over him."[53]

Yūsī also opined that if Suyūṭī's intention had been merely to reject the extreme view that studying logic is the individual duty of every Muslim then there would be no disagreement. Yūsī also took no issue if Suyūṭī's aim was merely to warn against excessive study of logic (*tawaghghul* or *ifrāṭ*) to such an extent that one neglects or denigrates the study of Quran and hadith.[54]

This last concession would be taken up in defense of Suyūṭī by the eighteenth-century scholar Zabīdī (whose complaints about Maghrebī scholars' enthusiasm for logic were quoted at the beginning of Chapter 4). Zabīdī's argument was precisely that Yūsī and his students were preoccupied with logic to an excessive degree, at the expense of the study of hadith. And he had a point, insofar as Yūsī's oeuvre included a number of logical works but apparently none that can be classified as contributions to the science of hadith. One of Yūsī's own students noted that his teacher had been well versed in the rational sciences (*dirāya*) but not in the traditional sciences (*riwāya*).[55] A later Moroccan scholar expressed astonishment that Yūsī, when he went on pilgrimage toward the end of his life, did not take the trouble to "hear" hadith from some of the prominent scholars of Egypt and the Hejaz and obtain from them their

53 Yūsī, *Ḥawāshī*, 282–283. For the source of the Arabic saying attributed to Aristotle, see Gutas, *Avicenna and the Aristotelian Tradition*, 201, 206.

54 Yūsī, *Ḥawāshī*, 283.

55 Kattānī, *Fihris al-fahāris*, 1155–1156.

prestigious certificates with particularly short lines of transmission for canonical collections of hadith.[56]

Zabīdī, perhaps wisely, shifted the discussion from the question of the extramental existence of universals to the religious uses of logic. Even if one were to concede, he wrote, that basic logic could serve as an aid to the acquisition of other sciences, the greater part of the discussions in logic handbooks were of no use at all. They were simply examples of immersion in the intellectual vanities of the nether world:

As for its being a means to the other sciences, this is conceded, but most of its discussions and issues are superfluous and the knowledge and understanding of the Divine Address (*al-khiṭāb*) is in no need of them. Rather, most of them are trifles and constitute delving into matters that have no relation to religion at all... You do not find in the books of these people any mention whatsoever of God and His Prophet except in the preamble and all you find in their sessions is blameworthy dispute, proscribed enmity, belittlement, accusation and scorn.[57]

Yūsī would certainly not have agreed that logic is of little or no use for the understanding of the "Divine Address." His own treatment of theological issues is replete with the concepts and principles of logic. In one of his major theological works, dealing with an issue that had caused a good deal of controversy in Morocco in the sixteenth and seventeenth centuries, he explicitly stated that confusion had arisen due to insufficient attention to the principles of logic. It is to this work that the following section is devoted.

Ḥasan al-Yūsī on the Controversy Concerning the Islamic Profession of Faith

It may perhaps be recalled that Yūsī, in the quotation given near the beginning of this chapter, mentioned that the debate about "imitation" in creedal matters was the second major theological controversy he had witnessed in his own time. The first controversy he described thus:

In the years of the 1070s [= 1660s] I... passed by the town of Sijilmāsa and found that a great controversy had arisen amongst students and teachers concerning the meaning of "There is no god but Allah." One of them had explained the discourse of al-Sanūsī to the effect that what is denied [in this statement] is a presumed equal [to God]. Some of those who were prominent in legal matters but not in the

56 Ibid., 1156–1157.

57 Zabīdī, *Itḥāf al-sāda al-muttaqīn*, I, 180 (l.18ff).

ratiocinative sciences accused him of what al-Habṭī [d. 1555] had been accused in his well-known controversy with his contemporaries, and he was flogged.[58]

The controversy to which Yūsī referred was about what is denied (*al-manfī*) by the first part of the well-known Islamic profession of faith, "There is no god but Allah." The controversy had apparently first arisen in Morocco in the mid-sixteenth century.[59] A scholar from Algiers by the name of Muḥammad al-Kharrūbī al-Ṭarābulusī (d. 1555) had presented an ethical treatise to the court of the Moroccan Sultan Maḥammad al-Shaykh al-Mahdī (r. 1517–1557) in Fes. Kharrūbī claimed therein, among other things, that it is most appropriate when uttering the profession "There is no god but Allah" to understand in one's heart by the term "god" the false gods of the polytheists, not the one and true God. This elicited a retort by the Mufti of Fes Muḥammad al-Yassīthnī (d. 1552), who objected that what is denied by the phrase "There is no god" is not particular gods but the generic "god" that includes both the false gods of the unbelievers and the one and true god, Allah. After all, Yassīthnī pointed out, the Arabic phrase "There is no god" (*lā ilāha*) is a categorical negation that negates the entire category (*jins*), not this or that particular idol that polytheists happen to worship. Furthermore, the overall statement "There is no god but Allah" is grammatically an exception (*istithnā'*) and the default understanding of an exception is that what is excepted (in this case Allah) is of the same kind as what is denied (god). In turn, Yassīthnī's position was criticized by the local scholar 'Abdullāh al-Habṭī (d. 1555) – the person mentioned by Yūsī in the above-quoted lemma. Habṭī insisted that what is denied by the phrase "There is no god" is not the false gods of the polytheists and idolaters at all. Such false gods exist aplenty, Habṭī wrote, and to deny their existence is simply incorrect. Habṭī's position was treated as scandalous by many of his contemporaries who took him to be perversely denying that the Islamic profession implies a rejection of polytheism and idolatry. A debate was

58 Yūsī, *Muḥāḍarāt*, I, 226.

59 On the controversy, see especially Muḥammad Ibn 'Askar (d. 1578), *Dawḥat al-nāshir li-maḥāsin man kāna bi-l-Maghrib min mashāyikh al-qarn al-'āshir*, edited by Muḥammad Ḥajjī (Rabat: Dār al-Maghrib, 1976), 9–11. Ibn 'Askar was a student and disciple of one of the protagonists, 'Abdullāh al-Habṭī, and his account is accordingly partisan. For the actual arguments of the main protagonists, see Yūsī, *Mashrab*, 331–332 and Mayyāra, *al-Durr al-thamīn*, 47–48. The account in M. Ḥajjī, *al-Ḥaraka al-fikriyya*, I, 282–284 recapitulates those of Ibn 'Askar and Yūsī. The controversy must have occurred after Maḥammad al-Shaykh al-Mahdī moved his court to Fes in 1549 and before Yassīthnī's death in 1552.

held in front of the aforementioned Sultan, during which an enraged Yassīthnī called for Habṭī's execution. Habṭī was apparently stunned by the demand and may even have fainted. He then reportedly left the hall without saying anything in his own defense – it is possible that he was helped out in order to recover. The Sultan was not willing to execute him without first hearing what he had to say, and in the meantime Habṭī was prevailed upon to sign a written retraction. He then quietly left Fes for his home near Chefchaouen in northern Morocco, where he died a few years later. Nevertheless, the controversy did not die with him. Sanūsī's widely studied Commentary on the Short Creed (*al-Ṣughrā*) seemed to advocate the same position as Habṭī – indeed Habṭī explicitly invoked Sanūsī's position in his altercation with Yassīthnī. Sanūsī wrote that the term "god" (*ilāh*) in the statement "There is no god but Allah" cannot be understood to be equivalent in meaning to "object of worship" (*maʿbūd*) because there are evidently many objects of worship in existence besides Allah. Rather, it should be taken to be equivalent in meaning to "true object of worship" (*maʿbūd bi-ḥaqq*).[60] This seems to amount to the position that Habṭī was later to defend: What is denied by the statement "There is no god but Allah" is not the false objects of worship of the unbelievers but rather true objects of worship (except Allah). But Sanūsī's discussion merely suggested such a conclusion, whereas Habṭī defended it explicitly and emphatically in a public dispute with the Mufti of Fes, and it is this that got him into serious trouble. His position became infamous in later generations and was often denounced by Moroccan theologians for around a century after his death.

In response to the renewal of the controversy in the 1660s, Yūsī wrote an extended work, entitled *Mashrab al-ʿāmm wa-l-khāṣṣ min kalimat al-ikhlāṣ* (The fountainhead for commoners and scholars concerning the statement of singular devotion), in which he sought to vindicate Habṭī's view. Though its exact date of composition is not known, Yūsī must have written the work some time between the late 1660s and mid-1670s.[61] It is perhaps the lengthiest and most detailed intervention in the controversy, and appears to have been esteemed in later times – it was lithographed in Fes in 1327/1909.

Yūsī began his work by expounding and defending at some length a number of points derived from logic and the closely related discipline

60 Sanūsī, *Sharḥ Umm al-barāhīn*, 125 (Darwīsh edition).

61 The earliest dated manuscript of the work is from 30 Rajab 1088/28 September 1677 and is not an autograph; see the editor's introduction to Yūsī, *Mashrab*, 237.

of semantics (*'ilm al-ma'ānī*).[62] The very first section is devoted to an analysis of judgment (*ḥukm*).[63] A categorical judgment, Yūsī explained, presupposes a subject and a predicate. The subject can be an actually existent entity, as, for example, in the judgment "Abū Ḥanīfa is a scholar," or a supposed entity, for example "A partner of God does not exist." In the latter case, the mind possesses the concept "Partner of God" and then judges that there is nothing corresponding to this concept in extramental reality. We can, in other words, possess in our minds universal quiddities (*māhiyyāt kulliyya*) or mental ideas (*ṣuwar dhihniyya*) of nonexistents and make truthful negative claims about them.

A related, and crucial, principle that Yūsī was at pains to establish is that negation should properly be understood to be neither of the subject nor of the predicate but of a proposed propositional nexus (*nisba*) between the two. The subject and the predicate are both objects of conception (*taṣawwur*) and it is senseless to affirm or deny conceptions. To affirm is to declare true, to deny is to declare false, and only propositions are true or false. Yūsī quoted the following from the standard commentary by Taftāzānī on a widely studied manual of semantics-rhetoric:

> There is no doubt that affirmation and negation are directed at the propositional nexus (*al-nisba al-ḥukmiyya*). [...] If a reasonable person considers the matter introspectively it will become clear that if you conceive the notion "Zayd" or "human" without conceiving anything further such as "existence" or its [i.e., the notion's] relation to something else, then there is certainly no negation or affirmation.[64]

Arabic lacks the copulative "is," and a literal translation of the Islamic profession is "No god except Allah." Yūsī pointed out that we nevertheless must understand the negation to be not of the subject "god" but of a proposition consisting of the subject "god" and an implicit predicate. This implicit predicate could be "exists," for example, so that the meaning would be "No god *exists* except Allah."[65] What is negated on this

62 Yūsī, *Mashrab*, 245–284. The first eight sections of the lengthy introduction are devoted to logical, semantic, and grammatical principles. In the ninth section, Yūsī explains word for word the statement *lā ilāha illā Allāh*. In the tenth, he offers a syntactical analysis of it. Only then does Yūsī end the introduction and begin to present the controversy, his solution, and his replies to real or anticipated objections.

63 Yūsī, *Mashrab*, 245–256.

64 Ibid., 255–256.

65 Yūsī noted that classical Arabic lexicographers differed on whether "god" (*ilāh*) means "object of worship" or "true object of worship." In the former case, the implicit predicate would be "deserves being worshipped"; see Yūsī, *Mashrab*, 293–301, 324.

account is not the conception "god" but rather the existence of god, that is, a proposed propositional nexus between the subject "god" and the predicate "exists." Yūsī wrote:

> Essences (*dhawāt*) are not denied or affirmed... so when we say: this quiddity has been denied or its instances have been denied, it should be understood that something has been left unsaid that is nevertheless part of the meaning, viz. their existence has been denied. The negation governs existence (*maṣabbu l-nafyi huwa l-wujūd*).[66] [...] This is the case in the honorable statement [i.e. "There is no god except Allah"], for it denies the existence of what is preceded by the negative particle with the exception of God the Exalted.[67]

Some people, Yūsī noted, seem to think that negation means annihilating something, so that by saying "No god" I do something to certain entities – deprive them of their existence. This is pure confusion, he noted. A true negative statement does not *do* anything. It simply registers that a certain conceived nexus between a subject and a predicate does not correspond to anything in the extramental world.[68]

The statement "No god exists" has as its subject a universal (*kullī*), viz. "god." In other words, "god" (in Arabic *ilāh*) is not a proper name that denotes a single individual, but a general term that in principle may be true of more than one individual. Of course, as a matter of fact there is only one individual who falls under this general term, viz. Allah. But one cannot know, Yūsī explained, that there is only one individual merely from contemplating the concept "god." The fact that there is only one god is something that is established through rational proof, not something that follows simply from understanding the term "god." Although the subject of the negative proposition is a universal, any particular individual falling under that universal is within the scope of the negative judgment. The universal is "more general" (*aʿamm*) and the particulars falling under it are "more specific" (*akhaṣṣ*), and it is a principle of logic that negating the more general entails negating the more particular.[69] If, for example, I say "No man is in the house" then I am also denying that Zayd and ʿAmr and Bakr are in the house. If any one of these individual men should be in the house then the universal-negative statement would be false.

As noted in the preceding section, Yūsī was not a realist with respect to universals. He believed that universals only exist in the mind and that

66 Yūsī, *Mashrab*, 259 (ll.13–16).
67 Ibid., 284 (ll.10–12).
68 Ibid., 271–272.
69 Ibid., 257.

anything that exists extramentally is a particular. Nevertheless, universals can be predicated truly or falsely of particulars. When I say "Abū Ḥanīfa is a scholar" I am claiming that the universal "scholar" (*ʿālim*) is predicated truly of a particular entity in the extramental world. If what I say is true then Abū Ḥanīfa has a particular instance or portion (*ḥiṣṣa*) of the universal "scholar" as an attribute (*ṣifa* or *maʿnā*). A general term such as "scholar" is in this sense potentially confusing because it may refer to either the universal concept (*mafhūm*) in the mind or to the particular instances that fall under it (*maṣdūq*). Keeping the two senses distinct could, Yūsī maintained, help avoid serious misunderstanding. For example, the whole controversy had been ignited by Kharrūbī's claim that what is denied in the profession of faith is "what polytheists claim to be divine" (*mā iddaʿāhu l-mushrikūn*). His contemporaries understood this to mean that what is denied are particular instances in the extramental world that polytheists worship, to which they objected that (1) the negation is categorical and thus universal, and (2) that it is false to deny the existence of particulars that idolaters and polytheists worship. But the phrase "what polytheists claim to be divine" could also be taken to mean, not the particular extramental idols worshipped by the polytheists, but the universal concept (*al-mafhūm al-kullī*) that is common to all the different objects of worship of polytheists, viz. "partner of God." The Islamic profession indeed denies that such a universal applies to anything in the extramental world, including the particulars that polytheists and idolaters happen to worship. In this sense, Kharrūbī's statement is entirely correct.[70]

Having established these preliminary logical and semantic principles, Yūsī presented his own position concerning the profession of faith. He wrote:

> If you say: That which is denied, is it the true god (*al-ilāh al-ḥaqq*) or the false god (*al-ilāh al-bāṭil*)? I say: It is the true god, not the false god. This is the correct position, for false gods such as idols and graven images exist, and it is incorrect to deny them. The honorable statement, as you know, is a declaration that any supposed particular of "god" does not exist except for one particular and this is Allah the Exalted. There is no doubt that the [universal] of whom Allah is the only existing instance is "god deserving to be worshipped," and that if any other instances [of this universal] were to exist then they would be equals to God the Exalted. But such instances do not exist and are impossible of existence. As for instances of "false god" these do exist.[71]

[70] Ibid., 335–337.
[71] Ibid., 325 (ll. 8ff).

In other words, what is denied in the Islamic profession is the existence of any true god besides Allah. The intention is not to deny the existence of false gods for these undoubtedly exist and, moreover, to say "There is no false god except Allah" would obviously be tantamount to unbelief.[72] Habṭī, despite the widespread denunciations to which he had been subjected, had been right after all.

At this point, someone might object that if false gods are not denied, then one would have to suppose – incredibly – that the Islamic profession does not include an explicit rejection of the false gods of idolaters and polytheists. This objection obviously runs afoul of the principle that entities are not denied, only assertions or propositions. What claim, Yūsī asked, does the objector want the profession to deny? Is it the claim that idols and false objects of worship exist? Surely not, since they manifestly do exist. It must be the claim that the idols and gods of the polytheists are true gods that deserve to be worshipped. But this *is* denied by the Islamic profession that there is no true god worthy of worship other than Allah.[73] Yūsī conceded that Habṭī had expressed himself incautiously by insisting that the idols of the polytheists are not included in what is denied in the Islamic profession, without making it clear in what sense this is true.[74] It is true that there is no denial of their essences (*dhawāt*) or of their existence, as some existent objects are improper objects of worship – for example, graven images or planets or Jesus. Nor is there a denial that these existent entities are false objects of worship. What is denied is that these existent entities are true gods or proper objects of worship.[75] Because the profession denies that any true god other than Allah exists, it thereby also denies that graven images, planets, or Jesus are true gods. This is analogous to an everyday situation in which one denies that there is any man in the house except Zayd; one thereby also denies that Bakr, ʿAmr, and so on are in the house. Yūsī wrote:

> Because in the honorable statement the existence is denied of a god deserving of worship other than our Lord (to whom be Might and Glory), it is known that the idols and everything else worshipped besides God the Exalted are not deserving of worship. If some of these were gods deserving of worship then the universal negation in the honorable statement would be falsified, for the universal-negative proposition is falsified if something that has been negated by it should obtain.[76]

72 Ibid., 344–345.
73 Ibid., 328–329.
74 Ibid., 347.
75 Ibid., 343–347.
76 Ibid. (ll.10ff).

Yūsī went on to disarm another objection that had been made to Habṭī's thesis. The objection is as follows: to claim that what is denied in the Islamic profession is the existence of true gods leads to absurdity. A true god is necessary of existence, and to deny the existence of a necessary existent is an outright contradiction.[77] But this objection, Yūsī countered, is based on confusing conception (*taṣawwur*) and assent (*taṣdīq*). To deny the existence of anything, one must first have a concept of that thing. To deny the existence of true gods other than Allah, one must first have a conception of the universal "true god" (*ilāh ḥaqq*) and then deny that such a universal is true of existing or imagined particulars other than Allah. Similarly, to deny the existence of necessary existents other than Allah, one must first have in mind the universal concept "necessary existent" and then make the judgment that such a universal concept is not true of anything other than Allah. There is no contradiction between a conception ("true god" or "necessary existent") and a judgment ("there is no true god other than Allah" or "there is no necessary existent other than Allah") – contradictions obtain only between two judgments. Yūsī wrote:

> Contradiction obtains when two judgments (*taṣdīqayn*) differ with respect to affirmation and negation, not when a judgment (*taṣdīq*) and a conception (*taṣawwur*) differ as in this case. For we conceive the [universal] "true god" in our minds – since one cannot judge affirmatively or negatively concerning anything except after conceiving it – and then we judge it not to exist extramentally. By conceiving it in our minds, we do not affirm that it exists extramentally, and hence it is not contradictory to negate its existence extramentally. [...] The objection of this person arises from ignorance and overlooking the difference between (1) conceiving something and its mental existence, and (2) making it the subject of an affirmative or negative judgment. [...] The "true god" is conceived in the mind as a universal quiddity (*bi-māhiyyatihi l-kulliya*) and then one inquires whether it exists or does not exist in extramental reality (*fī l-khārij*).[78]

On Yūsī's account, the universal "true god" has mental existence (*wujūd dhihnī*) in the sense that it is present to our mind as a universal quiddity or mental idea.[79] The Islamic profession denies that this quiddity has any correlate in the extramental world besides one existing particular, viz. Allah. Yūsī thus agreed that the exception in the Islamic profession is grammatically of the normal, so-called *muttaṣil* kind: what is excepted

[77] Ibid. 357. The objector is identified by the editor as Muḥammad al-ʿArabī al-Fāsī.

[78] Yūsī, *Mashrab*, 358–359.

[79] For Yūsī's defense of "mental existence," traditionally denied by theologians and upheld by philosophers, see *Mashrab*, 261–266.

(Allah) belongs to the same category as what is denied (true god). An earlier Moroccan scholar had rejected this understanding of the exception on the following grounds: To assume that Allah is of the same genus (*jins*) as what is denied is to assume that Allah consists of a genus (*jins*) and a differentia (*faṣl*). But it is generally agreed that this cannot be the case because Allah's essence (*dhāt*) cannot be composite in any way; hence the exception cannot be of the *muttaṣil* type.[80] Yūsī rejected this line of thinking for a number of reasons. Grammarians, he noted, use the term "genus" (*jins*) in a different way from logicians. Grammarians use it of any universal with instances; logicians use it only of universals that give the common essence of a number of distinct species. In the grammatical sense, Allah is part of a *jins*, as He is a particular instance of a universal ("object of worship," "true god," or "necessary existent"). In the logical sense, Allah is not part of a *jins* because He is a particular, not a species.[81] From a logical point of view, it is not sufficient for an entity being considered part of a genus that it falls under a general term. The general term must in addition indicate the essence of the entity that it has in common with other species.[82] Moreover, the fact that a number of universals can be predicated truly of God does not entail that God's essence is composite, for one must distinguish between being composite in extramental reality (*al-tarkīb al-khārijī*) and being composite in conception (*al-tarkīb al-dhihnī al-iʿtibārī*). It is only the former that is impossible, not the latter.[83]

The foregoing account cannot do justice to all aspects of Yūsī's lengthy, densely argued, and somewhat sprawling work. (He seems to have made a special effort to make his arguments accessible, leading to some repetitiveness and prolixity.) The purpose has rather been to give the reader a sense of the controversy and the extent to which rational theology and logic were interwoven in the later North African Ashʿarī tradition. When Zabīdī complained about excessive interest in logic in eighteenth-century Egypt, he was well aware of this fact. He noted that the impetus for this interest had come from Maghrebī scholars standing in the tradition of Sanūsī, and he lamented the resulting prominence of "theologian-logicians" (*al-mutakallimīn al-manāṭiqa*) in Cairo in his own time.[84]

80 Yūsī, *Mashrab*, 416–417. The scholar is identified by the editor as ʿAbd al-Raḥmān al-ʿĀrif al-Fāsī (d. 1626).
81 Yūsī, *Mashrab*, 418.
82 Ibid., 419.
83 Ibid., 418.
84 Zabīdī, *Itḥāf al-sāda al-muttaqīn*, I, 181 (l.23).

Epilogue: Zabīdī's Criticism

The radical party in Sijilmāsa who denied the faith of the imitator insisted that the ordinary believer should know the meaning of the Islamic profession in the sense that he or she should know and be able to explain what it denies and what it affirms. Yūsī explicitly distanced himself from this position. The common believers understand in a general way that the profession affirms *tawḥīd*, i.e., the principle that God is the only proper object of worship, and this is sufficient.[85] They are not charged with being able to expound the meaning in detail and using the technical terms of logic, semantics and grammar. Nor should they be expected to answer questions such as "Is it false gods or true gods that are denied?" Still, Yūsī clearly did not think that such questions are in principle illegitimate or that there is nothing to be gained from attempting to answer them. Had he thought so, he would hardly have devoted one of his longer works to an exhaustive discussion of the issue.[86] On the contrary, in the introduction he clearly stated that the profession of faith is of such central importance that it deserves the kind of careful attention that he was about to give to it. He also explicitly stated that he had two aims in mind: (1) to lay down what is absolutely essential for all Muslims to know concerning the profession, and (2) to clarify the issue to the intellectual elite who wished to go beyond the minimum requirement and develop a fuller understanding. Hence the title "The fountainhead of commoners and elite concerning the declaration of singular devotion." The fact that the finer points of the topic are beyond the ken of unlearned commoners did not, for Yūsī, mean that it is illegitimate to explore them. To that end, he believed that the tools of logic, semantics and grammar are relevant, and that ignorance of such disciplines leads to misapprehensions and misplaced worries. He wrote:

> The words of these objectors [to Habṭī] suggest that they believe that existents may be negated, or that they do not comprehend generalities and negative-universal propositions, or that they do not know what is the object of affirmation or negation. And the person of whom this is true, how can he presume to throw himself into a discussion that requires abundant understanding?[87]

85 Yūsī, *Mashrab*, 476–477.

86 Yūsī's account in *al-Muḥāḍarāt* might at first sight suggest that he found the controversy inappropriate, as he described the slightly later controversy concerning the faith of the imitator as "more disagreeable" (*absha*ʿ) and "more untoward" (*ashna*ʿ). But what he seems to have found unpleasant was the acrimony and the flogging of a person for having what Yūsī considered the correct view, not that the issue was being discussed.

87 Yūsī, *Mashrab*, 356 (l. 14ff).

Zabīdī would hardly have been impressed by this example of the "usefulness" of logic. For him, the entire discipline of rational theology (*kalām*) is illegitimate and had been declared to be so by the venerable earliest generations of Islam (*al-salaf*). In other words, the very raising of questions such as "Is it false gods or true gods that are denied by the first part of the profession of faith?" is a reprehensible innovation – an illicit departure from the pristine faith of early Islam. When Yūsī objected to Suyūṭī that his arguments for the proscription of logic could equally be raised against *kalām*, Zabīdī simply replied: "Yes, and that is why those who have warned against *kalām* have done so."[88] Yūsī had also objected that to claim that logic is useless for theology, as Suyūṭī did, is to contradict what is evident to the senses (*inkārun li-l-maḥsūs*).[89] Indeed, theology and logic in the North African Ashʿarī tradition of Sanūsī were so closely intertwined that Suyūṭī's claim must have seemed bizarre to someone standing in that tradition. Zabīdī, by contrast, held that the only legitimate "science of creed" (*ʿilm al-ʿaqāʾid*) is a presentation of the articles of faith on the basis of traditional reports (*al-ḥujaj al-sharʿiyya wa l-barāhīn al-naqliyya*), not rational argument (*al-adilla al-ʿaqliyya*),[90] and he therefore considered Suyūṭī to be in the right. He wrote:

> Suyūṭī's claim that it [logic] is of no use for the science of *tawḥīd* is correct. For the faith that comes from the profession of the unity of God is not based on logical demonstration, contrary to what they [i.e. logicians and theologians] suggest, but on knowledge bringing the one who possesses it to the truth of the matter. Its sign is the opening of the heart to the stations of faith, and acceptance of the decree of God, and turning to the recollection (*dhikr*) of Him, and loving Him while turning away from the world of vanity. [...] If a problem should arise concerning the monotheist creed and a doubt should find its way to the heart of the believer... then, if you seek its removal from one of the theologian-logicians who are leaders in such matters in our day, he will give you a response according to what he conceives of the testimony of those who enjoy certainty, and according to rational extrapolations from the outward sense of revealed texts. But these [conceptions and extrapolations] are in turn doubtful, so how can what is doubtful remove doubts?[91]

As will be seen in the following chapters, Zabīdī's position was typical of the Ibn ʿArabī-inspired school of Sufism that became increasingly visible in the Arabic-Islamic East in the seventeenth and eighteenth centuries.

88 Zabīdī, *Itḥāf al-sāda al-muttaqīn*, I, 183 (l. 1).
89 Yūsī, *Ḥawāshī*, 280.
90 Zabīdī, *Itḥāf al-sāda al-muttaqīn*, I, 185 (ll. 12–14).
91 Zabīdī, *Itḥāf al-sāda al-muttaqīn*, I, 181 (ll. 7–11, 20–24).

PART III

THE IMAMS OF THOSE WHO PROCLAIM THE UNITY OF EXISTENCE

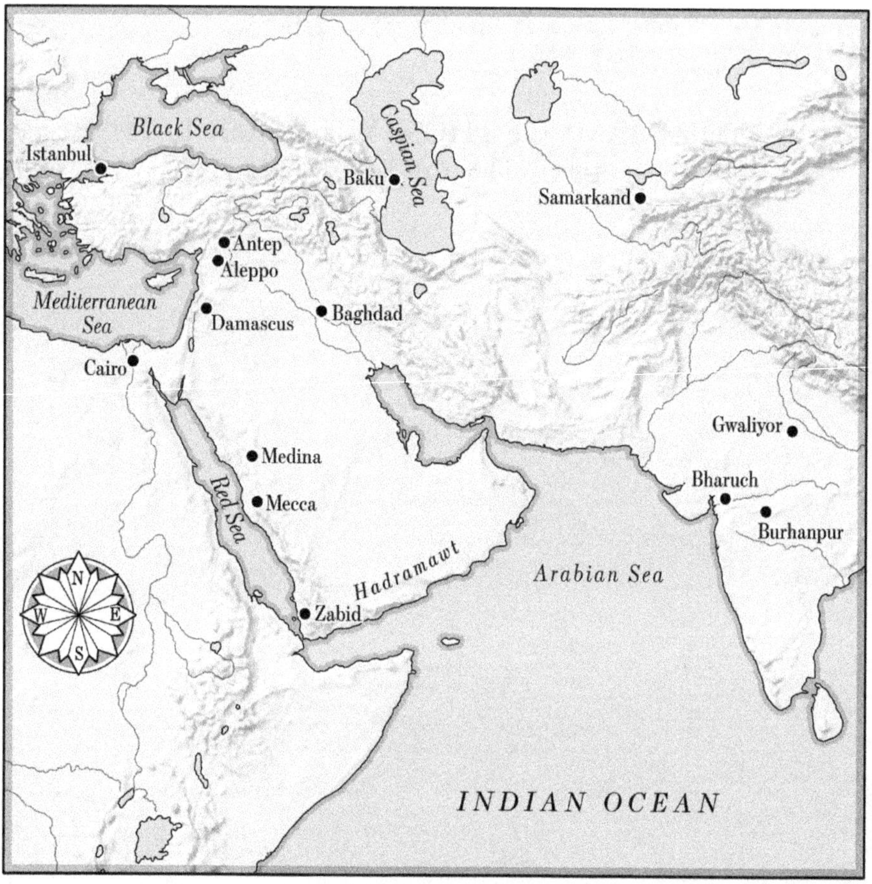

Map of India and Arabia

7

The Spread of Mystical Monism

The ideal of "verification" was, as has been seen in previous chapters, central to the Islamic scholarly tradition in the early modern period. It was also central to Sufism, but with a somewhat different connotation. In the context of the rational sciences, "verification" stood for a critical engagement with received scholarly views, often by applying the tools of logic or dialectic. In a Sufi context, "verification" typically denoted the mystical-experiential authentication of the truths to which ordinary believers – including exoteric theologians – abstractly assent. It is one thing, Sufis held, to assent to the proposition that God exists or even to prove that proposition rationally. It is another thing to experience directly the all-consuming presence of the divine being.

The centrality of the concept of "verification" in this sense is clear from a widely read manual on Sufism, entitled *al-Sayr wa-l-sulūk ilā malik al-mulūk*, by Qāsim al-Khānī (d. 1697) of Aleppo. The author invoked the concept from the outset when he gave the reason for writing the treatise:

> Since it is widely believed by those whom indolence and lethargy have rendered disinclined to pursue the path that leads to the highest stations, and who do not go beyond the external senses, that the path of the verifiers (*ṭarīq al-muḥaqqiqīn*) is wrecked, its traces vanished and its people dead, so that only the name remains, I have written this treatise and explicated therein how to pursue the Path, the states of the Seekers and the Trail, and what the Seeker will need in order to traverse the Path and reach Verification (*wa-l-wuṣūl ilā l-taḥqīq*).[1]

[1] Qāsim al-Khānī, *al-Sayr wa l-sulūk ilā malik al-mulūk*, edited by Muḥammad ʿĪd al-Shāfiʿī (Cairo: al-Jāmiʿa al-Ṣūfiyya al-Islāmiyya al-ʿĀlamiyya, no date), 23; edited by Saʿīd ʿAbd al-Fattāḥ (Cairo: Maktabat al-Thaqāfa al-Dīniyya, 2002), 40.

After the preface, Khānī proceeded to introduce the reader to the technical terminology (*iṣṭilāḥāt*) of what he called "the people of verification" (*ahl al-taḥqīq*).[2] These were the central concepts of the classical Sufi tradition: *ikhlāṣ*, *baqā'*, *taqwā*, *tajallī*, *taṣawwuf*, *jam'*, *jam' al-jam'*, and so forth. In the course of his ensuing discussion of the stages of the Sufi path, it is abundantly clear that Khānī understood "verification" to be closely related to "mystical unveiling" (*kashf*) and "mystical witnessing" (*shuhūd* and *mushāhada*). On one occasion, for instance, he referred to those who mistakenly consider themselves among "the verifiers, the people of unveiling (*al-muḥaqqiqīn ahl al-kashf*)."[3] When describing the most advanced stages of the mystical Path, he referred both to "verifying" that one's own self is naught, utterly impotent and dependent on the Lord, and to "witnessing" that indeed there is nothing in existence save God and His acts.[4]

The ideal of *taḥqīq* as direct mystical authentication was certainly not an innovation of Khānī's. It is attested in Sufi literature from much earlier centuries.[5] But despite the terminological continuity, there is reason to believe that the metaphysical truths that "verification" was supposed to authenticate underwent a subtle shift in the seventeenth century. A number of prominent mystics in the Arab East such as Aḥmad al-Qushāshī (d. 1661), Ibrāhīm Kūrānī (d. 1690), Muḥammad b. 'Abd al-Rasūl Barzinjī (d. 1691), the aforementioned Qāsim al-Khānī (d. 1697), 'Abd al-Ghanī al-Nābulusī (d. 1731), and Muṣṭafā al-Bakrī (d. 1749) all held that "verification" supports the controversial doctrine of "the unity of existence" (*waḥdat al-wujūd*), that is, that God *is* existence and, conversely, that existence is one and divine. This was not, or so it will be argued in the text that follows, the case prior to the seventeenth century in the Arab-Islamic world. The most prominent fifteenth- and sixteenth-century Arab mystics whose writings have come down to us were much more cautious about embracing ontological monism. This novel development in the seventeenth century seems largely to have been linked to the spread in the Arab East of Sufi orders such as the Khalwatiyya from Anatolia and the Shaṭṭāriyya and Naqshbandiyya from India.

[2] Khānī, *al-Sayr wa l-sulūk*, 25ff. [Shāfi'ī edition]; 43ff. ['Abd al-Fattāḥ edition].

[3] Khānī, *al-Sayr wa l-sulūk*, 95 (l. 9) [Shāfi'ī edition]. The passage is missing from the 'Abd al-Fattāḥ edition, cp. 166 (ll. 1–2).

[4] Khānī, *al-Sayr wa l-sulūk*, 114, 126 [Shāfi'ī edition]; 183 ['Abd al-Fattāḥ edition]. The ninth chapter has dropped out of my copy of the 'Abd al-Fattāḥ edition.

[5] W. Chittick, *The Sufi Path of Knowledge: Ibn 'Arabi's Metaphysics of Imagination* (Albany: SUNY Press, 1989), 4, 166–168; M. Profitlich, *Die Terminologie Ibn 'Arabīs im "Kitab wasa'il al-sa'il" des Ibn Saudakin: Text, Ubersetzung und Analyse* (Freiburg: Klaus Schwarz Verlag, 1973), 53–60.

Sixteenth-Century Arab Sufi Scholars on Ibn ʿArabī

The formula "the unity of existence" (*waḥdat al-wujūd*) has come to be intimately linked to the name of the Andalusian-born mystic Muḥyī al-Dīn Ibn ʿArabī (d. 1240). Nevertheless, as shown by William Chittick and James Morris, both the formula and the tendency to see it as encapsulating the entire worldview of Ibn ʿArabī derive, not from the writings of Ibn ʿArabī himself, but rather from a tradition of commentators stemming from his more philosophically inclined disciple Ṣadr al-Dīn al-Qūnawī (d. 1274).[6] This tradition included Qūnawī's students Saʿīd al-Dīn al-Farghānī (d. 1300) and Muʾayyid al-Dīn al-Jandī (d.ca.1296) and later influential commentators on Ibn ʿArabī's short and daring work *Fuṣūṣ al-ḥikam* such as ʿAbd al-Razzāq al-Qāshānī (d. 1335) and Dāʾūd al-Qayṣarī (d. 1350). It continued into the fifteenth century with, for example, the Ottoman Turkish scholar Meḥmed Fenārī (d. 1431), the Indo-Muslim scholar ʿAlāʾ al-Dīn al-Mahāʾimī (d. 1432), and the Persian scholar ʿAbd al-Raḥmān al-Jāmī (d. 1492). Both Chittick and Morris have suggested that this tradition tends toward an overly schematic presentation of Ibn ʿArabī's multifaceted thought. Chittick's own monumental reconstructions of this thought have accordingly been based largely on a direct engagement with Ibn ʿArabī's own works, and especially the voluminous *al-Futūḥāt al-makkiyya*, which is less systematic and philosophically involved than the works of the later commentators on the *Fuṣūṣ*.[7] Chittick's and Morris' suggestion is plausible, but for present purposes it is more to the point that their distinction between Ibn ʿArabī on the one hand and the later tradition of ontological monism (*waḥdat al-wujūd*) on the other was not foreign to the Islamic mystical tradition itself. As will be seen in the present section, there was a Sufi tradition that was especially strong in the Arabic-speaking world in the fifteenth and sixteenth centuries that esteemed Ibn ʿArabī as a saint, quoted approvingly from his *Futūḥāt*, and yet remained aloof from the ontological monism of the Qūnawī tradition. In fact, it would appear that the influence of the Persianate commentators on the *Fuṣūṣ* was somewhat marginal among Arab mystical scholars until the seventeenth century.

[6] Chittick, *The Sufi Path of Knowledge*, xvii–xiv; W. Chittick, "Ṣadr al-Dīn Ḳūnawī," *EI2*, XII, 753–755; W. Chittick, "Waḥdat al-Wujūd in Islamic Thought," *Bulletin of the Henry Martyn Institute of Islamic Studies* 10(1991): 7–27; W. Chittick, "Rūmī and Waḥdat al-Wujūd," in A. Banani, R. Hovannisian and G. Sadighi (eds.), *Poetry and Mysticism in Islam: The Heritage of Rumi* (Cambridge: Cambridge University Press, 1994), 70–111; J. W. Morris, "Ibn ʿArabī and His Interpreters: Part II: Influences and Interpretations," *Journal of the American Oriental Society* 106(1986): 733–756.

[7] Chittick, *The Sufi Path of Knowledge*, xx.

One may consider the case of the prominent Egyptian Sufi ʿAbd al-Wahhāb al-Shaʿrānī (d. 1565). There can be no question about Shaʿrānī's esteem for Ibn ʿArabī.[8] He wrote an abridgement of Ibn ʿArabī's *Futūḥāt* that he introduced with the following observation:

This [work] is a precious book that I have selected from my [longer] book *Lawāqiḥ al-anwār al-qudsiyya* which I summarized from [Ibn ʿArabī's] *al-Futūḥāt al-makkiyya*... I have entitled it *al-Kibrīt al-aḥmar fī bayān ʿulūm al-Shaykh al-Akbar* (The elixir of gold in explicating the sciences of the Greatest Master). I intend by the term *al-kibrīt al-aḥmar* the elixir of gold, and by "Greatest Master" Muḥyī al-Dīn Ibn ʿArabī, may God be pleased with him. I mean that the sciences of this book are to the books of other Sufis what the elixir of gold is to things that are merely coated with gold.[9]

Shaʿrānī's major theological work *al-Yawāqīt wa-l-jawāhir fī bayān ʿaqāʾid al-akābir* (Precious stones and jewels in explicating the creedal beliefs of the masters) is also replete with quotations from the works of Ibn ʿArabī. He wrote in the introduction to that work:

This is a book on the science of creeds that I have entitled *al-Yawāqīt wa-l-jawāhir fī bayān ʿaqāʾid al-akābir*. In it, I have attempted to reconcile the creed of the people of Unveiling [i.e. the Sufis] and the people of ratiocination [i.e. the rational theologians] to the limits of my ability... Know O brother that I have read from among the discourses of the people of Unveiling countless treatises and did not find in their wording anything more comprehensive than that of the Perfect Master, the Verifier (*al-muḥaqqiq*) and Spiritual Guide of Gnostics the Shaykh Muḥyī al-Dīn Ibn ʿArabī, may God have mercy on him. I have therefore supported this book with his discourse from *al-Futūḥāt* and other works rather than the discourse of other Sufis.[10]

Shaʿrānī in effect organized his *al-Yawāqīt* in a manner reminiscent of Sunni creedal treatises. For each creedal issue, he first expounded what he took to be the mainstream exoteric Sunni view, relying mainly on Ashʿarī authorities such as the Timurid scholar Saʿd al-Dīn al-Taftāzānī (d. 1390) and the Jerusalem-born Egyptian scholar Kamāl al-Dīn Ibn Abī l-Sharīf al-Maqdisī (d. 1500).[11] (Significantly, Shaʿrānī never referred to Sanūsī

[8] M. Winter, *Society and Religion in Early Ottoman Egypt: Studies in the Writings of ʿAbd al-Wahhāb al-Shaʿrānī* (New Brunswick, NJ: Transaction Publishers, 1982), 127–133.

[9] ʿAbd al-Wahhāb al-Shaʿrānī, *al-Kibrīt al-aḥmar fī bayān ʿulūm al-Shaykh al-Akbar*, printed on the margins of *al-Yawāqīt wa l-jawāhir fī bayān ʿaqāʾid al-akābir* (Cairo: al-Maṭbaʿa al-Muyammaniyya, 1317/1899), I, 2 (margin).

[10] ʿAbd al-Wahhāb al-Shaʿrānī, *al-Yawāqīt wa l-jawāhir fī bayān ʿaqāʾid al-akābir* (Cairo: al-Maṭbaa al-Muyammaniyya, 1317/1899), I, 2.

[11] On Ibn Abī l-Sharīf, see Ghazzī, *al-Kawākib al-sāʾira*, I, 11–13. Shaʿrānī regularly quoted from his gloss on Taftāzānī's commentary on the creed of Abū Ḥafṣ al-Nasafī (d. 1142); his gloss on the commentary of Jalāl al-Dīn al-Maḥallī (d. 1459) on *Jamʿ al-Jawāmiʿ* (a

whose influence in Egypt, as argued in Chapter 5 (section on "Sanusi's Influence in the East") was not particularly strong until the seventeenth century.) Sha'rānī then appended to each issue lengthy quotations from Sufi works, most often – but not invariably – by Ibn 'Arabī. It is striking that not once in the lengthy two-volume work did Sha'rānī quote from Ibn 'Arabī's controversial *Fuṣūṣ* or from the works of Qūnawī and the later *Fuṣūṣ* commentators. It is also striking that Sha'rānī was not concerned at all with the metaphysical discussions of essence and existence that so preoccupied the later Persianate tradition of ontological monism. He was obviously much more interested in the more visionary aspects of Ibn 'Arabī's oeuvre, for example quoting at great length Ibn 'Arabī's angelology and his hierarchy of the divine names.[12] The phrase *waḥdat al-wujūd* is never mentioned. Sha'rānī did note that Ibn 'Arabī was sometimes accused of holding the view that "there is no existent other than God (*lā mawjūda illā Allāh*)." He characteristically replied that what is meant by the formula is simply that there is no self-subsisting entity besides God and that all other entities are in need of something extrinsic, viz. God, to keep them in existence.[13] Sha'rānī's interpretation renders the formula innocuous and acceptable to practically all Islamic scholars; it is certainly not what the *Fuṣūṣ* commentators meant by *waḥdat al-wujūd*. Sha'rānī betrayed his own interpretation when he added that a phrase such as "there is no existent other than God" would have been uttered by Ibn 'Arabī in a state of mystical intoxication in which his heart "witnessed" God and nothing else.[14] Sha'rānī seems not to have noticed that his two points are incompatible: If Ibn 'Arabī had meant nothing more than the uncontroversial thesis that there is no self-sufficient entity other than God then why suppose he had made the utterance in a state of mystical intoxication? Be that as it may, it is quite clear that Sha'rānī had great esteem for Ibn 'Arabī but without committing himself to the idea of *waḥdat al-wujūd* as presented by Qūnawī and the later *Fuṣūṣ* commentators.

Sha'rānī's almost exclusive focus on the *Futūḥāt* also meant that he could dismiss some other controversial ideas that were widely attributed to Ibn 'Arabī on the basis of the latter's *Fuṣūṣ*. For example, he was adamant that Ibn 'Arabī did not, as some critics charged, believe that the Pharaoh who had opposed Moses died as a believer – an idea that is

handbook on jurisprudence by Tāj al-Dīn al-Subkī [d. 1370]); and his commentary on *al-Musāyara*, a work on theology by Ibn Humām (d. 1456).

12 Sha'rānī, *Yawāqīt*, I, 75–89; II, 44–50.

13 Ibid., I, 12 (ll. 1–4).

14 Ibid., I, 12 (ll. 4–6).

quite clearly set out in the *Fuṣūṣ*.[15] With respect to the charge that Ibn ʿArabī believed that the torments of infidels in hell would eventually come to an end, Shaʿrānī adopted another strategy: he managed to find passages in Ibn ʿArabī's extensive oeuvre that suggest that infidels will be consigned to hell forever, and he maintained that all passages that stated otherwise were heretical interpolations by later hands.[16] Shaʿrānī repeatedly insisted that the works of Ibn ʿArabī had been tampered with by heretics. At times he simply argued that Ibn ʿArabī was a saint who could not possibly have expressed such heretical views; at other times, he claimed that an acquaintance of his had collated the text of the *Futūḥāt* with the autograph manuscript in Konya and found that such problematic passages were absent from the original.[17]

Shaʿrānī's combination of attitudes – admiration for Ibn ʿArabī while resisting ontological monism and other controversial ideas expressed especially in the *Fuṣūṣ* and its later commentaries – appears to have been standard among sixteenth-century Arab mystical scholars. It is also in evidence in the works of Ibn Maymūn al-Maghribī (d. 1511), a North African Shādhilī mystic who settled in Damascus.[18] Ibn Maymūn wrote a strongly worded apology for Ibn ʿArabī, accusing detractors of being reprobates (*fussāq*) for calumniating an upright Muslim on the basis of insufficient knowledge of the technical terms and modes of expression of Sufism.[19] Ibn Maymūn nevertheless avoided any engagement with specific charges or ideas. There is nothing in his treatise about *waḥdat al-wujūd* or the faith of Pharaoh or the transience of hell. In a brief postscript to the treatise, Ibn Maymūn's disciple ʿAlī b. ʿAṭiyya al-Ḥamawī, better known as ʿAlwān al-Ḥamawī (d. 1530), cited the positive opinion of Ibn ʿArabi expressed by the widely respected Egyptian scholars Zakariyyā al-Anṣārī (d. 1519) and Jalāl al-Dīn al-Suyūṭī (d. 1505). But the main thrust of their defense was to emphasize that Sufis had a distinctive technical vocabulary and often used it to express their peculiar spiritual

15 Shaʿrānī, *Yawāqīt*, I, 12 (ll. 12ff.); II, 100 (ll. 3ff.), II, 106 (ll. 30ff.); II, 158 (ll. 18ff.) For the relevant passage in the *Fuṣūṣ*, see Ibn ʿArabī, *Fuṣūṣ al-ḥikam*, edited by Abū l-ʿAlāʾ al-ʿAfīfī (Cairo: ʿĪsā al-Bābī al-Ḥalabī, 1946), 201.

16 Shaʿrānī, *Yawāqīt*, II, 165 (ll. 13ff.).

17 Shaʿrānī, *Yawāqīt*, I, 2 (ll. 8ff); I, 6 (ll. 22ff.). Shaʿrānī invoked such heretical interpolations on numerous occasions in his *Yawāqīt*, e.g., I, 55 (l. 11); II, 21 (l. 23); II, 43 (l. 22).

18 On this Sufi and his immediate disciples, see M. Winter, "Sheikh Ali Ibn Maymun and Syrian Sufism in the Sixteenth Century," *Israel Oriental Studies* 7(1977): 281–308.

19 ʿAlī Ibn Maymūn al-Maghribī [*Risāla fī l-radd ʿalā munkirī l-Shaykh Muḥyī al-Dīn Ibn al-ʿArabī*] (MS: Berlin Staatsbibliothek: Wetzstein 1545), fols. 55a–59a.

experiences. Their expressions should not, they insisted, be judged by those who are unfamiliar with the terminology or spiritual experiences.[20] This line of defense falls short of a wholesale endorsement of *waḥdat al-wujūd* and other controversial ideas attributed to Ibn ʿArabī. Indeed, Suyūṭī decried what he saw as the infiltration into Sufism of Avicennan philosophical terminology and concerns, and firmly rejected the doctrine of what he called "absolute unity" (*al-waḥda al-muṭlaqa*) which he claimed was based on this infiltration. He also expressed a desire to ban the books of Ibn ʿArabī for all but accomplished mystics, and rejected other controversial ideas associated with the Ibn ʿArabī school – for example, that Pharaoh had died as a believer and that sainthood is a more elevated station than prophecy.[21] ʿAlwān al-Ḥamawī, in his aforementioned appendix to Ibn Maymūn's treatise, likewise stressed that Ibn ʿArabī's works were often invoked by heretics and should not be read except by upright Sufis who were familiar with the terminology of these works. He added that Ibn Maymūn, after writing his apology, had encountered some of the potentially problematic passages in Ibn ʿArabi's works and ordered these to be erased from manuscript copies "for fear of their effects on the minds of the commoners" (*khawfan ʿalā ʿuqūl al-ʿawāmm*).[22] A similar story is related of the southern Arabian Sufi Ḥusayn Bā-Faḍl al-Ḥadramī (d. 1571). In his lifetime, he was supposed to have eagerly collected the works of Ibn ʿArabī and to have owned the only copy of the *Futūḥāt* in all of Hadhramaut (in what is today southern Yemen). But on his deathbed, he destroyed his manuscript on the grounds that it was likely to be misunderstood. The source for this account, the Yemeni Sufi and chronicler

[20] Éric Geoffroy, in his seminal study of Egyptian and Syrian Sufism in the fifteenth and sixteenth centuries, devotes considerable attention to the defense of Ibn ʿArabī by scholars such as Suyūṭī; see *Le Soufisme en Egypte et en Syrie sous les derniers Mamelouks et les premiers Ottomans* (Damascus: Institut français de Damas, 1995), 452–476. Valuable as it is, Geoffroy's discussion suffers in my opinion from a sweeping use of the term "Akbarī," which elides the distinction between (1) defending the person of Ibn ʿArabi from the charge of heresy or unbelief and (2) wholesale adoption and defense of the most controversial aspects of the Qūnawī-inspired tradition, such as *waḥdat al-wujūd* and "the faith of Pharaoh." There is simply no evidence that Suyūṭī and other Egyptian and Syrian "Akbarīs" whom Geoffroy cites were engaged in the latter project.

[21] Jalāl al-Dīn al-Suyūṭī, *Taʾyīd al-ḥaqīqa wa tashyīd al-ṭarīqa al-Shādhilīyya*, edited by ʿAbdullah al-Ghamrī (Cairo: al-Matbaʿa al-Islāmiyya, 1934), 70–71, 80, 85–86. Suyūṭī (on pp. 30–43) cited in support of his position the writings of Quṭb al-Dīn al-Qasṭallānī (d. 1287), a conservative Sufi critic of the more speculative, monistic strands of Sufism in his time. On Qastallānī, see A. Knysh, *Ibn ʿArabī in the Later Islamic Tradition* (Albany: SUNY Press, 1999), 44–45.

[22] Ibn Maymūn, *Risāla*, fols. 59b–60b.

ʿAbd al-Qādir al-ʿAydarūsī (d. 1627), added another report in support of the same moral: The Yemenī Shādhilī Sufi Abū Bakr al-ʿAydarūsī (d. 1516) recounted to a disciple that his father had once beaten and severely rebuked him when he had found him reading a volume of Ibn ʿArabī's *Futūḥāt*. The father was of the opinion that Ibn ʿArabī was a great saint but that his works were likely to lead novices astray and should not be read except by fully accomplished Sufis. The historian ʿAydarūsī ended the account with the words "I too am of this creed, and this way is safer and God knows best."[23]

Another prominent representative of this current of thought in the sixteenth century was the Egyptian Muḥammad b. Abī l-Ḥasan al-Bakrī (d. 1586), one of the most prominent Arab Sufis and Sufi poets of his time.[24] Bakrī too expressed his respect for Ibn ʿArabī while at the same time firmly rejecting the idea of *waḥdat al-wujūd*. In a short treatise entitled *Taʾbīd al-minna fī taʾyīd al-sunna*, he quoted and endorsed the position of Taftāzānī who had distinguished between two Sufi positions, both of which could at first sight suggest the heretical idea that God is incarnate in or unified with creation (*ḥulūl wa ittiḥād*).[25] The first position was that the advanced mystic could be overwhelmed by the direct experience of God to such an extent that his or her consciousness of other things (including the mystic's own self) fades away. This stage, in which the mystic sees "nothing in existence but God," was traditionally termed "annihilation in divine unity" (*al-fanāʾ fī l-tawḥīd*). Taftāzānī expressed sympathy with this kind of mystical experience, and he was eager to distinguish it from another position that he denounced as contrary to both reason and religion. This was the position that God is identical to absolute, unconditioned existence (*al-wujūd al-muṭlaq*) and that this absolute existence is strictly one, whereas the phenomenal world is in truth nothing but an insubstantial shadow or mirage. As will be seen in greater detail in Chapter 9, the position that Taftāzānī denounced is precisely the position upheld by the Qūnawī tradition of ontological monism. Seventeenth century defenders of *waḥdat al-wujūd* such as Ibrāhīm Kūrānī and ʿAbd al-Ghanī al-Nābulusī were fully aware of this and accordingly

[23] ʿAbd al-Qādir al-ʿAydarūsī, *al-Nūr al-sāfir ʿan akhbār al-qarn al-ʿāshir*, edited by Aḥmad Ḥālū, Muḥammad al-Arnāʾūṭ and Akram al-Bashūshī (Beirut: Dar Sadir, 2006), 455–456.

[24] On Bakrī, see ʿAydarūsī, *al-Nūr al-sāfir*, 534–554; and Ghazzī, *al-Kawākib al-sāʾira*, III, 67–72.

[25] Taftāzānī, *Sharḥ al-Maqāṣid* (Istanbul: Matbaʿat al-Hajj Muharram al-Bosnawi, 1305/1888), I, 73–75; II, 69–70; edited by Ibrāhīm Shams al-Dīn (Beirut: Dār al-Kutub al-ʿIlmiyya, 2001), I, 176–179; III, 43–45.

tried to rebut Taftāzānī's arguments on this point. Bakrī, by contrast, wholeheartedly endorsed Taftāzānī's position. He wrote:

How good is this discourse [by Taftāzānī] about the first position, and how well it fits the experiences of the mystic knowers!... This to me is the true position upon which one should rely. As for the second position, it is waywardness and a rejection of religion and of evident truth. No one has adopted this position except a group of pseudo-Sufis and a party of pseudo-philosophers.[26]

Bakrī also touched on this issue in his collection (*Dīwān*) of mystical poetry. He prefaced the collection with the following disclaimer:

This *Dīwān* of ours includes some poems and ditties in the styles of those who propound *waḥdat al-wujūd* (*ʿalā asālīb al-qāʾilīn bi-waḥdat al-wujūd*). God forbid that this be our creed! Rather our creed is that of the people of the Sunni community. But pointers can be subtle while full expressions cannot do them justice (*lākin talṭufu l-ishārātu fa-taqṣuru ʿanhā l-ʿibārāt*), and the Sultan of the witnessing of the Worshipped obliterates His rivals from the field of witnessing, and these utterances are then used (*fa-tajrī hādhihī l-alfāẓ*) due to the subtlety of the witnessed meaning (*li-diqqat al-maʿnā al-shuhūdī*) and the divine secret that is more exalted than to be confined within existential distinctions *(al-farq al-wujūdī)*.[27]

Another poem in Bakrī's *Dīwān* takes up the condemnation of those who espouse ontological monism:

How many people have gone too far in their claims, alleging that they are among the reverent!
They proclaimed *waḥdat al-wujūd* and said that everything is God the Creator!
O my people! Is there no one who will come to the aid of the Prophet? Be damned the one who is not among his partisans!
Which person says "I believe in God" and yet is satisfied with the position of the dissolute?...[28]

Despite thus distancing himself from the idea of *waḥdat al-wujūd*, Bakrī's poetry conforms to the style canonized by the Arab mystic poet par excellence Ibn al-Fāriḍ (d. 1235), with its often ecstatic language of divine epiphany (*tajallī*) and mystic annihilation (*fanāʾ*) in the majesty and beauty (*jalāl wa jamāl*) of God. Such poetry easily lent itself to being interpreted as a poetic expression of the monist ideas of the Qūnawī tradition, and indeed some of the most prominent commentators on Ibn al-Fāriḍ's famous *Tāʾiyya* (Ode rhyming in the letter *t*) belonged to this

26 Muḥammad b. Abī l-Ḥasan al-Bakrī, *Taʾbīd al-minna fī taʾyīd al-sunna* (MS: Princeton University Library, Yahuda 253), fols. 106b–111b, at fol. 109a–b.

27 Muḥammad b. Abī l-Ḥasan al-Bakrī, *Tarjumān al-asrār wa-dīwān al-abrār* (MS: Berlin Staatsbibliothek, Wetzstein II, 227), fol. 3a.

28 Bakrī, *Tarjumān al-asrār*, fols. 112b–113a.

tradition, for example Qūnawī's student Farghānī or the *Fuṣūṣ* commentator Qayṣarī. Nevertheless, a number of modern scholars such as R. A. Nicholson, Muḥammad Muṣṭafā Ḥilmī, and Guiseppe Scattolin have protested this straightforward assimilation of Ibn al-Fāriḍ's poetry to the doctrines of *waḥdat al-wujūd*. Nicholson, for example, wrote:

> Neither the form nor the substance of the *Tā'iyya* suggests that it was inspired by Ibn ʿArabī, though some traces of his influence may perhaps be found in it. It differs in kind from poems indubitably so inspired, such as the *ʿAyniyya* of Jīlī [i.e. ʿAbd al-Karīm al-Jīlī (d. 1428)]. Above all, it is a mystic's autobiography, a poet's description of his inner life, and the terms which it employs belong to the psychological vocabulary of Sufism, with few exceptions. I have no quarrels with those who call Ibn al-Fāriḍ a pantheist; but his pantheism (unlike that of his commentators) is essentially a state of feeling, not a system of thought.[29]

Nicholson's claim may or may not be correct; in the present context it is more relevant that it was prefigured by Bakrī and other Sufis from the fifteenth and sixteenth centuries, who adopted Ibn al-Fāriḍ's poetic imagery but not the ontological monism of many of his commentators. Bakrī's rejection of *waḥdat al-wujūd* did not prevent him from thinking highly of Ibn al-Fāriḍ. One of his poems starts with the lines:

> O visitor to those parts! Convey to the Pole (*al-quṭb*) Ibn al-Fāriḍ my greetings,
> The Imam, complete and unique, who to the heights of truth with truth ascended . . .[30]

Bakrī summarized his own view toward the end of the aforementioned treatise *Ta'bīd al-minna* in the following words: "The unity is experiential, not ontological (*al-waḥdatu shuhūdiyyatun lā wujūdiyyatun*)."[31] This is a remarkable anticipation of the position expressed by the later Indo-Muslim Naqshbandi Sufi Aḥmad Sirhindī (d. 1624). Sirhindī's position has often been presented as a radical break with earlier Sufi thought and as ushering in a new period in which "neo-Sufis" abandoned the

[29] R. A. Nicholson, *Studies in Islamic Mysticism* (Cambridge: Cambridge University Press, 1921), vii–viii. A similar interpretation has more recently been put forward by Guiseppe Scattolin; see, e.g., his "L'expérience mystique de Ibn al-Fāriḍ à travers son Poème al-Tā'iyyat al-kubrā," *MIDEO* 19(1989): 203–223 and "Al-Farghānī's commentary on Ibn al-Fāriḍ's mystical poem al-Tā'iyyat al-kubrā," *MIDEO* 21(1993): 331–383. A generation after Nicholson, the Egyptian scholar Muḥammad Muṣṭafā Ḥilmī anachronistically presented Ibn al-Fāriḍ as a partisan of *waḥdat al-shuhūd* as opposed to Ibn ʿArabī's *waḥdat al-wujūd*; see his *Ibn al-Fāriḍ wa l-ḥubb al-ilāhī* (Cairo: Lajnat al-Ta'līf wa l-Tarjama wa l-Nashr, 1945) and *Ibn al-Fāriḍ: sulṭān al-ʿāshiqin* (Cairo: Wizārat al-Thaqāfa wa l-Irshād al-Qawmī, 1963).

[30] Bakrī, *Tarjumān al-asrār*, fol. 184b.

[31] Bakrī, *Ta'bīd al-minna*, fol. 110b. Bakrī's treatise was completed in Mecca in January 1552.

idea of "the unity of existence" (*waḥdat al-wujūd*) and exchanged it for the alternative formula "the unity of mystical witnessing/experience" (*waḥdat al-shuhūd*).[32] This narrative clearly ignores a powerful Sufi tradition in the Arab world in the fifteenth and sixteenth centuries that explicitly rejected (or explained away) *waḥdat al-wujūd* while at the same time endorsing classic Sufi notions of "annihilation" in the experience of the divine. One Meccan contemporary of Sirhindī even used the formula *waḥdat al-shuhūd* independently of Sirhindī, claiming that it was typical of the Shādhilī order that was so powerful a presence in the Arabic-speaking world in the sixteenth century.[33] As shown by the research of especially Paul Nwyia, John Renard, and Richard McGregor, the North African Shādhilī tradition, represented by figures such as Ibn ʿAṭāʾullāh al-Iskandarī (d. 1309) and his commentator Ibn ʿAbbād al-Rundī (d. 1390), typically avoided the terminology and concerns of the monist school of Ibn ʿArabī commentators, even while defending mainstream institutionalized Sufism from criticisms by the likes of the Ḥanbalī purist Ibn Taymiyya.[34]

32 Classic formulations of this idea are in Fazlur Rahman, *Islam*, 2nd ed. (Chicago: University of Chicago Press, 1979), 148, 164, 195, 202, and J. S. Trimingham, *The Sufi Orders in Islam* (Oxford: Oxford University Press, 1998 [first published in 1971]), 58, 95. For a more up-to-date survey of Sirhindī's views on this issue, see J. G. J. ter Haar, *Follower and Heir of the Prophet: Shaykh Aḥmad Sirhindī (1564–1624) as Mystic* (Leiden, the Netherlands: Het Oosters Institut, 1992), 119–136.

33 Muḥammad ʿAlī Ibn ʿAllān al-Ṣiddīqī (1588–1648), *al-ʿIqd al-farīḍ fī taḥqīq al-tawḥīd* (MS: Berlin Staatsbibliothek, Sprenger 677, fols. 107b–113a, at fol. 110b: *wa-ḥāṣiluhu waḥdatu l-shuhūdi wa-huwa ṭarīqu l-Shādhiliyya.* Ibn ʿAllān did not mention Sirhindī in his treatise and there is no reason to think that he obtained the formula from him. On Ibn ʿAllān, see Muḥibbī, *Khulāṣat al-athar*, IV, 184–189. The "sobriety" of mainstream Shādhilī thought and its affinities with the later Indian Naqshbandi tradition are noted by A. Schimmel in her classic *The Mystical Dimensions of Islam* (Chapel Hill: The University of North Carolina Press, 1975), 249–251. To my knowledge, there has been no modern study that acknowledges the pervasive influence of Taftāzānī on later efforts to distinguish between experiential and ontological monism. Sirhindī was familiar with Taftāzānī's theological works, which were widely studied in Mughal colleges; see ter Haar, *Follower and Heir of the Prophet*, 59n4.

34 Paul Nwyia, *Ibn ʿAṭāʾullāh (m.709/1309) et la naissance de la confrérie šādilite* (Beirut: Dar el-Machreq, 1972), 25–26; Paul Nwyia, *Ibn ʿAbbad de Ronda (1332–1390)* (Beirut: Imprimerie Catholique, 1961); J. Renard (trans. and intr.), *Ibn ʿAbbad of Ronda: Letters on the Sufi Path* (New York: Paulist Press, 1986), 43; R. A. McGregor, *Sanctity and Mysticism in Medieval Egypt: The Wafāʾ Sufi Order and the Legacy of Ibn ʿArabī* (Albany: SUNY Press, 2004), 31, 47, 157–158. McGregor's study points out that the fourteenth-century Egyptian Shādhilīs Muḥammad Wafāʾ (d. 1363) and his son ʿAlī Ibn Wafāʾ (d. 1405) adopted views that were much closer to Ibn ʿArabī-inspired monism than was common in the mainstream Shādhilī tradition. Nevertheless, the style of those two thinkers is markedly different from that of the Qūnawī tradition of *Fuṣūṣ* commentators: it is "ecstatic" rather than analytic, rarely includes quotations from other works, and makes little use of the conceptual scheme of philosophy and rational theology. In a

Bakrī's student Mullā ʿAlī al-Qāriʾ al-Harawī (d. 1604), who was born in Herat but was active in the Hejaz, wrote treatises severely criticizing ontological monism and the idea of the "faith of Pharaoh."[35] Yet, he ended his treatise against the idea of the "faith of Pharaoh" by citing the positive opinion that his own teacher Bakrī had expressed of Ibn ʿArabī and by quoting the fatwas of the prominent Egyptian scholars Suyūṭī and Ibn Ḥajar al-ʿAsqalānī (d. 1449), both of whom opined that Ibn ʿArabī was a saint but at the same time discouraged reading his works and warned against relying on them to establish points of exoteric law or creed.[36] Like Shaʿrānī, Harawī suggested that there had been heretical interpolations in Ibn ʿArabī's works. Also like Shaʿrānī, he preferred the views of the *Futūḥāt* to what he deemed to be the abhorrent views of "the commentators on the *Fuṣūṣ*" (*shurrāḥ al-Fuṣūṣ*).[37]

Yet other Arab Sufis of the fifteenth and sixteenth centuries simply avoided explicit references to Ibn ʿArabī altogether, preferring to cite

review of McGregor's book, Th. Emil Homerin points out that the extent of Ibn ʿArabī's influence on Muḥammad and ʿAlī Wafāʾ may have been overestimated by McGregor and that the issue requires more research – the two Wafāʾī mystics apparently never explicitly cite Ibn ʿArabī (see T. Emil Homerin, "Review of R. A. McGregor, *Sanctity and Mysticism in Medieval Egypt*," *Mamluk Studies Review* 9(2005), 238–241, at 241). In any case, the two fourteenth-century mystics were widely respected as saints and mystic poets in Egypt in subsequent centuries, but it is clear that *ulema* typically viewed the contents of their works ambivalently. Shaʿrānī, for example, included a lengthy and positive entry on ʿAlī Ibn Wafāʾ in his biographical dictionary of Sufis, including lengthy quotations from Ibn Wafāʾ's works. Nevertheless, Shaʿrānī repeatedly interrupted his quotations with remarks that explain away the apparent sense of some passages, for example, Ibn Wafāʾ's monistic ideas and blistering attacks on the religious authority of the *ulema*. See ʿAbd al-Wahhāb al-Shaʿrānī, *al-Ṭabaqāt al-kubrā* (Cairo: Muṣṭafā al-Bābī al-Ḥalabī, 1954), II, 22–65. See, e.g., Shaʿrānī's comments on p. 45 (l. 27) and p. 57 (l. 7).

35 His attack on *waḥdat al-wujūd* is printed along with that of pseudo-Taftāzānī (actually ʿAlāʾ al-Dīn al-Bukhārī) in *Majmūʿat rasāʾil fī waḥdat al-wujūd* (Istanbul: n.p., 1294/1877). His attack on the idea of the faith of Pharaoh has been printed along with Dawānī's defense in *Īmān firʿawn*, edited by Ibn al-Khaṭīb (Cairo: al-Maṭbaʿa al-Miṣriyya, 1964). On Harawī's vehement denial of the faith of Pharaoh while maintaining a veneer of respect for Ibn ʿArabī, see C. Ernst, "Controversy over Ibn ʿArabī's Fuṣūṣ: The Faith of Pharaoh," *Islamic Culture* 59(1985), 259–266.

36 Harawī, *Īmān firʿawn*, 84–92.

37 Ibid., 35–37. Harawī's attitude to Ibn ʿArabī appears to have hardened by the time he wrote his treatise condemning *waḥdat al-wujūd*. That treatise, written after and explicitly referring to his treatise on the faith of Pharaoh, unequivocally condemns the views expressed in both *al-Futūḥāt* and *al-Fuṣūṣ* as beyond the pale and adds that if Ibn ʿArabī did not repent from these views then he must be judged an unbeliever. But even in that work, Harawī carefully distinguished partisans of *waḥdat al-wujūd* from law-abiding and orthodox Sufis such as al-Qushayrī (d. 1074), al-Anṣārī al-Harawī (d. 1089), al-Ghazālī (d. 1111), and ʿUmar al-Suhrawardī (d. 1235). At one point, he even cited approvingly poetry of Ibn al-Fāriḍ describing ultimate Sufi experience; see *Majmūʿat rasāʾil fī waḥdat al-wujūd*, pp. 52–114, especially 87–89.

pre- or non-monist Sufis such as al-Qushayrī (d. 1074), al-Anṣārī al-Harawī (d. 1089), al-Ghazālī (d. 1111), ʿAbd al-Qādir al-Jīlānī (d. 1166), ʿUmar al-Suhrawardī (d. 1235), Yaḥyā al-Nawawī (d. 1277), and the aforementioned Ibn ʿAṭāʾullāh al-Iskandarī (d. 1309). This, for example, was the case with the prominent Damascene mystic and poetess ʿĀʾisha al-Bāʿūniyya (d. 1517), who belonged to the Qādirī order. As in the case of Bakrī, ʿĀʾisha's mystic poetry nevertheless clearly shows the influence of Ibn al-Fāriḍ.[38]

Enough evidence has been presented in this section to show that Shaʿrānī's combination of attitudes – admiration for Ibn ʿArabī while keeping a distance to the claims and concerns of the later Persianate tradition of ontological monism – was common in the Arabic-speaking lands in the fifteenth and sixteenth centuries.[39] This is emphatically not to deny that some of the works of Qūnawī and the later *Fuṣūṣ* commentators might have circulated in the Arab-Islamic lands in the fifteenth and sixteenth centuries or that individual Sufis may have adhered to their interpretation of Ibn ʿArabī. But there are no obvious examples from this period of Arab-Islamic scholars (*ulema*) who explicitly and unambiguously endorsed the outlook of the Qūnawī tradition.[40] The vehement

38 Th. Emil Homerin, *Emanations of Grace: Mystical Poems by ʿĀʾisha al-Bāʿūniyya (d.923/1517)* (Louisville, KY: Fons Vitae, 2011), 16–17, 129ff. See the list of authorities cited in her *al-Muntakhab fī uṣūl al-rutab*, edited and translated by Th. Emil Homerin with the title *The Principles of Sufism* (New York and London: New York University Press, 2014), 177–187. I am grateful to Professor Homerin for discussing this issue with me and for confirming that there are no explicit references to Ibn ʿArabī in ʿĀʾisha's works.

39 The attitudes of Ibn Maymūn, Shaʿrānī and Bakrī were broadly shared by, for example, the following prominent scholars and Sufis: In Egypt, Zakariyyā al-Anṣārī and ʿAbd al-Raʾūf al-Munāwī (1545–1622); on the former's attitude, see Ghazzī, *al-Kawākib al-sāʾira*, I, 203–204; on the latter's attitude, see his *Ṭabaqāt al-Ṣūfiyya*, II, 421–422, 442, 503, 515. In Damascus, Najm al-Dīn al-Ghazzī (1570–1651), for whose attitude see Ghazzī, *al-Kawākib al-sāʾira*, I, 152 (l. 2), 204 (ll. 3–11), 274 (l. 10); II, 10 (l. 10) and his *Luṭf al-samar*, 256.

40 Two persons who might at first sight appear to be exceptions are Shaʿrānī's Sufi master ʿAlī al-Khawwāṣ (d. 1532) and the Egyptian Khalwatī Sufi master Meḥmed Demirdāş (d. 1523). Judging from the quotations in especially Shaʿrānī's earlier works, it would appear that Khawwāṣ's ideas were quite similar to those of the monist tradition; see for example the many quotations in Shaʿrānī's *al-Mīzān al-dharriyya al-mubayyina li-ʿaqāʾid al-firaq al-ʿaliyya*, edited by Jawdat Muḥammad Abū l-Yazīd al-Mahdī (Cairo: al-Dār al-Jawdiyya, 2007). But it is important to note that Khawwāṣ was not a member of the *ulema* class – he was even reportedly illiterate – and that he appears never to have cited Qūnawī or the later *Fuṣūṣ* commentators (or anyone else for that matter). His aphoristic style appears much more similar to that of the independent monist tradition of the fourteenth-century Egyptian Shādhilī Sufis Muḥammad Wafāʾ and ʿAlī Ibn Wafāʾ. Meḥmed Demirdāş went to Tabriz where he was initiated into the Khalwatī order, before returning to Egypt as head of what came to be known as the Demirdāşī suborder

hostility toward Ibn ʿArabī's ideas expressed by, for example, the Damascene Ḥanbalī scholar Ibn Taymiyya, the prominent Yemenī Shāfiʿī jurist Ibn al-Muqriʾ (d. 1434), and the Egyptian Ashʿarī scholar and Quran exegete Burhān al-Dīn al-Biqāʿī (d. 1480) suggests that the intellectual climate among Arab-Islamic *ulema* was not conducive to such an open and wholehearted endorsement.[41] The aforementioned North African-born Ibn Maymūn portrayed the situation in Damascus in the last decade of the fifteenth century and the first decade of the sixteenth as bleak for supporters of Ibn ʿArabī: his grave in Damascus was neglected, most local religious scholars disapproved of him, and supporters did not dare to speak out or even ask for directions to his grave. Even allowing for some rhetorical exaggeration, Ibn Maymūn's portrayal does suggest that an outright defense of the most controversial aspects of Ibn ʿArabī's worldview was not a live option among Arab-Islamic religious scholars in the fifteenth and sixteenth centuries. Those who dissented from outright condemnations of Ibn ʿArabī were rather inclined to express respect for him as a Sufi saint while remaining uncommitted to – or explaining away – the contents of some of his works, especially the deeply divisive *Fuṣūṣ*.

This cautious outlook did not disappear in later centuries. For example, ʿAbdullāh Bā-ʿAlawī al-Ḥaddād (d. 1720), a prominent Sufi (and Ashʿarī) from Hadhramaut, extolled Ghazālī's *Iḥyāʾ ʿulūm al-dīn*, while warning against "most of the works" (*akthar muʾallafāt*) of Ibn ʿArabī, which he believed could easily lead readers into heresy (*zandaqa*) and belief in incarnation (*ḥulūl*). He cited in support of this view the prominent North African Shādhilī Sufi (and Ashʿarī) Aḥmad Zarrūq (d. 1493).[42]

in Cairo. He espoused monist views explicitly inspired by Ibn ʿArabī and Qūnawī, see, for example, his *al-Qawl al-farīd fī maʿrifat al-tawḥīd*, included in a collection of treatises edited by Muḥammad ʿAbd al-Qādir Naṣṣār (Cairo: Dār al-Karaz, 2008). But (1) he was a Turkish-speaking Circassian, (2) hardly a member of the *ulema* class, and (3) his Demirdāşī disciples in Cairo included a conspicuous proportion of Turkish speakers. His successor was Ḥasan Rūmī (d. 1548) and the later Egyptian scholar Munāwī was initiated into the suborder by a certain Meḥmed Türkī (d. 1598); see Munāwī, *al-Kawākib al-durriyya fī tarājim al-sāda al-ṣūfiyya*, edited by Muḥammad Adīb al-Jādir (Beirut: Dār Ṣādir, 1999), III, 359 and 509–510.

41 Knysh, *Ibn ʿArabī in the Later Islamic Tradition*, 87–111, 208–222, 256–267.

42 ʿAbdullāh b. ʿAlawī al-Ḥaddād, *Risālat al-muʿāwana wa l-muẓāhara wa l-muʾāzara li-l-rāghibīn min al-muʾminīn fī sulūk ṭarīq al-ākhira* (Beirut: al-Nāshir li-l-Ṭibāʿa wa-l-Nashr, 1993), 28–29. On al-Ḥaddād, see M. al-Badawi, *Sufi Sage of Arabia: Imam ʿAbdullah ibn ʿAlawī al-Ḥaddād* (Louisville, KY: Fons Vitae, 2005). On his attitude to Ibn ʿArabī, see al-Badawi, *Sufi Sage*, 100–101. On the relevant discussion by Zarrūq, see S. Kugle, *Rebel Between Spirit and Law: Ahmad Zarruq, Sainthood and Authority in Islam* (Bloomington, IN: Indiana University Press, 2006), 152–153.

The North African Shādhilī tradition, in which such an attitude was common, was also still a powerful force in the seventeenth century. The influence of Moroccan Shādhilī masters such as Qāsim al-Sufyānī (d. 1667), Muḥammad Ibn Nāṣir al-Dar'ī (d. 1674), and 'Abdullāh al-Sharīf al-Yimlaḥī (d. 1678) extended even beyond the Maghreb, to Egypt, Syria, and the Hejaz.[43] Their disciples included some of the most prominent Ash'arī theologians of North Africa and Egypt in the seventeenth and eighteenth centuries – theologians who had little sympathy for the monistic tradition's departures from standard Ash'arī doctrine. Ḥasan al-Yūsī, for example, was Ibn Nāṣir's disciple, and he insisted that those who believe that God is identical to absolute existence and that existence is one are infidels.[44] Nevertheless, as will be shown in the following sections, the seventeenth century also saw the emergence of a new intellectual trend in Arab Sufi and *ulema* circles that endorsed precisely the view that Yūsī so strongly rejected. Defenders of Ibn 'Arabī belonging to the newly introduced Shaṭṭārī, Naqshbandī, and Khalwatī Sufi orders were much less hesitant in adopting the outlook of the *Fuṣūṣ* commentators, and much bolder in espousing its most controversial elements: ontological monism (*waḥdat al-wujūd*), the "faith of Pharaoh" (*īmān fir'awn*), and the passing away of the torments of hell (*fanā' al-nār*). They accordingly had no use for more or less crude appeals to the possibility of later heretical interpolations in Ibn 'Arabī's works.

The Shaṭṭārī Order in the Hejaz

In the year 1597, the Indian Sufi and scholar Ṣibghatullāh Barūchī (d. 1606) came to the Hejaz on pilgrimage and settled in Medina for the last ten years of his life.[45] Barūchī ("al-Barwajī" in Arabic sources) was a second-generation disciple of the prominent and controversial Indian Sufi of the Shaṭṭārī order Muḥammad Ghawth Gwāliyārī (d. 1562). As was common at the time, he was also initiated into numerous other

[43] On Qāsim al-Sufyānī, see Qādirī, *Nashr al-mathānī*, II, 161. One of his disciples settled in Damascus and had success in spreading the Shādhilī order there; see Murādī, *Silk al-durar*, IV, 33. On 'Abdullāh al-Sharīf al-Yimlaḥī, see Qādirī, *Nashr al-mathānī*, II, 233–236. As mentioned in Chapter 4, his disciple 'Abdullāh al-Kinaksī initiated the Egyptian scholars Aḥmad al-Mallawī, Aḥmad al-Damanhūrī and Aḥmad al-Jawharī, three of the most prominent Azhari scholars of the early- to mid-eighteenth century. On Ibn Nāṣir, see ibid., II, 211–215. His disciples included al-Ḥasan al-Yūsī, Muḥammad al-Rūdānī, and Aḥmad al-Hashtūkī.

[44] Yūsī, *Mashrab al-'āmm wa l-khāṣṣ*, 449.

[45] Muḥibbī, *Khulāṣat al-athar*, II, 243–246.

orders – a fact that appears to have caused some confusion in later sources, which sometimes referred to him and his disciples as belonging to the Naqshbandī order even though it was merely one of several secondary affiliations that Barūchī transmitted.[46]

Barūchī came to enjoy considerable prominence in his new surroundings. He initiated a number of local scholars, and it was explicitly for their benefit that he prepared a translation from Persian into Arabic of the *Jawāhir-i khamsa* (The Five Jewels) of Muḥammad Ghawth. As its name indicates, the work is divided into five major sections: (1) On supererogatory bodily acts of worship; (2) On mental askesis by means of formulaic invocations and supplications; (3) On incantations involving, for example, the names of the zodiac and planets, the letters of the Arabic alphabet, and the divine names; (4) On the distinctive spiritual practices of the Shaṭṭārīs, including formulaic utterances, bodily postures, and detailed breathing and visualization techniques; (5) On the practices of adepts whom Muḥammad Ghawth termed the "inheritors of the Truth" and "verifiers" (*al-muḥaqqiqūn* in Barūchī's Arabic translation).[47] Certain elements in the work have been thought to betray Muḥammad Ghawth's well-attested interest in Indian yogic ideas and practices, though it has also been argued that the parallels are "superficial" and that the work is firmly rooted in the Islamic mystical and esoteric traditions.[48] Be that

[46] A. Copty, in a thorough discussion to which I am indebted, presents Barūchī as a Naqshbandī and nothing else, see his "The Naqshbandiyya and its offshoot the Naqshbandiyya-Mujaddidiya in the Haramayn in the 11th/17th Century," *Die Welt des Islams* 43(2003): 321–348. Muḥammad Ghawth Gwāliyārī was primarily a Shaṭṭārī, see Trimingham, *The Sufi Orders in Islam*, 97–98. In giving the Sufi chains into which he was initiated, Barūchī's second-generation disciple Aḥmad al-Qushāshī gave the Shaṭṭārī chain first, and the Naqshbandī line is given much later; see Aḥmad al-Qushāshī, *al-Simṭ al-majīd fī sha'n al-bay'a wa-l-dhikr wa talqīnihi wa salāsil ahl al-tawḥīd* (Hyderabad: Dā'irat al-Ma'ārif al-Niẓāmiyya, 1327/1909), 67, 78. Dina Le Gall in her valuable study *A Culture of Sufism: Naqshbandīs in the Ottoman World, 1450–1700* (Albany: SUNY Press, 2005) provides a good discussion of the multiple affiliations of Barūchī and his disciples; see pp. 100–101.

[47] C. Ernst, "Jawāher-e Kamsa," *Encyclopaedia Iranica*, XIV, 608–609.

[48] For Muḥammad Ghawth's interest in Indian yogic ideas and practices, see C. Ernst, "Sufism and Yoga according to Muḥammad Ghawth," *Sufi* 29(1996): 9–13. The question of possible yogic "influences" on the *Jawāhir* is controversial, partly owing to an understandable sensitivity among Sufis and sympathetic modern specialists to wildly exaggerated claims by earlier European scholars and modern anti-Sufi Muslim reformers that Sufism surreptitiously imported an essentially "un-Islamic" worldview. Carl Ernst is largely dismissive of the suggestion of yogic influences and characterizes parallels as "superficial"; see his "Situating Sufism and Yoga," *Journal of the Royal Asiatic Society* 15(2005): 15–43. In light of Muḥammad Ghawth's well-attested interest in yogism, this may be to go too far in the opposite direction. One might agree with Ernst's point that

as it may, Barūchī's translation enjoyed considerable popularity in some later Arab Sufi circles – it was lithographed in Fez in 1900 and has since been printed in Cairo.[49] It appears ironically to have been particularly popular among North African orders that have sometimes been presented in modern Western scholarship as "neo-Sufi," "this-worldly," "sober," and "reformist" such as the Tījāniyya and the Sanūsiyya.[50]

Barūchī was succeeded as head of the lodge in Medina by his Egyptian-born disciple Aḥmad al-Shinnāwī (d. 1619).[51] Shinnāwī is known to have taught Barūchī's translation of the *Jawāhir* and wrote an extensive commentary on it.[52] Shinnāwī was succeeded by his disciple and son-in-law Aḥmad al-Qushāshī, and Qushāshī was in turn succeeded by the Kurdish-born Ibrāhīm Kūrānī – a major figure in seventeenth-century Islamic intellectual history who will feature prominently in the following chapters. Shinnāwī, Qushāshī, and Kūrānī were all prominent exponents of *waḥdat al-wujūd* and the closely related idea that God is identical to absolute, unqualified existence (*al-wujūd al-muṭlaq*). Shinnāwī propounded the thesis in his treatise *al-Iqlīd al-farīd fī tajrīd al-tawḥīd*.[53] He also wrote a versification of *Risālat al-Zawrā'* by the fifteenth-century Persian philosopher and theologian Dawānī that expressed this view.[54] Qushāshī was described by a contemporary source as "the Imam of those who propound the unity of existence" (*imām al-qā'ilīn bi-waḥdat al-wujūd*).[55] Kūrāni wrote a number of influential works in which he defended the doctrine – treatises that are dealt with in greater detail in Chapter 9. Kūrānī's star pupil and fellow Kurd Muḥammad b. ʿAbd al-Rasūl Barzinjī wrote a considerably expanded Arabic translation of a Persian apologia for Ibn ʿArabī written by Shaykh-i Makkī Kāzarūnī

it is preposterous to suggest, as some earlier Western scholars did, that the *Jawāhir* is basically a Hindu-yogic work in Persian, and yet remain open to the possibility that Muḥammad Ghawth occasionally drew on his knowledge of yogic ideas and practices.

49 Edited by Aḥmad Ibn al-ʿAbbās (Cairo: Maṭbaʿat al-Ḥājj Muḥammad Rifʿat ʿĀmir, 1973).

50 The Cairo edition of 1973 was edited by a modern Tījānī scholar on the basis of a manuscript in the Tījānī lodge in Cairo.

51 Muḥibbī, *Khulāṣat al-athar*, I, 243–246.

52 More precisely, Shinnāwī wrote a commentary on the first three "jewels." The commentary on the last two was written by his student Sālim Ibn Shaykhān (d. 1637); see Muḥibbī, *Khulāṣat al-athar*, II, 201 (ll. 10–12).

53 See ʿAbd al-Ghanī al-Nābulusī's lengthy commentary on this work *Taḥrīk al-iqlīd fī fatḥ bāb al-tawḥīd*, edited by al-Sayyid Yūsuf Aḥmad (Beirut: Dār al-kutub al-ʿIlmiyya, 2012). The editor has conveniently printed Shinnāwī's short treatise on pp. 10–12.

54 Ibrāhīm Kūrānī, *al-Amam li-ʾīqāẓ al-himam* (Hyderabad: Matbaʿat Majlis dāʾIrat al-Maʿārif al-Niẓāmiyya, 1910), 128.

55 Muḥibbī, *Khulāṣat al-athar*, I, 345 (l. 13).

(d. 1519) and dedicated to the Ottoman Sultan Selīm I (r. 1512–1520).[56] Barzinjī rendered the Persian text into Arabic but added his own usually lengthy discussions of each of the topics covered in the original. The result is an extensive work – more than twice the length of the Persian original – almost half of which is dedicated to a defense of *waḥdat al-wujūd*. Barzinjī in the same work also defended the thesis of the "faith of Pharaoh" – the very thesis that Shaʿrānī had so adamantly insisted was falsely attributed to Ibn ʿArabī.[57]

It is important to emphasize that Kūrānī and Barzinjī were not just Sufi exponents of *waḥdat al-wujūd*, but also eminent members of the *ulema* class in Medina who taught and wrote works on a range of exoteric sciences: philosophy, rational theology, hadith, and Quran exegesis. Kūrānī had been born in the town of Shahrān in the Kurdish province of Shahrizor, and received a thorough training in especially the rational sciences from local teachers who traced their intellectual lineage back to Dawānī (see Chapter 1). He then traveled to Damascus and Cairo, before settling in Medina where he was initiated by Qushāshī. Kūrānī put his earlier scholastic training to use in his later apologies for Sufi positions. As one contemporary scholar noted, Kūrānī's works were written in a style that was immediately understandable by exoteric scholars, whereas his master Qushāshi had written in a more inspired and less analytic style with little attempt to make his theses commensurable with those of rational theologians and philosophers.[58] Apart from his apologies for *waḥdat al-wujūd*, Kūrānī's works include[59]

1. *al-Amam li-īqāẓ al-himam*, a work that collected his certificates for transmitting a range of books, especially in the science of hadith. The work was highly esteemed even beyond Sufi circles, as short chains of transmission were particularly valued and some of Kūrānī's chains were considered to be among the shortest (literally the "highest") available in his time. Incredibly, Kūrānī adduced a

[56] Shaykh-i Makkī Kāzarūnī, al-*Jānib al-gharbī fī ḥall mushkilāt al-shaykh Muḥyī al-Dīn Ibn Arabī*, edited by Najīb Māʾil Heravī (Tehran: Intishārāt-i Mevlā, 1985).

[57] Barzinjī, *al-Jādhib al-ghaybī min al-Jānib al-gharbī* (MS: www.yazmalar.gov.tr/45Hk6230), fols. 108a–130b (on the faith of Pharaoh – note the criticism of Shaʿrānī's position on fol. 111a), fols. 135b–201a (on *waḥdat al-wujūd*).

[58] ʿAyyāshī, *Riḥla*, I, 435.

[59] Works (1–4) have been used in the present study and are listed in the bibliography. For (5), see A. Guillaume, "al-Lumʿat al-saniya by Ibrahim al-Kurani," *Bulletin of the School of Oriental and African Studies* 20(1957): 291–303. For (6), see MS: Süleymaniye Kütüphanesı, Istanbul: Nuruosmaniye 2126, fols. 1–50.

chain of transmission that included only eight people between himself and the famous collector of hadith al-Bukhārī (d. 870). This made Kūrānī's chain as "high" as the chain of the famous Egyptian specialist on hadith Jalāl al-Dīn al-Suyūṭī who had died almost two centuries earlier.[60]

2. An extensive commentary, entitled *Qaṣd al-sabīl ilā tawḥīd al-ʿaliyy al-wakīl*, on the versified creed of his master Qushāshī. This work, probably Kūrānī's longest, was widely quoted in subsequent centuries.
3. A treatise entitled *Maslak al-sadād fī masʾalat khalq afʿāl al-ʿibād*. This is the longest of a number of treatises that Kūrānī wrote on the oft-discussed topic of how to reconcile divine omnipotence with the view that humans have an ability to bring about their own acts for which they are legally responsible. The following chapter will afford a closer look at this work.
4. A treatise entitled *Ifāḍat al-ʿallām fī masʾalat al-kalām*. This is devoted to an adjudication of the views of Ḥanbalīs and Ashʿarīs on the eternal Word of God. Ḥanbalīs traditionally considered the eternal Word of God to consist of letters and sounds whereas Ashʿarīs typically denied this and insisted that the Arabic words and letters of the Quran express God's eternal Word that is itself outside of space and time.
5. A treatise entitled *al-Lumʿa al-saniyya fī l-ilqāʾ bi-l-umniya*. This is a discussion of the incident of the "Satanic verses" and is based on an acceptance of the historicity of the early reports that related this incident. The virulent riposte to this treatise by the North African Ashʿarī scholar Yaḥyā al-Shāwī has already been mentioned in Chapter 4.
6. A gloss on the commentary of Dawānī on *al-ʿAqāʾid al-ʿAḍudiyya*.

Barzinjī (from the town of Barzinja, also in the province of Shahrizor) was also initiated into the Shaṭṭārī order by Qushāshī, but he was a

60 Kūrānī, *al-Amam*, 5. Kūrānī's chain came to be widely accepted and adopted by later scholars such as Muḥammad Murtaḍā al-Zabīdī (d. 1791), Ṣāliḥ al-Fūlānī (d. 1803), and Muḥammad al-Shawkānī (d. 1834), even though it featured one person – a certain Bābā Yūsuf al-Harawī – who supposedly lived more than 300 years. See the extensive and refreshingly skeptical discussion of this chain by ʿAbd al-Ḥayy al-Kattānī (d. 1962) in his *Fihris al-fahāris*, edited by Iḥsān ʿAbbās (Beirut: Dār al-Gharb al-Islāmī, 1982), II, 948–961. I do not mean to suggest that Kūrānī fabricated the chain: It is clear that he – like the eighteenth- and nineteenth-century scholars just mentioned – let himself be taken in by a chain forged in the eastern Islamic lands in the fifteenth century.

close student of Kūrānī in the exoteric religious and rational sciences. Apart from his expanded translation of Shaykh-i Makkī's apology for Ibn ʿArabī, he wrote[61]

1. *al-Ishāʿa fī ashrāṭ al-sāʿa*, on the signs of the Hour. This appears to have been Barzinjī's most widely disseminated work. It has been in print for the greater part of the twentieth century and has recently been translated into Urdu.
2. A lengthy defense of the controversial idea that the parents of the Prophet Muḥammad, who died prior to his prophecy, are among those who are saved in the hereafter.
3. *al-Nawāqiḍ li-l-rawāfiḍ*, an abridgement with additional material of an anti-Shiite tract by Mīrzā Makhdūm Ḥusaynī (d. 1587)
4. A treatise defending his teacher Kūrānī from the attacks of the aforementioned North African theologian Yaḥyā al-Shāwī on the issue of the Satanic verses.
5. Two polemical treatises condemning the ideas of the Indian Naqshbandī Sufi Aḥmad Sirhindī.
6. Glosses, commentaries, and abridgments that presumably reflect his teaching activities in Medina, for example a gloss on Bayḍāwī's esteemed exegesis of the Quran; a commentary on a didactic poem by al-Suyūṭī on the science of hadith; and an abridgment of the standard handbook on semantics and rhetoric by Jalāl al-Dīn al-Qazwinī (d. 1338) *Talkhīṣ al-Miftāḥ*.

The Moroccan scholar ʿAbdullāh al-ʿAyyāshī (d. 1679) left a vivid portrait of this Hejazi line of Shaṭṭārīs with whom he interacted during his pilgrimage to Mecca and subsequent sojourn in Medina in 1662–1664. ʿAyyāshī related that he used to frequent Ibrāhīm Kūrānī and studied a number of works with him, including works on philosophy such as *Hidāyat al-ḥikma* by al-Abharī (d. 1265) and *Ḥikmat al-ishrāq* by the Illuminationist philosopher Yaḥyā al-Suhrawardī (d. 1191). As noted in

[61] For (1), see the older printed edition from 1907 (Cairo: Maṭbaʿat al-Saʿādah) and the more recent edition edited by Ḥusayn Muḥammad ʿAlī Shukrī (Jeddah: Dār al-Minhāj lil-Nashr wa-al-Tawzīʿ, 1997). For the Urdu translation: *Qiyāmat kī nishāniyāṉ* (Lāhore: Zāviyah Pablisharz, 2007). For (2), see *Sadād al-dīn wa-sidād al-dayn fī ithbāt al-najāt wa-l-darajāt li-l-wālidayn*, edited by ʿAbbās Aḥmad Ṣaqr al-Ḥusaynī and Ḥusayn Muḥammad ʿAlī Shukrī (Cairo: Dār Jawāmiʿ al-Kalim, 2005). For (3), see Mach, *Catalog*, nr. 2630. For (4), see P. K. Hitti et al., *Descriptive Catalog of the Garrett Collection of Arabic Manuscripts in the Princeton University Library* (Princeton, NJ: Princeton University Press, 1938), 460–61. For (5–6), see Copty, "The Naqshbandiyya," 331–345. For (7–9), see Ḥamawī, *Fawāʾid al-irtiḥāl*, I, 478.

Chapter 1, ʿAyyāshī was impressed with Kūrānī's style of teaching that evidently corresponded to the characteristic style of seventeenth-century Kurdish specialists in the rational sciences by heeding the science of *ādāb al-baḥth*. ʿAyyāshī wrote:

> His lecture on a topic reminded one of discussion (*mudhākara*) and parley (*mufāwaḍa*), for he would say "Perhaps this and that" and "It seems that it is this" and "Do you see that this can be understood like that?" And if he was questioned on even the slightest point he would stop until the matter was established.[62]

ʿAyyāshī also read with Kūrānī some of the works of Ibn ʿArabī such as the *Futūḥāt* and the *Fuṣūṣ*. The *Fuṣūs* was clearly of particular importance to the Shaṭṭārīs of Medina. ʿAyyāshī mentioned that Kūrānī's master Qushāshī had in a dream received a copy of the work from Ibn ʿArabī himself, and that Ibn ʿArabī had in turn mentioned in the introduction to the work that he had in a dream received it from none other than the Prophet Muḥammad. Kūrānī then "received" the *Fuṣūṣ* from Qushāshī, and in turn ʿAyyāshī "received" it from Kūrānī in what seems to have been a waking-world continuation of this earlier transmission of the work via dreams.[63]

Another work that ʿAyyāshī studied with Kūrānī was a treatise entitled *al-Tuḥfa al-mursala* by the Indian Shaṭṭārī mystic Muḥammad b. Faḍlullāh Burhānpūrī (d. 1619). This gave a brief exposition of the cosmology of *waḥdat al-wujūd*: the idea that God is identical to "absolute, unqualified existence" (*al-wujūd al-muṭlaq*) and the various levels of qualifications or emanations of the divine. ʿAyyāshī was sufficiently impressed by the treatise that he reproduced it in his travelogue "since it is short and unfamiliar in the Maghreb."[64] Though he clearly did not disapprove of the thesis, ʿAyyāshī remained uncommitted to *waḥdat al-wujūd*. In general, his account of his studies with Kūrānī is quite revealing of the encounter between the explicitly monistic tradition represented by the Shaṭṭārīs in Medina and the more cautious North African Shādhilī tradition that respected Ibn ʿArabī but remained uncommitted to controversial ideas associated with the *Fuṣūṣ* and its later commentaries. ʿAyyāshī noted that Kūrānī repeatedly attempted to convince him of the truth of *waḥdat al-wujūd*. ʿAyyāshī, however, remained unconvinced by Kūrānī's arguments and preferred to maintain the uncommitted attitude to this issue

62 ʿAyyāshī, *Riḥla*, I, 396.
63 Ibid., I, 428–429.
64 Ibid., I, 401–409.

that he associated with his original Shādhilī order.[65] ʿAyyāshī noted that he would sometimes joke with Kūrānī that Qushāshī – whom ʿAyyāshī had met on a previous pilgrimage – had expressed his admiration for the Shādhilī order and thereby implicitly sanctioned ʿAyyāshī's insistence on retaining his typical Shādhilī reluctance to accept all of the ideas of Ibn ʿArabī. He wrote:

> This [the praise of Qushāshī for the Shādhilī order] was one of the things that I would invoke to our teacher Mullā Ibrāhīm [i.e. Kūrānī] in jest when he would insist on explaining to me some of the words of Ibn ʿArabī – may God be pleased with him – while I would not give in and would not accept this by imitation. I would say to him: "The Shaykh [i.e. Qushāshī] did not see in me a readiness to accept any order except that of the Shādhilīs, and this is why he praised it to me and commanded me to persist in it. Had he seen in me a readiness for another order then he would have commanded me to follow it." He [i.e. Kūrānī] would reply: "Rather, he saw that this [i.e. the Shādhilī order] had a hold on you then, so he commanded you to persevere in it until you would ascend by the blessing of this perseverance to an understanding of a higher level."[66]

As suggested by this exchange, relations between ʿAyyāshī and Kūrānī remained cordial despite their differences concerning *waḥdat al-wujūd*. Kūrānī issued ʿAyyāshī a certificate (*ijāza*) and gave him a number of his own works as a parting gift before ʿAyyāshī returned to Morocco. (These autograph manuscripts of Kūrānī are still extant in the Zāwiya ʿAyyāshiyya.)[67] ʿAyyāshī in turn gave his support to Kūrānī in his bitter polemics with North African theologians such as Shāwī.

Another work that Kūrānī is known to have taught in Medina is *al-Durra al-fākhira* by the fifteenth-century Persian mystic and poet Jāmī – a treatise that defends the position of monist Sufis on a range of issues vis-à-vis theologians and philosophers. ʿAyyāshī did not mention having studied the work, but Kūrānī wrote extant glosses on it and is known to have transmitted it to other, perhaps more pliable, students such as Yūsuf Tāj Maqāṣīrī (d. 1699) from the island of Sulawesi (in present-day Indonesia).[68]

[65] Ibid., I, 437–438, 440–442.
[66] Ibid., I, 497.
[67] Laḥmar, *al-Fihris al-waṣfī*, III, nrs. 1228, 1232, 1234, 1235, 1236.
[68] N. Heer, *The Precious Peal: al-Jāmī's al-Durra al-fākhira* (Albany: SUNY Press, 1979), 15. On Maqāṣīrī or Maqaṣṣārī (from Makassar in Sulawesi) see A. Azra, *The Origins of Islamic Reformism in Southeast Asia* (Hawaii: University of Hawaii Press, 2004), 87–108. Note, however, that Azra's overall interpretation of Maqāṣīrī is questionable: he assumes that he was a "neo-Sufi" who rejected the monism of Ibn ʿArabī, simply on the basis of his "activism," his distancing himself from the idea of "incarnation"

The Naqshbandī Order in the Hejaz and Syria

A sustained Naqshbandī presence among Arab *ulema* can be traced to the early seventeenth century. As mentioned previously, Ṣibghatullāh Barūchī initiated local disciples into a range of Sufi orders besides the Shaṭṭārī order to which he primarily belonged, and the Naqshbandī order featured prominently among these secondary affiliations. There were a number of other Sufi masters who were active in propagating the Naqshbandī order in the Hejaz in the early and mid-seventeenth century. One of the earliest who had a primary affiliation to the order was the Indian master Tāj al-Dīn ʿUthmānī (d. 1640).[69] Tāj al-Dīn performed the pilgrimage to Mecca twice, both times via Yemen. After his second pilgrimage in 1631 he settled in Mecca and remained there for the last years of his life. Like Barūchī, Tāj al-Dīn initiated a considerable number of local scholars from Yemen and the Hejaz. Also like Barūchī, he translated into Arabic some of the Persian works that were current in his order in India, specifically the hagiographical collections *Nafaḥāt al-uns* by Jāmī and *Rashaḥāt ʿayn al-ḥayāt* by Kāshifī (d. 1532).[70] Tāj al-Dīn also wrote a treatise in Persian on the principles of the Naqshbandī order that was translated into Arabic at least twice in the seventeenth century, the first time by his Meccan disciple Aḥmad Ibn ʿAllān al-Ṣiddīqī (d. 1624).[71] Other prominent disciples of Tāj al-Dīn included the Yemeni ʿAbd al-Bāqī al-Mizjājī (d. 1663), who headed the order in Zabid in Yemen, and ʿAbdullāh Bā-Qushayr (d. 1665), who initiated the prominent hadith scholar ʿAbdullāh b. Sālim al-Baṣrī (d. 1722) in Mecca.[72]

Until recently, scholars of Sufism assumed that the Naqshbandī order was "sober" and "strictly orthodox" and as such lukewarm toward Ibn

(*ḥulūl*), and his respect for Islamic law. This assumes what is surely a caricature of Ibn ʿArabī's thought. All major apologists for *waḥdat al-wujūd* – including Maqāṣirī's teachers and Sufi masters in the Hejaz and Syria – were eager to distance themselves from antinomianism and incarnation.

69 Muḥibbī, *Khulāṣat al-athar*, I, 464–470; Le Gall, *A Culture of Sufism*, 94–98; Copty, "The Naqshbandiyya," 325–330.

70 Tāj al-Dīn's translation of Jāmī's *Nafaḥāt* has been published (Cairo: al-Azhar al-Sharīf, 1989). For an extant manuscript of his translation of Kāshifī's *Rashaḥāt*, see Mach, *Catalogue*, nr. 4690.

71 On Ibn ʿAllān, see Muḥibbī, *Khulāṣat al-athar*, I, 157–158. A different Arabic translation of the treatise is embedded in the later commentary of ʿAbd al-Ghanī al-Nābulusī, as noted by the modern editors of the commentary; see ʿAbd al-Ghanī al-Nābulusī, *Miftāḥ al-maʿiyya fī ṭarīq al-Naqshbandiyya*, ed. by Jūda Muḥammad Abū l-Yazīd al-Mahdī and Muḥammad ʿAbd al-Qādir Naṣṣār (Cairo: al-Dār al-Jūdiyya, 2008), 10.

72 On Mizjājī, see Muḥibbī, *Khulāṣat al-athar*, II, 283. On Bā-Qushayr, see Muḥibbī, *Khulāṣat al-athar*, III, 42 and al-Baṣrī, *al-Imdād fī maʿrifat ʿuluw al-isnād*, 74.

ʿArabī and opposed to *waḥdat al-wujūd*. More recent research by especially Hamid Algar and Dina Le Gall has shown that this assumption is an illegitimate generalization of the views of the so-called "Mujaddidī" suborder of the Naqshbandiyya that goes back to the Indian master Aḥmad Sirhindī.[73] Pre- and non-Mujaddidī Naqshbandīs were typically adherents of *waḥdat al-wujūd* and deeply influenced by Ibn ʿArabī. A good example of this is the fifteenth-century Persian mystic and poet Jāmī, whose commentary on the *Fuṣūṣ*, hagiographical collection *Nafaḥāt al-uns*, and aforementioned *al-Durra al-fākhira* were studied in Shaṭṭārī and Naqshbandī circles in the seventeenth-century Hejaz. Tāj al-Dīn, whose leaving India may well have been prompted by losing out to Sirhindī in the struggle to succeed their common Indian master Khwāja Bāqībillāh (d. 1603), is known to have taught the works of Ibn ʿArabī, including the *Fuṣūṣ*, in the Hejaz.[74] His treatise on the principles of the Naqshbandī order explicitly expounds the claim that Shaʿrānī had tried to explain away: "There is no existent but God (*lā mawjūda illā Allāh*)." This, Tāj al-Dīn asserted, represents the highest level of understanding the basic Islamic profession: *lā ilāha illā Allāh*. The novice understands the profession to mean that there is no proper object of worship except Allah; the intermediate seeker understands it to mean that there is no reliance on anything except Allah; the advanced mystic understands it to mean that there is nothing in existence except Allah. The passage in the treatise elicits a footnote expressing dissent from this view by the modern editor who belongs to the Mujaddidī suborder of the Naqshbandiyya.[75]

Another Naqshbandī master who was active in the Hejaz in the seventeenth century was Muḥammad Ḥusayn Khwāfī (d. 1677).[76] Khwāfī belonged to a different Naqshbandī spiritual lineage than Tāj al-Dīn – the so-called "Dahbīdī" line stemming from the prominent Central Asian master Makhdūm-i Aʿẓam (d. 1542) who had set up a lodge in Dahbīd near Samarqand.[77] Khwāfī nevertheless sat at the feet of the older Tāj al-Dīn when he first arrived in Mecca and it may have been him who re-translated Tāj al-Dīn's Persian treatise on the principles of the

[73] H. Algar, "A Short History of the Naqshbandī Order," in M. Gaborieau, A. Popovic and T. Zarcone (eds.), *Naqshbandīs: cheminements et situations actuelle d'un ordre mystique musulman* (Paris: Editions Isis, 1990): 3–44, at 21; Le Gall, *The Culture of Sufism*, 4–7, 123–127.

[74] Muḥibbī, *Khulāṣat al-athar*, IV, 442.

[75] Nābulusī, *Miftāḥ al-maʿiyya*, 75–76 (and the editors' fn. 4 on p. 76).

[76] See Le Gall, *A Culture of Sufism*, 89–90, Copty, "The Naqshbandiyya," 330–331.

[77] H. Algar, "Dahbīdiyya," *Encyclopaedia Iranica*, VI, 585–586.

Naqshbandī order.[78] Khwāfī initiated among others the prominent local scholar Ḥasan Ibn al-ʿUjaymī (d. 1702), who became his successor (*khalīfa*) in Mecca.[79] Two other Dahbīdī Naqshbandīs who initiated prominent local scholars in the Arab East were Mīr Kalān Balkhī and Abū Saʿīd Balkhī (d. 1681). The former initiated the Meccan scholar Aḥmad al-Nakhlī (d. 1718).[80] The latter, after spells in the Hejaz and Istanbul, came to Damascus where he initiated ʿAbd al-Ghanī al-Nābulusī in 1676. Abū Saʿīd Balkhī asked his new Damascene disciple to write a commentary on Tāj al-Dīn's treatise on the principles of the Naqshbandī order.[81]

Like his older contemporaries Kūrānī and Barzinjī, Nābulusī was not merely a Sufi who espoused *waḥdat al-wujūd* (as will be shown in greater detail in Chapter 9) but also an esteemed scholar and teacher of a range of exoteric sciences such as law, hadith, and Quran exegesis. In the latter part of his life he was also Ḥanafī Muftī of Damascus. Some of his more influential works (which were printed in the nineteenth and early twentieth centuries) include[82]

1. A commentary on Ibn ʿArabī's *Fuṣūṣ al-ḥikam*. This was the first major commentary on this work by an Arab (as opposed to a Turkish, Persian or Indo-Muslim) scholar.
2. An extensive commentary on the *Dīwān* of Ibn al-Fāriḍ
3. An extensive commentary on *al-Ṭarīqa al-Muḥammadiyya* by Meḥmed Birgevī (d. 1573), a pietistic work particularly esteemed by the violently puritan Ḳāḍizādeli movement in the seventeenth century. Nābulusī, while maintaining a veneer of respect toward Birgevī, systematically softened the work's advocacy of moralist vigilantism and its criticisms of Sufi "innovations" by adding numerous conditions and qualifications to Birgevī's statements.[83]

78 Khwāfī reportedly authored and translated treatises on the Naqshbandī order; see Le Gall, *A Culture of Sufism*, 90. Given that the second translation of Tāj al-Dīn's treatise was the one commented upon by Nābulusī, it is tempting to think that it had come about in Naqshbandī-Dahbīdī circles in Mecca. Nābulusī's master Abū Saʿīd Balkhī also belonged to the Dahbīdī line and almost certainly met Khwāfī, for he had been in Mecca before coming to Damascus and initiating Nābulusī in 1676.

79 Copty, "The Naqshbandiyya," 330.

80 Aḥmad al-Nakhlī, *Bughyat al-ṭālibīn li-bayān al-mashāyikh al-muʿtamadīn* (Hyderabad, Deccan: Dāʾirat al-Maʿārif al-ʿUthmāniyya, 1328/1910), 73.

81 Ghazzī, *al-Wird al-unsī*, 148–149.

82 For a list of his works, see Murādī, *Silk al-durar*, III, 32–36. I have listed those works that were printed prior to 1920.

83 Michael Cook, *Commanding Right and Forbidding Wrong in Islamic Thought* (Cambridge: Cambridge University Press, 2000), 325–328.

4. A *Dīwān* of mystical poetry
5. A *Dīwān* of poetic eulogies of the Prophet, illustrating various rhetorical tropes
6. An extended defense of the permissibility of listening to music, a traditional point of contention between Sufis and their opponents
7. A treatise on the permissibility of tobacco, perhaps the most substantial such treatise written in the seventeenth century
8. A brief, introductory presentation, entitled *Kifāyat al-ghulām*, of the fundamentals of Islamic law according to the Ḥanafī school
9. An extensive and very popular work on dream interpretation. This has been in print throughout most of the nineteenth and twentieth centuries, both in the original Arabic and in Turkish translation.
10. An abridgment of a sixteenth-century work on agronomy (*ʿilm al-filāḥa*)

The Mujaddidī suborder of the Naqshbandiyya also made their presence felt in seventeenth-century Hejaz. A disciple of Aḥmad Sirhindī, Ādam Banūrī (d. 1663) settled in Mecca and translated a selection of Sirhindī's letters from Persian into Arabic.[84] Some of the ideas expressed therein were vehemently resisted by other local Sufis, especially the aforementioned Shaṭṭārī master Aḥmad al-Qushāshī.[85] The controversy seems to have died down when Aḥmad Sirhindī's son and successor Muḥammad Maʿṣūm (d. 1668) came to the Hejaz in 1657, stayed there for three years, and made conciliatory overtures to Qushāshī. But it flared up again in 1682 when a request arrived in Mecca from the Mughal court asking local scholars for their verdicts concerning some of Sirhindī's ideas. The most vociferous in condemning Sirhindī were Kūrānī's student Muḥammad b. ʿAbd al-Rasūl Barzinjī and Khwāfī's disciple and successor Ḥasan Ibn al-ʿUjaymī. The two critics were aware that the Mujaddidīs had a tendency to denigrate belief in *waḥdat al-wujūd* and this may well be part of the explanation of their hostility.[86] Nevertheless, the immediate focus of the controversy was on other topics, in particular the extravagant-sounding spiritual and millennial claims of Sirhindī and whether the "Reality of the Kaʿbah" is superior or inferior to the "Reality of Muḥammad." ʿAbd al-Ghanī al-Nābulusī, a prominent advocate of *waḥdat al-wujūd*, was willing to write in defense of Sirhindī, showing clearly that the

[84] Copty, "The Naqshbandiyya," 331–332.

[85] For the controversy, see especially Copty, 332–345 and Y. Friedmann, *Shaykh Aḥmad Sirhindī: An Outline of His Thought and His Image in the Eyes of Posterity* (New Delhi: Oxford University Press, 2000), 94–101.

[86] Copty, "The Naqshbandiyya," 335–336.

controversy had little to do with this particular doctrine.[87] Indeed there is some evidence that the Mujaddidīs in seventeenth-century Hejaz chose to deemphasize their distinctive ideas about *waḥdat al-wujūd* in their efforts to placate Qushāshī and other local Sufis.[88] Some of the most prominent Naqshbandīs in the Ottoman Empire in the eighteenth century were advocates of *waḥdat al-wujūd* – for example, Nābulusī in Damascus, Ebū Saʿīd Ḫādimī (d. 1762) in Konya, and Muḥammad Murtaḍā al-Zabīdī (d. 1791) in Cairo.[89] It may be that it was only with the spectacular spread of the so-called Mujaddidī-Khālidī suborder of Shaykh Khālid Shahrazūrī (d. 1827) that Naqshbandīs in the Near East eventually ended up with an almost emblematic rejection of *waḥdat al-wujūd*.

The Khalwatī Order in Syria

The Khalwatī order expanded considerably in the Ottoman Empire in the fifteenth and sixteenth centuries from its origins in the region of Azerbaijan and Shirwan.[90] By the early seventeenth century, when the puritan Ḳāḍīzādelī movement began to wage a fierce campaign against Sufi "innovations," the Khalwatīs were a major presence in the Turkish-speaking parts of the Empire and featured prominently among the orders that were targeted. Conversely, Khalwatī Sufis such as ʿAbd ül-Mecīd Sīvāsī (d. 1639) and ʿAbd ül-Aḥad Nūrī (d. 1651) were at the forefront of the defense of Sufi beliefs and practices against Ḳāḍīzādelī attack.[91] The latter's *Mirʾāt al-wujūd*, for example, includes an exposition of *waḥdat*

[87] S. Pagani, "Renewal before Reformism: ʿAbd al-Ghanī al-Nābulusī's Reading of Aḥmad Sirhindī's Ideas on *Tajdīd*," *Journal of the History of Sufism* 5(2007): 291–307.

[88] Copty, "The Naqshbandiyya," 335–336.

[89] On Ḫādimī's attitude to *waḥdat al-wujūd*, see Y. Sarıkaya, *Abū Saʿīd Muḥammad al-Ḫādimī*, 221–226. Ḫādimī was initiated by his father Muṣṭafā Ḫādimī (d. 1734), who in turn was initiated by Murād Bukhārī (d. 1720), a disciple of Aḥmad Sirhindī's son Muḥammad Maʿṣūm; see ibid., 55–59. On Zabīdī's sympathy for *waḥdat al-wujūd* (which he read back into Ghazālī's *Iḥyāʾ ʿulūm al-dīn*), see Reichmuth, *The World of Murtaḍā al-Zabīdī*, 37, 295, 322.

[90] For the history of the Khalwatī order, see B. G. Martin, "A Short History of the Khalwati Order of Dervishes," in N. R. Keddie (ed.), *Scholars, Saints and Sufis: Muslim Religious Institutions in the Middle East since 1500* (Berkeley, 1972), 275–305; F. de Jong, "Khalwatiyya," *EI2*, IV, 991–993; J. J. Curry, *The Transformation of Muslim Mystical Thought in the Ottoman Empire: The Rise of the Halveti Order, 1350–1650* (Edinburgh: Edinburgh University Press, 2010), 21–86. The attributive "al-Khalwatī" appears to go back to the fourteenth century, but all later Khalwatī chains pass through the Azeri master Yaḥyā al-Bākūbī al-Shirwānī (d. 1464 in Baku) and subsequent Khalwatī expansion can therefore be seen as stemming from fifteenth-century Azerbaijan and Shirwan.

[91] M. Zilfi, "The Kadizadelis: Discordant Revivalism in Seventeenth-Century Istanbul," *Journal of Near Eastern Studies* 45(1986): 251–269, esp. 255–256 and 261–262.

al-wujūd and an attack on moralists who busy themselves with what they take to be other people's wrongdoing instead of focusing on their own sins and spiritual imperfections.[92]

Up until around 1600, the Khalwatiyya was still largely an Azeri, Turkish, and (to a lesser extent) Kurdish order. Even the order's adherents in cities such as Cairo and Aleppo seem initially to have been mainly Turkish speaking.[93] In Syria, it is only in the course of the seventeenth century that a sustained line of Arab Khalwatī masters took root. In Egypt, this happened only in the eighteenth century. The present section will look closer at this process in Damascus, Aleppo, and Cairo.

The spread of the order in Damascus can be traced back to Aḥmad ʿUsālī (d. 1639), who was of Kurdish origin.[94] ʿUsālī was initiated into the order in Gaziantep by a certain Şāh Velī ʿAyntābī (d. 1605) before returning to Damascus. He first settled in the Ṣāliḥiyya suburb, though two years before he died he moved to a more centrally located lodge built for him by the Ottoman governor of Damascus Küçük Aḥmed Pāşā. His two major local disciples were Ayyūb al-ʿAdawī (d. 1660) and Muḥammad al-ʿAbbāsī (d. 1665), both important figures in the subsequent spread of the Khalwatī order in Damascus. Ayyūb was a prolific mystical writer and poet.[95] According to the Damascene historian Muḥibbī, who was writing toward the end of the seventeenth century, Ayyūb's writings were numerous, his mystical poetry in wide circulation, and his maxims on verification (*taḥqīq*) "well-known." These, added Muḥibbī, were based on "unadulterated unveiling which is the tongue of Ibn ʿArabī" (*al-kashf*

92 For extant manuscripts of the work along with the commentary of ʿAbd al-Ghanī al-Nābulusī, see www.yazmalar.gov.tr/ 06Hk74 and W. Ahlwardt, *Verzeichnis der Arabischen Handschriften* (Berlin: Georg Olms Verlag, 1887–1899), nr. 3244.

93 In Cairo, the two major Khalwatī suborders in the sixteenth and seventeenth centuries, the Gülşenī and Demirdāşī suborders, were primarily popular among the Turkish-speaking minority in the city; see F. de Jong, "Mustafa Kamal al-Din al-Bakrī (1688–1749): Revival and Reform of the Khalwatiyya Tradition?" in N. Levtzion and J. Voll (eds.), *Eighteenth-Century Renewal and Reform in Islam* (Syracuse: Syracuse University Press, 1987), 117–132 (at 122), and M. Winter, *Society and Religion in Early Ottoman Egypt*, 83–88. The Egyptian scholar ʿAbd al-Raʾūf al-Munāwī was primarily a Shādhilī but, as was common at his time, was also initiated into other orders, including at least two suborders of the Khalwatiyya. Both times, he was initiated by Turkish masters, first by a Cairene Demirdāşī master named Meḥmed Türkī and the other time by a visiting Khalwatī from Turkey (*al-diyār al-rūmiyya*) named Muḥarrem Meḥmed; see ʿAbd al-Raʾūf al-Munāwī, *al-Kawākib al-durriyya*, III, 509–510 and III, 512–514.

94 Muḥibbī, *Khulāṣat al-athar*, I, 248–250. In the secondary literature, the attributive العسالي is sometimes erroneously vocalized as "al-ʿAssālī." The correct vocalization is given by Muḥibbī; see *Khulāṣat al-athar*, I, 249 (l. 16).

95 Muḥibbī, *Khulāṣat al-athar*, I, 428–433.

al-ṣarīh wa-huwa lisān Ibn 'Arabī) – the meaning is presumably that Ayyūb's own mystical experiences confirmed to him the truth of the discourse of Ibn ʿArabī. Ayyūb had, according to Muḥibbī, once dreamt that he had managed to uncover approximately forty veils to get to Ibn ʿArabī, whereupon the latter said: "O Ayyūb, you are on my path and I do not know anyone else who has managed to enter my presence." Ayyūb was on good terms with the Shaṭṭārī Sufis of Medina and exchanged cordial letters with Aḥmad al-Qushāshī.[96] It may have been on the recommendation of Qushāshī that the aforementioned Sulawesi student Yūsuf Tāj Maqāṣīrī went to Damascus and was initiated into the Khalwatī order by Ayyūb.[97]

ʿUsālī's other main disciple, Muḥammad al-ʿAbbāsī, seems not to have left behind a comparable oeuvre but to have been focused primarily on practical Sufi training.[98] The seventeenth-century Meccan scholar Aḥmad al-Nakhlī described ʿAbbāsī as "the one at whose hands God most High brought forth the Khalwatī order in Damascus" (*man aẓhara Allāhu taʿālā ʿalā yadayhi ṭarīqata l-Khalwatiyyati fī l-Shām*).[99] The historian Muḥibbī, who was himself initiated by ʿAbbāsī, wrote:

> Novices flocked to him and the good people of the Path trained under his guidance. The many who derived benefit from him cannot be counted, and God most High favored them all with an excellent path and reception, and He cast a glow on their spiritual conditions by means of his [i.e. ʿAbbāsī's] blessings and prayers.[100]

Perhaps surprisingly, followers of the Ḥanbalī school of law featured conspicuously among the adherents of the order in the seventeenth century. ʿAbbāsī himself was a Ḥanbalī, as was his main disciple and successor ʿĪsā Ibn Kannān al-Ṣāliḥī (d. 1682).[101] Ayyūb al-Khalwatī's disciples included his deputy (*khalīfa*) Aḥmad Ibn Sālim al-Ḥanbalī (d. 1675), the eminent historian Ibn al-ʿImād al-Ḥanbalī (d. 1679), and the illustrious scholar and Ḥanbalī Mufti of Damascus Abū l-Mawāhib b. ʿAbd al-Bāqī al-Ḥanbalī (d. 1714).[102] To some extent, this may have been due

96 See the letter quoted in Muḥibbī, *Khulāṣat al-athar*, I, 244–245.
97 Azra, *The Origins of Islamic Reformism in Southeast Asia*, 92.
98 Muḥibbī, *Khulāṣat al-athar*, IV, 103.
99 Nakhlī, *Bughyat al-ṭālibīn*, 76.
100 Muḥibbī, *Khulāṣat al-athar*, IV, 103.
101 Ibid., III, 243–244.
102 On Ibn Sālim al-Ḥanbalī, see Muḥibbī, *Khulāṣat al-athar*, I, 253–256. On Ibn al-ʿImād al-Ḥanbalī as an initiate of Ayyūb al-Khalwatī, see Ḥamawī, *Fawāʾid al-irtiḥāl*, IV, 517 (l. 2). On Abū l-Mawāhib as an initiate of Ayyūb al-Khalwatī, see Abū l-Mawāhib al-Ḥanbalī, *Mashyakha*, edited by Muḥammad Muṭīʿ al-Ḥāfiẓ (Damascus: Dār al-Fikr, 1990), 88–90.

to the accident that the order initially established itself in the Ṣāliḥiyya district, which then had a significant Ḥanbalī presence. Nevertheless, the phenomenon of Ḥanbalī Khalwatīs calls for some comment.[103] Modern historians have often supposed that the Ḥanbalī school was "strict" and "traditionalist" and as such inimical to the supposedly speculative and esoteric mysticism of Ibn ʿArabī. One would, on this account, have expected Ḥanbalīs to have been sympathetic to the Turkish Ḳāḍīzādelīs in their campaign against Sufi "innovations." As with the case of the Naqshbandīs, it would seem that such an assumption is the result of anachronistically back-projecting attitudes that prevail among modern Ḥanbalīs. Modern Ḥanbalism has been profoundly shaped by the eighteenth-century Wahhābī movement, which vehemently condemned Ibn ʿArabī and all aspects of institutionalized Sufism. The seventeenth-century Ḥanbalī Khalwatīs are a salutary reminder that things were not always thus. The two most prominent Damascene Ḥanbalī religious scholars of the seventeenth century were ʿAbd al-Bāqī al-Baʿlī (d. 1661) and his aforementioned son Abū l-Mawāhīb. ʿAbd al-Bāqī had been initiated into Sufism by a master from Jerusalem and had cordial relations with Aḥmad al-Qushāshī and Ibrāhīm Kūrānī, the two prominent Medinan advocates of *waḥdat al-wujūd*.[104] He also acted as foster father to ʿAbd al-Ghanī al-Nābulusī – who would become an equally prominent defender of Ibn ʿArabī and *waḥdat al-wujūd* – when Nābulusī lost his own father at the age of eleven.[105] ʿAbd al-Bāqī's son Abū l-Mawāhib, whom Nābulusī considered a "foster brother" (*akhūnā min al-riḍāʿ*), was – as has just been mentioned – initiated by Ayyūb al-Khalwatī.[106] A somewhat later Ḥanbalī Khalwatī, ʿAbd al-Raḥmān al-Baʿlī (d. 1778), studied with Nābulusī Ibn ʿArabī's *Fuṣūṣ* and *Futūḥāt* as well as Nābulusī's commentary on the *Dīwān* of Ibn al-Fāriḍ.[107] The prominent Ḥanbalī scholar from Nablus in Palestine, Muḥammad al-Saffārīnī (d. 1774), whose numerous works have been studied in Ḥanbalī circles until the present, also studied

[103] The connection between Damascene Ḥanbalīs and the Khalwatī order was noted by John Voll in his valuable article "The Non-Wahhābī Ḥanbalīs of Eighteenth-Century Syria," *Der Islam* 49(1972): 277–291, at 285. But I do not agree with Voll that the Damascene Ḥanbalīs preferred "conservative" forms of Sufism. There was nothing "conservative" about the Khalwatī order in seventeenth-century Syria: It was only just beginning to spread in the area and tended to have a more positive attitude to the ideas of Ibn ʿArabī than had been usual in Arab-Islamic *ulema* circles in previous centuries.

[104] Abū l-Mawāhib, *Mashyakha*, 32–38; Muḥibbī, *Khulāṣat al-athar*, II, 283–285.

[105] Voll, "The Non-Wahhābī Ḥanbalīs," 286–287.

[106] Nābulusī's description of Abū l-Mawāhib as a "foster-brother" is quoted in the editor's introduction to the latter's *Mashyakha*, 15.

[107] Murādī, *Silk al-durar*, II, 304–308, at 305.

Sufi works with Nābulusī and was initiated into the Khalwatī order – to the chagrin of some of his modern Salafi editors.[108] As will be shown in the following chapter, Ḥanbalism and the views of Ibn ʿArabī were not as far apart as one might think – a Ḥanbalī scholar arguably had less reason to be perturbed by Ibn ʿArabī's positions on a range of central issues than someone committed to Ashʿarī or Māturīdī theology.

The northern Syrian city of Aleppo is closer to the Turkish- and Kurdish-speaking areas of Anatolia and Upper Mesopotamia, and the Khalwatī order appears to have made some inroads there already in the sixteenth century. The local historian Abū l-Wafāʾ al-ʿUrḍī (d. 1660) noted in passing that there was a lodge that had been established in the city toward the end of the sixteenth century or early in the seventeenth belonging to the Gülşenī branch of the Khalwatiyya. The lodge was an extension of the Gülşenī suborder in Cairo – ʿUrḍī mentioned that new masters were appointed from there. The suborder in Cairo is known to have used Persian and Turkish in their rites, which must have limited its appeals to local Arabs. ʿUrḍī described the lodge as having been somewhat marginal and even disreputable in Aleppo, though he added that in his own lifetime the master, a certain Ismāʿīl Gülşenī (d. 1665), was well liked and that people used to come to the lodge to listen to his recitation of the Quran during the month of Ramadan. He also taught Persian to young boys. There is no indication, however, that even this Ismāʿīl Gülşenī had a substantial following among the local Arabic-speaking population.[109] ʿUrḍī also mentioned a prominent Kurdish Khalwatī master named Aḥmad b. ʿAbdū Quṣayrī (d. 1560) who was based in a village near Antioch but often came to Aleppo and had close contacts with the religious notables there. ʿUrḍī noted that he attracted scores of disciples from "the people of the East, Kurds and others," and this suggests that not only the head of the order but also a conspicuous proportion of its early initiates were Kurds or Turcomans.[110] Nevertheless, he is also known to have attracted followers from nearby Arab towns such as Hama.[111]

108 Saffārīnī, *Thabat*, edited by Muḥammad al-ʿAjamī (Beirut: Dār al-Bashāʾir al-Islāmiyya, 2004), 172–175, 192–193. Note the editor's comments on p. 173 (fn. 1) and p. 193 (fn. 1).

109 Abū l-Wafāʾ al-ʿUrḍī, *Maʿādin al-dhahab fī l-aʿyān al-musharrafa bi-him Ḥalab*, edited by ʿĪsā Sulaymān Abū Salīm (Amman: al-Jāmiʿa al-Urduniyya, Manshūrāt markaz al-wathāʾiq wa-l-makhṭūṭāt, 1992), 416–418.

110 ʿUrḍī, *Maʿādin al-dhahab*, 285 (l. 6). In the same entry, ʿUrḍī related a story of Turcomans petitioning Quṣayrī, see pp. 281–282.

111 For one such disciple, see ʿUrḍī, *Maʿādin al-dhahab*, 396–399; Muḥibbī, *Khulāṣat al-athar*, I, 154–156.

A more substantial Khalwatī presence in Aleppo stems from Şāh Velī ʿAyntābī (d. 1605), the aforementioned master of the Aḥmad ʿUsālī who introduced the order to Damascus. Şāh Velī visited Aleppo on a number of occasions from nearby Gaziantep. Under his influence, the local head of the ʿAlwāniyya – a branch of the Shādhilī order whose eponym was ʿAlwān al-Ḥamawī, the aforementioned disciple of Ibn Maymūn al-Maghribī – embraced the Khalwatī order and ordered his disciples to do so as well. The former ʿAlwānī master's hopes of succeeding his new master were frustrated, though, when Şāh Velī on his deathbed insisted on appointing a certain Ḳāyā Çelebī as his successor in Aleppo.[112] The personal name "Ḳāyā" ("rock" in Turkish) indicates that he was a Turk, as does the absence of a reference to the father's name (biographical entries on Arab notables almost always include the father's name). The same applies to Ḳāyā's successor Iḫlāṣ (d. 1663).[113] In 1634, the Ottoman Grand Vizier Arnaʾūt Meḥmed Pāşā built the so-called Ikhlāṣiyya lodge in the city for Iḫlāṣ and his disciples.[114] This, incidentally, was just a couple of years before Küçük Aḥmed Pāşā built a lodge for Aḥmad ʿUsālī in Damascus – there was clearly a pattern of Ottoman sponsorship of the Khalwatī order in Syria in the 1630s, presumably as part of a broader reconsolidation of Ottoman control over the area during the reign of Murād IV (r. 1623–1640) after the troubles associated with the renegade governor of Aleppo ʿAlī Jānpūlād (d. 1611) and the powerful Druze emir of Mt. Lebanon Fakhr al-Dīn al-Maʿnī (d. 1635).[115] Iḫlāṣ was succeeded by his disciple Meḥmed Ġāzī (d. 1671), of whom the historian Muḥibbī wrote, "We have not seen in our time a Sufi master who had as many initiates as him." When Meḥmed Ġāzī visited Damascus, the sheer number of people around him was such that he could not shake their hands individually (to receive their pledge of allegiance) and instead held out a long cloth for the crowds to touch.[116] After his death, the leadership of the lodge in Aleppo passed, in what may have been something of a "coup," to a disciple of Ayyūb al-Khalwatī in Damascus, Muḥammad al-Bakhshī

112 ʿUrḍī, *Maʿādin al-dhahab*, 306–310.

113 Ibid., 411–413.

114 H. Z. Watenpaugh, *The Image of an Ottoman City: Imperial Architecture and Urban Experience in Aleppo in the Sixteenth and Seventeenth Centuries* (Leiden, the Netherlands: Brill, 2004), 148ff.

115 For these troubles, see J. Hathaway, *The Arab Lands under Ottoman Rule, 1516–1800* (Harlow, UK: Pearson Education, 2008), 70–72.

116 Muḥibbī, *Khulāṣat al-athar*, IV, 312–313. Muḥibbī was himself one of those who pledged his allegiance to Meḥmed Ġāzī, though he had already been initiated into the Khalwatī order by the aforementioned Muḥammad al-ʿAbbāsī.

al-Bakfalūnī (d. 1687), who originally hailed from a village near Idlib in northwestern Syria.[117] Bakfalūnī's successors came to be known as the "Bakhshiyyah" in following centuries.

Besides Bakfalūnī, two other figures indicate that by the second half of the seventeenth century the order in Aleppo was no longer associated with non-Arabs. One of these was Qāsim al-Khānī, whose influential *al-Sayr wa-l-sulūk ilā malik al-mulūk* was mentioned at the beginning of this chapter.[118] This widely copied and emulated work gave an outline of the seven stations of the mystic path as conceived by the Khalwatī tradition.[119] Khānī accepted the formula of *waḥdat al-wujūd*, though he stressed that the mystic seeker should not just assent to the truth of this doctrine but also come to the direct experience of its truth (*shuhūd waḥdat al-wujūd*) after strenuous ascetic and spiritual exercise.[120] Like Kūrānī, Barzinjī, and Nābulusī, Khānī was not merely a Sufi but also one of the prominent religious scholars of his city. He wrote an introductory manual on logic that appears to have been studied in Syrian scholarly circles in later centuries, and a commentary on a didactic creedal poem by the North African Ashʿarī theologian Aḥmad al-Jazāʾirī (d. 1479).[121] He was also authorized to issue fatwas according to both the Shāfiʿī and Ḥanafī schools of law.

Another prominent local Khalwatī master was ʿAbd al-Laṭīf b. Ḥusām al-Dīn al-Ḥalabī (d. 1709) who had been initiated into the order by a son of the eminent Turkish Sufi Ḳarabāş ʿAlī Velī (d. 1686).[122] ʿAbd al-Laṭīf in turn initiated the Damascene Muṣṭafā al-Bakrī (d. 1749), one of the most prominent Khalwatī Sufis of the eighteenth century.[123] Bakrī

117 Ibid., 208–211. Muḥibbī explicitly stated that Bakfalūnī went to Istanbul to receive the appointment as head of the lodge of Iḫlāṣ.

118 On Khānī, see Murādī, *Silk al-durar*, IV, 9–10. For the influence of his work, see B. Radtke, "Sufism in the 18th Century: An Attempt at a Provisional Appraisal," *Die Welt des Islams* 36(1996): 326–364, at 330–331.

119 Some manuscripts give Khānī the attributive "al-Qādirī" suggesting that he belonged to that order, see Ahlwardt, *Verzeichnis*, nr. 2498. Nevertheless, his *al-Sayr wa-l-sulūk* is explicitly written as a Khalwatī work so one must assume that its author was initiated into that order as well; see *al-Sayr wa-l-sulūk*, 120–121 [Shāfiʿī edition], 191 [ʿAbd al-Fattāḥ edition]. He was reportedly a disciple of a certain Aḥmad al-Ḥimṣī who appears to have escaped the notice of contemporary biographers – it is not clear whether he initiated Khānī into the Qādirī or the Khalwatī order.

120 Khānī, *al-Sayr wa-l-sulūk*, 62–63 [Shāfiʿī edition], 122 [ʿAbd al-Fattāḥ edition].

121 Mach, *Catalogue*, nr. 3317, Mach and Ormsby, *Handlist*, nr. 959.

122 Murādī, *Silk al-durar*, III, 123. On Ḳarabāş Velī, see N. Clayer, "Shaʿbāniyya," *EI2*, IX, 155.

123 Ibid., IV, 190–200.

played a central role in spreading the order in Egypt and the Hejaz. His disciples included Muḥammad b. Sālim al-Ḥafnī (d. 1767) in Egypt and Muḥammad b. ʿAbd al-Karīm al-Sammān (d. 1775) in the Hejaz, both of whom were in turn important influences on some of the most successful African Sufi movements in the nineteenth century such as the Tījāniyya, the Sanūsiyya, and the Mīrghaniyya.[124]

The later religious scholar and Sufi apologist Yūsuf al-Nabahānī (d. 1932) once wrote that Bakrī "revived" (*aḥyā*) the Khalwatī order.[125] From a Syrian – let alone a Turkish – perspective, such a description makes little sense. From an Egyptian perspective, on the other hand, it is understandable. Prior to the eighteenth century, the order in Egypt had been confined mainly to Turkish speakers, and there are indications that local Egyptian scholars often disparaged it.[126] The Egyptian Sufi and scholar ʿAbd al-Raʾūf al-Munāwī (d. 1622), for example, wrote that in his own day:

> It [the Khalwatī order] is merely presumption and foolery with the utter absence of either exoteric or esoteric knowledge, to such an extent that the clever and eminent amongst scholars laugh at this faction, ridicule them, and regard their ignorance as proverbial.[127]

Bakrī started a process whereby the order became one of the most influential and respected among Egyptian *ulema* in the eighteenth and nineteenth centuries. For example, in the second half of the eighteenth century no less than three Rectors of the Azhar had a primary affiliation to the order (all of them direct or indirect disciples of Bakrī).[128]

124 Radtke, "Sufism in the 18th Century," 331–332; N. Levtzion, "Islamic Revolutions in West Africa," in N. Levtzion and J. Voll (eds.), *Eighteenth-Century Renewal and Reform in Islam*, 21–38, at 32–33.

125 Cited by de Jong, "Mustafa Kamal al-Din al-Bakri," 119.

126 For the Arab-Turkish tensions underlying Egyptian scholars' suspicions of the Khalwatī order in the sixteenth century, see E. S. Ohlander, ""He Was Crude of Speech": Turks and Arabs in the Hagiographical Imagination of Early Ottoman Egypt," in J. Hathaway (ed.), *The Arab Lands in the Ottoman Era* (Minnesota: Center for Early Modern History, 2009), 111–135.

127 Munāwī, *al-Kawākib al-durriyya*, III, 510. As noted previously, Munāwī was initiated by the Demirdāşī master Meḥmed Türkī (d. 1598). His remarks were intended to buttress this master's own pessimistic remarks about the state of the Khalwatī order in Egypt in his time.

128 These are Muḥammad b. Sālim al-Ḥafnī (d. 1767), Aḥmad al-ʿArūsī (d. 1793) and ʿAbdullāh al-Sharqāwī (d. 1812). See Jabartī, *ʿAjāʾib al-āthār*, I, 289–291; II, 252–255; IV, 159–163.

Unfortunately, some modern historians have taken Nabahānī's characterization of Bakrī "reviving" the Khalwatī order in a different sense – they have speculated that he was a "reformer" who abandoned the doctrine of *waḥdat al-wujūd* and imposed a stricter organizational structure on his followers, thus allowing for a more worldly and politically effective movement – in effect prefiguring later, so-called "neo-Sufi," movements. But as shown by both Frederick De Jong and Ralf Elger, there is little substance to such suggestions. There is simply no evidence that Bakrī made any "reforms" other than introducing a particular litany (known as *wird al-saḥar*) among his followers.[129] Furthermore, Bakrī belonged to the Ḳarabāşī suborder that was particularly devoted to Ibn ʿArabī: Ḳarabāş ʿAlī Velī had authored a commentary on the *Fuṣūṣ* and his disciples believed that Ibn ʿArabī had predicted their master's appearance.[130] Bakrī was also a close student of ʿAbd al-Ghanī al-Nābulusī, studied with him numerous works by Ibn ʿArabī, including the *Fuṣūṣ*, and himself upheld the doctrine of *waḥdat al-wujūd* in his treatise *al-Mawrid al-ʿadhb li-dhawī l-wurūd fī kashf maʿnā waḥdat al-wujūd*.[131] Bakrī is moreover known to have taught an exposition of *waḥdat al-wujūd* by the prominent fourteenth-century *Fuṣūṣ* commentator ʿAbd al-Razzāq al-Qāshānī to a disciple in Mecca.[132] His son and disciple Kamāl al-Dīn al-Bakrī (d. 1782) is also known to have taught Nābulusī's commentary on the *Fuṣūṣ* in Gaza where he settled and died.[133] The most that can be said is that Bakrī's oeuvre suggests that he may have been less interested in mystical metaphysics than Nābulusī and more focused on the devotional life and on initiating and training disciples. He was also eager to distance himself from antinomian Sufis who understood the ideas of Ibn

129 De Jong, "Mustafa Kamal al-Din al-Bakri," esp. 121, 125–127.

130 Ibid., 126–127.

131 R. Elger, *Muṣṭafā al-Bakrī: Zur Selbstdarstellung eines syrischen Gelehrten, Sufis und Dichters des 18. Jahrhunderts* (Schenefeld: EB-Verlag, 2004), 163–164.

132 Murādī, *Silk al-durar*, IV, 239 (ll. 3–4). Murādī's text states that Bakrī taught his disciple "*waḥdat al-wujūd li-Munlā Jāmī*." This is probably a reference to a short treatise on the cosmology of *waḥdat al-wujūd* falsely attributed to Jāmī but actually by Qāshānī. Bakrī's teacher Nābulusī wrote a commentary on this work, attributing it to Jāmī; see his *al-Ẓill al-mamdūd fī maʿnā waḥdat al-wujūd* (MS: Princeton University Library, Yahuda 1901), fols. 45b–64a. Rudolf Mach has shown that the work cannot be by Jāmī, as there are extant manuscripts of it that predate Jāmī's birth; see Mach, *Catalogue*, nr. 2785. The treatise in question has recently been edited along with other treatises by Qāshānī; see ʿAbd al-Razzāq al-Qāshānī, *Majmūʿah-yi rasāʾil va musannafāt*, edited by Mājid Hādīzāde (Tehran: Mirās-i Maktūb, 2000), 595–603.

133 Murādī, *Silk al-durar*, IV, 239 (ll. 12–14).

ʿArabī as a license to disregard Islamic law, but this theme was already in place in the writings of Nābulusī and Qāsim al-Khānī.[134] To interpret such concerns in Bakrī's writings as an effort to "reform" a wayward or decadent order is to overlook clear evidence that the Khalwatī order had enjoyed a period of dramatic expansion in the generations prior to Bakrī, at least in Aleppo and Damascus, and was already thoroughly respectable in *ulema* circles – indeed it counted among its members some of the major religious scholars of the two cities.

Conclusion

Attitudes to Ibn ʿArabī in later Islamic history were complex, and a good deal of nuance is lost by reducing them to a simple opposition between "for" and "against." As has become clear from the foregoing discussion, there were numerous and historically influential shades of opinion within a generally favorable attitude to the Andalusian mystic. Some later Sufis and scholars considered him to have been a saint but largely avoided a direct engagement with his works, preferring to rely on the works of, for example, earlier Sufis and the later North African Shādhilī tradition. Others esteemed and cited the *Futūḥāt* but avoided committing themselves to the more controversial theories expounded in the *Fuṣūṣ* and its later commentaries, such as *waḥdat al-wujūd*, "the faith of Pharaoh" and the transience of the punishments of hell. Both of these attitudes are abundantly in evidence among Arab-Islamic scholars with Sufi affiliations in the fifteenth and sixteenth centuries. An explicit endorsement of the monistic tradition stemming from Qūnawī and the later *Fuṣūṣ* commentators appears by contrast to have been rare in the Arab-Islamic world in the fifteenth and sixteenth centuries, especially if one confines one's attention to *ulema* circles and prominent, learned Sufis. The spread of support for monism in the seventeenth century appears to have been linked to the introduction of the Shaṭṭārī, Naqshbandī, and Khalwatī mystical orders in Syria and the Hejaz. (In North Africa the process occurred a century later with the spread of the Khalwatī order and its offshoots.)

As will be shown in the following chapter, the consequences of this development were both important and surprising. A widely held belief

[134] For Khānī's criticism of antinomian Sufis, see my "Heresy and Sufism in the Arabic-Islamic World, 1550–1750: Some Preliminary Observations," *Bulletin of the School of Oriental and African Studies* 73(2010): 357–380, at 369–370. For Bakrī's criticism, see ibid., 370–373. For Nābulusī's criticisms, see Chapter 9 below.

among critics of Ibn ʿArabī, from Ibn Taymiyya in the thirteenth century to Fazlur Rahman in the twentieth, is that his "pantheism" leads naturally to esotericism, antinomianism, and a blurring of the boundaries between Islam and other religions.[135] There is little evidence of such inclinations among prominent seventeenth-century scholars who espoused ontological monism. It is, to be sure, undeniable that Ibn ʿArabī's ideas were often invoked by groups widely condemned as antinomian – there is abundant evidence for this even from the works of his supporters in the sixteenth and seventeenth centuries.[136] But the ideas of Ibn ʿArabī and the later *Fuṣūṣ* commentators were also making inroads among eminent members of the *ulema* class in the seventeenth century, including muftis of some of the major Arab cities of the Ottoman Empire, and there is no evidence that these scholars drew antinomian consequences from Ibn ʿArabī's writings – indeed they were eager to dissociate themselves from antinomian groups. The consequences of the increased influence of monistic interpretations of Ibn ʿArabī were in fact very different. Scholars such as Kūrānī and Nābulusī were critical of several aspects of established Ashʿarī theology, and they formulated alternative positions on these issues that were akin to those of the long-submerged Ḥanbalī tradition of thought. Nābulusī was personally close to the most eminent Ḥanbalī scholars of Damascus in his lifetime, and his positions on a range of traditional theological issues were very similar to theirs. Kūrānī in fact seems to have played an important role in rehabilitating the thought of the Ḥanbalī purists Ibn Taymiyya and Ibn Qayyim al-Jawziyya (d. 1350) – long deemed problematic or even outright heretical by the later Ashʿarī tradition. This may appear paradoxical at first sight. The mystical worldview of the *Fuṣūṣ* commentators and the fiercely anti-esoteric outlook of traditionalist Ḥanbalism have for understandable reasons often been seen as antithetical. The following chapter will attempt to show that matters are a good deal more complicated.

[135] Knysh, *Ibn ʿArabī in the Later Islamic Tradition*, 106, 109; Rahman, *Islam*, 146–147.
[136] El-Rouayheb, "Heresy and Sufism," 369–373.

8

Monist Mystics and Neo-Ḥanbalī Traditionalism

In September 1660, the prominent Damascene Ḥanbalī scholar ʿAbd al-Bāqī al-Baʿlī completed a creedal work entitled *al-ʿAyn wa-l-athar fī ʿaqāʾid ahl al-athar* (The eye and the trace concerning the creeds of the people of tradition). In the introduction, he mentioned that he had been asked to compose a work that presented the Ḥanbalī position on the articles of faith (*ʿaqāʾid*), with special attention to the points on which Ḥanbalīs differed from Ashʿarīs and in particular the question of God's Speech.[1] He duly penned a treatise that outlined the Ḥanbalī creed, including a defense of distinctive Ḥanbalī positions such as the illegitimacy of prying into divine matters with unaided reason; the rejection of figurative interpretation of apparent anthropomorphic expressions in the Quran and hadith; and the insistence that God's eternal and uncreated Speech consists of Arabic sounds and letters (Ashʿarīs tended to believe that the Arabic sounds and letters of the Quran express the eternal Speech of God that is itself beyond time and space and hence not spatially or aurally ordered).

Introductions in which an author claims that he is writing at the request of someone else are so frequent in premodern Islamic scholarship that one might suspect such claims to be nothing more than literary commonplaces. In this particular case, though, it is possible to determine that ʿAbd al-Bāqī had in fact been asked to write the treatise. The Moroccan scholar ʿAbdullāh al-ʿAyyāshī, whose account of his pilgrimage and subsequent stay in Mecca and Medina in 1662–1664 has already been

[1] ʿAbd al-Bāqī al-Ḥanbalī, *al-ʿAyn wa l-athar fī ʿaqāʾid ahl al-athar*, edited by ʿIṣām Rawwās al-Qalʿajī and ʿAbd al-ʿAzīz Rabāḥ (Damascus and Beirut: Dār al-Maʾmūn li-l-turāth, 1987), 26.

cited on a number of occasions in previous chapters, wrote that his Medinan teacher Ibrāhīm Kūrānī had attempted to adjudicate the views of the Ashʿarīs and the Ḥanbalīs on the question of God's Speech, and that Kūrānī had sent a letter to Damascus asking ʿAbd al-Bāqī to present the Ḥanbalī case. ʿAyyashi wrote:

> One of these [works by Kūrānī] is *Ifāḍat al-ʿallām fī masʾalat al-kalām*... The starting point of this work is critically appraising (*taḥqīq*) the dispute between the Ashʿarīs and Ḥanbalīs concerning [God's] Speech... Much has been said on this issue between the later Shāfiʿīs and the Ḥanbalīs to such an extent that each party pronounced the other wayward. Because of this issue and others concerning which the Ḥanbalīs held on to the apparent (*ẓāhir*) meaning of the Quran and the hadith, such as God's being seated on the throne, descending to the lower heavens, and having feet, a face and two eyes... Ibn Taymiyya and his disciples such as Ibn Qayyim al-Jawziyya were declared wayward by their Shāfiʿī contemporaries such as Taqī al-Dīn al-Subkī [d. 1355] and Tāj al-Dīn al-Subkī [d. 1370]... Our teacher [i.e. Kūrānī], when he resolved to investigate these issues, wrote at the suggestion of his own master Ṣafī al-Dīn [al-Qushāshī] to Shaykh ʿAbd al-Bāqī al-Ḥanbalī al-Baʿlī who was at the time the most prominent and learned Ḥanbalī in Damascus, asking him to write an exposition of the beliefs of the Ḥanbalīs along with their evidential grounds... The Shaykh ʿAbd al-Bāqī wrote for him a treatise that included everything that he had been asked to explicate, and then he [i.e. Kūrānī] began to write this work.[2]

As indicated in ʿAyyāshī's account, relations between Ḥanbalīs and Ashʿarīs had often been tense. In the early fourteenth century, the iconoclastic Damascene Ḥanbalī scholar Ibn Taymiyya had attacked several Ashʿarī positions as heretical deviations from the pristine beliefs of the earliest generations of Islam (*al-salaf*). In turn, a number of Ashʿarī and Shāfiʿī scholars roundly condemned Ibn Taymiyya's positions as crassly anthropomorphic. Ashʿarī/Shāfiʿī critics of Ibn Taymiyya included such prominent scholars as Taqī al-Dīn al-Subkī, Tāj al-Dīn al-Subkī, Taqī al-Dīn al-Ḥisnī (d. 1426), Aḥmad al-Qasṭallānī (d. 1517), Ibn Ḥajar al-Haytamī (d. 1565), and Aḥmad al-Khafājī (d. 1658). Both Ashʿarīs and Māturīdīs in later centuries often condemned the Ḥanbalīs – or at least anti-Ashʿarī Ḥanbalīs such as Ibn Taymiyya and his followers – as so-called *Ḥashwiyya* who were beyond the pale of Sunni Islam altogether.[3] Kūrānī wished to depart from such views even though they

[2] ʿAyyāshī, *Riḥla*, I, 474–475.

[3] K. El-Rouayheb, "From Ibn Ḥajar al-Haytamī (d. 1566) to Khayr al-Din al-Ālūsī (d. 1899): Changing Views of Ibn Taymiyya amongst Sunni Islamic Scholars," in S. Ahmed and Y. Rapoport (eds.), *Ibn Taymiyya and His Times* (Karachi: Oxford University Press, 2010), 269–318.

were widespread among adherents of his own Shāfiʿī school of law. He told ʿAyyashi:

When I looked carefully at the treatises and works of these people [i.e. the Ḥanbalīs], I found them innocent of many of the charges that had been brought against them by my fellow Shāfiʿīs, such as corporealism (*tajsīm*) and anthropomorphism (*tashbīh*). Rather, they adhere to the position of the great hadith scholars – as is known from the case of their Imam [Ibn Ḥanbal], may God be pleased with him – which is to believe in Quranic verses and hadith reports as they stand, while entrusting [to God] the meaning of passages that seem anthropomorphic. This position is not condemned by any Ashʿarī.[4]

In his glosses on Dawānī's commentary on the creed of ʿAḍud al-Dīn al-Ījī, Kūrānī also went out of his way to defend Ibn Taymiyya against the charge of anthropomorphism. In his discussion of the Aristotelian thesis of the eternity of the world, Dawānī claimed that something similar had been proposed by antirationalist traditionalists such as Ibn Taymiyya: God is seated on a throne that is constantly being recreated, so that the throne is eternal in kind. An earlier glossator on Dawānī's commentary had suggested that this position of Ibn Taymiyya was based on his being an anthropomorphist (*mujassim*) who believed that God is literally seated on a throne and that because God is eternal the throne must be eternal in some sense as well.[5] Kūrānī demurred, writing

Ibn Taymiyya is not an anthropomorphist. He explicitly stated in a treatise on God's descent to the lower heavens every night that God is not a body. He stated in another treatise: "One who claims that God is like a human body or that God resembles a creature is fabricating lies of God." Rather, his is the position of the earliest generations of Islam, which is to believe in the apparently anthropomorphic passages [in the Quran and hadith] while at the same time clearing (*tanzīh*) God of resemblance to creatures by [asserting] "There is nothing like Him" (Quran 42:11).[6]

It may at first sight appear surprising that Kūrānī, an ardent follower of Ibn ʿArabī and advocate of *waḥdat al-wujūd*, should have gone out of his way to defend Ibn Taymiyya against charges of anthropomorphism. Ibn ʿArabī and Ibn Taymiyya have often been viewed as antithetical expressions of Islam: the former a speculative mystic and monist, the

4 ʿAyyāshī, *Riḥla,* I, 475–476.

5 The glossator in question is Yūsuf Kawsaj Qarabāghī (d. 1625), an eminent student of Mīrzā Jān Bāghnavī (d. 1586); see his *al-Ḥāshiya al-Khānqāhiyya ʿalā Sharḥ al-ʿAqāʾid al-ʿAḍudiyya* (MS: British Library: Bijapur 213), fol. 16a.

6 Khayr al-Dīn al-Ālūsī, *Jalāʾ al-ʿaynayn fī muḥākamat al-Aḥmadayn* (Cairo: Maṭbaʿat al-Madanī, 1961), 339.

latter a strict traditionalist opposed to anything that smacked of esotericism, Neo-Platonism and pantheism. As will be seen in this chapter, Ibn ʿArabī and his commentators in fact shared some important but often overlooked commonalities with Ḥanbalī traditionalists. Both camps were united in opposition to mainstream Ashʿarī and Māturīdī theology on a range of central issues: the rejection of rationalistically motivated figurative interpretations of apparent anthropomorphisms in the Quran and hadith; the denigration of the discipline of rational theology; and the rejection of mainstream Ashʿarī views on secondary causality and the creation of human acts. The following sections explore each of these issues in turn.

Kūrānī on Figurative Interpretation (*Taʾwīl*)

Ibn ʿArabī has often been associated in modern scholarship with a speculative esotericism that ignores or twists the plain text of the Quran and hadith to fit the exigencies of a mystical, pantheist worldview. Even some modern admirers have contributed to this misconception. The French scholar Henry Corbin, for example, emphasized what he saw as the pivotal role of nonliteral interpretation (*taʾwīl*) in Ibn ʿArabī's thought, thus explicitly aligning him with a largely Shiite tradition of esotericism. As William Chittick has pointed out, this emphasis is misleadingly one sided. It is of course true that Ibn ʿArabī and his followers regularly proposed hidden meanings in the Quran and hadith – meanings that were discoverable only through mystic "unveiling" or "verification." But Ibn ʿArabī was also adamant that the apparent sense of the Quran and hadith should be accepted, and he castigated rational theologians and philosophers for their refusal to do so when they deemed the apparent sense to be rationally impossible.[7] This is an important aspect of Ibn ʿArabī's thought that has often been missed by modern scholars, and it goes some way toward showing the common ground between Ibn ʿArabī-inspired Sufism and Ḥanbalī antirationalist traditionalism.

Another widespread misconception that is relevant in the present context concerns the Ashʿarī view of apparent anthropomorphisms in the Quran and hadith. It is often mistakenly believed that the Ashʿarī position can be summed up with the formula *bilā kayf*: apparently anthropomorphic passages should be accepted "without asking how." In fact, the mainstream Ashʿarī position from at least the eleventh century was

[7] Chittick, *The Sufi Path of Knowledge*, 199–202.

that such passages in the Quran and hadith should *not* be interpreted literally. This was the view propounded in such standard handbooks of Ashʿarī theology as *Sharḥ al-ʿAqāʾid al-Nasafiyya* by Taftāzānī, *Sharḥ al-Mawāqif* by al-Sayyid al-Sharīf al-Jurjānī (d. 1413), the creedal works of Sanūsī (d. 1490) and the *Jawharat al-tawḥīd* of Ibrāhīm al-Laqānī (d. 1631).[8] In these widely studied works, the correct position concerning apparent anthropomorphisms in the Quran and hadith is held to be the following: Such passages should not be taken in their apparent (*ẓāhir*) sense. Rather, one should either reinterpret them figuratively (*taʾwīl*) or entrust their meaning to God (*tafwīḍ*). The latter option was held to be the position of the earliest generations of Islam (*al-salaf*); the former option was that of most later Ashʿarī theologians (*al-khalaf*). The aforementioned Ashʿarī handbooks emphasized that both positions involved rejecting the apparent sense. It is just that later theologians ventured to give suggestions as to which of the many possible non-literal meanings was intended, largely because they had to contend with the challenge of newfangled anthropomorphist groups who appealed to the superficial sense of the Quran and hadith in support of their heresies. To minimize the difference between the two approaches, some later Ashʿarī authors characterized the earlier approach of *tafwīḍ* (or entrusting the meaning to God) as nonspecific figurative interpretation (*taʾwīl ijmālī*). What the later Ashʿarī theologians had done was – on this account – simply to specify which of many possible figurative interpretations is most plausible (*taʾwīl tafṣīlī*).

Some Ḥanbalī thinkers were satisfied with the position of *tafwīḍ*: we should leave off reinterpreting apparent anthropomorphisms and instead entrust their meaning to God.[9] But more radical Ḥanbalīs like Ibn Taymiyya – at least in his more combative moods – rejected *tafwīḍ* and denied that it had been the position of the venerable earliest generations. At one point he wrote:

[8] Taftāzānī, *Sharḥ al-ʿAqāʾid al-Nasafiyya*, edited by Klūd Salama (Damascus: Wizārat al-Thaqāfa, 1974) 42–44; Jurjānī, *Sharḥ al-Mawāqif* (Istanbul: Hācī Muḥarrem Būsnavī Maṭbaʿasī, 1286/1869), 501; Sanūsī, *Sharḥ al-Kubrā*, 276–277; Laqānī, *Hidāyat al-murīd bi-sharḥ Jawharat al-tawḥīd*, I, 488ff. Whether Taftāzānī was an Ashʿarī or a Māturīdī is not entirely clear. He may have held that the disagreements between the two schools were less than the scope for individual disagreement within either of the schools. In any case, his commentary on the creed of Nasafī was regularly studied and glossed in later Ashʿarī circles.

[9] This appears to have been the position of the Ḥanbalī Ibn Qudāma (d. 1233); see his *Censure of Speculative Theology*, ed. and trans. G. Makdisi (London: Luzac, 1962), par. 55, 73.

The unacceptable figurative interpretation (*taʾwīl*) is to divert discourse from its apparent sense to what goes against the apparent sense (*ṣarfu l-kalāmi ʿan ẓāhirihi ilā mā yukhālifu ẓāhirahu*). If it is said... that only God knows its *taʾwīl* then we concede to the Jahmiyya[10] that the Quranic verse has a true *taʾwīl* that is other than its [plain] signification (*yukhālifu dalātahā*), but that this is only known to God. This is not the position of the *salaf* and the Imams. Rather, their position is to deny and reject *taʾwīl*, not to suspend judgment.[11]

Ibn Taymiyya thus insisted that the apparent (*ẓāhir*) sense of passages that state that God has eyes, hands, and feet, and that He occasionally descends to the lowest heavens, should simply be accepted – in the same way that one should accept passages that state that God knows or wills or speaks. Why should the latter passages be interpreted in accordance with their plain sense but not the former? After all, a rational theologian would have to say that God's Knowledge, Will, and Speech are very unlike human knowledge, will, and speech. But why can one not similarly say that God has eyes, feet, and hands but that these are very unlike human eyes, feet, and hands? Or that God descends but that this is very different from creatures descending?

As mentioned, Ibn ʿArabī and his followers tended to adopt a position on this issue that was close to that of Ḥanbalī traditionalists: One should accept descriptions of God in the Quran and hadith in their apparent (*ẓāhir*) sense and refrain from rationalistically motivated *taʾwīl*. And like Ḥanbalī traditionalists, they were sometimes accused by opponents of falling into the heresy of *tajsīm* or *tashbīh* (corporealism or anthropomorphism). This can be seen from a treatise by Ibrāhīm Kūrānī, completed in January 1682 and entitled *Tanbīh al-ʿuqūl ʿalā tanzīh al-ṣūfiyya ʿan iʿtiqād al-tajsīm wa l-ʿayniyya wa l-ittiḥād wa l-ḥulūl*.[12] The treatise is a defense of Ibn ʿArabī and his followers against the charges of anthropomorphism, pantheism, immanentism, and incarnationism. Kūrānī began his treatise by outlining the basic features of the cosmology of Ibn ʿArabī and his followers:[13] God is identical to pure, absolute existence (*al-wujūd*

10 The Jahmiyya were an early theological sect who, among other beliefs, interpreted apparent anthropomorphisms in the Quran figuratively. The sect had long died out by the fourteenth century but Ibn Taymiyya continued to use the term derogatorily of those who endorse figurative interpretation of apparent anthropomorphisms.

11 Ibn Taymiyya, *al-Iklīl fī l-mutashābah wa l-taʾwīl*, in *Majmūʿat al-rasāʾil al-kubrā* (Cairo: Muḥammad ʿAlī Ṣubayḥ, 1966), II, 5–36, at 22–23.

12 Ibrāhīm Kūrānī, *Tanbīh al-ʿuqūl ʿalā tanzīh al-ṣūfiyya ʿan iʿtiqād al-tajsīm wa l-ʿayniyya wa l-ittiḥād wa l-ḥulūl*, edited by Muḥammad Ibrāhīm al-Ḥusayn (Damascus: Dār al-Bayrūtī, 2009).

13 Kūrānī, *Tanbīh al-ʿuqūl*, 33–48.

al-muṭlaq or *al-wujūd al-maḥḍ*), in the sense that God has no quiddity (*māhiyya*) apart from unqualified existence as such. Only for contingent entities is there a distinction between quiddity (*what* it is) and existence (*that* it is). The quiddities of contingent entities are eternal in the sense that they are determinate objects of God's eternal knowledge. The quiddities are therefore not "made" (*maj'ūla*), that is, there is no cause for an entity being the kind of entity it is (a horse being a horse, for example, or a human being a human). There is a cause, though, for quiddities becoming realized as more than mere possibilities. Such a realization or actualization (*ta'ayyun*) of quiddities is equivalent to God/Existence making Himself manifest in them. The concept of divine manifestation or epiphany (*tajallī*) is rooted in the Quran and hadith, but it assumes a central importance in the cosmology of Ibn 'Arabī and his followers. God in Himself is utterly different from anything that may be conceived or sensed, but He manifests Himself in the phenomenal world. Such divine manifestation is constrained by the eternal and unmade quiddities of contingent entities, so that the manifestations of God will be in accordance with the limitations and distinct characteristics of the contingent loci.

All passages in the Quran and hadith that suggest that God has bodily or human form or spatial location should, on this account, be understood as descriptions of the manifestations or epiphanies of God. As such, they should not be interpreted figuratively, because doing so would be to deny the manifestation or epiphany. On that basis, Kūrānī disagreed with, for example, the interpretation of the story of Moses and the burning bush put forward by al-Bayḍāwī (fl. 1284), by far the most influential Quran exegete during the Ottoman period. In the Quranic version of this story (27:8), God says to Moses: "Blessed be the one who is in the fire and the one who is around it; Glory be to God, Lord of the Worlds. O Moses, it is I, God, the Mighty and Wise." An early exegetical tradition purporting to go back to Ibn 'Abbās (d. 687) interpreted "the one who is in the fire" (*man fī l-nār*) as God. Bayḍāwī, and most later exegetes, resisted such an interpretation, and proposed instead that "in the fire" (*fī l-nār*) meant "in the vicinity of the fire" (*fī makān al-nār*) so that "the one who is in the fire" would be Moses and possibly also other humans and angels in the vicinity.[14] Kūrānī held such an interpretation to be an illegitimate departure from the apparent sense (*al-ẓāhir*) simply to avoid conceding that it is God who is in the fire. There is, he insisted,

14 Bayḍāwī, *Anwār al-tanzīl wa-asrār al-ta'wīl*, edited by 'Abd al-Qādir Ḥassūna (Beirut: Dār al-Fikr, 2011), IV, 259–260.

no reason to avoid the plain, literal sense. God, in His Wisdom, has freely chosen to manifest Himself in the form (*ṣūra*) of that particular fire, even though He is in Himself devoid of any sensible or limited form.[15] Bayḍāwī and other exoteric scholars would worry that such a position implies that God comes to dwell or inhere in (*ḥalla bi-*) the fire, but this is to confuse manifestation (*tajallī*) with inherence or indwelling (*ḥulūl*). To bring out this point, Kūrānī availed himself of an analogy much used by the monist tradition: Phenomenal appearances (*maẓāhir*) are like a manifold of mirrors reflecting one thing. These appearances delimit the reflection in accordance with their own limited natures, without this implying any delimitation or multiplicity or defect in the reflected object.

Kūrānī summed up his position as follows:

> The truth of the Prophet has been established by miracles, and in what he – peace and blessings upon him – has conveyed to us there are descriptions of the Truth that liken Him to creatures (*al-mutashābihāt*). The venerable earliest generations – the companions (*al-ṣaḥāba*), those who followed them (*al-tābiʿūn*), and those who in turn followed them (*atbāʿ al-tābiʿūn*) – by consensus granted their apparent sense while also affirming "There is nothing like Him" . . . The consensus of the first three generations which are the best generations as attested by the truthful one – peace and blessing be upon him – establishes that God manifests Himself in appearances (*al-maẓāhir*), while at the same time clearing (*tanzīh*) Him of likeness to His creatures. This necessitates the knowledge that there is in fact no rational objection that contradicts traditional reports of divine manifestation in appearances . . . This was shown by the Shaykh Muḥyī al-Dīn [Ibn ʿArabī] – may God make us benefit from him – when he explained that the Truth – may He be exalted – is absolute existence and is not delimited by other entities, and that He who is not delimited by others may manifest Himself in appearances without this precluding His freedom from likeness to creatures.[16]

Kūrānī ended his treatise with a lengthy quotation from the monumental commentary on Bukhārī's esteemed collection of hadith by Ibn Ḥajar al-ʿAsqalānī on the question of apparent anthropomorphic expressions in the Quran and hadith.[17] Ibn Ḥajar had gathered an impressive barrage of quotations from earlier sources in favor of the view that one should leave off reinterpreting such passages. Some of the authorities quoted by Ibn Ḥajar explicitly commended the position of *tafwīḍ*, that is, leaving the meaning of such passages to God. Other authorities quoted seem to have upheld the more radical position that the apparent sense should be

15 Kūrānī, *Tanbīh al-ʿuqūl*, 54–56.
16 Ibid., 44, 45–46.
17 Ibn Ḥajar al-ʿAsqalānī, *Fatḥ al-bārī bi-sharḥ Ṣaḥīḥ al-Bukhārī* (Cairo: Muṣṭafā al-Bābī al-Ḥalabī, 1959), XVII, 176–179.

affirmed. Kūrānī may at times have glossed over the distinction between these two approaches, for example when he – as quoted previously – told the North African Ashʿarī scholar ʿAyyāshī that the position of the Ḥanbalīs amounted to refraining from figurative interpretation of problematic passages and leaving their meaning (*tafwīḍ*) to God – a position that "is not condemned by any Ashʿarī." It is nevertheless important to note that the interpretive strategy Kūrānī defended in his *Tanbīh al-ʿuqūl* is more radical than the *tafwīḍ* option that mainstream contemporary Ashʿarism recognized as legitimate. This can be brought out by contrasting his position with that of the Ashʿarī theologian Sanūsī who was also suspicious of figurative reinterpretation. Sanūsī explicitly stated that the apparently anthropomorphic passages should *not* be taken in their apparent (*ẓāhir*) sense. Indeed, he was scathing in his condemnation of those heretics who accept the apparent sense, and are therefore led to crude anthropomorphic and corporealist notions of God. In his commentary on his own Short Creed (*al-Ṣughrā*), Sanūsī wrote that refusing to go beyond the apparent senses of the Quran and hadith in matters of creed (*al-tamassuku fī uṣūli l-ʿaqāʾidi bi-mujarradi ẓawāhiri l-kitābi wa l-sunna*) is one of the roots of unbelief (*kufr*).[18] In his major creed (*al-Kubrā*), he wrote: "As for that whose apparent sense is impossible such as "He sat Himself on the throne," we divert it from its apparent sense by common agreement" (*wa ammā mā istaḥāla ẓāhiruhu naḥwa "ʿalā l-ʿarshi istawā" fa-innā naṣrifuhu ʿan ẓāhirihi ittifāqan*). The only disagreement among Ashʿarīs, he added, was whether to put forward a specific figurative interpretation or, as the earliest generations preferred, to leave the meaning of such passages to God. Sanūsī preferred the latter option because there would normally be a number of possible figurative interpretations of an anthropomorphic passage, and he held it to be foolhardy and presumptuous to specify one of these as correct.[19] By contrast, Kūrānī described the correct position as "refraining from diverting apparent anthropomorphisms from their apparent sense" (*min ghayri ṣarfihā ʿan ẓawāhirihā*) but rather "granting their apparent sense (*ijrāʾihā ʿalā ẓāhirihā*) while simultaneously affirming: "There is nothing like Him" (*maʿa l-tanzīhi bi-laysa ka-mithlihi shayʾ*).[20] To that extent, Kūrānī was in agreement with Ibn Taymiyya, rather than with the Ashʿarī partisans of *tafwīḍ*.

[18] Sanūsī, *Sharḥ al-Ṣughrā*, 81–82 (1351 edition), 134–136 (Darwīsh edition).
[19] Sanūsī, *Sharḥ al-Kubrā*, 276–277.
[20] Kūrānī, *Tanbīh al-ʿuqūl*, 44 (l. 9), 45 (l. 2).

It should be pointed out, though, that Kūrānī did not present himself as abandoning Ashʿarism, but as returning to the original teachings of al-Ashʿarī expressed in the latter's *al-Ibāna*. Following Ibn Taymiyya, Kūrānī thought that this work was al-Ashʿarī's last and that it included his most considered and authoritative positions.[21] Not all modern historians agree with this dating of the work. Some see it instead as a relatively early overture to the Ḥanbalīs of Baghdad – an overture that was spurned, after which Ashʿarī wrote a number of other works in which he felt less inclined to attempt to phrase his positions in a manner that would be acceptable to the Ḥanbalīs.[22] Be that as it may, Kūrānī's view of *al-Ibāna* allowed him to present himself as an Ashʿarī, even though on a number of central issues he was clearly departing from mainstream Ashʿarism as it had developed in later centuries, in the direction of traditional Ḥanbalī positions.

Kūrānī's rejection of figurative reinterpretation was very much in line with that of the tradition of Ibn ʿArabī and his later commentators. Indeed, a large portion of his treatise consists of quotations from the works of Ibn ʿArabī (especially the *Futūḥāt*) and his students Ibn Sawdakīn al-Nūrī (d. 1248) and Ṣadr al-Dīn al-Qūnawī (d. 1274). What is less typical is Kūrānī's explicit attempt at aligning the Ḥanbalī and monistic Sufi attitudes. This concern is less prominent in the works of the earlier Persianate exponents of *waḥdat al-wujūd* and commentators on the *Fuṣūṣ* such as Farghānī, Jandī, Qāshānī, Qayṣarī, and Jāmī, perhaps because there was little or no Ḥanbalī presence in the Persianate world in later centuries. Kūrānī, by contrast, was active in the Arabic-speaking Near East, where Ḥanbalism was still alive. Because – as was seen in the previous chapter – seventeenth-century Ḥanbalīs were not in any way anti-Sufi, he would have had a good reason both to defend their position on apparent anthropomorphisms and to invoke their

21 See his commentary on Burhānpūrī's *al-Tuḥfa al-mursala*, ed. O. Fathurahman, *Itḥāf al-dhakī: Tafsīr Wahdatul Wujūd bagi Muslim Nusantra* (Jakarta: Penerbit Mizan, 2012), 220.

22 R. Frank, "Elements in the Development of the Teaching of al-Ashʿarī," *Le Museon* 104(1991): 141–190, at 170–172; R. Frank, "al-Ashʿarī's *al-Ḥathth ʿalā l-baḥth*," *MIDEO* 18(1988): 83–152, at 99–100. M. Allard differs from Frank, estimating that the work was written around 315/927–928, some eight or nine years before the death of al-Ashʿarī; see his *Le probleme des attributs divins dans la doctrine d'al-Ashʿarī et de ses premiers grands disciples* (Beirut: Imprimerie Catholique, 1965), 250–251. D. Gimaret is agnostic about dating the work but agrees that it was part of an unsuccessful attempt to conciliate the Ḥanbalīs of Baghdad rather than indicating a significant change of heart on any major issue; see D. Gimaret, *La doctrine d'al-Ashʿarī* (Paris: CERF, 1990), 10.

literature while defending his own very similar position. The result was at times a surprising and farfetched assimilation of Ibn Taymiyya's thought to that of Ibn ʿArabī. Kūrānī's most sustained defense of Ibn Taymiyya against the charge of corporealism and anthropomorphism occurs toward the end of his aforementioned treatise on God's Speech, completed in July 1661.[23] Kūrānī quoted extensively from some of the works of Ibn Taymiyya and his student Ibn Qayyim al-Jawziyya to show that they explicitly distanced themselves from corporealism and anthropomorphism. He then refuted one of the later critics of the two Ḥanbalī thinkers, the prominent sixteenth-century Shāfiʿī jurist Ibn Ḥajar al-Haytamī. Ibn Ḥajar al-Haytamī had quoted (from Ibn Qayyim al-Jawziyya) Ibn Taymiyya's view that the Prophet had let down the end of his turban (*ʿadhaba*) to mark the spot between his shoulder blades that God had touched with His own hand. He then angrily commented: "This is among their abhorrent and wayward views, since it is based on what they affirmed, tried at length to prove, and castigated Sunnis for rejecting, namely that God is a body and is in a certain direction, may He be exalted above what the unjust say!"[24]

Kūrānī countered Ibn Ḥajar's charge as follows:

> As for the charge that they claim that God is a body and is in a certain direction, this has already been seen for what it is. They have not affirmed that God is a body at all. Rather, they have explicitly rejected this in a number of passages in their works. They have also not affirmed that God is in a direction in a way that implies anything illegitimate. Rather, they have granted His statement "He seated Himself on the throne" in an apparent sense that is suitable for the majesty of God the Exalted, not in an apparent sense that is a characteristic of creatures.[25]

Kūrānī then moved seamlessly from a defense of Ibn Taymiyya's position regarding apparent anthropomorphisms in the Quran and hadith to an affirmation of Ibn ʿArabī's ontology:

> The words of Ibn Taymiyya – both the general thrust and more specific passages – show that the Truth – may He be Exalted – manifests Himself to whom He chooses and in whatever way He chooses while being clear of any likeness to creatures by virtue of "There is nothing like Him" even in the state of manifesting Himself in phenomenal appearances. This is indeed the ultimate in both religious belief and knowledge. The verification (*taḥqīq*) of this position ... is that the Truth – may

[23] Ibrāhīm Kūrānī, *Ifāḍat al-ʿallām fī taḥqīq masʾalat al-kalām* (MS: Süleymaniye Kütüphanesi, Istanbul: Halet Efendi 787), fols. 36b–67a.

[24] Ibn Ḥajar al-Haytamī, *Ashraf al-wasāʾil ilā fahm al-Shamāʾil*, edited by Aḥmad Farīd al-Mazyadī (Beirut: Dār al-Kutub al-ʿIlmiyya, 1998), 172–173.

[25] Kūrānī, *Ifāḍat al-ʿallām*, fol. 66b.

He be exalted – is pure existence (*al-wujūd al-maḥḍ*) which is compatible with any manifestation, for He is the general and all-encompassing (*al-wāsi ʿ al-muḥīṭ*) who is free of likeness to any of these [appearances] even in the state of manifesting Himself.[26]

It is astonishing that Ibn Taymiyya was invoked in this effortless way to buttress a worldview to which he was so hostile. Did Kūrānī not know that Ibn Taymiyya had condemned the view that God is identical to absolute existence as a pernicious heresy, if not outright unbelief, and had charged Ibn ʿArabī and his followers with believing in divine indwelling (*ḥulūl*) in created things?[27] Bio-bibliographical evidence suggests that the works of Ibn Taymiyya were not widely read outside Ḥanbalī circles in the sixteenth, seventeenth, and eighteenth centuries. Kūrānī seems to have made a special effort to find at least some of Ibn Taymiyya's works but may not have succeeded in seeing more than a handful, and it is possible that he never directly encountered his virulent condemnations of Ibn ʿArabī and his followers.[28] From the perspective of Kūrānī and other early modern defenders of ontological monism, the most prominent and formidable opponent of the view that God is identical to absolute existence was not Ibn Taymiyya but Taftāzānī – as will be seen in the following chapter.

It is of course also possible that Kūrānī was aware of Ibn Taymiyya's hostility to the ideas of Ibn ʿArabī but was simply not concerned. His aforementioned treatise on the question of God's Speech reveals that he was perfectly willing to criticize – sometimes in sharp tones – Ḥanbalī thinkers when they departed from what he considered the truth. Kūrānī advanced a position on God's Speech that was intermediate between mainstream Ashʿarism and traditionalist Ḥanbalism. Mainstream Ashʿarism held that God's eternal Speech is a "spiritual speech" (*kalām nafsī*) that does not consist of sounds and letters (*ṣawṭ wa ḥarf*) and that the Arabic Quran that is recited, written, and memorized is an expression of this eternal spiritual speech that in itself is not ordered

[26] Ibid., fol. 67a.

[27] See Knysh, *Ibn ʿArabī in the Later Islamic Tradition*, chapter 4.

[28] In his *Ifāḍat al-ʿallām*, Kūrānī did refer to Ibn Taymiyya's *al-Risāla al-Tadmuriyya* which in passing condemns those heretics who believe that the existence of God is identical to the existence of created things and that existence is in that sense one; see Ibn Taymiyya, *al-Risāla al-Tadmuriyya*, edited by Muḥammad Zuhrī al-Najjār (Cairo: Maṭbaʿat al-Imām, 1949), 129. Ibn Taymiyya's uncharitable phrasing of the doctrine may have suggested to Kūrānī that he was condemning crudely pantheist and antinomian Sufis rather than Ibn ʿArabī and his major followers.

spatially or aurally.[29] Opposed to this, Ḥanbalī thinkers insisted that God's eternal Speech is ordered precisely as in the Quran that is recited, written, and memorized – refusing to concede the argument that the eternal, uncreated Speech of God cannot possibly be spatially and temporally arranged into letters and sounds that precede or follow each other. Kūrānī's position – which was typical of the Ibn ʿArabī tradition – was that the ordered and revealed Quran must have some primordial arrangement into constituent parts insofar as this arrangement is the object of God's eternal foreknowledge. To that extent, he rejected the mainstream Ashʿarī position.[30] Nevertheless, against the Ḥanbalīs he argued that this primordial arrangement was of the spiritual speech (*al-kalām al-nafsī*) and not an arrangement of audible sounds and extended letters – the latter being a manifestation or "descent" (*tanazzul*) of the eternal Speech into the phenomenal world. A portion of Kūrānī's treatise is therefore devoted to arguing against the Ḥanbalīs that it does indeed make sense to speak of speech or discourse (*kalām*) that does not consist of audible sounds or spatially extended letters.[31] At one point, he quoted Ibn Qayyim al-Jawziyya as saying that his teacher Ibn Taymiyya had refuted the very idea of "spiritual speech" in nine ways. Kūrānī's response was sharp:

As for Ibn al-Qayyim saying that al-Shaykh Taqī al-Dīn [Ibn Taymiyya] refuted "the spiritual speech" in nine ways, I say [in reply]: Even if he claimed to have refuted it in nine hundred ways, or nine thousand ways, or as many ways as he likes, he would only thereby refute himself and bear witness to his misunderstanding of the Quran, the Sunna, and the arguments of those who affirm it [i.e., spiritual speech].[32]

It is clear that Kūrānī was willing to go along with Ḥanbalī traditionalists such as Ibn Taymiyya and Ibn Qayyim al-Jawziyya only to the extent that their ideas were in line with those of Ibn ʿArabī. This alignment, though of greater extent than most modern historians have suspected,

29 See Taftāzānī, *Sharḥ al-ʿAqāʾid al-Nasafiyya*, 52–54; Sanūsī, *Sharḥ al-Kubrā*, 139–146; Laqānī, *Hidāyat al-murīd*, I, 388–395. Māturīdī handbooks agree on this point; see Dāvūd Ḳārṣī, *Sharḥ al-Qaṣīda al-Nūniyya* (Istanbul: Meḥmed Ṭālib, 1318/1900–1901), 40–41; Beyāżīzāde, *Ishārāt al-marām*, 138–144. On this point, Ījī was at variance with the dominant position of the Ashʿarī school and advanced a position closer to that of the Ḥanbalīs; see Jurjānī, *Sharḥ al-Mawāqif*, 499.

30 Kūrānī, *Ifāḍat al-ʿallām*, fols. 45a ff. On fols. 47a–b, Kūrānī quoted Ījī's position with approval, and on fols. 48b–50a defended it against the criticisms of Dawānī.

31 Kūrānī, *Ifāḍat al-ʿallām*, fol. 55b ff.

32 Ibid., fol. 58b (ll. 23–24).

was certainly not perfect, and when the two traditions differed, Kūrānī's primary allegiance became clear.

Kūrānī and Nābulusī on the Value of Rational Theology (*Kalām*)

In the Islamic religious tradition, attitudes to the question of anthropomorphism and figurative reinterpretation have historically been strongly correlated to the question of the value of the discipline of rational theology. Those Islamic religious scholars who believed that apparent anthropomorphisms in the Quran and hadith should be left as they are without any figurative reinterpretation also tended to have a dim view of *kalām*. By contrast, scholars who extolled *kalām* overwhelmingly held that apparent anthropomorphisms in the Quran and hadith could easily lead believers to corporealist and anthropomorphic notions of God unless the proper and improper senses of such passages were made clear.

The former combination of attitudes – opposition to *kalām* as well as figurative reinterpretation – is often associated with Ḥanbalī traditionalism, but it was in fact also shared by Ibn ʿArabī and his later followers. In his voluminous *al-Futūḥāt al-makkiyya,* Ibn ʿArabī repeatedly denigrated both the science of *kalām* and the urge to engage in nonliteral interpretation (*taʾwīl*) of scripture, while at the same time defending the simple, unquestioning faith of the common people. The tone is set already in the introduction to the work, in which Ibn ʿArabī wrote:

> Let us now turn to the reasons for which we prohibit one who readies himself for the manifestations of God in his own heart from looking into the creed from the perspective of the science of *kalām*. One of these is that the creedal beliefs of the commoners are correct – there is no disagreement on this point among right-thinking religious scholars – and they are Muslims even though they have not perused anything of the science of *kalām* and are unaware of the positions of opponents. Rather, God has preserved in them the sound instinctual attitude (*siḥḥat al-fiṭra*), which is knowledge that God the Exalted exists, this having been imparted to them by a righteous parent or teacher. With respect to the knowledge of Truth the Exalted and of His being free of any likeness, they [i.e., the common people] . . . are – thanks to God – in the right as long as they do not begin to engage in figurative reinterpretation (*taʾwīl*). If one of them should engage in figurative reinterpretation then he ceases to be judged as a commoner and becomes one of the people of ratiocination (*ahl al-naẓar*).[33]

33 Ibn ʿArabī, *al-Futūḥāt al-makkiyya* (Beirut: Dār Ṣādir, 1968 [reprint of Būlāq edition of 1911]), I, 34 (l. 16ff).

As mentioned in Chapter 5, Ashʿarī theologians such as Sanūsī would worry that simple appeals to the Quran and hadith are insufficient to establish the creed beyond doubt. They held that there is a need for a foundational rational science that (1) distinguishes between cases in which the apparent sense of the creedal pronouncements of the Quran and hadith is binding and cases in which the apparent sense is misleading, and (2) can explain why appeal to the Islamic scriptural texts is legitimate while appeals to the scriptural texts of other religious traditions (e.g., the Torah or the Gospels) are not. Ibn ʿArabī clearly had no sympathy whatsoever with such claims. The truth of the Quran is, on his account, so obvious that there is no need to worry about constructing rational proofs in support of its contentions. He wrote:

> It has been established for us by means of numerous, independent lines of transmission that the glorious Quran was brought forth by a person claiming to be a prophet of God, and that this person brought what proves his veracity and this is the Quran itself and that no one else was able to bring forth anything like it. In this way, it becomes established for us that this person is indeed the prophet of God, and that he brought forth this Quran that we have with us today and told us that it is the word of God. All of this has been established through numerous, independent lines of transmission, and thus the knowledge is established that it is a true message and the decisive statement... One who readies himself [for witnessing divine manifestations] does not need rational proof alongside this, for the indisputable evidence upon which [the threat of] the sword is based is already there.[34]

Muslims, Ibn ʿArabī opined, have not been charged with arguing with doubters or opponents, nor with constructing elaborate rational proofs. Rather, the evidence is already there for all to see, and the way to deal with doubt and opposition is simply the sword:

> In the glorious Quran there is sufficiency to the rational person, a cure for the ill... and conviction for one who is determined to walk the path of salvation and ascend the spiritual ranks and abandon the sciences that deal with doubts and objections that lead to the wasting of time and fear of perdition. This is because one who takes that path is almost never free of disturbing thoughts and rarely preoccupies himself with exercising and taming the soul, being instead engaged in arguing against opponents who do not even exist and refuting objections that may or may not have occurred to anyone. If these objections do occur then the sword of the religious law can deal with this better and more decisively. "I was ordered to fight people until they say 'There is no god but Allah' and until they believe in me and the message I bring." These are his [the Prophet Muḥammad's] words,

[34] Ibid., I. 34 (l. 25ff).

may God bless him and grant him salvation. He has not urged us to dispute with them if they are present. Rather, if they are intransigent then there is nothing but religious war and the sword. This is all the more so in the case of an imagined opponent whom we waste our time refuting even though we have never seen him in reality . . .[35]

Indeed, Ibn ʿArabī's attitude to the science of *kalām* and to belief by imitation (*taqlīd*) is about as far removed from that of Sanūsī as one can imagine. As seen in Chapter 5, Sanūsī held that someone who affirms the Islamic creed out of unthinking conformism to elders and peers is either a sinner or not truly a believer at all, and that it is the individual duty of Muslims to acquaint themselves with the rational grounds for the articles of faith. By contrast, Ibn ʿArabī held the exact opposite thesis: The faith of the common "imitator" is superior to that of the rational theologian; the former is firm and unquestioning, whereas the latter is liable to be disturbed by counterarguments and refutations. Ibn ʿArabī wrote:

One whose faith is categorical and based on imitation is more secure and unflinching in his faith than one who takes faith from rational proof, since the latter, if he is intelligent and adept, is more prone to perplexity, to recognizing inadequacies (*dakhl*) in his proofs, and to objections or doubts (*shubah*). Hence, he will not remain steadfast and secure, and one fears for him.[36]

A detailed discussion of the question of "the faith of the imitator" is contained in Ibrāhīm Kūrānī's lengthiest theological work, his commentary on a creedal poem by his Sufi master al-Qushāshī. The section-heading containing the discussion reveals Kūrānī's position on the issue: "On showing the correctness of the faith of the imitator, that ratiocination (*naẓar*) is not incumbent on everyone, and that proper imitation leads to knowledge in a sense that will be explained in what follows."[37] Kūrānī began by quoting the sixteenth-century Shāfiʿī jurist Ibn Ḥajar al-Haytamī (the aforementioned critic of Ibn Taymiyya) as expressing the opinion that the faith of the imitator is valid as long as it is firm and unwavering.[38] It is not, on this view, a condition of faith that it be derived from ratiocination and rational proof. This is clear, added Ibn Ḥajar, from the fact that the companions of the Prophet conquered large swathes of land and accepted

35 Ibid., I, 35 (l. 27ff).
36 Ibid., II, 616 (l. 23ff).
37 Kūrānī, *Qaṣd al-sabīl ilā tawḥīd al-ʿaliyy al-wakīl* (MS: Princeton University Library: New Series, 1139), fol. 61bff.
38 Ibn Ḥajar al-Haytamī, *al-Fatḥ al-mubīn li-sharḥ al-Arbaʿīn* (Cairo: ʿĪsā al-Bābī al-Ḥalabī, 1352/1933), 74.

the conversion of unlearned Arabs and non-Arabs, many of whom had converted simply out of fear or in imitation of a tribal leader. They did not ask these converts to engage in ratiocination or supply rational proofs. Ibn Ḥajar went on to say that one might argue that an imitator is nevertheless a sinner (*āthim*) insofar as he can make an effort to acquire such rational proofs but refrains from doing so. This, he opined, is because the faith of the imitator is weak and liable to be shaken by even the simplest objections. At this point, Kūrānī demurred.[39] If providing rational proofs for religious belief is not an individual duty, then refraining from doing so cannot be a sin. Furthermore, the whole discussion is about the imitator whose faith is firm and unwavering – everyone agreed that someone who wavered or hesitated is not a believer at all. But if the imitator's faith is firm then it is implausible in the extreme to hold that he is nevertheless a sinner on the ground that his faith might be disturbed by some future objection. After all, the person whose faith is based on reasoning might similarly be disturbed by some future counterargument or refutation. Indeed, Kūrānī, like Ibn ʿArabī, held that someone whose religious faith is based on rational reflection is much more liable to be disturbed by objections than someone whose faith is not so based. He wrote:

> The room for doubt is in the rational proof, not imitation. If someone categorically affirms [the creed] on the basis of a rational argument, then he is susceptible to doubts in the form of an objection to one of the premises of his proof. As for the imitator, his categorical affirmation is not based on rational proof but on the unveiling (*kashf*) of the truth of the Prophet by a light that God casts into his breast... and hence there is no room for doubt as long as the light remains in the heart.[40]

Kūrānī was here alluding to the Quranic verse "One whom God desires to guide He will open up his breast to Islam" [6:125] and to an exegetical tradition according to which the Prophet was asked how God would open up the breast and replied: "It is a light that is cast into it and so it opens up and receives it."

Kūrānī went on to develop this point while refuting the position of the prominent fourteenth-century Ashʿarī theologian ʿAḍud al-Dīn al-Ījī (d. 1355). Ījī had argued that an "imitator" cannot be described as having knowledge of God because knowledge is either evident (*ḍarūrī*) or acquired through ratiocination (*naẓarī*), and the imitator has neither

[39] Kūrānī, *Qaṣd al-sabīl*, fol. 63a–63b.
[40] Ibid., fol. 63b.

kind of knowledge.[41] Kūrānī replied that Ījī had overlooked the fact that knowledge can be evident to someone even though it is not evident to others.[42] The category of evident knowledge was standardly thought to include things such as knowledge through perception, repeated experience, and introspection, and these are not necessarily shared. In other words, what is evident to one person may not be evident to another. This being so, Kūrānī went on to argue that the knowledge of the imitator is evident *to himself*. He wrote:

Correct imitation leads to knowledge in the sense that one who imitates correct authorities does not assent to creedal beliefs except after their truth has been unveiled to him without a proof [. . .]. We choose the position that the [imitator's] knowledge that the one who is reporting to him speaks truly is evident to him, in the sense that knowledge of this occurs to him without depending on ratiocination and rational proof, though it depends on something else . . . The way to this is clear from His statement – may He be Exalted – "One whom God desires to guide He will open up his breast to Islam."[43]

From this perspective, the imitator is clearly at a higher spiritual stage than the one who seeks to base religious belief on rational proof. The former already has, by the grace of God, the firm and certain belief that the latter seeks through reasoning. Kūrānī wrote:

Ratiocination is not incumbent on everyone. It is only incumbent on the person who cannot find a way to belief except this, so that if the message of Islam reaches him and firm belief does not come to him from the outset by imitation then he must reason so that the truth of Islam becomes clear . . . As for the imitator who believes firmly without any hesitation what the Prophet brought forth as soon as it reaches him . . . he does not sin by not reasoning, since the aim for which reasoning is sought has already been achieved without it and so there is no need for it.[44]

It may be instructive to compare Kūrānī's position with that of his Moroccan contemporary al-Ḥasan al-Yūsī (d. 1691). As seen in Chapter 6, Yūsī dissented from Sanūsī's radical view that an imitator is either a sinner or not strictly a believer at all. He argued that true and firm conviction is all that is incumbent on commoners, not constructing rational proofs for these convictions. Nevertheless, Yūsī held belief by imitation to be clearly

41 ʿAḍud al-Dīn al-Ījī, *Sharḥ Mukhtaṣar Ibn al-Ḥājib* (Cairo: al-Maṭbaʿa al-Azhariyya, 1973–1974), II, 305 (main text).
42 Kūrānī, *Qaṣd al-sabīl*, fol. 65a–66a.
43 Ibid., fol. 66a.
44 Ibid., fol. 62b.

inferior to the "verified" belief enjoyed by learned theologians. The latter could give an account of the rational justification for their beliefs, engage with and disarm heretical doubts and objections, and correct vulgar misconceptions, such as anthropomorphism, that are rife among the unlearned. In Kūrānī's discussion, faith based on imitation appears in a more positive light than belief based on reasoning. The imitator has, by means of a divine light cast into his breast, the true and unshakeable conviction that makes rational proof redundant. The person who bases his assent on rational proof is hazarding a notoriously dangerous road simply to reach a station that the imitator already enjoys.

A similar denigration of faith based on reasoning is characteristic of the other great exponent of the ideas of Ibn ʿArabī in the Arabic-speaking lands in the seventeenth century, the Damascene Naqshbandī Sufi ʿAbd al-Ghanī al-Nābulusī. Indeed, in Nābulusī's writings the fideist, antirationalist rhetoric is even more accentuated and equals or even exceeds anything that a Ḥanbalī traditionalist might have produced. In his commentary on Birgevī's *al-Ṭarīqa al-muḥammadiyya* Nābulusī dealt at some length with the question of the status of studying logic.[45] He too took his point of departure from a discussion of the issue by the prominent sixteenth-century Shāfiʿī jurist Ibn Ḥajar al-Haytamī. Ibn Ḥajar had opined that logic is a legitimate instrumental science that is particularly helpful in legal reasoning and in refuting heresies such as those of the Aristotelian philosophers. Earlier jurists who had condemned logic, Ibn Ḥajar added, were thinking of the logic of the early philosophers, not the kind of logic that was studied in Muslim colleges and had been defended by venerable scholars such as Ghazālī and Taqī al-Dīn al-Subkī.[46] Nābulusī vehemently rejected this position. There are not, he insisted, two kinds of logic; the logic studied in colleges *is* the logic of the philosophers. Even apart from this point, logic is not a helpful science at all. The earliest generations of Islam were innocent of it and yet were able to engage in legal reasoning. Anyone who dares to suggest that the venerable Companions knew and taught logic should be charged, Nābulusī wrote, with unbelief (*kufr*) for denigrating the Companions and their knowledge.[47] Nābulusī was also scathing about the idea that logic can help refute the heresies of the

45 ʿAbd al-Ghanī al-Nābulusī, *al-Ḥadīqa al-nadiyya sharḥ al-Ṭarīqa al-muḥammadiyya* (Lalpur: al-Maktaba al-Riḍwiyya al-Nūriyya [reprint of Cairo edition of 1276/1860]), I, 335–340.

46 Ibn Ḥajar al-Haytamī, *al-Fatāwā al-kubrā al-fiqhiyya* (Beirut: Dār Ṣādir [reprint of Cairo edition of 1308/1891), I, 49–51.

47 Nābulusī, *al-Ḥadīqa al-nadiyya*, I, 337–338.

philosophers. Logic is the gateway to infidel philosophy, and the believer has no need to know the foundations of unbelief. Rather, ignorance of such foundations is praiseworthy in the believer. To think otherwise is due to nothing but a vainglorious ambition to take pride in a science of the infidel Greeks and look down upon the upholders of traditional Islamic learning. Nābulusī wrote:

Logic is pure harm for Muslims. There is no other reason for those who study it to do so except the desire to distinguish themselves by a science of which Muslims are ignorant, and in this way achieve prominence over contemporaries. That is the only reason that someone [Ibn Ḥajar al-Haytamī] should write, as was quoted above, that it is sufficient [for it to be deemed a praiseworthy science] that the person who is ignorant of it cannot discuss with a philosopher or anyone else who knows it. He thus made this science, the studying of which leads to the complete uprooting of Islamic principles, a perfection . . . even though it is rather a perfection for a believer to be ignorant of the foundations of infidelity and waywardness.[48]

Furthermore, Nābulusī wrote, the root of the heresies of the philosophers is the reliance on unaided reason, and it is absurd to imagine that one might rely on reason to refute them. On the contrary, to use logic is to engage with philosophers on a level at which they are bound to win, for reason is on their side. Nābulusī wrote:

It is evident that one who attempts to refute the doctrines of the philosophers, and other ideas that are based on the principles of logic, by making use of these same logical principles, is not refuting them by means of that upon which the Muḥammadan religion is based, but by means of that upon which these false doctrines are based, namely reason. It is not possible to do this, and if one tries to do so then they will reply to him, and reason is on their side for their religion is based on it (*wa l-ʿaqlu maʿahum liʾanna mabnā dīnihim ʿalayhi*), and the principles of logic will assist them, and they will reply to each refutation . . . False doctrines are not refuted except by true religion and Muḥammadan, Islamic principles, and these are not reason, rather reason does not have anything to do with them at all. One should instead receive these [principles] from the Book and the Tradition without using its [i.e. reason's] principles but instead have faith, submit and acquiesce. This is why the Damascene mystic master al-Shaykh Arslān said: "People are led away from the truth by reason."[49]

[48] Ibid., I, 339 (l. 13ff.).

[49] Nābulusī, *al-Ḥadīqa al-nadiyya*, I, 339 (l. 19ff.). Arslān al-Jaʿbarī was a Damascene mystic. Estimates of his date of death vary wildly but the earlier sources place it in the middle of the twelfth century; see ʿAbd al-Raʾūf al-Munāwī, *al-Kawākib al-durriyya*, II, 414 (editor's footnote).

Nābulusī wrote that even if there were no harm in logic other than that it strengthens the faculty of reason in a person this would suffice for condemning it:

It is not incumbent on the legally responsible person to strengthen his rational side, for strengthening that side will harm his religion. For the Muḥammadan religion cannot be known through reason . . . and this part of logic, even if we say that it is free of philosophy, will strengthen reason at the expense of faith and submission to religious law. Thus, due to the strengthening of the rational side, the side of submissive faith will weaken or be entirely destroyed or transformed into reason. This can be seen in the case of many people. You see them resisting a religious decree when it is not rational or reason has no role in ascertaining it. Therefore, the people inclined toward figurative reinterpretation have discoursed about the apparent anthropomorphisms [in the Quran and hadith], have indulged in finding rationally acceptable meanings, and are unable to believe in them as they stand.[50]

The discipline of *kalām*, which Sanūsī and Yūsī considered the most important of the religious sciences, fared no better in Nābulusī's estimation. His condemnation of the discipline is as vehement as anything penned by Ḥanbalī traditionalists such as Ibn Taymiyya. The following poem by him is a case in point. It is a scathing attack on the rationalism of philosophical theologians such as Fakhr al-Dīn al-Rāzī (d. 1210) and Sa'd al-Dīn al-Taftāzānī, which is contrasted with a salutary reliance on revelation and mystic unveiling:[51]

Where would Sa'd al-Dīn or Rāzī obtain what we know from [mystic] unveiling and what we attempt to express?
They speak on the basis of their reason regarding God, trying to measure monuments by the span of their arms (*hindāz*) . . .
They fancy that what they indulge in is pure righteousness and that anything else is taunts and gibes.
But their knowledge is but a drop of ours, and they have adulterated it with the statements of those who transgress and make sport of religion,
From the opinions of an idiotic and deceitful philosophy that has been rendered wobbly by the sword of Islam.
The science of *kalām*, with which they have bought and sold words like a peddler,
The earliest generations [*al-salaf*] have prohibited it, but they have not desisted, having escaped the notice of religious warriors.
Had it not been for the part [of *kalām*] dealing with traditional reports, the entirety of its discourse would be mockery.

50 Nābulusī, *al-Ḥadīqa al-nadiyya*, I, 338 (l. 26)–339 (l. 4).
51 'Abd al-Ghanī al-Nābulusī, *al-Wujūd al-ḥaqq wa-l-khiṭāb al-ṣidq*, edited by Bakrī 'Alā' al-Dīn (Damascus: Institute Francais de Damas, 1995), 147–148.

They even called it "the principles of religion" (*uṣūl al-dīn*) since they briefly touch on issues dealt with in traditional reports.
Rather, the principles of religion are nothing but the Book and what is contained in the sunna of the Prophet of promises of things to come!
So take from God what is in the Book regarding creedal matters, and with it a lofty religious belief,
And what has been related in the noble sunna as it is intended – with the certainty of the blessed,
And you will obtain all the principles of religion and be rid of *kalām* in which there is nothing but babble.

In another poem, Nābulusī struck a similar note:[52]

Repent to God from the sciences of *kalām*, and purify yourself and enter into Islam!
Submit your religion to the speech (*kalām*) that God has revealed, for that is the best of speech.
It is a most luminous Quran, so believe in what it contains with full submission!
And ask understanding of it from your God, for it is for Him to make it clear to human understanding.
And know the sunna that has come down from the chief of prophets and the best of mankind.
Contemplate what your Lord has revealed therein, and you will find the truth and full-fledged verity.
If you do not understand, then believe nonetheless and do not be in doubt nor enamored of your reason (*ʿaql*) . . .
Beware of the opinions of the people of reason who, in what they say, have followed the blind!
The science of *kalām* is nothing but speech concerning accidents and bodies.
It is an affront to religion (*jarḥun li-l-dīn*) and there is nothing in it apart from mere names.
The view of reason (*naẓaru l-ʿaql*) has above it the view of religious law; and in the latter there is an overturning of the former order.
How far is the light of religious faith (*īmān*) from the "light" of a reason that investigates judgments with mere imaginings?
The people of faith are bathed in the light of the transcendent, and the people of reason (*dhawū l-ʿuqūl*) are all of them in darkness . . .
Imitate God, o son of my people, and imitate the prophets, the most veracious of peoples!
If you are a believer in God, then submit to the sciences of the Omniscient Master!
Do not think that rational proof (*al-dalīl*) will lead to Him, or will arouse the sleepers or enable them to see! . . .

52 ʿAbd al-Ghanī al-Nābulusī, *Dīwān al-ḥaqāʾiq wa majmūʿ al-raqāʾiq* (Būlāq: Dār al-Ṭibāʿa al-Bāhira, 1270/1854), II, 104–106.

In Chapter 1, it was noted that even though the anti-Sufi Ḳāḍīzādelī movement is often assumed by modern historians to have been opposed to the rational sciences, there is remarkably little evidence for this. In fact, Birgevī – by all accounts one of the major intellectual inspirations of the movement – held that logic and rational theology are commendable sciences. He believed, as did later Turkish Ḥanafī-Māturīdī critics of Sufism such as Ḥasan Kāfī, Aḥmed Rūmī Āḳḥiṣārī, and Dāvūd Ḳārṣī, that it is incumbent on Muslims to strengthen their faith by ascertaining the rational-theological grounds for the creed, and that it is a sin not to do so and to remain content with "imitation."[53] It is rather among the seventeenth-century followers of Ibn ʿArabī that one encounters fierce opposition to logic and rational theology, and a valorization of religious belief that is not grounded in rational proof at all.

Kūrānī and Nābulusī on Occasionalism and Human Acts

One of the central features of Ashʿarī and Māturīdī theology, which claimed the allegiance of most Sunni scholars in the early modern period, is its commitment to what is now often referred to as "occasionalism," that is, the belief that only God has causal powers. When we touch fire and experience a burning sensation we are inclined to believe that the fire caused the burning sensation. Ashʿarī and Māturīdī theologians would insist that, strictly speaking, fire has no causal powers, but that God brings about the effect (the burning sensation) in conjunction with the contact with fire. They accepted that God is in the habit of creating burning sensations in us when we touch fire, and that for all practical purposes we can be confident that this will happen the next time this occurs. They nevertheless insisted that, strictly speaking, there is no natural necessity and no contradiction in supposing that we might touch fire without having the usual burning sensation. Ashʿarīs and Māturīdīs claimed support for their position in the Quran, in which the power to bring things into existence is often claimed to be God's alone. They also typically relied on a range of rational arguments, for example, anticipating Hume in arguing

[53] For the opinion of Birgevī, see Chapter 1. For the opinions of Ḥasan Kāfī and Aḥmed Rūmī, see Chapter 5. For the opinion of Dāvūd Ḳārṣī (fl. 1739–1755) on the sin of being content with imitation in matters of creed and not acquainting oneself with the rational proofs of kalām, see his *Sharḥ al-Nūniyya*, 121–122. For Ḳārṣī's overall outlook, see his condemnation of the "unbelieving heretics" (*al-malāḥida al-kafara*) who claim that God is identical to absolute existence (*al-wujūd al-maḥḍ*) on p. 17 of the same work, and his praise of Birgevī on p. 131.

that sense perception only reveals constant conjunction between events, not any necessary connection between them.[54] One worry that animated at least some theologians in this tradition was that acknowledging causes other than God would rule out miracles and also undercut the carefully constructed theological arguments for the existence of a single, omniscient, and omnipotent creator. Admitting that causes could be mindless and limited would make it more difficult to infer from our changing world an omniscient and omnipotent Cause; and admitting that there might be a plurality of independent causes in the world made it more difficult to rule out by pure reason the possibility that there might be a multiplicity of gods.[55]

One widely acknowledged problem for occasionalism was voluntary human actions. Ashʿarī and Māturīdī theologians had to accommodate a distinction between voluntary actions (such as praying) and involuntary bodily changes and movements (such as graying), as Islamic law holds humans responsible only for the former. It is not immediately clear, though, how to reconcile this distinction with an occasionalist worldview. For example, one might be tempted to say that voluntary actions are "up to us," or that "we bring them about," or that "we are capable of doing or refraining from doing them." But how can one make sense of such locutions if one is also committed to the principle that God is the direct cause of all things, including human acts? The standard theological response, presented in widely studied theological handbooks from the fourteenth, fifteenth, and sixteenth centuries such as Taftāzānī's *Sharḥ al-ʿAqāʾid al-Nasafiyya,* Jurjānī's *Sharḥ al-Mawāqif*, Sanūsī's creedal works, and Laqānī's *Jawharat al-tawḥīd*, was in outline as follows:[56] In the case of involuntary bodily movements or changes, God simply creates them. In the case of voluntary actions, God likewise creates them but in

54 See Ghazālī, *Tahāfut al-falāsifa*, ed. and trans. M. Marmura (Provo, UT: Brigham Young Press, 1997), 167.

55 For example, Sanūsī explicitly applies the argument against the existence of more than one God to also rule out the idea that anything other than God can bring something into existence; see Sanūsī, *Sharḥ al-kubrā*, 180ff. Another standard argument was that if humans brought about their own acts then they would know all there is to know about these acts, and that to reject this conditional would be to reject standard proofs for the creator of the world being omniscient.

56 Taftāzānī, *Sharḥ al-ʿAqāʾid al-Nasafiyya,* 85–89; Taftāzānī, *Sharḥ al-Maqāṣid* (Istanbul: Hāc Muḥarrem Būsnavī Maṭbaʿasī, 1305/1888), II, 125ff; Jurjānī, *Sharḥ al-Mawāqif*, 515ff.; Sanūsī, *Sharḥ al-kubrā*, 180–203; Laqānī, *Hidāyat al-murīd*, I, 538–544, 562–590. For an excellent survey of Ashʿarī views on voluntary action until the fifteenth century, see D. Gimaret, *Théories de l'acte humain en théologie musulmane* (Paris: J. Vrin, 1980), 79–170.

conjunction with the agent's intention (*irāda*) and capacity (*istiṭā'a*). To that extent, one might acknowledge a difference between voluntary and involuntary behavior – the former occurs in conjunction with the agent's intention and capacity, whereas the latter does not. The agent's intention and capacity are thus analogous to other ordinary "causes" such as fire – there is a regular and for all practical purposes predictable conjunction between the so-called "cause" (intention and capacity) and the so-called "effect" (voluntary action). Nevertheless, intentions and capacities are, like anything else besides God, causally inefficacious. They have no effect (*ta'thīr*) on the existence of the action, but are simply occasions for God's direct creation of the action.

The response was arguably ingenious but nevertheless left a number of critics unimpressed. Two recurrent criticisms were (1) that it is incoherent to speak of a "capacity" or "power" (*qudra* or *istiṭā'a*) that has no effect on the action, and (2) that regarding God as the direct cause of human actions would make divine command and prohibition – the very basis of Islamic law – senseless, amounting to God commanding and prohibiting humans who cannot bring about actions.[57] Such lingering dissatisfaction with the mainstream Ash'arī position fueled the attempt to find alternative positions on the question of "the creation of human acts" (*khalq al-af'āl*). One suggestion had already been made by Ghazālī's teacher, the prominent Ash'arī theologian Imām al-Ḥaramayn al-Juwaynī (d. 1085).[58] In his major work *al-Irshād*, Juwaynī had defended at some length the standard Ash'arī position on this issue, but in the later *al-'Aqīda al-Niẓāmiyya* he had advanced an alternative suggestion: Human ability does have an effect on the action "by God's permission" (*bi-idhni Allah*). This does not, Juwaynī stressed, amount to the unacceptable position of the early Mu'tazilī theologians that humans bring about their own

[57] Many modern observers seem to think that the main problem with the Ash'arī view of human action is that it would be "unfair" for God to create actions and then reward and punish humans for these actions. This was not a problem for Ash'arīs because they explicitly rejected the idea that there are objective standards of goodness or fairness that God must respect, insisting instead that the good and the fair are simply what God does. The problem as seen by premodern Sunni scholars was rather that God's creation of actions seems to contravene the Quranic principle that God imposes only obligations that humans are able to fulfill. One may note that the alternatives to the mainstream Ash'arī view proposed by Juwaynī, Rāzī, and Ibn Taymiyya agree that God has predetermined the beliefs and acts of humans and yet punishes them and rewards them. They merely sought to make space for a genuine human capacity to act, even while conceding that humans cannot act contrary to God's Will and Decree.

[58] Gimaret, *Theories de l'acte humain*, 120–128.

acts with complete independence of God and indeed often act contrary to God's Will. By the same token, it is not clear that Juwaynī's later position amounted to what we might today call "free will" – a term that is foreign to the *kalām* tradition – for Juwaynī seems to have maintained that God preordains everything that happens and that He creates all the incentives and inclinations in us that lead to the action.[59] Nevertheless, he believed that by making space for humans to have an effect on their actions, he had (1) avoided appealing to a mysterious "capacity" that has no effect whatsoever, and (2) safeguarded the basic principle of human legal responsibility (*taklīf*). Juwaynī's *al-ʿAqīda al-Niẓāmiyya* was not widely copied and studied in later centuries, but reports of his alternative position survived in the works of the later Ashʿarī theologian Shahrastānī (d. 1153) and, as will be seen later, Ibn Taymiyya's student Ibn Qayyim al-Jawziyya.

A closely related view – often conflated by premodern observers with Juwaynī's later position – was that of the Islamic Aristotelian–Neo-Platonic philosophers who upheld a deterministic system in which God is the first or ultimate cause but not the direct cause of every effect. On their account, at least according to standard interpretations, human voluntary actions are caused by humans agents themselves, but human agents are only intermediate or "secondary" causes that are themselves determined by preceding causes ultimately deriving from God. This kind of determinist but non-occasionalist view remained an alternative – albeit minority – opinion in later centuries. It was defended by, for example, the philosophically inclined theologian Fakhr al-Dīn al-Rāzī and by Ḥanbalī thinkers such as Ibn Taymiyya and Ibn Qayyim al-Jawziyya.[60]

Ibn ʿArabī's position on this and a number of other theological controversies is often difficult to pin down, but was arguably close to that of the philosophers and later traditionalist Ḥanbalīs. In a number of passages, he apparently advocated the view that there are secondary causes; that they have causal efficacy (*taʾthīr*); that they reflect God's Wisdom (*ḥikma*) in creation; and that to deny secondary causality is to detract

[59] Gimaret notes that Juwaynī's later view was understood by later theologians to be non-occasionalist but determinist, but that there is some ambiguity in Juwaynī's account concerning whether the given inclinations and motives fully determine the resultant action; see *Theories de l'acte humain*, 124–126.

[60] For Rāzī's view, see Gimaret, *Theories de l'acte humain*, 134–153. For Ibn Taymiyya's very similar view, see J. Hoover, *Ibn Taymiyya's Theology of Perpetual Optimism* (Leiden, the Netherlands: Brill, 2007), 136–176.

from this divine Wisdom.[61] Some of the more systematic and philosophically inclined followers of Ibn ʿArabī, such as the *Fuṣūṣ* commentator ʿAbd al-Razzāq al-Qāshānī, unambiguously rejected occasionalism in favor of a deterministic system of secondary causes similar to that of the Aristotelian–Neo-Platonic philosophers.[62]

Ibrāhīm Kūrānī wrote a number of works on the issue of "the creation of human acts" in which he expounded a position that was inspired by both the tradition of Ibn ʿArabī and the works of the Ḥanbalī traditionalists. His most extensive discussion is contained in his *Maslak al-sadād fī masʾalat khalq afʿāl al-ʿibād* (The correct path concerning the issue of the creation of the acts of servants of God), completed in September 1674.[63] Kūrānī's position involved rejecting two common views: (1) the view attributed to the early Muʿtazilīs according to which humans create their acts independently of God (*bi-l-istiqlāl*) and sometimes even act against God's Will and Decree, and (2) the view of most later Ashʿarīs that human acts are direct creations of God and that human intentions and abilities have no effect (*taʾthīr*) on the created act. Kūrānī was careful to use the locution "the common opinion of the later Ashʿarīs" (*al-mashhūr ʿan mutaʾakhkhirī l-Ashāʿira*)[64] because he believed that this was not the position of al-Ashʿarī himself. Again, he relied on al-Ashʿarī's *al-Ibāna*, which he considered his last and most authoritative work, to show that al-Ashʿarī had only denied the Muʿtazilī position, not endorsed the position that human power has no effect whatsoever on the action.[65] On the contrary, al-Ashʿarī had in that work expressed his commitment to deriving the creed from the Quran and hadith, and both of these sources are replete with passages that suggest that God often acts in the world through secondary causes, and that humans may be considered the secondary causes of their own actions. To support his point, Kūrānī repeatedly quoted from a work by Ibn Qayyim al-Jawziyya that argues at length that the plain sense of the Quran and hadith supports the belief in

61 Chittick, *Sufi Path of Knowledge*, 44–46, 174–179.

62 ʿAbd al-Razzāq al-Qāshānī, *Risāla fī l-qaḍāʾ wa l-qadar*, in *Majmūʿah-i rasāʾil va muṣannafāt*, edited by Majīd Hādīzāde (Tehran: Mirās-i maktūb, 2000), 565–593, esp. 577–582.

63 Ibrāhīm Kūrānī, *Maslak al-sadād fī masʾalat khalq afʿāl al-ʿibād* (MS: Princeton University Library: Yahuda 3867). Kūrānī also wrote a lengthy postscript to the work, completed three years later, in which he clarified a number of points at the request of some of his contemporaries. The postscript is often bound with *Maslak al-sadād* in extant manuscripts.

64 Kūrānī, *Maslak al-sadād*, fol. 4a (ll. 15–16).

65 Ibid., fol. 15b.

secondary causality – including the belief that humans have been granted the power to bring about their own acts as long as this is in accord with God's Decree and Will.[66] A radical Ashʿarī such as Sanūsī considered the view that God has instilled causal "powers" (*qiwā*) into created entities a dangerous heresy that verged on outright unbelief (*kufr*).[67] An influential Ashʿarī creedal work written by Kūrānī's Tunisian contemporary ʿAlī al-Nūrī al-Safāqisī (d. 1706) reiterated the point in equally uncompromising terms:

> The one who believes that any of the customary "causes" (*al-asbāb al-ʿādiyya*) has an effect by its very nature (*bi-ṭabʿihi*) is an infidel without any disagreement. The one who believes that it has an effect by a power (*quwwa*) instilled in it by God – such that were God to remove this power it would not have an effect – is [at least] a wayward innovator (*fāsiq bidʿī*) without any disagreement, and opinions are divided concerning whether he is an infidel. As for the one who believes that these "causes" (*asbāb*) have no effect whatsoever, but that God creates what He wants concurrently with them and not by means of them (*ʿindahā lā bihā*)... he is a monotheist believer.[68]

For Kūrānī, the uncompromising occasionalism of Sanūsī and his followers was baseless and amounted to denying God's Wisdom in governing creation.[69] God could, he argued, bring about effects without a secondary cause, but He has freely and in His Wisdom chosen not to do so and instead to produce effects through the intermediacy of secondary causes. Kūrānī quoted the following from Ibn al-Qayyim's aforementioned work:

> The truth, compared to which no other suggestion is acceptable, is that He – may He be exalted – acts by His Will, Power and Wish and that He does what He does by means of secondary causes and in view of wise and beneficial aims. He has instilled in the world powers and instincts upon which the creation and the [divine] command are grounded.[70]

66 Kūrānī, *Maslak al-sadād*, fols. 9b–12a. On this work, entitled *Shifāʾ al-ʿalīl fī masāʾil al-qaḍāʾ wa l-qadar wa al-ḥikma wa-l-taʿlīl*, see I. Perho, "Man chooses his destiny: Ibn Qayyim al-Jawziyya's Views on Predestination," *Islam and Christian-Muslim Relations* 12(2001): 61–70.

67 Sanūsī, *Sharḥ al-ṣughrā*, 81 (1351 edition), 133 (Darwīsh edition).

68 ʿAlī al-Nūrī al-Safāqisī, *al-ʿAqīda al-Nūriyya fī iʿtiqād al-aʾimma al-Ashʿariyya*, edited by al-Ḥabīb Ben Ṭāhir (Beirut and Damascus: al-Yamāma, 2008), 156–157. The cited words are by Nūrī's student ʿAlī al-Tamīmī al-Safāqisī (fl. 1706).

69 Kūrānī, *Maslak al-sadād*, fol. 21a.

70 Ibn Qayyim al-Jawziyya, *Shifāʾ al-ʿalīl fī masāʾil al-qaḍāʾ wa l-qadar wa l-ḥikma wa l-taʿlīl*, edited by al-Ḥassānī Ḥasan ʿAbdullāh (Cairo: Dār al-Turāth, 1975), 434–435.

Kūrānī then added:

> It is well known that Wisdom does not decree that someone is commanded who has no ability to obey, or that someone is prohibited who has no ability to desist. Wisdom, which God the Exalted has freely and mercifully respected in His Creation and Command, therefore dictates that legal responsibility (*taklīf*) be in accordance with capacity.[71]

Radical occasionalism, Kūrānī added, also involves denying the plain sense of a host of passages in the Quran and hadith, and – as was seen in the previous sections – respecting the plain or apparent (*ẓāhir*) sense of the Quran and hadith was a fundamental principle for Ibn ʿArabī and his followers, just as it was for Ḥanbalī traditionalists. Accordingly, Kūrānī angrily rejected the suggestion of the fourteenth-century Ashʿarī theologian ʿAḍud al-Dīn al-Ījī – author of the widely studied handbook *al-Mawāqif* – that the question of the creation of human acts should be resolved on the basis of rational argumentation rather than by appeal to the Quran and hadith. Ījī had advanced this suggestion because he believed that the scriptural passages that support the view that humans have choice and the ability to bring about their own actions can be answered by other scriptural passages that support the view that God is the sole creator and that God has predetermined everything.[72] How, responded Kūrānī, could a pious person suggest that there is a less than perfect consistency in the Quran and on that basis recommend that the Book of God – which has been sent down to guide mankind – simply be set aside in favor of rational argumentation?[73] There is, he insisted, not even an apparent contradiction in the Quran. All passages support the correct view, which is that humans bring about their own actions but that they do so "with God's permission," not independently (*bi-l-istiqlāl*) or contrary to God's Will and Decree. This, as mentioned previously, was the view of the later Juwaynī in his *Niẓāmiyya*. Kūrānī did not have direct access to this work, but he found a lengthy quotation from it in Ibn Qayyim al-Jawziyya's aforementioned work on secondary causality and reproduced it in his treatise.[74]

Even though Kūrānī endorsed the view of the later Juwaynī and of Ibn Qayyim al-Jawziyya, his basic point of departure was that of the

[71] Kūrānī, *Maslak al-sadād*, fol. 14a.
[72] Jurjānī, *Sharḥ al-Mawāqif*, 520 (ll. 10–12).
[73] Kūrānī, *Maslak al-sadād*, fols. 8a–8b.
[74] Ibid., fols. 23b–25b.

monist-mystical tradition of Ibn ʿArabī and his disciples and commentators. Kūrānī began his treatise by emphasizing what he called "the unity of attributes" (*tawḥīd al-ṣifāt*).[75] According to this doctrine, there is but a single unqualified power in existence, and that is God's Power. Instances of power in our lower world are appearances (*maẓāhir*), specifications (*taʿayyunāt*), or descents (*tanazzulāt*) of this divine Power. The human power that causes an action is on this account not independent of God's Power, as the early Muʿtazilīs wrongly supposed, but rather a manifestation of God's absolute Power. The human act results from a certain manifestation or instance of Power and can to that extent be seen as the act of a particular created agent, and yet human power is not independent of God's Power but rather the medium or vehicle for its working. Kūrānī wrote:

> Among the perfections are power (*qudra*) and this belongs to God essentially (*bi-l-dhāt*), and if some of it accrues to a servant (*ḥaṣala li-ʿabdin*) then this is by God (*bi-llāh*).... It is as the Exalted has said "Power is God's in its entirety" [Quran 2:165], i.e., power that is apparent in the forms of powerful servants – and that is as manifold as they are – "is God's in its entirety" not theirs.... So it is clear that power is one in essence but manifold in its specifications. Whenever that is the case, then it is correct to say that actions are one while also affirming acquisition (*kasb*) to the servant by means of the effect of his power by God's permission and not independently.... Thus is repudiated the assumption that there is a conflict between saying that the power of the servant has an effect by God's permission and saying that there is no creator other than God.[76]

Kūrānī also invoked Ibn ʿArabī's cosmology to address the issue of how God can condemn and reward humans even though He has from eternity predetermined everything, including who is a believer and who is not. The quiddities, Kūrānī reiterated, are not "made" (*majʿūla*) – there is no cause for an entity being the kind of entity it is, though there is a cause for a contingent entity coming to exist as more than a mere possibility. Quiddities are on this account fixed and unchanging objects of God's foreknowledge. God's Will follows God's Knowledge, and in turn God's Knowledge follows the fixed and "unmade" objects of knowledge. For Kūrānī, this means that God's eternal foreknowledge simply follows or tracks the independent and primordial fact that, for example, Abū Jahl – the Prophet Muḥammad's archenemy – is an unbeliever. In turn, God's Will follows this foreknowledge in the sense that God Wills and Decrees

[75] Ibid., fols. 3a–3b.
[76] Ibid., fol. 3b.

that what He knows from all eternity will come to pass. But Abū Jahl is in no position to object to God's Willing and Decreeing that he be a damned unbeliever, for God Wills this on the basis of His eternal Knowledge that Abū Jahl is primordially an unbeliever, and that fact is not "made" but simply registered by God's eternal Knowledge.[77]

To say that Kūrānī was inspired by Ibn ʿArabī to develop his position on the creation of human acts is of course not to say that such a position was straightforwardly read off Ibn ʿArabī's works. As mentioned previously, the task of extracting from Ibn ʿArabī's writings a clear and unambiguous position on established theological controversies can be difficult. Kūrānī's particular thesis could be and was challenged by other followers of Ibn ʿArabī, such as his younger Damascene contemporary ʿAbd al-Ghanī al-Nābulusī. Nābulusī sent a letter to Kūrānī, dated October 4, 1678, in which he respectfully but incisively raised some problems for the position defended in *Maslak al-sadād*.[78] Nābulusī questioned what exactly Kūrānī meant by saying that human power has an effect "by permission of God, not independently." Surely, he could not have meant that, with God's permission, human power exerts an effect on its own, as that is precisely the Muʿtazilī position that Kūrānī explicitly ruled out by adding the qualification "not independently."[79] Nor could he have meant that human power has an effect in partnership with God, as no one would claim that God's Power is not by itself sufficient. But if human power does not bring about an effect on its own or in partnership with God, then the only remaining option is that God's Power brings about the action. If it is supposed that God's Power is entirely distinct from human power then it follows that the latter has no effect on the action, which is precisely the mainstream Ashʿarī position. If, on the other hand, God's power and human power are not distinct, but the latter is a "specification" or "descent" of the former, then there is no need for the qualification "not independently" because God's Power most certainly does act "independently."[80] Nābulusī shared Kūrānī's allegiance to Ibn ʿArabī's mystical monism, and had no objection to speaking of God's Power manifesting itself in the phenomenal world. But he insisted that God's manifest or "descended" Power strictly speaking remains God's Power and not the power of a human creature. To

[77] Ibid., fol. 12a.

[78] ʿAbd al-Ghanī al-Nābulusī, *Wasāʾil al-taḥqīq wa rasāʾil al-tawfīq*, edited by Bakrī ʿAlāʾ al-Dīn (Damascus: Dār Nīnawī, 2010), 49–75; edited by Samer Akkach (Leiden, the Netherlands: Brill, 2010), 61–108.

[79] Nābulusī, *Wasāʾil al-taḥqīq*, 50 (ʿAlāʾ al-Dīn edition), 63 (Akkach edition).

[80] Ibid., 51 (ʿAlāʾ al-Dīn edition), 64 (Akkach edition).

suppose otherwise is precisely the mistake of confusing manifestation (*tajallī*) with "indwelling" (*ḥulūl*), that is, assuming that God's absolute Power "descends" to a human creature who then possesses God's Power but remains distinct in all other respects from God. One can only speak of "descent" in the sense that all human attributes are collectively manifestations or "descents" of God and His attributes.[81] Nābulusī's main objection may thus be summarized as follows: Insofar as human power is different from God's Power it is inefficacious, just as mainstream Ashʿarīs believe, and insofar as it is not distinct from God's Power but rather a manifestation or "descent" of that Power, it cannot be correctly characterized as operating "with permission" and "not independently."[82]

Nābulusī also challenged Kūrānī's readings of a number of proof texts. The Quran and hadith cannot, he insisted, be adduced in support of the recognition of secondary causality since they do not explicitly state that God acts *by means of* secondary causes (*bi-l-asbāb*) rather than, as Ashʿarī occasionalists would have it, *in conjunction with* occasional causes (*ʿinda l-asbāb*).[83] The quotations that Kūrānī adduced from Ashʿarī's *al-Ibāna* only include a rejection of the Muʿtazilī thesis, not an explicit claim that human power has an effect.[84] Nābulusī also adduced a number of quotations from Ibn ʿArabī himself in support of the view that contingent existents do not have causal powers and that God creates in conjunction with occasional causes (*ʿinda l-asbāb*) rather than by means of secondary causes (*bi-l-asbāb*).[85] The respectful tone of the beginning and end of the

[81] Ibid., 54–55 (ʿAlāʾ al-Dīn edition), 70 (Akkach edition).

[82] Nābulusī's objections to Kūrānī have been discussed by Samer Akkach in the introduction to his edition of *Wasāʾil al-taḥqīq*, 90–95. Akkach's discussion is based on a misunderstanding of Kūrānī's position; for a corrective, see Stearns, "All Beneficial Knowledge is Revealed," 66-72.

[83] Nābulusī, *Wasāʾil al-taḥqīq*, 60–64 (ʿAlāʾ al-Dīn), 80–87 (Akkach).

[84] Ibid., 64–65 (ʿAlāʾ al-Dīn), 88–90 (Akkach). Whether al-Ashʿarī denied any effect (*taʾthīr*) to created human power remains a controversial point. Richard Frank has argued that he did not deny this outright (and thus would agree with Kūrānī's reading); see his "The Structure of Created Causality according to al-Ashʿarī: An Analysis of *al-Lumaʿ*, §§82–164," *Studia Islamica* 25(1966): 13–75. Binyamin Abrahamov rejects Frank's interpretation (and would thus agree with Nābulusī); see his "A Re-examination of al-Ashʿarī's Theory of *kasb* According to *al-Lumaʿ*," *Journal of the Royal Asiatic Society* 2(1989): 210–221.

[85] Nābulusī, *Wasāʾil al-taḥqīq*, 56–59 (ʿAlā al-Dīn), 72–79 (Akkach). The difficulty in pinning down Ibn ʿArabī's views on occasionalism and secondary causality is reflected in Chittick's magisterial studies. In *The Sufi Path of Knowledge* (1989), Chittick translates the Arabic term *asbāb* as "secondary causes," suggesting that Ibn ʿArabī accepted secondary causality. In the later *The Self-Disclosure of God* (Albany: SUNY Press, 1998), Chittick translates *asbāb* as "occasions," suggesting that he was an occasionalist.

letter could not hide the fact that Nābulusī disagreed profoundly with Kūrānī's position and had launched a comprehensive attack on it. Kūrānī apparently never responded to him, and the relations between the two seem not to have been particularly close or cordial in later years. Nābulusī and Kūrānī likewise took opposing positions on the controversial issue of the permissibility of tobacco, a hotly debated topic in the seventeenth and eighteenth centuries.[86] It is also conspicuous that Nābulusī did not cite Kūrānī's apologies for *waḥdat al-wujūd* when he wrote his own apologies on the same topic, and that he chose to write his own commentaries on works that Kūrānī had already commented on.

Nābulusī's own position on the question of the "creation of human acts" appears to have been in line with his strikingly dim view of rational theology and the capacity of pure reason. His major treatise on the topic, entitled *al-Kawkab al-sārī fī ḥaqīqat al-juzʾ al-ikhtiyārī* (The wandering planet concerning the nature of the voluntary part) and completed in January 1689, includes a strongly worded attack on the tendency to rationalize in matters of creed. In legal matters, some degree of reasoned extrapolation (*ijtihād*) from the Quran and hadith is unavoidable. But in matters of creed one should resist this temptation and rest content with submissive acceptance, for failure to do so led inexorably to empty disputatiousness and heresy.[87] Nābulusī went on to present the major positions that had been advanced on the issue of the creation of acts:[88] the early Muʿtazilī view that humans bring about their own actions independently of God; the early "Jahmī" view that humans are entirely devoid of intention and capacity; and the three views that were still current among the Sunni Muslims of his own time:

1. The view of the later Juwaynī and the later Ḥanbalīs that humans create their actions by permission of God, in the sense that God has granted humans the power to act but only in accordance with His Decree and Will
2. The view of the later Ashʿarī theologians that God creates human actions and that human intentions and abilities are merely occasions for God's direct creation

86 Compare Nābulusī's *al-Ṣulḥ bayna l-ikhwān fī ḥukm ibāḥat al-dukhkhān* (printed in abridged form in Damascus: Maṭbaʿat al-Iṣlāḥ, 1343/1924) with the condemnations of tobacco by Kūrānī and his student Barzinjī (see Ahlwardt, *Verzeichniss*, nr. 5492).

87 ʿAbd al-Ghanī al-Nābulusī, *al-Kawkab al-sārī fī ḥaqīqat al-juzʾ al-ikhtiyārī*, edited by Muḥammad Rāghib al-Ṭabbākh (Aleppo: al-Maṭbaʿa al-ʿIlmiyya, 1931), 8–10.

88 Nābulusī, *al-Kawkab al-sārī*, 4–8, 13–18.

3. The view of some Māturīdī scholars that humans have the ability to bring about a choice (*ikhtiyār*) or firm determination (*ʿazm muṣammam*) in their minds, though it is God who, as the sole cause in the physical realm, creates the consequent action

Having presented these views, Nābulusī concluded his treatise by outlining his own position. He made it plain that he accepted occasionalism – the view that "since God has created everything, as has been expounded in general creedal works, nothing has any effect whatsoever on anything else" (*inna Allāha taʿālā ḥaythu khalaqa kulla shayʾin kamā huwa l-muqarraru fī ʿaqāʾidi l-ʿumūmi lam yakun shayʾun min al-ashyāʾi yuʾaththiru aṣlan fī shayʾin min al-ashyā*).[89] He added that the complete truth concerning human voluntary acts and divine predetermination could not be expressed discursively and was only accessible by mystical "verification" (*taḥqīq*) through spiritual exercise and "unveiling" (*kashf*).[90]

Conclusion

In the 1960s, 1970s, and 1980s, historians of early modern Islamic religious thought tended to believe that the influence of Ibn ʿArabī was on the wane, and that a number of so-called "Neo-Sufi" movements

89 Ibid., 19. A treatise by Nābulusī entitled *Radd al-jāhil ilā l-ṣawāb fī jawāz iḍāfat al-taʾthīr ilā l-asbāb*, completed in March 1680, might suggest at first sight that Nābulusī vacillated regarding occasionalism (see MS: Berlin Staatsbibliothek, Sprenger 853: fols. 67a–79a). The title appears to allow for some sort of "effect" (*taʾthīr*) to secondary causes, and this has been adduced by S. Akkach (in the introduction to his edition of *Wasāʾil al-taḥqīq*, pp. 94–95) as indicating Nābulusī's concern with making room for the "relative autonomy of natural processes." But the treatise begins by explicitly advocating occasionalism: secondary causes (*al-asbāb*) have no effect whatsoever (*lā taʾthīra lahā aṣlan*) and God creates in conjunction with them (*ʿindahā*) not by means of them (*bihā*) (see fol. 67b). Nābulusī merely emphasizes that it is nevertheless permissible in everyday discourse to attribute effects to secondary causes in a loose, figurative sense (*majāz*), for example, saying that "Zayd helped me," or "I wrote this work," or "the doctor's treatment cured me." Even radical Ashʿarīs such as Sanūsī would not object to this, as Nābulusī correctly states. The main (and more controversial) purpose of Nābulusī's treatise is to argue on that basis that it is legitimate to seek spiritual favors from living and dead saints, just as one would seek a physical cure from a physician. There is nothing in this treatise to suggest that Nābulusī was particularly concerned with the "autonomy" of the natural world. Rather, he seems to have been worried about the attacks on saint- and grave-veneration by Ḳāḍīzādelīs such as Aḥmed Rūmī Āḳḥiṣārī; see the latter's treatise that was published (with a misattribution to Birgevī) under the title *Ziyārat al-qubūr al-sharʿiyya wa l-shirkiyya* (Cairo: Matbaʿat al-Imām, n.d).

90 Nābulusī, *al-Kawkab al-sārī*, 23–24.

in the seventeenth, eighteenth, and nineteenth centuries abandoned his "pantheism" and "quietism" in favor of a more "orthodox" and "activist" stance inspired by earlier, nonmonistic Sufis such as Ghazālī.[91] This thesis has come in for criticism in recent decades, for assuming what is surely a caricature of Ibn ʿArabī's thought and for underestimating the extent of Ibn ʿArabī's influence on a number of movements considered Neo-Sufi (such as the Tījāniyya and Sanūsiyya).[92] The previous chapter suggested that the discussion should take into account differences between various parts of the Islamic world. The influence of Ibn ʿArabī in the Arab-Islamic world, far from being on the wane, grew much stronger in the course of the seventeenth and eighteenth centuries. In the fifteenth and sixteenth centuries, Sufi scholars from North Africa, Egypt, and geographic Syria tended to esteem Ibn ʿArabī as a saint but were still largely resistant to adopting wholesale the outlook of his monist commentators and interpreters. This began to change in the seventeenth century in the Arab East, and in the eighteenth century in the Arab West. Prominent Sufi scholars such as Ibrāhīm Kūrānī, ʿAbd al-Ghanī al-Nābulusī and Muṣṭafā al-Bakrī were much more willing to align their terminology and concerns with those of the monist, Ibn ʿArabī-inspired tradition than their forebears from the fifteenth and sixteenth centuries such as ʿĀʾisha al-Bāʿūniyya, ʿAlwān al-Ḥamawī, ʿAbd al-Wahhāb al-Shaʿrānī, and Muḥammad b. Abī l-Ḥasan al-Bakrī.

The present chapter has dealt with one notable consequence of this development. The nonmonistic Sufism that prevailed in the Arab-Islamic world in the fifteenth and sixteenth centuries had largely made its peace with Ashʿarism and included in its ranks some of the most prominent Ashʿarī theologians of the period.[93] By contrast, prominent upholders of mystical monism in the seventeenth and eighteenth centuries opposed established Ashʿarī theology on a range of central issues. They attacked the value of the discipline of *kalām*; upheld the validity of the religious beliefs of the "imitator" (*muqallid*); rejected the figurative

[91] Rahman, *Islam*, 205–211; Trimingham, *The Sufi Orders in Islam*, chapter IV; J. Voll, *Islam: Continuity and Change in the Modern World* (Boulder, CO: Westview Press, 1982), 36–37; N. Levtzion and J. Voll, "Introduction" in N. Levtzion and J. Voll (eds), *Eighteenth-Century Renewal and Reform in Islam* (Syracuse, NY: Syracuse University Press, 1987), 3–20, at 9–10.

[92] A classic critique is R. S. O'Fahey and B. Radtke, "Neo-Sufism Reconsidered," *Der Islam* 70(1993): 52–87.

[93] For the synthesis of Ashʿarism and Sufism evident in the works of Qushayrī, Ghazālī, ʿUmar al-Suhrawardī, and Ibn ʿAṭāʾullāh al-Iskandarī, see T. Meyer, "Theology and Sufism," in T. Winter (ed.), *The Cambridge Companion to Classical Islamic Theology* (Cambridge: Cambridge University Press, 2008), 258–287, at 270–274.

reinterpretation of apparent anthropomorphisms in the Quran and hadith; challenged the mainstream Ashʿarī view of the nature of God's eternal Speech; rejected occasionalism and the mainstream Ashʿarī view of the creation of human voluntary acts; and emphasized that God acts in accordance with what is objectively good and wise (as opposed to the mainstream Ashʿarī view that there are no objective standards of goodness that God must respect and that what is good and wise is simply what God chooses to do).[94] Contrary to what one might expect, their position on most of these issues was quite close to that of traditionalist Ḥanbalīs such as Ibn Taymiyya and his student Ibn Qayyim al-Jawziyya. Monist mystics who were eager to overturn or at least radically redefine Ashʿarism unearthed and cited the writings of these Ḥanbalīs, long held in disrepute in Ashʿarī and Māturīdī circles.

Ibrāhīm Kūrānī played an important role in this process. Widely esteemed not just as a mystic but also as an exoteric scholar and teacher, Kūrānī launched a comprehensive assault on established Ashʿarī theology – the kind of Ashʿarism represented by Ījī, Taftāzānī, Jurjānī, Sanūsī, and Dawānī – and advocated a return to the more traditionalist Ashʿarism of the *Ibāna*. He went out of his way to find and read the works of Ibn Taymiyya and Ibn Qayyim al-Jawziyya, and on a number of occasions defended them from the charge of anthropomorphism. He also cultivated close personal ties with prominent Ḥanbalī scholars in his own time, for example, asking the leading Damascene Ḥanbalī of his day, ʿAbd al-Bāqī al-Baʿlī, for an exposition of the Ḥanbalī creed. A surviving manuscript copy of Kūrānī's main work on the creation of human acts includes autograph certificates to two other prominent Damascene Ḥanbalī scholars: ʿAbd al-Bāqī's son Abū l-Mawāhib (d. 1714) and the jurist ʿAbd al-Qādir al-Taghlibī (d. 1723). (See Figures 8.1 and 8.2.)

Kūrānī's influence in subsequent centuries was substantial. The great Indian Naqshbandi scholar Shāh Waliyullāh Dihlavī (d. 1762) was profoundly influenced by his studies with Kūrānī's son Abū l-Ṭāhir Muḥammad (d. 1733) in Medina.[95] Shāh Waliyullāh exhibited the same curious and fascinating combination of adherence to Ibn ʿArabī-inspired

94 Further departures from mainstream Ashʿarism by monist Sufis include the beliefs that: (1) there are non-existent entities (*shayʾiyyat al-maʿdūm*); (2) God's attributes are not superadded to God's Self; (3) the punishment of hell-fire is not eternal; and (4) reports about the Satanic verses are historical. On the first two points, monist Sufis were much closer to classical Muʿtazilī doctrine. On the last two points, they were again in agreement with Ibn Taymiyya and Ibn Qayyim al-Jawziyya.

95 J. M. S. Baljon, *Religion and Thought of Shāh Walī Allāh Dihlawi, 1703–1762* (Leiden, the Netherlands: Brill, 1986), 5–6.

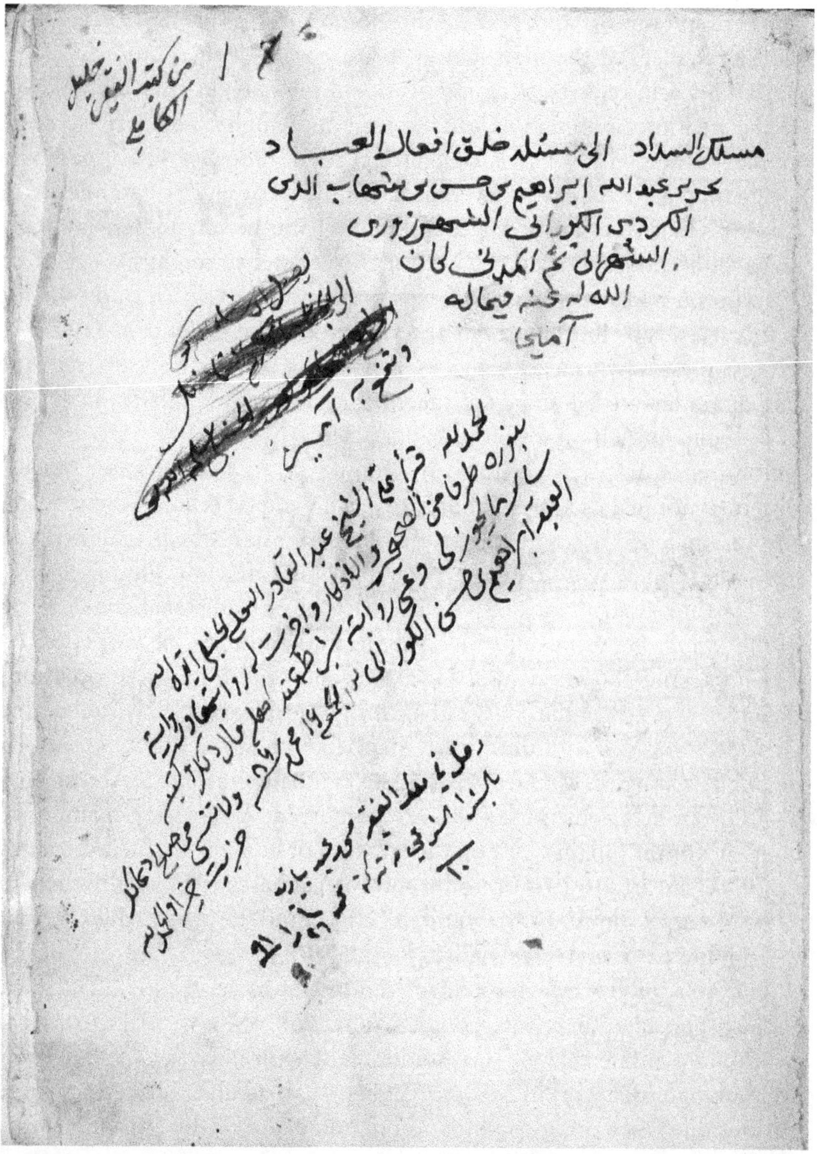

FIGURE 8.1 Autograph certificate by Ibrāhīm Kūrānī, dated 1089/1678, to the Damascene Ḥanbalī scholar ʿAbd al-Qādir al-Taghlibī (d. 1723), written on the title page of a manuscript copy of Kūrānī's *Maslak al-sadād fī masʾalat khalq afʿāl al-ʿibād*. (Ibrāhīm Kūrānī, *Maslak al-sadād fī masʾalat khalq afʿāl al-ʿibād*, fol. 1a. Islamic Manuscripts, Garrett Y3867. Department of Rare Books and Manuscripts, Princeton University Library. Reproduced with permission).

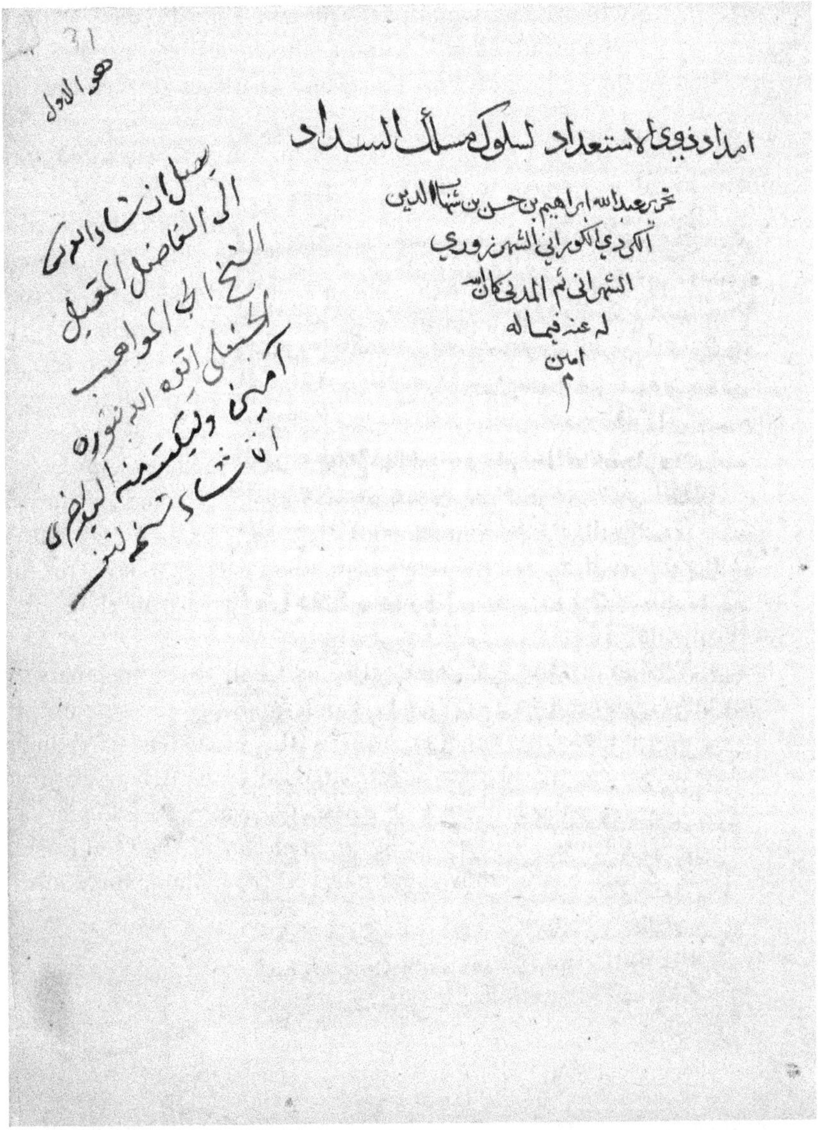

FIGURE 8.2 Autograph dedication by Kūrānī to the Damascene Ḥanbalī scholar Abū l-Mawāhib al-Ḥanbalī (d. 1714), written on the title page of a manuscript copy of Kūrānī's postscript to his *Maslak al-sadād fī mas'alat khalq af'āl al-'ibād*. (Ibrāhīm Kūrānī, *Maslak al-sadād fī mas'alat khalq af'āl al-'ibād*, fol. 31a. Islamic Manuscripts, Garrett Y3867. Department of Rare Books and Manuscripts, Princeton University Library. Reproduced with permission).

mystical monism (*waḥdat al-wujūd*) and respect for Ibn Taymiyya's position in matters of creed and law.[96] Kūrānī's theological works continued to be cited in the eighteenth and nineteenth centuries throughout the Islamic world. His rehabilitation of the view of the later Juwaynī and Ibn Qayyim al-Jawziyya on the creation of human acts was cited with approval by, for example, Muḥammad Murtaḍā al-Zabīdī (d. 1791) in his voluminous commentary on Ghazālī's *Iḥyāʾ ʿulūm al-dīn*.[97] It was also cited with approval by the Ḥanbalī scholar from Nablus Muḥammad al-Saffārīnī (d. 1774) in his lengthy and influential work on the creedal beliefs of non-Ashʿarī traditionalists – a work that was printed in the early twentieth century with the support of the well-known Salafi reformer Rashīd Riḍā (d. 1935).[98] The prominent Iraqi scholar and Quran exegete Maḥmūd al-Ālūsī (d. 1854) relied heavily on Kūrānī's works in his own treatment of a range of theological issues such as *waḥdat al-wujūd*, occasionalism and the creation of human acts, and the justice of God's Willing that certain humans be damned.[99] Maḥmūd al-Ālūsī's son Khayr al-Dīn (d. 1899), in his lengthy and influential apology for Ibn Taymiyya, also cited Kūrānī's defense of Ibn Taymiyya from the charge of anthropomorphism.[100]

Saffārīnī, Zabīdī, and Maḥmūd al-Ālūsī – all three members of Sufi orders introduced into the Arab-Islamic world in the seventeenth century – are indicative of the strengthening of a current of thought in the Arab-Islamic world that distanced itself from Ashʿarism as it had developed over the centuries, in favor of a more traditionalist or "neo-Ḥanbalī" outlook. By the time of Khayr al-Dīn al-Ālūsī and Rashīd Riḍā, a self-styled "Salafi" movement had become a major force in the

96 Baljon, *Religion and Thought of Shāh Walī Allāh*, 56–63, 200–201.

97 Zabīdī, *Itḥāf al-sāda al-muttaqīn bi-Sharḥ Iḥyāʾ ʿulūm al-dīn*, II, 168–171.

98 Muḥammad al-Saffārīnī, *Lawāmiʿ al-anwār al-bahiyya wa-sawāṭiʿ al-asrār al-athariyya fī sharḥ al-Durra al-muḍīʾa fī ʿaqd al-firqa al-marḍiyya* (Cairo: Maṭbaʿat al-Manār, 1328/1907), I, 314 (l. 25) ff. In Vol. II, 137 (l. 2), Saffārīnī refers to Kūrānī as "the teacher of our teachers" (*shaykh mashāyikhinā*).

99 In his *al-Ajwiba al-ʿIrāqiyya ʿalā l-asʾila al-Īrāniyya*, printed on the margins of ʿAlī Dedeh, *Ḥall al-rumūz wa kashf al-kunūz* (Cairo: al-Maṭbaʿa al-Sharafiyya, 1314/1896), Ālūsī relies heavily on Kūrānī in his treatment of *waḥdat al-wujūd* (pp. 3–23), the "thingness of the non-existent" (pp. 57–70), and the creation of human acts (pp. 70–85). See also the explicit mentions of Kūrānī on p. 6 (ll. 31–32), p. 14 (l. 25), p. 69 (l. 11), and p. 78 (n. 1). In his Quran commentary *Rūḥ al-maʿānī*, there are more than two dozen references to Kūrānī; see the index prepared by Ibrāhīm Shams al-Dīn and Sanāʾ Shams al-Dīn, *Fahāris Rūḥ al-maʿānī fī tafsīr al-Qurʾān* (Beirut: Dār al-Kutub al-ʿIlmiyya, 1996) under "Kūrānī" and "Ibrāhīm Kūrānī."

100 Khayr al-Dīn al-Ālūsī, *Jalāʾ al-ʿaynayn*, 339, 406, 415, 569.

Arab-Islamic world.[101] In the course of the twentieth century, professed Salafis overwhelmingly adopted Ibn Taymiyya's hostility to Ibn ʿArabī and monist mysticism, and they tended to trace their own intellectual lineage to Ibn Taymiyya and his Ḥanbalī followers, as well as to a number of traditionalist Yemeni Zaydī religious thinkers such as Ibn al-Wazīr (d. 1436), Ibn al-Amīr (d. 1768), and Muḥammad al-Shawkānī (d. 1834). Nevertheless, there is surely a story to be told about how ideas that had long survived amongst Ḥanbalīs and traditionalist Zaydīs in the highlands of Yemen began in the eighteenth and nineteenth centuries to infiltrate mainstream Sunni thinking in the core areas of the Arab-Islamic world. The present chapter has presented reasons for thinking that such a "genealogy"[102] of the emergence and early spread of modern Salafism would, paradoxical as this may sound, feature the activities of monist mystics such as Kūrānī, Shāh Waliyullāh and Zabīdī and, via them, the ideas of Ibn ʿArabī himself.[103]

101 An up-to-date history of the emergence of Salafism is an urgent desideratum. For informative partial accounts, see B. M. Nafi, "Abu l-Thanaʾ al-Alusi: An Alim, Ottoman Mufti, and Exegete of the Qurʾan," *International Journal of Middle East Studies* 34(2002): 465–494; B. Abu-Manneh, "Salafiyya and the Rise of the Khālidiyya in Baghdad in the Early Nineteenth Century," *Die Welt des Islams* 43(2003), 349–372; D.D. Commins, *Islamic Reform: Politics and Social Change in Late Ottoman Syria* (Oxford: Oxford University Press, 1990); I. Weismann, *Taste of Modernity: Sufism, Salafiyya, and Arabism in Late Ottoman Damascus* (Leiden, the Netherlands: Brill, 2001). For a very welcome disentanglement of some of the conceptual and historical confusions in modern scholarship concerning Salafism in the late nineteenth and early twentieth centuries, see H. Lauzière, "The Construction of *Salafiyya*: Reconsidering Salafism from the Perspective of Conceptual History," *International Journal of Middle East Studies* 42(2010): 369–389.

102 On Nietzsche's idea of a "genealogy," see R. Geuss, "Nietzsche and Genealogy," *European Journal of Philosophy* 2(1994): 274–292. The core idea is precisely that an intellectual or cultural movement may have roots in ideas and values that are very different and even antithetical to those that exponents of the full-fledged movement espouse. In this sense, a critical "genealogy" will differ from a *post facto* sanitized intellectual pedigree given by apologists.

103 Another important figure in the prehistory of Salafism is ʿAbd al-Qādir al-Jazāʾirī (d. 1883), a follower of Ibn ʿArabī, defender of *waḥdat al-wujūd*, and critic of established theological and legal schools. As shown by I. Weismann, the earliest professed "Salafis" in Damascus were students or associates of ʿAbd al-Qādir, see *Taste of Modernity*, 6, 275ff. For a helpful exposition of ʿAbd al-Qādir's thought, see ibid., 155–192. In my opinion, though, Weismann overestimates the extent to which ʿAbd al-Qādir's position was advanced with the problem of "modernity" in mind. ʿAbd al-Qādir seems very much to have been in the tradition of Kūrānī and Shāh Waliyullāh, neither of whom were particularly concerned with "modernity." Ibn ʿArabī-inspired monism also seems to have played a part in the intellectual formation of Muḥammad ʿAbduh (d. 1905), as attested by his early work *al-Wāridāt*; see M. Sedgwick, *Muḥammad ʿAbduh* (Oxford: Oneworld, 2010), 11–12.

9

In Defense of *Waḥdat al-Wujūd*

In the previous two chapters, it was argued that the monist, Qūnawī-inspired interpretation of Ibn ʿArabī became markedly more influential among religious scholars (*ulema*) in the Arab East in the seventeenth and eighteenth centuries, and that this development tended to weaken the hold of Ashʿarī theology, at least as it had developed since the twelfth century, and to rehabilitate a more traditionalist Ḥanbalī position on a number of core theological issues: occasionalism and secondary causation; the creation of human acts; the value of rational theology; the faith of the "imitator"; the eternity of the letters and sounds of the Quran; and the interpretation of apparent anthropomorphisms in the Quran and hadith. The very idea that followers of Ibn ʿArabī could have had such an effect might appear odd to the modern reader accustomed to think of mystical advocates of "the unity of existence" (*waḥdat al-wujūd*) and anti-esoteric Ḥanbalī traditionalists as polar opposites. One might accordingly wonder if there is any truth to the suggestion – made by Fazlur Rahman in the 1960s and repeated by some more recent scholars – that Ibrāhīm Kūrānī and ʿAbd al-Ghanī al-Nābulusī were advancing a novel, more restrained and less "pantheistic" version of "mystic theosophy" that avoided the "extravagant intellectual and spiritual consequences" of the ideas of Ibn ʿArabī and took seriously the demands of religious law.[1] On this account, the rapprochement between Ibn ʿArabī-inspired mysticism

[1] Rahman, *Islam*, 148–149. More recent portrayals of Ibrāhīm Kūrānī as a "reformist" or "neo-Sufi" who was opposed to "extreme" monism or "extravagant" Sufism include B. Nafi, "Taṣawwuf and Reform in Pre-Modern Islamic Culture: In Search of Ibrāhīm al-Kūrānī," *Die Welt des Islams* 43(2002): 307–355 and A. Azra, *The Origins of Islamic Reformism in Southeast Asia*, 32–51, esp. 49–51.

and traditionalist Ḥanbalism would have been made possible by scholars such as Kūrānī and Nābulusī quietly abandoning the most controversial and provocative aspects of the monistic worldview of Ibn ʿArabī and his disciples. Rahman's bare suggestion has not been elaborated and defended at any length, but it nevertheless raises the serious point that by simply characterizing a scholar as having been an advocate of Ibn ʿArabī or even of *waḥdat al-wujūd* we may be overlooking the possibility that the interpretation advanced by this scholar was in important ways novel, more moderate, and less offensive to mainstream exoteric scholars than previous interpretations. Whether this was the case or not can, of course, be determined only on the basis of careful scrutiny of primary sources. Accordingly, relevant works by Kūrānī and Nābulusī will be investigated in some detail in the present chapter. The conclusion will be that both mystics stood firmly in the tradition of Ibn ʿArabī, Qūnawī and the later *Fuṣūṣ* commentators, and that both scholars endorsed the very same doctrine of *waḥdat al-wujūd* that had been so passionately condemned by antimonist scholars in the fourteenth and fifteenth centuries. There is, in other words, nothing to support the suggestion that their interpretation was less "pantheistic" and more "orthodox" than those of earlier mystics in the tradition of Ibn ʿArabī and Qūnawī.

Taftāzānī's Criticism of *Waḥdat al-Wujūd*

The ideas of Ibn ʿArabī, Qūnawī, and the latter's disciples and epigones elicited passionate rejoinders in the fourteenth and fifteenth centuries from, for example, the Ḥanbalī scholar Ibn Taymiyya, the Timurid theologian Saʿd al-Dīn al-Taftāzānī, Taftāzānī's student ʿAlāʾ al-Dīn al-Bukhārī (d. 1438), and the Egyptian scholar Burhān al-Dīn al-Biqāʿī. Though such critics typically denounced a number of ideas that they attributed to Ibn ʿArabī and his followers, it was that of *waḥdat al-wujūd* that caused the greatest offense and elicited the lion's share of denunciations. As was seen in Chapter 7, even a number of Sufis either rejected the thesis outright or studiously avoided embracing it. An early example is the Persian mystic of the Kubrawī order ʿAlāʾ al-Dawla al-Simnānī (d. 1336), but a hostile or uncommitted attitude was not unusual among North African Shādhilī mystics.[2] It would of course later become

[2] On Simnānī, see J. Elias, *The Throne Carrier of God: The Life and Thought of ʿAlāʾ al-Dawla al-Simnānī* (Albany: SUNY Press, 1995). For his views on *waḥdat al-wujūd*, see H. Landolt, "Simnānī on waḥdat al-wujūd," in H. Landolt and M. Mohaghegh (eds.), *Collected Papers on Islamic Mysticism and Philosophy* (Tehran: Institute of Islamic Studies, 1971), 91–112.

the prevalent idea among mystics of the Naqshbandī order due to the influence of Aḥmad Sirhindī.

By far the most influential criticism of the idea of *waḥdat al-wujūd* in early modern Islamic scholarly circles was that penned by Taftāzānī in his widely studied handbook of theology *Sharḥ al-Maqāṣid*. It was accordingly this criticism that seventeenth-century defenders of *waḥdat al-wujūd* tried to disarm, as will be seen later. It has been suggested that Taftāzānī's criticisms were in turn influenced by Ibn Taymiyya's criticisms two generations earlier, but this does not stand up to closer scrutiny.[3] Taftāzānī's voluminous writings do not indicate any acquaintance whatsoever with Ibn Taymiyya's works. Furthermore, even a cursory glance at the relevant discussions in *Sharḥ al-Maqāṣid* shows that Taftāzānī's attack was written in a very different register from that of Ibn Taymiyya. One conspicuous difference is that Taftāzānī's refutation is preceded by a sustained and dispassionate presentation of the idea that he wished to criticize – indeed, it will be seen later that seventeenth-century advocates of *waḥdat al-wujūd* accepted his presentation of the doctrine (though not his criticisms of it). By contrast, Ibn Taymiyya seems to have been averse to giving a sustained exposition of ideas with which he disagreed – he rarely attributed more than isolated, single-sentence assertions to his opponents, shorn of any supporting arguments, before attacking them. Another conspicuous difference is that Taftāzānī's criticism is through and through metaphysical, whereas Ibn Taymiyya's denunciations of *waḥdat al-wujūd* are less focused, with numerous asides on the supposed historical roots of the heretical idea and its supposed antinomian consequences. Taftāzānī's criticism is much more akin in spirit to the less rambling and more cerebral criticisms of the Aristotelian–Neo-Platonist philosophers by Persianate theologians such as Ghazālī and Fakhr al-Dīn al-Rāzī – the latter especially gained notoriety in some circles for the care and detail with which he presented the views of "heretics."[4]

[3] The suggestion of Ibn Taymiyya's influence on Taftāzānī is made in A. Knysh, *Ibn ʿArabī in the Later Islamic Tradition*, 141–165, esp. 147, 149, 163. Knysh was misled by an Istanbul printing from 1877 that falsely attributed a treatise against *waḥdat al-wujūd* to Taftāzānī; see *Majmūʿat rasāʾil fī waḥdat al-wujūd* (Istanbul: n.p. 1294/1877), 2–47. Bakri Aladdin has shown conclusively that the treatise is not by Taftāzānī but by ʿAlāʾ al-Dīn al-Bukhārī; see the introduction to his edition of ʿAbd al-Ghanī al-Nābulusī, *al-Wujūd al-ḥaqq wa l-khiṭāb al-ṣidq*, 15–19. Aladdin also correctly brought out the differences between Ibn Taymiyya's and Taftāzānī's criticisms of *waḥdat al-wujūd*; see ibid., pp. 28–29.

[4] Abū Shāma (d. 1267), *al-Dhayl ʿalā l-Rawḍatayn*, edited by Muḥammad Zāhid al-Kawtharī and ʿIzzat al-ʿAṭṭār al-Ḥusaynī (Cairo: Dār al-Kutub al-Mālikiyya, 1947), 48.

On the level of content, too, there are important differences between the criticisms of Taftāzānī and Ibn Taymiyya. The latter regularly accused Ibn ʿArabī and his followers of believing in *ittiḥād* and *ḥulūl*, i.e., that God is unified with or immanent in creation.[5] By contrast, Taftāzānī held that the partisans of *waḥdat al-wujūd* are not guilty of the stock charge of believing in *ittiḥād* or *ḥulūl*. In his discussion of various Christian and extremist Shiite notions of "immanence" and "unification," he noted that there are two further positions that at first sight might appear to be guilty of the same heresy but are not so. The first position, with which he expressed sympathy, is that an advanced mystic overwhelmed with the experience of God will temporarily become blind to anything else and may make ecstatic utterances that – if taken out of context – could suggest a belief in *ḥulūl* or *ittiḥād*. The second position is that God is identical with absolute existence and that the phenomenal world is nothing but a phantasm or mirage that does not strictly speaking exist at all. Even though Taftāzānī had rejected this position in an earlier section of his *Sharḥ al-Maqāṣid*, considering it contrary to both religion (*sharʿ*) and reason (*ʿaql*), he did not deem it an example of *ḥulūl* or *ittiḥād* since according to this kind of ontological monism there are not two different existents one of which can dwell in or become unified with the other.[6]

In the earlier section of *Sharḥ al-Maqāṣid*, Taftāzānī had discussed the view, which he attributed to some "pseudo-Sufis" (*mutaṣawwifa*), that God is absolute existence (*al-wujūd al-muṭlaq*) which accordingly is not a universal attribute (*maʿnan kullī*) but a single individual (*wāḥid bi-l-shakhṣ*) that exists necessarily.[7] Their reasoning, as reconstructed by Taftāzānī, is as follows: The Necessary Existent cannot have existence superadded to its quiddity, but rather its existence must be identical to its quiddity. In other words, there can be no real distinction between *what* the Necessary Existent is (its quiddity) and *that* it is (its existence). Furthermore, the Necessary Existent cannot be a particular existent (*wujūd khāṣṣ*), that is an instance of general, absolute existence (*al-wujūd al-muṭlaq*) because this would imply (1) a composite nature (composed of

[5] Knysh, *Ibn ʿArabī in the Later Islamic Tradition*, 90.

[6] Taftāzānī, *Sharḥ al-Maqāṣid* (Istanbul: Haci Muharrem Bosnavi Matbaʿasi, 1305/1888), II, 69–70 [Shams al-Dīn ed. III, 41–45]. Modern editions of Taftāzānī's *Sharḥ al-Maqāṣid* are very unreliable. Nevertheless, since they are more readily available than the older Istanbul edition, I have added references to the edition of Ibrāhīm Shams al-Dīn (Beirut: Dār al-Kutub al-ʿIlmiyya, 2001) in square brackets here and in the text that follows.

[7] Taftāzānī, *Sharḥ al-Maqāṣid*, I, 73 (ll. 18–28) [Shams al-Dīn ed. I, 176–177].

specific plus general existence) that as such could not be necessary, and (2) that the Necessary Existent depends on general existence for its existence. Rather, the Necessary Existent must be existence as such, that is, absolute existence, which therefore is a concrete entity that exists by virtue of an existence that is identical with itself. Existence is simply not a universal (like "white" or "human") with many distinct instances, but a particular, viz. God. The claim that someone – say Zayd – exists should therefore not be understood analogously to "Zayd is white," for the latter implies that Zayd possesses a particular instance of the universal attribute "white," whereas Zayd cannot possess a particular instance of God. Rather, the statement "Zayd exists" (*Zayd mawjūd*) should be understood in the sense of "Zayd is lorded" (*Zayd ma'lūh*; *Zayd marbūb*). In other words, a possible entity can be said to "exist" insofar as it stands in a certain relationship to Existence, not insofar as it has a particular share or instance of a universal "existence."

Against this view, Taftāzānī insisted that the multiplicity of existents is evident (*ḍarūrī*), and equally evident is the principle that absolute existence is a universal concept (*mafhūm kullī*) that does not exist extramentally apart from its particular instances. The assumption of the "pseudo-Sufis" is that if the Necessary Existent were an instance of the universal "existence" then it would be dependent on this universal and would not be necessary. But this, replied Taftāzānī, is to get things the wrong way round: If the Necessary Existent were an instance of general existence then general existence would depend on the Necessary Existent (among other things) for its instantiation in the extramental world. Taftāzānī, like almost all Islamic theologians, assumed that only particulars have extramental existence and that universals can only be said to exist insofar as their particular instances exist.[8]

The "pseudo-Sufis," Taftāzānī stated, also claim that general, absolute existence is necessarily existent. They argue for this in one of two ways:

1. If general, absolute existence did not exist then nothing would exist, but all parties agree that the Necessary Existent exists; hence general, absolute existence necessarily exists. This, Taftāzānī protests, is sophistry. The argument does not show that general, absolute existence is necessary in itself, as opposed to being derivatively necessary in the sense that it depends on there being a God who is necessarily existent. One may consider the analogous and

[8] Taftāzānī, *Sharḥ al-Shamsiyya*, 31.

fallacious argument: If knowledge in general did not exist then there would be no knowledge, but God is conceded by all parties to have knowledge necessarily; therefore knowledge in general is a Necessary Existent.[9]

2. Existence is necessary in and of itself, for it is absurd to think that its contrary, viz. nonexistence, could be true of it. Taftāzānī responded that what is impossible is that something is not identical with itself, as in "Existence is not existence (*wujūd*)" or "Existence is nonexistence (*ʿadam*)." This does not show that it is self-contradictory to say "Existence does not exist (*mawjūd*)" or "Existence is a nonexistent (*maʿdūm*)."[10] Taftāzānī refused, in other words, to concede that there is something special about the case of the concept of existence. It is a universal concept like any other and whether or not it has a referent in the extra-mental world is something that can only be established through sense perception or rational proof. Like the majority of philosophers in both the European and Islamic traditions, he dismissed any attempt at showing that a concept must have an extra-mental referent merely by considering the concept itself.

According to Taftāzānī, the "pseudo-Sufis" claim that their position is prefigured in the views of the philosophers, for the latter claim that God's quiddity is identical to God's existence and that He has no contrary, no analogue, no genus and no differentia. Taftāzānī thought that the philosophers' claims were questionable, but that in any case they did not establish what the "pseudo-Sufis" wish, for what these arguments establish is that something is true both of absolute existence and God, and it does not follow from this that absolute existence and God are identical. Taftāzānī here invoked the logical principle that a syllogism in the second figure (in which the predicates of the two premises are identical) does not produce a conclusion when both premises are affirmative or negative (it must be the case that one premise is affirmative and the other negative).[11] His point is that an argument of the following form is fallacious:

Absolute existence has no genus.
God has no genus.
Absolute existence is God.

[9] My example, not Taftāzānī's.
[10] Taftāzānī, *Sharḥ al-Maqāṣid*, I, 74 (ll. 4–10) [Shams al-Dīn ed. I, 177].
[11] Taftāzānī, *Sharḥ al-Maqāṣid*, I, 74 (l. 29) [Shams al-Dīn ed. I, 177–178].

Compare the evidently fallacious argument:[12]

> Ibn Taymiyya does not accept *waḥdat al-wujūd*.
> Taftāzānī does not accept waḥdat al-wujūd.
> ---
> Ibn Taymiyya is Taftāzānī.

Taftāzānī added that the attempt of the "pseudo-Sufis" to invoke the philosophers in support of their views is doomed, for the philosophers take it as axiomatic that general, absolute existence is (1) an attribute (*ʿaraḍ*) rather than a substance, and (2) not even a real attribute (like shape or color) but rather a mental or virtual predicate (*maḥmūl ʿaqlī* or *maḥmūl iʿtibārī*).[13] A mental or virtual predicate is true of a subject but without denoting an additional, mind-independent feature of the object in the extramental world. A standard example given by theologians is the attribute of being possible: it arguably makes little sense to suppose that "Unicorns are possible beings" means that unicorns in the extramental world have the attribute of being possible (since there are no unicorns in the extramental world).[14] Another example was encountered in Chapter 5 in the discussion of the Ashʿarī creed of the Moroccan scholar Ibn ʿĀshir. It was there mentioned that Ashʿarī theologians tended to consider existence (*wujūd*) a so-called *ṣifa nafsiyya* rather than a superadded attribute of the Divine Self (*dhāt*), since existence is simply equivalent to being a self, not an attribute that a self has. The distinction between a self and its existence is, on this account, merely mental or virtual and does not correspond to a real distinction in the extramental world. Another way of putting the same point is that existence is a "second intention" (*maʿqūl thānī*), that is, a concept that is true of things insofar as they are apprehended by the mind, not insofar as they exist extramentally.[15]

Taftāzānī added that the view that general, absolute existence is God also goes against the philosophers' division of existence into necessary and contingent, and uncreated and created. It also goes against their assumption that existence is a universal common to all things, and that it is said of things in a "modulatory" or "gradational" way (*bi-l-tashkīk*, that is, admitting of more or less, like "tall" and "white"). Finally, and perhaps most seriously, the equation of God and existence is incompatible

[12] My example, not Taftāzānī's.

[13] Taftāzānī, *Sharḥ al-Maqāṣid*, I, 74 (l. 30)–I, 75 (l. 3) [Shams al-Dīn ed. I, 178–179].

[14] Ibid., 119 (l. 23)–123 (l. 21) [Shams al-Dīn ed. I, 273–277].

[15] On "second intentions," see A. I. Sabra, "Avicenna on the Subject-Matter of Logic," 753–757.

with the view that God is the creator of the world who has personal qualities such as knowledge, will, and power.[16]

Taftāzānī's *Sharḥ al-Maqāṣid* came to be studied throughout the Sunni Islamic world, from Morocco to India, in subsequent centuries. His criticism of *waḥdat al-wujūd* reappears in the antimonist polemic of his student ʿAlāʾ al-Dīn al-Bukhārī – a polemic that to judge from the number and location of extant manuscripts was popular among later Turkish Ḥanafī opponents of Ibn ʿArabī.[17] Bukhārī, though much more vehement in tone than Taftāzānī, retained his teacher's sympathy for what he considered nonmonistic Sufism, citing with approval the writings of, for example, Qushayrī and Ghazālī and arguing that these older and venerable Sufis were innocent of the heresies of the "partisans of existence" (*wujūdiyya*).[18] Taftāzānī's criticisms were also cited with approval in the fifteenth century by the Egyptian scholar al-Biqāʿī, in the sixteenth century by the Egyptian Shādhilī Sufi Muḥammad b. Abī l-Ḥasan al-Bakrī, and in the late seventeenth century by the Moroccan Ashʿarī theologian and Shādhilī Sufi Ibn Yaʿqūb al-Wallālī (d. 1716).[19] The theological writings of Taftāzānī were also well known in India in the seventeenth century.[20] It is therefore very likely that Aḥmad Sirhindī knew of Taftāzānī's rejection of *waḥdat al-wujūd* combined with sympathy for mystic experiences of "annihilation" (*fanāʾ*) in God. More surprisingly perhaps, Taftāzānī's arguments against *waḥdat al-wujūd* reappear in later Shiite Iranian works. The philosophers Ghiyāth al-Dīn Dashtakī (d. 1542) and Mullā Ṣadrā Shīrāzī (d. 1635) both helped themselves (without acknowledgment) to the relevant discussion from *Sharḥ al-Maqāṣid* to buttress their own disagreement with the received doctrine of *waḥdat al-wujūd*.[21]

16 Taftāzānī, *Sharḥ al-Maqāṣid*, I, 75 (ll. 8–24) [Shams al-Dīn edition I, 179].

17 See the list of extant manuscripts in Bakri Aladdin's introduction to his edition of Nābulusī, *al-Wujūd al-ḥaqq*, 18. Nine out of the sixteen listed manuscripts are in Turkish libraries.

18 Bukhārī, *Faḍīḥat al-mulḥidīn* [printed in *Majmūʿat rasāʾil fī waḥdat al-wujūd* and attributed to Taftāzānī] (Istanbul: n.p. 1294/1877), 3, 8–9, 30–38.

19 Burhān al-Dīn al-Biqāʿī, *Tanbīh al-ghabī ilā takfīr Ibn ʿArabī*, edited [with the title *Maṣraʿ al-taṣawwuf*] by ʿAbd al-Raḥmān al-Wakīl (Cairo: Matbaʿat al-Sunna al-Muḥammadiyya, 1953), 81–83; Muḥammad b. Abī l-Ḥasan al-Bakrī, *Taʾbīd al-minna fī taʾyīd al-sunna*, fols. 106b–111b, at fol. 109a–b; Ibn Yaʿqūb al-Wallālī, *Falsafat al-tawḥīd [=Ashraf al-maqāṣid fī sharḥ al-Maqāṣid]*, 137–141.

20 ter Haar, *Follower and Heir of the Prophet*, 59n4.

21 Ghiyāth al-Dīn Dashtakī, *Ishrāq hayākil al-nūr li-kashf ẓulumāt shawākil al-ghurūr*, edited by ʿAlī Owjabī (Tehran: Mirās-i Maktūb, Tehran 2003), 189–190; Mullā Ṣadrā Shīrāzī, *al-Ḥikma al-mutaʿāliya fī l-asfār al-ʿaqliyya al-arbaʿa*, edited and annotated

Kūrānī's Defense of *Waḥdat al-Wujūd*

Ibrāhīm Kūrānī discussed the issue of *waḥdat al-wujūd* in a number of his works, most extensively in his commentary on the didactic creedal poem of his Sufi master Qushāshī; in his treatise *Maṭlaʿ al-jūd bi-taḥqīq al-tanzīh fī waḥdat al-wujūd*; and in his commentary on the treatise *al-Tuḥfa al-mursala* by the Indian Shaṭṭārī mystic Burhānpūrī. The present section offers a closer look at the latter work, recently edited from an autograph manuscript by Oman Fathurahman.[22] Kūrānī began writing the work on November 9, 1665 and stopped writing around a month later.[23] For unknown reasons, he never completed the commentary, which covers only the preamble and the first few passages of Burhānpūrī's treatise.

In the introduction, Kūrānī wrote that he had been asked to write the commentary by some of his Javanese students who told him that Burhānpūrī's treatise was popular in their home region and was sometimes invoked by antinomian Sufis.[24] This might at first sight be taken as support for the view that Kūrānī was working out a novel, "orthodox" interpretation of ontological monism. But this is to ignore the fact that there was nothing at all new or remarkable about monist mystics in the tradition of Ibn ʿArabī and Qūnawī insisting on following Islamic law and condemning those Sufis who did not do so. Both Kūrānī and Nābulusī could quote a number of earlier monist mystics who made this point, including of course Ibn ʿArabī himself.[25] Furthermore, as will be seen later, Kūrānī's concerns in the work were not exclusively or even mainly with antinomian Sufis, but more with defending the worldview of Ibn ʿArabī and his followers against the attacks of antimonist religious scholars.

by Ḥasanzāde Āmolī (Tehran: Vizārat-i Farhang va Arshād-i Islāmī, 1383/2004), I, 406–409.

22 O. Fathurahman, *Itḥāf al-dhakī: Tafsīr Wahdatul Wujūd bagi Muslim Nusantra* (Jakarta: Penerbit Mizan, 2012), 175–250.

23 See the title page of the autograph manuscript reproduced in Fathurahman, *Itḥāf al-dhakī*, 39.

24 Kūrānī, *Itḥāf al-dhakī*, 176. The Javanese students would have included ʿAbd al-Raʾūf Singilī (d. 1693) and Yūsuf Tāj Maqāṣīrī (d. 1699), both of whom studied with Kūrānī in the 1660s; see Azra, *The Origins of Islamic Reformism*, 74–77, 90–91. Maqāṣīrī hailed from the island of Sulawesi, not Java, but he spent time in Java before embarking on his western travels and used the attributive "al-Jāwī" of himself when signing a manuscript he copied in Medina in 1075/1664; see Nicholas Heer's introduction to his edition of Jāmī, *al-Durra al-fākhira*, 17.

25 Kūrānī, *Itḥāf al-dhakī*, 213–215.

Kūrānī ended his introduction by expressing his hope that the work would be of assistance to those who are sincere in the "pursuit of verification" (*ṭalab al-taḥqīq*) and that God would bestow "verification" (*taḥqīq*) upon them and upon the author himself. Kūrānī regularly thereafter used the terms "verifiers" (*al-muḥaqqiqūn*), "the people of verification" (*ahl al-taḥqīq*), and "the seeker of verification" (*ṭālib al-taḥqīq*) of those who possess or seek higher mystical insight.[26] As mentioned in Chapter 7, this sense of "verification" is attested already in Ibn ʿArabī's works, if not earlier.

Though formally a commentary, only a small part of Kūrānī's work is in fact an explication of what Burhānpūrī had written. Of the seventy-five pages of Fathurahman's edition, three are devoted to Kūrānī's own introduction, forty-three to a discussion of seven preliminary points that Kūrānī wanted to establish before embarking on his commentary, and nineteen to an excursus in which Kūrānī argued at some length that absolute existence exists in the extramental world (and is not simply a universal concept in the mind) and refuted in detail Taftāzānī's arguments against *waḥdat al-wujūd*.

Kūrānī's discussion of preliminary matters follows the first substantive thesis in Burhānpūrī's treatise: "Know O brothers, may God grant you and me true happiness, that the Truth – May He be exalted – is existence." Before commenting on the statement, Kūrānī proceeded to present and defend seven points.

1. It is imperative that one not deviate from the Quran and the Sunna. In his brief discussion of this point, Kūrānī cited scriptural passages stating that revelation affords infallible guidance, and he concluded therefrom that revelation – the Quran and hadith – is the measure of both rational investigation and mystical experiences. The point was buttressed by a quotation from Ibn ʿArabī to the effect that authentic mystical knowledge accords with the revelation vouchsafed to the Prophet Muḥammad.[27]

2. The Quran and hadith have both an exoteric and an esoteric meaning, and it is legitimate for Sufis to find hidden meanings as long as these are in accord with the principles of the Arabic language and do not contravene the exoteric creed and law. Kūrānī invoked widely respected Sufis such as Ghazālī in support of the idea that, for instance, the Prophetic saying "Angels do not enter a home with a dog" could legitimately be interpreted as an injunction to cleanse one's soul of baser inclinations

[26] Ibid., 177.
[27] Kūrānī, *Itḥāf al-dhakī*, 183–185.

and desires, as long as one did not reject the former, plain meaning. In this context, Kūrānī rejected the view of Ibn Taymiyya (as reported in a later source) that any interpretation other than the plain, exoteric meaning is illegitimate, even if that interpretation is in accord with generally accepted legal and creedal principles. This, countered Kūrānī, would be to constrict the meaning of the Quran and betray the scripturally attested view that the Word of God is inexhaustible and all-encompassing.[28]

3. The earliest generations of Islam (*al-salaf*) accepted the apparently anthropomorphic passages (*mutashābihāt*) of the Quran and hadith without figurative reinterpretation (*taʾwīl*), and this position is preferable to the misplaced trust in reason and the consequent refusal to accept the plain sense of a number of scriptural passages due to the mistaken view that these lead to anthropomorphism.[29] Kūrānī wrote:

> The earnest seeker... should from the beginning follow the creed of the venerable *salaf* who were free from the two evils of anthropomorphism and figurative reinterpretation on the basis of mere ratiocination and non-demonstrative syllogisms. He should believe in apparent anthropomorphic passages [in the Quran and hadith] and affirm them of God in accordance with God's intention and knowledge, while also holding God free of similarity to created things on the basis [of the Quranic statement] "There is nothing like Him."[30]

Kūrānī's point here is clearly not aimed at esoteric, antinomian Sufis. The little that is known about antinomian Sufis suggests that they did not consider the apparently anthropomorphic passages a problem. On the contrary, they were typically accused of believing that God is immanent in the world and can unite with or dwell in physical objects. Kūrānī doubtless had in mind mainstream rational theologians of the Ashʿarī school who, as shown in Chapter 8, tended to hold that apparently anthropomorphic passages should not be understood literally and should be either interpreted figuratively (*taʾwīl*) or not interpreted at all (*tafwīḍ*).

4. One should not reject outright the theses of accomplished, law-abiding mystics even if one has not had any mystical experience oneself. At the very least, one should remain open to the possibility that they may be in the right.[31]

5. There is no contradiction between the view that existence is one and that humans have religious-legal responsibility (*taklīf*) for what they do

[28] Ibid., 190–191.
[29] Ibid., 196–202.
[30] Kūrānī, *Itḥāf al-dhakī*, 196.
[31] Ibid., 202–203.

and believe. On the contrary, Kūrānī argued, the doctrine of *waḥdat al-wujūd* is the only one that can give a satisfactory account of religious-legal responsibility. It is generally agreed that God has not imposed obligations that humans do not have the power to fulfill, and there is also abundant scriptural support for the view that all power is God's. It follows, or so Kūrānī argued, that human power is not entirely different from God's power but rather a concretization or specification (*ta'ayyun*) of it, and that humans act "by God" and not independently. This, insisted Kūrānī, is the proper middle path between two unsatisfactory extremes: (1) that humans have no power at all, and (2) that human power to act is entirely independent of God's Power, Decree, and Will.[32] He wrote:

> It does not follow from the unification of existence (*tawḥīd al-wujūd*) – which implies that those who are addressed by religious-legal demands are specifications of absolute existence and manifestations of the Names of God most High – that they are not legally responsible... For this is not incompatible with religious-legal responsibility. Rather, if one verifies the matter it is clear that religious-legal responsibility is only in accord with wisdom if it [the unity of existence] is true. For God most High does not impose upon a self except what it is able to do, and so He does not impose obligations except upon one who has the power to do what is imposed... And He most High has said "And God is the Powerful"... and "All Power is God's", i.e., that the power that appears in the forms of those with power is God's, since they are forms that concretize the essential and divine power... In this way it is clear that the fact that concretizations are manifestations of the Divine Names is what makes it proper to impose religious-legal obligations and to hold servants accountable for what they do by God's permission.[33]

6. Religious-legal responsibility does not cease until death. The law does not apply only to those who are at a lower stage of spiritual insight. This, according to Kūrānī, is clear from the fact that all legal obligations were instituted *after* the Prophet Muḥammad had undergone extensive spiritual training and achieved the highest spiritual station; indeed many laws were instituted relatively late in the Prophet's career.[34]

7. The unity of existence does not contravene the principle that one should respect God's transcendence vis-à-vis creation and avoid the twin perils of anthropomorphism (*tashbīh*) and denying God's attributes (*ta'ṭīl*).[35] The identification of God with absolute existence – that is, with existence free of any further qualification (*qayd*) – means that God is in

[32] Ibid., 203–206.
[33] Ibid., 204–205.
[34] Ibid., 210–215.
[35] Kūrānī, *Itḥāf al-dhakī*, 215–227.

Himself utterly different from any created entity. In this sense, God is transcendent and anthropomorphism is false. Nevertheless, the fact that God is pure existence and in Himself devoid of any sensible or conceivable form does not rule out that He can manifest Himself in sensible and conceivable forms, and both revelation (*shar*ʿ) and mystic unveiling (*kashf*) testify that this is what He does. Numerous hadith state that God appeared to the Prophet Muḥammad in sensory form, for example, in the form of a young man with curly hair, and that God will appear to believers in Paradise in more than one sensory form, some of which they will recognize and some of which they will not. In this sense, one can affirm the divine attributes that are grounded in revelation and mystic unveiling, including attributes that rational theologians tended to explain away such as laughing, wondering, running and descending. Such an attitude, Kūrānī pointed out, was shared by al-Ashʿarī himself: affirming the apparently anthropomorphic passages in the Quran and hadith without figurative reinterpretation while simultaneously affirming that "There is nothing like him." As mentioned in the previous chapter, Kūrānī appealed to al-Ashʿarī's most traditionalist work *al-Ibāna,* following Ibn Taymiyya in believing that this was al-Ashʿarī's last and most authoritative work.[36]

After this lengthy preliminary discussion, Kūrānī resumed his commentary on Burhānpūrī's treatise. But after briefly discussing a handful of Burhānpūrī's statements – that God is existence; that existence is one; that the manifestations of this one existence are many; that existence is the underlying reality of all these manifestations; and that divine existence is not identical to the abstract notion of "obtaining" – Kūrānī interrupted the commentary once again to embark on another lengthy excursus. Because the question of "absolute existence" is "the principle of principles" (*aṣl al-uṣūl*), he wrote, it is important to give the proofs for the thesis that it exists in the extramental world and is not merely an abstract notion in the mind.[37] Burhānpūrī had not done so, and Kūrānī went on to adduce some of the proofs given by the fifteenth-century defenders of monism Meḥmed Fenārī, ʿAlāʾ al-Dīn al-Mahāʾimī, and Jāmī. The latter, for example, had argued that there must be a Necessary Existent and that this Necessary Existent must be identical to the reality of existence (*ḥaqīqat al-wujūd*) because otherwise the Necessary Existent

36 Kūrānī, *Itḥāf al-dhakī*, 220. Kūrānī appears not to have had a copy of *al-Ibāna* but to have used the extracts quoted from it in the apology for al-Ashʿarī by Ibn ʿAsākir (d. 1176) entitled *Tabyīn kadhib al-muftarī fī-mā nasaba ilā l-Imām Abī l-Ḥasan al-Ashʿarī.*

37 Kūrānī, *Itḥāf al-dhakī*, 231.

would depend for His existence on something else, viz. Existence, which is absurd. Jāmī then carefully distinguished this "reality of existence" from the abstract "concept of existence" (*mafhūm al-wujūd*). The former exists extramentally whereas the latter is a universal in the mind. The reality of existence is identical to God; the concept of existence is a mental predicate that is true of this single divine reality.[38] As will be seen later, this distinction will play a crucial role in Kūrānī's refutation of Taftāzānī.

Kūrānī then, in what seems to have been an original aside, tried to show that the view that absolute existence exists extramentally can be reconciled with the view of al-Ashʿarī himself.[39] Of course, Ashʿarī in the early tenth century had lived in a different conceptual universe innocent of the Avicennan and post-Avicennan discussions of quiddity and existence. Kūrānī did not attempt to deny the distinctness of terminology but argued that there was an underlying substantive agreement. Later theological sources attributed to al-Ashʿarī the view that "the existence of anything is identical to its reality" (*wujūdu kulli shayʾin ʿaynu ḥaqīqatihi*). From the perspective of modern historians, there can be little doubt that this is an (indirect) report of the view of early Ashʿarī theologians who maintained, against some early Muʿtazilī theologians, that the "nonexistent" (*al-maʿdūm*) is not a "thing" (*shayʾ*) – rather "thing" and "existent" are coextensive.[40] Mystics of the Ibn ʿArabī/Qūnawī school were usually understood to have been in agreement with the Muʿtazilīs on this point, as they were committed to nonexistent entities (viz. the eternal archetypes) and to the unity of existence and the plurality of entities.[41] The claim that Ashʿarī's view can be reconciled with that of the monist Sufis is prima facie surprising and required some skillful hermeneutic maneuvering from Kūrānī. He argued that because Ashʿarī identified a thing's existence and a thing's "reality," he must – in substance – have held the view that there is no distinction between God's quiddity and God's existence. *What* God is, on this account, is identical to *that* God is. This, of course, was also the view of both the Islamic philosophers and the monist Sufis.[42]

At this point, one might wonder how Kūrānī dealt with the following problem: Ashʿarī's principle ("the existence of anything is identical to its

38 See Jāmī, *al-Durra al-fākhira*, 3–4.

39 Kūrānī, *Itḥāf al-dhakī*, 235–238.

40 See R. Frank, "The Non-Existent and the Possible in Classical Ashʿarīte Teaching," *Mélanges de l'Institut Dominicain d'Études Orientales* 24(2000): 1–37.

41 Chittick, *The Sufi Path of Knowledge*, 83a; Chittick, *The Self-Disclosure of God*, 52a.

42 Kūrānī, *Itḥāf al-dhakī*, 235.

reality") was clearly meant to apply to contingent entities as well, but the Islamic philosophers and monist Sufis were usually understood to have denied that the quiddities of contingent entities are identical to their existences. Kūrānī appears to have tackled this difficulty by invoking the concept of relative existence (*al-wujūd al-muḍāf*). Pure, Divine Existence manifests Himself in numerous quiddities. When He does so, contingent entities can be said to "exist" in a derivative sense – one may recall Taftāzānī's statement (which Kūrānī held to be accurate) that for monist mystics a certain contingent entity can be said to "exist" when it stands in a certain relationship to Existence. Because numerous contingent entities manifest Existence, they can all be said to "exist" in this sense. This derivative sense of "exist" that is true of created things, that is, relative existence, is not something over and above their quiddities but simply identical to their quiddities. In other words, relative existence is shared by quiddities in name only (*mushtarak lafẓī*) – there is no real attribute shared by all "existing" quiddities. In this way, Ashʿarī's principle that existence is not a superadded attribute of things is respected.[43]

Kūrānī next turned to the argument of Taftāzānī against the identification of God with absolute existence. It may be recalled from the previous section that Taftāzānī considered such an identification to be contrary to both reason (*ʿaql*) and religion (*sharʿ*). Kūrānī countered that it is contrary to neither. The claim that it is contrary to reason is false, he noted, as it can be proven that a Necessary Existent exists in the extramental world, that it has no quiddity besides existence as such, and that it is unique (for there cannot be several concrete entities each of which is nothing but pure existence and yet different from the others). Existence is therefore one, and what are often supposed to be a multitude of existents are nothing but different realities (*ḥaqāʾiq mukhtalifa*) that stand in certain relations to the One Existence as concrete objects of divine knowledge (*taʿayyunāt ʿilmiyya*) and as appearances of the divine tasks (*maẓāhir al-shuʾūn al-dhātiyya*).[44] There is nothing contrary to reason, Kūrānī added, in postulating a single Necessary Existent of whom a series of relational and negative predicates are true, and who therefore can be said to stand in a number of relations (*iḍāfāt*) to other things. In support of this contention, Kūrānī cited a passage from the book on *Metaphysics* from Avicenna's philosophical summa *al-Shifāʾ* in which it is stated that the Self (*dhāt*) of the Necessary Existent is one and without attributes

[43] Kūrānī, *Itḥāf al-dhakī*, 235–236.
[44] Ibid., 239–240.

but that a number of relations and privations are nevertheless true of It.[45] Kūrānī also cited a passage from the fifteenth-century Persian philosopher and theologian Jalāl al-Dīn al-Dawānī in which it is argued that the term "existent" (*mawjūd*) is true both of that which exists by virtue of its own self and of that which exists by virtue of another. This general (*ʿāmm*) concept of existence is not identical to (*ʿayn*) any extramental entity and is always mentally superadded (*zāʾid*) to that of which it is true. What makes it true to predicate this general concept of the Necessary Existent is the Necessary Existent Itself. By contrast, what makes it true to predicate the general concept of existence of contingent realities is their being derived (*muktasaba*) from the Necessary Existent.[46]

Following the lead of Jāmī and Dawānī, Kūrānī emphasized that it is crucial to distinguish between *al-wujūd al-mushtarak*, that is, the general concept that is common to the Necessary Existent and the contingent realities, and *al-wujūd al-mujarrad*, that is, pure, quiddity-less existence. It is the latter that Sufis claim to exist in the extramental world. Again, Kūrānī quoted from Avicenna's *Shifāʾ* a passage that emphasizes this distinction: The pure (*mujarrad*) existence that is identical to the quiddity of the Necessary Existent is not the absolute (*muṭlaq*) existence that is common to many things. The former is existence with a negative condition (*bi-sharṭ al-salb*), that is, existence insofar as it is devoid of quiddity, not the existence that is common to all quiddities.[47] Having invoked that particular passage by Avicenna, Kūrānī had to confront the problem that it seems to say that God is *not* "absolute existence" (*wujūd muṭlaq*). Undaunted, he argued that this was a terminological difference, not a substantive disagreement. Avicenna meant by "absolute" (*muṭlaq*) what defenders of monism meant by "common" (*mushtarak*), and there can be no question of God being identical to existence in that sense. On the other hand, Avicenna identified God with "pure" (*mujarrad*) existence, and this was precisely what defenders of monism meant by "absolute" (*muṭlaq*) existence – existence that is devoid of any quiddity.[48]

Kūrānī also quoted passages from the final mystical section of Avicenna's short epitome *al-Ishārāt* and the commentary on it by Naṣīr

[45] Ibid., 240–241. The passage quoted by Kūrānī can be found in Avicenna, *The Metaphysics of The Healing*, edited and translated by M. Marmura (Provo, UT: Brigham Young University Press, 2005), 273.

[46] Kūrānī, *Itḥāf al-dhakī*, 241; Kūrānī was quoting from Dawānī's gloss on Qūshjī's commentary on Ṭūsī's *Tajrīd al-kalām*.

[47] Kūrānī, *Itḥāf al-dhakī*, 242; Avicenna, *The Metaphysics of the Healing*, 276.

[48] Kūrānī, *Itḥāf al-dhakī*, 242.

al-Dīn al-Ṭūsī (d. 1274) in which it is held possible for the mystic seeker's power, will, and knowledge to become absorbed in (*mustaghriqatan fī*) God's Power, Will, and Knowledge – so that God would, as a well-known hadith put it, become the sight with which the servant sees, the hearing with which the servant hears, and the hand with which the servant strikes.[49] For Kūrānī, this showed that Avicenna too held that God manifests Himself in phenomenal forms that in turn are "concretizations" of pure existence. He wrote:

> If you understand that the appearances of multiplicity from the essential one, and their return to Him, is a matter for which there is evidence among the people of ratiocination among the verifiers, then saying this is not contrary to reason. From this the meaning of their saying "The concretizations are like phantasms and mirages" becomes clear rationally... for extra-mental forms appear in your imagination as independent existents that are other than their [divine] ground. Then if you look closer it will be clear to you that there is no essential existence to anything but God most High... just as a mirage will appear to the imagination of the thirsty person as water until he reaches it and does not find what he expected but rather finds God there.[50]

Having established that the identification of God and absolute existence is not contrary to reason, Kūrānī argued that it is not contrary to religious law either. He reiterated the earlier point that the doctrine of the unity of existence alone can do justice to the plethora of scriptural passages that suggest that God is utterly transcendent and independent and yet is in whatever direction one faces and is with His servants wherever they are. As Kūrānī never tired of repeating, Ashʿarī also believed that apparent anthropomorphisms in the Quran and hadith should be accepted literally while maintaining that "There is nothing like Him," and this shows that Ash'arī – regardless of his distinct terminology – also believed that God, whose quiddity and existence are identical, is both distinct from all contingent quiddities and manifests Himself in them.[51]

At the core of Taftāzānī's argument against *waḥdat al-wujūd*, Kūrānī suggested, is a confusion of pure, quiddity-less existence with the universal concept of existence that is true of both the Necessary Existent and the contingent realities. When Sufis identify God with *wujūd muṭlaq* they identify Him with quiddity-less and unqualified existence, not with the abstracted universal "existence" that only exists outside the mind within

49 Ibid., 243. The relevant passage can be found in Ṭūsī, *Sharḥ al-Ishārāt* (Tehran: Maṭbaʿat al-Ḥaydarī, 1377/1958–1379/1959), III, 388–389.
50 Kūrānī, *Itḥāf al-dhakī*, 244.
51 Ibid., 244–245.

particular instances. This pure existence is necessary by virtue of itself and is an "individual" (*shakhṣ*) and "concretized" (*muta'ayyan*), but it is nevertheless not a "particular" (*juz'ī*), for a particular is an instance of a more general quiddity, whereas Pure Existence is *sui generis*. Pure Existence is also not a universal, for it has no instances (if we were to suppose, counterfactually, that there are two instances of Pure Existence then we would see that there is no difference between these supposed instances to justify the claim that they are *different* instances).[52]

Having made this clarification, Kūrānī claimed that it is easy to dismantle Taftāzānī's arguments. Taftāzānī objected, for example, that absolute existence cannot be identical to the Necessary Existent because the former is a universal that is true of a plurality of things whereas the latter is one and unique. However, this objection does not get off the ground if we take "absolute existence" to be a unique and concrete entity. On this account, there is no plurality of existences (*lā takaththura fī l-wujūdāt*). There are instances of existence only if "existence" is understood in the sense of *mawjūdiyya,* that is, the common abstracted concept of "existentiality" that is true of both the Necessary Existent and contingent entities.[53]

As mentioned in the previous section, Taftāzānī attributed to the pseudo-Sufis the argument that God cannot be a specific existence (*wujūd khāṣṣ*) because such a specific existence would be dependent on absolute existence and hence would not be necessary-of-existence by itself. This, he claimed, gets things the wrong way round. Absolute existence, like any common universal, would not exist if it were not for specific existences. It is indeed absurd to suppose that absolute existence has no instances, but this is simply because one of its instances, namely God, is necessary. Kūrānī again replied that this objection rests on the mistaken assumption that absolute existence (*wujūd muṭlaq*) is the same as common existence (*wujūd 'āmm*). Sufis mean by absolute existence concrete existence with no qualification. When they claim that a specific existence is dependent on *wujūd muṭlaq* this should be understood as follows: Unqualified, pure existence is a concrete entity in the extramental world. Any specific existence is on this account a qualification of this unqualified existence, and a qualification presupposes that which it qualifies (*wa-kullu qaydin fa-huwa amrun lāḥiqun lā budda lahu min amrin sābiqin huwa mā lā qayda fīhi*). By contrast, Taftāzānī mistakenly took the relation between *wujūd muṭlaq* and *wujūd khāṣṣ* to be the relation between universal and

[52] Ibid., 245–246.
[53] Ibid., 248.

particular and on that basis pressed the point that the universal only exists within the particular.[54]

Taftāzānī argued that it is not contradictory to say "Existence is a nonexistent" (*al-wujūdu ma'dūmun*). In fact, he added, philosophers and theologians agree that "existence" is a concept of "second intention" that does not have a correlate in the extramental world. Kūrānī countered that something is nonexistent (*ma'dūm*) when its existence (*wujūd*) is negated. To negate the existence of existence is a straightforward contradiction.[55] The appeal to the agreement of philosophers is, he added, to no avail once a position has been established rationally, religiously, and mystically. In any case, the agreement of philosophers is that the existence that is common to the Necessary and the contingents is a second-intention, not that quiddity-less unqualified existence is a second-intention.[56]

To sum up, Kūrāni repeated once again that the rejection of *waḥdat al-wujūd* by both theologians such as Taftāzānī and by other mystics such as 'Alā' al-Dawla al-Simnānī is based on a conflation between the universal concept of existence (*wujūd mushtarak*) and quiddity-less existence (*wujūd mujarrad*), both often being called *wujūd muṭlaq*. Once the different senses are heeded, it becomes easy – or so Kūrānī claimed – to dispel the objections of such people to *waḥdat al-wujūd*.[57]

Was Kūrānī developing a novel interpretation of *waḥdat al-wujūd*, or was he defending an already established interpretation? Perhaps the answer to this question is not hard and fast, as the very fact of defending a received doctrine against new challenges may involve subtle changes of emphases and even substantial modifications of certain points. But there can nevertheless be little doubt that Kūrānī was defending the view that Taftāzānī had presented and condemned in the fourteenth century. Despite Kūrānī's suggestions to the contrary, Taftāzānī was clearly not guilty of simply confusing the concept and reality of existence. He had

54 Ibid., 248.

55 Kūrānī did not justify the premise that something is *ma'dūm* when its *wujūd* is negated, and it would presumably be rejected by Taftāzānī in favor of, for example, "something is *ma'dūm* when its *wujūd* in the extramental world (*fī-l-khārij*) is negated," and it is not clear that it is a straightforward contradiction to negate *wujūd fī l-khārij* of *wujūd*. Kūrānī's argument also appears to fall afoul of the distinction that he is otherwise keen on emphasizing between the concept and reality of existence. Is it self-contradictory to say that the *concept* of existence has no correlate in the extramental world apart from the entities of which it is true? It would seem not (as otherwise the concept of existence would be a necessary existent), but this is presumably exactly what Taftāzānī claimed.

56 Kūrānī, *Itḥāf al-dhakī*, 249.

57 Ibid., 250.

explicitly stated that when the "pseudo-Sufis" were faced with the objection that existence is a universal concept in the mind they responded that it is rather a concrete individual in the extramental world – and this is indeed precisely how Kūrānī responded. He wrote:

What he [Taftāzānī] reported in answer to the objection when he said "They reply that it [absolute existence] is a single individual that exists with an existence that is its own self and that the multiplicity of existents is due to [multiple] relations [to Absolute Existence], not due to a multiplicity of existences..." is a correct response.[58]

The pivotal difference was rather that Taftāzānī – like numerous theologians and philosophers before and after – thought that it is simply nonsense to speak of "the reality of existence," that is, pure existence that is not the existence of *something*, and was unimpressed by the philosophers' identification of God's quiddity and God's existence.[59] It is clearly not the case that Taftāzānī was condemning one view and Kūrānī defending another.

Kūrānī's works are also replete with approving quotations from the canonical line of Sufi monists: Ibn ʿArabī himself, Qūnawī, Farghānī, Qāshānī, Fenārī, Mahāʾimī, and Jāmī.[60] This is not to say that he was "unoriginal." His detailed refutation of Taftāzānī appears not to have been simply lifted from previous authors. He was also on occasion willing to signal his departure from other interpreters of Ibn ʿArabī on certain points. For example, he took Jāmī to task for denying that Absolute Existence is "concretized" (*mutaʿayyan*) by itself, and he cited passages from Ibn ʿArabī that suggest otherwise.[61] Furthermore, his emphasis on reconciling mystical monism, Avicennan philosophy, and the traditionalist Ashʿarism of *al-Ibāna* was certainly distinctive and invites comparisons with the synthesis of mysticism, philosophy and Shiism worked out by the Iranian scholar Mullā Ṣadrā Shīrāzī, who died when Kūrānī was nineteen.[62] But whereas Mullā Ṣadrā's synthesis proved highly

58 Ibid., 247.

59 Taftāzānī, *Sharḥ al-Maqāṣid*, I, 76 (ll. 11–14).

60 See, for example, Kūrānī, *Itḥāf al-dhakī*, 180 (Qūnawī), 182 (Mahāʾimī), 182 (Fenārī), 183 (Ibn ʿArabī), 194 (Farghānī), 201 (Qāshānī), 232 (Jāmī).

61 Kūrānī, *al-Taḥrīrāt al-bāhira ʿalā l-Durra al-fākhira* (MS: Princeton University Library: Yahuda 4049), fols. 5b–7b.

62 Much has been written on Mullā Ṣadrā's life and philosophy. For two good general surveys, see F. Rahman, *The Philosophy of Mulla Sadra (Sadr al-Din al-Shirazi)* (Albany: SUNY Press, 1975) and S. Rizvi, *Mullā Ṣadrā Shīrāzī: His Life and Works and the Sources for Safavid Philosophy* (Oxford and New York: Oxford University Press on behalf of the University of Manchester, 2007).

influential, especially since the nineteenth century, Kūrānī's proved less enduring. As mentioned in the previous chapter, his works exerted a strong influence on Shāh Waliyullāh in the eighteenth century and Maḥmūd al-Ālūsī in the early nineteenth. Even in the late nineteenth century, Kūrānī was still considered by a prominent Indian scholar to have been the "renewer" (*mujaddid*) at the end of the eleventh Islamic century and the beginning of the twelfth.[63] But his works fell into oblivion thereafter, perhaps because of the rising tide of antimonist sentiments in Sunni religious circles in the twentieth century. (Had the antiphilosophical and antimystical trends of Safavid Iran emerged victorious in the modern period chances are that Mullā Ṣadrā would have been as little known today as Kūrānī is.) It is only in recent years that Kūrānī's works have begun to be edited and printed, though his magnum opus – his lengthy commentary on Qushāshī's creedal poem – remains unpublished and still awaits serious study. The preceding discussion and those of the previous chapter strongly suggest that it would be worthwhile to rediscover the writings of this scholar – surely one of the giants of Islamic intellectual history in the seventeenth century.

Nābulusī's Defense of *Waḥdat al-Wujūd*

The death of Kūrānī in Medina in 1690, and the death of his star pupil Muḥammad b. ʿAbd al-Rasūl Barzinjī in the following year, left the Damascene scholar and Naqshbandī mystic ʿAbd al-Ghanī al-Nābulusī as undoubtedly the most prominent advocate of *waḥdat al-wujūd* in the Arab provinces of the Ottoman Empire. His major exposition and defense of the doctrine is his *al-Wujūd al-ḥaqq wa l-khiṭāb al-ṣidq*, completed in March 1693. The work has been superbly edited by Bakri Aladdin, with a thorough introduction and helpful indexes, including an index of works cited by Nābulusī. It is noteworthy that Nābulusī did not explicitly cite Kūrānī, even though it can be established that he was familiar with Kūrānī's commentary on Burhānpūrī's *al-Tuḥfa al-mursala* and helped himself to some passages from it.[64] As mentioned in the previous chapter, the relationship between the two mystics appears not to have been

[63] Muḥammad Shams al-Ḥaqq ʿAẓīmābādī (d. 1911), *ʿAwn al-maʿbūd Sharḥ sunan Abī Dāʾūd* (Delhi: 1323/1905), IV, 181 (ll. 25–26). Quoted in Azra, *The Origins of Islamic Reformism in Southeast Asia*, 18.

[64] For example, two passages in Kūrānī, *Itḥāf al-dhakī*, 190 (l. 10–13) and 196 (l. 17)–197 (l. 11) are reproduced literally in Nābulusī's work; see Nābulusī, *al-Wujūd al-ḥaqq*, 85 (l. 3–6) and 171 (l. 1–18).

particularly cordial, at least not after Nābulusī in 1678 sent Kūrānī a letter with objections to the latter's views on the creation of human acts.

Nābulusī's style is somewhat different from Kūrānī's. The latter's careful prose tends toward the ponderous and repetitive – even obvious premises of an argument tend to be spelled out, and claims and qualifications are constantly reiterated. It is with some justice that one seventeenth-century scholar complained of "tedious repetition" in Kūrānī's writings.[65] Nābulusī's style is more audacious and smooth, and he regularly added often lengthy poems that express a point he had just made – poems by himself or by earlier mystical poets such as Ibn al-Fāriḍ or ʿAfīf al-Dīn al-Tilimsānī (d. 1291). (Kūrānī apparently never composed a line of verse.) Nābulusī also appears to have been the more temperamental of the two – his claims are often expressed more boldly and his polemic against Taftāzānī is somewhat sharper in tone.

Nābulusī's emphases also do not always align with those of Kūrānī. He was less invested in reconciling mystical monism with the traditionalist Ashʿarism of *al-Ibāna,* perhaps because he belonged to the Ḥanafī school of law that traditionally adhered to Māturīdī rather than Ashʿarī theology. His discussion is also less philosophically involved than Kūrānī's. He did cite philosophically inclined authors such as Shams al-Dīn al-Iṣfahānī (d. 1348) and Jalāl al-Dīn al-Dawānī, but only their less demanding works that are known to have been taught in Damascus in Nābulusī's time, not the more advanced works cited by Kūrānī such as Avicenna's *al-Shifāʾ*, Naṣīr al-Dīn al-Ṭūsī's commentary on Avicenna's *Ishārāt*, or Dawānī's gloss on ʿAlī al-Qūshjī's commentary on Ṭūsī's *Tajrīd*.[66]

There are also indications of substantial differences on some minor points. As mentioned previously, Kūrānī took issue with Jāmī's

[65] Ṣāliḥ al-Maqbalī (d. 1696), *al-ʿAlam al-shāmikh fī tafḍīl al-ḥaqq ʿalā l-ābā wa-l-mashāyikh* (Sanaa: Maktabat al-jīl al-jadīd, 2009) 437 (l. 5). Maqbalī was a traditionalist Zaydī in the tradition of Ibn al-Wazīr and, later, Ibn al-Amīr and Shawkānī. As such, his positions tend to be close to those of modern Salafism. Unlike modern scholars who wish to cast Kūrānī as a "reformist" and "neo-Sufi," Maqbalī was very critical of Kūrānī and Kūrānī's student Barzinjī, denouncing their position on Ibn ʿArabī and *waḥdat al-wujūd*; see, e.g., pp. 70–72, 437–438, 697.

[66] Nābulusī quoted Iṣfahānī's commentary on Bayḍāwī's *Ṭawāliʿ al-anwār* and Dawānī's commentary on *al-ʿAqāʾid al-ʿAḍudiyya*; see Nābulusī, *al-Wujūd al-ḥaqq*, 25, 59, 69, 98, 129, 216. The former work was taught by Ibrāhīm al-Fattāl (d. 1687) to the biographer Muḥibbī; see Muḥibbī, *Khulāṣat al-athar*, I, 52 (l. 23). The latter work was taught by ʿUthmān al-Qaṭṭān (d. 1704) to the chronicler Ibn Kannān al-Ṣāliḥī (d. 1740), see Ibn Kannān al-Ṣāliḥī, *al-Ḥawādith al-yawmiyya,* 84. Fattāl and Qaṭṭān were, along with Nābulusī, students of Mullā Maḥmūd Kurdī, the scholar mentioned in Chapter 1 as having introduced to Damascus new Persianate works on the rational sciences.

statement that Absolute Existence is not "concretized" (*muta'ayyan*) by itself, whereas Nābulusī cited Jāmī's statement without comment.[67] There are also some interesting variations in Sufi authorities quoted by Nābulusī and Kūrānī. For example, the former was fond of quoting 'Abd al-Karīm al-Jīlī, whereas the latter appears not to have done so in any of his works – and presumably not by coincidence because his master Qushāshī had written a treatise critical of certain ideas of Jīlī's, prompting Nābulusī to write a riposte.[68] Such differences – intriguing as they are – will not be pursued in the present context, and they should not obscure the fact that Nābulusī and Kūrānī both stood firmly in the monist tradition of Ibn 'Arabī and Qūnawī. Both regularly cited previous writers in this tradition without any hint of disapproval: Ibn 'Arabī himself, Qūnawī, Farghānī, Qāshānī, and Jāmī.[69] Both were committed to defending the doctrine of *waḥdat al-wujūd* against the criticisms of theologians such as Taftāzānī. Both invoked the Islamic philosophers in support of the view that God is identical with pure existence. Both believed that God manifests Himself in phenomenal forms and on that basis rejected figurative reinterpretation of apparent anthropomorphisms in the Quran and hadith. Both stressed the dangers of overreliance on reason at the expense of revelation and mystic "unveiling."

Nābulusī's work begins with a series of clarifications aimed at correcting what he saw as standard misunderstandings of the doctrine of *waḥdat al-wujūd* by exoteric scholars. We defenders of the doctrine, Nābulusī explained, do not believe that God is identical to existents (*mawjūdāt*) but to existence (*wujūd*). The distinction between existence and existents is accordingly foundational for avoiding misunderstandings. Nābulusī wrote:

> Know that the difference between existence and existents is something necessary and certain, for existents are many and different, whereas existence is one without differentiation or multiplicity and is, for us, a single reality that is not divisible and multiple despite the multiplicity of existents.[70]

In what is clearly an argument similar to that attributed to "pseudo-Sufis" by Taftāzānī, Nābulusī argued that existence cannot be an attribute

[67] Nābulusī, *al-Wujūd al-ḥaqq*, 140–141.

[68] Ibid., 212, 215, 251 (Jīlī's *Sharḥ Risalat al-khalwa*), 172 (Jīlī's *Marātib al-wujūd*). The treatise in which Nābulusī responded to Qushāshī's criticisms of Jīlī is entitled *al-Kashf wa l-bayān 'an asrār al-adyān*; for an extant copy, see Mach, *Catalogue*, nr. 2801.

[69] Nābulusī, *al-Wujūd al-ḥaqq*, 25 (Jāmī), 56 (Farghānī), 140 (Jāmī), 141–146 (Qūnawī), 235 (n2) (Qāshānī).

[70] Nābulusī, *al-Wujūd al-ḥaqq*, 19.

of God, for this would mean that God is composite and dependent on something else (viz. existence) and as such He would not be a Necessary Existent. Furthermore, God is radically different from creation, and this would not be the case if He were one of many things that have the attribute of existence. If God exists but does not have the attribute of existence, then He must be existence itself. If God were not existence, He would be a specific qualification (*qayd*) or delimitation (*ḥadd*) of existence, but the latter is impossible since it would imply that God is (1) composite, (2) not necessarily existent, and (3) similar to created things. Hence, God must be identical to existence and must be "absolute" or "unqualified" (*muṭlaq*) by any determination or form.[71]

The very fact that Absolute Existence is entirely free of any qualification or delimitation and is entirely unlike anything else means that He cannot be the object of human conception or perception. Anything that humans conceive or perceive is rather a particular qualification or delimitation of Divine Existence. Nābulusī wrote:

> The intelligible and sensible existents are confined to those that are known by reason or the senses. All of these are created in time, since they can be observed by the mind and senses to change and alter, and what changes and alters is created in time without any doubt. As for the Creator, uncreated and most High, He is outside both divisions – the intelligible and the sensible – and is beyond both, and there is nothing at all in common between Him and any of these things in any respect. As for our acquaintance with Him – implied by our being Muslim and believing in Him and obeying Him – this is directed at His epiphanies and appearances in the form of every intelligible and sensible form, without making any differentiation between His appearing in one form and His appearing in another – for all are for us epiphanies in [delimited] forms.[72]

In other words, God is accessible to humans only when He manifests Himself in phenomenal form. Nābulusī took rational theologians to task for their assumption that God is just one particular among many that partake of the universal attribute of existence, and that it is possible to differentiate God from other existents and thus attain a determinate conception or mental idea of God. We cannot, argued Nābulusī, have mental conceptions or ideas of God. Any human conception or idea is created and, as such, utterly unlike the Uncreated. Without any similarity at all between a human idea and God Himself, what, asked Nābulusī, made the idea an idea of God? This would be like a person having a mental image of water and yet claiming that it represents a stone.[73]

71 Ibid., 23, 31.
72 Ibid., 39.
73 Ibid., 75.

The line of argument is curiously similar to that of Nābulusī's younger British contemporary Bishop Berkeley (1685–1753) for the impossibility of having an idea of matter.[74]

Nābulusī noted that the term "the party of existence" (*al-firqa al-wujūdiyya*), was sometimes applied disparagingly to mystical monists – the term is used in ʿAlāʾ al-Dīn al-Bukhārī's diatribe against Ibn ʿArabī and his followers, and repeated by later Ḥanafī Turkish critics with a broadly "Kāḍīzādelī" orientation.[75] Nābulusī turned the tables on such critics, accusing them of being worshippers of their own delimited mental images and conceptions of God, and he accordingly called them "the party of imagining and conceptualization" (*al-ṭāʾifa al-khayāliyya al-taṣawwuriyya*).[76] By refusing to equate God with pure, unqualified existence, such critics are committed to the view that God is one of many entities that exists; that He is similar to other entities in some ways (e.g., He exists and they exist); and that He differs from other entities in other ways (e.g., He is a necessary existent whereas they are contingent existents); and that He, like other entities, can be the object of conception and predication – thereby betraying God's utter transcendence and sheer incommensurability with anything that may be conceived or perceived. Nābulusī wrote:

> Know that one of the false accusations of exoteric scholars against the mystic knowers of God is that they call them "the party of existence" (*al-firqa al-wujūdiyya*)... You see one of them avoiding the belief that the true existence by which everything is existent – i.e. is judged to be existent by reason – is God, and believing instead that a mental image that his mind has fashioned and an idea that he has conceived within himself is God.[77]

One might wonder how Nābulusī reconciled this accusation with the aforementioned principle that God is accessible to humans only insofar as He manifests Himself in delimited forms that we conceive and perceive. If God is entirely inaccessible to us apart from His epiphanies in the phenomenal and intelligible world, then one would think that we must all be "worshippers of mental images," not only the antimonist theologians. Nābulusī did not directly address such an objection, but he appears to have believed that the monist mystics carefully avoid equating

[74] G. Berkeley, *Principles of Human Knowledge*, part 1, par. 8. In G. Berkeley, *Principles of Human Knowledge and Three Dialogues*, edited by H. Robinson (Oxford: Oxford University Press, 1996).

[75] Bukhārī, *Faḍīḥat al-mulḥidīn*, 3; Dāvūd Ḳārṣī, *Sharḥ al-Qaṣīda al-Nūniyya*, 17.

[76] Nābulusī, *al-Wujūd al-ḥaqq*, 72.

[77] Ibid., 63.

the ultimate object of their devotion with any particular mental image or intelligible conception. These images and conceptions are avenues unto God, but mystics do not claim that these images and conceptions resemble God in any way and are uniquely appropriate to Him. The theologians, by comparison, firmly identify – or so Nābulusī claimed – the object of their devotion with certain ideas and not with others. Monist mystics are not guilty of the same offense when they identify God with Absolute Existence because, for Nābulusī, we do not have an idea of pure, unqualified existence at all. It is simply the designation that best captures the fact that God is radically different from anything that we conceive or perceive but at the same time is the ground or mainstay (*qiwām*) of everything that we conceive or perceive.

> If God most High were not existence then it would follow that He is one of the sensible or intelligible forms that subsist by virtue of existence, and this contradicts His being unqualified and unlike created things . . . It therefore must be the case that what we mean by Him most High is what is meant by the term "existence" if it is not qualified in relation to all sensible and intelligible existents and if it is said that these [existents] become existent by it. This is why we use the term "existence" of Him.[78]

Nābulusī's replies to Taftāzānī's critique are quite similar to those of Kūrānī before him, though with some variation in emphasis and tone. He distinguished the pure, unqualified existence that is God from the universal concept of existence that exists extramentally only insofar as its particular instances exist. He noted that exoteric theologians tend to use the term "absolute existence" (*wujūd muṭlaq*) exclusively of the universal concept and on that basis deride the monist mystics' equation of God with absolute existence. This, noted Nābulusī, is at the heart of Taftāzānī's criticisms of the idea that God is absolute existence. "All his discourse from this point on," Nābulusī wrote, "is based on confining absolute existence to the universal mental concept."[79]

Like Kūrānī before him, Nābulusī argued that, contrary to Taftāzānī's assertion, the identification of God with absolute existence does not conflict with religion or reason. Religiously, the view that God is utterly transcendent and incommensurable with anything that we conceive and perceive is preferable to Taftāzānī's own view that would make of God one of many existents who is differentiated from other existents by

[78] Ibid., 37.
[79] Ibid., 123.

being necessarily existent.[80] Rationally, the view that God's existence is not superadded to God's quiddity but identical to it is fully defensible. Indeed even mainstream exoteric theologians, Nābulusī added, concede that existence is not a real, superadded attribute and that it is only attributed "mentally" or "virtually" to the divine self.[81] As with Kūrānī's criticisms of Taftāzānī, Nābulusī's arguably do not go to heart of the matter. Yes, theologians such as Taftāzānī held that existence is a mental predicate and not a real attribute, but they meant this principle to apply across the board, not just to God. They did not intend this to mean that God is pure existence whereas other existents are not pure existence – the whole idea of an existence in the extramental world that is not the existence of *something* struck them as incoherent, like claiming that there is pure movement that is not the movement of some thing or pure knowledge that is not the knowledge of some thing. Such a position is stated quite clearly by Nābulusī's antimonist Moroccan contemporary Ibn Yaʿqūb al-Wallālī in his commentary on Taftāzānī's *Maqāṣid*.[82]

It was seen in the previous section that Kūrānī argued, against Taftāzānī, that it is a contradiction to say that existence does not exist. Nābulusī adopted the same argument and concluded: (1) existence exists necessarily and (2) there can be no such thing as contingent or created existence (*wujūd ḥādith*).[83] To suppose that there is contingent existence is to suppose that existence can begin to exist after not existing, but this is absurd. Existence exists necessarily and cannot come to be or pass away. The supposition that existence divides into necessary existence and contingent existence has a number of unpalatable consequences. It would imply that existents exist by a created existence and not by God – in other words that God is not the direct support or mainstay of things. Furthermore, one could ask what maintains this created existence in existence. It is surely not existent by virtue of itself, and so the only acceptable answer would be that contingent existence exists by virtue of God. But this makes contingent existence an idle wheel that fulfills no function whatsoever. We might as well, pressed Nābulusī, dispense with it altogether and hold that there are only existents (*mawjūdāt*) and God/Existence (*wujūd*), with the latter being the mainstay of the former.[84]

80 Ibid., 126.
81 Ibid., 126–127.
82 Ibn Yaʿqūb, *Falsafat al-tawḥīd*, 134 (ll. 6–13 [central rubric]).
83 Nābulusī, *al-Wujūd al-ḥaqq*, 153–155.
84 Ibid., 33, 51–54.

Nābulusī admitted that human reason willy-nilly attributes existence to what it perceives and conceives, but he insisted that this is an illusion that is unmasked in mystical experience. He wrote:

Know that it is reason that relates existence to things, making it dependent on things just as all attributes are dependent on what they inhere in. But in fact matters are not like this. Rather the quiddities of all things – intelligible and sensible – are dependent on existence and subsist in it while existence is not dependent on them and does not subsist in them.[85]

The idea that God is the existence of things had, of course, been condemned by earlier critics such as Ibn Taymiyya, Simnānī, Taftāzānī, ʿAlāʾ al-Dīn al-Bukhārī and Biqāʿī. Among other objections, such critics asked about the existence of excrement and other impurities – is God really to be thought of as the existence of these as well?[86] Nābulusī was unapologetic and challenged such critics: Do they themselves not believe that God created excrement and impurity and that He maintains them in existence? What is objectionable in saying that excrement and impurity, like all phenomenal forms, are distinct from God but grounded in God's existence rather than their own independent and created existence?[87]

In any case, Nābulusī thought that such criticisms were aimed at the view that contingent existents exist by the existence of God and not by a created, contingent existence. This view Nābulusī considered partial and incomplete, and he associated it with more philosophically inclined defenders of ontological monism. Such defenders identify God with absolute existence and deny contingent existences, but their reason leads them to believe that all intelligible and perceivable things exist by God's existence (*fa-l-jamīʿu ʿindahum mawjūdun bi-wujūdihi taʿāla lā bi-wujūdin ghayra wujūdihi taʿāla*).[88] The "verifiers" (*muḥaqqiqūn*) among the mystics realize that contingent existents do not exist at all, that nothing exists but the one divine existence. He wrote:

All things insofar as they are sensible and intelligible quiddities do not in fact exist and have not smelled the whiff of existence at all apart from the epiphany and unveiling of the one absolute true existence in it and to it. Rational knowledge

85 Ibid., 149.

86 Ibn Taymiyya, *Ḥaqīqat madhhab al-ittiḥādiyyīn*, in *Majmūʿ fatāwā Shaykh al-Islām Aḥmad Ibn Taymiyya,* edited by ʿAbd al-Raḥmān al-Najdī (Riyad: no publisher, 1381/1961), II, 134–285, at 142; Landolt, "Simnani on wahdat al-wujud," 99; Taftāzānī, *Sharḥ al-Maqāṣid*, I, 73 (l. 29)–74 (l. 1) [Shams al-Dīn edition I, 175 (l. 5)]; Bukhārī, *Faḍīḥat al-mulḥidīn*, 3 (l. 11); Biqāʿī, *Tanbīh al-ghabī*, 123.

87 Nābulusī, *al-Wujūd al-ḥaqq*, 123.

88 Ibid., 212.

(*idrāk ʿaqlī*) judges these to exist due to this aforementioned epiphany... but it does not know what it sees.[89]

The distinction here seems to be similar to the one advanced by Nābulusī's contemporary, the Khalwatī mystic from Aleppo Qāsim al-Khānī, who insisted that it is one thing to affirm "the unity of existence" and another to experience this unity first-hand (*shuhūd waḥdat al-wujūd*). The former theoretical assertion could also be found among heretics and antinomians, whereas the latter experience was the outcome of proper ascetic and spiritual exertion.[90] This distinction between *waḥdat al-wujūd* and *shuhūd waḥdat al-wujūd* adds an interesting twist to the hackneyed distinction between *waḥdat al-wujūd* and *wahdat al-shuhūd* in the secondary literature concerning Sufism.

Nābulusī's views here might at first sight appear inconsistent with what he wrote in earlier parts of the work. In a number of earlier passages, he insisted that mystics do not deny that there are existents. For example, he wrote: "Know that we do not say that all things – perceptible and intelligible – are non-existents. Rather we say that they are existents by the existence of God most High, not by another existence apart from God's existence."[91] How does this square with his assertion that the "verifying" Sufis realize the nothingness of all beside the one True Existence? The passage just quoted should be read alongside other passages such as the following two:

[1] We are in agreement with all those of reason in affirming the existence of sensible and intelligible things without any difference between us and them. But apart from the perspective of reason and sense, nothing at all exists alongside absolute existence; indeed there is not even reason and sense in the view of the people of verification. This is why we say that our knowledge is above the station of reason since it is beyond reason.[92]

[2] There is no existence except Absolute, Divine Existence. What is other than Him is pure non-existence (*ʿadam maḥḍ*)... and has nothing of existence and nothing of the whiff of existence. Rather, the aforementioned True Existence is the One who manifests Himself by Himself to Himself in all of this. This is the direct experience (*mashhad*) of the accomplished verifiers (*al-muḥaqqiqīn*) among the people of God most High, insofar as they are accomplished verifiers in divine knowledge. Insofar as they are rational and have reason with which to reason and senses with which to perceive, their experience is the same as that of other rational

89 Ibid., 129.
90 Khānī, *al-Sayr wa l-sulūk*, 62–63 (Shāfiʿī edition), 122 (ʿAbd al-Fattāḥ edition).
91 Nābulusī, *al-Wujūd al-ḥaqq*, 47.
92 Ibid., 203.

people who are ignorant and heedless [of mystical truth]. They thus know what others know but others do not know what they know.[93]

Nābulusī clearly wanted to differentiate between what monist Sufis espouse in a sober state and what they "verify" during mystical experience. In a sober state, they affirm the plurality of existents like everyone else but merely insist that these existents do not exist by virtue of their own distinct existences but rather by virtue of the one divine existence. In mystical experience, they realize that entities have "not smelled the whiff of existence" and that all but God is a vapid illusion.

Nābulusī's point may not have been original – the idea that quiddities have not "smelled the whiff of existence" is topical in monist-mystical literature – but what is striking about it is that he squarely stated that the illusion of a plurality of existents is central to religious-legal obligation. The entire edifice of religious law is, he conceded, based on reason and the senses being confronted with a plurality of distinct existents. He wrote:

This second existence that we have called "created in time" (*ḥādith*) in accordance with the view of reason alone, and which we make an attribute of things, just as common believers do, is the basis (*manāṭ*) of religious law and judgments in this world and the next. There is no doubt that all the rulings of the law are imposed on the servant and he is responsible for them in view of the prevalence of this illusion (*wahm*).[94]

He reiterated the point in a later passage:

The possession by things of the attribute of existence is what reason knows. Religious-legal responsibility (*taklīf*) is imposed in consideration of this rational view that existence is an attribute of things, and on this basis have been erected the rulings and details of religious laws, as has been mentioned. It is thus incumbent to affirm this [i.e., the possession by things of the attribute of existence] in general and affirm that it means that God has made things exist, as reason and the senses tell the commonality of mankind. As for the spiritual elite (*ahl al-khuṣūṣ*), they believe that God creates things in the sense of determining them (*taqdīrihā*) not causing them to exist (*ījādihā*), since existence is for them a single reality distinct from things and things do not possess it as an attribute.[95]

In such passages, Nābulusī came very close to saying that the "verifying" mystics see through the falsity of the basic premise of religious law. This is nothing if not daring. Indeed, toward the end of the work Nābulusī wrote that some groups that invoke Ibn ʿArabī in his time are led to

93 Ibid., 219.
94 Ibid., 56.
95 Ibid., 104.

heresy and antinomianism (*zandaqa* and *ilḥād*) precisely because they refuse to take seriously the plurality of existent entities and claim to be in a state of "seeing everything as one" (*jamʿ*).[96] Yet, he himself stated that "verifying" Sufis also come to the realization that there are no existent entities at all, only Existence. It appears that Nābulusī thought that "verifying" Sufis can only experience this truth momentarily, and that outside their states of mystic ecstasy, when their reason and senses are fully functional, they must affirm the illusion of plurality like everyone else. By contrast, antinomian Sufis deceive themselves into thinking that they can maintain the insights gained in direct mystical experience after they – as they must – return to their senses. He wrote:

> Abandoning everything that is other than God is not possible at all, especially with [the possession of] reason and the senses. Each one of them [i.e., the antinomian Sufis] knows himself and others and is aware of what he eats and drinks, and knows other people, and seeks worldly fortune and the satisfaction of his instincts and desires . . . and all of these are created entities that subsist in God.[97]

Nābulusī was certainly not condoning antinomianism, but it seems far-fetched to sum up his enterprise as that of effecting a novel reconciliation between Ibn ʿArabī-inspired mysticism and religious law. Rather, he was boldly expressing one of the most controversial aspects of mystical monism and drawing a very fine line indeed between ultimate mystic "verification" and sheer antinomianism.

Nābulusī's point that overreliance on reason tends to magnify the importance of quiddities and belittle the importance of existence, and that the truth of the matter is that quiddities are as naught and only existence exists, has led some observers to suggest that he was echoing debates in Safavid Persia on whether existence or quiddity is "primary" (*aṣīl*), and that he must somehow have been influenced by Mullā Ṣadrā Shīrāzī (the major exponent of the "primacy of existence") even though he never mentioned or cited him.[98] Though perhaps understandable, the suggestion is not sustainable. Mullā Ṣadrā in fact rejected the formula of *waḥdat al-wujūd* expounded by Kūrānī and Nābulusī, a fact that was deemphasized by the influential modern scholars Henry Corbin and Seyyed Hossein Nasr who, presumably due to their own sympathies for "perennial philosophy," were inclined to deemphasize the disagreements between

[96] Ibid., 256–257.
[97] Ibid., 250.
[98] Bakri Aladdin in his introduction to Nābulusī, *al-Wujūd al-ḥaqq*, 58.

Mullā Ṣadrā and the later followers of Ibn ʿArabī.[99] It has already been mentioned that Mullā Ṣadrā reproduced – without acknowledgment – Taftāzānī's attack on the "pseudo-Sufi" identification of God with absolute existence, and clearly endorsed the very criticisms that Kūrānī and Nābulusī were so concerned to refute. In other passages too, Mullā Ṣadrā explicitly distanced himself from the view that would later be defended by Kūrānī and Nābulusī. For example, he wrote:

> A group have maintained that true existence is one individual which is the essence of God most High and the quiddities are realities whose existence consists in their being related to Necessary Existence and connected to Him most High. For them, "existence" (*wujūd*) is one individual, and "existent" (*mawjūd*) is a universal that has numerous instances, viz. the existents. And they attribute this position to the spiritual tasting of the theosophists (*dhawq al-mutaʾallihīn*). I say: There are a number of objections to this...[100]

The target of Mullā Ṣadrā's critique was Dawānī whose works were cited with approval by both Kūrānī and Nābulusī.[101] There is no need to speculatively posit indirect and unmentioned sources for Nābulusī's views on quiddity and existence when the sources that he actually cited (especially Jāmī and Dawānī) already formulate a very similar view. The suggestion, famously expressed by Corbin, that Mullā Ṣadrā was the first philosopher to advance the thesis that existence is *aṣīl*, that is, exists extramentally, overlooks the importance of figures such as Jāmī and Dawānī – Sunni Persian thinkers who have been largely expunged from the prevalent narrative of Islamic philosophy in the Shiite Iranian scholarly circles from which Corbin derived his account.

There is also no indication that Kūrānī or Nābulusī accepted the idea that is central to Mullā Ṣadrā's metaphysics, viz. the "modularity" (*tashkīk*) of existence. Both appear to have assumed, along with older mystics in the Qūnawī tradition, that "modularity" is not characteristic of Absolute Existence. Nābulusī, for example, wrote: "Existence as is known and experienced... does not vary in being the mainstay and

99 Mullā Ṣadrā's rejection of *waḥdat al-wujūd* is noted in Rahman, *The Philosophy of Mulla Sadra*, 37–41. Sajjad Rizvi has noted the continued existence in Iran up until the nineteenth century of a strand of mystical philosophy that opposed Mullā Ṣadrā in the name of a more traditional understanding of *waḥdat al-wujūd*; see his *Mullā Ṣadrā and Metaphysics: Modulation of Being* (Abingdon and New York: Routledge, 2009), 133.

100 Mullā Ṣadrā Shīrāzī, *al-Ḥikma al-mutaʿāliya*, I, 111.

101 See T. Izutsu, *The Concept and Reality of Existence* (Tokyo: Keio Institute of Cultural and Linguistic Studies, 1971), 204.

fixation of created things. It is hence not more in some thing and less in another, nor is it stronger or weaker."[102]

Conclusion

We *do* have an idea of what a moderate reinterpretation of Ibn ʿArabī that makes his central ideas less controversial to exoteric theologians would look like. This is the reinterpretation advanced by the sixteenth-century Egyptian Sufi ʿAbd al-Wahhāb al-Shaʿrānī. As mentioned in Chapter 7, Shaʿrānī's voluminous *al-Yawāqīt wa-l-jawāhir fī bayān ʿaqāʾid al-akābir* is an exposition of creedal theology in which Ibn ʿArabī is regularly cited approvingly, though Shaʿrānī carefully omitted citing the controversial *Fuṣūṣ* or works by Qūnawī and his followers. The abstruse, philosophically influenced discussions of quiddity and existence to be found in the Qūnawī tradition are also conspicuously absent from Shaʿrānī's discussion, in favor of the more visionary aspects of Ibn ʿArabī's worldview, such as his angelology and his hierarchy of the divine names. Shaʿrānī also insisted that Ibn ʿArabī had not claimed that Pharaoh was a believer or that the torments of hellfire would eventually pass away – two theses that were defended by the Qūnawī-inspired tradition and that were regularly condemned by critics of monist mysticism. On one point, namely the issue of whether God's core attributes (such as Power, Knowledge, and Will) are superadded to the Divine Self or identical to the Divine Self, Shaʿrānī even admitted that Ibn ʿArabī's view conflicted with that of Ashʿarī theologians and carefully added that the position of the latter is preferable (*awlā*).[103] Though Shaʿrānī avoided the formula *waḥdat al-wujūd*, he did note that Ibn ʿArabī was often accused of believing that "there is no existent but God." He explained the formula as follows:

> Among the claims of critics is that the Shaykh [Ibn ʿArabī] repeatedly says in his books that there is no existent other than God. The answer is that this – assuming it is correctly attributed to him – means there is no existent that subsists by itself other than Him the Exalted. What is other than Him subsists by another, as

[102] Nābulusī, *al-Wujūd al-ḥaqq*, 30. It is also revealing that at one point when quoting (without acknowledgment) from Dāʾūd al-Qayṣarī's commentary on Ibn ʿArabī's *Fuṣūṣ*, Mullā Ṣadrā broke off the quotation just before Qayṣarī wrote that existence "does not admit of strengthening or weakening in itself" (*lā yaqbalu l-ishtidāda wa l-ḍuʿfa li-dhātihi*); compare Mullā Sadrā, *al-Ḥikma al-mutaʿāliya*, I, 415 (l. 2) with Qayṣarī, *Sharḥ Fuṣūṣ al-ḥikam*, ed. and ann. by Ḥasanzāde Āmolī (Qom: Bustān-i Kitāb, 1382/2003), I, 28 (l. 4).

[103] Shaʿrānī, *al-Yawāqīt wa l-jawāhir*, I, 73 (ll. 22–23).

indicated in the hadith "Verily everything but God is naught." Something whose reality is like this is closer to non-existence, since its existence is preceded by non-existence and, in the state of existing, wavers between existence and non-existence and is not secure in either alternative.[104]

Sha'rānī's reinterpretation makes ontological monism innocuous. It is difficult to imagine any exoteric theologian taking issue with the claims that only God exists by virtue of His own Self, whereas created things exist by virtue of something other than their own selves, or that created things are preceded by nonexistence and while existing are not secure in their existence but remain as if suspended between existence and nonexistence. This is most certainly not the thesis that Taftāzānī condemned in the fourteenth century, nor is it the thesis that Kūrānī and Nābulusī defended in the seventeenth.

On other issues too, the apologies of Kūrānī and Nābulusī differ from that of Sha'rānī. They defended the theses of "the faith of Pharaoh" and the passing away of the torments of hellfire.[105] They both accepted the Avicennan view that God's quiddity is identical with His existence and the closely related view that the Divine Essence does not have numerous and distinct superadded attributes. Their works are also full of quotations from Qūnawī, Farghānī, Tilimsānī, Qāshānī, Jīlī and Jāmī – all authorities that Sha'rānī studiously avoided quoting.

Fazlur Rahman was not wrong in suggesting that there were Sufis who attempted to dilute or explain away Ibn 'Arabī's monism, making it less objectionable to those who accepted the criticisms of the likes of Ibn Taymiyya, Taftāzānī, and 'Alā' al-Dīn al-Bukhārī. But Kūrānī and Nābulusī were most certainly not engaged in such a project. They were rather defending the Qūnawī-inspired interpretation of Ibn 'Arabī, including its most controversial aspects, and they were doing so in a region – the Arabic-speaking provinces of the Ottoman Empire – in which this interpretation had not hitherto gained much support within the *ulema* class. To be sure, both Kūrānī and Nābulusī took care to emphasize the

104 Ibid., I, 12 (ll. 1–4).

105 Nābulusī, *al-Radd al-matīn 'alā muntaqiṣ al-'ārif Muḥyī al-Dīn* (MS: British Library: Or. 1033), fols. 10a–17a (on the passing away of the torments of hell); Nābulusī, *al-Ḥadra al-unsiyya fī l-riḥla al-Qudsiyya*, edited by Akram al-'Ulabī (Beirut: al-Maṣādir, 1990), 206 (on the faith of Pharaoh); Barzinjiī, *al-Jādhib al-ghaybī min al-jānib al-gharbī*, fols. 73a–108a (on the passing away of the torments of hell) and fols. 108a–130b (on the faith of Pharaoh – note the criticism of Sha'rānī's position on fol. 111a). Barzinjī was a disciple and student of Kūrānī; his discussion, written during Kūrānī's lifetime, is replete with quotations from his teacher's writings and there can be no doubt that Kūrānī was in agreement with Barzinjī on these points.

importance of adhering to the precepts of Islamic law, and they condemned antinomianism among some Sufi groups in their time. But this was far from being a novel feature of the writings of Kūrānī and Nābulusī, neither of whom had any difficulty finding passages from earlier partisans of *waḥdat al-wujūd* and indeed from Ibn ʿArabī himself that warned against antinomianism.[106] The necessity of respecting the law was not a novel, "neo-Sufi" idea but rather a familiar refrain in writings of the most prominent advocates of *waḥdat al-wujūd* from the thirteenth century onward.

[106] Kūrānī, *Itḥāf al-dhakī*, 213–215 (quoting Ibn ʿArabī); Nābulusī, *al-Wujūd al-ḥaqq*, 251–252 (quoting al-Jīlī).

Conclusion

> The idea of dynamic Europe versus stagnating Asia is both old and well-entrenched, and it underlies much literature to the effect that Europe won the race because comparable developments in Asia were 'blocked' by this or that: both were traveling in the same direction (so it is tacitly assumed), but Europe was less encumbered than its Asian counterparts. It should be clear from what has been said so far that this approach cannot be right... Europe and the different civilizations of Asia were *all* travelling along paths of their own.
>
> – Patricia Crone

Until recently, historians assumed that the intellectual life of the *ulema* in the Ottoman Empire was moribund or stagnant. In the Turkish-speaking parts of the Empire, the cultural and intellectual florescence of the fifteenth and sixteenth centuries was supposed to have given way to a reassertion of narrow-minded religious fanaticism that destroyed observatories and put an end to the study of philosophy and natural science. In the Arabic-speaking provinces, the culture of the *ulema* was supposed to have been inward- and backward-looking, isolated not only from the West but also from intellectual currents in other parts of the Islamic world and "living off its own past."[1] Scholarly interests were supposedly confined to the religious and linguistic sciences, and even these were thought to have been cultivated in an uncompromisingly conservative and dogmatic way, assuming the form of "mere" commentaries and glosses on earlier work.

[1] The phrase is used in H. A. R. Gibb and H. Bowen, *Islamic Society and the West* (London: Oxford University Press, 1957), Vol. 1, part II, 163.

The present study has presented a very different picture of intellectual and scholarly life in the Ottoman Empire and North Africa in the seventeenth century. By no means all scholarly works took the form of commentaries and glosses, and in any case the idea that commentaries and glosses are simply uncritical explications of received views does not stand up to scrutiny. The idea of a seventeenth-century "triumph of fanaticism" in the Turkish-speaking parts of the Empire is a myth. The Arabic parts of the Empire were not isolated at all from other currents in the Islamic world. Indeed the number of Persian works that were translated into Arabic in the seventeenth century is striking: Aḥmed Müneccimbāşī translated ʿIṣām al-Dīn Isfarāyinī's treatise on figurative usage; Ṣibghatullāh Barūchī translated Gwāliyārī's *Jawāhir-i khamsah*; Tāj al-Dīn ʿUthmānī translated Jāmī's *Nafaḥāt al-uns* and Kāshifī's *Rashaḥāt ʿayn al-ḥayāt*; Tāj al-Dīn's own treatise on the principles of the Naqshbandī order was translated twice; Ādam Banūrī translated a selection of Sirhindī's letters; and Muḥammad Barzinjī translated Kāzarūnī's *al-Jānib al-gharbī*. The cosmopolitan towns of Mecca and Medina seem to have been a center for such translation activity, though the translations subsequently spread throughout the Arabic-speaking world.

In the preceding chapters, three major seventeenth-century intellectual trends among Ottoman and North African *ulema* were identified and explored. The first of these was the westward transmission by Kurdish and Azeri scholars of a range of scholarly works in the rational sciences by fifteenth- and sixteenth-century Persian scholars, along with a scholarly and didactic style that emphasized dialectic (*ādāb al-baḥth*) and "deep reading." This development had a profound influence on especially Turkish scholars of Anatolia and Istanbul. From the middle of the seventeenth century until the end of the Empire, it became usual for such scholars to trace their intellectual lineage not to fifteenth- and sixteenth-century Ottoman scholars but rather to Kurdish and Azeri figures active in the early to mid-seventeenth century and – via these – to Persian specialists in the rational sciences such as Mīrzā Jān Bāghnavī and Jalāl al-Dīn al-Dawānī. Ottoman Turkish *ulema*, rather than turning away from the study of philosophy, dialectics, and logic in a fit of "fanaticism," actually displayed an increased interest in these fields in the seventeenth and eighteenth centuries.

This development was not a matter of simply absorbing influences from the east. As shown in Chapter 2, the field of dialectics underwent important developments at the hands of Turkish-speaking Anatolian scholars such as Ḥüseyn Adanavī and Meḥmed Sāçaḳlīzāde. In Chapter 3, it was seen that another Turcophone scholar, Aḥmed Müneccimbāşī, penned a pioneering work on "the proper manner of reading" – a work that marks a shift away from the focus on teacher–student interaction in older Arabic educational manuals toward a self-conscious model of the acquisition of knowledge through close reading of texts. By the eighteenth century, there is evidence that Turkish scholarly culture had outgrown its dependence on teachers from the east. Indeed, the works of prominent eighteenth-century Turkish scholars such as Sāçaḳlīzāde and Gelenbevī themselves came to be studied and commented upon by later Kurdish scholars.

The second intellectual trend parallels the first to a striking extent. In the course of the seventeenth century, scholars from the Maghreb transmitted to Egypt and the Hejaz the works of the fifteenth-century theologian and logician Sanūsī and his North African commentators and glossators. This intellectual tradition, strangely ignored in modern scholarship, promoted radical Ashʿarism, denigrated "imitation" in matters of faith, and valorized rational theology and formal logic. It came to dominate the teaching of theology and logic at al-Azhar college in Cairo from the middle of the seventeenth century until the late nineteenth. Chapter 5 discussed Sanūsī's condemnation of "imitation" in creedal matters and his consequent insistence that ordinary believers master the basic rational arguments for the articles of faith. This was seen to have inspired a genre of popular creeds that aimed at imparting the central arguments of Ashʿarī rational theology to the commonality of believers, explicitly including illiterates and women. Chapter 6 presented some seventeenth-century Moroccan controversies elicited by Sanūsī's hostility toward "imitation": over the status of the ordinary believer who is unable to give an account of the rational justification for his or her beliefs, and over the proper understanding of the basic Islamic profession of faith, "There is no god but Allah." The chapter went on to discuss in some detail the contributions to these debates by the eminent Moroccan theologian and logician al-Ḥasan al-Yūsī. His sophisticated interventions reveal the extent to which this North African tradition of Islamic theology was intertwined with Greek-inspired formal logic, leading one eighteenth-century critic to bemoan the prominence of "theologian-logicians" in Cairo in his time.

Again, this was not merely a matter of a more central region of the Islamic world absorbing intellectual trends emanating from a more peripheral region. Eighteenth-century Egyptian scholars such as Aḥmad al-Mallawī, Aḥmad al-Damanhūrī, Aḥmad al-Jawharī, and Muḥammad al-Bulaydī in turn produced works on logic, philosophy, and rational theology that were not merely derivative and whose influence extended beyond Egypt and beyond the eighteenth century. It was precisely in the eighteenth and nineteenth centuries that the Azhar college emerged as preeminent in the Sunni, Arabic-speaking world, attracting students from far and wide (including the Maghreb). If Sanūsī's influence eventually reached the Malay Archipelago, this was largely due to the influence of eighteenth-century Egyptian scholars on students from that region such as ʿAbd al-Ṣamad Palimbānī (d. 1788) and Muḥammad Arshad Banjārī (d. 1812).[2]

The third current was the introduction of the mystical-monist outlook of Ibn ʿArabī's student Qūnawī and his Persianate epigones to the Arab lands that had hitherto kept this tradition at arm's length. This was largely the result of the influence of Khalwatī Sufis from Anatolia and Shaṭṭārī and Naqshbandī Sufis from India and Central Asia. The idea that the influence of Ibn ʿArabī-inspired mystical monism was receding in the seventeenth and eighteenth centuries, giving way to "neo-Sufi" currents, is untenable. On the contrary, Arab Sufis from the fifteenth and sixteenth centuries tended to subscribe to Ashʿarī theology and, while defending Ibn ʿArabī from the charge of heresy, often ignored, explained away, or rejected the controversial theories of his Persianate commentators and interpreters – including the theory of *waḥdat al-wujūd*. By contrast, seventeenth- and early eighteenth-century Shaṭṭārī and Naqshbandī mystics such as Ibrāhīm Kūrānī and ʿAbd al-Ghanī al-Nābulusī were much more vocal and wholehearted about espousing the most controversial ideas of Ibn ʿArabī's Persianate commentators and interpreters. Chapter 8 presented some surprising consequences of the increased influence of this tradition of mystical monism. Rather than leading to antinomianism and syncretism, it appears to have lead to an assault on established Ashʿarī and Māturīdī theology in favor of more traditionalist, near-Ḥanbalī positions on a range of issues: the status of the "imitator" in the Islamic creed; the value of rational theology; the nonliteral interpretation of apparent anthropomorphisms in the Quran and hadith; occasionalism and the creation of human acts; and the eternity of the sounds and letters of the Quran. Especially Kūrānī seems to have played an important role in rehabilitating the ideas of the fourteenth-century

[2] On these two scholars and their intellectual formation, see Azyumardi, *The Origins of Islamic Reformism in Southeast Asia*, 112–122.

Ḥanbalī purists Ibn Taymiyya and Ibn Qayyim al-Jawziyya who were in agreement with the school of Ibn ʿArabī on these points. Chapter 9 attempted to show that there is no truth to the suggestion that Kūrānī and Nābulusī were distancing themselves from the more "extravagant" and controversial aspects of the teachings of Ibn ʿArabī. On the contrary, both scholars were outspoken defenders of *waḥdat al-wujūd* against the criticisms of that idea by earlier Ashʿarī theologians such as Taftāzānī. Especially Kūrānī developed a striking defense that drew on the ideas of philosophers such as Avicenna and Dawānī, mystical monists such as Qūnawī and Jāmī, and Ḥanbalī thinkers such as Ibn Taymiyya and Ibn Qayyim al-Jawziyya.

Again, it should be emphasized that Kūrānī and Nābulusī did not merely assimilate ideas originating elsewhere. The very fact that they differed on a number of points shows that, though standing squarely in an intellectual tradition, they could reach individual conclusions on a number of issues by emphasizing various elements of this tradition at the expense of others, or by resolving tensions between earlier authorities in different ways. In turn, their influence extended well beyond the central Arab lands in later generations. Nābulusī's writings came to be widely read and studied in Turkish-speaking Anatolia and Istanbul.[3] Kūrānī's influence extended from Morocco and Istanbul to Sulawesi during his lifetime; in later centuries it appears to have been especially strong in South Asia (mostly via his influence on Shāh Waliyullāh).

These three intellectual trends were independent of each other and sometimes even at loggerheads. The keen interest in dialectics (*ādāb al-baḥth*) was much stronger among Kurdish and Turkish than among Arab *ulema*. North African scholars did not cultivate the discipline, and there is also little evidence of its influence on the writings of an antirationalist Syrian mystic such as Nābulusī. Staunchly Ashʿarī North African scholars such as al-Ḥasan al-Yūsī and Yaḥyā al-Shāwī, though by no means anti-Sufi, had little sympathy for the ideas of Ibrāhīm Kūrānī and his monist-mystical inspired attempts at rethinking Ashʿarism and reasserting the more traditionalist, pro-Ḥanbalī positions of Ashʿarī's *Ibāna*. In turn, monist mystics such as Kūrānī and Nābulusī had little sympathy with the North African Ashʿarī tradition's valorization of logic and rational theology. These were no trifling quibbles: Yūsī wrote that those who equate God with absolute existence are infidels; Shāwī accused Kūrānī of

[3] See B. Kellner-Heinkele, "ʿAbd al-Ghanī al-Nābulusī and His Turkish Disciples," *Revue d'Histoire Maghrébine* 50–60(1990): 107–112.

being a calumniating heretic; Kūrānī's student Barzinjī dismissed Sanūsī as someone who was taken seriously only in the Maghreb; Nābulusī vehemently condemned logic and the reliance on unaided reason in theological matters.

What was common to the three intellectual currents was the rhetorical emphasis on "verification" (*taḥqīq*). To be sure, the ideal was not new; Islamic scholars and mystics were called "verifiers" (*muḥaqqiqūn*) long before the seventeenth century. Nevertheless, there is evidence that each of the three intellectual traditions understood this ideal in distinct and sometimes novel ways. For the scholarly tradition brought to the Ottoman Empire by Kurdish and Azeri scholars, verification was associated with dialectic and "deep reading." For the scholarly tradition that emanated from the Maghreb, the ideal was associated with the explicit use of the argument schemes of formal logic to transcend the stage of "imitation" in matters of theology. For the Sufi tradition associated with Khalwatī, Shaṭṭārī and non-Mujaddidī Naqshbandīs, "verification" was closely related to the concepts of mystical "witnessing" and "unveiling," and was thought to support the views of Ibn ʿArabī as interpreted by his student Qūnawī and the later monist commentators on *Fuṣūṣ al-ḥikam*. The nominal ideal of "verification" might have been single, but its concrete historical manifestations were many and varied (pun intended).

In the preceding chapters, the political, social, and economic contexts of intellectual activity were largely bracketed. This was done from the conviction that it is legitimate to reconstruct self-standing narratives of intellectual history, just as political, social, and economic historians of the Ottoman Empire can legitimately go about their business while bracketing the scholarly preoccupations of the *ulema*. I believe the foregoing chapters have shown that this can be done, and that the results of doing so can be surprising and worthwhile. It should also be emphasized that the institution of the endowed madrasa or *zāwiya* gave the *ulema* an autonomous economic base, and made them less dependent on direct patronage by the political and economic elite than, say, belletrists, astrologers, and physicians. The fact that the intellectual concerns of the *ulema* enjoyed some degree of autonomy vis-à-vis the surrounding society was itself grounded in socioeconomic realities.

Having said this, once narratives of intellectual history have been established it would certainly be legitimate to ask how they relate to received narratives of political, social, and economic history. This is, of course, not a topic that can be treated exhaustively here. Moreover, there appears to be no consensus on the nature of broader developments in the seventeenth-century Ottoman Empire. Until the 1970s, the dominant position among Ottomanists was that the Empire declined on all fronts after the sixteenth century: demographically and economically as well as politically and militarily. Some still think that this picture is basically correct, but this is no longer the only or even predominant view among specialists. A number of historians have in recent decades questioned the tendency to reduce all aspects of the period after 1600 to the overarching narrative of decline. While conceding that the Empire went through serious dislocations and crises in the early decades of the seventeenth century and then again in the final decades of the eighteenth, they portray the intervening period in more nuanced and less uniformly dark colors.[4] The period witnessed the resurgence of the power of the imperial center at the time of Murad IV (r. 1623–1640) and the Köprülü viziers (1656–1683), and the artistic and literary efflorescence of the reign of Ahmed III (1703–1731).[5] The number of madrasas in the central parts of the Empire seems to have risen dramatically in the second half of the seventeenth century and the early decades of the eighteenth.[6] The same period witnessed the pioneering establishment of endowed, self-standing libraries.[7] Militarily, the Empire was expanding in the 1660s and 1670s, conquering Crete and the western part of the Ukraine. The

[4] For an insightful and wide-ranging discussion of the question of the decline of the Ottoman Empire, see C. Kafadar, "The Question of Ottoman Decline," *Harvard Middle Eastern and Islamic Review* 4 (1997–1998): 30–75. For two recent monographs that move beyond the decline narrative of Ottoman history in the seventeenth and eighteenth centuries, see S. Faroqhi, *Artisans of Empire: Crafts and Craftspeople under the Ottomans* (London: IB Tauris, 2009) and B. Tezcan, *The Second Ottoman Empire: Political and Social Transformation in the Early Modern World* (Cambridge: Cambridge University Press, 2010). For recent overviews of economic and social developments in this period, see S. Faroqhi, "Crisis and Change, 1590–1699" and B. McGowan, "The Age of the *Ayans*," in H. Inalcik & D. Quataert (eds.), *An Economic and Social History of the Ottoman Empire* (Cambridge: Cambridge University Press, 1997), II, 411–636 and II, 637–758. For a recent study that challenges notions of overall economic stagnation in Ottoman Egypt, see N. Hanna, *Artisan Entrepreneurs in Cairo and Early-Modern Capitalism (1600–1800)* (Syracuse: Syracuse University Press, 2011).

[5] It is remarkable that a period that witnessed the composer ʿIṭrī (d. 1712), the historian Naʿīmā (d. 1716), the poet Nedīm (d. 1730), and the miniaturist Levnī (d. 1732) should be considered one of cultural and intellectual decline.

[6] Zilfi, *The Politics of Piety*, 205.

[7] İ. Erünsal, *Ottoman Libraries: A Survey of the History, Development, and Organization of the Ottoman Foundation Libraries* (Cambridge, MA: The Department of Near Eastern Languages & Literatures, Harvard University, 2008), 43–62.

failure of the attempt at capturing Vienna in 1683 and the ensuing military debacle was the result of a combination of overreach and an unprecedented alliance of Austria, Russia, Poland, Venice and the Papacy – and one wonders whether *any* army at the time could have withstood such an alliance.[8] Even in the first half of the eighteenth century, the Ottomans continued to enjoy modest military successes, defeating the Russians in 1710–11, the Venetians in 1714–18, and the Austrians in 1737–39. It was only with the later disastrous wars with Russia, starting in 1768 and continuing intermittently throughout the nineteenth century, that it became clear that the Ottoman Empire was no longer able to meet novel military challenges. Even then, it is an open question whether the term "decline" effectively captures this development, as opposed to speaking of the dramatic and inexorable rise of Russia in the eighteenth and nineteenth centuries at the expense of not only the Ottoman Empire but also Poland, Sweden, Persia and the Central Asian khanates.

The history of Morocco in the early modern period, too, cannot plausibly be summed up with the word "decline." Sultan Aḥmad al-Manṣūr (r.1578–1603) conquered Touat (in what is now southern Algeria) and Timbuktu (in northern Mali); his resultant control over the Saharan trade in gold earned him the epithet "the Golden." In the first half of the seventeenth century, Morocco was plunged into civil war, but this period of turmoil ended with the establishment of the Alaouite dynasty in the 1660s. Under Mawlāy Ismāʿīl (r. 1672–1727), Moroccan forces reasserted control over the entrepots of the Saharan trade and managed to dislodge the Spanish and the English from their outposts on the Atlantic coast of Morocco. As mentioned in Chapter VI, a number of Moroccan scholars writing toward the end of the seventeenth century associated their era with the revival of learning.

From the perspective of the Ottoman provinces, André Raymond has attempted to show that the major Arab cities of the Empire – Cairo, Aleppo, Damascus, Tunis, and Algiers – on the whole grew and prospered in the period between the crises of the early seventeenth century and the late eighteenth, notwithstanding the inevitable occurrence from

8 According to Rhoads Murphey, the military difficulties experienced by the Ottomans in the late seventeenth century were *not* the result of "military, and still less technological, advances among western European armies that left them lagging behind, but shifting diplomatic patterns that forced them to confront a better-organized and financed, as well as more determined, adversary (or group of adversaries) than ever before"; see his *Ottoman Warfare, 1500–1700* (New Brunswick, NJ: Rutgers University Press, 1999), 10–11.

time to time of harvest failures and epidemics.[9] Important contributing factors were the trans-Saharan trade in gold, salt, and slaves; Barbary piracy (which peaked in the seventeenth century); the influx of skilled Moriscos from Spain after the expulsions of 1609–1614; the coffee trade (particularly important in Yemen and Egypt); the Iranian silk trade (particularly important for Mosul and Aleppo); and the Hajj (which is generally thought to have been facilitated by the political unification of much of the Middle East and North Africa under Ottoman rule).[10] The Kurdish areas of southeastern Anatolia and northeastern Iraq were important centers for the production of dyed fabrics, and there is some evidence that they also experienced a boom in the production and sale of gall in the seventeenth century.[11] The relative underdevelopment of that region would seem to be a later phenomenon, linked to the increased importance of economic interaction with Europe in the eighteenth and nineteenth centuries, and the concomitant rise of Izmir and its western Anatolian hinterland.[12]

9 See especially his "The Ottoman Conquest and the Development of the Great Arab Towns," *International Journal of Turkish Studies* 1(1980): 84–101; *The Great Arab Cities in the 16th–18th Centuries: An Introduction* (New York: New York University Press, 1984), 5–9; *Cairo* (Cambridge, MA: Harvard University Press, 2000), 216–25. A similar view is presented in Hathaway, *The Arab Lands under Ottoman Rule, 1516–1800*, 144–165. For a more pessimistic view, see B. Masters, *The Arabs of the Ottoman Empire, 1516–1918: A Social and Cultural History* (Cambridge: Cambridge University Press, 2013), 75–79. But Masters' claim that the major Arab cities stagnated or declined after the sixteenth century contradicts his own account in other works of the growth of Aleppo in the seventeenth century; see his "Aleppo: The Ottoman Empire's Caravan City," in E. Eldem, D. Goffman, and B. Masters, *The Ottoman City between East and West: Aleppo, Izmir, and Istanbul* (Cambridge: Cambridge University Press, 1999), 17–78, at 36–40.

10 For the trans-Saharan trade, see Abun-Nasr, *A History of the Maghreb in the Islamic Period*, 215–217, 230–232. For the importance of the coffee trade, see the works of André Raymond cited previously. For the Hajj and its economic significance, see S. Faroqhi, *Pilgrims and Sultans: The Hajj under the Ottomans, 1517–1683* (London: I. B. Taurus, 1996). For the expulsion of the Moriscos, see L. P. Harvey, *Muslims in Spain, 1500–1614* (Chicago: University of Chicago Press, 2005). For the Barbary corsairs, see A. G. Jamieson, *Lords of the Sea: A History of the Barbary Corsairs* (London: Reaktion Books, 2012). For the Iranian silk-trade, see R. P. Matthee, *The Politics of Trade in Safavid Iran: Silk for Silver, 1600–1730* (Cambridge: Cambridge University Press, 1999).

11 M. van Bruinessen and H. Boeschoten, *Evliya Çelebī in Dıyarbekır: The Relevant Section of the Seyahatname, edited with translation, commentary and introduction* (Leiden, the Netherlands: Brill, 1988), 40.

12 On the rise of Izmir, see D. Goffman, "Izmir: From Village to Colonial Port City," in E. Eldem, D. Goffman, and B. Masters, *The Ottoman City between East and West*, 79–134.

This revisionist view of political, social, and economic developments from approximately the accession of Murad IV in 1623 to the Russian-Ottoman war of 1768–1774 fits well with the account of intellectual flourishing presented in the present study. However, it should be emphasized that a narrative of intellectual developments does not stand or fall with the findings of political, social, and economic historians. After all, some historians characterize the seventeenth century in Western Europe as a time of general "crisis" with demographic decline, epidemics, religious wars, political turmoil, witch crazes, steep inflation, and disruptions to established trade routes.[13] No one would infer from this that it would not be worthwhile to reconstruct that century's intellectual developments – this was, after all, the century of Galileo, Torricelli, Descartes, Kepler, Harvey, Hobbes, Locke, Huygens, Spinoza, Leibniz, and Newton.

There are at least two other points that have been of some concern to modern historians and with which I have not engaged in the foregoing chapters. One is the extent to which early modern Ottoman *ulema* were open to Western ideas; the other is the question whether the door of *ijtihād* was closed or open in this period. Both topics are certainly deserving of attention, and I hope that future research will expand our knowledge of both points. Nevertheless, they should not be allowed to overshadow other legitimate questions that may be asked of Islamic intellectual history in the early modern period. Some modern authors have treated the lack of engagement with Western ideas as sufficient proof of hidebound obscurantism among the *ulema*.[14] Others have pointed out that some Ottoman scholars did indeed engage with Western ideas: Kātib Çelebī translated *Atlas Minor*; Ebū Bekr Dimaşḳī (d. 1691) translated *Atlas Major*; the Ottoman court physician Ṣāliḥ Ibn Sallūm (d. 1670) translated Paracelsus, Sennert, and Crollius; Esʿad Yānyavī (d. 1729) translated works by the Renaissance Aristotelian Ioannes Cottunius. Some have countered that this activity was sporadic, narrowly confined to court circles, and failed to have a sufficient impact on the *ulema* class as a whole.[15] The entire

[13] See G. Parker and L. M. Smith (eds.), *The General Crisis of the Seventeenth Century* (New York and London: Routledge, 1997). Geoffrey Parker, in his recent *Global Crisis: War, Climate Change and Catastrophe in the Seventeenth Century* (New Haven, CT: Yale University Press, 2013), includes (in Chapter 7) the Ottoman Empire in his narrative of dramatic economic and demographic decline linked to the "little Ice Age."

[14] Abū l-Ḥasan Nadwī, *Mādhā khasira al-ʿālam bi-inḥiṭāṭ al-muslimīn* (Cairo: Maktabat Dār al-ʿUrūba, 1964), 150–151; Aḥmad Amīn, *Zuʿamāʾ al-iṣlāḥ fī l-ʿaṣr al-ḥadīth* (Cairo: Maktabat al-Nahḍa al-Miṣriyya, 1965), 7.

[15] L. Berger, *Gesellschaft und Individuum in Damaskus, 1550–1791*, 286–288.

premise of this debate seems to me questionable. Did seventeenth-century Western European philosophers and scientists engage with the ideas of the Ottoman ulema? Did they translate or discuss seventeenth-century Ottoman, Safavid, or Mughal scientific or philosophical works? Does the fact that they did not do this (or did so sporadically and in narrowly confined circles) mean that Western European philosophers and scientists were hidebound obscurantists? Why has no one suggested that Ottoman scholars were hidebound and dogmatic for not being open to seventeenth-century *Chinese* thought? One need not ponder such questions for long to see that there is a hidden teleological assumption at work, according to which human scientific and philosophical development really could develop only in one direction – the direction that western Europe actually took since the seventeenth century.[16] On this account, the only route to genuine intellectual development for seventeenth-century Ottoman *ulema* would have been to receive new scientific and philosophical ideas from Western Europe, and the only alternative to this was for them to remain where they were or to backslide into obscurantism and religious fanaticism. What this assumption elides is that there could have been genuine development in the realm of ideas that was neither derived from Western Europe nor paralleled Western European developments. It is this overlooked possibility that I have attempted to flesh out in the present study.

Debates about *ijtihād* have also sometimes been conducted on the basis of hidden and questionable assumptions. For one thing, both parties to the debate have assumed that a great deal is at stake. Muhammad Iqbal (d. 1938), in his influential *The Reconstruction of Religious Thought in Islam* (written in English but translated into all major Islamic languages), described *ijtihād* as "the principle of movement in Islam," and this is a sentiment that has been widely shared by self-styled Islamic "reformists" and "revivalists" in the twentieth century.[17] On that account, the absence of *ijtihād* is tantamount to blind imitation (*taqlīd*) of earlier fallible human authorities. If indeed the gate of *ijtihād* was closed after around the twelfth century, then this would have meant that *taqlīd* became the order of the day, causing Islamic thought to enter a prolonged period of stagnation. Conversely, if one does not want to accept that the "post-classical" period of Islamic thought was marked by stagnation and decadence, then one

16 For a brilliant critique of this assumption, see P. Crone, *Pre-Industrial Societies: Anatomy of the Pre-Modern World* (Oxford: Oneworld, 2003), 170–175.

17 Muhammad Iqbal, *The Reconstruction of Religious Thought in Islam* (London: Oxford University Press, 1934), chapter VI.

would try to show that *ijtihād* in some form or other continued to be practiced in later centuries. Again, there are a number of problems with the premise of this debate. *Ijtihād* was a concept in Islamic jurisprudence. It is defined in standard premodern dictionaries of technical terms as the effort of a jurist (*faqīh*) to reach a preponderant belief (*ẓann*) concerning a legal judgment (*ḥukm*).[18] In practice, it meant legal reasoning that engages directly with the acknowledged sources of Islamic law (primarily the Quran and hadith) without being bound by legal precedent.[19] As such, it is not at all clear what significance *ijtihād* would have had for a philosopher, logician, physician, mathematician, astronomer, grammarian, belletrist, theologian, and mystic. Indeed, we have seen that the seventeenth-century scholars discussed in this book tended to contrast "uncritical imitation" (*taqlīd*) with "verification" (*taḥqīq*), not with *ijtihād.* When the Moroccan scholar al-Ḥasan al-Yūsī compared an imitator (*muqallid*) to a pack animal, he was not a lone hero advocating *ijtihād*, as a number of modern historians have assumed.[20] Rather, he was repeating a slogan that is to be found in Sanūsī's *Commentary on the Short Creed*, which was studied by practically all students in Islamic Africa in the seventeenth century, and in that work *taqlīd* is contrasted with "verification" (*taḥqīq*) by mastering rational theology, not with *ijtihād* and legal reform.

Even in the field of law, recent scholarship has suggested that *ijtihād* was not the only tool available for jurists who wished to critically evaluate or go beyond received legal positions.[21] Nor is it at all clear that a legal system that obliges jurists to respect the precedent of previous verdicts must be irrational and inflexible, as it will often not be a straightforward matter to establish which precedent is relevant to a particular case. A jurist who did not see himself as engaged in *ijtihād* would still need to exercise considerable ratiocinative and interpretive skill to reach a judgment, with the concomitant scope for disagreement and controversy. There is nothing at all to suggest that the field of positive Islamic law became "easy" or "straightforward" in later centuries – if anything, the reverse is true.[22]

[18] Jurjānī, *al-Taʿrīfāt* (Beirut: Librarie du Liban, 1969 [reprint of Flügel edition of 1845]), 8; Munāwī, *al-Tawqīf ʿalā muhimmāt al-taʿrīf*, 35.

[19] B. Weiss, *The Spirit of Islamic Law* (Athens and London: University of Georgia Press, 2006), 134.

[20] ʿAbbās b. Ibrāhīm al-Marrākushī al-Samlālī (d. 1959), *al-Iʿlām bi-man ḥalla Marrākush wa-Aghmāt min al-aʿlām* (Rabat: al-Maṭbaʿa al-Malakiyya, 1975), III, 162; Berque, *Al-Yousi: Problèmes de la culture marocain au XVIIème siècle*, 37–38.

[21] Gerber, *Islamic Law and Culture, 1600–1840*, 92–104.

[22] Weiss, *The Spirit of Islamic Law*, 134–135.

Narratives of Islamic decline that revolve around the supposed closing of the door of *ijtihād* also ignore the fact that *ijtihād* continued to be operative within Shiite law in later centuries, without this resulting in Shiite law being in any obvious sense more "flexible" or "progressive" than Sunni law on the eve of modernity, or Shiite areas of the Islamic world being any less "backward" in comparison to Europe.[23]

The assumptions that *ijtihād* is equivalent to "creative, original thinking" as such, and that it is "the principle of movement in Islam" therefore have little basis in historical fact. The roots of the assumption would seem to derive instead from the rhetoric of Muslim self-styled "revivers" and "reformers" in the modern period, especially Muḥammad ʿAbduh and the Salafi movement in Iraq, Syria, and Egypt in the early decades of the twentieth century. These Sunni thinkers tended to have little sympathy with rational theology or Sufism. For them, Islamic law was the heart of the Islamic religious experience, and the task was primarily to reform the law in a direction that was more "modern" or "pure" (or both). To that end, the force of legal precedent in postformative Sunni law had to be challenged through claiming the right of *ijtihād*, and opponents had to be portrayed as hidebound exponents of "unthinking imitation." It is quite striking to what extent modern historians – both Western and native – have been taken in by this partisan perspective. Hence the widespread assumption that the only alternative to *taqlīd* is *ijtihād*, notwithstanding the fact that nonjurists from at least the tenth and eleventh centuries (e.g., Avicenna and the early Ashʿarīs) typically considered the opposite of *taqlīd* to be *taḥqīq*. Hence also the idea that law rather than theology is "Islam's ideal religious science"; that orthopraxy is more important in Islam than orthodoxy; that theology in Islam was of marginal importance and fulfilled a purely defensive and apologetic role. Though such statements masquerade as obvious historical truths, they are in fact based on a highly selective and biased reading of Islamic history – on the identification of "Islam" with the Islam of modern (Sunni) reformers, rather than, for example, the Islam of the Ashʿarī theologians or the Sufis or the Shiites.

A lot of attention has been given in recent decades to the question of "Orientalism" and the ways in which Western scholars have constructed a tendentious image of Islamic history. The foregoing observations point

[23] This is in effect conceded by Fazlur Rahman in his *Islam and Modernity: Transformation of an Intellectual Tradition* (Chicago and London: University of Chicago Press, 1982), 107.

to a current of influence that has received much less attention and that flows in the opposite direction: the ways in which Western scholarship on Islamic intellectual history mirrors contemporary trends in the Islamic world and inherits the partisan historical narratives of such contemporary trends. A case in point is the manner in which the self-presentation of Muḥammad ʿAbduh and his followers was largely accepted at face value in influential works such as Charles C. Adams' *Islam and Modernism in Egypt* (1933) and H. A. R. Gibb's *Modern Trends in Islam* (1947).[24] The bad habit of taking ʿAbduh's own assessment of the immediately preceding past at face value is still with us today, leading even an otherwise excellent recent survey of his life and work to assert that "the necessity of *taqlīd* was then generally accepted by all at the Azhar" and that in Sunni Islam in this period believers were not required to possess "an understanding of the logical proofs behind belief."[25] As was seen in Chapter 5, such assertions are inaccurate and rest on not reading the works of eminent Azharī scholars in the generations prior to ʿAbduh, such as Faḍālī, Bājūrī and ʿIllaysh.

Further examples are not hard to come by. Nineteenth- and early twentieth-century Western scholars of Islam gave some attention to the fourteenth- or fifteenth-century Ashʿarī theologians Ījī, Jurjānī and Sanūsī.[26] After all, these were the figures whose works were studied in Ottoman and North African colleges at the time. But such interest waned in the course of the twentieth century, in step with the waning influence of such figures in the Islamic world. At the same time, Western scholarly interest in Ibn Taymiyya has increased dramatically in the course of the twentieth century, in step with his increased resonance in modern Sunni Islam.[27] Yet another example is the prevalent Western narrative of the

[24] This tendency is noted and deplored in E. Kedourie, *Afghani and ʿAbduh: An Essay on Religious Unbelief and Political Activism in Modern Islam* (London: Frank Cass, 1966), 1–6.

[25] Sedgwick, *Muḥammad ʿAbduh*, 12–13, 41.

[26] See T. Soerensen (ed.), *Statio quinta et sexta et appendix libri Mevakif. Auctore ʿAdhad-ed-Dîn el-Îgî cum comentario Gorgânii* (Leipzig: Engelmann, 1848); M. Wolff (ed. and trans.), *El-Senusi's Begriffsentwicklung des muhammedanischen Glaubensbekenntnisses* (Leipzig: F. C. W. Vogel, 1848); J. D. Luciani (ed. and trans.), *Les prolégomènes théologiques de Senoussi* (Algiers: Fontana, 1908); M. Horten, "Sanusi und die griechische Philosophie," *Der Islam* 6(1915): 178–188; M. Horten (trans.) *Muhammedanische Glaubenslehre: Die Katechismen des Fudali und des Sanusi* (Bonn: Marcus & Weber, 1916).

[27] The pioneering Western study is H. Laoust, *Essai sur les doctrines sociales et politiques de Takī-d-Dīn Ahmad b. Taimīya* (Cairo: Institut Français d'Archéologie Orientale, 1939).

course of later Islamic philosophy, which tends to reflect quite closely the dominant narrative in Iranian scholarly circles since the nineteenth century, especially in the prominence given to Mullā Ṣadrā. This is hardly surprising given that two of the most eminent scholars of later Islamic philosophy in the West, Henry Corbin and Seyyed Hossein Nasr, both studied in Iran. As a result, these narratives largely pass over Mughal and Ottoman philosophers such as Mīr Zāhid Haravī (d. 1689) and Ismāʿīl Gelenbevī, earlier and extremely influential Sunni Persian philosophers such as Jalāl al-Dīn al-Dawānī and Mīrzā Jān Bāghnavī, and even later Iranian philosophers who were critical of Mullā Ṣadrā but whose influence declined over the course of the nineteenth century, such as Rajab ʿAlī Tabrīzī (d. 1669) and Āqā Ḥusayn Khwānsārī (d. 1687).

This is of course not to deny that Western scholars have sometimes been driven by their own peculiar prejudices when writing about Islam and Islamic history. But it is clearly not only "Orientalists" who have constructed partisan and self-serving historical narratives; so have Islamic "reformers" and "revivers," Arab nationalists, modern Iranian theosophists, and Turkish Kemalists. Recognizing this fact should help historians keep a critical distance from ideologically motivated and largely armchair presentations of the Islamic past. Western medievalists succeeded in the course of the twentieth century in overturning received Renaissance and Enlightenment assessments of the Middle Ages as a period of barbarism, obscurantism, superstition, clericalism, and scholastic pedantry.[28] Historians of Islamic and Ottoman thought are in the early stages of a similar reassessment of their own "dark ages." As older narratives of "decline," "decadence," and "the triumph of fanaticism" lose their hold, previously unsuspected horizons of research appear, and important but forgotten thinkers and intellectual traditions come into view. Exciting times lie ahead.

[28] Important figures in this scholarly reassessment included Pierre Duhem (1861–1916), Charles Haskins (1870–1937), Lynn Thorndike (1882–1965), Etienne Gilson (1884–1978), and Anneliese Maier (1905–1971). For a lively if opinionated survey of the rise of medieval studies in the twentieth century, see N. Cantor, *Inventing the Middle Ages: The Lives, Works and Ideas of the Great Medievalists of the Twentieth Century* (New York: Harper, 1991).

References

Unpublished Primary Sources

Āḳḥiṣārī, Aḥmad Rūmī. *Risāla fī l-Taqlīd*. MS, Manisa İl Halk Kütüphanesi 2937, fols. 53b–62b. Available online at www.yazmalar.gov.tr (Arşiv Numarası: 45 Hk 2937/6).

ʿĀkifzāde, ʿAbd al-Raḥmān. *Al-Majmūʿ fī l-Mashhūd wa-l-Masmūʿ*. MS, Süleymaniye Kütüphanesi, Istanbul, Ali Emiri Arabi 2527.

Āmidī, ʿUmar b. Ḥusayn. *Sharḥ al-Waladiyya*. MS, Milli Kütüphane, Ankara, Tokat Zile İlçe Halk Kütüphanesi 231, fols. 71b–115b. Available online at www.yazmalar.gov.tr (Arşiv Numarası: 60 Zile 231).

Bakrī, Muḥammad b. Abī al-Ḥasan. *Taʾbīd al-Minna fī Taʾyīd al-Sunna*. MS, Princeton University Library, Yahuda 253, fols. 106b–111b.

Bakrī, Muḥammad b. Abī al-Ḥasan. *Tarjumān al-Asrār wa Dīwān al-Abrār*. MS, Staatsbibliothek zu Berlin, Wetzstein II, 227.

Barzinjī, Muḥammad b. ʿAbd al-Rasūl. *Al-Jādhib al-Ghaybī min al-Jānib al-Gharbī*;. MS, Manisa İl Halk Kütüphanesi 6230. Available online at www.yazmalar.gov.tr (Arşiv Numarası: 45 Hk 6230).

Bertizī, Ḥüseyn. *Jāmiʿ al-Kunūz*. MS, Milli Kütüphane, Ankara, Yazmalar 4812. Available online at www.yazmalar.gov.tr (Arşiv Numarası: 06 Mil Yz A 4812).

Chillī, ʿUmar. *Ḥāshiya ʿalā Mīr al-Ādāb*. MS, Milli Kütüphane, Ankara, Tokat Müzesi 115, fols. 67b–102a. Available online at www.yazmalar.gov.tr (Arşiv Numarası: 60 Mü 115/4).

Damanhūrī, Aḥmad. *Al-Laṭāʾif al-Nūriyya fī l-Minaḥ al-Damanhūriyya*. MS, Princeton University Library, Garrett 797H.

Damanhūrī, Aḥmad. *Al-Qawl al-Mufīd bi-Sharḥ Durrat al-Tawḥīd*. MS, British Library, Or. 11023, fols. 61a–70a.

Damanhūrī, Aḥmad. *Al-Qawl al-Mufīd bi-Sharḥ Durrat al-Tawḥīd*. MS, Princeton University Library, Yahuda 2798, fols. 6b–13a.

Damanhūrī, Aḥmad. *Al-Qawl al-Mufīd fī Sharḥ Durrat al-Tawḥīd*. MS, Staatsbibliothek zu Berlin, Wetzstein 1734.

Dārendevī, Ḥamza. *Ḥāshiya 'alā Mīr al-Ādāb*. MS, Milli Kütüphane, Ankara, Nevşehir Ortahisar İlçe Halk Kütüphanesi 70, fols. 94b–112a. Available online at www.yazmalar.gov.tr (Arşiv Numarası: 50 Or His 70/6).

Dārendevī, Meḥmed. *Sharḥ al-Risāla al-Ḥusayniyya*. MS, Manisa İl Halk Kütüphanesi, Akhisar Zeynelzade 672. Available online at www.yazmalar.gov.tr (Arşiv Numarası: 45 Ak Ze 672).

Dashtakī, Ghiyāth al-Dīn. *Ta'dīl al-Mīzān*. MS, Mashhad, Kitābkhānah-i Āstān-i Quds-i Rażawī, 23596.

Ferdī Ḳayṣerī, 'Alī (d. 1715). *Ḥāshiya 'alā Sharḥ al-Ḥusayniyya*. MS, Milli Kütüphane, Ankara, Yazmalar 2614. Available online at www.yazmalar.gov.tr (Arşiv Numarası: 06 Mil Yz A 2614).

Ghaffārī, Ḥāmid. *Ḥāshiyah 'alā Sharḥ Mas'ūd*. MS, Çorum Hasan Paşa İl Halk Kütüphanesi 2328. Available at www.yazmalar.gov.tr (Arşiv Numarası: 19 Hk 2328).

Ghaffārī, Ḥāmid. *Risālah fī Ādāb al-Muṭāla'a*. MS, Manisa İl Halk Kütüphanesi, Zeynelzade 822, fols. 63a–65b. Available at www.yazmalar.gov.tr (Arşiv Numarası: 45 Ak Ze 822/2).

Ghaffārī, Ḥāmid. *Risālah fī Ādāb al-Muṭāla'a*. MS, Harvard University, Houghton Library, MS Arab SM4335-39, fols. 1v–6v.

Ḫōca 'Abd ül-Raḥīm. *Ajwiba 'an Tis' Masā'il*. MS, Princeton University Library, Yahuda 4070.

Ibn 'Allān, Muḥammad 'Alī. *Al-'Iqd al-Farīḍ fī Taḥqīq al-Tawḥīd*. MS, Staatsbibliothek zu Berlin, Sprenger 677.

Ibn Maymūn, 'Alī. *Risāla fī l-Radd 'alā Munkirī l-Shaykh Muḥyī al-Dīn Ibn al-'Arabī*;. MS, Staatsbibliothek zu Berlin, Wetzstein 1545, fols. 55a–59a.

Kūrānī, Ibrāhīm. *Al-Taḥrīrāt al-Bāhira 'alā l-Durra al-Fākhira*. MS, Princeton University Library, Yahuda 4049.

Kūrānī, Ibrāhīm. *Ifāḍat al-'Allām fī Taḥqīq Mas'alat al-Kalām*. MS, Süleymaniye Kütüphanesi, Istanbul, Halet Efendi 787, fols. 36b–67a.

Kūrānī, Ibrāhīm. *Maslak al-Sadād fī Mas'alat Khalq Af'āl al-'Ibād*. MS, Princeton University Library, Yahuda 3867.

Kūrānī, Ibrāhīm. *Qaṣd al-Sabīl ilā Tawḥīd al-'Aliyy al-Wakīl*. MS, Princeton University Library: New Series 1139.

Mallawī, Aḥmad. *Thabat*. MS, Princeton University Library, Yahuda 3786, fols. 1–29.

Müneccimbāşī, Aḥmad. *Fayḍ al-Ḥaram fī Ādāb al-Muṭāla'a*. MS, Istanbul, Süleymaniye Kütüphanesi, Laleli 3034.

Müneccimbāşī, Aḥmad. *Fayḍ al-Ḥaram*. MS, Istanbul, Süleymaniye Kütüphanesi, Nafiz Pāşā 1350.

Nābulusī, 'Abd al-Ghanī. *Al-Radd al-Matīn 'alā Muntaqiṣ al-'Ārif Muḥyī al-Dīn*. MS, British Library, Or. 1033.

Nābulusī, 'Abd al-Ghanī. *Radd al-Jāhil ilā l-Ṣawāb fī Jawāz Iḍāfat al-Ta'thīr ilā l-Asbāb*. MS, Staatsbibliothek zu Berlin, Sprenger 853, fols. 67a–79a.

Qarabāghī, Yūsuf Kawsaj. *Al-Ḥāshiya al-Khānqāhiyya 'alā Sharḥ al-'Aqā'id al-'Aḍudiyya*. MS, British Library, Bijapur 213.

Sāçaḳlīzāde, Meḥmed. *Ḥāshiya 'alā Risālat al-Ādāb*. MS, Manisa İl Halk Kütüphanesi 2007, fols. 53b–63b. Available online at www.yazmalar.gov.tr (Arşiv Numarası: 45 Hk 2007/6).

Samarqandī, Shams al-Dīn. *Sharḥ Qistās al-Afkār*. MS, Yale University Library, Beinecke, Arabic 11.

Shāwī, Yaḥyā. *Ḥāshiya ʿalā Sharḥ Umm al-Barāhīn*. MS, Milli Kütüphane, Ankara, Afyon Gedik Aḥmet Paşa 17879. Available online at www.yazmalar.gov.tr (Arşiv Numarası: 03 Gedik 17879).

Sugtānī, ʿĪsā. *Ḥāshiya ʿalā Sharḥ Umm al-Barāhīn*. MS, Princeton University Library, Yahuda 5500.

Tājī, Muḥammad Hibatullāh. *Al-ʿIqd al-Farīd fī Ittiṣāl al-Asānīd*. MS, Princeton University Library, Yahuda 3723.

Tilimsānī, Muḥammad al-Sharīf (d. 1370). *Sharḥ Jumal*. MS, British Library, Add. 9617.

Yūsī, al-Ḥasan. *Nafāʾis al-Durar fī Ḥawāshī al-Mukhtaṣar*. MS, Bibliotheque Nationale, Paris, Arabe 2400.

Yūsī, al-Ḥasan. *Nafāʾis al-Durar fī Ḥawāshī l-Mukhtaṣar*. MS, Princeton University Library, Garrett 485 H.

Published Primary Sources

ʿAbbādī, Aḥmad b. Qāsim. *Al-Āyāt al-Bayyināt ʿalā Sharḥ Jamʿ al-Jawāmiʿ*;. Cairo: n.p., 1289/1872.

ʿAbduh, Muḥammad. *Risālat al-Tawḥīd*. Edited by Bassām ʿAbd al-Wahhāb al-Jābī. Beirut and Limassol: Dār Ibn Ḥazm and al-Jaffan wa-l-Jābī, 2001.

Abū Shāma. *Al-Dhayl ʿalā al-Rawḍatayn*. Edited by Muḥammad Zāhid al-Kawtharī and ʿIzzat al-ʿAṭṭār al-Ḥusaynī;. Cairo: Dār al-Kutub al-Mālikiyya, 1947.

Adanavī, Ḥüseyn. *Ḥusayniyya*. Lithograph, Istanbul: n. p., 1267/1850.

Āghā Buzurg Tehrānī, Muḥammad Muḥsin. *Al-Dharīʿa ilā Taṣānīf al-Shīʿa*. Beirut: Dār al-Aḍwāʾ, 1983.

Ālūsī, Khayr al-Dīn Abū al-Barakāt. *Jalāʾ al-ʿAynayn fī Muḥākamat al-Aḥmadayn*. Cairo: Maṭbaʿat al-Madanī, 1961.

Ālūsī, Maḥmūd. *Al-Ajwiba al-ʿIrāqiyya ʿalā al-Asʾila al-Īrāniyya*. Printed on the margins of ʿAlī Dedeh, *Ḥall al-Rumūz wa Kashf al-Kunūz*. Cairo: al-Maṭbaʿa al-Sharafiyya, 1314/1896.

Ālūsī, Maḥmūd. *Fahāris Rūḥ al-Maʿānī fī Tafsīr al-Qurʾān*. Edited by Ibrāhīm Shams al-Dīn and Sanaʾ Bazīʿ Shams al-Dīn. Beirut: Dār al-Kutub al-ʿIlmiyya, 1996.

Āmidī, ʿAbd al-Wahhāb. *Sharḥ al-Waladiyya*. Cairo: Maṭbaʿat al-Khānjī, 1329/1911.

ʿĀmilī, Zayn al-Dīn. *Munyat al-Murīd fī Adab al-Mufīd wa-l-Mustafīd*. Edited by Riḍā al-Mukhtārī. Beirut: Dār al-Amīra, 2006.

ʿAṭṭār, Ḥasan *Ḥāwāshī ʿalā Maqūlāt al-Bulaydī wa-l-Sijāʿī*. Cairo, al-Maṭbaʿa al-Khayriyya, 1328/1910–1911.

ʿAydarūsī, ʿAbd al-Qādir. *Al-Nūr al-Sāfir ʿan Akhbār al-Qarn al-ʿĀshir*. Edited by Aḥmad Ḥālū, Muḥammad al-Arnāʾūṭ, and Akram al-Bashūshī. Beirut: Dār Ṣadir, 2006.

ʿAyyāshī, ʿAbdullāh (d. 1679). *Itḥāf al-Akhillāʾ bi-Ijāzāt al-Mashāyikh al-Ajillāʾ*. Beirut: Dār al-Gharb al-Islāmī, 1999.

ʿAyyāshī, ʿAbdullāh. *Riḥla*. Edited by Aḥmad Farīd al-Mazyadī. Beirut: Dār al-Kutub al-ʿIlmiyya, 2011.
ʿAẓīmābādī, Shams al-Ḥaqq Muḥammad. *ʿAwn al-Maʿbūd Sharḥ Sunan Abī Dāʾūd*. Delhi: n.p. 1323/1905.
Bā-ʿAlawī al-Ḥaddād, ʿAbdallāh. *Risālat al-Muʿāwana wa-l-Muẓāhara wa-l-Muʾāzara li-l-Rāghibīn min al-Muʾminīn fī Sulūk Ṭarīq al-Ākhira*. Beirut: al-Nāshir li-l-Ṭibāʿa wa-l-Nashr, 1993.
Baghdādī, Ismāʿīl. *Hadiyyat al-ʿĀrifīn: Asmaʾ al-Muʾallifīn wa Athar al-Muṣannifīn*. Istanbul: Milli Eğetim Basımevi, 1951–1955.
Bājūrī, Ibrāhīm. *Ḥāshiya ʿalā Matn al-Sanūsiyya*. Būlāq: Dār al-Ṭibāʿa al-ʿĀmira, 1283/1866.
Baʿlī, ʿAbd al-Bāqī. *Al-ʿAyn wa-l-Athar fī Aqāʾid Ahl al-Athar*. Edited by ʿIṣām Rawwās Qalʿajī. Damascus and Beirut: Dār al-Maʾmūn, 1987.
Baṣrī, Sālim b. ʿAbdullāh. *Al-Imdād bi-Maʿrifat ʿUluw al-Isnād*. Hyderabad, Deccan: Maṭbaʿat Majlis Dāʾirat al-Maʿārif, 1328/1910.
Bāʿūniyya, ʿĀʾisha. *Kitāb al-muntakhab fī uṣūl al-rutab*. Edited and translated by Th. Emil Homerin with the title *The Principles of Sufism*. New York and London: New York University Press, 2014.
Bayḍāwī, ʿAbdullāh b. ʿUmar. *Anwār al-Tanzīl wa Asrār al-Taʾwīl*. Edited by ʿAbd al-Qādir Ḥassūna. Beirut: Dār al-Fikr, 2011.
Behisnī, Meḥmed b. Ḥüseyn. *Sharḥ al-Waladiyya* [printed with the commentary of ʿAbd al-Wahhāb Āmidī]. Cairo: Maṭbaʿat al-Khānjī, 1329/1911.
Beyāżīzāde, Aḥmed. *Ishārāt al-Marām min ʿIbārāt al-Imām*. Edited by Yūsuf ʿAbd al-Razzāq. Cairo: Muṣṭafā al-Bābī al-Ḥalabī, 1949.
Biqāʿī, Burhān al-Dīn. *Tanbīh al-Ghabī ilā Takfīr Ibn ʿArabī;*. Edited [with the title *Maṣraʿ al-Taṣawwuf*] by ʿAbd al-Raḥmān al-Wakīl. Cairo: Matbaʿat al-Sunna al-Muḥammadiyya, 1953.
Bukhārī, ʿAlāʾ al-Dīn Muḥammad. *Faḍīḥat al-Mulḥidīn* [printed in *Majmū;ʿat Rasāʾil fī Waḥdat al-Wujūd* and attributed to Taftāzānī]. Istanbul: n. p., 1294/1877.
Būrīnī, Ḥasan. *Tarājim al-Aʿyān min Abnāʾ al-Zamān*. Edited by S. al-Munajjid. Damascus: al-Majmaʿ al-ʿIlmī al-ʿArabī, 1959–1963.
Būrsalī, Meḥmed Ṭāhir. *ʿOthmānlı Müellifleri*. Istanbul: Matbaʿah-i ʿĀmire, 1333/1914–1342/1928.
Damanhūrī, Aḥmad. *Īḍāḥ al-Mubham min Maʿānī al-Sullām*. Cairo: Muṣṭafā al-Bābī al-Ḥalabī, 1948.
Dashtakī, Ghiyāth al-Dīn. *Ishrāq Hayākil al-Nūr li-Kashf Ẓulumāt Shawākil al-Ghurūr*. Edited by ʿAlī Owjabī. Tehran: Mirās-i Maktūb, 2003.
Dawānī, Jalāl al-Dīn. *Sharḥ al-ʿAqāʾid al-ʿAḍudiyya*. Istanbul: ʿĀrif Efendī Maṭbaʿası, 1316/1899.
Dawānī, Jalāl al-Dīn. *Sharḥ Tahdhīb al-Manṭiq*. Istanbul: Hācı Muḥarrem Bōsnavī Maṭbaʿası, 1305/1887.
Demirdāş, Meḥmed. *Al-Qawl al-Farīd fī Maʿrifat al-Tawḥīd*. Included in a collection of treatises edited by Muhammad ʿAbd al-Qādir Naṣṣār. Cairo: Dār al-Karaz, 2008.
Erżurūmī [= Ṭāvūskārī], Meḥmed. *Sharḥ al-Risāla al-Qiyāsiyya al-Mūsawiyya*. Istanbul: Maṭbaʿah-i ʿAmire, 1281/1864–1865.

Fenārī, Meḥmed b. Ḥamza. *Sharḥ Īsāghūjī*. Istanbul: Maṭba'at Aḫter, 1294/1877.

Fındıḳlılī, 'İsmet Efendī. *Tekmiletü l-Şeḳā'iḳ*. In *Şaḳaiḳ-i Nu'maniye ve Zeyilleri*. Istanbul: Çağrı Yayinları, 1989.

Gelenbevī, Ismā'īl. *Al-Burhān fī 'Ilm al-Mīzān*. Cairo: Maṭba'at al-Sa'āda, 1347/1928–1929.

Gelenbevī, Ismā'īl. *Ḥāshiya 'alā Ḥāshiyat al-Lārī*. Istanbul: Maṭba'ah-i 'Āmire, 1270/1853–1854.

Gelenbevī, Ismā'īl. *Ḥāshiya 'alā Mīr al-Ādāb*. Istanbul: Maṭba'ah-i 'Āmire, 1234/1818–1819.

Ghazālī, Abū Ḥāmid. *Al-Mustaṣfā min 'Ilm al-Uṣūl*. Cairo: al-Maṭba'a al-Tijāriyya al-Kubrā, 1937.

Ghazālī, Abū Ḥāmid. *Iḥyā' 'Ulūm al-Dīn*. Cairo: Mu'assasat al-Ḥalabī, 1967.

Ghazālī, Abū Ḥāmid Muḥammad. *Tahāfut al-Falāsifa*. Edited and translated by M. Marmura. Provo, UT: Brigham Young Press, 1997.

Ghazzī, Badr al-Dīn. *Al-Durr al-Naḍīd fī Adab al-Mufīd wa-l-Mustafīd*. Edited by Nash'at al-Miṣrī. Giza: Maktabat al-Taw'iya al-Islāmiyya, 2006; edited by 'Abdallāh al-Kandarī. Beirut: Dār al-Bashā'ir al-Islāmiyya, 2006.

Ghazzī, Kamāl al-Dīn. *Al-Wird al-Unsī wa-l-Wārid al-Qudsī fī Tarjamat al-'Ārif 'Abd al-Ghanī al-Nābulusī*. Edited by S. Akkach. Leiden, the Netherlands: Brill, 2012.

Ghazzī, Najm al-Dīn. *Al-Kawākib al-Sā'ira fī Akhbār al-Mi'a al-'Āshira*. Edited by J. Jabbūr. Beirut: American University of Beirut Publications, 1945–1958.

Gūrānī, Zayn al-'Ābidīn. *Al-Yamāniyyāt al-Maslūla*. Edited by M. M. al-Murābiṭ. Cairo: Maktabat al-Imām al-Bukhārī, 2000.

Ḫādimī, Ebū Sa'īd. *Barīqa Maḥmūdiyya fī Sharḥ al-Ṭarīqa al-Muḥammadiyya*. Cairo: Muṣṭafā al-Bābī al-Ḥalabī, 1348/1929–1930.

Ḥamawī, Muṣṭafā b. Fatḥullāh. *Fawā'id al-Irtiḥāl wa Natā'ij al-Safar fī Akhbār al-Qarn al-Ḥādī 'Ashar*. Edited by 'Abdallāh al-Kandarī. Damascus, Beirut and Kuwait: Dār al-Nawādir, 2011.

Ḥāmidī, Ismā'īl. *Ḥawāshin 'alā Sharḥ al-Kubrā*. Cairo: Muṣṭafā al-Bābī al-Ḥalabī, 1936.

Ḥanbalī, Abū al-Mawāhib. *Mashyakha*. Edited by M. M. al-Ḥāfiẓ. Damascus: Dār al-Fikr, 1990.

Ḥudaygī, Muḥammad. *Ṭabaqāt*. Edited by A. Bū-Mazgū. Casablanca: Maṭba'at al-Najāḥ al-Jadīda, 2006.

Ibn Abī al-Sharīf, Kamāl al-Dīn. *Al-Musāmara fī Sharḥ al-Musāyara fī al-'Aqā'id al-Munjiya fī al-Ākhira*. Edited by Ṣalāh al-Dīn al-Ḥimṣī. Damascus: Ṣalāḥ al-Dīn al-Ḥimṣī, 2009.

Ibn al-Akfānī, Muḥammad b. Ibrāhīm. *Irshād al-Qāṣid ilā Asnā al-Maqāṣid*. Edited by J. J. Witkam. Leiden, the Netherlands: Ter Lugt Pers, 1989.

Ibn 'Arabī, Muḥyī al-Dīn. *Al-Futūḥāt al-Makkiyya*. Beirut: Dār Ṣādir, 1968 [reprint of Būlāq edition of 1911].

Ibn 'Arabī, Muḥyī al-Dīn. *Fuṣūṣ al-Ḥikam*. Edited by Abū al-'Alā' al-'Afīfī. Cairo: 'Īsā al-Bābī al-Ḥalabī, 1946.

Ibn 'Askar, Muḥammad. *Dawḥat al-Nāshir li-Maḥāsin man kāna bi-l-Maghrib min Mashāyikh al-Qarn al-'Āshir*. Edited by Muḥammad Ḥajjī. Rabat: Dār al-Maghrib, 1976.

Ibn Ḥajar al-ʿAsqalānī. *Fatḥ al-Bārī bi-Sharḥ Ṣaḥīḥ al-Bukhārī*. Cairo: Muṣṭafā al-Bābī al-Ḥalabī, 1959.

Ibn Ḥajar al-Haytamī. *Ashraf al-Wasāʾil ilā Fahm al-Shamāʾil*. Edited by Aḥmad Farīd al-Mazyadī. Beirut: Dār al-Kutub al-ʿIlmiyya, 1998.

Ibn Ḥajar al-Haytamī. *Al-Fatāwā al-Kubrā al-Fiqhiyya*. Beirut: Dār Ṣādir [reprint of Cairo edition of 1308/1891], 1403/1983.

Ibn Ḥajar al-Haytamī. *Al-Fatḥ al-Mubīn li-Sharḥ al-Arbaʿīn*. Cairo: ʿĪsā al-Bābī al-Ḥalabī, 1352/1933.

Ibn Ḥajar al-Haytamī. *Al-Taʿarruf fī al-Aṣlayn wa-l-Taṣawwuf*. Printed on the margin of Muḥammad ʿAlī Ibn ʿAllān al-Ṣiddīqī, al-Talaṭṭuf fī al-Wuṣūl ilā al-Taʿarruf. Mecca and Cairo: Maṭbaʿat al-Taraqqī and Muṣṭafā al-Bābī al-Ḥalabī, 1912–1936.

Ibn al-ʿImād al-Ḥanbalī. *Shadharāt al-Dhahab fī Akhbār man Dhahab*. Cairo: Maktabat al-Qudsī, 1351/1932–1933.

Ibn Jamāʿa, Badr al-Dīn. *Tadhkirat al-Sāmiʿ wa-l-Mutakallim fī Adab al-ʿĀlim wa-l-Mutaʿallim*. Edited by Muḥammad al-ʿAjamī. Beirut: Dār al-Bashāʾir al-Islāmiyya, 2008.

Ibn Kannān al-Ṣāliḥī, Muḥammad. *Al-Ḥawādith al-Yawmiyya min Tārīkh Iḥdā ʿAshar wa-Alf wa-Miʾa*. Edited by A. Ḥ. al-ʿUlabi. Damascus: Dār al-Ṭabbāʿ, 1994.

Ibn Khaldūn, ʿAbd al-Raḥmān. *Al-Taʿrīf bi-Ibn Khaldūn wa Riḥlatihi Gharban wa Sharqan*. Edited by M. al-Ṭanjī. Cairo: n. p., 1951.

Ibn Nāṣir al-Dīn, Muḥammad. *Al-Radd al-Wāfir ʿalā man Zaʿama anna man Sammā Ibn Taymiyya Shaykh al-Islām Kāfir*. Edited by Z. al-Shāwīsh. Damascus: al-Maktab al-Islāmī, 1393/1973–1974.

Ibn Qayyim al-Jawziyya. *Shifāʾ al-ʿAlīl fī Masāʾil al-Qaḍāʾ wa-l-Qadar wa-l-Ḥikma wa-l-Taʿlīl*. Edited by al-Ḥassānī Ḥasan ʿAbdallāh. Cairo: Dār al-Turāth, 1975.

Ibn Qudāma, Mawaffaq al-Dīn. *Censure of Speculative Theology*. Edited and translated by G. Makdisi. London: Luzac, 1962.

Ibn Rushd (Averroes). *Faṣl al-Maqāl wa Taqrīr mā Bayna al-Sharīʿa wa-l-Ḥikma min al-Ittiṣāl*. Edited by G. Hourani. Leiden, the Netherlands: Brill, 1959.

Ibn Sanad al-Baṣrī. *Maṭāliʿ al-Suʿūd*. Edited by ʿImād Raʾūf and Suhayla Qubaysī. Baghdad: Wizārat al-Thaqāfa, 1991.

Ibn Sīnā (Avicenna). *al-Shifāʾ: al-Qiyās*. Edited by S. Zāyid and I. Madkour. Cairo: n. p., 1964.

Ibn Sīnā (Avicenna). *The Metaphysics of The Healing*. Edited and translated by M. Marmura. Provo, UT: Brigham Young University Press, 2005.

Ibn Taymiyya, Aḥmad. *Al-Iklīl fī al-Mutashābah wa-l-Taʾwīl*. In *Majmūʿat al-Rasāʾil al-Kubrā*, II: 5–36. Cairo: Muḥammad ʿAlī Ṣubayḥ, 1966.

Ibn Taymiyya, Aḥmad. *Al-Risāla al-Tadmuriyya*. Edited by Muḥammad Zuhrī al-Najjār. Cairo: Maṭbaʿat al-Imām, 1949.

Ibn Taymiyya, Aḥmad. *Ḥaqīqat Madhhab al-Ittiḥādiyyīn*. In *Majmūʿ Fatāwā Shaykh al-Islām Aḥmad Ibn Taymiyya*. Edited by ʿAbd al-Raḥmān al-Najdī, II: 134–285. Riyad: n. p., 1381/1961.

Ibn al-Tilimsānī, Sharaf al-Dīn. *Sharḥ Maʿālim Uṣūl al-Dīn*. Edited by Nizār Ḥammādī. Beirut: Dār Maktabat al-Maʿārif, 2009.

Ibn Yaʿqūb al-Wallālī, Aḥmad. *Falsafat al-Tawḥīd* [= *Ashraf al-maqāṣid fī sharḥ al-Maqāṣid*]. Cairo: al-Maṭbaʿa al-Khayriyya, n. d.

Ifrānī, Muḥammad al-Ṣaghīr. *Rawḍat al-Taʿrīf bi-Mafākhir Mawlānā Ismāʿīl ibn al-Sharīf*. Rabat: al-Maṭbaʿa al-Malakiyya, 1962.

Ifrānī, Muḥammad al-Ṣaghīr. *Ṣafwat man Intashara fī Akhbār Ṣulaḥāʾ al-Qarn al-Ḥādī ʿAshar*. Edited by ʿAbd al-Majīd Khayālīf. Casablanca: Markaz al-Turāth al-Thaqāfī al-Maghribī, 2004.

Ījī, ʿAḍud al-Dīn. *Sharḥ Mukhtaṣar Ibn al-Ḥājib*. Cairo: al-Maṭbaʿa al-Azhariyya, 1973–1974.

ʿIllaysh, Muḥammad. *Al-Futūḥāt al-Ilāhiyya al-Wahbiyya ʿalā l-Manẓūma al-Maqqariyya*. Printed on the margins of Muḥammad ʿIllaysh, *Hidāyat al-Murīd li-ʿAqīdat Ahl al-Tawḥīd*. Cairo: Maṭbaʿat Muḥammad Efendī Muṣṭafā, 1306/1888.

ʿIllaysh, Muḥammad. *Ḥāshiya ʿalā Sharḥ Īsāghūjī*. Cairo: Maṭbaʿat al-Nīl, 1329/1911.

ʿIllaysh, Muḥammad. *Hidāyat al-Murīd li-ʿAqīdat Ahl al-Tawḥīd*. Cairo: Maṭbaʿat Muṣṭafā Efendī, 1306/1888.

Īmān Firʿawn. Edited by Ibn al-Khaṭīb. Cairo: al-Maṭbaʿa al-Miṣriyya, 1964.

ʿIṣāmī, ʿAbd al-Malik. *Simṭ al-Nujūm al-ʿAwālī fī Anbāʾ al-Awāʾil wa-l-Tawālī*. Cairo: al-Maṭbaʿa al-Salafiyya, 1960–1961.

Isfarāyinī, ʿIṣām al-Dīn. *Ḥāshiya ʿalā Sharḥ al-Jāmī*. Istanbul: Hācı Muḥarrem Bōsnavī Maṭbaʿası, 1281/1864.

Jabartī, ʿAbd al-Raḥmān. *ʿAjāʾib al-Āthār fī al-Tarājim wa-l-Akhbār*. Būlāq: n. p., 1297/1880.

Jawnpūrī, ʿAbd al-Rashīd. *Sharḥ al-Risāla al-Sharīfiyya*. Cairo: Muḥammad ʿAlī Ṣubayḥ, 1929.

Jurjānī, al-Sayyid al-Sharīf. *Al-Taʿrīfāt*. Beirut: Maktabat Lubnān, 1969 [reprint of the Flügel edition of 1895].

Jurjānī, al-Sayyid al-Sharīf. *Ḥāshiya ʿalā Sharḥ Mukhtaṣar Ibn al-Ḥājib*. Būlāq: al-Maṭbaʿa al-Amīriyya, 1316–1317/1898–1900.

Jurjānī, al-Sayyid al-Sharīf. *Sharḥ al-Mawāqif*. Istanbul: Hācī Muḥarrem Būsnavī Maṭbaʿasī, 1286/1869.

Jurjānī, al-Sayyid al-Sharīf. *Sharḥ al-Mawāqif*. Istanbul: Maṭbaʿa-yi ʿĀmire, 1239/1824.

Kāfī, Ḥasan. *Azhār al-Rawḍāt fī Sharḥ Rawḍāt al-Jannāt*. Edited by ʿAlī Akbar Ḍiyāʾī;. Beirut: Dār al-Kutub al-ʿIlmiyya, 2012.

Kānḳirī, ʿAbdallāh. *Nafāʾis ʿArāʾis al-Anẓār wa Laṭāʾif Fawāʾid al-Afkār*. Istanbul: Maṭbaʿah-i ʿAmire, 1313/1896.

Ḳara Ḫalīl Tīrevī. *Al-Risāla al-ʿAwniyya fī Īḍāḥ al-Ḥāshiya al-Ṣadriyya*. Istanbul: Maṭbaʿah-i ʿĀmire, 1288/1871.

Ḳara Ḫalīl Tīrevī. *Ḥāshiya ʿalā Ḥāshiyat al-Lārī*. Istanbul: Maṭbaʿah-i ʿĀmire, 1271/1855.

Ḳara Ḫalīl Tīrevī. *Ḥāshiya ʿalā Ḥāshiyat Ḳūl Aḥmed ʿalā Sharḥ Īsāghūjī*. Istanbul: Maṭbaʿah-i ʿĀmire, 1279/1862–1863.

Ḳārṣī, Dāvūd. *Sharḥ al-Qaṣīda al-Nūniyya*. Istanbul: Meḥmet Ṭālib b Ḥüseyn, 1318/1900–1901.

Kātib Çelebī. *Kashf al-Ẓunūn ʿan Asāmī al-Kutub wa-l-Funūn*. Istanbul: Maarif Matbaasi, 1941–1943.

Kātib Çelebī. *Mīzān ül-Ḥaḳḳ fī Ịḫtiyār il-Eḥaḳḳ*. Istanbul: Ebū l-Żiyā' Maṭbaʿası, 1306/1888–1889.

Kātib Çelebī, *Sullam al-wuṣūl ilā ṭabaqāt al-fuḥūl*, edited by Ekmeleddin İhsanoğlu, Maḥmūd ʻAbd al-Qādir al-Arnā'ūṭ, and Ṣāliḥ Sa'dāwī Ṣāliḥ. Istanbul: IRCICA, 2010.

Kāzarūnī, Shaykh Makkī. *Al-Jānib al-Gharbī fī Ḥall Mushkilāt al-Shaykh Muḥyī al-Dīn Ibn ʿArabī*. Edited by Najīb Mā'il Heravī. Tehran: Intishārāt-i Mawlā, 1985.

Kefevī, Ebū al-Beḳā. *Al-Kulliyyāt*. Edited by M. al-Miṣrī and ʿA. Darwīsh. Damascus: Wizārat al-Thaqāfa, 1975.

Kefevī, Meḥmed. *Ḥāshiya ʿalā Ḥāshiyat al-Lārī*. Istanbul: Şirket-i Ṣeḥāfiye-yi ʿOsmāniye, 1309/1891–1892.

Khafājī, Aḥmad. *Rayḥānat al-Alibbā wa Zahrat al-Ḥayāt al-Dunyā*. Edited by ʿAbd al-Fattāḥ Muḥammad al-Ḥilū. Cairo: Muṣṭafā al-Bābī al-Ḥalabī, 1967.

Khalkhali, Husayn. *Sharḥ al-Dā'irah al-Hindiyyah*. Edited by D. ʿA. Nūrī Baghdad: Wizārat al-Awqāf, 1981.

Khānī, Qāsim. *Al-Sayr wa-l-Sulūk ilā Malik al-Mulūk*. Edited by Muḥammad ʿĪd al-Shāfiʿī. Cairo: al-Jāmiʿa al-Ṣūfiyya al-Islāmiyya al-ʿĀlamiyya, n. d.; edited by Saʿīd ʿAbd al-Fattāḥ. Cairo: Maktabat al-Thaqāfa al-Dīniyya, 2002.

Khiyārī, Ibrāhīm. *Tuḥfat al-Udabā' wa Salwat al-Ghurabā'*. Edited by R. M. al-Sāmarrā'ī. Baghdad: Wizārat al-Thaqāfa, 1969.

Khūnajī, Afḍal al-Dīn. *Kashf al-Asrār ʿan Ghawāmiḍ al-Afkār*. Edited by K. El-Rouayheb. Tehran and Berlin: Iranian Institute of Philosophy and Institute for Islamic Studies, 2010.

Kūrānī, Ibrāhīm. *Al-Amam li-Īqāẓ al-Himam*. Hyderabad, Deccan: Matbaʿat Majlis Dā'irat al-Maʿārif al-Niẓāmiyya, 1328/1910.

Kūrānī, Ibrāhīm. *Tanbīh al-ʿUqūl ʿalā Tanzīh al-Ṣūfiyya ʿan Iʿtiqād al-Tajsīm wa-l-ʿAyniyya wa-l-Ittiḥād wa-l-Ḥulūl*. Edited by Muḥammad Ibrāhīm al-Ḥusayn. Damascus: Dār al-Bayrūtī, 2009.

Laqānī, Ibrāhīm. *Hidāyat al-Murīd bi-Sharḥ Jawharat al-Tawḥīd*. Edited by Marwān al-Bajawī;. Cairo: Dār al-Baṣā'ir, 2009.

Majmūʿ min Muhimmāt al-Mutūn al-Mustaʿmala min Ghālib Khawāṣṣ al-Funūn. Cairo: al-Maṭbaʿa al-Khayriyya, 1306/1888–1889.

Majmūʿal-Mutūn al-Kabīr. Cairo: al-Maṭbaʿa al-ʿUthmāniyya al-Miṣriyya, 1347/1928.

Majmūʿat Rasā'il fī Waḥdat al-Wujūd. Istanbul: n. p., 1294/1877.

Mallawī, Aḥmad. *Sharḥ al-Samarqandiyya*. Printed on the margins of Muḥammad al-Khuḍarī, *Ḥāshiya ʿalā Sharḥ al-Samarqandiyya li-l-Mallawī*. Būlāq: Dār al-Ṭibāʿa al-ʿĀmira, 1287/1870.

Mallawī, Aḥmad. *Sharḥ al-Sullam*. Printed on the margins of Muḥammad b. ʿAlī al-Ṣabbān, *Ḥāshiya ʿalā Sharḥ al-Sullam li-l-Mallawī*. Cairo: al-Maṭbaʿa al-Azhariyya, 1319/1901.

Maqbalī, Ṣāliḥ. *Al-ʿAlam al-Shāmikh fī Tafḍīl al-Ḥaqq ʿalā al-Ābā' wa-l-Mashāyikh*. Sanaa: Maktabat al-Jīl al-Jadīd, 2009.

Marrākushī al-Samlālī, ʻAbbās. *Al-Iʻlām bi-man Ḥalla Marrākush wa Aghmāt min al-Aʻlām*. Rabat: al-Maṭbaʻa al-Malakiyya, 1975.
Mayyāra, Muḥammad b. Aḥmad. *Al-Durr al-Thamīn fī Sharḥ al-Murshīd al-Muʻīn*. Cairo: Maṭbaʻat al-Taqaddum al-ʻIlmiyya, 1323/1905.
Mayyāra, Muḥammad b. Aḥmad. *Mukhtaṣar al-Durr al-Thamīn*. Rabat: Wizārat al-Awqāf, 1981.
Mīr Abū al-Fatḥ b. Makhdūm Ḥusaynī. *Miftāḥ al-Bāb*. Edited by M. Mohaghegh. Tehran: Institute of Islamic Studies, 1986.
Mīr Dāmād, Muḥammad Bāqir. *Al-Qabasāt*. Edited by M. Mohaghegh. Tehran: Tehran University Publications, 1988.
Muḥibbī, Muḥammad Amīn. *Khulāṣat al-Athar fī Aʻyān al-Qarn al-Ḥādī ʻAshar*. Cairo: al-Maṭbaʻa al-Wahbiyya, 1284/1867–1868.
Mullā Ṣadrā Shīrāzī. *Al-Ḥikma al-Mutaʻāliya fī al-Asfār al-ʻAqliyya al-Arbaʻa*. Edited and annotated by Ḥasanzāde Āmolī. Tehran: Vizārat-i Farhang valrshād-i Islāmī, 1383/2004.
Mullā Ṣadrā Shīrāzī. *Al-Shawāhid al-Rubūbiyya*. In *Majmāʻah-i Rasāʼil-i Falsafī-yi Ṣadr al-Mutaʼallihīn*. Edited by Ḥ. N. Iṣfahānī. Tehran: Ḥikmat, 1996.
Munāwī, ʻAbd al-Raʼūf. *Al-Kawākib al-Durriyya fī Tarājim al-Sāda al-Ṣūfiyya*. Edited by Muḥammad Adīb al-Jādir. Beirut: Dār Ṣādir, 1999.
Munāwī, ʻAbd al-Raʼūf. *Al-Tawqīf ʻalā Muhimmāt al-Taʻārīf*. Edited by M. R. al-Dāya. Beirut and Damascus: Dār al-Fikr, 1990.
Murābiṭ, Muḥammad. *Natāʼij al-Taḥṣīl fī Sharḥ al-Tashīl*. Edited by Muṣṭafā al-Ṣādiq al-ʻArabī. Tripoli: al-Kitāb wa-l-Tawzīʻ wa-l-Iʻlān wa-l-Maṭābiʻ, 1980.
Murādī, Muḥammad Khalīl. *Silk al-Durar fī Aʻyān al-Qarn al-Thānī ʻAshar*. Istanbul and Cairo: al-Maṭbaʻa al-Mīriyya al-ʻĀmira, 1291/1874–1301/1883.
Nābulusī, ʻAbd al-Ghanī. *Al-Ḥadīqa al-Nadiyya Sharḥ al-Ṭarīqa al-Muḥammadiyya*. Lalpur: al-Maktaba al-Riḍwiyya al-Nūriyya [reprint of Cairo edition of 1276/1860].
Nābulusī, ʻAbd al-Ghanī. *Al-Ḥaḍra al-Unsiyya fī al-Riḥla al-Qudsiyya*. Edited by Akram al-ʻUlabī. Beirut: al-Maṣādir, 1990.
Nābulusī, ʻAbd al-Ghanī. *Al-Kawkab al-Sārī fī Ḥaqīqat al-Juzʼ al-Ikhtiyārī*. Edited by Muḥammad Rāghib al-Ṭabbākh. Aleppo: al-Maṭbaʻa al-ʻIlmiyya, 1931.
Nābulusī, ʻAbd al-Ghanī. *Al-Ṣulḥ Bayna al-Ikhwān fī Ḥukm Ibāḥat al-Dukhkhān*. Printed in abridged form in Damascus: Maṭbaʻat al-Iṣlāḥ, 1343/1924.
Nābulusī, ʻAbd al-Ghanī. *Al-Wujūd al-Ḥaqq wa-l-Khiṭāb al-Ṣidq*. Edited by Bakri Aladdin. Damascus: Institute Francais de Damas, 1995.
Nābulusī, ʻAbd al-Ghanī. *Dīwān al-Ḥaqāʼiq wa Majmūʻ al-Raqāʼiq*. Būlāq: Dār al-Ṭibāʻa al-Bāhira, 1270/1854.
Nābulusī, ʻAbd al-Ghanī. *Miftāḥ al-Maʻiyya fī Tarīq al-Naqshbandiyya*. Edited by Jūda Muḥammad Abū al-Yazīd al-Mahdī and Muḥammad ʻAbd al-Qādir Naṣṣār. Cairo: al-Dār al-Jūdiyya, 2008.
Nābulusī, ʻAbd al-Ghanī. *Rāʼiḥat al-Janna bi-Sharḥ Iḍāʼat al-Dujunna*. Cairo: Muṣṭafā al-Bābī al-Ḥalabī, 1958.

Nābulusī, ʿAbd al-Ghanī. *Taḥrīk al-Iqlīd fī Fatḥ Bāb al-Tawḥīd*. Edited by al-Sayyid Yūsuf Aḥmad. Beirut: Dār al-Kutub al-ʿIlmiyya, 2012.

Nābulusī, ʿAbd al-Ghanī. *Wasāʾil al-Taḥqīq wa Rasāʾil al-Tawfīq*. Edited by Bakrī ʿAlā al-Dīn. Damascus: Dār Nīnawī, 2010; edited by Samer Akkach. Leiden, the Netherlands: Brill, 2010.

Nakhlī, Aḥmad. *Bughyat al-Ṭālibīn li-Bayān al-Mashāyikh al-Muʿtamadīn*. Hyderabad, Deccan: Dāʾirat al-Maʿārif al-ʿUthmāniyya, 1328/1910.

Qādirī, Muḥammad b. al-Ṭayyib. *Nashr al-Mathānī li-Ahl al-Qarn al-Ḥādī ʿAshar wa-l-Thānī*. Edited by Ḥajjī and Ṭawfīq. Rabat: Maktabat al-Ṭālib, 1977–1986.

Qāshānī, ʿAbd al-Razzāq. *Risāla fī al-Qaḍāʾ wa-l-Qadar*. In *Majmūʿah-yi Rasāʾil va Muṣannafāt*. Edited by Majīd Hādīzāde. Tehran: Mirās-i Maktūb, 2000, 565–593.

Qayṣarī, Dāʾūd. *Sharḥ Fuṣūṣ al-Ḥikam*. Edited and annotated by Ḥasan Ḥasanzāde Āmulī. Qom: Bustān-i Kitāb, 1382/2003.

Qushāshī, Aḥmad. *Al-Simṭ al-Majīd fī Shaʾn al-Bayʿa wa-l-Dhikr wa Talqīnihi wa Salāsil Ahl al-Tawḥīd*. Hyderabad: Dāʾirat al-Maʿārif al-Niẓāmiyya, 1327/1909.

Rāzī, Fakhr al-Dīn. *Manṭiq al-Mulakhkhaṣ*. Edited by A. F. Karamaleki and A. Asgharinezhad. Tehran: ISU Press, 2003.

Rāzī, Quṭb al-Dīn (d. 1365). *Sharḥ Maṭāliʿ al-Anwār*. Istanbul: Maṭbaʿah-i ʿAmire, 1277/1860–1861.

Rāzī, Quṭb al-Dīn. *Sharḥ al-Shamsiyya*. Cairo: al-Maṭbaʿa al-Amīriyya, 1323–1329/1905–1909.

Rāzī, Quṭb al-Dīn. *Taḥrīr al-Qawāʿid al-Manṭiqiyya bi-Sharḥ al-Risāla al-Shamsiyya*. Istanbul: Aḥmed Efendī Maṭbaʿasī, 1325/1907.

Rūdānī, Muḥammad. *Jamʿ al-Fawāʾid min Jāmiʿ al-Uṣūl wa Majmaʿ al-Zawāʾid*. Medina: Maṭbaʿat al-Sayyid ʿAbdallāh Hāshim al-Yamanī, 1961; Kuwait and Beirut: Maktabat Ibn Kathīr and Dār Ibn Ḥazm, 1998.

Rūdānī, Muḥammad. *Ṣilat al-Khalaf bi-Mawṣūl al-Salaf*. Edited by Muḥammad al-Ḥajjī. Beirut: Dār al-Gharb al-Islāmī, 1988.

Ṣabbān, Muḥammad b. ʿAlī. *Ḥāshiya ʿalā Sharḥ al-Mallawī*. Cairo: Muṣṭafā al-Bābī al-Ḥalabī, 1938.

Sabzavārī, Mullā Hādī. *Sharḥ al-Manẓūma*. Edited by Masʿud Ṭālibī and with annotations by Ḥasan Ḥasanzade Āmulī. Qom: Nashr-i Nāb, 1416/1995.

Sāçaḳlīzāde, Meḥmed. *Al-Risāla al-Waladiyya*. Cairo: Maṭbaʿat al-Khānjī, 1329/1911.

Sāçaḳlīzāde, Meḥmed. *Taqrīr al-Qawānīn al-Mutadāwala fī ʿIlm al-Munāẓara*. Istanbul: n. p., 1289/1872–1873.

Sāçaḳlīzāde, Meḥmed. *Tartīb al-ʿUlūm*. Edited by Muḥammad b. Ismāʿīl al-Sayyid Aḥmad. Beirut: Dār al-Bashāʾir al-Islāmiyya, 1988.

Ṣadrüddīnzāde, Meḥmed Emīn. *Risālat Jihat al-Waḥda*. Istanbul: Maṭbaʿa-i Ḥāci Muḥarrem Bōsnavī, 1288/1871.

Safāqisī, ʿAlī al-Nūrī. *al-ʿAqīda al-Nūriyya fī iʿtiqād al-aʾimma al-Ashʿariyya*. Edited by al-Ḥabīb Ben Ṭāhir. Beirut and Damascus: al-Yamāma, 2008.

Saffārīnī, Shams al-Dīn Muḥammad. *Lawāmiʿ al-Anwār al-Bahiyya wa Sawāṭiʿ al-Asrār al-Athariyya li-Sharḥ al-Durra al-Muḍīʾa fī ʿAqīdat al-Firqa al-Marḍiyya*. Beirut and Riyadh: al-Maktab al-Islāmī and Dār al-Khānī, 1991; Cairo: Maṭbaʿat al-Manār, 1328/1907.

Saffārīnī, Shams al-Dīn Muḥammad. *Thabat*. Edited by Muḥammad al-ʿAjamī. Beirut: Dār al-Bashāʾir al-Islāmiyya, 2004.

Sanūsī, Muḥammad b. Yūsuf. *Sharḥ al-Muqaddimāt*. Edited by Salīm Fahd Shaʿbāniya. Damascus: Dār al-Bayrūtī, 2009.

Sanūsī, Muḥammad b. Yūsuf. *Sharḥ al-Wusṭā*. Tunis: Maṭbaʿat al-Taqaddum al-Waṭaniyya, 1327/1909.

Sanūsī, Muḥammad b. Yūsuf. *Sharḥ Mukhtaṣar al-Manṭiq*. Cairo: n. p., 1292/1875.

Sanūsī, Muḥammad b. Yūsuf. *Sharḥ Ṣughrā al-Ṣughrā*. Edited by Saʿīd Fūda. Amman: Dār al-Rāzī, 2006.

Sanūsī, Muḥammad b. Yūsuf. *Sharḥ Umm al-Barāhīn* [= *Sharḥ al-Ṣughrā*;]. Cairo: Maṭbaʿat al-Istiqāma, 1934.

Sanūsī, Muḥammad b. Yūsuf. *Sharḥ Umm al-Barāhīn* [= *Sharḥ al-Ṣughrā*]. Edited by Muḥammad Ṣādiq Darwīsh. Damascus: Dār al-Bayrūtī, 2009.

Sanūsī, Muḥammad b. Yūsuf. *ʿUmdat Ahl al-Tawfīq wa-l-Tasdīd fī Sharḥ ʿAqīdat Ahl al-Tawḥīd* [= *Sharḥ al-Kubrā*]. Cairo: Maṭbaʿat Jarīdat al-Islām, 1316/1898.

Şeyḫī Meḥmed. *Veḳāʾiʿ ül-Fużalāʾ*. In *Şaḳaiḳ-i Nuʿmaniye ve Zeyilleri*. Istanbul: Çağrı Yayinları, 1989.

Shaʿrānī, ʿAbd al-Wahhāb. *Al-Kibrīt al-Aḥmar fī Bayān ʿUlūm al-Shaykh al-Akbar*. Printed on the margins of *al-Yawāqīt wa-l-Jawāhir fī Bayān ʿAqāʾid al-Akābir*. Cairo: al-Maṭbaʿa al-Muyammaniyya, 1317/1899.

Shaʿrānī, ʿAbd al-Wahhāb. *Al-Mīzān al-Dharriyya al-Mubayyina li-ʿAqāʾid al-Firaq al-ʿAliyya*. Edited by Jawdat Muḥammad Abū al-Yazīd al-Mahdī. Cairo: al-Dār al-Jawdiyya, 2007.

Shaʿrānī, ʿAbd al-Wahhāb. *Al-Ṭabaqāt al-Kubrā*. Cairo: Muṣṭafā al-Bābī al-Ḥalabī, 1954.

Shaʿrānī, ʿAbd al-Wahhāb. *Al-Yawāqīt wa-l-Jawāhir fī Bayān ʿAqāʾid al-Akābir*. Cairo: Muṣṭafā al-Bābī al-Ḥalabī, 1959.

Shaʿrānī, ʿAbd al-Wahhāb. *Al-Yawāqīt wa-l-Jawāhir fī Bayān ʿAqāʾid al-Akābir*. Cairo: al-Maṭbaa al-Muyammaniyya, 1317/1899.

Shāwī, Yaḥyā. *Al-Muḥākamāt Bayna Abī Ḥayyān wa Ibn ʿAṭiyya wa-l-Zamakhsharī*. Edited by M. ʿUthmān. Beirut: Dār al-Kutub al-ʿIlmiyya, 2009.

Shāwī, Yahyā. *Al-Tuḥaf al-Rabbāniyya fī Jawāb al-Asʾila al-Lamadāniyya*. Edited by J. M. Faytūrī. Beirut: Dār al-Madār al-Islāmī, 2002.

Shāwī, Yahyā. *Irtiqāʾ al-Siyāda fī Uṣūl Naḥw al-Lugha al-ʿArabiyya*. Edited by ʿA. al-Saʿdī. Damascus: Dār Saʿd al-Dīn, 2010.

Shawkānī, Muḥammad. *Adab al-Ṭalab*. Beirut: Dār al-Kutub al-ʿilmiyya, 2008.

Sinjārī, ʿAlī b. Tāj al-Dīn. *Manāʾiḥ al-Karam fī Akhbār Makka wa-l-Bayt wa Wulāt al-Ḥaram*. Edited by Mājida Fayṣal Zakariyyā. Mecca: Jāmiʿat Umm al-Qurā, 1998.

Subkī, Tāj al-Dīn. *Ṭabaqāt al-Shāfiʿiyya al-Kubrā*. Edited by Ṭanāḥi and al-Ḥilū;. Cairo: ʿĪsā al-Bābī al-Ḥalabī, 1964–1976.

Subkī, Taqī al-Dīn. *Al-Sayf al-Saqīl fī l-Radd ʿalā Ibn Zafīl*. In *al-Rasāʾil al-Subkiyya fī l-Radd ʿalā Ibn Taymiyya*. Beirut: ʿĀlam al-Kutub, 1983.

Suyūṭī, Jalāl al-Dīn. *Al-Ḥāwī li-l-Fatāwā*. Cairo: Idārat al-Ṭibāʿa al-Munīriyya, 1352/1933.

Suyūṭī, Jalāl al-Dīn. *Ṣawn al-Manṭiq wa-l-Kalām ʿan Fannay al-Manṭiq wa-l-Kalām*. Edited by ʿA. S. al-Nashshar. Cairo: Maktabat al-Saʿāda, 1947.

Suyūṭī, Jalal al-Dīn. *Taʾyīd al-Ḥaqīqa wa Tashyīd al-Ṭarīqa al-Shādhiliyya*. Edited by ʿAbdallah al-Ghamrī. Cairo: al-Matbaʿa al-Islāmiyya, 1934.

Taftāzānī, Saʿd al-Dīn. *Sharḥ al-ʿAqāʾid al-Nasafiyya*. Edited by Klūd Salāma. Damascus: Wizārat al-Thaqāfa, 1974.

Taftāzānī, Saʿd al-Dīn. *Sharḥ al-Maqāṣid*. Edited by ʿA. ʿUmayra. Cairo: Maktabat al-Kulliyyāt al-Azhariyya, 1984.

Taftāzānī, Saʿd al-Dīn. *Sharḥ al-Maqāṣid*. Istanbul: Matbaʿat al-Hajj Muḥarram al-Bosnawi, 1305/1888; edited by Ibrāhīm Shams al-Dīn. Beirut: Dār al-Kutub al-ʿIlmiyya, 2001.

Taftāzānī, Saʿd al-Dīn. *Sharḥ al-Shamsiyya*. Lucknow: al-Maṭbaʿal-Yūsufī, 1317/1899.

Ṭarsūsī, ʿOthmān b. Muṣṭafā. *Risāla-yi Istidlāliyya*. Istanbul: Maṭbaʿat Dār al-Khilāfa, 1258/1842.

Ṭāşköprīzāde, Aḥmed. *Al-Shaqāʾiq al-Nuʿmāniyya fī ʿUlamāʾ al-Dawla al-ʿUthmāniyya*. Edited by Sayyid Muḥammad Ṭabaṭabāʾī Behbehānī. Tehran: Kitābkhāne-yi Majlis-i Shūrā-yi Islāmī, 1389/2010.

Ṭāşköprīzāde, Aḥmed. *Miftāḥ al-Saʿāda wa Miṣbāḥ al-Siyāda*. Edited by Kāmil Kāmil Bakrī and ʿAbd al-Wahhāb Abū l-Nūr. Cairo: Dār al-Kutub al-Haditha, 1968.

Ṭāşköprīzāde, Aḥmed. *Sharḥ al-Risāla fī Ādāb al-Baḥth*. Lithograph, Istanbul: n. p., 1313/1895.

Ṭihrānī, Muḥammad Yūsuf. *Naqḍ al-uṣūl wa talkhīṣ al-fuṣūl*. Edited by A. Faramarz Karamaleki, S. Kavandi, and M. Jahed. Zanjan, Iran: Dānishgāh-i Zanjān, 1389/2010.

Timbuktī, Aḥmad Bābā. *Nayl al-Ibtihāj bi-Taṭrīz al-Dībāj*. Cairo: ʿAbbās b. ʿAbd al-Salām b. Shaqrūn, 1351/1932.

Ṭūsī, Naṣīr al-Dīn. *Sharḥ al-Ishārāt wa-l-Tanbīhāt*. Tehran: Maṭbaʿat al-Ḥaydarī, 1377/1958–1379/1959.

ʿUmarī, ʿUthmān. *Al-Rawḍ al-Naḍir fī Tarjamat ʿUlamāʾ al-ʿAṣr*. Edited by S. al-Nuʿaymī. Baghdad: al-Majmaʿ al-ʿIlmī, 1975.

ʿUrḍī, Abū al-Wafāʾ. *Maʿādin al-Dhahab fī al-Aʿyān al-Musharrafa bi-him Ḥalab*. Edited by ʿĪsā Sulaymān Abū Salīm. Amman: al-Jāmiʿa al-Urduniyya, Manshūrāt Markaz al-Wathāʾiq wa-l-Makhṭūṭāt, 1992.

Yemlīḥāzāde, Ḫalīl Esʿad. *Jilāʾ al-ʿUyūn: Sharḥ al-Qiyāsiyya min Naẓm al-Funūn*. Istanbul: Cemal Efendī Maṭbaʿasī, 1308/1890.

Yūsī, al-Ḥasan. *Al-Muḥāḍarāt*. Edited by Muḥammad Ḥajjī and Aḥmad al-Sharqāwī Iqbāl. Beirut: Dār al-Gharb al-Islāmī, 1982.

Yūsī, al-Ḥasan. *Al-Qānūn fī Aḥkām al-ʿIlm wa Aḥkām al-ʿĀlim wa Aḥkām al-Mutaʿallim*. Edited by Ḥ;. Ḥammānī. Rabat: Maṭbaʿat Shāla, 1998.

Yūsī, al-Ḥasan. *Ḥawāshī ʿalā Sharḥ Kubrā al-Sanūsī*. Edited by Ḥamīd Ḥammānī. Casablance: Dār al-Furqān, 2008.
Yūsī, al-Ḥasan. *Mashrab al-ʿĀmm wa-l-Khāṣṣ min Kalimat al-Ikhlāṣ*. Edited by Ḥamīd Ḥammānī;. Casablanca: Dār al-Furqān, 2000.
Zabīdī, Muḥammad Murtaḍā. *Al-Muʿjam al-Mukhtaṣṣ*. Edited by Yaʿqūbī and ʿAjamī;. Beirut: Dār al-Bashāʾir al-Islāmiyya, 2006.
Zabīdī, Muḥammad Murtaḍā. *Itḥāf al-Sāda al-Muttaqīn bi-Sharḥ Iḥyāʾ ʿUlūm al-Dīn*. Cairo: al-Maṭbaʿa al-Muyammaniyya, 1311/1894.
Zabīdī, Muḥammad Murtaḍā. *Tāj al-ʿArūs fī Sharḥ Jawāhir al-Qāmūs*. Edited by ʿA. Farrūj, et al. Kuwait: Maṭbaʿat Ḥukūmat Kuwayt, 1965–2001.
Zarnūjī, Burhān al-Dīn. *Taʿlīm al-Mutaʿallim Ṭuruq al-Taʿallum*. Cairo: Dār Iḥyāʾ al-Turāth al-ʿArabī, n. d.

Secondary Literature

"Ādāb al-Baḥth." In *Dāʾirat al-Maʿārif-i Buzurg-i Islāmī*, edited by Kāẓim Mūsawī Bujnūrdī, I: 159–160. Tehran, 1991.
ʿĀbid al-Fāsī, Muḥammad. *Fihris Makhṭūṭāt Khizānat al-Qarawiyyīn*. Casablanca: Dār al-Kitāb, 1979–1989.
Abou El-Hajj, Rifaat. *Formation of the Modern State: The Ottoman Empire, Sixteenth to Eighteenth Centuries*. Albany: SUNY Press, 1991.
Abrahamov, Binyamin. "A Re-Examination of al-Ashʿarī's Theory of *Kasb* According to al-Lumaʿ." *Journal of the Royal Asiatic Society* 2 (1989): 210–221.
Abu-Manneh, B. "Salafiyya and the Rise of the Khālidiyya in Baghdad in the Early Nineteenth Century." *Die Welt des Islams* 43 (2003): 349–372.
Abun-Nasr, J. M. *A History of the Maghrib in the Islamic Period*. Cambridge: Cambridge University Press, 1987.
Adang, C. "Islam Is the Inborn Religion of Mankind: The Concept of Fiṭra in the Works of Ibn Ḥazm." *Al-Qantara* 21 (2000): 391–410.
Ağırakça, A. "Müneccimbāşī, Aḥmed Dede." *İslam Ansiklopedisi*. Istanbul: Türkiye Diyanet Vakfı, 2006, XXXII, 4–6.
Ahlwardt, W. *Verzeichnis der Arabischen Handschriften*. Berlin: Georg Olms Verlag, 1887–1899.
Ahmed, S. "Satanic Verses." In *Encyclopaedia of the Quran*, edited by J. D. McAuliffe, V, 531–536. Leiden, the Netherlands: Brill, 2001–2006.
Ahmed, S., and N. Filipovic. "The Sultan's Syllabus: A Curriculum for the Ottoman Imperial Medreses Prescribed in a Fermān of Qānūnī I Süleymān, Dated 973/1565." *Studia Islamica* 98/99 (2004): 183–218.
Akkach, S. *ʿAbd al-Ghanī al-Nābulusī: Islam and the Enlightenment*. Oxford: Oneworld Publications, 2007.
Algar, H. "A Short History of the Naqshbandī Order." In *Naqshbandīs: Cheminements et Situations Actuelle d'un Ordre Mystique Musulman*, edited by M. Gaborieau, A. Popovic, and T. Zarcone, 3–44. Paris: Editions Isis, 1990.
Algar, H. "Dahbīdiyya." *Encyclopaedia Iranica*. Edited by E. Yarshater. New York: Bibliotheca Persica Press, 2001. VI, 585–586.

Allard, M. *Le Probleme des Attributs Divins dans la Doctrine d'al-Ash'arī et de ses Premiers Grands Disciples*. Beirut: Imprimerie Catholique, 1965.

Amīn, Aḥmad. *Zu'amā' al-Iṣlāḥ fī al-'Aṣr al-Ḥadīth*. Cairo: Maktabat al-Nahḍa al-Miṣriyya, 1965.

Assmann, A. *Cultural Memory and Western Civilization: Functions, Media, Archives*. Cambridge: Cambridge University Press, 2011.

Azra, A. *The Origins of Islamic Reformism in Southeast Asia*. Hawaii: University of Hawaii Press, 2004.

Badawi, M. *Sufi Sage of Arabia: Imam 'Abdallāh ibn 'Alawī al-Ḥaddād*. Louisville, KY: Fons Vitae, 2005.

Baljon, J. M. S. *Religion and Thought of Shāh Walī Allāh Dihlawi, 1703–1762*. Leiden, the Netherlands: Brill, 1986.

Bencheneb, H. "al-Sanūsī, Muḥammad b. Yūsuf." In *Encyclopaedia of Islam*, 2nd ed. Leiden, the Netherlands: Brill, 1960–2002. IX, 21a.

Berger, L. *Gesellschaft und Individuum in Damaskus, 1550–1791*. Würzburg: Ergon, 2007.

Berkeley, G. *Principles of Human Knowledge and Three Dialogues*. Edited by H. Robinson. Oxford: Oxford University Press, 1996.

Berkey, J. *The Transmission of Knowledge in Medieval Cairo: A Social History of Islamic Education*. Princeton, NJ: Princeton University Press, 1988.

Berque, J. *Al-Yousi: Problèmes de la Culture Marocaine au XVIIème Siècle*. Paris: Mouton, 1958.

Bingöl, A. *Gelenbevi İsmail*. Ankara: Kültür ve Turizm Bakanliği, 1988.

Brenner, L. "Muslim Thought in Eighteenth-Century West Africa; The Case of Shaykh Uthman b. Fudi." In *Eighteenth-Century Renewal and Reform in Islam*, edited by N. Levtzion, and J. Voll, 39–67. Syracuse, NY: Syracuse University Press, 1987.

Brockelmann, C. *Geschichte der Arabischen Litteratur*. Leiden, the Netherlands: Brill, 1937–1949.

Brustad, K. "Jirmānus Jibrīl Farḥāt." In *Essays in Arabic Literary Biography, 1350–1850*, edited by J. E. Lowry and D. Stewart, 242–251. Wiesbaden: Otto Harrassowitz, 2009.

Calverley, E. E., and J. W. Pollock, trans. *Nature, Man and God in Medieval Islam*. Leiden, the Netherlands: Brill: 2002.

Cantor, N. *Inventing the Middle Ages: The Lives, Works and Ideas of the Great Medievalists of the Twentieth Century*. New York: Harper, 1991.

Cantwell Smith, W. *On Understanding Islam: Selected Studies*. The Hague and New York: Mouton Press, 1981.

Cantwell Smith, W. *The Meaning and End of Religion*. New York: Macmillan, 1962.

Carter, M. G. "al-Baghdādī, 'Abd al-Qādir b. 'Umar." In *Essays in Arabic Literary Biography, 1350–1850*, 69–77.

Çavuşoğlu, S. "The Ḳāḍīzādelīs: An Attempt at Şerī'at-Minded Reform in the Ottoman Empire." Unpublished PhD dissertation, Department of Near Eastern Studies, Princeton University, 1990.

Chamberlain, M. *Knowledge and Social Practice in Medieval Damascus, 1190–1350*. Cambridge: Cambridge University Press, 1994.

Chittick, W. "Rūmī and Waḥdat al-Wujūd." In *Poetry and Mysticism in Islam: The Heritage of Rumi*, edited by A. Banani, R. Hovannisian, and G. Sadighi, 70–111. Cambridge: Cambridge University Press, 1994.

Chittick, W. "Ṣadr al-Dīn Ḳūnawī." In *EI2*, XII, 753–755.

Chittick, W. "Waḥdat al-Wujūd in Islamic Thought." *Bulletin of the Henry Martyn Institute of Islamic Studies* 10 (1991): 7–27.

Chittick, W. *Science of the Cosmos, Science of the Soul: The Pertinence of Islamic Cosmology in the Modern World.* Oxford: Oneworld Publication, 2007.

Chittick, W. *The Self-Disclosure of God.* Albany: SUNY Press, 1998.

Chittick, W. *The Sufi Path of Knowledge: Ibn ʿArabi's Metaphysics of Imagination.* Albany: SUNY Press, 1989.

Clayer, N. "Shaʿbāniyya." *EI2*, IX, 155.

Commins, D. D. *Islamic Reform: Politics and Social Change in Late Ottoman Syria.* Oxford: Oxford University Press, 1990.

Cook, Michael. *Commanding Right and Forbidding Wrong in Islamic Thought.* Cambridge: Cambridge University Press, 2000.

Copty, A. "The Naqshbandiyya and Its Offshoot the Naqshbandiyya-Mujaddidiya in the Haramayn in the 11th/17th Century." *Die Welt des Islams* 43 (2003): 321–348.

Crone, P. *Pre-Industrial Societies: Anatomy of the Pre-Modern World.* Oxford: Oneworld Publication, 2003.

Curry, J. J. *The Transformation of Muslim Mystical Thought in the Ottoman Empire: The Rise of the Halveti Order, 1350–1650.* Edinburgh: Edinburgh University Press, 2010.

Dale, S. F. *The Muslim Empires of the Ottomans, Safavids, and Mughals.* Cambridge: Cambridge University Press, 2010.

De Jong, F. "Khalwatiyya." *EI2*, IV, 991–993.

De Jong, F. "Mustafa Kamal al-Din al-Bakri (1688–1749): Revival and Reform of the Khalwatiyya Tradition?" In *Eighteenth-Century Renewal and Reform in Islam*, edited by N. Levtzion, and J. Voll, 117–132. Syracuse, NY: Syracuse University Press, 1987.

Dunlop, D. M. "Fārābī's Paraphrase of the Categories of Aristotle." *Islamic Quarterly* 4 (1957): 168–197 and 5 (1959): 21–54.

Eickelman, D. *Knowledge and Power in Morocco: The Education of a Twentieth-Century Notable.* Princeton, NJ: Princeton University Press, 1985.

Elder, E. E., trans. *A Commentary on the Creed of Islam: Sa ʿd al-Dīn al-Taftāzānī on the Creed of Najm al-Dīn al-Nasafī.* New York: Columbia University Press, 1950.

Elgar, R. "Adab and Historical Memory: The Andalusian Poet/Politician Ibn al-Khaṭīb as Presented in Aḥmad al-Maqqarī, Nafḥ al-Ṭīb." *Die Welt des Islams* 43 (2002): 289–306.

Elger, R. *Muṣṭafā al-Bakrī: Zur Selbstdarstellung eines Syrischen Gelehrten, Sufis und Dichters des 18. Jahrhunderts.* Schenefeld: EB-Verlag, 2004.

Elias, J. *The Throne Carrier of God: The Life and Thought of ʿAlāʾ al-Dawla al-Simnānī;.* Albany: SUNY Press, 1995.

Elman, Benjamin. *On Their Own Terms: Science in China, 1550–1900*. Cambridge, MA: Harvard University Press, 2005.

El-Rouayheb, K. "Aḥmad al-Mallawī (d. 1767): The Immediate Implications of Hypothetical Propositions." In *Oxford Handbook of Islamic Philosophy*, edited by K. El-Rouayheb and S. Schmidtke. Oxford: Oxford University Press, forthcoming.

El-Rouayheb, K. "From Ibn Ḥajar al-Haytamī (d.1566) to Khayr al-Dīn al-Alūsī (d.1899): Changing Views of Ibn Taymiyya amongst Sunni Islamic Scholars." In *Ibn Taymiyya and His Times*, edited by S. Ahmed and Y. Rapoport, 269–318. Karachi: Oxford University Press, 2010.

El-Rouayheb, K. "Heresy and Sufism in the Arabic-Islamic World, 1550–1750: Some Preliminary Observations." *Bulletin of the School of Oriental and African Studies* 73 (2010): 357–380.

El-Rouayheb, K. "Sunni Muslim Scholars on the Status of Logic, 1500–1800." *Islamic Law and Society* 11 (2004): 213–232.

El-Rouayheb, K. "Theology and Logic." In *The Oxford Handbook of Islamic Theology*, edited by S. Schmidtke. Oxford: Oxford University Press, forthcoming. Available on Oxford Handbooks Online at http://www.oxfordhandbooks.com/view/10.1093/oxfordhb/9780199696703.001.0001/oxfordhb-9780199696703-e-009

El-Rouayheb, K. *Relational Syllogisms and the History of Arabic Logic, 900–1900*. Leiden, the Netherlands: Brill, 2010.

El-Shayyal, G. "Some Aspects of Intellectual and Social Life in Eighteenth-Century Egypt." In *Political and Social Change in Modern Egypt*, edited by P. M. Holt, 117–132. Oxford: Oxford University Press, 1968.

Ephrat, D. *A Learned Society in a Period of Transition: The Sunnī 'Ulama' of Eleventh-Century Baghdad*. Albany: SUNY Press, 2000.

Ernst, C. "Controversy over Ibn 'Arabī's Fuṣūṣ: The Faith of Pharaoh." *Islamic Culture* 59 (1985): 259–266.

Ernst, C. "Jawāher-e K̲amsa." *Encyclopaedia Iranica*, XIV, 608–609.

Ernst, C. "Situating Sufism and Yoga." *Journal of the Royal Asiatic Society* 15 (2005): 15–43.

Ernst, C. "Sufism and Yoga according to Muhammad Ghawth." *Sufi* 29 (1996): 9–13.

Erünsal, İ. *Ottoman Libraries: A Survey of the History, Development, and Organization of the Ottoman Foundation Libraries*. Cambridge, MA: The Department of Near Eastern Languages and Literatures, Harvard University, 2008.

Fagnon, E. *Catalogue Generale des Manuscrits des Bibliotheque Publiques d'Alger*. Paris: Bibliothèque Nationale, 1893.

Fahd, T. "Zā'irdja." *EI2*, XI, 404.

Faroqhi, S. "Crisis and Change, 1590–1699." In *An Economic and Social History of the Ottoman Empire*, edited by H. Inalcik, and D. Quataert, II: 411–636. Cambridge: Cambridge University Press, 1997.

Faroqhi, S. *Artisans of Empire: Crafts and Craftspeople under the Ottomans*. London: I. B. Tauris, 2009.

Faroqhi, S. *Pilgrims and Sultans: The Hajj under the Ottomans, 1517–1683*. London: I. B. Taurus, 1996.

Fathurahman, O. *Itḥāf al-Dhakī: Tafsīr Wahdatul Wujūd bagi Muslim Nusantra*. Jakarta: Penerbit Mizan, 2012.

Fihris al-kutub al-ʿarabiyya al-maḥfūẓa bi-l-kutubkhāneh al-khedīviyya al-miṣriyya. Cairo: Maṭba'at 'Uthmān 'Abd al-Razzāq, 1305/1888 – 1311/1893.

Fihris al-Kutub al-Mawjūda bi-l-Maktaba al-Azhariyya ilā Sanat 1366/1947. Cairo: al-Maṭbaʿa al-Azhariyya, 1947.

Ferrari, C. *Der Kategorienkommentar von Abū l-Farağ 'Abdallāh ibn aṭ-Ṭayyib: Text und Untersuchungen*. Leiden, the Netherlands: Brill, 2006.

Fierro, M., and L. Molina. "Al-Maqqarī." *EALB, 1350–1850*, 273–283.

Floor, W. "Art (Naqqāshī;) and Artists (Naqqāshān) in Qajar Iran." *Al-Muqarnas: An Annual on the Visual Culture of the Islamic World* 16 (1999): 125–154.

Frank, R. "Al-Ashʿarī's Kitāb al-Ḥathth ʿalā l-Baḥth." *Mélanges de l'Institut Dominicain d'Études Orientales* 18 (1988): 83–152.

Frank, R. "Al-Ustādh Abū Isḥāḳ: An ʿAḳīda together with Selected Fragments." *Mélanges de l'Institut Dominicain d'Études Orientales* 19 (1989): 129–202.

Frank, R. "Elements in the Development of the Teaching of al-Ashʿarī." *Le Museon* 104 (1991): 141–190.

Frank, R. "Knowledge and Taqlīd: The Foundation of Religious Belief in Classical Ashʿarism." *Journal of the American Oriental Society* 109 (1989): 37–62.

Frank, R. "The Non-Existent and the Possible in Classical Ashʿarīte Teaching." *Mélanges de l'Institut Dominicain d'Études Orientales* 24 (2000): 1–37.

Frank, R. "The Structure of Created Causality According to al-Ashʿarī: An Analysis of al-Lumaʿ, §§82–164. *Studia Islamica* 25 (1966): 13–75.

Friedmann, Y. *Shaykh Aḥmad Sirhindī: An Outline of His Thought and His Image in the Eyes of Posterity*. New Delhi: Oxford University Press, 2000.

Gardet, L., and G. Anawati. *Introduction à la Théologie Musulmane: Essai de Théologie Compare*. Paris: J. Vrin, 1948.

Geach, P. T. *Reference and Generality*. Ithaca and London: Cornell University Press, 1980.

Geoffroy, Éric. *Le Soufisme en Egypte et en Syrie sous les Derniers Mamelouks et les Premiers Ottomans*. Damascus: Institut Français de Damas, 1995.

Gerber, H. "Rigidity versus Openness in Late Classical Islamic Law: The Case of the Seventeenth-Century Palestinian Muftī Khayr al-Dīn al-Ramlī." *Islamic Law & Society* 5 (1998): 165–195.

Gerber, Haim. *Islamic Law & Culture, 1600–1840*. Leiden, the Netherlands: Brill, 1999.

Geuss, R. "Nietzsche and Genealogy." *European Journal of Philosophy* 2 (1994): 274–292.

Gibb, H. A. R., and H. Bowen. *Islamic Society and the West*. London and New York: Oxford University Press, 1957.

Gimaret, D. *La Doctrine d'al-Ashʿarī*. Paris: CERF, 1990.

Gimaret, D. *Théories de l'Acte Humain en Théologie Musulmane*. Paris: J. Vrin, 1980.

Goffman, D. "Izmir: From Village to Colonial Port City." In *The Ottoman City between East and West*, edited by E. Eldem, D. Goffman, and B. Masters, 79–134. Cambridge: Cambridge University Press, 1999.

Goichon, A. M. *Avicenne: Livre des Definitions*. Cairo: Institut Français d'Archéologie Orientale, 1963.
Gran, P. *The Islamic Roots of Capitalism, Egypt 1760–1840*. Syracuse, NY: Syracuse University Press, 1st ed., 1979; 2nd ed., 1998.
Greetham, D. C. *Textual Scholarship: An Introduction*. New York and London: Garland, 1994.
Grehan, J. *Everyday Life & Consumer Culture in 18th-Century Damascus*. Seattle and London: University of Washington Press, 2007.
Guillaume, A. "Al-Lum'at al-Saniya by Ibrahim al-Kurani." *Bulletin of the School of Oriental and African Studies* 20 (1957): 291–303.
Gunter, M. *Historical Dictionary of the Kurds*. Landham, MD: Scarecrow Press, 2011.
Gutas, D. *Avicenna and the Aristotelian Tradition*. Leiden, the Netherlands: Brill, 1988.
Gutelius, D. "Sufi Networks and the Social Contexts for Scholarship in Morocco and the Northern Sahara, 1660–1830." In *The Transmission of Learning in Islamic Africa*, edited by S. Reese, 15–38. Leiden, the Netherlands: Brill, 2004.
Gutelius, D. "The Path is Easy and the Benefits Large: The Nāṣiriyya, Social Networks and Economic Change in Morocco, 1640–1830." *Journal of African History* 43 (2002): 27–49.
Hadj-Sadok, M. "Ibn Zākūr." *EI2*, III, 971–972.
Ḥajjī, Muḥammad. *Al-Ḥaraka al-Fikriyya bi-l-Maghrib fī 'Ahd al-Sa'diyyīn*. Rabat, Maṭba'at Faḍāla, 1977.
Ḥajjī, Muḥammad. *Al-Zāwiya al-Dilā'iyya wa Dawruhā al-Dīnī wa-l-'Ilmī wa-l-Siyāsī*. Casablanca: Maṭba'at al-Najāḥ al-Jadīda, 1988.
Hallaq, W. "Ibn Taymiyya on the Existence of God." *Acta Orientalia* 52 (1991): 49–69.
Hallaq, W. "Logic, Formal Arguments and Formalization of Arguments in Sunni Jurisprudence." *Arabica* 87 (1990): 315–358.
Hallaq, W. *Ibn Taymiyya against the Greek Logicians*. Oxford: Clarendon Press, 1993.
Halverson, J. R. *Theology and Creed in Sunni Islam: The Muslim Brotherhood, Ash'arism and Political Sunnism*. New York: Palgrave Macmillan, 2010.
Hanna, N. *Artisan Entrepreneurs in Cairo and Early-Modern Capitalism (1600–1800)*. Syracuse, NY: Syracuse University Press, 2011.
Hanna, N. *In Praise of Books: A Cultural History of Cairo's Middle Class, Sixteenth to the Eighteenth Century*. Syracuse, NY: Syracuse University Press, 2003.
Harrak, F. "State and Religion in Eighteenth Century Morocco: The Religious Policy of Sidi Muḥammad b. 'Abd Allāh, 1757–1790." PhD dissertation, University of London: School of Oriental and African Studies, 1989.
Harvey, L. P. *Muslims in Spain, 1500–1614*. Chicago: University of Chicago Press, 2005.
Ḥasan, 'A. *Fihris Makhṭūṭāt Dār al-Kutub al-Ẓāhiriyyah: al-Falsafa, al-Manṭiq, Ādāb al-Baḥth*. Damascus: Majma' al-Lugha al-'Arabiyya, 1970.

Ḥasanī, ʿAbd al-Ḥayy. *Al-Thaqāfa al-Islāmiyya fī al-Hind*. Damascus: al-Majmaʿ al-ʿIlmī al-ʿArabī, 1958.

Hathaway, J. *The Arab Lands under Ottoman Rule, 1516–1800*. Harlow, UK: Pearson Education Limited, 2008.

Heer, N. *The Precious Peal: al-Jāmī's al-Durra al-Fākhira*. Albany: SUNY Press, 1979.

Heinen, A. H. *Islamic Cosmology: a Study of as-Suyūṭī's* al-Hayʾa as-Sanīya fī l-Hayʾa as-Sunnīya, *with critical edition, translation, and commentary*. Beirut: Orient-Institut, 1982.

Hess, A. C. *The Forgotten Frontier: A History of the Sixteenth-Century Ibero-African Frontier*. Chicago: University of Chicago Press, 1978.

Ḥilmī, Muḥammad Muṣṭafā. *Ibn al-Fāriḍ: Sulṭān al-ʿĀshiqīn*. Cairo: Wizārat al-Thaqāfa wa-l-Irshād al-Qawmī, 1963.

Ḥilmī, Muḥammad Muṣṭafā. *Ibn al-Fāriḍ wa-l-Ḥubb al-Ilāhī*. Cairo: Lajnat al-Taʾlīf wa-l-Tarjama wa-l-Nashr, 1945.

Hirschler, K. *The Written Word in the Medieval Arabic Lands: A Social and Cultural History of Reading Practices*. Edinburgh: Edinburgh University Press, 2012.

Hitti, P. K., N. A. Faris, and B. ʿAbd al-Malik. *Descriptive Catalog of the Garrett Collection of Arabic Manuscripts in the Princeton University Library*. Princeton, NJ: Princeton University Press, 1938.

Hodgson, Marshall. *The Venture of Islam*. Chicago: Chicago University Press, 1974.

Holt, P. M. "The Later Ottoman Empire in Egypt and the Fertile Crescent." In *The Cambridge History of Islam*, edited by P. M. Holt, A. K. Lambton, and B. Lewis, I: 374–393. Cambridge: Cambridge University Press, 1977.

Homerin, Th. E. "Review of R. A. McGregor, Sanctity and Mysticism in Medieval Egypt." *Mamluk Studies Review* 9 (2005), 238–241.

Homerin, Th. E. *Emanations of Grace: Mystical Poems by ʿĀʾisha al-Bāʿūniyya (d.923/1517)*. Louisville, KY: Fons Vitae, 2011.

Honerkamp, K. L. "Al-Yūsī, al-Ḥasan b. Masʿūd." In *EALB, 1350–1850*, 410–419.

Hoover, J. *Ibn Taymiyya's Theology of Perpetual Optimism*. Leiden, the Netherlands: Brill, 2007.

Horten, M. "Sanusi und die Griechische Philosophie." *Der Islam* 6 (1915): 178–188.

Horten, M., trans. *Muhammedanische Glaubenslehre: Die Katechismen des Fudali und des Sanusi*. Bonn: Marcus & Weber, 1916.

Howard, D. A. "Ottoman Historiography and the Literature of 'Decline' of the Sixteenth and Seventeenth Centuries." *Journal of Asian History* 22 (1988): 52–77.

Huff, T. *The Rise of Early Modern Science: Islam, China, and the West*. Cambridge: Cambridge University Press, 1993.

Ḥurayshī, ʿAbd al-Raḥmān. *Al-Fihris al-Mūjaz li-Makhṭūṭāt Muʾassasat ʿAllāl al-Fāsī*. Rabat: Muʾassasat ʿAllāl al-Fāsī, n. d.

İhsanoğlu, E., ed. *Osmanlı Matematik Literaturu Tarihi*. Istanbul: IRCICA, 1999.

İnalcik, Halil. *The Ottoman Empire: The Classical Age, 1300–1600*. London: Weidenfeld & Nicholson, 1973.
Iqbal, Muhammad. *The Reconstruction of Religious Thought in Islam*. London: Oxford University Press, 1934.
Izutsu, T. *The Concept and Reality of Existence*. Tokyo: Keio Institute of Cultural and Linguistic Studies, 1971.
Jamieson, A. G. *Lords of the Sea: A History of the Barbary Corsairs*. London: Reaktion Books, 2012.
Janin, Louis. "Un Texte d'ar-Rudani sur l'Astrolabe Sphérique." *Annali dell'Istituto e Museo di Storia Della Scienza di Firenze* 3 (1978): 71–75.
Jolivet, J. and R. Rashed. "Al-Kindī." EI2, V, 122–123.
Kafadar, C. "The Question of Ottoman Decline," *Harvard Middle Eastern and Islamic Review* 4 (1997–1998): 30–75.
Kafadar, C. "A Rome of One's Own: Reflections on Cultural Geography and Identity in the Lands of Rum." *Muqarnas* 24 (2007): 7–25.
Kafadar, C. "Self and Others: The Diary of a Dervish in Seventeenth Century Istanbul and First-Person Narratives in Ottoman Literature." *Studia Islamica* (1989): 121–150.
Karabela, Mehmet. "The Development of Dialectic and Argumentation Theory in Post-Classical Islamic Intellectual History." Unpublished PhD dissertation, McGill University, 2010.
Kattānī, ʿAbd al-Ḥayy. *Fihris al-Fahāris*. Edited by Iḥsān ʿAbbās. Beirut: Dār al-Gharb al-Islāmī, 1982.
Kawtharī, Muḥammad Zāhid. *Maqālāt*. Cairo: al-Maktaba al-Azhariyya li-l-Turāth, 1994.
Kawtharī, Muḥammad Zāhid. *Al-Taḥrīr al-Wajīz fīmā Yabtaghīhi al-Mustajīz*. Edited by ʿAbd al-Fattāḥ Abū Ghudda. Aleppo: Maktab al-Maṭbūʿāt al-Islāmiyya, 1993.
Kawtharī, Muḥammad Zāhid. "Tarjamat al-ʿAllāma Ismāʿīl al-Kalanbawī wa-Lumʿa min Anbāʾ baʿḍ Shuyūkhihi." In Muḥammad Zāhid al-Kawtharī, *Maqālāt* [see al-Kawtharī, 1994], 553–561.
Kawtharī, Muḥammad Zāhid. "Ṭuraf min Anbāʾ al-ʿIlm wa-l-ʿUlamāʾ. In Muḥammad Zāhid al-Kawtharī, *Maqālāt* [see al-Kawtharī, 1994], 572–578.
Kedourie, E. *Afghani and ʿAbduh: An Essay on Religious Unbelief and Political Activism in Modern Islam*. London: Frank Cass, 1966.
Kellner-Heinkele, B. "ʿAbd al-Ghanī al-Nābulusī and His Turkish Disciples." *Revue d'Histoire Maghrébine* 50–60 (1990): 107–112.
Khaṭṭāb, Muḥammad. *Fahāris al-Khizāna al-Ḥasaniyya bi-l-Qaṣr al-Malakī bi-l-Rabāṭ*. Rabat: n. p., 1985.
Khwānsārī, Mīrzā Muḥammad Bāqir. *Rawḍāt al-Jannāt fī Aḥwāl al-ʿUlamāʾ wa-l-Sādāt*. Qum, 1391/1971–1972.
Kirmili, A. M. "Le Programme des etudes chez les chiites et principalement ceux de Nedjef." *Revue du Monde Musulman* XXIII (1913): 268–279.
Laḥmar, Ḥamīd. *Al-Fihris al-Waṣfī li-Makhṭūṭāt Khizānat al-Zāwiya al-Ḥamziyya al-ʿAyyāshiyya*. Rabat: Wizārat al-Awqāf, 2009.
Makhlūf, Muḥammad. *Shajarat al-Nūr al-Zakiyya fī Ṭabaqāt al-Mālikiyya*. Edited by ʿA. ʿUmar. Cairo: Makatabt al-Thaqāfa al-Dīniyya, 2006.

Manūnī, M. *Dalīl Makhṭūṭāt Dār al-Kutub al-Nāṣiriyya bi-Tamagrūt*. Rabat: Wizārat al-Awqāf, 1985.
King, D. A. "Taḳī al-Dīn b. Muḥammad b. Ma'rūf." *EI2*, X, 132–133.
Klein, D. *Die Osmanischen Ulema des 17. Jahrhunderts. Eine Geschlossene Gesellschaft?* Berlin: Klaus Schwartz Verlag, 2007.
Klima, G. *John Buridan*. Oxford: Oxford University Press, 2008.
Knysh, A. *Ibn 'Arabī in the Later Islamic Tradition*. Albany: SUNY Press, 1999.
Kramers, J. "Münedjdjim Bashi." *EI2*, VII, 572.
Kratschkowsky, I. "Farḥāt, Djarmānus." *EI2*, II, 795.
Kugle, S. *Rebel between Spirit and Law: Ahmad Zarruq, Sainthood and Authority in Islam*. Bloomington: Indiana University Press, 2006.
Lakhder, M. *La vie littéraire au Maroc sous la Dynastie 'Alawide (1664–1894)*. Rabat: Editions Techniques Nord-Africaines, 1971.
Landolt, H. "Simnānī on Waḥdat al-Wujūd." In *Collected Papers on Islamic Mysticism and Philosophy*, edited by H. Landolt, and M. Mohaghegh, 91–112. Tehran: Institute of Islamic Studies, 1971.
Laoust, H. *Essai sur les Doctrines Sociales et Politiques de Takī-d-Dīn Ahmad b. Taimīya*. Cairo: Institut Français d'Archéologie Orientale, 1939.
Lauzière, H. "The Construction of Salafiyya: Reconsidering Salafism from the Perspective of Conceptual History." *International Journal of Middle East Studies* 42 (2010): 369–389.
Le Gall, D. *A Culture of Sufism: Naqshbandīs in the Ottoman World, 1450–1700*. Albany: SUNY Press, 2005.
Le Tourneau, R. "Al-Djazā'ir." *EI2*, II, 519.
Levi-Provencal, E. "Tamgrūt." *EI2*, X, 170.
Levtzion, N. "Islamic Revolutions in West Africa." In *Eighteenth-Century Renewal and Reform in Islam*, edited by N. Levtzion, and J. Voll, 21–38. Syracuse, NY: Syracuse University Press, 1987.
Levtzion, N., and J. Voll. "Introduction." In *Eighteenth-Century Renewal and Reform in Islam*, 3–20.
Lewis, G. L., trans. *The Balance of Truth by Kātib Chelebī*. London: George Allen & Unwin, 1957.
Ljubovic, A. *The Works in Logic by Bosniac Authors in Arabic*. Leiden, the Netherlands: Brill, 2008.
Luciani, J. D., ed. and trans. *Les Prolégomènes Théologiques de Senoussi*. Algiers: Fontana, 1908.
Mach, R. *Catalogue of Arabic Manuscripts (Yahuda Section) in the Garrett Collection*. Princeton, NJ: Princeton University Press, 1977.
Mach, R., and E. L. Ormsby. *Handlist of Arabic Manuscripts (New Series) in the Princeton University Library*. Princeton, NJ: Princeton University Press, 1987.
Madelung, Wilfrid. *Religious Sects in Early Islamic Iran*. Albany, NY: Persian Heritage Foundation, 1988.
Makdisi, G. "Law and Traditionalism in the Institutions of Learning of Medieval Islam." In *Theology and Law in Islam*, edited by G. von Grunebaum, 75–88. Wiesbaden: Otto Harrassowitz, 1971.
Martin, B. G. "A Short History of the Khalwati Order of Dervishes." In *Scholars, Saints and Sufis: Muslim Religious Institutions in the Middle East since 1500*,

edited by N. R. Keddie, 275–305. Berkeley: University of California Press, 1972.
Maslūtī, Muṣṭafā. *Muḥammad b. Sulaymān al-Rūdānī: Ḥakīm al-Islām wa Mafkharat al-Maghrib*. Rabat: Markaz al-Dirāsāt wa-l-Abḥāth wa-Iḥyā' al-Turāth, 2010.
Masters, B. "Aleppo: The Ottoman Empire's Caravan City." In *The Ottoman City between East and West: Aleppo, Izmir, and Istanbul*, edited by E. Eldem, D. Goffman, and B. Masters, 17–78. Cambridge: Cambridge University Press, 1999.
Masters, B. *The Arabs of the Ottoman Empire, 1516–1918: A Social and Cultural History*. Cambridge: Cambridge University Press, 2013.
Matthee, R. P. *The Politics of Trade in Safavid Iran: Silk for Silver, 1600–1730*. Cambridge: Cambridge University Press, 1999.
McGowan, B. "The Age of the Ayans." In *An Economic and Social History of the Ottoman Empire*, edited by H. Inalcik, and D. Quataert, II: 637–758. Cambridge: Cambridge University Press, 1997.
McGregor, R. A. *Sanctity and Mysticism in Medieval Egypt: The Wafā' Sufi Order and the Legacy of Ibn 'Arabī*. Albany: SUNY Press, 2004.
McMahon, D. M. "The Return of the History of Ideas?" In *Rethinking Modern European Intellectual History*, edited by D. M. McMahon, and S. Moyn, 13–31. Oxford and New York: Oxford University Press, 2014.
McMahon, D. M., and S. Moyn, eds. *Rethinking Modern European Intellectual History*. Oxford and New York: Oxford University Press, 2014.
Messick, B. *The Calligraphic State: Textual Domination and History in a Muslim Society*. Berkeley: University of California Press, 1993.
Meyer, T. "Theology and Sufism." In *The Cambridge Companion to Classical Islamic Theology*, edited by T. Winter, 258–287. Cambridge: Cambridge University Press, 2008.
Michot, Yahya, ed. and trans. *Against Smoking: An Ottoman Manifesto*. Markfield: Kube Publishing, 2010.
Miller, L. "Islamic Disputation Theory: A Study of the Development of Dialectic in Islam from the Tenth through the Fourteenth Centuries." Unpublished PhD dissertation, Princeton University, 1984.
Miquel, A. "Ibn Baṭṭūṭah." *EI2*, III, 735.
Morris, J. W. "Ibn 'Arabī and His Interpreters: Part II: Influences and Interpretations." *Journal of the American Oriental Society* 106 (1986): 733–756.
Moyn, S., and A. Sartori, eds. *Global Intellectual History*. New York: Columbia University Press, 2013.
Murphey, R. *Ottoman Warfare*, 1500–1700. New Brunswick, NJ: Rutgers University Press, 1999.
Murphy, J. H. "Aḥmad al-Damanhūrī (1689–1778) and the Utility of Expertise in Early Modern Egypt." *Osiris* 25 (2010): 85–103.
Nadwī, Abū al-Ḥasan. *Mādhā Khasira al-'Ālam bi-Inḥiṭāṭ al-Muslimīn*. Cairo: Maktabat Dār al-'Urūba, 1964.
Nafi, B. "Abu l-Thana' al-Alusi: An Alim, Ottoman Mufti, and Exegete of the Qur'an." *International Journal of Middle East Studies* 34 (2002): 465–494.

Nafi, B. "Taṣawwuf and Reform in Pre-Modern Islamic Culture: In Search of Ibrāhīm al-Kūrānī." *Die Welt des Islams* 42 (2002): 307–355.

Naficy, S. "al-Ghaffārī, Aḥmad b. Muḥammad." *EI2*, II, 994–995.

Nagel, Tilman. *A History of Islamic Theology: From Muhammad to the Present.* Princeton, NJ: Markus Wiener, 2000.

Nicholson, R. *A Literary History of the Arabs.* Cambridge: Cambridge University Press, 1930.

Nicholson, R. A. *Studies in Islamic Mysticism.* Cambridge: Cambridge University Press, 1921.

Nwyia, Paul. *Ibn ʿAbbad de Ronda (1332–1390).* Beirut: Imprimerie Catholique, 1961.

Nwyia, Paul. *Ibn ʿAṭāʾullāh (m.709/1309) et la Naissance de la Confrérie Šādilite.* Beirut: Dar el-Machreq, 1972.

O'Fahey, R. S., and B. Radtke. "Neo-Sufism Reconsidered." *Der Islam* 70 (1993): 52–87.

Ohlander, E. S. "'He Was Crude of Speech': Turks and Arabs in the Hagiographical Imagination of Early Ottoman Egypt." In *The Arab Lands in the Ottoman Era*, edited by J. Hathaway, 111–135. Minnesota: Center for Early Modern History, 2009.

Ohlander, E. S. "Ibn Kathīr." In *Essays in Arabic Literary Biography, 1350–1850*, edited by J. E. Lowry, and D. J. Stewart, 147–159. Wiesbaden: Harrassowitz Verlag, 2009.

Özyılmaz, Ömer. *Osmanlı Medreselerinin Eğetim Programları.* Ankara: Kültür Bakanlığı, 2002.

Pagani, S. "Renewal before Reformism: ʿAbd al-Ghanī al-Nābulusī's Reading of Aḥmad Sirhindī's Ideas on Tajdīd." *Journal of the History of Sufism* 5 (2007): 291–307.

Parker, G., and L. M. Smith, eds. *The General Crisis of the Seventeenth Century.* New York and London: Routledge, 1997.

Parker, Geoffrey. *Global Crisis: War, Climate Change and Catastrophe in the Seventeenth Century.* New Haven, CT: Yale University Press, 2013.

Pellat, Ch. "Al-Dilāʾ." *EI2*, XII, 223.

Pellat, Ch. "Al-Nāqiʿa ʿalā al-Āla al-Jāmiʿa li-l-Rūdānī." *Bulletin d'Études Orientales* 26 (1973): 7–82.

Pellat, Ch. "L'Astrolabe Sphérique d'ar-Rūdānī." *Bulletin d'Études Orientales* 28 (1975): 83–165.

Perho, I. "Man Chooses His Destiny: Ibn Qayyim al-Jawziyya's Views on Predestination." *Islam and Christian-Muslim Relations* 12 (2001): 61–70.

Perry, J. "Forced Migration in Iran during the Seventeenth and Eighteenth Centuries." *Iranian Studies* 8 (1975): 199–215.

Pocock, J. G. A. *Barbarism and Religion, Volume One: The Enlightenments of Edward Gibbon, 1737–1764.* Cambridge: Cambridge University Press, 1999.

Pourjavady, R. *Philosophy in Early Safavid Iran: Najm al-Dīn Maḥmūd al-Nayrīzī and His Writings.* Leiden, the Netherlands: Brill, 2011.

Profitlich, M. *Die Terminologie Ibn ʿArabīs im "Kitab Wasaʾil al-Saʾil" des Ibn Saudakin: Text, Ubersetzung und Analyse.* Freiburg: Klaus Schwarz Verlag, 1973.

Quiring-Roche, Rosemarie. *Verzeichnis der Orientalischen Handschriften in Deutschland: Arabischen Handschriften, Teil III*. Stuttgart: Franz Steiner Verlag, 1994.

Radtke, B. "Sufism in the 18th Century: An Attempt at a Provisional Appraisal." *Die Welt des Islams* 36 (1996): 326–364.

Rahman, F. *Islam*. Chicago: University of Chicago Press, 1st ed., 1966; 2nd ed., 2002.

Rahman, F. *Islam & Modernity: Transformation of an Intellectual Tradition*. Chicago and London: University of Chicago Press, 1982.

Rahman, F. *The Philosophy of Mulla Sadra (Sadr al-Din al-Shirazi)*. Albany: SUNY Press, 1975.

Raymond, A. "The Ottoman Conquest and the Development of the Great Arab Towns." *International Journal of Turkish Studies* 1 (1980): 84–101.

Raymond, A. *Cairo*. Cambridge, MA: Harvard University Press, 2000.

Raymond, A. *The Great Arab Cities in the 16th–18th Centuries: An Introduction*. New York: New York University Press, 1984.

Reichmuth, S. "Bildungskanon und Bildungreform aus der Sicht eines Islamischen Gelehrten der Anatolischen Provinz: Muḥammad al-Sajaqlī (Saçaqlızāde, gest. um 1145/1733) und sein Tartīb al-ʿUlūm." In *Words, Texts and Concepts Cruising the Mediterranean Sea*, edited by R. Arnzen and J. Thielmann, 493–522. Leuven, Belgium: Peeters, 2004.

Reichmuth, S. *The World of Murtaḍā al-Zabīdī (1732–91): Life, Networks, and Writings*. Cambridge: Gibb Memorial Trust, 2009.

Renard, J., trans. and intr. *Ibn ʿAbbad of Ronda: Letters on the Sufi Path*. New York: Paulist Press, 1986.

Repp, R. C. *The Müfti of Istanbul: A Study in the Development of the Ottoman Learned Hierarchy*. London: Ithaca Press, 1986.

Rescher, N. *The Development of Arabic Logic*. Pittsburgh: University of Pittsburgh Press, 1964.

Rizvi, S. *Mullā Ṣadrā and Metaphysics: Modulation of Being*. Abingdon, UK and New York: Routledge, 2009.

Rizvi, S. *Mullā Ṣadrā Shīrāzī: His Life and Works and the Sources for Safavid Philosophy*. Oxford and New York: Oxford University Press on behalf of the University of Manchester, 2007.

Robinson, F. "Ottomans-Safavids-Mughals: Shared Knowledge and Connective Systems." *Journal of Islamic Studies* 8 (1997): 151–184.

Rosenthal, F. *Knowledge Triumphant: The Concept of Knowledge in Medieval Islam*. Leiden, the Netherlands: Brill, 1970.

Rosenthal, F., trans. *The Muqaddima of Ibn Khaldun*. New York: Pantheon Books, 1958.

Rosenthal, F. *The Technique and Approach of Muslim Scholarship*. Rome: Pontificium Institutum Biblicum, 1947.

Sabra, A. I. "Avicenna on the Subject Matter of Logic." *Journal of Philosophy* 77 (1980): 746–764.

Sabra, A. I. "Science and Philosophy in Medieval Islamic Theology: The Evidence of the Fourteenth Century." *Zeitschrift für Geschichte der Arabisch-Islamischen Wissenschaften* 9 (1994): 1–42.

Sajdi, D. *The Barber of Damascus: Nouveau Literacy in the Eighteenth Century Ottoman Levant*. Stanford: Stanford University Press, 2013.

Sarıkaya, Yaşar. *Abū Saʿīd Muḥammad al-Ḫādimī (1701–1762): Netwerke, Karriere und Einfluss eines Osmanischen Provinzgelehrten*. Hamburg: Verlag Kovač, 2005.

Savory, R. *Iran under the Safavids*. Cambridge: Cambridge University Press, 1980.

Sayılı, A. "Alā al-Dīn al-Manṣūr's Poems on the Istanbul Observatory." *Belleten* 20 (1956): 429–484.

Sayılı, A. *The Observatory in Islam*. Ankara: Türk Tarih Kurumu Basimevi, 2nd ed., 1988.

Sayyid, Fuʾād. *Dār al-Kutub al-Miṣriyyah: Fihris al-Makhṭūṭāt al-latī Iqtanathā al-Dār min Sanat 1936 ilā 1955*. Cairo: n. p., 1961.

Scattolin, G. "L'expérience mystique de Ibn al-Fāriḍ à travers son Poème al-Tāʾiyyat al-kubrā." *Mélanges de l'Institut Dominicain d'Études Orientales* 19 (1989): 203–223.

Scattolin, G. "Al-Farghānī's commentary on Ibn al-Fāriḍ's mystical poem al-Tāʾiyyat al-kubrā." *Mélanges de l'Institut Dominicain d'Études Orientales* 21 (1993): 331–383.

Schimmel, A. *The Mystical Dimensions of Islam*. Chapel Hill: The University of North Carolina Press, 1975.

Schlegell, B. von. "Sufism in the Ottoman Arab World: Shaykh ʿAbd al-Ghanī al-Nābulusī (d.1143/1731)." Unpublished PhD dissertation, University of California, Berkeley, 1997.

Schultze, R. "Das Islamischen Achtzehnte Jahrhundert." *Die Welt des Islams* 30 (1990): 140–159.

Schultze, R. "Was ist die Islamischen Aufklärung?" *Die Welt des Islams* 36 (1996): 276–325.

Schwarz, F. "Writing in the Margins of Empires: the Ḥusaynābādī Family of Scholiasts in the Ottoman-Safawid Borderlands." In *Buchkultur im Nahen Osten des 17. und 18. Jahrhunderts*, edited by T. Heinzelmann, and H. Sievert. Bern: Peter Lang, 2010, 151–198.

Sebag, P. "Tūnis."*EI2*, X, 629.

Sedgwick, M. *Muḥammad ʿAbduh*. Oxford: Oneworld Publication, 2010.

Shapin, S. *The Scientific Revolution*. Chicago: University of Chicago Press, 1996.

Shaw, S. J. *History of the Ottoman Empire and Modern Turkey, Vol. 1: Empire of the Gazis: The Rise and Decline of the Ottoman Empire, 1280–1808*. Cambridge: Cambridge University Press, 1976.

Shihadeh, A. "The Existence of God." In *The Cambridge Companion to Classical Islamic Theology*, edited by T. Winter, 197–217. Cambridge: Cambridge University Press, 2008.

Slane, M. Le Baron de. *Catalogue des Manuscrits Arabes*. Paris: Imprimerie Nationale, 1883–1895.

Soerensen, T., ed. *Statio quinta et sexta et Appendix libri Mevakif. Auctore 'Adhad-ed-Dîn el-Îgî cum Comentario Gorgânii*. Leipzig: Engelmann, 1848.

Spade, P. V., ed. *The Cambridge Companion to Ockham*. Cambridge: Cambridge University Press, 1999.

Spevack, A. "Apples and Oranges: The Logic of the Early and Later Arabic Logicians." *Islamic Law and Society* 17 (2010): 159–184.

Stearns, J. "All Beneficial Knowledge is Revealed: The Rational Sciences in the Maghrib in the Age of al-Yūsī (d.1102/1691)." *Islamic Law and Society* 21 (2014): 49–80.

Strawson, P. F. "Singular Terms and Predication." In *Logico-Linguistic Papers*, edited by P. F. Strawson, 41–56. Aldershot, UK: Ashgate, 2004.

Süssheim, K., and J. Schacht. "Āḳ Ḥiṣārī." *EI2*, I, 310a.

Suter, H. "Ibn al-Bannā' al-Marrākushī." *EI2*, III, 731.

Tādilī, Ṣāliḥ, and Sa'īd al-Murābiṭ, eds. and rev. *E. Levi-Provencal: Fihris al-Makhṭūṭāt al-'Arabiyya al-Maḥfūẓa fī l-Khizāna al-'Āmma bi-l-Rabāṭ, al-juz'. 1*. Rabat: al-Khizāna al-'Āmma li-l-Kutub wa l-Wathā'iq, 1997–1998.

ter Haar, J. G. J. *Shaykh Aḥmad Sirhindī: An Outline of His Thought and His Image in the Eyes of Posterity*. New Delhi: Oxford University Press, 2000.

Terzioglu, D. "Sufi and Dissent in the Ottoman Empire: Niyazî-i Mısrî (1618–1694)." Unpublished PhD dissertation, Harvard University, 1999.

Tezcan, B. *The Second Ottoman Empire: Political and Social Transformation in the Early Modern World*. Cambridge: Cambridge University Press, 2010.

Thackston, W., trans. and ed. *Khwandamir: Habibu l-Siyar*. Cambridge, MA: The Department of Near Eastern Languages and Civilizations, Harvard University, 1994.

Thom, Paul. "Termini Obliqui and the Logic of Relations." *Archiv für Geschichte der Philosophie* 59 (1977): 143–155.

Thorpe, J. *Principles of Textual Criticism*. San Marino, CA: The Huntington Library, 1972.

Tolmacheva, M. "Ibn Baṭṭūṭah." *EALB, 1350–1850*, 126–137.

Trimingham, J. Spencer. *The Sufi Orders in Islam*. New York and Oxford: Oxford University Press, 1st ed., 1971; 2nd ed., 1998.

Uğur, A. *The Ottoman Ulema in the Mid-17th Century: An Analysis of the Veḳā'i' ül-Fużalā' of Meḥmed Şeyḫī Efendī*. Berlin: Klaus Schwarz Verlag, 1986.

Van Bruinessen, M. *Mullas, Sufis and Heretics: The Role of Religion in Kurdish Society*. Istanbul: Isis Press, 2000.

Van Bruinessen, M., and H. Boeschoten, *Evliya Çelebī in Dıyarbekır: The Relevant Section of the Seyahatname*. Edited with translation, commentary, and introduction. Leiden, the Netherlands: Brill, 1988.

Van den Boogert, N. *The Berber Literary Tradition of the Sous: With an Edition and Translation of the "Ocean of Tears" by Muḥammad Awzāl (d. 1749)*. Leiden: Nederlands Instituut voor het Nabije Oosten, 1997.

Van Ess, J. "The Logical Structure of Islamic Theology." In *Logic in Classical Islamic Culture*, edited by G. E. von Grünebaum, 21–50. Wiesbaden: Otto Harrassowitz, 1970.

Van Ess, J. *The Flowering of Muslim Theology*. Cambridge, MA: Harvard University Press, 2006.

Voll, J. "ʿAbdallāh ibn Sālim al-Baṣrī and 18th Century Hadith Scholarship." *Die Welt des Islams* 42 (2002): 356–372.

Voll, J. "The Non-Wahhābī Ḥanbalīs of Eighteenth-Century Syria." *Der Islam* 49 (1972): 277–291.

Voll, J. *Islam: Continuity and Change in the Modern World*. Boulder, Colorado: Westview Press, 1982.

Von Grunebaum, G. E., and T. M. Abel. *Az-Zarnūjī's Instruction of the Student: The Method of Learning*. New York: King's Crown Press, 1947.

Walbridge, J. "Suhrawardī and Illuminationism." In *The Cambridge Companion to Arabic Philosophy*, edited by P. Adamson, and R. C. Taylor, 201–223. Cambridge: Cambridge University Press, 2005.

Watenpaugh, H. Z. *The Image of an Ottoman City: Imperial Architecture and Urban Experience in Aleppo in the Sixteenth and Seventeenth Centuries*. Leiden, the Netherlands: Brill, 2004.

Watt, W. M. *Islamic Creeds: A Selection*. Edinburgh: Edinburgh University Press, 1994.

Watt, W. M. *Islamic Philosophy and Theology: An Extended Survey*. Edinburgh: Edinburgh University Press, 1985.

Weismann, I. *Taste of Modernity: Sufism, Salafiyya, and Arabism in Late Ottoman Damascus*. Leiden, the Netherlands: Brill, 2001.

Weiss, B. *The Spirit of Islamic Law*. Athens and London: University of Georgia Press, 2006.

Wensinck, A. J. *The Muslim Creed: Its Genesis and Historical Development*. Cambridge: Cambridge University Press, 1932.

Winter, M. "Sheikh Ali Ibn Maymun and Syrian Sufism in the Sixteenth Century." *Israel Oriental Studies* 7 (1977): 281–308.

Winter, M. *Egyptian Society under Ottoman Rule 1517–1798*. London and New York: Routledge, 1992.

Winter, M. *Society & Religion in Early Ottoman Egypt: Studies in the Writings of ʿAbd al-Wahhāb al-Shaʿrānī*. New Brunswick, NJ: Transaction Publishers, 1982.

Wisnovsky, R. "The Nature and Scope of Arabic Philosophical Commentary in Post-Classical (ca. 1100–1900 AD) Islamic Intellectual History." In *Philosophy, Science and Exegesis in Greek, Arabic and Latin Commentaries*, edited by P. Adamson, H. Balthussen, and M. W. F. Stone, II, 149–191. London: Institute of Advanced Studies, 2004.

Wolff, M., ed. and trans. *El-Senusi's Begriffsentwicklung des Muhammedanischen Glaubensbekenntnisses*. Leipzig: F. C. W. Vogel, 1848.

Zaydān, Jurjī. *Tārīkh Ādāb al-Lugha al-ʿArabiyya*. Cairo: Maṭbaʿat al-Hilāl, 1911–1914.

Zaydān, Y., and M. Zahrān. *Fihris Makhṭūṭāt Baladiyyat al-Iskandariyya: al-Manṭiq*. Alexandria: n. p., 2001.

Ziai, H., and J. Walbridge, eds. and trans. *Suhrawardī: The Philosophy of Illumination*. Provo, UT: Brigham Young Press, 1999.

Zilfi, M. "A Medrese for the Palace: Ottoman Dynastic Legitimation in the Eighteenth Century." *Journal of the American Oriental Society* 113 (1993): 184–191.

Zilfi, M. "Elite Circulation in the Ottoman Empire: Great Mollas of the Eighteenth-Century." *Journal of the Economic and Social History of the Orient* 26 (1983): 309–327.

Zilfi, M. "Sultan Süleymān and the Ottoman Religious Establishment." In *Süleymān the Second and his Time*, edited by H. Inalcik and C. Kafadar. Istanbul: The Isis Press, 1993.

Zilfi, M. "The Diary of a Müderris: A New Source for Ottoman Biography." *Journal of Turkish Studies* 1 (1977): 157–173.

Zilfi, M. "The ʿIlmiye Registers and the Ottoman Medrese System Prior to the Tanzimat." In *Contributions à l'Histoire Économique et Sociale de l'Empire Ottoman*, edited by J-L. Bacqué-Grammont, and P. Dumont. Louvain, Belgium: Peeters, 1983.

Zilfi, M. "The Kadizadelis: Discordant Revivalism in Seventeenth-Century Istanbul." *Journal of Near Eastern Studies* 45 (1986): 251–269.

Zilfi, M. *The Politics of Piety: The Ottoman Ulema in the Postclassical Age, 1600–1800*. Minneapolis: Bibliotheca Islamica, 1988.

Ziriklī, Khayr al-Dīn. *Al-Aʿlām*. Beirut: Dār al-ʿIlm li-l-Malāyīn, 1995.

Index

'Abbāsī, Muḥammad, 262, 263, 266n
'Abd al-Qādir Ibn 'Abd al-Hādī, 29, 165–166
'Abduh, Muḥammad, 2n, 202, 311n, 359, 360
Abharī, Athīr al-Dīn
His *Hidāyat al-ḥikma*, 22–23, 28, 49, 51, 77, 99, 147, 157, 254
His *Īsāghūjī*, 29, 122n, 134, 138, 139, 142
Abū 'Inān Fāris al-Mutawakkil, 148
Adāb al-baḥth, 4, 34, 35n, 36, 44n, 45, 56n, 60–96, 98, 106–109, 142, 147n, 255, 348
Adams, Charles C., 360
Adanavī, Ḥüseyn, 22, 63, 67n, 68, 71, 74–85, 86, 90, 349
'Adawī, Ayyūb, 262–264, 266
Aḥmed III. *See* Sultan Aḥmed III
Akhḍarī, 'Abd al-Raḥmān, 134, 137, 139, 140, 141, 142, 155, 170, 170n, 171n
'Ākıfzāde, 'Abd ül-Raḥīm, 90, 91
Aladdin, Bakri, 2n, 16n, 314n, 319n, 332, 342n
Aleppo, 5, 160, 235, 262, 265–267, 340, 354–355
Algiers, 144, 153, 155, 156, 157, 161, 222, 354
Ālūsī, Khayr al-Dīn, 310
Ālūsī, Maḥmūd, 310
Āmidī, 'Abd al-Raḥmān, 55, 123
Āmidī, Mullā Çelebī. *See* Mullā Çelebī Āmidī
Āmidī, Rajab, 19n, 55, 55n
Anawati, George, 173–174, 202
Anṣārī, Zakariyyā, 28, 35, 66, 134, 138, 140, 142, 189n, 240, 247n
Anṭākī, Şāh Ḥusayn. *See* Adanavī, Hüseyn
'Arabī al-Fāsī, Muḥammad, 141, 149, 228n
Arna'ūt Meḥmed Pāşā, 266
Ash'arī, Abū l-Ḥasan, 180n, 281, 298, 303, 303n, 324, 325, 326, 328, 351
Ash'arī (theological school); *see also* individual Ash'arī theologians
on essence and existence, 196, 318, 325–326
on letters and sounds of the Quran, 192, 196, 211, 253, 272, 283–284
on occasionalism and the creation of human acts, 294–300
on *ta'wīl*, 275–276, 280–281, 322
on *taqlīd*, 176–188, 204–205, 207–212, 289–290
Astrolabe, 163, 166, 168, 170
Astronomy; *see also* Ulugh Beg
Ottoman observatory (1577–1580), 14, 18, 26
religious scholars' attitude to, 17–18, 25, 116, 170n, 213
Rūdānī's expertise in, 161–165
teaching of, 15, 47, 99, 162
works on, 24, 42, 46, 47n, 166–168
'Aṭṭār, Ḥasan, 7n, 66, 67, 139, 145
Averroes, 70, 94, 148, 180

Avicenna, 21, 28, 45, 70, 94–95, 114, 140n, 144, 148, 326–328, 333, 351, 359
'Aydarūsī, 'Abd al-Qādir, 242
'Ayntāb. *See* Gaziantep
'Ayyāshī, Abū Sālim 'Abdullāh, 35, 51, 143n, 151, 156–159, 162–166, 168, 205, 254–256, 272–274, 280
Awzāl, Muḥammad, 152
Azhar (college), 4, 126, 136, 137n, 158, 175, 189, 200, 201n, 202, 268, 349, 350, 360

Bā-'Alawī al-Ḥaddād, 'Abdullāh, 248
Baghdad, 1, 46, 97, 143, 281
Baghdādī, Ismā'īl Pāşā, 75, 77, 86n, 90–91
Bāghnawī. *See* Mīrzā Jān Bāghnawī
Bājūrī, Ibrāhīm, 175, 201, 360
Bakfalūnī, Muḥammad al-Bakhshī, 266–267
Bakrī, Muḥammad b. Abī l-Ḥasan, 242–244, 246–247, 247n, 306, 319
Bakrī, Muṣṭafā, 236, 267–270, 306
Ba'lī, 'Abd al-Bāqī, 192, 264, 272–273, 307
Balkhī, Abū Sa'īd, 259
Balkhī, Mīr Kalān, 259
Banūrī, Ādam, 260, 348
Barūchī, Ṣibghatullāh, 249–251, 257, 348
Barzinji, Muḥammad, 5, 27, 159, 236, 251–254, 259, 260, 267, 304n, 332, 333n, 345n, 348, 352
Baṣrī, 'Abdullāh b. Sālim, 164, 257
Bā'ūniyya, 'Ā'isha, 247, 306
Bayḍāwī, al-Qāḍī Nāṣir al-Dīn, 55, 118, 139n, 140n, 142, 144, 254, 278–279, 333n
Bāyezīd II. *See* Sultan Bāyezīd II
Bertizī, Ḥüseyn, 64, 86–87, 89–90, 92, 96
Beyāżīzāde, Aḥmed, 16, 186n
Biqā'ī, Burhān al-Dīn, 248, 313, 319, 339
Birgevī, Meḥmed, 13, 15–18, 19, 25, 35, 52, 65, 91n, 190, 193, 259, 290, 294, 305n
Brockelmann, Carl, 39n, 40n, 45n, 66, 69, 75n, 171n, 175
Bukhārī, 'Alā' al-Dīn, 16, 193, 313, 319, 336, 339, 345
Bulaydī, Muḥammad, 144–145, 147, 350
Burhānpūrī, Muḥammad b. Fażlullāh, 255, 320–321, 324, 332
Būrīnī, Ḥasan, 29
Būrsalī, Meḥmed Ṭāhir, 74–75, 86n

Cairo, 4, 5, 20, 32, 37, 66, 67, 97, 99, 100, 126, 131–147 passim, 149, 154–155, 158, 161, 172, 175, 180, 189, 200, 201, 229, 251, 252, 261, 262, 265, 349, 354
Categories (*maqūlāt*), 116, 143–147
Causality. *See* Secondary Causality; Occasionalism
Chillī, 'Umar, 62, 75, 76n
Chittick, William, 7n, 237, 275, 303n
Corbin, Henry, 275, 342, 343, 361
Cottunius, Ioannes, 356
Crone, Patricia, 347

Dahbīdī (Naqshbandī suborder), 258–259
Damanhūrī, Aḥmad, 66, 133, 136–137, 141–143, 200–201, 249n, 350
Damascus, 26–30, 32, 36–38, 42, 47, 58, 97, 154–155, 165, 240, 248, 249n, 252, 259, 261–263, 266, 270–271, 273, 311n, 333, 354
Dashtakī, Ghiyāth al-Dīn, 39, 69, 319
Dashtakī, Ṣadr al-Dīn, 45, 69n, 88
Dawānī, Jalāl al-Dīn, 30–31, 37–42, 45–47, 49, 56, 59, 78, 84, 88, 116, 123–124, 143, 171, 189, 246n, 252–253, 274, 284n, 307, 333, 348, 351, 361
  in Ottoman scholarly genealogies, 43, 48, 50, 52–55
  on *taḥqīq*, 32–34, 78
  on *waḥdat al-wujūd*, 251, 327, 343
De Jong, Frederick, 269
Dialectics. *See ādāb al-baḥth*
Dilā'ī. *See* Zāwiya al-Dilā'iyya
Dilā'ī, Muḥammad al-Murābiṭ, 151, 161
Dimaşḳī, Ebū Bekr b. Behrām, 356
Diyarbakır, 46, 47, 58n, 62, 75, 77n

Ebū l-Su'ūd Efendī, 44, 52, 126
Eight Colleges (Istanbul), 57, 58
Elger, Ralf, 2n, 269
Examinations, 20, 127–128

Faḍālī, Muḥammad, 201, 360
Fārābī, Abū Naṣr, 21, 70, 144n
Farang-i Mahall (college), 67

Farghānī, Sa'īd al-Dīn, 237, 244, 281, 331, 334, 345
Farḥāt, Jirmānus, 160
Fathurahman, Oman, 2n, 320, 321
Fenārī, Meḥmed b. Ḥamza, 43, 52, 122n, 157, 237, 324, 331
Figurative interpretation. *See Ta'wīl*
Free will. *See* Human acts, creation of

Gancī, Sinān al-Dīn, 71
Gardet, Louis, 173–174, 202
Gaziantep, 47, 91n, 262, 266
Gelenbevī, Ismā'īl, 23, 39, 49, 54, 56, 62–63, 64, 66, 68, 76, 89, 218, 349, 361
Ghaffārī, Ḥāmid, 106–109
Ghazālī, Abū Ḥāmid, 9n, 17, 117–119, 132, 174, 176n, 178, 180, 187–188, 202, 207, 216, 247–248, 261n, 290, 296, 306, 310, 314, 319, 321
Ghazzī, Badr al-Dīn, 29, 105, 120–121, 125
Ghazzī, Najm al-Dīn, 30, 247n
Ghunaymī, Aḥmad, 37, 66, 138n
Gibb, H.A.R., 5n, 347n, 360
Gülşenī (Khalwatī suborder), 262n, 265
Gūrānī, Zayn al-'Ābidīn, 22, 27, 39, 47, 48, 53, 54, 62, 88
Gwaliyārī, Muḥammad Ghawth, 249–250, 348

Habṭī, 'Abdullāh, 222–223, 227, 228, 230
Ḥaddād, 248; *see also* Bā-'Alawī al-Ḥaddād, 'Abdullāh
Ḫādimī, Ebū Sa'īd, 49, 52–53, 261
Ḥadīth, study of, 103, 115, 117, 132, 142, 156, 163–165, 220–221, 252–253
Halvetī. *See* Khalwatī
Ḥamawī, 'Alwān, 240, 241, 266, 306
Ḥanbalī, Abū l-Mawāhib, 29, 263, 264, 307, 309
Ḥanbalī (school of law); *see also* individual Ḥanbalī thinkers
  on the letters and sounds of the Quran, 192, 196, 211, 253, 272, 283–284
  relation to Sufism, 263–265, 272–311
  on *ta'wīl*, 110, 186, 272, 275, 276–277, 280
Ḥasanī, 'Abd al-Ḥayy, 68
Hashtūkī, Aḥmad, 135, 137, 140, 144, 145n, 148n, 151, 171, 249n
Ḥashwīs (anthropomorphists), 110, 185–186, 192, 212, 273
Ḫayālī, Aḥmed, 39n, 43–44, 52
Ḥikma. See Philosophy
Hindī, Badr al-Dīn, 156–157
Ḫōca 'Abd ül-Raḥīm, 42–43, 44, 46, 58, 59, 62
Horten, Max, 201, 360n
Human acts, creation of, 194, 275, 294–305, 307, 308, 310, 312, 333, 350
Ḥusaynābādī, Aḥmad, 5, 27, 39n, 40, 49, 50, 53, 58, 59
Ḥusaynābādī, Ḥaydar, 5, 22, 40, 41, 49–50
Ḥużūr Dersleri, 158

Ibn 'Allān, Aḥmad, 257
Ibn 'Allān, Muḥammad 'Alī, 19, 21, 245n
Ibn al-'Arabī, Abū Bakr, 180
Ibn 'Arabī, Muḥyī al-Dīn, 4, 16, 231, 237–346 passim
  on *kalām*, 285–287
  on occasionalism, 297–298, 302–303
  on *ta'wīl*, 275
  and *waḥdat al-wujūd*, 237
Ibn 'Arafa al-Tūnisī, 138, 139, 140, 158n, 180, 186n
Ibn 'Āshir, 'Abd al-Wāḥid, 149, 194–200, 318
Ibn 'Aṭā'ullāh al-Iskandarī, 142, 245, 247, 306n
Ibn Dihāq, 180
Ibn al-Fāriḍ, 243, 244, 246n, 247, 259, 264, 333
Ibn Ḥajar al-'Asqalānī, 53n, 181n, 189n, 246, 279
Ibn Ḥajar al-Haytamī, 188, 273, 282, 287–288, 290–291
Ibn Ḥazm, 210
Ibn Humām, 166n, 181, 189n, 208, 239n
Ibn al-'Imād al-Ḥanbalī, 30, 263
Ibn Jamā'a, Badr al-Dīn, 100, 103–106, 114–115, 117, 118, 120, 125
Ibn Kannān, 'Īsā, 263
Ibn Kathīr, 119
Ibn Khaldūn, 35n, 70, 174, 182, 183, 186n, 210
Ibn Maymūn al-Maghribī, 'Alī, 240, 241, 247n, 248, 266
Ibn Nāṣir al-Dar'ī, Muḥammad, 152, 249
Ibn Nujaym, Zayn al-Dīn, 26

Ibn Qayyim al-Jawziyya, 15, 17, 22, 26, 192, 271, 273, 282, 284, 297, 298–300, 307, 310, 351
Ibn Rushd al-Ḥafīd. *See* Averroes
Ibn Sallūm, Ṣāliḥ, 356
Ibn Sīnā. *See* Avicenna
Ibn Taymiyya, 5, 132, 175, 201–202, 210, 245, 271, 281, 287, 292, 307, 310, 318, 324, 345, 351, 360
  criticism of *waḥdat al-wujūd*, 248, 283, 311, 313–315, 339
  Kūrānī's criticism of, 283–285, 321–322
  Kūrānī's defense of, 273–275, 282–283
  on logic, 217–218
  relation to Ḳāḍīzādelīs, 15–17, 191–193
  on *ta'wīl*, 276–277
Ibn al-Tilimsānī, Sharaf al-Dīn, 180
Ibn al-'Ujaymī, Ḥasan, 259, 260
Ibn Ya'qūb al-Wallālī, Aḥmad, 135, 137, 140–141, 148n, 149, 150n, 151, 171, 209, 319, 338
Ifrānī, Muḥammad al-Ṣaghīr, 209–210
Iḫlāṣ (Khalwatī shaykh), 266
Ījī, 'Aḍud al-Dīn, 14, 31, 32, 33, 62, 99, 274, 288, 300
Ijtihād, 7–8, 192, 219, 304, 356, 357–359
'Illaysh, Muḥammad, 140n, 155, 175, 360
'Ilm al-kalām. See Kalām
'Ilm al-ma'ānī. See Semantics-Rhetoric
'Ilm al-munāẓara. See Ādāb al-baḥth
Iqbal, Muhammad, 357
Irbil, 49, 58n
'Iṣāmī, Jamāl al-Dīn, 37
'Iṣāmī, Ṣadr al-Dīn, 37
Isfarāyinī, Abū Isḥāq, 179–180
Isfarāyinī, 'Iṣām al-Dīn, 30, 31–32, 33, 36, 37, 43–45, 51n, 52, 59, 99, 143, 171, 348
Istanbul, 14, 16, 18, 19–20, 23, 24, 32, 35, 37–59 passim, 63, 66, 71, 76, 90n, 99, 115, 131, 158, 161, 165, 166, 175, 189n, 191, 259, 267n, 348, 351

Jāmī, 'Abd al-Raḥmān, 31, 33, 34, 36, 37, 60, 143, 237, 256, 257, 258, 269n, 281, 324, 327, 331, 333, 334, 343, 345, 348, 351
Java, 175, 200, 320
Jawharī, Aḥmad, 133, 135, 137, 137n, 141n, 200, 201, 249n, 350
Jīlī, 'Abd al-Karīm, 244, 334, 345, 346n
Jurjānī, al-Sayyid al-Sharīf, 14, 18, 25, 36, 39n, 43, 44, 51, 57, 67, 117, 118, 122, 142, 189n, 276, 295, 307, 360
Juwaynī, Imām al-Ḥaramayn, 180, 181, 182n, 197n, 207, 296–297, 300, 304, 310

Kābulī, 'Abd al-Raḥīm, 28
Ḳāḍīzādelī (movement), 13, 14–17, 18, 24, 25, 26, 57n, 166, 175, 191–193, 259, 261, 264, 294, 305n, 336
Ḳāḍīzāde, Meḥmed, 13, 191
Kāfī, Ḥasan, 190, 294
Kahramanmaraş, 64n, 115
Kalām. See individual theologians, schools, and themes
  Ibn 'Arabī on, 285–287
  Kūrānī on, 287–290
  Nābulusī on, 290–294, 304–305
  Sanūsī on, 175–188
  supposedly dialectical nature of, 173–175
  Yūsī on, 210–214, 289–290
  Zabīdī on, 230–231
Kānḳirī, 'Abdullāh, 23, 39, 71n, 76, 77
Ḳara Ḫalīl Tīrevī, v, 5, 22, 23–24, 38, 39, 64, 88, 122–125, 128
Ḳarabāş 'Alī Velī, 267, 269
Ḳārsī, Dāvūd, 16, 64, 284, 294, 336n
Kasb. See Human acts, creation of
Kāshifī, Fakhr al-Dīn Vā'iẓ, 257, 348
Kātī, Ḥusām al-Dīn, 29
Kātib Çelebī, 14, 15, 19, 32, 33, 38, 39n, 40n, 41n, 44n, 45n, 49n, 50n, 56–59, 61, 64, 65, 68, 69, 71, 106n, 143, 160, 189, 356
Kātibī, Najm al-Dīn
  his *Ḥikmat al-'ayn*, 45, 49
  his *al-Risāla al-Shamsiyya*, 32, 82, 138–140, 157, 218, 219n
Kawtharī, Muḥammad Zāhid, 50n, 56, 59
Ḳāzābādī, Aḥmed, 41, 53, 54
Kāzarūnī, Shaykh-i Makkī, 251–252, 254, 348
Kefevī, Ebū l-Beḳā' Eyyūb, 28
Kefevī, Meḥmed b. Ḥamīd, 22, 38, 39, 41, 62, 63, 64, 65
Kemālpāşāzāde, Aḥmed, 40n, 44, 65
Khafājī, Aḥmad, 19–20, 21, 37, 46–47, 273

Khalkhālī, Ḥusayn, 39, 40, 43, 45–46, 55, 58, 75, 88
Khalwatī, Ayyūb. *See* ʻAdawī, Ayyūb
Khalwatī (Sufi order), 236, 247n, 249, 261–270, 340, 350, 352
Khānī, Qāsim, 235, 236, 267, 270, 340
Kharrūbī al-Ṭarābulusī, Muḥammad, 222, 226
Kharrūf al-Anṣārī, Muḥammad, 148–149
Khiyārī, Ibrāhīm, 43, 49n
Khūnajī, Afḍal al-Dīn, 70, 137, 139–140, 141, 156–158, 162, 171
Khwāfī, Muḥammad Ḥusayn, 258–259, 260
Khwānsārī, Āqā Ḥusayn, 69, 361
Kinaksī, ʻAbdullāh, 135–137, 141–143, 144, 189, 249n
King, David A., 18
Ḳonevī, Ismāʻīl, 55
Köprülü (Viziers), 22, 47n, 59, 165–166, 353
Küçük Aḥmed Pāşā, 262, 266
Kūrānī, Ibrāhīm
  on Ashʻarism, 281, 298, 306–307, 350–351
  on the letters and sounds of the Quran, 283–284
  on Ibn Taymiyya, 273–275, 282–285, 321–322
  on occasionalism and the creation of human acts, 294–302
  relations to Ḥanbalīs, 264, 273, 281, 308–309
  on Satanic verses, 159, 253–254, 307n
  style of lecturing, 35, 255
  on *taqlīd* in theology, 287–290
  on *ta'wīl*, 277–285
  teachers and studies, 51–52, 252
  on *waḥdat al-wujūd*, 255–256, 320–332
  works, 252–253

Laqānī, Ibrāhīm, 188, 189n, 276, 295
Lārī, Muṣliḥ al-Dīn, 22, 39, 47n, 49, 77, 99
Logic; *see also* Syllogisms and Universals
  Birgevī on, 17
  handbooks of, 29, 32, 45, 46, 52, 68, 77, 94n, 137–140, 142, 155, 157, 162, 170–171, 218
  Nābulusī on, 290–292
  Sāçaḳlīzāde on, 25–26
  Sanūsī on, 176–177, 215–216
  Yūsī on, 216–221, 223–229
  Zabīdī on, 132–133, 220–221

Mahā'imī, ʻAlā' al-Dīn, 237, 324, 331
Makdisi, George, 202
Mallawī, Aḥmad, 66, 133–135, 137, 138n, 141, 145n, 200–201, 218, 249n, 349–350
Manjūr, Aḥmad, 149
Manṣūr, Aḥmad. *See* Sultan Aḥmad al-Manṣūr
Maqāṣīrī, Yūsuf Tāj, 256, 263, 320n
Maqqarī, Aḥmad, 5, 151, 154–155, 156, 189
Marʻaş. *See* Kahramanmaraş
Māturīdī (theological school), 4, 5, 15, 16, 143, 181, 186, 189, 190, 193, 218, 265, 273, 275, 284n, 294, 295, 305, 307, 333, 350
Maybudī, Qāḍī Mīr Ḥusayn, 22, 46, 49, 59, 77, 99, 147
Maymūnī, Ibrāhīm, 37
Mayyāra, Muḥammad, 195–199, 200, 222n
Māwarān, 49, 58n
Mawlāy Ismāʻīl, 153, 170, 209, 354
Mawlāy al-Rashīd, 151, 153
McGregor, Richard, 245
Mecca, 37, 99–100, 104, 151, 153–154, 156, 164–166, 172, 244n, 254, 257–260, 269, 272, 348
Medina, 35, 37, 51, 143n, 151, 154, 156, 162, 164–166, 172, 249, 252, 254–256, 263, 272, 307, 320n, 332, 348
Meḥmed IV. *See* Sultan Meḥmed IV
Meḥmed Ġāzī (Khalwatī shaykh), 266
Minḳārīzāde, Yaḥyā, 42–44, 62, 75, 99, 127, 158
Mīr Abū l-Fatḥ ʻArabshāhī, 39, 41, 43, 44–45, 47n, 59, 62, 63, 66, 67n, 68, 75, 84, 91n
Mīr Dāmād, 69, 169n
Mirightī, Muḥammad b. Saʻīd, 150, 161
Mīrzā Jān Bāghnawī, 41, 43, 45–46, 48–55, 59, 88, 139n, 274n, 348, 361
Mīrzā Makhdūm Ḥusaynī, 49n, 254
Mollā Fenārī. *See* Fenārī, Meḥmed

Morocco, 4, 131, 135, 147–154, 161, 170–172, 183, 204–231 passim, 256, 319, 351, 354
Morris, James, 237
Muḥibbī, Muḥammad Amīn, 27–29, 32–35, 47, 51n, 58n, 60, 61, 74, 99, 108–109, 158, 163, 166, 262–263, 266, 267n
Mujaddidī (Naqshbandī suborder), 258, 260–261
Mujalī, Aḥmad, 48, 48n, 50, 53, 54, 58
Mullā Çelebī Āmidī, 42, 46–47, 55, 58, 62
Mullā Ḥanafī Tabrīzī, 41, 45, 49, 62, 69, 75, 84, 123
Mullā Maḥmūd Kurdī, 26–30, 40n, 333n
Mullā Ṣadrā Shīrāzī, 69, 169n, 319, 331–332, 342–344, 361
Munāwī, 'Abd al-Ra'ūf, 28, 66, 247n, 248n, 262n, 268
Müneccimbāşī, Aḥmed, 5, 22, 99–100, 106–107, 109–115, 119, 120–122, 125, 128, 166, 348, 349
Muqallid, 180, 189n, 204–209, 306, 358; *see also Taqlīd*
Murād IV. *See* Sultan Murād IV
Mu'tazilī (theological school), 20n, 34, 174, 186, 201, 216, 296–298, 301–304, 307n, 325

Nabahānī, Yūsuf, 268, 269
Nābulusī, 'Abd al-Ghanī
  initiated into the Naqshbandī order, 259
  on logic and rational theology, 290–293
  on occasionalism and the creation of human acts, 302–305
  relation to Kūrānī, 302–304, 332–334
  on Sirhindī, 260–261
  on *waḥdat al-wujūd*, 261, 332–344
  works, 155, 259–260, 262n, 269n
Na'īmā, Muṣṭafā, 14, 353n
Nakhlī, Aḥmad, 259, 263
Naqshbandī (Sufi order), 156, 236, 244, 245n, 249, 250, 254, 257–261, 264, 270, 290, 307, 314, 332, 348, 350, 352
Naqshbandī, Khālid, 261
Naqshbandī, Tāj al-Dīn. *See* 'Uthmānī, Tāj al-Dīn
Narāqī, Mahdī, 69
Nasr, Seyyed Hossein, 342, 361
Nietzsche, Friedrich, 169, 311
Nīthārī, 'Alī, 22, 55, 56, 76n
Nominalism. *See* Universals
Nūrī, 'Abd ül-Aḥad, 261–262
Nwyia, Paul, 245

Occasionalism, 169, 294–305, 307, 310, 312, 350

Paracelsus, 356
Pehlivānī, Mūsā, 90–96
Philosophy; *see also* Logic
  Birgevī on, 17–18
  handbooks of, 22–23, 45, 46, 47n, 49, 51, 77, 99, 143–147, 254
  teaching of, 19–25, 51

Qaddūra, Sa'īd, 137, 155, 157, 161, 171n
Qādirī (Sufi order), 247, 267n
Qarabāghī, Yūsuf Kawsaj, 40, 41, 274n
Qārī' al-Harawī, Mullā 'Alī, 246
Qāshānī, 'Abd al-Razzāq, 237, 269, 298, 331, 334, 345
Qaṣṣār al-Gharnāṭī, Muḥammad, 149
Qaṭṭān, 'Uthmān, 29, 333n
Qayṣarī, Dā'ūd, 244, 281, 344n
Qazwīnī, Jamāl al-Dīn, 29, 31, 37, 106, 142, 150n, 254
Qūnawī, Ṣadr al-Dīn, 237, 239, 241n, 242–244, 245n, 247, 270, 281, 312, 313, 320, 325, 331, 334, 343–345, 350–352
Quran, letters and sounds of, 192, 196, 211, 253, 272, 283, 284, 312, 350
Quṣayrī, Aḥmad b. 'Abdu, 265
Qushāshī, Aḥmad, 236, 250n, 251–256, 260–261, 263–264, 273, 287, 320, 332, 334
Qushayrī, 'Abd al-Karīm, 178, 180n, 246n, 247, 306n, 319

Rahman, Fazlur, 2n, 245, 271, 312, 345, 359n
Rashīd Riḍā. *See* Riḍā, Muḥammad Rashīd
Raymond, Andre, 354
Rāzī, Fakhr al-Dīn, 70, 88, 117, 180, 185, 202, 292, 297, 314
Rāzī, Quṭb al-Dīn, 32, 45, 82–83, 94n, 138, 139, 140, 157, 219n
Reichmuth, Stefan, 2n, 8, 115n
Renard, John, 245

Riḍā, Muḥammad Rashīd, 2n, 119n, 202, 310
Rosenthal, Franz, 100n, 120
Rūdānī, Muḥammad, 5, 152, 161–170, 249n
Rūmī Āḳḥiṣārī, Aḥmed, 15, 191, 305

Sabzavārī, Hādī, 69, 70n
Sāçaḳlīzāde, Meḥmed, 76, 91n
 on the acquisition of knowledge, 115–120, 121–122
 on dialectics, 36, 60, 63–65, 67–68, 74, 84–89, 95, 109, 349
 on philosophy, 21–22
 on the rational sciences, 25–26, 36, 116–117
Ṣadrüddīnzāde, Meḥmed Emīn, 39, 42n, 50n, 88, 122, 169
Safāqisī, ʿAlī al-Nūrī, 153, 299
Safavids, 3n, 4, 19, 27, 31, 41n, 46, 68–70, 107, 139, 169, 332, 342, 357
Saffārīnī, Muḥammad, 181n, 192n, 264–265, 310
Şāh Ḥusayn Antāḳī. *See* Adanavī, Hüseyn
Şāh Ḥusayn Urfalī, 65, 67n, 77
Şāh Velī ʿAyntābī, 262, 266
Ṣaḥn-i Themān. *See* Eight Colleges
Salafī (theological school), 15n, 118, 119n, 191, 201–202, 265, 310–311, 333n, 359
Ṣāliḥ Żihnī "Ders-i ʿāmm," 47, 58n, 99
Samarqand, 44n, 258
Samarqandī, Abū l-Qāsim, 32, 168
Samarqandī, Shams al-Dīn, 35, 61, 65, 66, 67n, 69, 71–72, 77, 84, 106, 218
Sammākī, Fakhr al-Dīn, 39, 68
Sammān, Muḥammad b. ʿAbd al-Karīm, 268
Sanūsī, Muḥammad b. Yūsuf
 Barzinjī on, 352
 influence in Egypt, 131–133, 141, 175–176, 188–189, 349–350
 influence on Ḳāḍīzādelī movement, 189–193
 Kūrānī on, 299
 on logic, 176–177, 215–216
 popular creeds of, 176, 193–194
 on *taqlīd*, 176–188
 translations of, 175, 200
 Yūsī on, 207–209, 211
 Zabīdī on, 132
Sayılı, Aydin, 18
Secondary causality. *See* Occasionalism
Semantics-Rhetoric (*ʿilm al-maʿānī wa-l-bayān*), 13, 42, 44, 46, 109, 112, 115, 116, 118, 121, 122, 125, 126, 135, 136, 141, 143, 148n, 149, 156, 166, 213, 224, 230, 254
 Qazwīnī's handbook *Talkhīṣ al-Miftāḥ*, 29, 31, 32n, 37, 106, 142, 150n, 166n
Şeyḫī, Meḥmed, 42, 47, 47n, 58n
Schultze, Reinhardt, 8
Selīm I. *See* Sultan Selīm I
Shādhilī (Sufi order), 135n, 136, 143, 152, 156, 162, 164, 169, 240, 242, 245, 247n, 248–249, 255–256, 262n, 266, 270, 313, 319
Shāh ʿAbbās I, 4, 27
Shāh Waliyullāh, 131, 307–308, 311, 332, 351
Shaʿrānī, ʿAbd al-Wahhāb, 142, 188, 238–240, 246n, 306, 344–345
Shaṭṭārīs (Sufi order), 156, 236, 249–256, 258, 260, 263, 270, 320, 350, 352
Shāwī, Yaḥyā, 5, 137n, 157–160, 188, 253, 254, 256, 351
Shawkānī, Muḥammad, 85, 131, 253n, 311, 333n
Shaykh Khālid. *See* al-Naqshbandī, Khālid
Shaykh al-Mahdī, Maḥammad. *See* Sultan Maḥammad al-Shaykh al-Mahdī
Shinnāwī, Aḥmad, 251
Shīrāzī, Mullā Ṣadrā. *See* Mullā Ṣadrā Shīrāzī
Shirwan, 27, 261
Sīdī Muḥammad III, 170, 171n
Sijāʿī, Aḥmad, 145, 147
Sijilmasa, 205, 206, 207, 221, 230
Simnānī, ʿAlāʾ al-Dawla, 313, 330, 339
Sirhindī, Aḥmad, 244–245, 254, 258, 260–261, 314, 319, 348
Sivas, 48, 76
Sīvāsī, ʿAbd ül-Mecīd, 261
Siyālkūtī, ʿAbd al-Ḥakīm, 40, 156
Subkī, Tāj al-Dīn, 142, 180n, 239n, 273
Subkī, Tāqī al-Dīn, 132, 186n, 273, 290
Sugtānī, ʿĪsā, 141, 142, 149, 161, 206–207
Suhrawardī, ʿUmar, 246n, 247, 306n
Suhrawardī, Yaḥyā, 31, 51, 218, 254
Sulawesi, 256, 263, 320n, 351
Sultan Aḥmad al-Manṣūr, 152, 154, 354
Sultan Aḥmed III, 353

Sultan Bāyezīd II, 38
Sultan Maḥammad al-Shaykh al-Mahdī, 222
Sultan Meḥmed IV, 99, 160
Sultan Murād IV, 42, 46, 266, 353, 356
Sultan Selīm I, 252
Sultan Süleymān the Magnificent, 1, 57
Suyūṭī, Jalāl al-Dīn, 25, 36, 132, 160, 189n, 217–220, 231, 240–241, 246, 253, 254
Svevo, Italo, 202
Syllogism, 20, 134, 157, 322
  application to arguments, 92–96, 122
  relational, 34, 87–96
  use in dialectics, 80–85, 86–87
  use in *kalām*, 176, 183–184, 197–199, 207, 215–216, 317

Tabrīzī, Mullā Ḥanafī. *See* Mullā Ḥanafī Tabrīzī
Tabrīzī, Rajab 'Alī, 361
Taftāzānī, Sa'd al-Dīn
  criticism of *waḥdat al-wujūd*, 242–243, 245n, 283, 313–319
  Kūrānī's criticism of, 326–332
  Nābulusī's criticism of, 337–340
  on *taqlīd*, 181, 206–207, 208
  works, 29, 31, 32n, 37, 38, 39n, 45, 46, 51, 106, 116, 118, 122, 138, 139, 140n, 142, 144, 150n, 224, 276, 295, 314
Taḥqīq
  and *ādāb al-baḥth*, 35, 60–61
  Dawānī on, 32–33
  and "deep reading," 108–109, 112, 121–122
  and *kalām*, 176–183
  Ḳara Ḫalīl on, 124
  meaning of, 28
  and Sufism, 235–236, 321
Taqlīd
  Ibn 'Arabī on, 285–287
  in *kalām*, 176–203 passim, 204–207, 358
  Kūrānī on, 287–290
  in law, 192, 304, 357–359
  Sanūsī on, 176–188
  Nābulusī on, 293, 304
  Yūsī on, 204–205, 207–212, 289–290, 358
Ṭarsūsī, Meḥmed, 22, 24–25, 41, 53, 64
Ṭāşköprīzāde, Aḥmed, 14, 19, 35, 38, 40n, 44, 52, 64–66, 67n, 71–74, 77, 78, 83, 106, 160
Ta'wīl (nonliteral interpretation of anthropomorphisms), 110, 186, 192, 194, 272, 275–283, 285, 292, 306, 322, 324, 328, 334, 350
Ṭāvūskārī, Meḥmed, 90n, 91, 93n, 95
Tefsīrī Meḥmed, 47–49, 53, 54, 56, 58, 62, 76
Tha'ālibī, 'Īsā, 137n, 155–157, 162, 164–165
Theology. *See Kalām*
Ṭihrānī, Muḥammad Yūsuf, 69
Tilimsānī, 'Afīf al-Dīn, 333, 345
Tilimsānī, Aḥmad. *See* al-Maqqarī, Aḥmed
Tilimsānī, Muḥammad al-Sharīf, 137, 140, 148, 157n
Timbuktu, 152, 354
Tlemcen, 131, 150, 153, 154, 183
Tokat, 90
Touat, 152, 354
Translations, 23, 99, 175, 200, 250, 251–252, 257, 258–259, 260, 348, 356
Tunis, 148, 153, 171n, 180, 183, 189n, 299, 354
Ṭūsī, Naṣīr al-Dīn, 31, 45, 114, 202, 328

Ujhūrī, 'Alī, 138n, 162
Ulugh Beg, 44n, 168
Universals, 217–219, 221, 225–226, 229, 316
'Urḍī, Abū l-Wafā', 265
Urmawī, Sirāj al-Dīn, 45, 139, 140n
'Usālī, Aḥmad, 262–263, 266
'Uthmānī, Tāj al-Dīn, 257–258, 348

Van Ess, Josef, 173, 174, 202
Vānī Meḥmed, 15, 16, 24

Waḥdat al-shuhūd, 244n, 245, 340
Waḥdat al-wujūd
  'Alā' al-Dīn al-Bukhārī on, 16, 193, 313, 319, 336, 339, 345
  Barzinjī on, 236, 251–252, 345n
  Dawānī on, 251, 327, 343
  Ibn Taymiyya on, 248, 283, 311, 313–315, 339

Kūrānī on, 255–256, 320–332
Muḥammad b. Abī l-Ḥasan al-Bakrī on, 242–244, 306, 319
Mullā Ṣadrā on, 319, 342–343
Muṣṭafā al-Bakrī on, 236, 269
Nābulusī on, 261, 332–344
Naqshbandīs on, 257–258, 260–261, 313–314, 350, 352
Qāri' al-Harawī on, 246
Qāsim al-Khānī on, 267, 340
Shādhilīs on, 245, 248–249, 255–256, 313, 319
Sha'rānī on, 239, 246n, 306, 344–345
Taftāzānī on, 242–243, 245n, 283, 313–319
Yūsī on, 249, 351
Warzāzī, Muḥammad al-Ṣaghīr, 135, 137, 141, 144, 150n, 189
Watt, William Montgomery, 174, 188, 190n
Wisnovsky, Rob, 66, 69, 171n

Yānyavī, Es'ad, 62, 356
Yassīthnī, Muḥammad, 222–223
Yūsī, al-Ḥasan
defense of logic, 132, 217–220
influence in Egypt, 132–137, 141, 143–146
on the Islamic profession of faith, 221–229
on *kalām*, 210–214, 289–290
on *taqlīd*, 204–205, 207–212, 289–290, 358
on *waḥdat al-wujūd*, 249, 351

Zabid, 257
Zabīdī, Muḥammad Murtaḍā, 131–133, 135, 138, 141, 144n, 220–221, 229, 230–231, 253n, 261, 310, 311
Ẓāhirī (school of law), 110, 185
Zamakhsharī, Maḥmūd, 118, 160
Zarnūjī, Burhān al-Dīn, 100–102, 104–106, 114–118, 120
Zarrūq, Aḥmad, 148n, 189n, 248
Zaydī (sect), 311, 333n
Zāwiya al-'Ayyāshiyya (Morocco), 151, 156, 163, 256
Zāwiya al-Dilā'iyya (Morocco), 150–151, 154, 161
Zāwiya al-Ikhlāṣiyya (Aleppo), 266–267
Zāwiya al-Nāṣiriyya (Morocco), 151–152, 161
Zaydān, Jurjī, 155